Vasta / Haith / Miller

Child Psychology

The Modern Science

Third Edition
Abridged

prepared for use by
Stratford Career Institute Student #
E940598

WILEY
CUSTOM SERVICES

Printed in the United States of America.

ISBN 0-471-26797-X

Development in Context

This book follows a contextualist approach to human development. Each chapter examines the role that family, school, and culture play in a child's development. In addition, special Development in Context sections highlight specific examples of these three major contextual forces. The following summary of contextual material is not exhaustive—it merely identifies some of the most important such passages.

Chapter 1: Introduction and Perspective

- (pp. 4–7) "Historical Views of Childhood"—Discusses the treatment of children in cultures from Greece and Rome through the Reformation, highlighting the importance not only of cultural but of historical context in shaping ideas about the nature of childhood and accepted practices for treating children.

Chapter 2: Theories of Child Development

- (pp. 32–33) "Cognitive/Developmental Models"— Provides an initial treatment of Vygotsky's influential sociocultural model.
- (pp. 39–43) "Environmental/Learning Approaches"— Introduces Bandura's notion of reciprocal determinism, or the interaction of person, behavior, and environmental context.
- (pp. 49–52) ■ *Development in Context:* The Ecological Approach—Introduces the theoretical rationale for a focus on context, drawing especially from the theorizing of Urie Bronfenbrenner.

Chapter 3: Research Methods

- (p. 70) "Cross-Sectional Studies"—Considers cohort effects.
- (pp. 72–73) "Cross-Cultural Research"— Lays the methodological groundwork for one important form of contextual research.
- (p. 69) ■ *Development in Cultural Context:* Studying the Life Course

Chapter 4: Genetics: The Biological Context of Behavior

- (pp. 97–102) "Models of Gene-Environment Interaction"—Presents four models of the interplay of genes and environmental context, including Plomin's concept of nonshared environmental factors and Bronfenbrenner and Ceci's Bioecological Model.
- (pp. 102–109) "Studying Gene Effects on Behavior"—Reviews evidence (including various kinds of family studies) that indicates both genes and environments contribute to most psychological outcomes.

Chapter 5: Prenatal Development

- (pp. 120–121) ■ *Development in Family Context:* Families Created by Alternative Methods of Conception
- (p. 134) ■ *Development in Cultural Context:* Ganja Use in Jamaica

Chapter 6: Physical Development: Birth, Motor Skills, and Growth

- (pp. 154–158) "Neonatal Risk"—Includes data on the contribution of family factors.
- (pp. 172–175) "Motor Development"—Illustrates the importance of cultural factors in the comparison of rates of development for African and American infants.
- (pp. 158–160) ■ *Development in Family Context:* Infants at Risk: The Environment Holds the Key
- (pp. 188–189) ■ *Development in Cultural Context:* Social Class and Poverty

Chapter 7: Sensory and Perceptual Development

- (pp. 206–207) ■ *Development in Cultural Context:* Music to Our Ears: Cultural Influences on Perception of Tunes

Chapter 8: Cognitive Development: The Piagetian Approach

- (pp. 261,264–265, 278) Cross-Cultural material—Includes the appearance/reality distinction, children's cosmologies, and formal operations.
- (pp. 282–283) Applications section—Discusses the relevance of Piaget's work for education.
- (pp.274–275) ■ *Development in Cultural Context:* Cross-Cultural Research and Piaget

Chapter 9: Cognitive Development: The Information-Processing Approach

- (pp. 309–310) Applications section—Discusses learning to study.
- (pp. 330–335) Academic Abilities—Applies information-processing principles to the school setting.
- (pp. 308, 323, 333) Cross-Cultural material—Includes mnemonic strategies, memory talk in the home setting, and arithmetical strategies in school.
- (pp. 321–324) ■ *Development in Family Context:* How Parents Teach Their Children to Remember

Chapter 10: Cognitive Development: The Intelligence-Test Approach

- (pp. 365–370) "Contributions of the Family"—Provides one of the most extended treatments of the role of the family.
- (pp. 370–374) "Contributions of the School"—Provides the text's most extended coverage of the contribution of schooling to children's intellectual development, including cross-cultural material.
- (pp. 377–378) Applications section—Discusses Project Head Start's intervention efforts for at-risk children.
- (pp. 381–386) "Alternatives to IQ"—Adds to the theoretical basis for an understanding of context through discussions of the Vygotskian approach and Ceci's Bioecological Theory.
- (pp. 369–370) ■ *Development in Cultural Context:* Families and Achievement: The Message from Cross-Cultural Research
- (pp. 383–384) ■ *Development in Cultural Context:* Mathematics in the School and on the Streets— Brazilian Candy Vendors

CHILD PSYCHOLOGY

THE MODERN SCIENCE

l'école

CHILD PSYCHOLOGY

THE MODERN SCIENCE

THIRD EDITION

Ross Vasta
State University of New York at Brockport

Marshall M. Haith
University of Denver

Scott A. Miller
University of Florida

John Wiley & Sons, Inc.
New York Chichester Weinheim Brisbane Singapore Toronto

Acquisitions Editor	Ellen Schatz
Developmental Editor	Rachel Nelson
Senior Marketing Manager	Charity Robey
Senior Production Editor	Elizabeth Swain
Senior Designer	Kevin Murphy
Photo Editor	Kim Khatchatourian
Illustration Editor	Anna Melhorn

Cover photo by Charles Thatcher/Tony Stone Images, NYC.

Special thanks to Photo Researchers, a New York City photo agency, for their various contributions to this book, including consulting on the stock and location photography.

This book was set in 10/12 New Baskerville by LCI Design, and printed and bound by Von Hoffman Press. The cover was printed by Lehigh.

This book is printed on acid-free paper.

The paper in this book was manufactured by a mill whose forest management programs include sustained yield harvesting of its timberlands. Sustained yield harvesting principles ensure that the numbers of trees cut each year does not exceed the amount of new growth.

Library of Congress Cataloguing in Publication Data:

Vasta, Ross.

Child Psychology: the modern science / Ross Vasta, Marshall M. Haith, Scott A. Miller. — 3rd ed.

p. cm.

Includes bibliographical references and index.

ISBN 0-471-19221-X

1. Child psychology. I. Haith, Marshall M., 1937– . II. Miller, Scott A., 1944– . III Title.

Printed in the United States of America

10 9 8 7 6 5

Preface

The major goals of the first two editions of *Child Psychology: The Modern Science* were to serve instructors' needs, to maximize student learning, and to reflect accurately and comprehensively the discipline of developmental psychology as it exists today. In preparing the third edition, we expanded these goals to include a greater integration of contextual material, an increased emphasis on cross- and multicultural research, and even more real-world applications. In so doing, we have created a truly new edition of this textbook that captures the excitement and relevance of child psychology as the discipline enters the 21st century.

A Contextualist Approach

The most important and distinctive feature of *Child Psychology* remains its emphasis on the contextualist view of human development. Inspired by Urie Bronfenbrenner's seminal work, and fueled by the rediscovery of Lev Vygotsky's writings, modern developmental psychology has increasingly adopted a contextualist perspective. The child is not viewed as a passive recipient of environmental influences, but as an active producer of those influences. From the very beginning, the infant engages in a transactional "dance" with the caregiver, each regulating the behavior of the other. As the child grows, development interacts in critical ways with the social contexts in which it occurs, the three most important being the family system, the school, and the cultural environment.

Unfortunately, textbooks of child psychology have not kept pace with this trend. Too often, contextual material has been included simply in the form of separate chapters on family and school influences, appended to the end of the book. As such, the discussion of these influences comes too late to be of maximal pedagogical value. We feel strongly that determinants residing in these and other contextual settings should instead be interwoven in the study of child development and considered at the point where the relevant aspect of development is being discussed. If we wish to discuss, for example, the effects of junior high school practices and policies on the self-esteem of preadolescents, the place to present that material is in the chapter on the development of the self, not in a chapter on schools near the end of the course. One solution to this problem—undoubtedly employed by many instructors—is to extract pieces of material from the later chapters and insert them where they belong. This, however, is awkward and unsatisfying.

Here, as in the first two editions, *Child Psychology* offers a better solution. *Material on the family, school, and culture is integrated into the appropriate chapters of the text.* This allows the course to move from one area of development to another in a topical manner, while including the broad tapestry of variables that affect each area. In the third edition, we have increased our coverage of contextual influences and also presented detailed examples of them in separate sections titled "Development in Family Context," "Development in School Context," and "Development in Cultural Context" (see Pedagogical Features).

As in the previous editions, Chapter 2 introduces the contextualist theme in the presentation of Urie Bronfenbrenner's ecological systems model. Thereafter, each chapter includes one or more Development in Context sections relevant to the topic under consideration. For example, in Chapter 5 (Prenatal Development) we consider what life is like in families created by alternative methods of conception. In Chapter 7 (Sensory and Perceptual Development) we describe how cultural experiences can affect a baby's perception of music. And in Chapter 15 (Gender-Role Development) we examine whether the typical school environment and curriculum favors boys over girls. Even more importantly, we weave contextual material throughout the entire text, examining pertinent specific influences in every chapter.

Topical Organization

We have chosen to organize the book topically. By considering each topic area in a single chapter, we believe we can most effectively present and critique the full body of research and theorizing relevant to that area.

The 16 chapters can be grouped into four general parts:

- Chapters 1–3 provide the foundation of the discipline, covering history, theory, and research methods. In keeping with the research-oriented approach of the text, these topics are presented in some detail.
- Chapters 4–6 focus on biological and physical development, including genetics, prenatal development, birth, growth, and motor development.
- Chapters 7–11 cover sensory and perceptual development, three approaches to cognitive development, and language.
- Chapters 12–16 describe social and personality development, including emotional development, attachment, the self-system, moral reasoning, prosocial and antisocial behavior, gender-role development, and peer relations.

Although the overall organization is topical, the internal presentation of Chapters 7–16 is developmental. The topic area—be it language, gender roles, or whatever—begins with the newborn and describes development through adolescence. This approach helps the student to appreciate the continuity of growth within each area and also to understand the ongoing interactions between biological processes and contextual influences.

Cultural Diversity

The dramatic increase in cross-cultural and multicultural research within the discipline prompted us to expand even further our discussion of these influences. For example, we discuss cross-culture investigations of Piaget's theory (Chapter 8), we describe how different cultures foster different approaches to language learning (Chapter 11), we examine ethnic differences in infant temperment (Chapter 12), and we describe cross-cultural variations in early play (Chapter 16).

Scientific Orientation

In this text we treat child psychology as a natural science and present it in a way that reflects its scientific underpinnings. In addition to providing a full chapter on research methods (Chapter 3), we discuss specific methodological issues frequently throughout the book, such as comparing research designs for examining genetic influences on development in Chapter 4, describing computer simulations in Chapter 9, and considering contrasting approaches to assessing infant–caregiver attachment in Chapter 12.

State-of-the-Art Coverage

Information is being generated in developmental psychology at a staggering rate. To prepare a textbook of manageable proportions, authors must make some tough decisions. We have chosen to present a state-of-the-art treatment of child psychology that focuses on the very latest issues and findings. For example, Chapter 4 discusses Ceci and Bronfenbrenner's new model of gene–environment interactions; Chapter 6 describes Thelen's dynamic systems approach to motor development; Chapter 8 discusses the newest developments in theory of the mind; and Chapter 13 presents Dweck's latest model of motivational processes and academic achievement.

Some chapters include boxed sections titled "*On the Cutting Edge*" that describe new and exciting research developments (see Pedagogical Features). Also, to keep the third edition as up-to-date as possible, we have added hundreds of new references, many from 1995 through 1998.

Although our focus is on current work, we recognize that some truly classic studies should be known by every student of human development. In such cases, the material is presented in boxed sections titled "*Classics of Research*" (see Pedagogical Features).

Balanced Theoretical Presentation

Rather than emphasizing any single theoretical orientation, our book examines child psychology from the perspectives of the three principal traditions that characterize the discipline today—*the cognitive-developmental approach, the environmental/learning approach,* and *the ethological approach.* The fundamental tenets of these three orientations are first presented in Chapter 2. Then, most of the remaining chapters begin by examining what the three traditions have to say about that topic area and go on to consider relevant research findings and applications. As a consequence, the student can approach the substantive material in these chapters with a conceptual structure that facilitates interpretation, comparison, and critical analysis. For example, Chapter 14, on moral development, begins by outlining the theoretical models of Piaget, Kohlberg, and Turiel and then examines recent studies designed to test the validity and scope of these models.

Readability and Simplicity

We have worked hard to make our text, above all, interesting and accessible to the student reader. We believe that the text's comfortable writing style and the clarity with which concepts are introduced, discussed, and interrelated will enable students to read and understand a rigorous treatment of the issues.

In addition, rather than presenting long and tedious discussions of research findings that are likely to overwhelm students, we first decided what concepts and principles we wished students to come away with and then carefully selected research findings and real-world examples to illustrate and support this material. As a consequence, we believe that we have produced a text that communicates the essence and excitement of developmental psychology simply and efficiently.

Pedagogical Features

In our effort to be complete and up-to-date, we have not forgotten that this is a textbook whose audience includes college sophomores. We have designed into the book a number of features—some new to the third edition (designated by ** below)—to maximize the likelihood that students will learn the material.

Chapter-Opening Vignettes Most of the chapters begin with a brief story or anecdote designed to capture the student's interest and to introduce the topic under consideration. In Chapter 4, for example, we open with the story of Dolly, the Scottish sheep that was cloned from a single cell, and we consider some of the intriguing ethical questions posed by the research. Or in Chapter 15, we describe a fascinating case study in which a male newborn is surgically altered and raised as a female.

"On the Cutting Edge" Boxes We use boxes selectively in this text. The "On the Cutting Edge" boxes are designed to make students aware of recent research findings—such as the latest studies of newborn facial perception (Chapter 7), Goldin-Meadow's work on using gestures to assess cognitive status (Chapter 9), and Bem's new theory of sexual orientation (Chapter 15)—or important ongoing research programs—such as the Human Genome Project (Chapter 4).

"Classics of Research" Boxes A highly praised feature of the first two editions was retained for this edition. The "Classics of Research" boxes present studies of enduring historical value, even though they are no longer of immediate relevance to contemporary thinking in the area. Examples include Arnold Gesell's research on motor development in twins (Chapter 6), Harlow's work with attachment in infant monkeys (Chapter 12), and Hartshorne and May's studies of moral character (Chapter 14).

"Applications" Sections These sections present examples of research findings and programs that have been applied to work in schools, homes, hospitals, and other real-world settings. Whereas previous editions had this material separated out as boxes, here we integrated it into the main body of the text at the points where we felt it was most relevant and labeled them as Applications. Examples of these sections include caring for cocaine-exposed babies (Chapter 5), using picture-book reading to encourage language development (Chapter 11), and controlling gang violence (Chapter 16).

"Development in Context" Sections In addition to describing the influences of contextual factors throughout the text, we also include more detailed discussions in separate sections labeled "Development in Family Context" (e.g., growing up in a single-parent household, in Chapter 15), "Development in School Context" (e.g., do schools depress adolescents' self-concept, in Chapter 13), and "Development in Cultural Context" (e.g., the effects of exposure to real-life violence, in Chapter 14). Like the Applications sections, these are integrated into the body of the text but are denoted by special headings and icons.

✓ ***"To Recap" Sections*** At the end of each major section in a chapter, a brief summary of the material is presented. This organization encourages students to pause and reflect on what they have just read and helps set the stage for the sections that follow. Feedback from the previous editions indicated that students found these sections very helpful.

Visual Summaries Each chapter ends with a summary of the major points and issues. Using a visual layout, much like a flow chart, these summaries help students organize and review the chapter's material.

Running Glossary Bold-faced glossary items in the text highlight terms of continuing importance to students. These items are defined in the margin on the same page, as well as at the end of the book, providing a convenient guide for reviewing the material.

Illustration Program We reworked many of the figures and drawings from the previous edition to create new, effective illustrations in a full-color format. We also carefully selected many color photos that depict situations and events described in the text, along with some that illustrate laboratory techniques and other research methods.

Supplementary Materials

Accompanying the text is a full package of materials to support student learning and classroom teaching. The package includes the following:

The Student Study Guide contains chapter outlines, learning objectives, key terms, application exercises, critical thinking exercises, self-test questions, and practice exams. The study guide was again prepared by Alastair Younger of the University of Ottawa.

The Instructor's Resource Guide contains guidelines for the first-time instructor, chapter outlines, learning objectives, key terms, lecture topics, discussion questions, in-class and out-of-class activities, supplemental readings, videoguide, and media materials. It was prepared by Susan Siaw of the California State Polytechnic University, Pomona.

The Test Bank provides approximately 120 questions for each chapter, keyed to the text in a multiple-choice, true/false, and essay format. Each question notes the text page on which the answer can be found, and whether the question is factual or conceptual.

The Computerized Test Bank is available in IBM and Macintosh versions.

Overhead Transparencies present approximately 100 figures and tables from the text.

Video Library Instructor's can choose from a variety of videos and clips for class presentation from the Child Psychology Video Library. Please contact your local Wiley representative for more details about the different video options.

Web Site Using the Vasta Web site, located at http://www.wiley.com/college/vasta, students will be able to sample the study guide, and instructors can download the text supplements directly to their computers.

Ross Vasta
Marshall M. Haith
Scott A. Miller

Acknowledgments

A project of this size requires the participation of many people. We would like to thank the helpful staff at Wiley, especially Ellen Schatz, for all their advice and assistance. We are especially grateful to Alastair Younger, who prepared the Visual Summaries, and to Beverly Peavler, who helped create the vignettes. Thanks also to M. Jeffrey Farrar for his input on Chapter 11.

We would like to acknowledge the contributions of the following reviewers, whose many comments and suggestions were extremely helpful in preparing this revision of the text.

Linda Baker
University of Maryland, Baltimore County

Marie T. Balaban
John Hopkins University

Byron Barrington
University of Wisconsin-Marathon County

Sarah Bengston
Augustana College

Cynthia Berg
University of Utah

Rebecca Bigler
University of Wisconsin-Madison

Theodore Bosack
Providence College

Kristine Brady
Rider University

Stewart Cohen
University of Rhode Island

Jodi Compton
Framingham State University

K. Laurie Dickson
Northern Arizona University

Shelly Drazen
SUNY Binghamton

Shirlee Fenwick
Augustana College

Barry Ghoulson
University of Memphis

Yolanda Harper
University of Tulsa

Yvette R. Harris
Miami University

Melissa Heston
University of Northern Iowa

Kenneth I. Hoving
University of Oklahoma

Janice Kennedy
Georgia Southern University

Katherine Kipp
University of Georgia

Gerald Larson
Kent State University

Gary Levy
University of Wyoming

Pamela Ludeman
Framingham State University

Patricia McKane
Augustana College

Tammy A. Marche
University of Saskatchewan

Carolyn Mebert
University of New Hampshire

Morton J. Mendelson
McGill University

Derek Montgomery
Bradley University

Lynn Okagaki
Purdue University

Jeff Parker
Pennsylvania State University

Catherine Raeff
Indiana University of Pennsylvania

Jane Rysberg
California State University, Chico

Greg Simpson
University of Kansas

Kathy Stansbury
University of New Mexico

Laura Thompson
New Mexico State University

Beth Wildman
Kent State University

Martha Zlokovich
Southeast Missouri State University

We would also like to thank the following reviewers for their expert reviews of the cross-cultural coverage in the third edition and for their many suggestions.

Xinyin Chen
University of Western Ontario

Catherine Raeff
Indiana University of Pennsylvania

Marite Rodriguez-Haynes
Clarion University

We would like to thank the following consultants for their suggestions and feedback on the video selections to accompany the text.

Michelle Boyer
Middle Tennessee State University

Kristine Brady
Rider University

A group of students at Nassau Community College participated in a focus group to help us develop the design and pedagogy of the third edition, and we thank them for their time and feedback.

Amy Brooks
Olivia Figueras
Marianne Gobek-Craven
Linda Machado
Shaun Smith

We would also like to thank the following reviewers of the previous editions of this text.

Brian P. Ackerman
University of Delaware

Karen Bauer
University of Delaware

Dan Bellack
College of Charleston

Dana Birnbaum
University of Maine

Fredda Blanchard-Fields
Louisiana State University

Cathryn L. Booth
University of Washington

Theodore Bosack
Providence College

Gordon F. Brown
Pasadena City College

Harriet Budd

Roger V. Burton
SUNY at Buffalo

Bruce D. Carter
Syracuse University

Stephen J. Ceci
Cornell University

Ed Cornell
University of Alberta

James Dannemiller
University of Wisconsin-Madison

Beverly D. Eckhardt
Albuquerque Technical Institute

Melissa Faber
University of Toledo

Beverly I. Fagot
University of Oregon

Mary Ann Fischer
Indiana University-Northwest

Katherine W. Gibbs
University of California, Riverside

Gail S. Goodman
University of California, Davis

Terry R. Greene
Franklin & Marshall College

Vernon Hall
Syracuse University

William S. Hall
University of Maryland at College Park

Vernon Haynes
Youngstown University

Erika Hoff-Ginsburg
University of Wisconsin-Parkside

Marsha Ironsmith
East Carolina University

Jane Jakoubek
Luther College

Boaz Kahana
Cleveland State University

Kenneth Kallio
SUNY Geneseo

Christine Kenitzer
Texas Tech University

Wallace Kennedy
Florida State University

Marguerite D. Kermis
Canisius College

Elizabeth Lemerise
Western Kentucky University

Gary Levy
University of Wyoming

Angeline Lillard
University of San Francisco

Barbara Manning
University of Nebraska-Omaha

John C. Masters
Vanderbilt University

Kevin MacDonald
California State University, Long Beach

Robert G. McGinnis
Ancilla College

Margie McMahan
Cameron University

Richard Metzger
Mercer University

Barbar Moely
Tulane University

Ernst L. Moerk
California State University, Fresno

Derek Montgomery
Bradley University

Lisa Oakes
University of Iowa

Cynthia O'Dell
Indiana University

Vicky Phares
University of South Florida

Harvey A. Pines
Canisius College

Dina Raval
Towson State University

D. Dean Richards
University of California, Los Angeles

William L. Roberts
York University

Marite Rodriguez-Haynes
Clarion University

Karl Rosengren
University of Illinois

Nicholas R. Santilli
John Carroll University

Ellin Scholnick
University of Maryland

Frederick M. Schwantes
Northern Illinois University

Gayle Scroggs
Cayuga Community College

Kathleen Sexton-Radek
Elmhurst College

Harriet Shaklee
University of Iowa

Cecilia Shore
Miami University

Susan Siaw
California Polytechnic State University

Robert S. Sigeler
Carnegie Mellon University

Gregory Simpson
University of Kansas

Frank J. Sinkavich
York College of Pennsylvania

Rita Smith
Millersvile University of Pennsylvania

Thomoas R. Sommerkamp
Central Missouri State College

Debra Cowart Steckler
Mary Washington University

Nanci Stewart Woods
Austin Peay State University

Katherin Van Giffen
California State University, Long Beach

Diane N. Villwock
Moorehead State University

Leonard Volenski
Seton Hall University

Amye Warren-Leubecker
University of Tennessee at Chattanooga

Alastair Younger
University of Ottawa

About the Authors

Ross Vasta

is Distinguished Professor of Psychology at the State University of New York at Brockport. He received his undergraduate degree from Dartmouth College in 1969 and his Ph.D. in clinical and developmental psychology from the State University of New York at Stony Brook in 1974. He is a Fellow in the American Psychological Society and the American Psychological Association (Division 7). In 1987 he was awarded the SUNY Chancellor's Award for Excellence in Teaching. His previous books include *Studying Children: An Introduction to Research Methods, Strategies and Techniques of Child Study,* and *Six Theories of Child Development.* He is currently editor of the annual series *Annals of Child Development.*

Marshall M. Haith

is Professor of Psychology at the University of Denver. He earned his B.A. in 1959 from the University of Missouri and received his masters degree and Ph.D. from the University of California, Los Angeles, in 1964. After completing postdoctoral work at Yale University, he held positions at Harvard University, University of Geneva, and Rene Descartes University in Paris. He has been a Guggenheim Fellow and a Fellow at the Center for Advanced Study in the Behavioral Sciences. He has previously authored *Day Care and Intervention Programs for Infants Under Two Years of Age* and *Rules That Babies Look By: The Organization of Newborn Visual Activity.* Along with J.J. Campos, he edited Volume 2 of Mussen's *Handbook of Child Psychology.* His research interests include infant perception, the formation of expectations in early infancy, and the development of information-processing skills.

Scott A. Miller

is Professor of Psychology at the University of Florida. After completing his undergraduate work at Stanford University in 1966, he entered the Institute of Child Development at the University of Minnesota, where he earned his Ph.D. in 1971. His initial appointment was at the University of Michigan. He is a Fellow in the American Psychological Association (Division 7). He has previously authored *Developmental Research Methods,* 2nd edition, and coauthored (with John Flavell and Patricia Miller) *Cognitive Development,* 3rd edition. His research has been in the cognitive area, focusing on Piaget's work, children's understanding of logical necessity, theory of mind, and parents' beliefs about children.

Brief Contents

Contents

7 Sensory and Perceptual Development 195

8 Cognitive Development: The Piagetian Approach 241

10 Cognitive Development: The Intelligence-Test Approach 345

11 Language Development 395

15 Gender-Role Development and Sex Differences 571

16 Peer Relations 613

Chapter 1

Introduction and Perspective

This book presents the modern science of child psychology. In it, we trace the growing child's development from the embryo's earliest beginnings in the mother's womb to the child's eventual ascent into adolescence. We also describe the many factors that affect children's development, as well as how researchers go about the work of identifying them.

Attempts to explain children's development go as far back as history can trace. But child psychology as a science is only about 100 years old. What distinguishes our efforts during this past century is psychologists' use of the scientific method. *This approach involves rules that specify, for example, how research evidence should be gathered, how it may be analyzed, and what sorts of conclusions researchers may draw from their findings. Scientists have used this method to study an endless number of phenomena, from stars to starfish. In this book, we examine how they use it to study children.*

At first glance, understanding child development may not appear to be very difficult. Certainly the typical behaviors of infants and young children–including their physical abilities, their interactions with others, and even the ways they think–are simpler than those same behaviors in adults. But it is a mistake to conclude that the processes *involved are simple. Psychologists have learned that human development is a complex and intricate puzzle, and unraveling its mysteries has proved to be a major challenge. Since the methods of science were first applied to the study of children 100 years ago, we have learned a great deal. Yet the more we learn, the more apparent it becomes that we have only scratched the surface.*

Developmental Psychology

To begin, it is important to understand exactly what psychology is and what psychologists study. Psychology is the scientific study of behavior. The behavior that most psychologists study is human behavior. But any species—from mice to mynah birds to monkeys—can be examined legitimately from a psychological (and developmental) perspective.

Developmental psychology The branch of psychology devoted to the study of changes in behavior and abilities over the course of development.

Developmental psychology, one of the largest of psychology's many subfields, is concerned with *the changes in behavior and abilities that occur as development proceeds.* Developmental researchers examine both what the changes are and why they occur. To put it another way, developmental research has two basic goals. One is *description*—to identify children's behavior at each point in their development. This involves such questions as, When do babies begin to detect colors? What are the typical mathematical abilities of a 5-year-old? or How do sixth graders usually resolve conflicts with their peers? The second goal is *explanation*—determining the causes and processes that produce changes in behavior from one point to the next. This involves examining the effects of such factors as the genes children inherit from their parents, the biological characteristics of the human brain, the physical and social environment in which children live, and the types of experiences they encounter.

Developmental psychologists study behavior changes at all phases of the life cycle. Most, though, have focused on the childhood period, ending at adolescence. For this reason, *developmental psychology* and *child psychology* have traditionally referred to the same body of scientific knowledge. That situation has changed somewhat in recent years as increasing research is being directed toward issues of adulthood and old age. This book, however, focuses on the traditional early period (and so we have chosen the title *Child Psychology*).

Why Study Children?

If developmental psychologists can study any species of animal and any period in the life cycle, why has so much of their research traditionally concentrated on humans during the childhood years? We have at least five answers to this question.

Period of Rapid Development Because developmental researchers are interested in studying change, it makes sense for them to focus on a period when much change occurs. During the first part of the life of most species, more developmental changes take place than during any other period. In humans, changes involving physical growth, social interactions, the acquisition of language, memory abilities, and virtually all other areas of development are greatest during childhood.

Long-Term Influences Another important reason for studying children is that the events and experiences of the early years strongly affect an individual's later development. As the poet Wordsworth once noted (and many psychologists have since reiterated), "The child is father to the man." Almost all psychological theories suggest that who we are today depends very much on our development and experiences as children.

Insight into Complex Adult Processes Not all psychologists are primarily concerned with early development. But even researchers who are attempting to understand complex adult behaviors often find it useful to examine those behaviors during periods when they are not so complex. For example, humans are capable of sophisticated communication because our languages follow systems of rules. But determining what these rules are has proved very difficult for researchers.

One approach to this problem is to study our language system as it is being acquired. Thus in language development, as well as in many other areas, the growing child is a "showcase" of developing skills and abilities, and researchers interested in different aspects of human development have taken advantage of this fact to help them understand adult behavior.

Real World Applications Developmental psychologists often conduct their research in laboratory settings, where they investigate theoretical questions regarding basic psychological processes. Nevertheless, the products of this research can sometimes benefit children with real world problems, such as poverty, illiteracy, drugs, and crime. Legislators and other policy makers often turn to psychologists to provide them with usable knowledge regarding the effects of these problems on children and possible ways to treat them (Fisher & Lerner, 1994; Zigler & Finn-Stevenson, 1992). Developmental research is also being extended to such areas as the effects of day care, classroom teaching methods, and parental disciplinary techniques, among others. Simply put, one reason we study children is to make their lives better.

Children's fascinating behavior and inherent appeal undoubtedly contribute to their being of great interest to developmental researchers.

Interesting Subject Matter A final and important reason so many developmental psychologists have directed their efforts toward understanding children is that the human child is an intriguing and wondrous creature. When we consider that children have attracted attention from artists, writers, and scholars in many other fields of study, it is perhaps not surprising that psychologists, too, have found this subject matter appealing. Our own interest in pursuing this area of science reflects our personal love of children and our fascination with their behavior and development.

✓ To Recap...

Developmental psychologists use the scientific method to study changes in behavior and abilities. The two basic goals of their research are to describe children's behaviors at each point in development and to explain the changes that occur from one point to the next. Although any species at any age level is legitimate subject matter for developmental psychology, most research has involved children, for five reasons: childhood is a period of rapid development; early experiences have long-term effects; complex processes are easier to understand as they are forming; knowledge of basic processes can help solve some of the problems of childhood; and children are inherently interesting to study.

Historical Views of Childhood

Modern psychology considers childhood an extremely important period of human development. Western culture views children as vulnerable and requiring a great deal of attention, care, and shelter from harm. Many laws are designed to protect children from dangerous toys, dangerous substances, and even dangerous parents. Our belief that all children deserve a free public education and that they should remain in school until adolescence similarly reflects the view that childhood is a special and important time.

In contrast to earlier historical periods, children today are viewed as physically and psychologically vulnerable, and are accorded a special place in Western society.

But these attitudes toward children reflect a relatively recent conception of early development (Greenleaf, 1978; Hart, 1991). To understand our modern view of the child, it is helpful to examine briefly some views of childhood from earlier points in history. Because child psychology is a science whose roots are in Western culture, this survey will focus on that tradition. In the remainder of the text, however, we consider contemporary aspects of child development in cultures throughout the world.

Ancient Greece and Rome

The Greek and Roman civilizations, which extended from about 600 B.C. to about A.D. 400, are usually regarded as periods of great enlightenment. Yet the status of children during these times was hardly enviable.

Although such great Greek thinkers as Plato and Aristotle wrote of the importance of education, they also defended practices that today would seem unthinkable. *Infanticide*, the killing of newborns, was routine and viewed as an appropriate way to deal with babies who were illegitimate, unhealthy, or simply unwanted (Breiner, 1990; Langer, 1974).

Severe punishment and the sexual exploitation of children were neither uncommon nor considered wrong or cruel. The Romans, for example, bought and sold children for various purposes, including domestic work and service in brothels for the sexual pleasure of adults (Mounteer, 1987). And in neighboring Carthage, children were killed and buried in the foundations of public buildings as sacrifices to the gods (Weld, 1968). So although the ancient world recognized the importance of the childhood years, it clearly did not display the caring and protective attitudes toward children that exist today.

The Medieval and Renaissance Periods

Following the collapse of the Roman Empire, the Catholic Church attempted to improve the lives of children by promoting an image of them as pure and innocent. The Church took a strong stand against infanticide and offered parents of unwanted children the alternative of shipping them away to convents and monasteries—an arrangement that benefited both parties. (The Church, however, remained generally powerless in preventing the killing of twins, who were considered to be the obvious products of adultery.) Although educational training during this period reached one of its lowest levels in recorded history, the Church did provide simple reading and writing instruction to children involved in religious studies (Sommerville, 1982).

As the medieval period progressed, the view of childhood continued to improve. In the 12th century, for example, December 6 was set aside to honor the patron saint of all children, St. Nicholas. That holiday was later moved to coincide with the celebration of the birth of Christ and became the modern Christmas.

Unfortunately, the abuse and exploitation of children remained commonplace during this period of history. It has even been suggested that childhood as we know it did not exist during the Middle Ages. Once children were old enough to participate in household and community labor (at about the age of 7), they became a part of the larger society and were, according to some historians, treated simply as less experienced adults (Aries, 1962; McCoy, 1988). Although not all scholars agree entirely with this theory, there is little doubt that children of the medieval period had a very difficult life (Kroll, 1977; Pollock, 1983).

The Renaissance began early in the 14th century and extended into the 17th. It was marked by a revival of interest in Greco-Roman art, literature, and philosophy, which in turn prompted a general rebirth of Western civilization. This era also brought an increased concern for the welfare of children. In Florence, Italy—generally considered the birthplace of the Renaissance—charitable institutions known as *foundling homes* were set up by wealthy individuals to take in sick, lost, and unwanted children. Foundling homes, which eventually spread throughout western Europe, were significant in that they represented a new and growing belief that society had some responsibility for the care and protection of its youngsters (Trexler, 1973).

The Renaissance also saw the reemergence of scientific investigation in such fields as astronomy, medicine, and physics. The science of psychology did not yet exist, so the study of human development was primarily the concern of philosophers and religious scholars. Some early scientific thinkers, such as Galileo, believed that physical and biological mechanisms were the basis for understanding human behavior. The Church, however, disagreed with any nonspiritual explanations of behavior and, as it was a powerful social force at the time, was effective in discouraging their study.

The Reformation and the Puritans

Throughout the medieval period and much of the Renaissance, "the Church" referred to the Roman Catholic Church. But early in the 16th century, a variety of Protestant groups broke away. From the perspective of child development, the most important of these groups was the Puritans, led by John Calvin (1509–1564).

The Puritans were perhaps the first to offer a comprehensive model of child development. In many ways, their view was a rejection of the earlier belief in the child's purity. Instead of seeing them as innocents, Calvin argued that children are born with original sin and are naturally inclined toward evil unless given the proper guidance and instruction (Pollock, 1987). Yet he also believed that children have a great capacity for learning at an early age and that parents therefore have the opportunity (and the obligation) to train them properly.

The Puritans took child rearing very seriously. They were the first to write manuals to aid parents in this task. The Calvinist approach was to encourage the child to become independent and self-reliant and, most of all, to develop self-control. Because sin and evil were seen as ever-present problems, it was crucial that the child learn to resist temptations early and effectively.

The Puritans also put great emphasis on education, particularly on reading (Moran & Vinovskis, 1985), and were the first to write books specifically for children. Although most of the books had religious or moral themes, a few were somewhat entertaining in an attempt to make the task of learning a bit more pleasant.

Descartes's Dualistic Model

To understand the views of child development that emerged in the 17th century and beyond, we must take a short side trip to discuss the contribution of René Descartes (1596–1650). Descartes, a French mathematician and philosopher, was not specifically interested in child development, but his model of human behavior laid the groundwork for what would eventually become the science of psychology.

The essence of Descartes's philosophy is that the mind and the body are separate from each other. The human mind, he argued, is God given and therefore does not have a material form or follow the physical laws of nature. Its function is to reason and make decisions and then carry out these decisions by commanding the body—which is earthly and physical—to perform whatever is required.

Descartes's description of the human mind as nonphysical and dominant over people's material bodies was consistent with the Church's views, and so his ideas met with little religious opposition. This was important for science in general—and eventually for psychology—because it allowed Descartes to develop a theoretical model of the human body that was based solely on mechanical and physical principles.

In essence, then, Descartes divided the investigation of human behavior into two separate realms—one concerned with the psychological functioning of the mind and the other with the physical workings of the body. The concept that the mind exists independently of the body, referred to as **Cartesian dualism**, remains a matter of debate even today. But the historical importance of Descartes's mind–body division was that it removed the scientific investigation of the body from the scrutiny of the Church, thus permitting researchers to pursue whatever questions they saw fit to study. This new view of human behavior ushered in the modern study of psychology.

Cartesian dualism
René Descartes's idea that the mind and body are separate, which helped clear the way for the scientific study of human development.

✓ To Recap...

The concept of childhood has changed dramatically over time. The ancient Greeks and Romans viewed children largely as property that was both exchangeable and expendable. During the medieval period, the Church helped elevate the image of children by stressing their purity and innocence. At the same time, the Church hindered scientific study, which reemerged as an area of interest during the Renaissance, by permitting only religious explanations of human behavior. The Puritans, who arose out of the Reformation, constructed the first comprehensive model of child development. This model was based on the idea of the child's inherent evil and inclination toward sin. René Descartes cleared the way for the scientific study of human behavior by proposing a dualistic system in which the nonphysical mind governs the mechanical functioning of the physical body.

Early Theorists

Descartes's mind–body distinction fueled debate over the nature of human development, and several very different points of view emerged. Three early scholars—John Locke, Jean-Jacques Rousseau, and Charles Darwin—offered theories of human behavior that are the direct ancestors of the three major theoretical traditions found in child psychology today. These three modern traditions include one model that focuses on the influence of the child's environment, a second that emphasizes the role of the child's cognitive development, and a third that is most concerned with the evolutionary origins of behavior.

JohnLocke, a 17th-century British philosopher, foreshadowed later environmentalists by proposing that a newborn's mind was like a blank sheet of paper on which environment and experiences wrote the script of the child's life.

John Locke (1632–1704)

In 17th-century England, Descartes's theory was taken up by a group of philosophers. The most famous of these, John Locke, was a physician as well as a leading political figure of the time. Locke espoused the belief that "all men are created equal" in the eyes of the law. This principle eventually became the cornerstone of the new government developed by the colonists in America. It also found its way into Locke's views regarding human development.

According to Locke's theory, all children are created (born) equal, and the mind of a newborn infant is like a piece of white paper—a **tabula rasa** ("blank slate"). All knowledge comes to the child only through experience and learning. Children are therefore neither innately good nor innately evil; they are simply the products of their environment and upbringing. This environmentalist point of view also means that any child theoretically is capable of becoming anything—a surgeon, an actor, or a skilled artisan—if given the proper rearing and training. Similarly, the wrong environment can produce a scoundrel, beggar, or thief.

Tabula rasa
Latin phrase, meaning "blank slate," used to describe the newborn's mind as entirely empty of inborn abilities, interests, or ideas.

Locke's writings were not all scholarly. He also offered advice to parents on the best methods for raising their children. Although he stressed the use of rewards and punishments, Locke did not favor material rewards (e.g., candy and toys) or physical punishment. Discipline, he believed, should involve praise for appropriate behaviors and scolding for inappropriate behaviors. Locke also discussed the importance of stimulating children to begin learning at a very early age. Locke's ideas gained wide acceptance among British and European scholars as well as the general public. But in less than 100 years, this strong environmentalist model was to be replaced by a very different conception of the child.

Jean-Jacques Rousseau (1712–1778)

Jean-Jacques Rousseau was born in Switzerland but spent most of his life in France, where he became the leading philosopher of his day. He is considered the father of French romanticism, a movement in which artists and writers emphasized themes of sentimentality, naturalness, and innocence. These ideas were reflected in Rousseau's conception of the child.

Jean Jacques Rousseau, an 18th-century French philosopher, described his nativistic views of human development in *Émile*, a novel about the growth and upbringing of a young French boy.

Rousseau's views on development are presented in his well-known novel *Émile* (1762), in which he describes the care and tutoring of a male child from infancy to young adulthood. Using this literary vehicle, Rousseau outlined his views of human development and offered suggestions on the most appropriate methods of child rearing and education (Mitzenheim, 1985).

In contrast to Locke, Rousseau believed that children are born with knowledge and ideas, which unfold naturally with age. Development, in this view, follows a predictable series of stages that are guided by an inborn timetable. The child's innate knowledge includes such things as the principles of justice and fairness and, above all, a sense of conscience. In effect, Rousseau returned to the theme of the inborn goodness and purity of the child. Rousseau also believed that whatever knowledge the child does not possess innately is acquired gradually from interactions with the environment, guided by the child's own interests and level of development. Thus the wisest approach to child rearing is not to instruct children formally, but to have them learn through a process of exploration and discovery. By clearly emphasizing innate processes as the driving forces in human development, Rousseau's theory contrasted with the environmentalistic ideas of Locke and would today be referred to as **nativism**.

Rousseau further believed that the development of the child repeats the cultural history of the human race. Émile, he said, was a *noble savage*, much as the primitive cave dwellers were: they were noble because they possessed an innate goodness that characterizes all humans; they were savage because their ideas were simple and unsophisticated.

Rousseau's suggestions for educating Émile contain at least three ideas that are promoted by many educators today. First, children should be exposed to a new body of knowledge only after they display a cognitive "readiness" to learn it. Second, children learn best when they are allowed to acquire ideas or information through their own discovery process. Finally, both education and child rearing should encourage a permissive style that allows children to follow their own natural inclinations (Thomas, 1979).

Nativism
The theory that human development results principally from inborn processes that guide the emergence of behaviors in a predictable manner.

Rousseau's ideas had a major impact in Europe, and his nativistic view of development was hailed by both scientific and political writers. His ideas, like Locke's, were both revolutionary and ahead of their time. And, as we will see, they would reappear 200 years later in the work of another Swiss theorist, Jean Piaget.

Charles Darwin (1809–1882)

The third major ancestor of modern developmental thought was the English biologist Charles Darwin. Although best known for his theory of evolution, presented in *The Origin of Species* (1859), Darwin was also a keen observer of child development. Indeed, his detailed record of the growth and behavior of his infant son, "Doddy," was one of the first developmental studies (Darwin, 1877).

Charles Darwin's theory of evolution, developed in the mid-19th century, was quickly adopted by the early developmental psychologists and laid the foundation for the modern fields of ethology and sociobiology.

Darwin's evolutionary theory begins with the assumption that individual members of a species vary in many characteristics, so that some are faster, some are stronger, some are lighter, and so on. A second assumption is that most species produce more offspring than their environment can support, which means that the individual members must compete for survival. Depending on the environment, some variations may increase the chances for survival, such as providing better ways of avoiding danger or acquiring food. If so, individuals possessing these traits are more likely to survive and so pass them along to future generations. Through this process, which Darwin called **natural selection**, the species continually evolves to evermore adaptive forms. At the same time, less useful variations gradually disappear. The evolutionary model thus suggests that some of the present-day behaviors of humans (or of any other animal) had their origins countless years ago, when they were important for the survival of an earlier form of our species.

Natural selection
An evolutionary process proposed by Charles Darwin in which characteristics of an individual that increase its chances of survival are more likely to be passed along to future generations.

Darwin's theory of evolution did not directly address the issue of child development, but his views led other biologists of the time, such as Ernst Haeckel, to propose the principle of **recapitulation** (Haeckel, 1906/1977). According to this theoretical notion, the development of the individual—that is, *ontogeny*—proceeds through stages that parallel the development of the entire species—that is, *phylogeny*. This principle is often stated as "ontogeny recapitulates phylogeny." As applied to our species, it means that human development—beginning with its earliest embryonic and prenatal forms and continuing with the physical, motor, and social development of the growing child—follows a progression similar to that which evolved through the various prehuman species (Wertheimer, 1985).

Recapitulation theory
An early biological notion, later adopted by psychologist G. Stanley Hall, that the development of the individual repeats the development of the species.

Although the recapitulation theory is no longer scientifically supported, the idea that the child's development repeats that of the species had great appeal for some early developmentalists. And by providing a theory that both explained the developing behaviors observed by Rousseau and others and served as a framework for future research on human development, Darwin's writings helped launch the scientific study of the child (Charlesworth, 1992).

✓ To Recap...

Even before psychology emerged as a discipline, three early scholars presented important models of human development. John Locke based his approach on the strict environmentalist position that all knowledge is acquired through experience. Jean-Jacques Rousseau proposed a nativistic model in which development unfolds according to inborn processes. Charles Darwin's theory of evolution suggested that many human behaviors have their origins in the past, when they were valuable for our ancestors' survival.

Pioneers of Child Psychology

The belief that the development of the child is related to the evolution of the species gave birth to the science of developmental psychology. But the evolutionary perspective was soon joined by other theoretical models as child development quickly became the focus of increasing amounts of scientific debate and research. Only a few of the individuals who contributed to the rise of this movement are discussed here. Our purpose is not to provide a detailed history of child study, but to point out the origins of some important ideas and controversies that remain a part of modern developmental science.

G. Stanley Hall (1846–1924)

Referred to as the father of child psychology, G. Stanley Hall is credited with founding the field of developmental psychology (Appley, 1986). He conducted and published the first systematic studies of children in the United States.

Hall received his Ph.D. from Harvard in 1878 under the direction of the famous psychologist William James. He spent the next 2 years working in Germany, where he became interested in a child study project being conducted in Berlin. On his return to the United States, Hall administered questionnaires to all the first-grade children in the Boston school district to determine precisely what sorts of everyday knowledge American children usually possessed when they began school. The questions included such items as, What season is it? Where are your elbows? and Where does butter come from? Hall published the results of this research in 1883 under the title "The Contents of Children's Minds." Although interesting, the findings contained nothing particularly new or surprising.

In 1891, he began a larger project designed to gather data on children of all ages and from all regions of the country. Once again Hall used questionnaires, but this time he sent them to parents, teachers, and other adults who had frequent contact with children. Unfortunately, Hall's research was not well conceived. The information that poured in from these questionnaires took many forms, as the respondents approached the questions in a wide variety of ways. In the end, Hall was left with a vast accumulation of data that were difficult to interpret and impossible to summarize (White, 1992).

Hall's attempts to make a theoretical contribution to psychology were also not particularly successful. Excited by Darwin's writings, he adopted the view that children's development recapitulates the evolution of the species. Hall also felt that education and child rearing should encourage the "natural" tendencies of the child that reflect the behavior and development of earlier forms of the species. He was especially interested in the period of adolescence, which he believed marked the end of biological recapitulation and the first opportunity for the child to develop individual talents and abilities (Hall, 1904).

By the turn of the century, however, advances in biological research had made it clear that no simple recapitulation process exists in human development

Some of the pioneers of psychology invited by G. Stanley Hall to Clark University in 1909. Hall is seated front center, and Sigmund Freud is seated front left.

(Coleman, 1971). Furthermore, many American psychologists were beginning to favor the more environmentalist view that children acquire knowledge and skills through experience and that their behavior can be best explained by learning processes (Cairns, 1998).

Although neither his research nor his theoretical ideas ultimately had much impact, Hall did make some lasting contributions to the field (Hilgard, 1987; Ross, 1972). As an educator at Clark University in Worcester, Massachusetts, Hall trained the first generation of developmental researchers. He also established several scientific journals for reporting the findings of child development research, and he founded and became the first president of the American Psychological Association. Finally, a more indirect contribution was his invitation to Sigmund Freud to present a series of lectures in the United States—an event that, as we will see, led to the introduction of psychoanalytic theory into American psychology.

John B. Watson (1878–1958)

The theoretical idea that is generally shared by the scientists of a given period is referred to as its **Zeitgeist**—a German term meaning "the spirit of the times." When a science is very young, the Zeitgeist can change dramatically from one time to the next. Major shifts in thinking regarding one of the most basic issues of human development—what causes changes in behavior in growing children—had already occurred several times in the centuries before the science of developmental psychology emerged in the mid-1800s. We saw that the Zeitgeist of the 17th century was Locke's environmentalist view of human development. This model was replaced first by Rousseau's nativistic explanation and then by the evolutionary theories of Darwin and Hall. As the 20th century dawned, the pendulum began to swing away from biological interpretations of development and back toward the environmentalist position.

Zeitgeist
The spirit of the times, or the ideas shared by most scientists during a given period.

John B. Watson was the first major psychologist to adopt Locke's belief that human behavior can be understood principally in terms of experiences and learn-

Behaviorism
A theory of psychology, first advanced by John B. Watson, that human development results primarily from conditioning and learning processes.

ing. But his new approach, which he called **behaviorism**, also differed radically regarding what psychologists should study and which methods of investigation they should use (Horowitz, 1992).

Watson received his Ph.D. in 1903 from the University of Chicago. His early career was devoted to the study of animal psychology. Descartes's dualism was very evident among psychologists at this time. Some, like Watson, studied the physiological workings of the body. But many were exclusively concerned with the psychological functioning of the human mind and, in particular, with consciousness and such issues as how individual perceptions are combined to form ideas and thoughts. The most common research method was *introspection*, which involved engaging research participants in a task and then having them try to look inward and report on the processes occurring in their minds.

Watson found this approach unsatisfactory for a number of reasons. First, little agreement was ever found across participants' descriptions of their internal experiences. Further, Watson felt strongly that psychology should follow the example of the other natural sciences and deal only with objective, observable subject matter—in this case, observable behavior. Finally, his interest in animal psychology led him to reject any method that could not also be used to study other species.

These ideas were radical for the time, but Watson's persuasive writing style, combined with a bit of luck, soon propelled behaviorism into the forefront of psychological theory (Cohen, 1979). Watson joined the psychology faculty at Johns Hopkins University in 1908. Within several years he became chairman of the prestigious psychology department, president of the American Psychological Association, and editor of *Psychological Review*, the most important journal in the field. Watson used these positions as platforms from which to market behaviorism to the scientific community.

The basic tenet of behaviorism is that changes in behavior result primarily from conditioning processes. Watson argued that learning occurs through the process of association, as described in the work of the Russian physiologist Ivan Pavlov (1849–1936). Pavlov had shown that any simple reflex can be conditioned to many different stimuli—for example, he conditioned dogs to salivate to the sound of a bell.

Conditioned reflex method
John B. Watson's name for the Pavlovian conditioning process in which reflexive responses can be conditioned to stimuli in the environment.

Watson believed that this simple conditioning process, which he called the **conditioned reflex method**, explained how human behavior changes over time. All human behavior, he argued, begins as simple reflexes. Then, through an association process like the one Pavlov described, various combinations of simple behaviors become conditioned to many stimuli in the environment. Language ("verbal behavior," to Watson), for example, begins as simple infant sounds that grow in complexity as they continue to be conditioned to the objects and events in the surrounding environment. Furthermore, as speech grows more and more sophisticated, it gradually develops a subvocal (silent) form, which we know as thinking, reasoning, and problem solving. Watson therefore believed that it was crucial for psychologists to study infants and young children—not simply to observe early physical changes, but to study the first steps in the conditioning process that produces complex human behavior.

The Pavlovian conditioning process that formed the core of Watson's behavioristic theory was straightforward and easy to understand. And it was this simplicity, along with Watson's demand for strict experimental methods, that led American psychologists of the time to embrace behaviorism as a major advance in scientific thinking. A new Zeitgeist had emerged.

In 1920, however, Watson was forced to resign from Johns Hopkins when an affair with a graduate student and a divorce from his wife created a scandal. He left academic life and began writing magazine articles and books for the general public about his behavioristic approach. *Psychological Care of the Infant and Child*, published in 1928, presented his views on child rearing, and it proved to be a very successful and influential book. Watson's suggestions to parents were based on an almost pure environmentalism—that is, the belief that no abilities or personality characteristics are inborn, so children are entirely the products of their upbringing and environment. This view had great appeal for many parents, who delighted in believing that their children had the potential to become great athletes, scientists, or Supreme Court justices, if only given the proper training.

Watson's career was brief, but his contributions to psychology were significant. His call for objective methods of study, in particular, brought early experimental psychology in line with the other natural sciences. Today, virtually all experimental psychology is based on the methods that Watson espoused, including the precise specification of experimental procedures and the emphasis on observable and measurable behaviors. However, Watson's strict environmentalist views and the major role he assigned to conditioned reflexes are no longer taken very seriously.

Sigmund Freud (1856–1939)

In 1909, as Watson was introducing behaviorism to the scientific world, another important event took place. G. Stanley Hall invited some of the most eminent psychologists of the day, including Sigmund Freud and several other European scholars, to Clark University to celebrate the institution's 20th anniversary (Hall and Freud are seen seated together on page 11). It was on this occasion that Freud, in a series of five lectures, first outlined his grand theory of psychological development. American psychologists were not immediately receptive to Freud's model, and it proved to be no obstacle to Watson's emerging behavioral movement. But the seeds of psychoanalytic thought had been planted in U.S. soil, and in time Freud's views would attract a good deal of attention both inside and outside psychology.

Freud spent most of his early life in Vienna, Austria, where he trained as a medical student. In 1885, bored with medical practice, he traveled to Paris to learn the technique of hypnosis from the French physician Charcot. During this time Freud began to develop many of his ideas regarding the powerful role of the unconscious. On his return to Vienna, Freud established a private practice and began refining both his theory and the methods of psychoanalysis.

Freud made two major contributions to psychology. His greatest impact was in the area of clinical psychology, where his model of personality and his techniques of psychoanalysis continue to represent a major school of thought in psychotherapy. His contribution to developmental psychology was his stage theory of psychosexual development. Although he spent very little time observing children directly, he used his patients' and his own recollections of childhood experiences to construct a comprehensive model of child development.

The central theme of Freudian developmental theory is that each child is born with a certain amount of sexual energy, called **libido**, which is biologically guided to certain locations on the body, called the **erogenous zones**, as the child grows. Sexual energy, in this model, refers simply to the ability to experience physical pleasure. The arrival of the libido at each location marks a new stage in the child's psychosexual development, and during that stage the child receives the greatest physical pleasure in that erogenous zone.

Freud's model was not purely biological, however. He firmly believed that children's experiences during each stage strongly affect their later development. Successful movement from stage to stage requires that children receive the proper

Libido
Sigmund Freud's term for the sexual energy that he believed is possessed by all children from birth and then moves to different locations on the body over the course of development.

Erogenous zones
According to Freud's theory of psychosexual development, the areas of the body where the libido resides during successive stages of development. The child seeks physical pleasure in the erogenous zone at which the libido is located.

amount of physical pleasure from each erogenous zone. Freud therefore cautioned parents not to frustrate children by being overly strict, but he warned that being too indulgent or permissive could cause problems as well. In other words, children should experience enough pleasure, but not too much. Unfortunately, both Freud's advice and his theoretical predictions were always rather vague as to how much pleasure was enough.

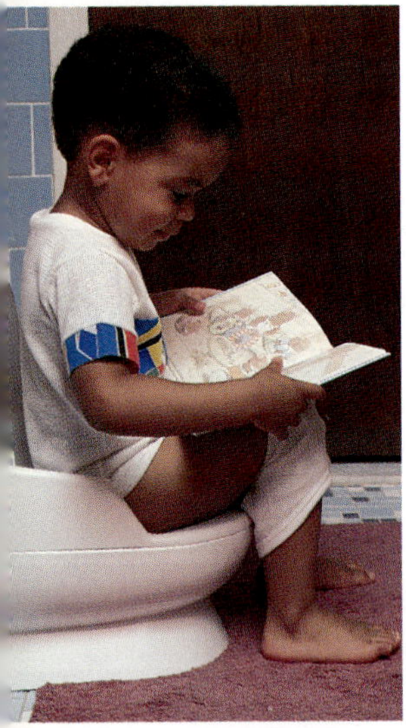

Freud proposed that, during the anal stage, successful toilet training is important to the child's psychosexual development.

According to the psychosexual model, human development unfolds in five stages. During the *oral stage*, from birth to about 18 months, the libido is located at the mouth. The infant's principal source of physical pleasure is sucking, and all objects tend to find their way into the child's mouth. When and how much infants are breast-fed and how they are eventually weaned are the events in this stage that, according to Freud, have the strongest long-term influence. The period from 18 months to 3 years marks the *anal stage*, in which the child attains physical pleasure first from having bowel movements and later from withholding them. Not surprisingly, positive toilet-training experiences are the major concern during this stage.

The most complex of Freud's stages is the *phallic stage*, which lasts roughly from age 3 to age 6 and the erogenous zone is the genital area. During this stage, according to Freud, children become sexually attracted to the parent of the opposite sex. But they soon experience feelings of conflict as they realize that the same-sex parent is a powerful rival. Children presumably resolve this conflict in two ways. First, they force their desires into the unconscious, a process called **repression**, which also wipes out their memory of these feelings. Then, they compensate for this loss by making a determined effort to adopt the characteristics of the same-sex parent, a process called **identification**.

Repression
Freud's term for the process through which desires or motivations are driven into the unconscious, as typically occurs during the phallic stage.

Identification
The Freudian process through which the child adopts the characteristics of the same-sex parent during the phallic stage.

The *latency stage* occurs in the middle and later childhood years, from age 6 to age 12. During this stage, the libido remains repressed and inactive. It reemerges at puberty in the *genital stage*, when once again the child develops an attraction toward the opposite sex. Now, however, it is more appropriately directed toward peers, rather than parents.

Freud's theory of child development is actually a theory of personality formation. It assumes that many aspects of the adult personality result from events during the childhood psychosexual stages. If the child's experiences during a stage are not what they should be, some portion of the libido will remain *fixated* in that erogenous zone, rather than moving on to the next one. For example, if a child is not given the appropriate amount of oral gratification during the first stage, the libido will remain partially fixated at the mouth. Later in life, this fixation will be manifested in the adult's continually seeking physical pleasure in this erogenous zone—perhaps by smoking, chewing on pencils, or having an unusual interest in kissing. Many everyday behaviors of this sort were explained by Freud as symptoms of early developmental difficulties.

Although Freud's theory had some influence on American developmentalists, they never fully accepted it, for several reasons. First, it is vague and its key elements cannot be scientifically verified or disproved. Furthermore, Freud's heavy reliance on unobservable mechanisms, such as unconscious motives, is not consistent with American psychology's belief that science should be based on measurable and verifiable observations.

In spite of its failings, though, Freud's theory of child development includes two fundamental concepts that are generally accepted today. The first is the rejection of both a purely nativistic and a strictly environmentalist explanation of human behavior. Freud was the first major developmentalist to argue for an **interactionist perspective**, which views both inborn processes and environmental factors as significant contributors to the child's development. Today almost all child psycholo-

Interactionist perspective
The theory that human development results from the combination of nature and nurture factors.

gists subscribe to an interactionist position. The second fundamental concept is Freud's suggestion that early experiences can have important effects on behavior in later life. Again, most contemporary developmentalists agree with this idea, although few would explain these effects in terms of unresolved childhood conflicts hidden in the adult's unconscious (Beier, 1991; Emde, 1992).

Perhaps a third positive outcome of Freud's theory is that it inspired a number of related models of development that have achieved somewhat greater acceptance in developmental psychology. One of these, proposed by Erik Erikson, is described shortly.

Arnold Gesell (1880–1961)

In science, the pendulum of philosophical thought swings back and forth. Just as scientists begin to accept a particular way of looking at things, someone seems to come along with an important criticism of that view or with new evidence that supports some earlier position. So when the Zeitgeist swings back toward a prior point of view, it is usually because of new research findings or a more complete theoretical explanation of the facts. Accordingly, when developmentalists began returning to the biological model of child development in the 1930s, it was not because they once again accepted recapitulation theory. Rather, they were persuaded to reconsider the nativistic viewpoint by the research and ideas of one of G. Stanley Hall's most successful students, Arnold Gesell.

Gesell completed his doctoral work at Clark University in 1906 and obtained a medical degree at Yale University. In 1911, he established the Yale Clinic of Child Development, where he spent almost 50 years studying and describing the development of the typical child.

Although he did not agree with Hall's view that human development mirrors the evolution of the species, Gesell did believe that development is guided primar-

Among Arnold Gesell's most important contributions to developmental psychology were his innovative research techniques, including an observation dome that permitted photographing the child unobtrusively from any angle.

ily by biological processes. He therefore felt that growth and the emergence of motor skills (crawling and sitting, for example) should follow very predictable patterns. In his scheme, the environment plays only a minor role, perhaps affecting the age at which certain skills appear but never affecting the sequence or pattern of development. The complex of biological mechanisms that guide development Gesell described simply as **maturation**. The resulting patterns of growth and development were as yet unknown, and Gesell set about to identify them.

Maturation
The biological processes assumed by some theorists to be primarily responsible for human development.

Using observational methods and hundreds of children of many different ages as research participants, Gesell conducted the first large-scale study to examine children's behavior in great detail. This research revealed a high degree of uniformity in children's development. They did not all develop at the same rate—some walked earlier and others later—but the pattern of development was very consistent. For example, almost all children walked before they ran, ran before they skipped, and skipped before they hopped. From his work, Gesell established statistical **norms**—a sort of developmental timetable that describes the usual order in which children display various early behaviors and the age range within which each behavior normally appears (Gesell & Thompson, 1938). These norms proved very valuable to physicians and parents as general guidelines for evaluating developmental progress—so much so that they continue to be revised and used today.

Norms
A timetable of age ranges indicating when normal growth and developmental milestones are typically reached.

To acquire this sort of descriptive information, Gesell did not rely on the outdated research methods of the past. In fact, the sophisticated research techniques he developed for observing and recording children's behavior are among his most important contributions to psychology (Thelen & Adolph, 1992). Gesell pioneered in the use of film cameras to record children's behavior. He also developed one-way viewing screens, and he constructed a photographic dome that allowed observations from all angles without disturbing the child under study.

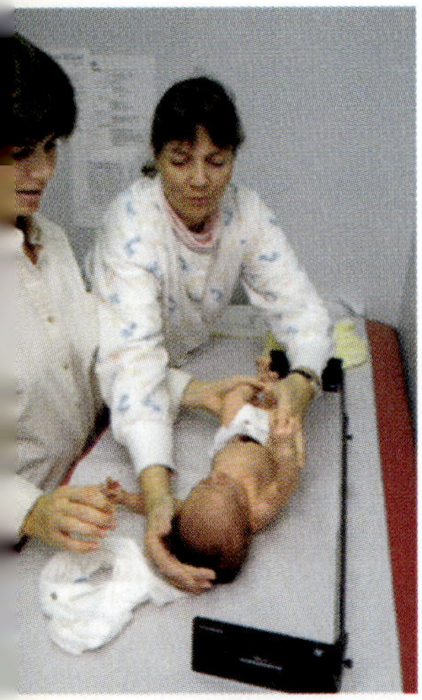

Gesell's method of comparing children's development to norms representing the average range of development continues to be used today.

Gesell wrote books containing advice for parents that could have been given by Rousseau 200 years earlier. He suggested, for instance, feeding babies only when they display signs of hunger and allowing them to sleep, play, and explore according to their own natural schedules. Parents should be patient, enjoying their children's current abilities and behaviors rather than trying to hurry them along toward more mature skills. Gesell did believe that parents need to include some limits and structure in the child's life, but he felt strongly that, if largely left alone, children will develop naturally and properly, according to their inborn biological plans (Gesell & Ilg, 1943).

Gesell's innovative methods of study and his establishment of developmental norms greatly expanded our knowledge of children's everyday skills and behavior. But his strongly biological philosophy, like most extreme viewpoints, was an oversimplification, because it largely neglected the crucial role of environmental factors. As a result, Gesell's theoretical model failed to have a long-term impact on developmental thought (Hilgard, 1987). His emphasis on patterns of unfolding behavior and his focus on similarities in children's development, however, may have helped prepare American psychologists to accept the more influential views of another of Rousseau's theoretical descendants, Jean Piaget.

Jean Piaget (1896–1980)

If we had to select the one psychologist whose work has had the greatest influence on the study of child development, we would have to consider Jean Piaget a very strong candidate. His ideas have inspired more research than those of any other theorist, and his conception of human development revolutionized thinking about children and their behavior. Piaget differs from the other pioneers discussed here in that his theoretical views are still widely accepted in some form by many of today's developmental psychologists. For this reason, we discuss Piaget in several places in this text. This chapter briefly describes his background and overall approach to psychology. Later chapters cover his theoretical views and the research that addresses them.

Jean Piaget is one pioneer of child psychology whose early ideas remain largely accepted today by many researchers.

Piaget was born and raised in Switzerland. From boyhood, he was interested in science, particularly biology and animal behavior. Although he eventually left this area of study, his background in biology is reflected in his theory of child development. Piaget had always been drawn to the study of psychology, and after earning his doctorate in 1918, he moved from Switzerland to Paris, where he became involved in the development of intelligence tests for children.

Intelligence testing was a new field at this time, and two of its founders, Alfred Binet and Theodore Simon, were attempting to develop questionnaires that could predict children's success in school. Binet and Simon first devised questions that represented the knowledge typical of children at a given age. Then they developed norms so that any child's test performance—the number of correct answers—could be compared with the average performance of other children of the same age. These tests improved on Hall's early questionnaires by including precise testing and scoring procedures that did not allow for subjective interpretations.

Piaget was hired by Simon to administer the tests, which gave him his first real experience with developmental work. But unlike his employers, Piaget became less interested in the number of test items children answered correctly than in the reasons for their incorrect responses. Children of different ages, he observed, not only knew different amounts of information but also looked at the world in very different ways. Their answers revealed *qualitative* (style related) differences in thinking, beyond the *quantitative* (amount related) differences in factual information.

After two years in Paris, Piaget returned to Switzerland and began his own research on the development of children's knowledge. Piaget called his area of interest **genetic epistemology**, by which he meant the study of the nature of knowledge in young children and how it changes as they grow older. Unlike Hall, Piaget was interested not in the precise knowledge and facts that children possess—for example, *what* children know when they enter school—but rather in how they go about acquiring and using that knowledge—that is, *how children think.*

Genetic epistemology Jean Piaget's term for the study of children's knowledge and how it changes with development.

To find support for his theory, Piaget developed his own research technique. Whereas Gesell's methods involved observing children without interfering with them, Piaget challenged children (including three of his own) with simple tasks and verbal problems that required solutions and explanations. His technique, known as the **clinical method**, involved a loosely structured interview in which he asked a question or posed a problem and then, depending on the child's response, followed up with other questions that might reveal the child's reasoning or problem-solving approach.

Clinical method Piaget's principal research method, which involved a semistructured interview with questions designed to probe children's understanding of various concepts.

Piaget's research initially attracted some attention in the United States during the 1920s and 1930s. But his writings were difficult for American psychologists to understand because they contained many terms and concepts that differed from the scientific language the Americans were using. And Piaget's somewhat informal methods of investigation were viewed as a problem by more rigorous experimental researchers. During the 1940s and 1950s, as American child psychology once again turned toward environmental and conditioning models, interest in Piaget's theory disappeared.

Beginning in the late 1950s, however, American psychologists began to rediscover Piaget's work. His theoretical writings were translated into more familiar concepts, and his studies were replicated under controlled experimental conditions (Flavell,

1963). Among the first to endorse Piaget's theories were educators, who began to develop school curricula based on his ideas. Research psychologists also became interested in Piaget's theoretical views. Their own experiments supported his predictions and confirmed the existence of qualitative differences in the thinking of children of different ages. In addition, his theory generated many new questions that psychologists felt could and should be investigated, questions about children's understanding of time, logic, causality, and other kinds of fundamental knowledge.

Piaget died in 1980 at the age of 84. As late as 1975, he was revising his model in response to new data and findings generated by his research team in Geneva (Beilin, 1989). Piaget's many books on child psychology remain the greatest contribution to the field by a single scholar (Beilin, 1992a).

Erik Erikson (1902–1994)

Freud's psychoanalytic theory had problems that made it unacceptable to many American experimental psychologists. Some of Freud's ideas, nevertheless, were provocative enough to spur other child researchers to extend and refine them into new models of development. One of the most important of these *neo-analytic* models was that of Erik Erikson.

Erikson grew up in Germany just after the turn of the century. As a young man, he was a skilled artist, and he spent his early life wandering through Europe pursuing this work. His travels eventually took him to Vienna, where he began teaching art to children of Americans who had come to train with Freud and his colleagues. In time, Erikson also entered psychoanalytic training and studied under Freud's daughter, Anna, an accomplished analyst in her own right.

In 1933, Erikson traveled to the United States and accepted a position at Harvard Medical School. He was principally interested in children and became Boston's first child psychoanalyst. More important, he constructed a comprehensive model of human development that continues to be of interest to many psychologists.

Erikson's model, although based on Freud's theory, differed from it in some major ways. For one, he believed that development continues throughout life. He thus replaced Freud's five stages of development—which end in late adolescence—with an eight-stage model that continues into old age. Erikson also believed that personality development cannot be understood without considering the environment in which it develops. After studying a number of diverse cultures—including Native American tribes in California and South Dakota, inner-city youth, and the people of India—Erikson developed a psycho*social* model (in contrast to Freud's psycho*sexual* model) of personality that included a major role for social and cultural influences. Finally, Erikson's model was based on the study of normal individuals and emphasized the positive, healthy aspects of personality.

Epigenetic principle
According to Erikson, the genetic process that guides personality formation through its stages of development.

Identity
In Erikson's theory, the component of personality that develops across the eight stages of life and that motivates progress through the stages.

Like Freud, Erikson believed that all children progress through a predictable series of stages. This progression, he argued, is guided by an **epigenetic principle**, meaning that personality development is not random but follows a blueprint or timetable built into our genes. According to Erikson, each individual's ultimate goal is the quest for **identity**, which is accumulated gradually across the eight stages. But, at each stage, a positive personality characteristic associated with the search for identity conflicts with a negative one resulting from interaction with the social world. For example, in Erikson's second stage, the toddler's newfound physical abilities—such as walking and controlling bladder and bowel functions—lead to the positive feelings of *autonomy* as the child begins to exert more control over his or her life. But these new abilities also tend to cause conflict in the child's social world—with parents, for instance—leading to feelings of *shame* and *doubt*. According to Erikson, the best resolution of these conflicts would have the child leaving the stage with a strong

Table 1.1
Stages of Development: Erikson and Freud

Ages (yrs)	*Erikson*	*Freud*
Birth–1.5	Basic Trust vs. Mistrust	Oral
1.5–3	Autonomy vs. Shame	Anal
3–6	Initiative vs. Guilt	Phallic
6–12	Industry vs. Inferiority	Latency
12–18	Identity vs. Role Confusion	Genital
Young adult	Intimacy vs. Isolation	
Adult	Generativity vs. Stagnation	
Older adult	Ego Integrity vs. Despair	

sense of the positive personality characteristic, but also with a small degree of the negative characteristic. The eight stages are presented in Table 1.1, which includes a comparison with the stages proposed by Freud.

Erikson's theory is thus also interactionist, combining nature and nurture factors. Each person is guided through the psychosocial stages by genetic processes, but the individual's social and cultural surroundings help determine how the conflicts are resolved at each stage and so also contribute heavily to personality development.

Lev Vygotsky (1896–1934)

Another pioneer of child psychology whose ideas continue to find considerable acceptance is Lev Vygotsky. As with Piaget, we present Vygotsky's background and general theoretical approach here, and in later chapters we discuss his ideas in more detail.

Lev Vygotsky's sociocultural theory of cognitive development, originally published more than fifty years ago, has generated great interest in modern developmentalists.

Vygotsky was born in Russia in the same year as Piaget, and their early work occupied the same period. Yet their backgrounds were very different. These differences are reflected in the contrasting models of human development they constructed (Glassman, 1994; Kozulin, 1990).

Unlike Piaget, Vygotsky was not trained in science but instead received a law degree from Moscow University. He went on to study literature and linguistics and eventually received a Ph.D. for a book he wrote on the psychology of art.

A similarity between the two scholars, however, is that both received little attention from Western scientists until the 1960s, when their work was translated into English and their theories began to be tested experimentally. Piaget, of course, was still active at this time and continued to contribute to the scientific advances brought about by his theory. Vygotsky, however, had died at 37 and never saw his ideas pursued by other researchers. Initially, his writings were misunderstood, and they were banned in the former Soviet Union for over 20 years. Thus his work remained unknown even to many of his contemporary Soviet psychologists.

To understand Vygotsky's theory, it is important to appreciate the political environment of the time. Vygotsky began working in psychology shortly after the Russian Revolution, which replaced the rule of the czar with Marxism. The new philosophy stressed socialism and collectivism; individuals were expected to sacrifice their personal goals and achievements for the betterment of the larger society. Sharing and cooperation were encouraged, and the success of any individual was seen as reflecting the success of the culture. Marxists also placed a heavy emphasis on history, believing that any culture could be understood only through examination of the ideas and events that had shaped it.

Vygotsky's model of human development incorporated these elements and so has been termed a *sociocultural* approach. It holds that the individual's development is a product of his or her culture. In this theory development refers largely to mental development, such as thought, language, and reasoning processes. Vygotsky assumed that these abilities develop through social interactions with others (especially parents) and thus represent the shared knowledge of the culture. Whereas Piaget believed that all children's cognitive development follows a very similar pattern of stages, Vygotsky saw intellectual abilities as much more specific to the culture in which the child was reared.

Today, the sociocultural approach has become one of the most influential movements in developmental psychology (Valsiner, 1998). We discuss the specific psychological mechanisms proposed by Vygotsky and others of this tradition in later chapters.

✓ To Recap...

The scientific study of children began with the questionnaire research of G. Stanley Hall, who also proposed a theory of development based on the principle of evolutionary recapitulation. John B. Watson helped make child psychology a natural science by introducing objective research methods based on observable and measurable behaviors. His behavioristic theory of development held that the conditioned reflex was the fundamental unit of development and that environmental and experiential factors were primarily responsible for changes in behavior. Sigmund Freud proposed a stage theory of child development that grew out of his clinical work in psychoanalysis. Modern developmentalists have little interest in Freud's theory, but his interactionist viewpoint and his emphasis on early experiences remain important concepts. Arnold Gesell's research with children renewed interest in the biological perspective by offering evidence that inborn maturational processes account for developmental changes. His observational studies produced age-related norms of behavior that have been valuable to both professionals and parents.

Jean Piaget is perhaps the most influential developmental theorist to date. His genetic epistemology was concerned with understanding the form of children's knowledge and the qualitative changes it undergoes as they develop. Erik Erikson offered a neo-analytic, stage model of development that similarly combined nature and nurture processes. Unlike Freud's theory, this model extended through adulthood, assigned a major role to social factors, and focused on the healthy aspects of personality. Lev Vygotsky proposed a sociocultural model of human, and especially mental, development that reflected Marxist beliefs in the social and cultural basis of individual development.

Issues in Developmental Psychology

As we described the views of some of the pioneers of developmental psychology, a number of questions arose repeatedly. Three issues in particular have run through scientific thinking about development almost from the very beginning, and they remain a source of debate today. These issues revolve around the questions of nature versus nurture, continuity versus discontinuity, and normative versus idiographic development.

Nature versus nurture debate
The scientific controversy regarding whether the primary source of developmental change rests in biological (nature) factors or in environmental and experiential (nurture) factors.

Nature versus Nurture

The most basic and long-standing issue in child psychology (and perhaps in all of psychology) involves the degree to which behavior and development result from inborn, biological, **nature** factors and the degree to which they reflect environmental, experiential, **nurture** factors. This debate has existed at least since Locke and Rousseau first proposed their rather pure environmental and nativistic models of child development. The nurture view was later taken up by Watson and other learning theorists, while the nature position formed the basis of the theories of Hall and Gesell. The modern debate, however, is far more complex than it was in these early days of psychology (Plomin & McClearn, 1993).

We noted earlier that virtually all child researchers today subscribe to some form of interactionist position, in which both nature and nurture are assumed to contribute to human development. Several theoretical models describing how our genes and environment may work together to guide our behavior are discussed in Chapter 4.

Nevertheless, the nature–nurture debate has not ended. There is still little agreement as to how and how much nature and nurture factors contribute to many areas of development. For example, when a kindergartner hits a classmate who has just taken away a toy, some psychologists are likely to believe that the child's aggressive response is principally a biological reaction to frustration and that it may have its roots in our evolutionary past. Others might argue that it probably represents a behavior the child learned by watching and interacting with others.

Another example can be found in the area of gender-role development. Once a sex difference in behavior has been identified—such as the finding that males are generally more adept than females at certain spatial tasks—explanations for the difference can take at least three different forms. The difference can be attributed to nature, as in the contention that the brains of males and females are structured differently. It can be attributed to environmental factors, as in the argument that boys receive more encouragement from parents and teachers to engage in activities that promote spatial skills. Or it can involve an interactionist explanation, such as the possibility that boys innately prefer activities involving spatial relations and, as a result, spend more time improving these skills.

Nature versus nurture questions arise in almost every topic we consider in this text. At times, however, they appear under different labels, such as heredity versus environment, maturation versus learning, or emergent abilities versus acquired skills. Whatever the name, these debates tend to involve the same fundamental issue.

The role of nature and nurture factors in human development has been at the heart of many theoretical debates in developmental psychology.

Continuity versus Discontinuity

Continuity versus discontinuity debate
The scientific controversy regarding whether development is constant and connected (continuous) or uneven and disconnected (discontinuous).

A second long-standing issue in child psychology is whether development displays **continuity** or **discontinuity**. This debate actually has two components (Emde & Harmon, 1984). One involves the *pattern* of development. Is development smooth and stable, with new abilities, skills, and knowledge gradually added at a relatively uniform pace (continuous)? Or does development occur at different rates, alternating between periods of little change and periods of abrupt, rapid change (discontinuous)? The second component involves the *connectedness* of development. Continuity theorists contend that many of the behaviors and abilities we see in adolescents and adults can be traced directly back to development early in life. Discontinuity theorists, in contrast, suggest that some aspects of development emerge relatively independently of what has come before and cannot be predicted from the child's previous behavior (Clarke & Clarke, 1976).

The continuity model is often associated with the belief that human behavior consists of many individual skills that are added one at a time, usually through learning and experience. As children acquire more and more of these skills, they combine and recombine them to produce increasingly complex abilities. This approach emphasizes quantitative change—the simpler elements are essentially added together to produce the more advanced capabilities—and tends to characterize environmentalist models of development. In contrast, psychologists who favor the discontinuity model usually hold that development is guided primarily by internal biological factors. Stage theorists, for example, argue that the unevenness of children's development—relatively stable periods followed by abrupt changes—reflects the discontinuous nature of the changes taking place in the underlying structures of the body and brain. Thus, development is thought to involve qualitative changes in previous abilities or behaviors.

Like the nature versus nurture issue, the question of continuity versus discontinuity is not all-or-nothing. Psychologists on both sides of the debate agree that some developmental processes are more accurately described by one model and others by the competing model (Rutter, 1987).

Normative versus Idiographic Development

Normative versus idiographic development
The question of whether research should focus on identifying commonalities in human development (normative development) or on the causes of individual differences (idiographic development).

Universals of development
Aspects of development or behavior that are common to children everywhere.

Cultural relativism
The idea that certain behaviors or patterns of development vary from one culture to another.

A third issue that commonly arises in child psychology is not a matter of debate so much as it is a description of a researcher's focus of study. Some psychologists are concerned with **normative** development, meaning what children have in common or how development is similar across them. Others focus on **idiographic** development, meaning the differences in development from one child to the next.

Normative research, such as the work of Gesell and, to a lesser degree, of Piaget, is often based on a biological view of development. This perspective thus focuses on the "average" child, with the primary goal of identifying and describing how normal development proceeds from step to step. A related issue involves the search for **universals of development**—behaviors or patterns of development that characterize all children, everywhere (which Piaget sought to identify).

Idiographic research centers on the individual child and the factors that produce human diversity. Genes are certainly responsible for some of the individual differences among people, but the idiographic perspective also considers the environmental and experiential processes that serve to mold and shape children into unique individuals. Researchers use this approach to study aspects of development that display **cultural relativism**—the way in which such aspects differ from one culture to another.

Research on language development illustrates these two approaches. Some theorists believe that language abilities develop in the same way for all children because they are controlled mainly by specific mechanisms in the brain. These

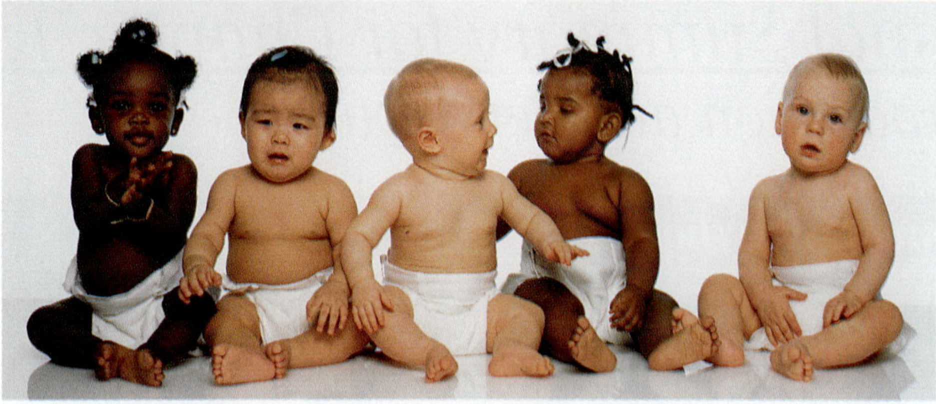

Normative research attempts to identify commonalities among children, whereas idiographic research is concerned with why one child is different from the next.

researchers therefore search for common patterns of linguistic development both in children who speak the same language and in children who speak different languages. Theorists concerned with individual differences in speech development are more apt to study environmental influences on language acquisition, such as the type of speech adults use when talking with children, in order to determine which factors cause language to develop differently from one child to the next.

✓ *To Recap...*

Three issues arise frequently in child psychology research. The nature versus nurture issue focuses on whether the primary source of developmental change is inborn and biological or environmental and experiential. The continuity versus discontinuity issue concerns whether the pattern of development is constant or uneven and whether development shows connectedness between early and later characteristics. The normative versus idiographic issue involves the researcher's preference for focusing either on the commonalities of children's development and the search for universals or on the factors that produce individual differences among children, such as cultural influences.

Conclusion

Our brief look backward in this chapter should have made one point clear—the more scholars have observed children and learned about early development, the more they have come to appreciate the importance of the childhood years for understanding all human behavior. As this fact became increasingly obvious, two things happened. First, we realized that because children are not fully developed organisms they are more vulnerable than adults, so we began to treat them better. Second, we began to study children much more closely, using all the available tools of science. Today, children are accorded a very special status in our society, and developmental psychology has taken its place among the other natural sciences.

Although child study is still young compared with other physical and biological sciences, our understanding of developmental processes is progressing so rapidly that it is difficult to keep up with the information that is being generated by researchers. The remainder of the text, therefore, focuses on the current state of the field rather than on historical issues and research. And yet, as we proceed from topic to topic, you may be struck by how familiar some of the recurring controversies sound, reminiscent of the fundamental differences that arose between Locke and Rousseau, Watson and Gesell, or Binet and Piaget.

Visual Summary for Chapter 1: Introduction and Perspective

Developmental Psychology

Two Basic Goals of Developmental Research →	1. To describe children's behavior at each point in development.
→	2. To explain developmental changes that occur from one point to the next.

Why Study Children?

Five reasons why developmental psychology has traditionally involved children

Period of rapid development →	More developmental changes take place in childhood than at any other time.
Long-term influences →	Experiences of early years may affect the individual's later development.
Insight into complex adult processes →	Complex processes are easier to understand as they are forming.
Real world applications →	Knowledge of basic process can be used to help solve some of children's problems.
Interesting subject matter →	Children are inherently interesting to study.

Historical Views of Childhood

Ancient Greece and Rome →	Medieval Period →	Renaissance →	The Reformation →	Descartes's Dualistic Model
Children were exchangeable, expendable property. →	The Church stressed children's purity and innocence. →	Foundling homes were set up to take in sick, lost, unwanted children. →	The Puritans constructed the first comprehensive model of child development, based on the notion of original sin. →	Descartes proposed a dualistic system, in which the nonphysical mind governed the mechanical functioning of the physical body.

Early Theorists

John Locke	*Based his approach on the strict environmentalist position that all knowledge is acquired through experience.*
Jean-Jacques Rousseau	*Proposed a nativistic model in which development unfolds according to inborn processes.*
Charles Darwin	*His theory of evolution suggested that some human behaviors may have had their origins in the past, when they were valuable to our ancestors' survival.*

Pioneers of Child Psychology

G. Stanley Hall	*Credited with founding the field of developmental psychology. Proposed a theory of development based on the principle of evolutionary recapitulation.*
John B. Watson	*Proposed a behaviorist theory of development which held that the conditioned reflex was the fundamental unit of development and that experiential factors were primarily responsible for changes in behavior.*
Sigmund Freud	*Proposed a 5-stage psychosexual theory of development that emphasized the combined importance of early experiences and inborn processes.*
Arnold Gesell	*Proposed a biological perspective that stressed inborn maturational processes. Produced valuable age-related norms of development.*
Jean Piaget	*His genetic epistemology was concerned with understanding the form of children's knowledge and the qualitative changes it undergoes as they develop.*
Erik Erikson	*Developed an 8-stage theory that differed from Freud's in that it extended through adulthood, assigned a major role to social factors, and focused on the healthy aspects of personality.*
Lev Vygotsky	*Proposed a sociocultural model of human, and especially cognitive, development that reflected Marxist beliefs in the social and cultural bases of individual development.*

Issues in Development Psychology

Nature versus nurture	*This issue focuses on whether the primary source of developmental change is inborn and biological or environmental and experiential.*
Continuity verus Discontinuity	*This issue focuses on whether the pattern of development is constant or uneven, and whether there is a connectedness between early and later characteristics.*
Normative versus Idiographic	*This issue relates to the researcher's preference for focusing on the commonalities of child development or on factors that produce individual differences among children.*

Chapter 2

Theories of Child Development

Developmental psychologists usually describe themselves in terms of their areas of research interest. One psychologist, for example, might concentrate on infants, studying how perceptual abilities develop during the first months of life. Another might be concerned with identifying the ways in which children's social skills affect their success in the classroom. But most psychologists also characterize themselves in terms of a particular theoretical orientation, that is, their view of how development occurs and which factors they believe are most responsible for changes in children's behavior.

Today, the large majority of child psychologists identify themselves with one of three general theoretical views: the cognitive-developmental approach, the environmental/learning approach, or the ethological approach. This chapter outlines the principal ideas and underlying assumptions of these three theories. Then, as we discuss various topics throughout the rest of the book, we will compare and contrast the approaches taken by each of the theories, including the types of questions they ask and the research methods they prefer.

Cognitive-Developmental Models

The cognitive-developmental approach actually includes several related theories. For years, it was most closely associated with the work of Piaget. Since the 1970s, however, information-processing and social models have also become very popular among cognitive developmentalists.

As we saw in Chapter 1, the roots of the cognitive-developmental tradition lie in the 18th-century writings of Jean-Jacques Rousseau. This early nativistic view suggested that human development unfolds predictably, with little or no environmental influence. Modern cognitive-developmental theorists assign a much greater role to environmental factors than did Rousseau, reflecting the interactionist perspective of all contemporary theories.

An important characteristic of this approach is its emphasis on cognition. According to these theories, the changes we witness in children's behaviors and abilities occur largely as a result of changes in their knowledge and intellectual skills. The major goals for psychologists of this tradition, therefore, are to specify what children know, how this knowledge is organized, and how it changes or develops.

Piaget's Theory

As a student of biology and zoology, Piaget learned that survival requires adaptation. Any individual organism, as well as any entire species, must adapt to constant changes in the environment. Piaget therefore viewed the development of human cognition (or intelligence) as the continual struggle of a very complex organism trying to adapt to a very complex environment (Piaget & Inhelder, 1968).

According to Piaget's theory, human development can be described in terms of *functions* and *cognitive structures.* The functions are inborn biological processes that are the same for everyone and remain unchanged throughout our lives. Their purpose is to construct internal cognitive structures. The structures, in contrast, change repeatedly as the child grows.

Schemes
Piaget's term for the cognitive structures of infancy. A scheme consists of a set of skilled, flexible action patterns through which the child understands the world.

Cognitive Structures The most fundamental aspect of Piaget's theory, and often the most difficult to understand, is the belief that intelligence is a process—not something that a child *has*, but something that a child *does*. Piaget's child does not possess knowledge passively, but understands the world by acting or operating on it.

For example, Piaget would describe an infant's knowledge of a ball in terms of the various actions the infant can perform with it—pushing the ball, throwing it, mouthing it, and so on. These actions represent the cognitive structures of infancy and are called **schemes**. Note that a scheme involves two elements: an object in the environment (such as a ball), and the child's reactions to the object. A scheme is therefore not a physical structure, but a psychological one. Early on, the infant has comparatively few of these schemes and they are related to one another in very simple ways. As development proceeds, however, schemes increase both in their number and in the complexity with which they are organized. These two characteristics of children's cognitive structures—number and complexity—define the child's intelligence at any point in development.

According to Piaget, babies' early schemes involve interactions with simple objects.

Schemes and other cognitive structures also display certain flexibilities. An infant does not perform exactly the same behavior with every ball she encounters—some may produce more squeezing, others more rolling—nor are the infant's reactions the same with every object. The way a ball is grasped may be somewhat different from the way a rattle is grasped, and the way either of these objects is sucked may be different from the way a nipple is sucked. Cognitive structures are flexible in another sense—they change over time. A particular scheme, such as grasping, reflects more and more skill as the infant applies it to more and more objects. In this way, schemes eventually become more individualized, or *differentiated*, so that a ball becomes primarily an object to be thrown, a rattle primarily an object to be shaken, and a nipple primarily an object to be sucked.

Beyond these simple schemes of infancy, new and higher-level cognitive structures gradually emerge. An 8-year-old confronted with a ball, for example, still has all the earlier schemes available (although sucking is not a very likely response), but the older child can also understand a ball by acting on it using mental operations, such as assigning it certain properties (color, size), actions (bouncing, hitting), or capabilities (being a member of the class "round things").

For Piaget, *development* referred to this continual reorganization of knowledge into new and more complex structures. Much of our discussion in Chapter 8 concerns what these structures are and how they change with development.

Organization
The tendency to integrate knowledge into interrelated cognitive structures. One of the two biologically based functions stressed in Piaget's theory.

Adaptation
The tendency to fit with the environment in ways that promote survival. One of the two biologically based functions stressed in Piaget's theory.

Assimilation
Interpreting new experiences in terms of existing cognitive structures. One of the two components of adaptation in Piaget's theory.

Functions The functions that guide cognitive development are also central to Piaget's theory. Piaget stressed two general functions, both of which reflect his training in biology. One is **organization**. Because an individual's cognitive structures are interrelated, any new knowledge must be fitted into the existing system. According to Piaget, it is this need for integrating new information, rather than simply adding it on, that forces our cognitive structures to become ever more elaborately organized.

The second function is **adaptation**, which in general terms refers to an organism's attempt to fit with its environment in ways that promote survival. In Piaget's model, cognitive adaptation involves two processes. **Assimilation** entails trying to make sense of new experiences in terms of our existing cognitive structures. The infant who brings everything to his mouth to suck is demonstrating assimilation, as is the toddler who calls all men "Daddy." Note that assimilation may require some

Accommodation
Changing existing cognitive structures to fit with new experiences. One of the two components of adaptation in Piaget's theory.

Constructivism
Piaget's belief that children actively create knowledge rather than passively receive it from the environment.

Periods
Piaget's term for the four general stages into which his theory divides development. Each period is a qualitatively distinct form of functioning that characterizes a wide range of cognitive activities.

Sensorimotor
Form of intelligence in which knowledge is based on physical interactions with people and objects. The first of Piaget's periods, extending from birth to about 2 years.

Preoperational
Form of intelligence in which symbols and mental actions begin to replace objects and overt behaviors. The second of Piaget's periods, extending from about 2 to about 6 years old.

Concrete operations
Form of intelligence in which mental operations make logical problem solving with concrete objects possible. The third of Piaget's periods, extending from about 6 to 11 years of age.

distortion of the new information in order to make it fit into the child's existing schemes. But trying to fit new things into what we already know is a necessary part of adapting to the world.

When new information is too different or too complex, **accommodation** occurs. Here, our cognitive structures change in order to integrate the new experiences. For example, the infant eventually learns that not all objects are to be sucked, just as the toddler learns that different labels or names need to be applied to different men. It is primarily through accommodation that the number and complexity of children's cognitive structures increase, that is, that intelligence grows.

Piaget assumed that assimilation and accommodation operate closely together. The growing child is continually making slight distortions of information to assimilate it into existing structures, while also making slight modifications in these structures to accommodate new objects or events. The interplay of these two functions illustrates another important aspect of Piaget's theory, the concept of **constructivism**. Children's knowledge of events in their environment is not an exact reproduction of those events—it is not like a perfect photograph of what they have seen or a precise recording of what they have heard. Children take information from the environment and bend, shape, or distort it until it fits comfortably into their existing cognitive organization. As we said earlier, they *operate* on it. Even when they accommodate structures to allow for new experiences, the accommodation is seldom complete, and some distortion of the information remains. Thus, when children 6, 8, and 10 years old watch a movie or hear a lecture, they come away with somewhat different messages, even though they may have seen or heard exactly the same stimulus input. Each child acts on the information somewhat differently, fitting it into his or her own existing set of structures. In this sense, the child *constructs* knowledge about the world, rather than simply receiving it.

The processes of assimilation, accommodation, and construction make the child's cognitive system increasingly more powerful and adaptive. However, these processes produce only small-scale changes. At certain points in development, Piaget argued, more major adjustments are required. At these points, the cognitive system, because of both biological maturation and past experiences, has completely mastered one level of functioning and is ready for new, qualitatively different challenges—challenges that go beyond what the current set of structures can handle. At such points, the child moves to a new stage of development.

Stages of Development Piaget was a stage theorist. In his view, all children move through the same stages of cognitive development in the same order. At each stage, the child's cognitive functioning is qualitatively different and affects the child's performance in a wide range of situations.

There are four such general stages, or **periods**, in Piaget's model. Chapter 8 discusses the four periods in detail and also evaluates the general claim that development is divided into stages.

The **sensorimotor** period represents the first 2 years of life. The infant's initial schemes are simple reflexes and knowledge of the world is limited to physical interactions with people and objects. During the **preoperational** period, from roughly 2 to 6 years, the child begins to use symbols, such as words and numbers, to represent the world cognitively. The preoperational child is not yet skilled at symbolic problem solving, however. The period of **concrete operations** lasts approximately from age 6 to age 11. Children in this stage are able to perform mental operations on the pieces of knowledge they possess, permitting a kind of logical problem solving that was not possible during the preoperational period. The final stage, the period of

formal operations, extends from about age 12 through adulthood. This period includes all the higher-level abstract operations, enabling the child to deal with events or relations that are only possible, as opposed to those that actually exist.

The accuracy of Piaget's theory has been studied extensively over the years. In Chapter 8 we consider the evidence psychologists have gathered that both supports and questions various aspects of this theory.

Formal operations
Form of intelligence in which higher-level mental operations make possible logical reasoning with respect to abstract and hypothetical events and not merely concrete objects. The fourth of Piaget's periods, beginning at about 11 years of age.

Information-Processing Models

A second type of cognitive-developmental model is the information-processing approach, which we describe in detail in Chapter 9. Information-processing theorists view cognition as a system composed of three parts. First, information in the world provides the input to the system. Stimulation enters our senses in the form of sights, sounds, tastes, and so on. Second, processes in the brain act on and transform the information in a variety of ways, including encoding it into symbolic forms, comparing it with previously acquired information, storing it in memory, and retrieving it when necessary. Most psychologists working in the information-processing tradition have concentrated on this middle part of the system, designing their experiments to reveal the nature of these internal processes and how they interact with one another. The third part of the system is the output, which is our behavior—speech, social interactions, writing, and so on.

As you have probably noticed, there is an inescapable connection between the information-processing approach to cognition and the operation of a computer. Some psychologists make this connection very strongly. Their goal is to construct computer programs that simulate human behavior, so that ultimately we will be able to specify our cognitive processes in precise mathematical and logical terms. More often, however, researchers use the computer analogy simply as a way of thinking about information flowing through a system, where it is processed, and then reemerging in a different form. This approach has been useful in guiding psychological research on children's problem solving, memory, reading, and other cognitive processes (Kail & Bisanz, 1992; Klahr & MacWhinney, 1998).

Information-processing models of development compare the functions of the human mind to those of a computer

In recent years, the information-processing view has probably become the leading approach to the study of human cognition. Its popularity reflects in part the growing interest in *cognitive science*, an interdisciplinary field in which researchers in biology, mathematics, philosophy, and neuroscience, among other disciplines, are attempting to understand the workings of the human mind (e.g., Keil, 1998; Osherson, 1990).

Not all information-processing research has been concerned with children, and much of it has not been directed toward developmental issues. Nevertheless, the approach has infused many areas of child psychology, and it will turn up throughout the text in topics as diverse as perception, language, gender roles, and aggression.

Social Models of Cognition

The cognitive-developmental tradition has always been most concerned with children's cognitive abilities, but in recent years it has also become involved with children's social development. This change has occurred for two reasons: On the one hand, cognitive processes have been shown to influence social experiences; on the other, social interactions are thought to influence cognitive development.

Social Cognition Many modern developmentalists believe that social development is affected by the nature and sophistication of the child's cognitive skills. How children interact with others depends, for example, on how they conceptualize interpersonal relationships, how accurately they interpret other children's behavior, how well they can apply information gained in previous situations to their current circumstances, and so forth. We will see in later chapters that such skills reflect fundamental aspects of children's emerging cognitive abilities.

This does not necessarily mean that the cognitive processes involved in social experiences are identical to those involved in nonsocial experiences. Although Piaget seemed to think they were (Piaget, 1964), most developmentalists today feel that the two are in some ways quite different. As a result, a new area of study, known as **social cognition,** has evolved (Flavell & Miller, 1998).

Social cognition Knowledge of the social world and interpersonal relationships.

How might understanding the social world differ from understanding the physical world? One major difference is that people possess certain characteristics not found in nonliving things. For example, people have motives and intentions that may lead them to choose one behavior or another, sometimes in ways that are difficult to predict. Also, people have feelings and emotions that influence their behaviors and that may be important components of those behaviors. And, perhaps most important, people interact—that is, when acted on, people act back. An inanimate object, such as a leaf or a cup, may respond when we act on it. But when we act on a cup, we need not be concerned about what mood it is in, or what it hopes will happen, or what it will say in response. Nor, of course, do we need to be concerned about how *it* may act on *us*.

Although modern theorists recognize that there are important similarities between physical cognition and social cognition (Marini & Case, 1989, 1994), their primary interest is in the kinds of differences just described. Much research is presently under way to investigate children's understanding of their social world. You will encounter examples of such studies when we discuss children's beliefs regarding how the mind works (theory of mind) (Chapter 8), children's concept of self (Chapter 13), the ways in which children reason about moral issues (Chapter 14), and children's understanding of what it means to be a friend (Chapter 16).

Sociocultural Models The kinds of research just described focus on how children's cognitive level enables them to understand their social world. But researchers have also been interested in the reverse process, that is, in how social experiences affect children's cognitive development.

The most influential contemporary theory of this type is that of the Soviet psychologist Lev Vygotsky, discussed briefly in Chapter 1. The theory itself is not new—as we saw, all of Vygotsky's work was conducted in the 1920s and 1930s—but only in recent years have developmental psychologists in the West begun to apply Vygotsky's ideas to children's cognitive and social development.

Tools of intellectual adaptation Vygotsky's term for the techniques of thinking and problem solving that children internalize from their culture.

Dialectical process The process in Vygotsky's theory whereby children learn through problem-solving experiences shared with others.

Vygotsky's theory emphasizes a number of related elements (Kozulin, 1990; Wertsch & Tulviste, 1992). Most important, it holds that culture is a major determinant of individual development. Humans are the only species that has created cultures, and every human child develops in the context of a culture. Culture makes two sorts of contributions to the child's intellectual development. First, children acquire much of the content of their thinking—that is, their knowledge—from the culture around them. Second, children acquire their thinking and reasoning processes—what Vygotskians call the **tools of intellectual adaptation**—from their culture. In short, culture teaches children both what to think and how to think.

How does culture exert its influences? Vygotsky believed that cognitive development results from a **dialectical process** in which the child learns through shared problem-solving experiences with someone else, usually a parent or teacher (Rogoff, 1998). Initially, the adult assumes most of the responsibility for guiding the

Vygotsky believed that children acquire cognition through shared experiences with others in their culture who are more knowledgeable.

problem they are working on. Gradually, however, the responsibility shifts partly and then completely to the child. Language plays a central role in this process in two ways. First, it describes and transmits to children the rich body of knowledge that exists in the culture. Second, it provides the means, or method, of problem solving, which is demonstrated by the adult and then adopted by the child, at first in vocal speech, and then in silent speech, to direct her own behavior.

This transfer of control from adult to child reflects the final Vygotskian theme, development as a process of **internalization** (Cox & Lightfoot, 1997). Bodies of knowledge and thinking tools at first exist outside the child, in the surrounding culture. Development, according to Vygotsky, consists of gradually internalizing them. This is what Vygotskians mean when they say that children's cognitive abilities grow directly out of their cultural experiences.

Internalization Vygotsky's term for the child's incorporation, primarily through language, of bodies of knowledge and tools of thought from the culture.

Undoubtedly much of the current popularity of this theory lies in its fit with contemporary ideas about the importance of contexts for understanding children's behavior. We have much to say about this issue throughout this book. And we return specifically to Vygotsky in Chapter 10, when we discuss theories of intelligence, and again in Chapter 13, when we examine the development of the self.

✓ To Recap...

The cognitive-developmental approach is based on the belief that cognitive abilities are fundamental and that they guide children's behavior. The key to understanding changes in behavior across development, then, lies in understanding how children's knowledge is structured at any given time.

Piaget described human development in terms of inborn functions and changing cognitive structures. With development, the structures increase in number and complexity. Changes in structures are guided by two functions—organization and adaptation. Adaptation, in turn, consists of assimilation and accommodation. These processes reflect Piaget's constructivist view of development—the belief that children construct their understanding of the world rather than passively receive it from the environment. As children do this, they pass through four stages, or periods, of development: the sensorimotor period, the preoperational period, the period of concrete operations, and the period of formal operations.

Information-processing models conceptualize cognition as a computer-like system with three parts. Stimulation from the outside world makes up input, the first part; mental processes act on that information and represent the second part; and behavior of various sorts makes up the output of the system, the third part.

Social cognition refers to children's knowledge about people and social processes. Cognitive researchers have increasingly come to believe that understanding the social world differs in important ways from understanding the physical world. Psychologists favoring a sociocultural approach contend that social processes are crucial in the development of children's cognitive abilities. Vygotsky's theory stresses the role of culture in the child's gradual internalization of bodies of knowledge and tools of thought, primarily through shared experiences with parents and teachers.

Environmental/Learning Approaches

Just as Rousseau was the ancestor of the cognitive-developmental approach, so John Locke was the great-grandfather of the learning tradition. Locke's belief that environment and experiences are the keys to understanding human behavior—a view that John B. Watson translated into behaviorism early in this century—continues to be the guiding principle for many child psychologists today.

The essence of the environmental/learning view is that a great deal of human behavior, especially social behavior, is acquired rather than inborn. Of course, modern behavioral psychologists, like cognitive-developmental psychologists, are interactionists. They accept that biological and cognitive factors make important contributions to human development. But they do not share the belief that our biology and evolutionary history largely dictate our development (a view discussed in the next part of this chapter). Nor do they accept the idea that cognition is the fundamental process in psychological development and that changes in behavior always reflect or require advances in cognitive abilities.

Defining Learning

Behavioral psychologists believe that the changes in behavior that occur as children develop often are *learned,* meaning they result from conditioning and learning principles. When psychologists use the term **learning**, they are not referring simply to what goes on in a classroom (although, one hopes, a good deal of it takes place there, too). Instead, they view learning in a much more general sense, defining it as *a relatively permanent change in behavior that results from practice or experience.* This definition has three distinct elements.

Learning
A relatively permanent change in behavior that results from practice or experience.

The first part of the definition, "relatively permanent," distinguishes learned changes in behavior from changes that are only temporary and that often reflect physiological processes—such as when behavior changes as a result of sleep, illness, or fatigue. The second part, "change in behavior," means that learning must always be demonstrated through changes in observable behavior. If a psychologist were interested in determining whether a child had learned a list of words, for example, the child would need to demonstrate this learning through some aspect of behavior, such as writing, reciting, or recognizing the words. The final part of the definition, "results from practice or experience," is meant to separate learned changes in behavior from changes caused by more general biological processes, such as growth, pregnancy, or even death.

B. F. Skinner and Behavior Analysis

In Chapter 1 we saw that John B. Watson's attempt to build a comprehensive theory of child development based on learning principles failed, in part, because human behavior was too complex to be explained by Pavlovian conditioning. Watson's model was based on the conditioning of reflexes. Except in very young infants, though, reflexes account for only a small part of human behavior. How, then, can a learning theory attempt to explain the whole range of typical child behaviors? One answer emerged in the work of another pioneer of behaviorism, B. F. Skinner (Gewirtz & Pelaez-Nogueras, 1992).

B. F. Skinner's revision of Watson's early behavioristic views down-played the role of Pavlovian processes in human development and introduced principles of operant conditioning.

Skinner accepted the role of Pavlovian conditioning of reflexes, but he added to learning theory a second type of behavior and, correspondingly, a second type of learning. According to his model, all behavior falls into one of two categories. The first involves reflexes. A **reflex** is composed of a stimulus that reliably elicits a response. This relation is biological and inborn. The responses involved in the simple reflexes that all organisms display Skinner called **respondent behaviors**. The salivation response of Pavlov's dogs is an example. The most important characteristic of a respondent behavior is that it is completely controlled by the stimulus that elicits it; quite simply, the response occurs when the stimulus is present and does not occur when the stimulus is absent. In humans, respondent behaviors are particularly obvious during infancy and include such reflexive behaviors as sucking in response to a nipple's being placed in the mouth and grasping in response to an object's touching the palm of the hand. Older children and adults also display a few respondent behaviors, usually in the form of simple physiological responses (blinking and sneezing) and emotional responses (some aspects of fear, anger, and sexual arousal).

Operant behaviors are very different. We can think of them roughly as voluntary responses, and they include the vast majority of all human behaviors. Operant behaviors are controlled by their effects, that is, by the consequences they produce. In general, pleasant consequences make the behaviors more likely to occur again, whereas unpleasant consequences have the opposite result (Skinner, 1953).

Skinner's model of learning has been applied to children's development by Sidney Bijou and Donald Baer (Bijou, 1995; Rosales-Ruiz & Baer, 1996), who pioneered the environmental/learning approach to developmental psychology known as **behavior analysis**. The goal of behavior analytic theory is to explain how children's innate capabilities interact with their experiences and environment to produce changes in their behavior and development—which is, of course, remarkably similar to the goal of cognitive-developmental theory and most other interactional theories of child development. What distinguishes behavior analysis is that (1) it relies heavily on learning processes as explanations for developmental change and (2) it avoids explanations based on unobservable cognitive processes, such as Piaget's mental operations and the computer-like mental mechanisms of the information-processing approach.

Reflex
A biological relation in which a specific stimulus reliably elicits a specific response.

Respondent behaviors
Responses based on reflexes, which are controlled by specific eliciting stimuli. The smaller category of human behaviors.

Operant behaviors
Voluntary behavior controlled by its consequences. The larger category of human behaviors.

Behavior analysis
B. F. Skinner's environmental/learning theory, which emphasizes the role of operant learning in changing observable behaviors.

Types of Learning

To understand environmental/learning accounts of child development, we must consider the various types of conditioning and learning that operate on the child. In this section, we examine three forms of learning: habituation, respondent conditioning, and operant learning.

Habituation The simplest form of learning, called **habituation**, involves respondent behaviors. Habituation begins with a reflex. For example, if we clap our hands

Habituation
The decline or disappearance of a reflex response as a result of repeated elicitation. The simplest type of learning.

loudly near an infant, the infant will display a full-body *startle reflex.* If we continue to clap our hands at frequent intervals (say, every 15 seconds), the size of the startle response will decrease steadily until it may be difficult to detect at all. This simple change in behavior caused by repeatedly presenting a stimulus illustrates learning through habituation.

Dishabituation
The recovery of a habituated response that results from a change in the eliciting stimulus.

Respondent (classical) conditioning
A form of learning, involving reflexes, in which a neutral stimulus acquires the power to elicit a reflexive response (UCR) as a result of being associated (paired) with the naturally eliciting stimulus (UCS). The neutral stimulus then becomes a conditioned stimulus (CS).

Unconditioned stimulus (UCS)
The stimulus portion of a reflex, which reliably elicits a respondent behavior (UCR).

Unconditioned response (UCR)
The response portion of a reflex, which is reliably elicited by a stimulus (UCS).

How do we know that habituation really represents some form of learning? Maybe the infant's muscles have simply become too fatigued to produce the response any longer—a change in behavior that, according to our earlier definition, we could not consider to be learned. To demonstrate that fatigue is not the reason for the decreased response, we need only change the stimulus. Assume, for instance, that the repeated hand clapping has reduced the startle to a very low level. Now, after waiting 15 seconds, we sound a loud buzzer instead of clapping our hands. With great reliability, the startle response will reappear at the same high level it showed when we first clapped our hands. The recovery of a habituated response that occurs as a result of a change in the eliciting stimulus is known as **dishabituation**.

Habituation plays only a small role in children's development. One common example is the way infants learn to sleep through routine household noises. If given enough exposure, babies habituate very quickly to slamming doors, ringing telephones, and similar sounds that might otherwise continually wake them. Unfortunately, many parents, unaware of the habituation process, try to keep everyone very quiet during nap times. The absence of typical household stimuli, however, may prevent the habituation process from occurring and, ironically, make the infant more likely to awaken at the first bark of the family dog.

Although habituation does not account for a great deal of children's development, psychologists have discovered that it can be a very useful technique for studying infants' sensory and memory abilities. We examine how this works in later chapters.

Respondent Conditioning **Respondent conditioning**—sometimes called **classical conditioning**—was developed by Pavlov and also involves reflexes. In this type of learning, the stimulus is termed the **unconditioned stimulus (UCS)** and the elicited response is called the **unconditioned response (UCR)**. Respondent conditioning involves having another stimulus, which previously did not elicit the UCR, acquire

Habituation is a simple learning process that explains why babies can sleep in noisy surroundings.

the power to do so. The neutral (new) stimulus is paired or associated with the UCS. After a number of such pairings, it elicits the UCR (or a response very similar to it), at which point the previously neutral stimulus is termed a **conditioned stimulus (CS)**.

We can illustrate this process with an example involving children's emotional responses, the aspect of human development in which respondent conditioning plays its largest role. Fear responses, for instance, can be naturally elicited by a number of stimuli, a very common one being pain. Suppose a child visits the dentist for the first time. The stimuli in that environment—the dentist, the office, the instruments, and so forth—are neutral to the child and so have no particular emotional effect on his behavior. During the visit, however, suppose that the child experiences pain (UCS), which elicits fear (UCR). The various neutral stimuli become associated with the UCS, because they are paired with it, and thus may become conditioned stimuli (CS) for the fear response. After that, the sight of the dentist or sound of the drill, for example, will also elicit the fear response (UCR). In the same way, many common fears of childhood can be learned responses to places or objects that previously were not frightening. (See Box 2.1 for a classic demonstration of the conditioning of fear.)

Note that in habituation, learning results in a change in the response, which gradually gets weaker. By contrast, in respondent conditioning, the response remains the same and learning involves a change in the stimulus, which begins as neutral but becomes effective in producing the response.

Respondent conditioning often produces **stimulus generalization**, which means that stimuli similar to the CS also become conditioned. In our example, the child may come to fear not only his own dentist but all dentists, or perhaps even anyone wearing a white medical coat. Fortunately, the conditioned association also can be unlearned, a process called **respondent extinction**. Suppose the child in our example returns to the dentist often without experiencing any more pain. The dentist and other conditioned stimuli in the situation will then gradually cease to elicit fear and return to being neutral.

Respondent conditioning is somewhat more influential in children's development than is habituation. It most commonly plays a role in aspects of the child's emotional behavior.

Operant Learning A third type of learning is called **operant learning**. Unlike habituation and respondent conditioning, operant learning is assumed by learning theorists to be very important for understanding the typical behavior of children.

Operant behaviors are influenced by their effects, and many of the everyday behaviors of children occur simply because they resulted in desirable consequences in the past. Any consequence that makes a response more likely to occur again is called a *reinforcer*. Consider the following examples. The same child may (1) share her toys with a friend because doing so often produces similar sharing by the other child, (2) throw a temper tantrum in the supermarket because this usually results in getting candy from her parent, (3) twist and shake the knob of the playroom door because this behavior is effective in getting it open, (4) work hard at skating lessons because the coach praises her when she performs well, and (5) put a pillow over her head when her baby brother is crying because this behavior helps reduce the unpleasant sound.

It should be obvious from this list that reinforcers can take many forms. Nevertheless, they all fall into one of two categories: those that involve getting something good are called **positive reinforcers** and those that involve getting rid of something bad are called **negative reinforcers**.

Conditioned stimulus (CS) A neutral stimulus that comes to elicit a response (UCR) through a conditioning process in which it is consistently paired with another stimulus (UCS) that naturally evokes the response.

Stimulus generalization A process related to respondent conditioning in which stimuli that are similar to the conditioned stimulus (CS) also acquire the power to elicit the response.

Respondent extinction A process related to respondent conditioning in which the conditioned stimulus (CS) gradually loses its power to elicit the response as a result of no longer being paired with the unconditioned stimulus (UCS).

Operant learning A form of learning in which the likelihood of an operant behavior changes as a result of its reinforcing or punishing consequences.

Positive reinforcer A consequence that makes the behavior it follows more likely through the presentation of something pleasant.

Negative reinforcer A consequence that makes the behavior it follows more likely through the removal of something unpleasant.

BOX 2.1

LITTLE ALBERT AND LITTLE PETER: CONDITIONING AND COUNTERCONDITIONING FEAR

Perhaps the most famous research conducted by John B. Watson involved the conditioning of a fear response in an 11-month-old child named Albert B. (Watson & Rayner, 1920). The study was designed to show that fear is an unconditioned response that can be easily conditioned to a variety of common stimuli.

Watson believed that children fear dogs, dentists, and the like because they associate these objects or persons with an unconditioned stimulus for fear, such as pain or a sudden loud noise. To illustrate this process, Watson first exposed Albert to a tame white laboratory rat, which produced only mild interest in the child. On several later occasions, Watson presented the rat to Albert and then made a loud noise (UCS) behind Albert. The noise elicited a pronounced fear response (UCR) in the form of crying and trembling. Very soon, the sight of the rat alone was enough to make Albert cry in fear—it had become a conditioned stimulus (CS) for that response. Watson demonstrated stimulus generalization by showing that objects similar to the rat, such as cotton or a white fur coat, also elicited the fear response.

A few years later, Watson and an associate named Mary Cover Jones applied the fear-conditioning process in reverse (Jones, 1924). A 3-year-old named Peter was brought to them with an intense fear of rabbits and other furry creatures. The researchers reasoned that if this fear had been learned (conditioned), it could be unlearned. They called their method for eliminating the fear response to the rabbit *counterconditioning*. It involved presenting the conditioned stimulus in such a way that it would not elicit the fear response but would instead elicit a competing emotional response—in this case, pleasure derived from eating.

On the first day of treatment, Peter was placed in a high chair and fed his lunch. At the same time, a caged rabbit was displayed on the other side of the room, far enough away so that the fear response did not occur. Each day, while Peter ate, the rabbit was moved slightly closer. In the end, Peter was not at all disturbed at having the rabbit sit next to him while he ate his lunch. The rabbit was no longer a conditioned stimulus for fear and had instead become associated with pleasure.

An experiment of the sort conducted with Little Albert, of course, would not be permitted today, because psychologists now have strict ethical guidelines for research that prohibit a child's being exposed to this type of fear experience (see Chapter 3). The experiment with Little Peter, however, is very similar to the type of fear-reduction therapy used today by clinical psychologists and would be considered a form of behavior modification.

It should also be apparent from our list of examples that the reinforcement process does not work only on desirable or beneficial responses. Reinforcement increases the likelihood of any behavior that leads to a pleasant consequence, whether we would typically view that behavior as appropriate (sharing toys), inappropriate (throwing a tantrum in a supermarket), or neutral (opening a door).

Punisher
A consequence that makes the behavior it follows less likely, either through the presentation of something unpleasant or the removal of something desirable.

Not all consequences are reinforcing, however. Behavior sometimes produces effects that are unpleasant, and these *reduce* the likelihood that the behavior will occur again. Such consequences are called **punishers**. We usually think of punishment as something that is delivered by parents or teachers for misbehavior, but the principle of punishment, like the principle of reinforcement, is simply part of nature's learning process. Punishment teaches organisms which responses are wise to repeat and which are better to avoid. Punishment, too, can entail either getting something bad (such as a spanking, a failing grade, or a scraped knee) or losing something good (such as a baseball, a chance to sit by a friend at lunch, or television privileges for a week). Either way, behaviors that lead to punishing consequences become less likely to occur again.

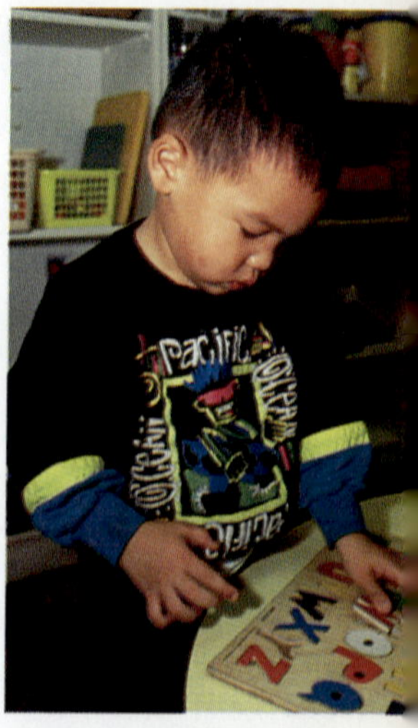

Some activities, like putting together a puzzle, are reinforced simply by the consequence of achieving the solution.

Applications

Effects and Side Effects of Punishment by Parents or Teachers

Punishment is a consequence that makes behavior less likely to occur again. We typically think of punishment as the discipline dispensed by parents, such as spanking or confining the child to his or her room. Most parents use these techniques in the hope that the punished behavior will disappear. Indeed, moderate to strong punishment, if delivered clearly and consistently, is effective in reducing undesirable behaviors.

At the same time, punishment can produce a number of side effects that parents may not anticipate. First of all, strong punishers can elicit aggression and other emotional behaviors in children, including crying, tantrums, and head banging. Second, the individual who delivers the punishment sometimes becomes so closely associated with punishment in general that the child may begin to avoid interacting with that person. Third, punishment can reduce an entire class of responses, sometimes including behaviors that are not a problem. For example, the child who is punished by the teacher for speaking out of turn may react by decreasing all verbal participation in class. Fourth, parents who use punishment may be serving as models for behavior that they do not want to see their children imitate. The fact that many delinquent children were exposed to physical punishment in childhood and that abused children frequently grow up to be abusing parents may reflect, in part, the children's imitation of aggression by the parents. Fifth, punishment is not a good teaching device because it tells children only what they did wrong, not what they should be doing instead. Finally, punishment has an addictive quality. Because it often is successful in temporarily ending the child's unwanted behavior, parents who are unaware of other disciplinary techniques may come to rely on it heavily.

Punishment should always be used in combination with reinforcement for the appropriate behaviors we wish the child to display. Even then, it should be used sparingly, and preferably as a negative consequence, such as removing something desirable, rather than as a positive consequence, such as slapping or spanking.

Punishment should be used sparingly as a disciplinary tool because it can produce side effects.

Social-Learning Theory

Over the years, the environmental/learning tradition has grown more like the other two major traditions (in fact, all three approaches continue to move closer together). In this section, we consider a second approach within the behavioral tradition, **social-learning theory**, which has become increasingly concerned with how cognitive factors influence development (Grusec, 1992).

Social-learning theory A form of environmental/learning theory that adds observational learning to respondent and operant learning as a process through which children's behavior changes.

The leading spokesperson for the social-learning viewpoint has been Albert Bandura (1986, 1992). Like other behavioral psychologists, Bandura believes that cognitive development alone does not explain childhood changes in behavior and that learning processes are responsible for much of children's development. But some learning processes, he feels, are affected by the child's cognitive abilities. This is especially true for the more complex types of learning that Bandura believes are involved in children's development beyond the infant years. We turn to one of these types next.

Observational Learning Skinner's addition of operant learning to Watson's Pavlovian conditioning greatly expanded learning theory's ability to explain children's behavior. Nevertheless, some problems remained. One was that children sometimes acquire new behaviors simply by seeing someone else perform them. A second was that children sometimes become more or less likely to perform a behavior after seeing another person experience reinforcing or punishing consequences for that behavior. Neither of these facts is easily explained by a type of learning in which changes in behavior occur only when children experience direct consequences for their actions.

Bandura solved this problem by proposing that as children grow, their development is increasingly based on a fourth type of learning—**observational learning**. Learning by observation occurs when the behavior of an *observer* is affected by witnessing the behavior (and often its consequences) of a *model*. In developmental psychology, the observers are children, and the models include parents, teachers, siblings, classmates, sports celebrities, television personalities, and even cartoon characters—in short, just about anyone in the child's world.

Observational learning A form of learning in which an observer's behavior changes as a result of observing a model.

Bandura and other researchers have studied three important questions regarding the modeling process: (1) Which models are most likely to influence a child's behavior? (2) Under what circumstances is this influence most likely to occur? (3) How does the child's behavior change as a result of observational learning?

The simple answer to the first question is that a model who possesses a characteristic that the child finds attractive or desirable—such as talent, intelligence, power, good looks, or popularity—is most likely to be imitated. Other issues can sometimes come into play, however, including the child's level of development and the types of behaviors being modeled.

The circumstances under which modeling is most effective also can vary, but one of the most important factors is whether the model receives reinforcing or punishing consequences for the behavior. One of Bandura's most significant contributions to social-learning theory was his demonstration that consequences of a model's behavior can affect the behavior of an observer. When a child sees a model receive reinforcement for a response, the child receives **vicarious reinforcement** and, like the model, becomes more likely to produce that same response. The opposite is true when the child receives **vicarious punishment** as a result of witnessing a model being punished. In some sense, then, observational learning is the same as operant learning, except that the child experiences the consequences vicariously rather than directly.

Vicarious reinforcement Reinforcing consequences experienced when viewing a model that affect an observer similarly.

Vicarious punishment Punishing consequences experienced when viewing a model that affect an observer similarly.

The most obvious and perhaps the most important result of modeling is **imitation**, which occurs when children copy what they have seen. Imitation can take such varied forms as eating the breakfast cereal a professional athlete claims to eat, climbing on a chair to steal a cookie from the shelf after seeing an older brother do it, or copying the problems a teacher is writing on the chalkboard.

Imitation Behavior of an observer that results from and is similar to the behavior of a model.

A second result of modeling occurs when the observer becomes less likely to perform a behavior that has just been modeled. This effect, known as **response inhibition**, is a common result of vicarious punishment. The teacher who publicly disciplines an unruly child in order to set an example for the rest of the class is counting on observational learning to inhibit similar behaviors in the other children.

Response inhibition The absence of a particular response that has just been modeled; often the result of vicarious punishment.

Children do not always immediately display behavior learned from models. A striking illustration of this point occurred in one of Bandura's early studies, in which one group of youngsters observed a model rewarded for displaying new aggressive behaviors toward an inflated toy clown, while a second group saw those same behaviors punished. When given an opportunity to play with the doll them-

Imitation is an important process by which children acquire new skills and behaviors.

selves, the children who witnessed the reinforcement imitated many of the model's aggressive acts toward the doll, whereas the group who observed punishment did not. But when later offered rewards for reproducing the aggressive behaviors, both groups were able to perform them quite accurately (Bandura, 1965). Obviously, all of the children had acquired (learned) the new behaviors, even though the vicariously experienced punishment had inhibited some children from performing them. This distinction between acquisition and performance has been of particular interest to researchers studying the potential effects of viewing television violence on children's aggressive behavior, which we discuss in Chapter 14.

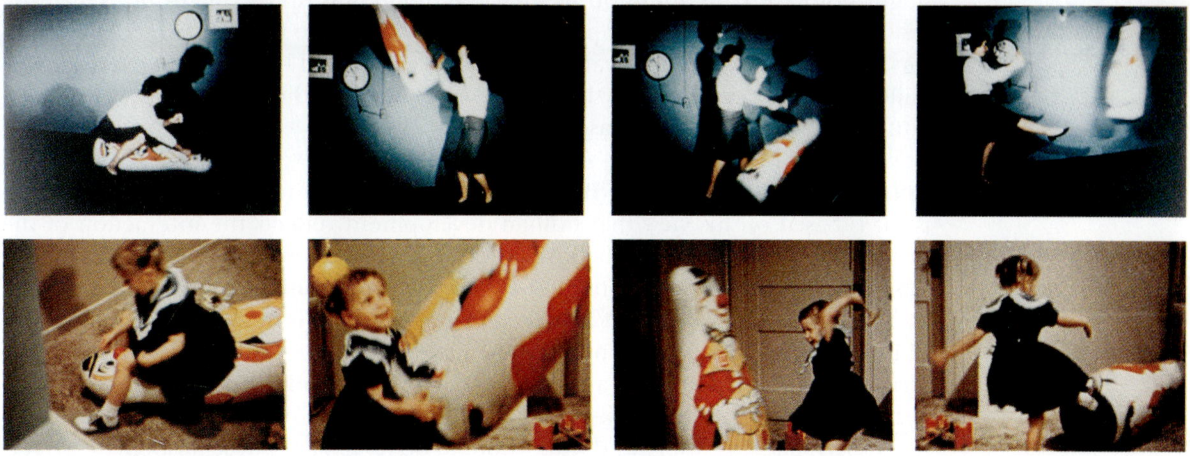

Albert Bandura's early research showed that children exposed to filmed violence were capable of very accurately imitating of the model's aggressive acts when given the opportunity to reproduce them.

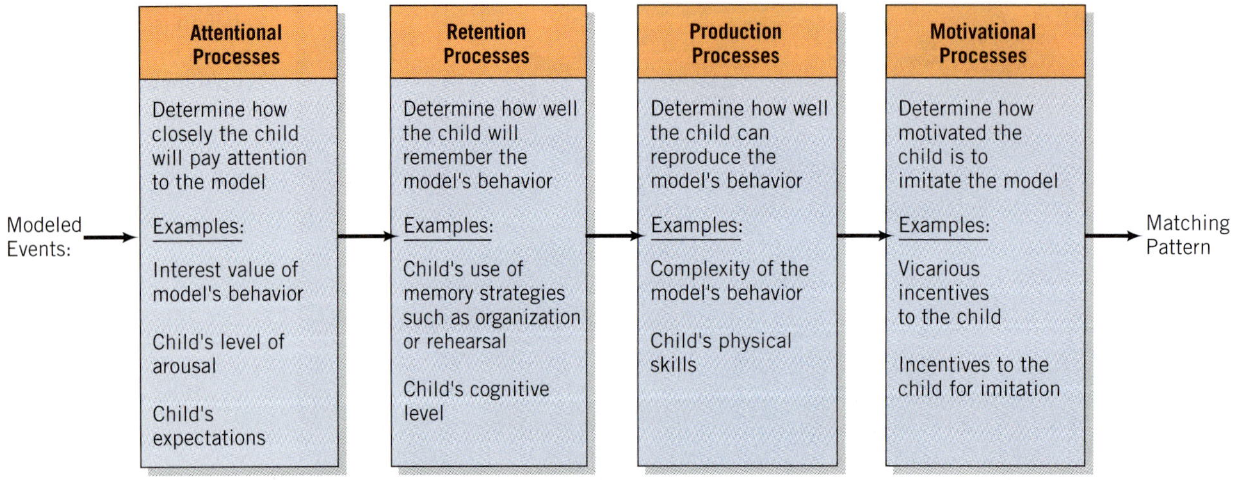

Figure 2.1
Bandura's model of observational learning. Adapted from Albert Bandura, *Social Learning Theory*, © 1977, p. 23. Reprinted by permission of Prentice-Hall, Inc., Upper Saddle River, New Jersey.

The acquisition–performance distinction is evident in Bandura's theoretical formulation of observational learning, depicted in Figure 2.1. Bandura believes that learning by observation involves four separate processes. The first two account for the acquisition, or learning, of a model's behavior, and the other two control the performance, or production, of these behaviors (Bandura, 1977b).

Attentional processes determine how closely the child pays attention to what the model is doing. *Retention processes* refer to how well the child can store the modeled information in memory for later use. *Production processes* control how well the child can reproduce the model's responses. *Motivational processes* determine who and what a child chooses to imitate.

One way to think of this formulation is to imagine a child viewing a model and then to consider why the child might *not* imitate the model's actions. The child might not have paid attention to what the model was doing, might not recall the model's responses, might not possess the physical skills to repeat the model's behaviors, or might feel little motivation to do what the model has done. In everyday life, children do not imitate everything they see. Bandura's theory suggests four important reasons why this is the case.

Reciprocal Determinism Bandura's social-learning analysis is truly interactionist. It is based on his view that human development reflects the interaction of the person (P), the person's behavior (B), and the environment (E). Bandura describes this process of interaction as **reciprocal determinism** (Bandura, 1978).

Reciprocal determinism Albert Bandura's proposed process describing the interaction of a person's characteristics and abilities (P), behavior (B), and environment (E).

As illustrated in Figure 2.2, the reciprocal determinism model forms a triangle of interactions. The person includes the child's cognitive abilities, physical characteristics, personality, beliefs, attitudes, and so on, which influence both the child's behavior and the child's environment. Children choose not only what they want to do (P→B), but also where and with whom to do it (P→E). These influences are reciprocal, however. Children's behavior (and the reactions it engenders) can affect their feelings about themselves and their attitudes and beliefs about other things (B→P). Likewise, much of children's knowledge about the world and other people

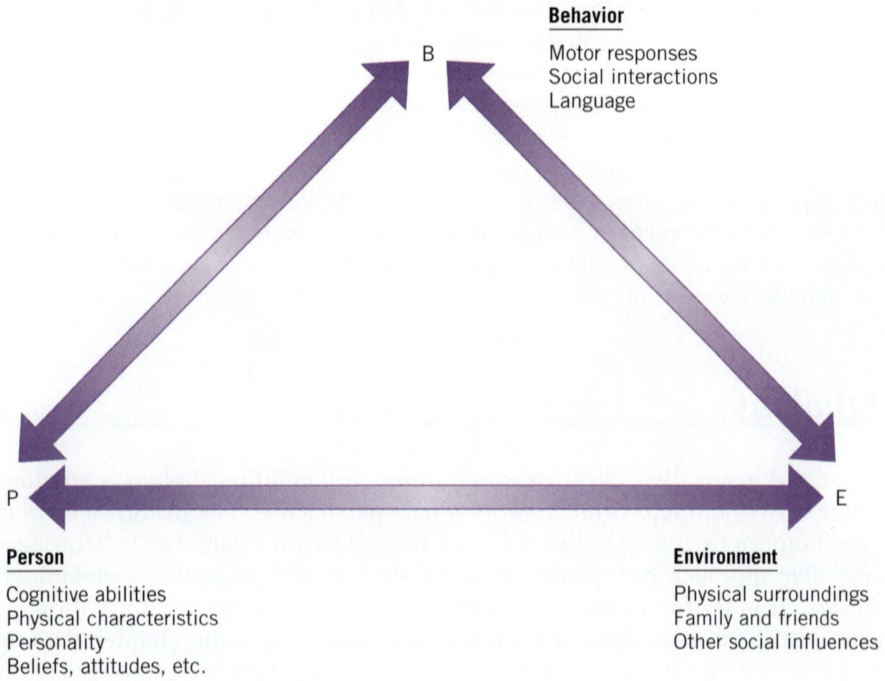

Figure 2.2
Bandura's model of reciprocal determinism. Adapted from "Self System in Reciprocal Determinism" by Albert Bandura, 1978, *American Psychologist, 33*, p. 345. Copyright © 1978 by the American Psychological Association. Adapted by permission.

results from information they receive from television, parents, textbooks, and other environmental sources (E→P).

Environment also affects behavior. The consequences of children's behavior and the models they observe can powerfully influence what they do (E→B). But children's behavior also contributes to creating their environment. A child who shares and cooperates with classmates is likely to attract many friends, whereas the opposite may be the case for a child who behaves selfishly or aggressively (B→E).

Bandura's addition of observational learning to the environmental/learning tradition, along with his willingness to incorporate cognitive aspects of development, has greatly increased the explanatory power of social-learning theory and has made it the most important learning-based approach. We consider the role of this model in many aspects of children's development throughout the text.

✓ *To Recap...*

Environmental/learning theories begin with the assumption that much of children's typical behavior is acquired through conditioning and learning principles. Learned behaviors are distinguished from behaviors that are temporary, unobservable, or based solely on biological processes.

Behavior analysis is one form of learning theory. In this view, three types of conditioning and learning are assumed to operate on children: habituation (and dishabituation), respondent conditioning, and operant learning. Habituation and respondent conditioning involve reflexes. In contrast, operant learning is controlled by the consequences of behavior. Consequences that make behavior more probable are called reinforcers; those that make behavior less probable are called punishers.

Social-learning theory, based largely on the ideas of Albert Bandura, proposes a greater role for cognitive factors than does behavior analysis. According to this theory, observational learning occurs when an observer's behavior changes as a result of viewing the behavior of a model. Consequences experienced when viewing a model, called vicarious reinforcement and vicarious punishment, can affect the behavior of an observer. The most important result of modeling is imitation. Response inhibition occurs when imitation of an observed behavior becomes less likely—usually because the model has received punishment for it. Acquisition of a modeled behavior is determined by the observer's attentional and retentional processes, whereas performance of the behavior is controlled by the observer's production and motivational processes.

Bandura's theoretical model, reciprocal determinism, holds that human development results from the complex interaction of characteristics of the person, the person's behavior, and the environment.

Ethology

Ethology
The study of development from an evolutionary perspective.

Sociobiology
A branch of biology that attempts to discover the evolutionary origins of social behavior.

The third major theoretical approach in modern child psychology is **ethology**, the study of development from an evolutionary perspective. The historical roots of this tradition can be traced to the work of Charles Darwin (1809–1882). More recently, a similar approach has sprung up in the field of biology. Called **sociobiology**, this approach looks for evolutionary origins of social behavior (E. O. Wilson, 1975). Among the three theoretical models we are discussing in this chapter, the ethological tradition has the fewest followers, but their numbers are growing rapidly, and the ideas and findings of ethology are being applied to more and more areas of child development (MacDonald, 1988a; Miller, 1993).

Behavior and Evolution

When trying to understand the ethological approach, it is important to keep in mind that from an evolutionary perspective, our species is the product of millions of years of change. What we are today represents only a small part of an enormous process. Ethology views human beings as only one of the 5 million or so species that presently inhabit the earth, and it considers human development within the context of the entire animal kingdom. It should not be surprising, then, that much of the research conducted within this tradition involves nonhuman species.

Like the other theoretical models, ethology attempts to explain the changes in behavior that occur across development. According to ethological theorists, these changes have two kinds of determinants, or causes—immediate and evolutionary. The immediate determinants are the more obvious and include the environment in which the behavior occurs, the animal's recent experiences, and the state or condition of the animal—whether it is hungry, tired, or angry, for example. The evolutionary determinants of behavior are less clear. Presumably the behavior at some point contributed to the animal's chances of survival and so became more likely to be passed along to future generations through the natural selection process. To explain such behaviors as hunting for prey or constructing a dam, then, ethologists consider both the immediate circumstances, such as the availability of prey or of appropriate building materials, and factors in the animal's evolutionary past, such as the climate and terrain in which the behaviors evolved.

Classical Ethology

Ethology first gained scientific recognition in the 1930s with the work of two pioneers in animal study, Konrad Lorenz and Niko Tinbergen. Both men were zoologists by training, and their early investigations focused exclusively on nonhuman animals. Nevertheless, their research laid the groundwork for the growing trend toward the application of ethological principles to child development, and in 1973 they were jointly awarded a Nobel Prize for their pioneering research.

Innate Mechanisms Ethologists have identified four qualities that characterize virtually all innate, or inborn, behaviors. First, they are *universal* to all members of the species. Second, since they are usually biologically programmed responses to very specific stimuli, they *require no learning or experience.* Third, they are normally *stereotyped,* meaning that they occur in precisely the same way every time they are displayed. Finally, they are only *minimally affected by environmental influences* (in the short run, that is; natural selection pressures affect them across generations) (Eibl-Eibesfeldt, 1989). Countless examples of these behaviors have been identified in virtually every known species, ranging from the nest-building behaviors of ants, to the pecking responses of chickens, to the herding behaviors of antelope.

In humans, such innate behaviors are most evident during infancy. An inborn response such as sucking, for example, is found in all babies, does not need to be learned, occurs in a stereotyped pattern, and is influenced very little by the environment (at least during the first weeks of life).

The idea of a stimulus that elicits a simple, reflexive, biological response, such as sucking, is neither new nor of interest only to ethologists (as the work of Pavlov and Watson clearly demonstrates). But ethologists have typically been interested in more complex *sequences* of innate behaviors, which they call **modal action patterns**. These are the chains of responses that we see, for example, when spiders spin webs, birds build nests, or bears care for newborn cubs. A modal action pattern is triggered by a specific stimulus in the animal's environment, what Lorenz called an **innate releasing mechanism**. A classic example of such a mechanism was demonstrated by Tinbergen (1973) in his work with the stickleback.

Modal action pattern
A sequence of behaviors elicited by a specific stimulus.

Innate releasing mechanism
A stimulus that triggers an innate sequence or pattern of behaviors.

The stickleback is a freshwater fish with three sharp spines. In winter, the males stay in schools and are relatively inactive. In spring, the rising water temperature sets off a distinctive pattern of mating behaviors. Each stickleback leaves the school and builds a tunnel-like nest in the sand, which he defends as his own territory against other males. When a female approaches the area above the nest, the male begins his courtship by stabbing her with one of his spines. He then swims down to the nest in an unusual zigzag pattern. The stabbing and swimming motion apparently excite the female, who follows him to his nest. When she enters it, the male places his face against her tail and begins to quiver. This stimulates the female to release her eggs, which the male fertilizes by releasing his sperm. He then chases her away and waits for another female to approach. This ritual continues until five or so females have released eggs in the nest. The male subsequently cares for the developing eggs, driving away intruders and fanning the water with his tail to provide the eggs with sufficient oxygen.

In addition to observing this mating process in the wild, Tinbergen studied sticklebacks in the laboratory. There he exposed the fish to wooden models of other sticklebacks of various colors and shapes to determine experimentally which stimuli are necessary to trigger and maintain the chain of behaviors. The details of these experiments are not crucial for our purposes, but the work does raise several important issues.

One issue concerns the relevance of these sorts of modal action patterns for human development. Although the mating rituals of humans are (fortunately) very different from those of sticklebacks, ethologists believe that many response patterns in humans are triggered by very specific stimuli. These may include, for example, maternal responses to newborn babies or certain forms of aggression. A related issue concerns the nature versus nurture question. The stickleback does not need to learn the complex courtship responses; they are elicited biologically by stimuli in the environment. This does not mean, however, that other aspects of the stickleback's behavior do not change in response to experiences or consequences. From the opposite perspective, even though many aspects of human behavior clearly result from learning processes, ethologists contend that this does not rule out the possibility that other aspects of human behavior—perhaps even complex behavior patterns—are controlled by innate evolutionary processes. Thus modern ethologists, too, are interactionists, assuming important roles for both nature and nurture processes.

Tinbergen's research strategy also illustrates how ethologists combine naturalistic and laboratory methods. The great majority of their investigations involve the observation of behaviors in the natural settings where they evolved. In this way, the researcher can examine how an animal's responses typically occur. But the behaviors are also studied in more structured settings, where the researcher can control the conditions under which events take place and can subject an animal's rituals and routines to various experimental tests.

Sensitive Periods An important issue in psychology concerns how an animal's genetic or biological makeup can influence the learning process (Bolles & Beecher, 1988), that is, how nature and nurture work together to change behavior. Ethologists argue that animals are biologically programmed so that some things are learned most easily during certain periods of development. A dramatic example of this is illustrated by Lorenz's research on **imprinting**, the process by which newborns of some species form an emotional bond with their mothers.

Imprinting
A biological process of some species in which the young acquire an emotional attachment to the mother through following.

In many bird species, whose young can walk almost immediately after hatching, baby birds soon begin to follow the mother as she moves about. Lorenz guessed that this simple act of following was responsible for the strong social bond that developed between the newborn and the parent. To confirm his suspicion, Lorenz removed just-hatched goslings from their mother and had them follow another animal, or various nonliving objects that he pulled along, or even himself. As he predicted, the young birds quickly imprinted to whatever they followed and thereafter treated it as their mother (Lorenz, 1937).

Lorenz further discovered that one of the most important influences on imprinting was the age of the chicks. If the act of following occurred during a period that began several hours after birth and lasted until sometime the next day, the attachment bond reliably developed. When the following occurred only before or after this period, however, little or no imprinting resulted. Ethologists now use the term **sensitive periods** to describe points in development when learning is much easier than it is at earlier or later points. Sensitive periods are not restricted to imprinting or even to the area of mother–infant attachment. Child researchers have applied the concept to areas as diverse as language acquisition (Newport, 1991) and gender-role development (Money & Annecillo, 1987), as we will see in later chapters.

Sensitive period
A period of development during which certain behaviors are more easily learned.

Applications to Human Development

Our main interest in ethological theory is its application to child development, and modern researchers are finding many areas of development in which evolutionary processes may be important (DeKay & Buss, 1992; Scarr, 1992).

Sociobiology We said earlier that some biologists have attempted to apply evolutionary principles to human social behavior. This new area of research began

Konrad Lorenz found that newly hatched goslings, when permitted to follow him around for a short time, would imprint to him and thereafter treat him as their mother.

rather dramatically in 1975 with the publication of a book by a Harvard biologist, E. O. Wilson, entitled *Sociobiology: The New Synthesis.* According to Wilson's radical and somewhat controversial theory, genes are very selfish structures whose only interest is to ensure their own survival from generation to generation.

Many specific physical characteristics (color of fur, size of ears, and so on) are carried in an animal's genes. When a characteristic is valuable for survival or reproduction, the genes that produce it are more likely to be passed along to the next generation—Darwin's natural selection process. Sociobiologists believe that genes produce not only physical traits, but social behaviors (although these theorists admit that the process by which a gene can produce a behavior is not yet completely understood). Social behaviors that are more adaptive for survival thus are assumed to undergo the same natural selection process as physical traits.

The sociobiological view can be illustrated by a frequently cited example. Consider a mother who risks her life to save her child from danger. According to the traditional ethological model, this response by the mother should not have an evolutionary basis, because natural selection would not favor behaviors that reduce an individual's chances of survival. Sociobiologists, however, contend that the mother's genes have in some way programmed her to do whatever she can to ensure that her genes are passed on to future generations. Because her child carries many of those same genes, and because he would have many reproductive years ahead, evolutionary mechanisms drive the mother to sacrifice her life to save that of her child (Dawkins, 1976; Porter & Laney, 1980).

Ethologists believe that evolutionary processes play some role in the behavior of all species.

Wilson suggests that genetic effects on social behavior are better understood at the level of the culture or society, rather than of the individual. He claims, for example, that many of our cultural practices, such as taboos against incest and laws against murder or assault, reflect an evolutionary process that favors individuals whose social behaviors are in line with what is best for the survival of the species. The behaviors of these individuals are thus more likely to be passed along to future generations, whereas undesirable behaviors are not. This new theory has been both praised and criticized (Lerner & von Eye, 1992). But it has sparked a great deal of debate and has drawn additional attention to the evolutionary perspective.

Human Ethology Ethological principles have increasingly been applied to our own species (Archer, 1992; Eibl-Eibesfeldt, 1989). As early as the 1940s, Lorenz suggested that physical characteristics of babies, such as the shape of their head and the sound of their cry, might serve as stimuli to trigger caregiving by mothers (Lorenz, 1950). Developmental psychologists likewise interpreted infants' early reflexive behaviors in terms of their evolutionary value to the species. Nevertheless, the scientific application of the ethological model to child development is usually considered to have begun in 1969, when John Bowlby published the first of his three volumes on the subject (Bowlby, 1969/1982, 1973, 1980).

Bowlby, an English physician and psychoanalyst, was the first to attract child psychologists to an evolutionary interpretation of human development. As a clinician, Bowlby had witnessed the emotional problems of children who had been raised in institutions. Such children often have difficulty forming and maintaining close relationships. Bowlby attributed this problem to the children's lack of a strong attachment to their mothers during infancy. His interest in this area eventually led him to an ethological explanation of how and why the mother–infant bond is established (Bretherton, 1995).

Bowlby's theory is an interesting mix of ethology and Freudian theory (Holmes, 1995; Sroufe, 1986). As did Freud, Bowlby believes that the quality of the early relationship (between baby and mother) is critical to later development and that these first experiences are carried forward by processes in the unconscious. Bowlby's theory also reflects the fundamental principle of classical ethology, that a close mother–infant bond is crucial in humans (and in most higher-level species) for the survival of the young. Infants who remain near the mother can be fed, protected, trained, and transported more effectively than can infants who stray from her side. The behaviors used by the mother and infant to keep the pair in close contact must therefore be innate and controlled by a variety of releasing stimuli (we discuss these behaviors in Chapter 12). Bowlby further maintains that the attachment bond develops easily during a sensitive period, but after this time it may become impossible for the child ever to achieve a truly intimate emotional relationship (Bowlby, 1988).

Bowlby's work has encouraged a great deal of additional research on attachment and bonding processes in humans. More important for this tradition, it began a general movement toward examining other aspects of child development within an evolutionary context (Blurton-Jones, 1972). Psychologists have since investigated children's aggression, peer interactions, cognitive development, and many other topics.

Ethologists have also influenced developmental research methods. Observational methods have always been used by child researchers, but there has been a renewed interest in studying children in their natural environments (Bronfenbrenner, 1979; McCall, 1977). Observational techniques that do not influence or intrude on children's normal social interactions are being added to more experimental approaches to studying these behaviors. The ethological tradition has clearly established itself as an important perspective in contemporary developmental psychology.

✓ To Recap...

Ethology is based on the principles of evolution as first proposed by Charles Darwin. Ethologists believe that behaviors have both immediate and evolutionary determinants. These scientists are primarily concerned with innate behaviors, and they attempt to explain complex response patterns in terms of their survival value for the species.

Lorenz and Tinbergen, two founders of the ethological movement, identified four characteristics of innate behavior: it is universal; it is stereotyped; it requires no learning; and it is minimally affected by the environment. Ethologists have described how complex sequences of inherited responses (modal action patterns) are triggered by stimuli in the environment and how innate mechanisms, such as imprinting, influence the learning process.

Sociobiology is a recent attempt to explain social behavior in terms of an evolutionary model in which the survival of the genes supersedes any other goal. This mechanism is believed to be principally expressed in cultural and social structures. Human ethology emerged largely as a result of Bowlby's research on the attachment process. Many aspects of child development now are being studied from an ethological perspective.

Development in Context

The Ecological Approach

The three approaches we have just described guide most of the research conducted by child psychologists. But a fourth perspective that has recently emerged is proving very influential. This perspective is not a new theoretical model. Instead, it represents a different way of thinking about human development and a different approach to studying the factors that influence it (Moen, Elder, & Luscher, 1995).

Scientific research on children's development traditionally has taken place in laboratory settings. There are good reasons for this. The most important is that scientific investigation demands careful experimental control and, until recently, the laboratory has afforded the only setting in which such control could be achieved.

Some researchers, however, have questioned the wisdom of this practice, pointing to an obvious fact—children's development does not generally take place in laboratories. It takes place at home, with the family; at school, with classmates and teachers; in the park, with neighbors and peers; and, more generally, within a larger social and cultural environment. In short, *development always occurs in a context.* And, more important, the context often influences the course of that development. This realization has produced a growing interest in studying children in the settings in which their development typically occurs and in examining how the context influences, and is influenced by, the children's behavior.

The idea of studying development in context—called the **ecological approach**—is not new. Darwin argued that to understand the evolutionary value of any behavior, we must consider the ecological niche in which it evolved.

Ecological approach An approach to studying development that focuses on individuals within their environmental contexts.

The recent resurgence of interest in the ecological perspective can be traced to two sources: the development of more sophisticated methods for studying behavior in the natural environment (Vasta, 1982a); and the publication of an influential book by Urie Bronfenbrenner, a psychologist at Cornell University. In *The Ecology of Human Development* (1979), Bronfenbrenner revitalized this field by providing researchers

Urie Bronfenbrenner's work has revitalized interest in the ecological approach to studying human development.

with a conceptual framework in which ecological issues could be studied. His approach, which he now describes as a *bioecological* model, has been revised several times (Bronfenbrenner, 1992; Bronfenbrenner & Ceci, 1994; Bronfenbrenner & Morris, 1998) and has generated a number of related efforts by other researchers (Leyendecker & Scholmerich, 1991; Moen et al., 1995).

The ecological approach is based on the notion that to understand development completely we must consider how the unique characteristics of a child interact with that child's surroundings. The child possesses a variety of personal characteristics; the most important of these are described by Bronfenbrenner as *developmentally generative*—capable of influencing other people in ways that are important to the child—and *developmentally disruptive*—capable of causing problems in the environment with corresponding negative effects on the child.

By instigating various responses and reactions from others, children in a sense become "producers" of their own environments—a concept we will come across again in later chapters. Examples of these characteristics include personality traits that are positive (sociability, cooperativeness, curiosity) or negative (impulsiveness, explosiveness, distractibility), physical appearance, and intellectual abilities. The environment, in this model, is viewed as a series of interrelated layers, with those closest to the child having the most direct impact and those farther away influencing the child more indirectly.

Transactional influence A bidirectional, or reciprocal, relationship in which individuals influence one another's behaviors.

Bronfenbrenner contends that the child and the environment continually influence one another in a bidirectional, or **transactional**, manner. For example, suppose a child has the developmentally generative characteristics of being bright and articulate. These may affect the child's environment by resulting in the parents' sending her to a better school, which in turn may influence the child by resulting in improved academic skills, which again may affect her environment by attracting friends who have high career aspirations, and so forth, in an ongoing cycle of interaction and development. These sorts of interactions, Bronfenbrenner argues, are very difficult to study if the child is removed from the natural environment in which they occur.

Ecological theory holds that development varies depending on the context in which it occurs, including the people and the physical resources.

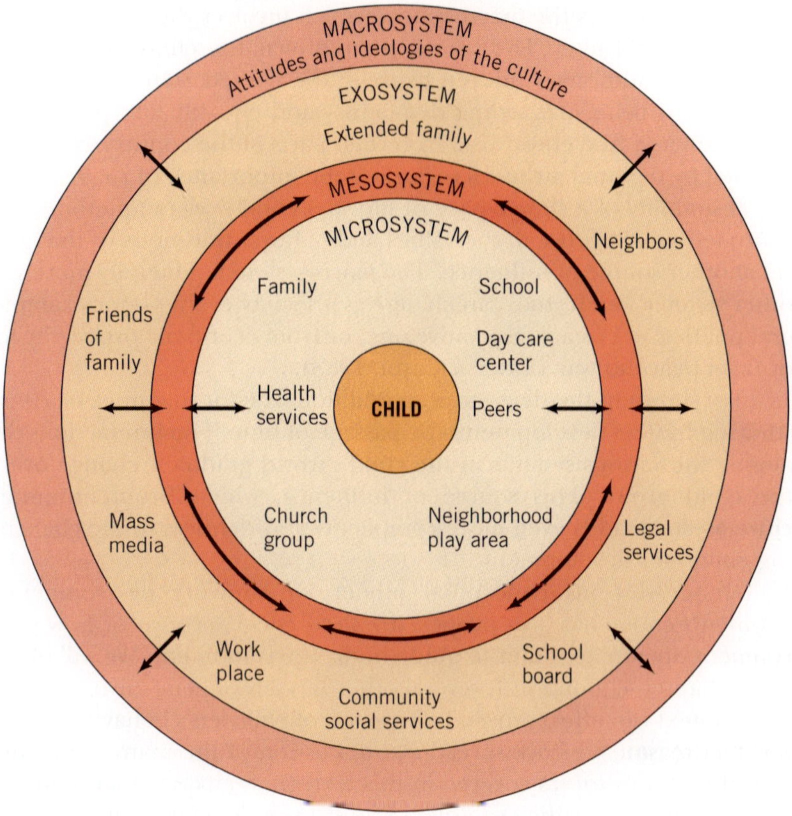

Figure 2.3 Bronfenbrenner's ecological model of the environment. U. Bronfenbrenner, from C. Kopp/Krakow, *Child Development in the Social Context* (figure 12.1), © 1982 by Addison-Wesley Publishing Co., Inc. Reprinted with permission of Addison Wesley Longman.

Figure 2.3 shows Bronfenbrenner's ecological model of development. At the center is the child and his or her physical and personal attributes. Nearest the child is the **microsystem**, which for most children includes the family, the school, the church, the playground, and so forth, along with the relationships that the child forms within these settings. The microsystem possesses physical characteristics, such as the size of the child's house, the amount of nearby playground equipment, and the number of books in the child's day-care center. It also consists of people, including the child's immediate family, the other children on the block, the child's teacher, and so on. These people, in turn, possess characteristics that may be relevant to the child's development, such as the socioeconomic status of the peer group, the educational background of the parents, and the political attitudes of the teacher. The microsystem is not constant, but changes as the child grows.

Microsystem The environmental system closest to the child, such as the family or school. The first of Bronfenbrenner's layers of context.

The **mesosystem** refers to the system of relationships among the child's microsystems. This might include the parents' relationship with the child's teacher and the relationship between the child's siblings and neighborhood friends. In general, the more interconnected these systems are, the more the child's development is likely to be supported in a clear and consistent way.

Mesosystem The interrelationships among the child's microsystems. The second of Bronfenbrenner's layers of context.

The **exosystem** refers to social settings that can affect the child but in which the child does not participate directly. Some examples are the local government, which decides how strictly air-pollution standards will be enforced or which families will be eligible for welfare payments; the school board, which sets teachers' salaries and recommends the budget for new textbooks and equipment; and the parents' places of employment, which establish policies regarding paid family leaves and on-site day-care facilities.

Exosystem Social systems that can affect children but in which they do not participate directly. Bronfenbrenner's third layer of context.

Macrosystem
The culture or subculture in which the child lives. Bronfenbrenner's fourth layer of context.

Finally, there is the **macrosystem**, which involves the culture and subculture in which the child lives. The macrosystem affects the child through its beliefs, attitudes, and traditions. Children living in the United States may be influenced, for example, by beliefs regarding democracy and equality and perhaps the virtues of capitalism and free enterprise. In certain parts of the country, children may also be affected by regional attitudes regarding the importance of rugged individualism or the desirability of a slower pace of life. If a child lives in an ethnic or racially concentrated neighborhood, the values and cultural traditions of that group may add yet another source of influence. The macrosystem is generally more stable than the other systems, but it, too, can change as a society evolves—for example, from a liberal political era to a conservative one, or from economic prosperity to depression, or from peace to war (Elder & Caspi, 1988).

Chronosystem
Bronfenbrenner's term for the passage of time as a context for studying human development.

Not shown in the diagram is an additional factor that must be considered when studying human development: the passage of time. The interactions that take place among the various systems in the child's world gradually change over time and as the child grows. This source of influence, which Bronfenbrenner terms the **chronosystem**, adds even more complexity and richness to the challenge of analyzing children's development.

Along with his conceptual model for studying development in context, Bronfenbrenner has also proposed a theoretical account of how genes and environment operate together to guide human development. We will discuss that theory in Chapter 4, along with several other models of gene-environment interaction.

Context can affect any and all aspects of children's behavior and development. For that reason, we have spread our discussion of the many contextual influences over the various topics covered in this text. Each chapter that follows includes sections discussing specific examples of *development in context*, which focus on the three most important contexts for children: the family, the school, and the culture.

Conclusion

It may seem that ideas regarding child development have not changed very much in the past few hundred years. Locke, Rousseau, and Darwin offered explanations of human behavior that are, in essence, still with us today. Modern theories of development, however, are different from these early models in several important ways.

The first is that today's viewpoints are much less extreme. There are no longer pure nature or nurture theories, for example. Thus, although each of the theories described in this chapter has its own ideas, philosophy, and methods, each also accepts many of the ideas of the other models. As psychologists continue to add to our knowledge of child development, the overlap among the three approaches will undoubtedly grow.

A second difference is that today's psychologists no longer attempt to explain human development with only a few principles or processes. We have come to realize that behavior has many causes and that the mechanisms through which they operate are intricate and often interrelated. Modern theoretical explanations reflect this increasing complexity, and this trend, too, is likely to continue.

The final difference is that today's models are based on a great deal of scientific data. Early theories of human development were mostly the products of philosophical debates and logical deductions. Modern explanations, in contrast, have grown out of research findings, and they are continually being modified and revised in response to new observations and experimental data. A particular child psychologist may prefer one theoretical approach over another. In the final analysis, however, the evidence provided by research will determine which theories will survive and which will be abandoned.

Visual Summary for Chapter 2:

Theories of Child Development

Cognitive-Developmental Models

Cognitive abilities are fundamental and guide children's behavior. The key to understanding children's behavior lies in how their knowledge is structured at any given time, and how it changes as they grow.

Major Approaches	Key Assumptions
Piaget's Theory	*Development can be described in terms of functions and cognitive structures. Changes in structures are guided by two functions: organization and adaptation. Adaptation consists of assimilation and accommodation. Development consists of movement through four stages: sensorimotor, preoperational, concrete operations, and formal operations.*
Information-processing	*Cognition is viewed in terms of a computer-like system with three parts: input from the senses, internal processes that act on and transform the information, output from the system in the form of behavior.*
Social Models	*Social cognition refers to children's knowledge about people and social processes. Vygotsky's sociocultural approach contends that social processes are crucial to the development of children's cognitive abilities and lead to the gradual internalization of culturally provided forms of knowledge and tools of adaptation.*

Environmental/Learning Approaches

Much of children's typical behavior is acquired through conditioning and learning principles.

Major Approaches	Key Assumptions
Behavior Analysis	*Three types of conditioning and learning are assumed to operate on children: habituation, respondent conditioning, and operant learning. Habituation and respondent conditioning involve reflexes, whereas operant learning is controlled by the consequences of behavior. Reinforcers are consequences that make behavior more probable; punishers are consequences that make behavior less probable.*
Social-Learning Theory	*Bandura's theory stresses the role of observational learning. Vicarious reinforcement and vicarious punishment can affect the behavior of an observer. The distinction is made between the acquisition of a modeled response and its performance. Reciprocal determinism holds that human development results from the interaction of characteristics of the person, the person's behavior, and the environment.*

Ethology

Ethology is based on the principles of evolution. Ethologists are primarily concerned with innate behaviors, and they attempt to explain complex response patterns in terms of their survival value for the species.

Major Approaches	Key Assumptions
Classical Ethology	*Lorenz and Tinbergen identified four characteristics of innate behavior: it is universal, it is stereotyped, it requires no learning, and it is minimally affected by the environment. Ethologists view complex sequences of inherited responses as modal action patterns that are triggered by innate releasing mechanisms in the organism's environment.*
Sociobiology	*Sociobiology is a recent attempt to explain social behavior in terms of an evolutionary model in which the survival of the genes supersedes any other goal.*
Human Ethology	*Human ethology emerged largely from the results of Bowlby's research on the attachment process. Many aspects of child development now are being studied from an ethological perspective.*

Ecological Approach

Human development should be studied in the various contexts in which it occurs. Developmental interactions are transactional.

Bronfenbrenner's Model

Microsystem	*Layer of the environment that most directly affects the child. Examples include family, school, and neighborhood.*
Mesosystem	*System of relationships among the child's microsystems.*
Exosystem	*Social settings that affect the child indirectly. Examples include community services, mass media, and family friends.*
Macrosystem	*Culture and subculture in which the child lives.*
Chronosystem	*Interactions among the various systems over time.*

Chapter 3

Research Methods

The developing child may seem quite different from atoms fusing to produce nuclear energy or leaf cells using light and carbon dioxide to make food. Yet the research methods used by developmental psychologists to study children are essentially the same as those used by physicists, biologists, and other researchers in the natural sciences. In this chapter, we examine some of these methods and the ways child researchers can use them to unlock the mysteries of human development.

We saw in Chapter 1 that the study of the child became scientific in the 19th century, when G. Stanley Hall began using questionnaires to reveal children's everyday knowledge. Since then, the research methods used by child psychologists have advanced in many different ways. These advances have contributed importantly to the enormous growth in our knowledge and understanding of developmental processes (Miller, 1998).

We begin by outlining some of the ideas and concepts that are basic to all scientific research. We then consider the principal research methods used in developmental psychology. Last, we discuss the sometimes thorny issue of research ethics.

Scientific Research

Scientific method
The system of rules used by scientists to conduct and evaluate their research.

Theory
A broad set of statements describing the relation between a phenomenon and the factors assumed to affect it.

Law (principle)
A predicted relation between a phenomenon and a factor assumed to affect it that is supported by a good deal of scientific evidence.

Hypothesis
A predicted relation between a phenomenon and a factor assumed to affect it that is not yet supported by a great deal of evidence. Hypotheses are tested in experimental investigations.

The approach scientists use to study any problem or issue is known as the **scientific method**. The method is really a system of rules that scientists use to design and conduct their research, to evaluate their results, and to communicate their findings to other scientists. These rules have evolved over hundreds of years, and they can be applied to the study of virtually anything.

The Role of Theory

In Chapter 2, we presented three major theories, but we did not actually define the term. In psychology, a **theory** is a set of statements describing the relation between behavior and the factors that influence it. A specific statement that is well supported by research evidence is called a **law** or **principle**—the principle of reinforcement is a good example. A statement that simply postulates, or proposes, a relation is called a **hypothesis**. Any individual study is usually designed to test a researcher's hypothesis regarding how some aspect of children's behavior is affected by some factor in their world.

Theories have two important roles in scientific research. The first is to *organize research findings*. As investigators acquire knowledge, they use theories to fit the information together into a coherent explanation of the behaviors and processes being studied. Once the knowledge is organized, it is sometimes obvious that certain questions remain to be answered or that specific relations probably exist even though they do not yet have substantial supporting evidence. A second role of theories, then, is to *guide new research* by indicating to investigators which hypotheses should be tested next.

Psychologists do not investigate children's development by randomly studying any question that pops into their heads. Research is typically guided by an underlying theory and theoretical orientation. Thus, cognitive-developmentalists tend to investigate characteristics of children's knowledge; environmental/learning theorists study ways in which behavior is acquired through experience; and ethologists examine various innate patterns of responses.

Objectivity

Children are not of interest only to psychologists, of course. Scholars in literature, music, and art, for example, have devoted much attention to the developing child. But in these fields, the emphasis frequently is on individual tastes, personal opinions, and other subjective judgments. In psychology and the other natural sciences, the emphasis is on **objectivity**.

Objectivity
A characteristic of scientific research; it requires that the procedures and subject matter of investigations should be formulated so that they could, in principle, be agreed on by everyone.

Objective methods of study have as their primary goal the opportunity for any other scientist, at least in principle, to conduct the same research in the same manner (and presumably arrive at the same results). In addition, objectivity helps to reduce potential sources of *bias* that may enter into the research, such as the experimenter's personal beliefs or preferences regarding what the results should be. These goals are achieved in a number of ways.

One is through a focus on *observable* behaviors. Recall that in child psychology our two primary goals—to describe children's behavior at each point in their development and to identify the causes and processes that produce changes in behavior from one point to the next—center on behavior. Even developmentalists who are concerned primarily with cognition observe the effects of internal cognitive processes on some aspect of behavior. For example, we study assimilation and accommodation by observing a child's reactions to new experiences; we study intelligence by calculating a child's performance on an IQ test; and we study self-esteem by examining how a child interacts in social situations.

A second requirement for ensuring objectivity is that the behaviors under study must be *measurable.* It is not enough that we can observe behavior; we must also feel confident as to when the behavior did or did not occur, when one behavior ended and the next one began, and so forth. Such confidence is achieved by defining and describing the behavior very precisely, so that independent observers would have no trouble agreeing on what happened in a given situation. For example, suppose we are interested in studying children's altruism—their willingness to help someone else. We might first define altruism in terms of sharing behaviors and then

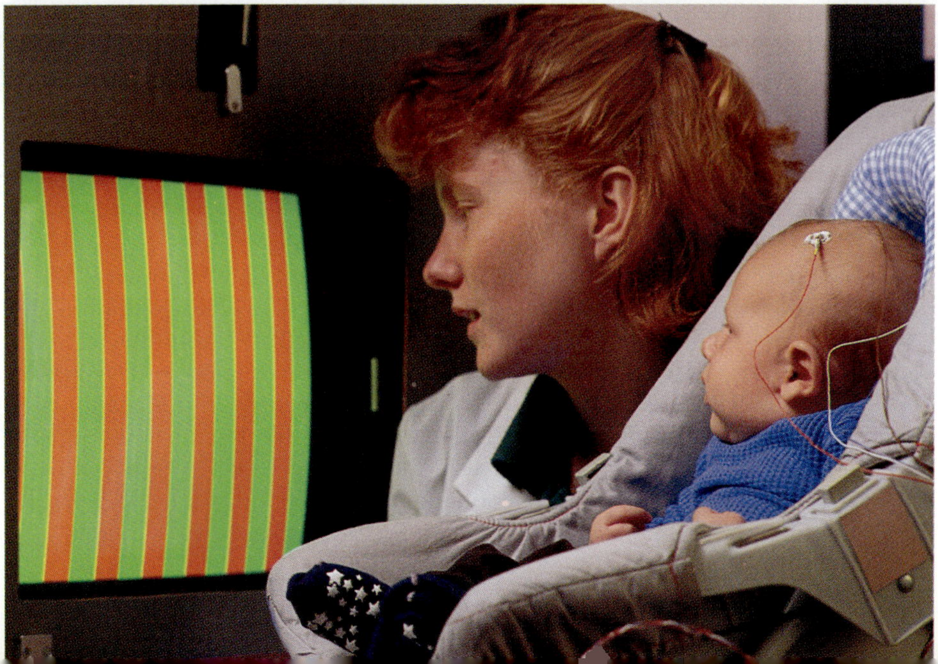

An important characteristic of psychological research is the focus on objective definitions and measurable behaviors.

develop a procedure that entails observing the number of pennies just won in a game that a child donates to a charity. Or, suppose we want to investigate an infant's attachment to her mother. We could define attachment in terms of specific behaviors, such as crying, smiling, and searching, and then measure the amount of time that elapses before the infant displays each of these behaviors after the mother has left the room. In this way, abstract concepts such as "altruism" and "attachment" become measurable in an objective, scientific way.

A third way to achieve objectivity is to make everything in the research study *quantifiable*, that is, able to be counted. The researcher must quantify not only the children's behaviors, but also the factors that the researcher hypothesizes may be affecting the behaviors. Usually such factors are physical. The number of children in a classroom, the length of time a child spends reading, or the amount of alcohol that a pregnant mother has consumed, for example, are relatively easy to define in this way. Factors that involve the behaviors of others—social approval, peer interactions, or modeling, for instance—are more difficult to deal with, but they, too, must be carefully defined so that they can be measured and counted.

Throughout this text, we describe many research studies. These studies vary greatly from one another in the issues under investigation, the methods used to collect data, and the types of research participants involved. All of them, however, share the characteristics we have just described. They focus on changes in observable responses, and they deal with behaviors and events that have been measured and quantified with as much precision as possible.

✓ To Recap...

The scientific method consists of the rules that researchers use to conduct and describe their investigations. Scientific theories play two important roles in the research process. First, they help to organize the information gathered from scientific studies. Second, they guide researchers to the important questions that need to be examined next.

Scientific research requires objectivity, which in psychology leads to a focus on observable behaviors and a need for behaviors and their determining factors to be described so that they are measurable and quantifiable.

Types of Research

Research in psychology generally falls into one of three categories: descriptive, correlational, or experimental. Here we briefly discuss each of these approaches as they apply to the study of children.

Descriptive Research

Descriptive research Research based solely on observations, with no attempt to determine systematic relations among the variables.

The oldest form of psychological research is the purely descriptive approach. When applied to children, **descriptive research** consists of simply observing children and recording what is seen. The psychologist makes no formal attempt to identify relations among the children's behaviors and any other factors. Early *baby biographies*, such as those in which Darwin and others kept daily records of the behaviors of their infants, provided the first systematic descriptive data on human development. G. Stanley Hall's questionnaire findings and, later, Arnold Gesell's norms—both of which described the typical skills and abilities of children of various ages—also used the descriptive method.

Today, descriptive research of this sort is not very common. Normally it is conducted only when very little is known about a topic. Even then, it is often only a first step in a research plan that will go on to use more sophisticated methods of investigation.

Correlational Research

The step beyond observing and describing behaviors is identifying any systematic relations in the observations. Specifically, researchers attempt to identify correlations among variables. A **variable** is any factor that can take on different values along some dimension. Common examples include human physical characteristics—height, weight, age, and so on—and aspects of the environment—temperature, room size, distance to the nearest library, and number of people in a family, for instance. Human behaviors, if properly defined, can also be variables and can vary along several types of dimensions—for example, how many times a child asks the teacher for help (*frequency*), how loudly a baby cries (*intensity*), or how long a child practices the piano (*duration*).

Variable
Any factor that can take on different values along a dimension.

A **correlation** is a statement that describes how two variables are related. Perhaps a psychologist would like to know whether children's ages are correlated with—systematically related to—their heights. The researcher might observe and record the heights of 100 children, aged 2 to 12, and examine whether changes in the one variable correspond to changes in the other. In this case, the psychologist could expect to find a clear relation between the variables of age and height—that is, as children increase in age, they generally increase in height as well. This type of relation, in which two variables change in the same direction, is described as a **positive correlation**.

Correlation
The relation between two variables, described in terms of direction and strength.

Positive correlation
A correlation in which two variables change in the same direction.

What about the relation between a child's age and the number of hours each day that the child spends at home? Here we would also discover a systematic relation, but the variables involved would move in opposite directions—as a child's age increases, the amount of time the child spends at home generally decreases. This sort of relation is called a **negative correlation.**

Negative correlation
A correlation in which two variables change in opposite directions.

Finally, we might investigate the relation between a child's height and the number of children in the child's classroom. In this case, we would likely find that the two variables are not related to one another at all and so have no correlation.

Correlations can be described not only in terms of their direction (positive or negative) but also in terms of their strength. A strong correlation means that two variables are closely related. In such cases, knowing the value of one gives us a good indication of the value of the second. As a correlation grows weaker, the amount of predictability between the two variables decreases. When the variables become completely unrelated, knowledge of the value of one gives us no clue as to the value of the other.

The direction of a correlation is indicated by a plus or minus sign, and its strength is indicated by a numerical value that can be calculated from a simple statistical formula. The result is called the **correlation coefficient (*r*)**, which can range between +1.00 and –1.00. A correlation coefficient of +.86 indicates a strong positive correlation, and +.17 indicates a weak positive correlation. Similarly, –.93, –.41, and –.08 denote, respectively, a strong, a moderate, and a weak negative correlation. A coefficient of 0.00 means that there is absolutely no correlation between two variables. Correlations can also be presented visually with a **scatter diagram**, some examples of which are shown in Figure 3.1.

Correlation coefficient (*r*)
A number between +1.00 and –1.00 that indicates the direction and strength of a correlation between two variables.

Scatter diagram
A graphic illustration of a correlation between two variables.

To illustrate both the usefulness and the limitations of correlational research, let us consider a hypothetical example. Suppose a research team is interested in learning whether a relation exists between children's reading ability and the amount of

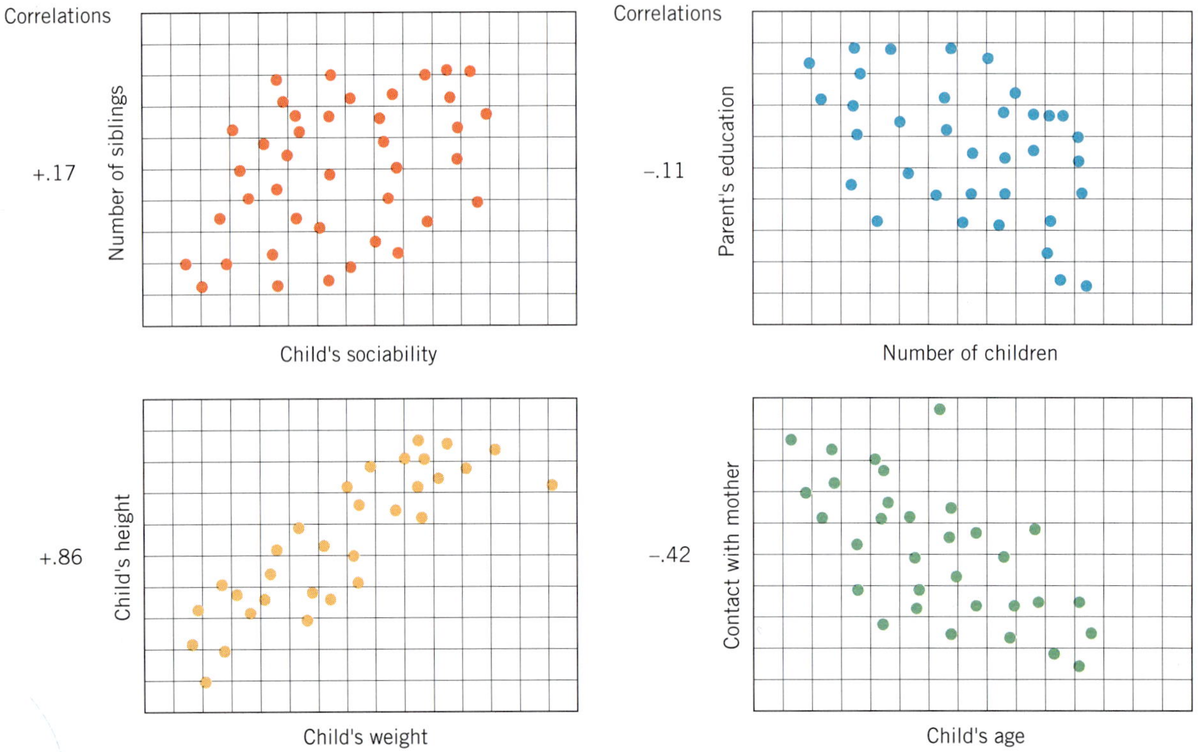

Figure 3.1
Scatter diagrams illustrating correlations between two variables. Each dot represents one child and shows the child's values for the two variables. One value is plotted from the vertical axis and the other from the horizontal axis. The left two graphs show positive correlations, and the right two graphs show negative correlations.

time they watch the educational television program *Sesame Street.* To begin, the researchers randomly select a number of children and measure each child's values on the reading-ability variable (perhaps by giving the children a reading test on which they can score between 0 and 100) and on the viewing variable (perhaps by having parents record the number of hours each week that the child watches *Sesame Street*). Then, the researchers calculate the correlation between the two sets of scores and discover that the variables have a correlation coefficient of +.78, as shown in Figure 3.2. What can the research team conclude from these findings?

Since the two variables display a strong positive correlation, we know that as one increases the other increases and also that knowing a child's value on one of the variables allows us to predict the child's value on the other variable fairly well. We therefore might be tempted to believe that the study shows that viewing *Sesame Street* leads to better reading skills, or in more general terms, that a change in one of the variables *causes* change in the other. Herein lies a major limitation of correlational research—*a correlation cannot be used to show causality between the variables.* The correlation in the example may accurately reveal the pattern and strength of the reading-viewing relation, but it cannot reveal cause and effect between the variables. Why not?

If we think carefully about the findings, we realize that some other conclusions cannot be ruled out. For example, rather than TV viewing's having an effect on the

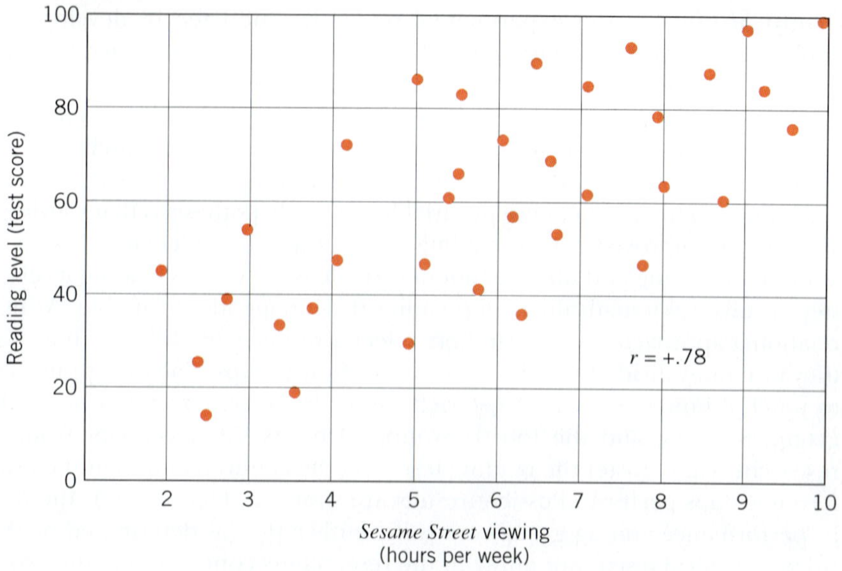

Figure 3.2
A scatter diagram of a hypothetical correlation between children's viewing of *Sesame Street* and their reading level. The correlation coefficient (*r*) shows a strong positive relation between the two variables.

reading, the reverse is equally plausible. That is, children who are better readers may watch *Sesame Street* more often than do children who are poorer readers (possibly because they enjoy it more). Another possibility is that the two variables are both influenced by some third variable that we have not measured. For instance, both might be affected by the educational background of the child's parents. Indeed, there is a good chance that the better educated a child's parents are, the more likely they are to encourage both reading and the viewing of educational television. Thus, although correlational research is a valuable tool for identifying and measuring systematic relations, it cannot be used to explain them. Explanation requires a more powerful research method—the experimental approach.

Nevertheless, correlational research can play an important role in the scientific research process. Like descriptive research, correlational studies sometimes raise interesting and provocative questions. These questions may be formed into specific research hypotheses that investigators can examine using more rigorous methods of research.

Experimental Research

The most popular and important type of research in developmental psychology is the experiment. A simple experiment often involves investigating the relation between just two variables, but, unlike correlational research, experimentation permits us to draw cause-and-effect conclusions about the variables.

The most important difference between a correlational study and an experimental study lies in how the information is gathered. Correlational research is usually based on simple observation. The two variables of interest are observed and recorded without any intrusion or interference by the researcher. In an experiment, however, the researcher systematically *manipulates*—changes—one variable and then looks for any effects (changes) in the second variable. The variable that is systematically manipulated is called the **independent variable**. The variable affected by the manipulation is called the **dependent variable**. In psychological research, the dependent variable is typically some aspect of behavior, whereas the independent variable is a factor the researcher suspects may influence that behavior.

Independent variable
The variable in an experiment that is systematically manipulated.

Dependent variable
The variable that is predicted to be affected by an experimental manipulation. In psychology, usually some aspect of behavior.

Group Studies Most experimental research conducted by developmental psychologists involves comparing the behavior of groups of research participants exposed to different manipulations of an independent variable.

Let us return to the previous example and consider how researchers might use the experimental method to address the question of whether watching *Sesame Street* affects reading level. First, the researchers need a hypothesis that clearly identifies the independent and dependent variables. If the hypothesis is that viewing the program *causes* improvements in reading ability, then the independent variable is the amount of viewing and the dependent variable is the child's reading level. The next step involves systematically manipulating the independent variable. As in the correlational approach, the researchers select a number of children, but in this case they randomly divide the children into, say, four groups. The first group is required to watch 2 hours of *Sesame Street* each week; the second group, 4 hours; the third group, 8 hours; and the fourth group, 10 hours. After perhaps 6 months, the researchers administer the reading test to all the children and examine how the different groups perform. Possible results are shown in Figure 3.3. If the differences in performance among groups are sufficiently large (as determined by the appropriate statistical tests), not only can the researchers conclude that the two variables are systematically related, but they can now also make the causal statement that viewing *Sesame Street* improves children's reading ability. That is, the psychologists' hypothesis now has been supported by experimental data.

Reversal-replication (ABAB) design
An experimental design in which the independent variable is systematically presented and removed several times. Can be used in studies involving very few research participants.

Reversal-Replication Studies Although experimental research most often involves exposing groups of subjects to different values of an independent variable, there is an alternative called the **reversal-replication design** (or sometimes the **ABAB design**). In this method, the independent variable is systematically presented and removed and effects on the dependent variable are noted. The main advantage of this design is that fewer subjects are needed; for instance, it can be used in an experiment involving a single child. Consider how we might use this method to test the hypothesis that the presence of the mother causes infants to smile more often. In this experiment, the independent variable would be the presence or absence of the mother, and the dependent variable would be the amount the infant

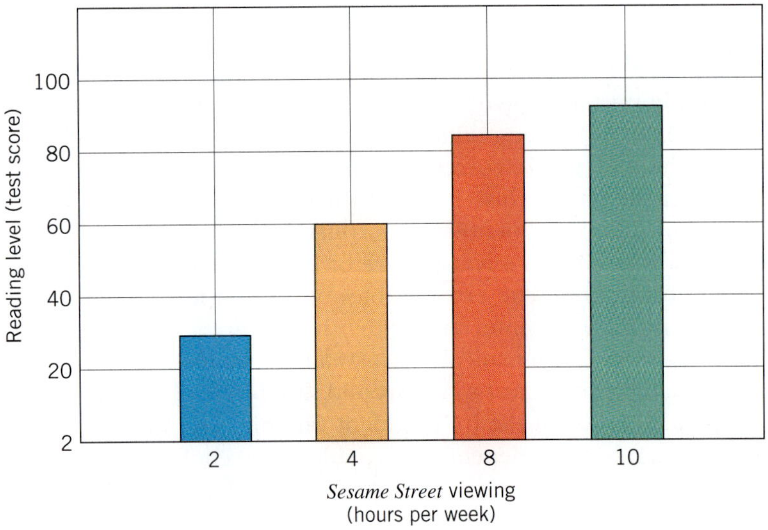

Figure 3.3
A bar graph illustrating an experimental test of the hypothesis that viewing *Sesame Street* improves reading test performance. Each bar shows the average test score for all the children in that experimental group.

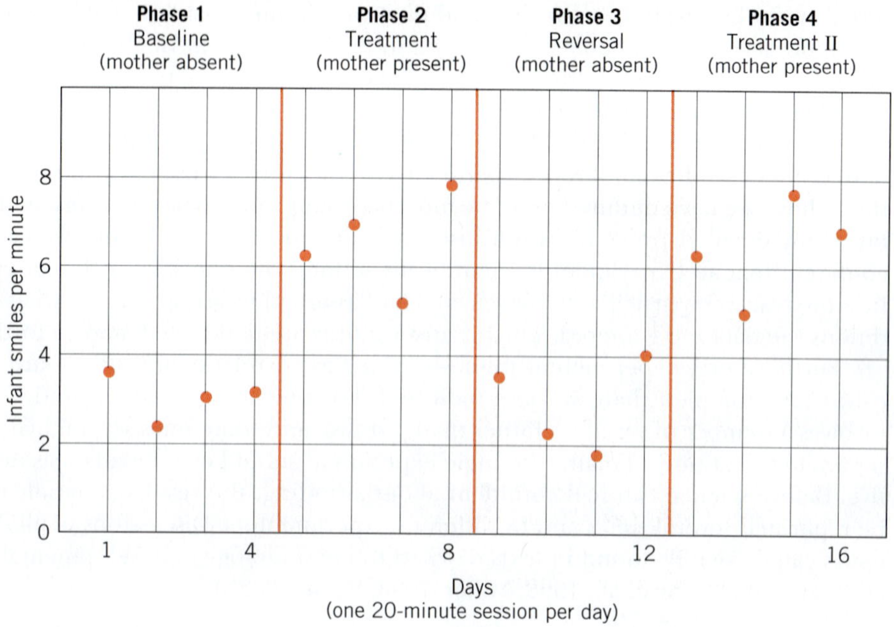

Figure 3.4
A reversal-replication design showing a causal relation between the presence of the mother (the independent variable) and the amount an infant smiles (the dependent variable). The third and fourth phases replicate the procedures and results of the first two phases.

smiles. As Figure 3.4 indicates, the basic procedure of the experiment involves counting the number of times the infant smiles per minute during a 20-minute daily session in which the mother is either present or absent.

To conduct the experiment, the researcher must first determine the *baseline*, or initial level of the behavior being observed. In this example, the baseline is the number of times the infant smiles when alone. In the second, or *treatment*, phase of the experiment, the independent variable is introduced. As shown in Figure 3.4, there is a clear increase in smiling when the mother is present. The change in the infant's behavior supports the researcher's hypothesis, but it is premature to conclude that a causal relation exists between the presence of the mother and the baby's smiling. Why? The change in the infant's behavior might have resulted from other factors—such as a better overall mood—that only coincidentally occurred when the mother was present.

To determine whether the change in behavior was only accidentally related to the change in the independent variable, the researcher attempts to *replicate* the procedure and results. In the next step, then, the independent variable is again removed. This is called the *reversal*, or withdrawal, phase. In our example, we can see that the infant's behavior returns to its baseline level. Finally, the independent variable is presented once more in a second treatment phase. If the subsequent change in behavior is the same as during the first treatment phase, then the researcher has enough evidence to infer a causal relation between the independent and dependent variables. Since the amount the infant smiles does indeed increase once again, the researcher can reasonably conclude that the baby's smiling is affected by the mother's presence.

Additional Considerations Experimental research is a powerful scientific tool, not only because it can reveal cause-and-effect relations, but also because it can be applied to a wide variety of problems and settings. Much of the experimentation conducted by child psychologists takes place in laboratories, especially when conditions must be carefully controlled and monitored. But consistent with an ecological approach, experimental studies can also be conducted in field settings—playgrounds, classrooms, or children's homes, for example—where the child's behavior is studied under more natural conditions.

The experimental approach is of paramount importance in the study of child development, and examples of experiments are described frequently in the pages that follow. We have outlined here the most basic concepts involved in this method, but many detailed procedures not discussed must be followed before we can be confident that an experiment is scientifically sound. These involve such matters as how the research participants are selected and assigned to groups, under what conditions the data are gathered, which statistical tests are conducted, and so forth.

Furthermore, experimental studies—as well as correlational studies—are typically more complex than we have indicated. For one thing, a single study often involves a number of variables rather than just two, and sometimes several hypotheses are tested at once. Finally, no single experiment should ever be taken as definitive. Before science can feel confident about a finding, the results generally must be replicated several times and by different experimenters. Discussions of all these issues can be readily found in texts devoted to methodology in developmental psychology (e.g., Cozby et al., 1998; Miller, 1998; Vasta, 1982b).

✓ To Recap...

The three major research methods used by child psychologists are descriptive research, correlational research, and experimentation. The descriptive approach involves simple observation and is used today primarily as a first step in exploring areas about which little is known. Correlational studies are used to identify relations between variables and to describe them in terms of their direction and strength. This method does not permit conclusions regarding cause and effect. The experimental approach involves testing hypotheses by systematically manipulating the independent variable and examining its effects on the dependent variable. It allows researchers to draw conclusions regarding cause and effect. Experimental studies may involve groups of subjects exposed to different values of an independent variable. They may also involve only a few subjects, who are exposed to the repeated presentation and removal of an independent variable in a reversal-replication design.

Studying Development

Development, as we have seen, involves changes in behavior over time. Many of the issues of interest to developmental researchers therefore focus on how children's behavior at one age differs from their behavior at another age. Sometimes these issues are mainly descriptive, such as how a child's speech progresses from the one-word utterances of the toddler, to the ill-formed sentences of the preschooler, to the reasonably accurate sentences of the preadolescent. At other times the issues concern the causes of behavior, such as the possible effects of day-care programs on children's later social adjustment to school. For either type of question, however, the psychologist needs a research method that will allow the comparison of behaviors at different ages. Four methods are available for this purpose: the longitudinal study, the cross-sectional study, a method that combines the two, and the microgenetic technique.

Longitudinal Research

Longitudinal design A research method in which the same individuals are studied repeatedly over time.

One approach to studying children's behavior at different ages is the **longitudinal design**. The logic of this approach is quite simple. The behaviors of interest are first measured when the child is very young and then measured again at various intervals as the child grows. The main advantage of this method is that it allows the researcher to study directly how each behavior changes as the child gets older (Menard, 1991).

The number of years required for a longitudinal study can vary considerably. Some questions can be explored within a relatively brief time frame. For example, determining whether different techniques of caring for premature infants have different effects on the age at which the babies begin to walk and talk should take only about 18 months to 2 years of observation. Other questions, such as whether a child's early disciplinary experiences influence his or her own use of punishment as a parent, may need to extend over decades.

Longitudinal studies can be either correlational or experimental. If we measure behaviors at one age and then again at a later age, we can determine the consistency of the behaviors by calculating the correlation between the two sets of measurements. Experimental longitudinal studies usually involve introducing a manipulation at one point in development and then examining its effects on the dependent variables of interest at some later point, or points, in development.

Two types of research questions are particularly well suited to the longitudinal approach (Magnusson et al., 1991). The first concerns the *stability*, or persistence, of behaviors. If, for instance, we wish to determine the extent to which a child's temperament (an aspect of personality) remains constant throughout life, the best approach is to measure this characteristic in the same children periodically and examine the correlations among the sets of scores.

The second type of question that works well with the longitudinal method involves the *effects of early experiences* on later behavior. If we wish to determine whether certain events or conditions that occur during a child's early years—divorce, an infant stimulation program, or the quality of diet, for instance—produce long-term effects, the clearest answers will be obtained with an experimental longitudinal approach. For example, we might identify children who have participated in an early stimulation program and children who have not and then follow both groups for a number of years to see whether differences emerge in their suc-

In longitudinal research, the same individuals are studied over a period of time, sometimes many years.

BOX 3.1

TERMAN'S STUDIES OF GENIUS

The first major longitudinal study in developmental psychology was Lewis Terman's investigation of intellectually gifted children. This classic research remains especially noteworthy because it followed a very large group of subjects for almost their entire lives and generated some fascinating findings (Cravens, 1992).

Terman was a psychologist at Stanford University and is best known for having developed one of the first IQ tests, the Stanford–Binet (which we will describe when we discuss intelligence testing in Chapter 10). In the course of administering his new test, Terman became interested in the children who scored at the very highest levels. In 1921 he selected approximately 1,400 extremely intelligent 11-year-olds in California to participate in a longitudinal project, which he titled *Genetic Studies of Genius* (Terman, 1925).

Terman was not interested only in the intelligence of these children. He also collected a great deal of information on their families, schools, physical characteristics, mental and medical health, personality traits, and more. At intervals of about 10 years, Terman readministered many of the same tests and measures to find out whether gifted children develop differently from their peers of normal intelligence.

The participants in this study, who became known as "Termites," proved to be quite different from what would have been predicted by the conventional wisdom of the time. They did not support the stereotype that genius children are sickly, meek, and social misfits. As they grew up, they were found to be healthier, wealthier, more successful professionally, and even happier than most of their peers in society.

Two of Terman's initial findings have been somewhat controversial. He reported that the gifted children came from wealthier, better educated families and that many more males than females had high IQ scores. Both of these findings today are regarded skeptically by psychologists and may have resulted from flaws or biases in the way in which Terman selected his research participants (Shurkin, 1992).

Terman died in 1957, but his research was continued by others, including Robert Sears, a Termite who became a developmental psychologist. In 1972, when the subjects had reached their 60s, they were asked to describe what aspects of their lives they had found most satisfying or rewarding. Interestingly, the majority of them pointed to their families—not their wealth, social status, or professional success—as having been their greatest source of happiness (Sears, 1977).

Although most of the Termites have now died, the vast amount of information collected by Terman's research team is still being studied, and scientists continue to generate new questions and better ways to look at the data (Friedman et al., 1995).

cess in school. Both questions also can be related to the more general issues of continuity and discontinuity, discussed in Chapter 1. (An early longitudinal study is presented in Box 3.1.)

Despite the obvious value of the longitudinal approach, the method does have certain disadvantages. One is the problem of *attrition*, the loss of individuals under study, which can occur for a variety of reasons. Families may move away, children may become ill or develop other problems that interfere with participation in the study, or parents may simply lose interest and withdraw from the project. Other problems may develop because of the repeated testing. For example, a study concerned with the stability of a child's intelligence requires that IQ tests be administered at regular intervals. But repeated experience with tests itself may make a child test wise to the types of responses that are expected and may thus artificially improve the child's performance.

A third disadvantage relates directly to the fact that longitudinal studies are often designed to last for many years. There is a very real possibility that the issues involved or the instruments used at the beginning of the study may become outdated. For example, the experimental questions posed at the outset of the project may become less important as the years pass and other research findings are published. Similarly, the tests and instruments used may become obsolete. Finally, there is a major practical disadvantage. Since it often requires a large research staff and many hours of observation or testing, longitudinal research can be very expensive.

Development in Cultural Context

Studying the Life Course

One interesting variation on longitudinal research is the study of the life course. Such investigations focus on how major personal and environmental events affect an individual. The dependent measures of interest here, however, are not the short-term impacts of these events, which psychologists usually study, but how these events can alter the course of the individual's entire life (Elder, 1998).

Generally such research is *archival* rather than experimental, that is, the investigators use existing longitudinal studies that have gone on for many years as their source of data. By examining the records of these studies—often tracing one individual's life at a time—the life-course researcher can study new questions of current interest that may not have been a specific focus of the original project. And, because the research uses data that have already been gathered, longitudinal issues can be studied in a fraction of the time normally required.

Studies of the life course have taken several forms. Some have examined the impact of major historical events or conditions on the lives of the people in a particular generation (Conger & Elder, 1994). Examples include the effects of the Great Depression of the 1930s and of World War II. Other studies have looked at the role of life transitions—for example, the age at which a woman decides to marry, to have her first child, or to enter the workforce (Elder, Caspi, & Downey, 1986); or the different effects of entering the military early or late, as reflected in the experiences of Terman's Termites (discussed in Box 3.1) (Elder, Shanahan, & Clipp, 1994).

Research on the life course has investigated the effects of major historical events, such as the Great Depression of the 1930s, on the lives of individuals involved.

A related interest of life-course researchers is the long-range effects of early personality characteristics (Caspi & Elder, 1988). A guiding assumption of research in this area is that an individual's relationship to his or her environment is transactional. Recall from Chapter 2 that this means that a person to some degree produces a certain type of environment to which he or she then continues to be exposed.

For example, studies have examined the lives of some shy children (Caspi, Elder, & Bem, 1988) and explosive children (Caspi, Elder, & Bem, 1987). Although few long-term effects of shyness in girls were identified, boys who were shy and unassertive later showed delays in marrying, fathering children, and establishing stable careers. Explosive, ill-tempered boys were more likely to drop out of school and ultimately to have poorer jobs, less job satisfaction, and more marital problems. Ill-tempered girls, too, tended to have less stable marriages as adults and to be married to men of lower socioeconomic status. The researchers believe these children, because of their shyness or explosiveness, engendered certain reactions in people and so gradually gravitated toward (or away from) certain social experiences and groups. These patterns, in turn, influenced the lives of these individuals for many years.

Cross-Sectional Research

Cross-sectional design A research method in which people of different ages are studied simultaneously to examine the effects of age on some aspect of behavior.

An alternative to longitudinal research is the **cross-sectional design**, which allows researchers to examine developmental differences in behavior by studying children of different ages at the same point in time. In this type of experiment, the age of the children becomes an independent variable in the research design. The major advantage of this approach is that it is much less time-consuming than is the longitudinal method. Rather than waiting 5 years to determine, say, how memory processes in 3-year-olds differ from memory processes in 8-year-olds, we can simply study a group of 3-year-olds and a group of 8-year-olds at the same time. The relatively short time required also means that such experiments are rarely plagued by the problems of attrition, repeated testing, outdated issues and instruments, and high cost.

Still, the cross-sectional approach has two significant disadvantages. First, this method cannot be used to investigate questions of behavior stability and early experience, as it is impossible to determine persistence of an early trait or the impact of an early event by examining those behaviors in *different* older children.

Cohort effect A problem sometimes found in cross-sectional research in which people of a given age are affected by factors unique to their generation.

Second is a problem known as the **cohort effect**, which occurs because certain aspects of people's behavior are influenced by the unique events and conditions experienced by their particular age group or generation. For example, suppose we were investigating the cognitive skills of individuals at ages 35, 45, and 65 and found that the 45-year-olds performed better on our various reasoning and problem-solving tests than did the younger or older groups. Would these results allow us to conclude that cognitive development improves into middle adulthood and then declines?

Such an interpretation is certainly consistent with our data, but another explanation arises when we consider the educational backgrounds of our three groups of subjects. The 65-year-olds were raised during the Depression, when many youngsters were forced to leave school early and find jobs. The 35-year-olds were raised during the late 1960s, when much greater emphasis was being placed on children's social and emotional development. But the 45-year-olds began attending school shortly after the launching of the Soviet satellite *Sputnik*, which stimulated a major U.S. effort to improve scientific and mathematical training. The point is that our research participants are members of three cohorts, or peer groups, which had different educational experiences. The performance differences we observe may not reflect the differences in their ages so much as their different life experiences.

Combining Longitudinal and Cross-Sectional Research

Cross-sequential design A research method combining longitudinal and cross-sectional designs.

To obtain the best features of the longitudinal and cross-sectional designs, researchers sometimes combine the two methods into a **cross-sequential design**. The combined approach begins with a simple cross-sectional investigation, during which groups of children of different ages are studied simultaneously. The same groups are then studied again at one or more later times to provide a longitudinal perspective on the question.

For instance, an investigator might begin by measuring the amount of competitiveness displayed by 4-year-olds, 7-year-olds, and 10-year-olds playing a game. Three years later, the investigator retests the children, who are now 7, 10, and 13. This procedure makes a number of data comparisons possible. For example, cross-sectional comparisons among the children can be made at both the initial testing and the later testing to see whether children at the different ages show different levels of competitiveness. In addition, the stability of each child's competitiveness can be examined by a comparison of the child's scores at the two ages.

The combined design also permits the investigator to check directly for two of the common problems associated with the individual designs. If the data for the groups at ages 7 and 10 during the first testing differ from the data for these groups during the second testing, then these differences are very likely the result of either a cohort effect (a cross-sectional design problem) or a repeated-testing effect (a longitudinal design problem). In either case, the investigator will need to exercise caution in drawing conclusions regarding age-related differences in competitiveness or the stability of the behavior over time. But if the data from these corresponding groups are very similar, the researcher can have considerable confidence in the results of the study.

Microgenetic Studies

A somewhat newer approach to examining developmental change involves the intensive study of a small number of children over a brief period of time. The purpose of this **microgenetic method** is to investigate changes in important developmental processes *as they are occurring* (Kuhn, 1995; Siegler, 1995).

Microgenetic method A research method in which a small number of individuals are observed repeatedly in order to study an expected change in a developmental process.

Recall from Chapter 1 that some aspects of human development are thought to be discontinuous—they are relatively stable for a period of time but then move abruptly to a higher level. Investigators attempting to understand the nature of such changes have used the microgenetic approach in the hope of examining the particular developmental process as it goes from one level to the next. Much of the research using this approach has been concerned with children's cognitive abilities, probably because the concept of discontinuous change is consistent with the view of development held by Piaget and most other cognitive-developmental psychologists.

A microgenetic study begins with several children who are about the age at which a developmental change is expected to occur. The behavior of interest is observed and measured repeatedly in these children. For example, if the experiment is concerned with the children's use of a particular cognitive strategy for solving a certain type of problem (a common focus of such research), the children may be asked to complete many such problems over a period of weeks. In such an experiment, the researcher not only notes the correctness of the children's solutions, but also examines precisely how they approach each problem, perhaps by asking them to describe what they are doing. In this way, the investigator attempts to identify when a child moves from the use of a simpler cognitive strategy to a more sophisticated one. By examining this process very carefully, the researcher may acquire a better understanding of exactly how it works.

Although the microgenetic method can yield a great deal of new information about a developmental process, it, too, has drawbacks. One practical problem is that making many observations over a compressed period of time can be expensive. Another consideration is that great care must be taken to ensure that the repeated assessment of the child's abilities does not itself cause changes in the behavior of interest (Pressley, 1992).

✓ *To Recap...*

Many developmental issues require comparisons of children's behavior at different ages. The longitudinal method assesses the behavior of the same children over a period of time. It is particularly useful for addressing the effects of early experience on later behavior and the stability of behavior. The longitudinal method commonly suffers from problems with attrition, the effects of repeated testing, and the fact that issues and instruments may become outdated. It is also expensive. Cross-sectional research is less time-consuming than longitudinal research because it involves simultaneously studying children of different ages. However, it is sometimes plagued by the cohort effect. The longitudinal and cross-sectional approaches can be combined into the cross-sequential design, which offers some of the advantages of both methods. The microgenetic method is used to study emerging developmental changes by intensive assessment of the behavior of a small number of children over a brief period of time.

Other Research Tactics

Many additional research methods are used by developmental psychologists. In this section we describe the case study, cross-cultural research, and comparative research, three popular approaches to investigating various developmental issues.

Case Studies

Case study
A research method that involves only a single individual, often with a focus on a clinical issue.

Sometimes research involves only a single individual who becomes the subject of a **case study**. Often these studies are concerned with clinical issues, such as when a child displays a rare disorder or when a new treatment approach is applied to a developmental problem. Occasionally, a child has encountered experiences so unusual as to attract the interest of psychologists for theoretical reasons.

Case study research can involve several different methods. At times it is purely descriptive, as with the early baby biographies we described in Chapter 1. But experimental research can also be conducted with only one child. We saw earlier, for example, that the reversal-replication design can be used in this way. At times case studies also represent natural experiments in the sense that a child has been exposed to a particular set of circumstances that could not have been otherwise arranged—usually for ethical reasons—but that offer researchers the opportunity to note the effects of these circumstances (independent variable) on one or more aspects of the child's behavior (dependent variable).

A dramatic example of such a situation is the case of "Genie," a child who was kept isolated by her parents and never spoken to until she was 14 years old (Curtiss, 1977). Genie presented language researchers with a unique opportunity to investigate whether being deprived from exposure to language early on can affect a child's ability to acquire verbal skills at an advanced age. Such a question, of course, could never have been studied in any conventional experimental way.

The major limitation of using only a single research participant is that the researcher must be very cautious about drawing conclusions from the case. Genie, for example, was not only deprived of language, but also experienced an extremely harsh and unusual childhood, because of her parents. Whether the data regarding her language abilities can be generalized to other children thus remains unclear.

Despite limitations, case studies can be valuable in the research process. They may raise new questions or issues that can be studied using more carefully controlled research methods.

Cross-Cultural Research

A major theme of modern child psychology is that development must be studied in context. We saw in Bronfenbrenner's model (Chapter 2) that an important context in which children develop is the culture of their people. How can we determine the influence of culture on a particular aspect of behavior or development?

Cross-cultural studies can sometimes help determine whether patterns of behavior among members of one culture are universal to humans or result from common environmental influences.

One approach is to study the same behavior in different cultures. **Cross-cultural studies** use the child's culture as an independent variable in the experiment and examine its effects on the dependent variable(s) of interest. Such studies have been conducted in areas as diverse as gender roles, moral reasoning, and perceptual abilities (Harkness & Super, 1987; Shweder et al., 1998).

Cross-cultural studies Research designed to determine the influence of culture on some aspect of development and in which culture typically serves as an independent variable.

An important use of this experimental method is to investigate nature–nurture questions. Language development again serves as a good example. English-speaking children generally follow a relatively predictable pattern of language acquisition. Certain grammatical structures are displayed before others (such as active sentences before passive sentences), and certain types of errors and omissions are common among all children of a given age. Do these similarities mean that language development is guided by inborn biological mechanisms and is therefore essentially the same for all humans? Or do they simply reflect the fact that most children in a given culture are exposed to similar language models in parents, teachers, and others?

One fruitful approach to answering this question is to examine patterns of language acquisition in several cultures. If children in different language environments display similar patterns in their development of grammar and speech distortions, we have good evidence that language development is genetically guided. If we find differences between cultural groups, however, we can conclude that environmental factors contribute to the language-acquisition process (an issue we pursue further in Chapter 11).

Comparative Research

Psychologists also study behaviors across species. Although **comparative research** of this sort has served many different purposes, developmentalists typically perform animal experiments for one of two reasons. First, researchers of the ethological tradition study animal behavior for clues to the evolutionary origins of similar human behaviors. For instance, determining how the imprinting process causes newborn birds to develop social attachments to their mothers may help child researchers

Comparative research Research conducted with nonhuman species to provide information relevant to human development.

Comparative research investigates similiar behaviors across different species.

understand the mechanisms involved in the development of attachment between human infants and their mothers. Similarly, studying the play fighting that commonly occurs among pups of many species may provide insights into the rough-and-tumble social interactions of young children.

More frequently, however, comparative research permits developmental psychologists to conduct studies that would be prohibited with humans for ethical reasons. What happens, for instance, to an infant who is reared for 6 months without a mother? Does the visual system develop normally in an infant raised in total darkness? Do injections of sex hormones during the mother's pregnancy affect the later social behavior of the offspring? These, as well as many other questions, would be impossible to address experimentally with humans. Using other species, however, researchers have studied each of these issues in the laboratory.

✓ To Recap...

Case studies involve a single individual and often are concerned with clinical issues. The generalizability of the findings is limited, but the results sometimes prompt more rigorous research on an issue. Cross-cultural research is useful for studying the influence of culture on development and for addressing some nature–nurture issues. Comparative research is conducted by ethologists to identify similarities in behavior processes of humans and non-human species. It also provides a way of experimentally addressing questions that would be unethical to investigate with humans.

Ethical Issues

No one would question the fact that psychological research often produces findings that benefit children, adults, and society as a whole. Nevertheless, almost any research involving humans can pose a variety of risks. Investigators have an obligation to determine exactly what potentially negative effects may result from their experiments and to consider whether these risks outweigh the potential value of the research findings (Fisher & Tryon, 1990; Rheingold, 1982a).

Concern over ethical issues has not always been as great as it is today. Early investigators had few restrictions on their research, as evidenced by such questionable experiments as John B. Watson's conditioning of 11-month-old Little Albert. Today, however, attention is increasingly focused on safeguarding children's rights and well-being (Sieber, 1992).

Potential Risks

An obvious concern in any experiment is the possibility of physical injury to the child, although this problem is relatively rare in developmental research. A more common, and often more subtle, issue involves potential psychological harm to the child. Some experimental hypotheses may require, for example, observing how children respond when they cannot solve a problem, are prohibited from playing with an attractive toy, or are exposed to violent behavior. These procedures may produce various negative emotions, such as feelings of failure, frustration, or stress. The concern is that the children may continue to experience these emotions for some time after leaving the experimental situation.

A less obvious category of problems involves violations of privacy. If a researcher secretly gains access to a child's school records, if observations are conducted without a child's knowledge, or if data regarding a child or a family become public knowledge, the legal and ethical rights of these individuals may be violated.

Safeguards

The concern for ethical research practices has led to the development of safeguards designed to avoid or eliminate potential risks. These safeguards have, by and large, become a routine part of modern research procedures. In addition, professional scientific organizations have developed codes of ethical standards to guide their members. *Ethical Principles in the Conduct of Research with Human Participants* (1982), published by the American Psychological Association, and "SRCD Ethical Standards for Research with Children" (1990), published by the Society for Research in Child Development and reproduced in part in Table 3.1, are two important examples.

Researchers who study children are required to ensure that neither physical nor psychological harm to the child is likely to result from their procedures.

Table 3.1
Ethical Standards for Research with Children, Society for Research in Child Development

Children as research participants present ethical problems for the investigator that are different from those presented by adult participants. Children are more vulnerable to stress than adults and, having less experience and knowledge than adults, are less able to evaluate the social value of the research and less able to comprehend the meaning of the research procedures themselves. In all cases, therefore, the child's consent or assent to participate in the research, as well as the consent of the child's parents or guardians, must be obtained.

In general, no matter how young children are, they have rights that supersede the rights of the investigator. The investigator is therefore obligated to evaluate each proposed research operation in terms of these rights, and before proceeding with the investigation, should obtain the approval of an appropriate Institutional Review Board.

The principles listed below are to be subscribed to by all members of the Society for Research in Child Development. These principles are not intended to infringe on the right and obligation of researchers to conduct scientific research.

Principle 1. Non-harmful Procedures:
The investigator should use no research operation that may harm the child either physically or psychologically. The investigator is also obligated at all times to use the least stressful research operation whenever possible. Psychological harm in particular instances may be difficult to define; nevertheless its definition and means for reducing or eliminating it remain the responsibility of the investigator. When the investigator is in doubt about the possible harmful effects of the research operations, consultation should be sought from others. When harm seems inevitable, the investigator is obligated to find other means of obtaining the information or to abandon the research.

Principle 2. Informed Consent:
Before seeking consent or assent from the child, the investigator should inform the child of all features of the research that may affect his or her willingness to participate and should answer the child's questions in terms appropriate to the child's comprehension. The investigator should respect the child's freedom to choose to participate in the research or not by giving the child the opportunity to give or not give assent to participation as well as to choose to discontinue participation at any time. Assent means that the child shows some form of agreement to participate without necessarily comprehending the full significance of the research necessary to give informed consent. Investigators working with infants should take special effort to explain the research procedures to the parents and be especially sensitive to any indicators of discomfort in the infant.

In spite of the paramount importance of obtaining consent, instances can arise in which consent or any kind of contact with the participant would make the research impossible to carry out. Nonintrusive field research is a common example. Conceivably, such research can be carried out ethically if it is conducted in public places, participants' anonymity is totally protected, and there are no foreseeable negative consequences to the participant.

Principle 3. Parental Consent:
The informed consent of parents, legal guardians or those who act in loco parentis (e.g., teachers, superintendents of institutions) similarly should be obtained, preferably in writing. Informed consent requires that parents or other responsible adults be informed of all the features of the research that may affect their willingness to allow the child to participate. Not only should the right of the responsible adults to refuse consent be respected, but they should be informed that they may refuse to participate without incurring any penalty to them or to the child.

Principle 4. Additional Consent:
The informed consent of any persons, such as school teachers for example, whose interaction with the child is the participant in the study, should also be obtained. As with the child and parents or guardians informed consent requires that the persons interacting with the child during study be informed of all features of the research which may affect their willingness to participate.

Perhaps the most important measure used to ensure that research is conducted ethically is *peer review*. Before beginning a research study, investigators are encouraged, and in many situations required, to submit the research plan to others for their comments and approval. This practice permits an objective examination of the procedures by knowledgeable individuals, including both scientists and community laypeople, who are not personally involved in the research. Peer review committees weigh the possible value of the research findings against potential risks. Sometimes they offer suggestions as to how negative effects might be prevented or minimized. Almost all research carried out at colleges and universities or funded by government organizations is subject to peer review.

Table 3.1
(Continued)

Principle 5. Incentives:
Incentives to participate in a research project must be fair and must not unduly exceed the range of incentives that the child normally experiences. Whatever incentives are used, the investigator should always keep in mind that the greater the possible effects of the investigation on the child, the greater is the obligation to protect the child's welfare and freedom.

Principle 6. Deception:
Although full disclosure of information during the procedure of obtaining consent is the ethical ideal, a particular study may necessitate withholding certain information or deception. Whenever withholding information or deception is judged to be essential to the conduct of the study, the investigator should satisfy research colleagues that such judgment is correct. If withholding information or deception is practiced, and there is reason to believe that the research participants will be negatively affected by it, adequate measures should be taken after the study to ensure the participant's understanding of the reasons for the deception.

Principle 7. Anonymity:
To gain access to institutional records, the investigator should obtain permission from responsible authorities in charge of records. Anonymity of the information should be preserved and no information used other than that for which permission was obtained.

Principle 8. Mutual Responsibilities:
From the beginning of each research investigation, there should be clear agreement between the investigator and the parents, guardians or those who act in loco parentis, and the child, when appropriate, that defines the responsibilities of each. The investigator has the obligation to honor all promises and commitments of the agreement.

Principle 9. Jeopardy:
When, in the course of research, information comes to the investigator's attention that may jeopardize the child's well-being, the investigator has a responsibility to discuss the information with the parents or guardians and with those expert in the field in order that they may arrange the necessary assistance for the child.

Principle 10. Unforeseen Consequences:
When research procedures result in undesirable consequences for the participant that were previously unforeseen, the investigator should immediately employ appropriate measures to correct these consequences, and should redesign the procedures if they are to be included in subsequent studies.

Principle 11. Confidentiality:
The investigator should keep in confidence all information obtained about research participants. The participants' identities should be concealed in written and verbal reports of the results, as well as in informal discussion with students and colleagues.

Principle 12. Informing Participants:
Immediately after the data are collected, the investigator should clarify for the research participant any misconceptions that may have arisen. The investigator also recognizes a duty to report general findings to participants in terms appropriate to their understanding.

Principle 13. Reporting Results:
Because the investigator's words may carry unintended weight with parents and children, caution should be exercised in reporting results, making evaluative statements, or giving advice.

Principle 14. Implications of Findings:
Investigators should be mindful of the social, political and human implications of their research and should be especially careful in the presentation of findings from the research. This principle, however, in no way denies investigators the right to pursue any area of research or the right to observe proper standards of scientific reporting.

Source: Excerpted from "SRCD Ethical Standards for Research with Children," 1990, *SRCD Newsletter*, winter, pp. 5–6.

Another basic measure for protecting children's rights is the requirement that researchers obtain the *informed consent* of the participants in the study. Any research conducted with children requires the written permission of both the parents and the institution (school, day-care center, and so on) where the research will take place. In addition, each child must be made aware of the general procedures of the study. Most important, the child has the right to refuse to participate or to withdraw from the study at any time, even though the parents have given their permission.

If the research procedures may produce negative feelings in the child, the investigator must provide some means of reducing those feelings before the child leaves. For example, if a child is participating in an experiment in which he or she experiences failure, the investigator might end the research session by having the child perform a relatively easy task that will ensure success. Also, to whatever extent seems reasonable, the investigator should at some point explain to the child the purpose of the study and the child's role in it, a procedure called *debriefing*.

Maintaining *confidentiality* is also a crucial aspect of ethical research. Whenever possible, the identities of the participants and information about their individual performance should be concealed from anyone not directly connected with the research. Anonymity often is achieved through the practice of assigning numbers to the participants and then using these numbers instead of names during the analysis of the data.

Finally, all research psychologists have some ethical responsibilities that go beyond the protection of the individuals participating in the research. For example, scientists who report data that may be controversial or that may affect social-policy decisions have an obligation to describe the limitations and degree of confidence they have in their findings. In addition, investigators should normally provide their research participants with some general information about the final results of the research, as an acknowledgment of the importance of their contribution to the overall research process.

✓ To Recap...

Research with humans always involves a balance between the potential value of the findings and any risks that may be involved. The most common categories of risk include physical and psychological harm to the child and violations of privacy. Certain safeguards are now routinely used. They include prior review of research plans by other scientists; obtaining the informed consent of parents, teachers, and children involved in a research study; elimination of any experimentally produced negative feelings through extra procedures; debriefing as to the purpose of the research; and strict maintenance of confidentiality. Additional ethical requirements include taking some responsibility for the social ramifications of research findings and providing feedback to participants about the outcome of the research project.

Conclusion

Our purpose in devoting an entire chapter to research methods is to emphasize the fact that effective methods are crucial for advancing scientific knowledge. Unlocking the secrets of child development requires several elements. It begins, of course, with the perceptive insights of an astute researcher. But even the brightest researcher cannot answer important theoretical questions without the necessary research techniques. For example, researchers suspected the existence of atoms and genes many years ago. But it was not until the advent of the particle accelerator and the electron microscope that scientists could confirm these suspicions. In the same way, psychologists have long debated the capabilities of the newborn. Only since the 1960s, however, have research techniques been developed that permit many related questions to be studied scientifically.

Another reason for including this chapter is that the remainder of the text presents a good deal of research evidence regarding developmental progress and processes. This evidence, for the most part, has been gathered through the methods described here, so it is helpful to approach it with an understanding of the differences between the correlational and experimental designs, longitudinal and cross-sectional experiments, and so on. These basics will also pave the way for the many more specific techniques and procedures used in various areas, which we describe as they come into play.

Visual Summary for Chapter 3: *Research Methods*

Scientific Research

Two roles of Theory

- *1. To organize research findings.*
- *2. To guide new research.*

Ways in which researchers ensure objectivity.

- *Focus on observable behaviors.*
- *Ensure that the behaviors to be studied are measurable and quantifiable.*

Types of Research

Method	Characteristics
Descriptive approach	*Involves simple observation. Used primarily as a first step in exploring areas about which little is known.*
Correlational Studies	*Used to identify relations between variables and to describe them in terms of their direction and strength. Cannot produce conclusions regarding cause and effect.*
Experimental Approach	*Involves systematically manipulating the independent variable and examining the effects produced on the dependent variable. Allows researchers to draw conclusions regarding cause and effect.*

Studying Development

Method	Characteristics
Longitudinal Research	*Assesses the behavior of the same children over a period of time. Useful for looking at questions concerning the long-term effects of early experience and the stability of behavior. Disadvantages: Subject attrition, effects of repeated testing, issues and instruments may become outdated, time- consuming and expensive.*
Cross-Sectional Research	*Involves simultaneously studying children of different ages. Less time-consuming than longitudinal research. Disadvantages: Cohort effects.*
Cross-Sequential Design	*A combination of longitudinal and cross-sectional research offering some of the advantages of both methods.*
Microgenetic Method	*Used to study emerging developmental changes by intensively assessing the behavior of small number of children over a brief period of time.*

Other Research Tactics

Method		Characteristics
Case Study	→	The study of a single individual, often focusing on clinical issues. Caution must be exercised in generalizing the findings to other individuals.
Cross-Cultural Research	→	Designed to determine the influence of culture on some aspect of development. Can also address some nature-nurture issues.
Comparative Research	→	Research conducted with nonhuman species in order to provide information relevant to human development.

Ethical Issues

Safeguards commonly used to reduce the risk of physical or psychological harm to the child and violations of privacy.

Peer review	→	Informed consent	→	Debriefing	→	Confidentiality
Have research plans reviewed by other individuals not personally involved in the research.	→	Obtain the informed consent of children, parents, and teachers involved in a study.	→	Explain to the child the purpose of the study and eliminate any experimentally produced negative feelings.	→	Conceal identities of participants and details of their individual performance.

Chapter 4

Genetics: The Biological Context of Development

In February 1997, newspapers around the world reported the birth in Edinburgh, Scotland, of a lamb named Dolly. Such an event would not normally be considered newsworthy. Even the fact that Dolly had an identical (although somewhat older) twin would not typically have added much to the story. But the event was truly a landmark in science, because this lamb was not born in the usual way. Dolly was the first mammal ever to be cloned. Rather than being the product of a sperm and an egg from two parents, Dolly came into existence when the genetic material from an adult sheep was transplanted into a cell that developed into an exact copy, or clone, of that sheep.

The implications of this accomplishment are staggering, both scientifically and ethically. For the moment, most scientists are talking about relatively noncontroversial applications of the technology—such as cloning cows that are especially good milk producers—but the possibilities involving humans cannot be ignored. By January 1998, a scientist in Chicago had announced that he would begin experiments on human cloning, prompting President Clinton to urge Congress to pass a law prohibiting such experimentation. Within days, 19 European nations had signed an agreement banning human cloning in their countries. But it is undoubtedly just a matter of time before the technology is in place to create copies of other humans from the DNA in the nucleus of a single cell. What would this mean?

On the one hand, consider the potential benefits to society. We could make perfect (but younger) copies of brilliant scientists, surgeons, or even chefs. Infertile couples could be helped to bear children, and genetic diseases could perhaps be cured or prevented by manipulating the structure of the genes that cause them.

But there is another side to this potential. Picture a basketball team on which every player is Michael Jordan, or any combination of players that the owners choose to have. Or imagine people deciding to create clones of themselves so that, in a sense, they can go on living indefinitely. The possibilities of human cloning are limited only by one's imagination, and many of them raise serious ethical questions.

For the moment, there is little to fear. It took over 400 attempts to create Dolly, and no laboratory has yet to replicate the feat. But science fiction is quickly becoming reality. And the extraordinary birth of a lamb named Dolly serves as an appropriate entry into the relatively new and fascinating world of human genetics, the topic of this chapter.

Now that we have presented some history, theory, and methodology of child development, it is time to turn to the development of the individual child. Where do we begin? People often think of birth as the beginning of life. We will see in the next chapter, however, that by the time a baby comes into the world, a good deal of development has already taken place inside the mother's womb. Perhaps, then, we should consider that development begins when the father's sperm fertilizes the mother's egg at conception. But even this event is a continuation, rather than the start, of the developmental process. To understand the development of the child, we must begin with genetic processes inside the child's parents that determine how they pass their heredity on to the next generation.

But this starting point is just that. Our genes guide, regulate, and influence development throughout our lives. Precisely how they do so, and exactly how much of our behavior is affected by our genes are two exciting and controversial issues in modern child psychology.

Unlike most of the other topics in this book, genetics will take us briefly into the fields of biology and biochemistry. But our primary emphasis will remain on the psychological perspective and how our behavior is influenced by genetic processes. First, we discuss the basic concepts surrounding genes and their functions. Then we consider genetic disorders and why they occur. Third, we present several models that attempt to explain how genes and environment interact to produce behavior. Finally, we examine the methods psychologists use to study gene-environment interactions and some of what they have learned.

Mechanisms of Inheritance

How does a baby inherit the characteristics of his or her parents—black or white skin, red or brown hair? How does a fertilized human egg know to develop into a person rather than a chimpanzee? How does a single cell give rise to trillions of other cells that become different parts of the body—the fingers, the heart, the brain, and so on? Such questions lie at the heart of the puzzle of inheritance, a mystery that scientists are now slowly beginning to solve.

Cell Division

All living things are composed of cells. Adult humans, on average, possess about 10 trillion of them. Cells have three major subdivisions, shown in Figure 4.1: the nucleus; the cytoplasm, which surrounds the nucleus; and the cell membrane, which encases the cell.

Inside the nucleus lies the body's genetic material, DNA, which is organized into chemical strands called **chromosomes**. In humans, each cell nucleus contains 23 pairs of chromosomes, 46 in all. For each pair, one chromosome came from the father, the other from the mother. Twenty-two of the pairs are called **autosomes**. The members of these pairs are similar to one another and carry the same genes in the same locations. The twenty-third pair comprises the **sex chromosomes** which come in two varieties. The *X* chromosome is of about average size and carries a good deal of genetic material, whereas the *Y* chromosome is much smaller and has

Chromosomes
Chemical strands in the cell nucleus that contain the genes. The nucleus of each human cell has 46 chromosomes, with the exception of the gametes, which have 23.

Autosomes
The 22 pairs of human chromosomes, other than the sex chromosomes.

Sex chromosomes
The pair of human chromosomes that determines one's sex. Females have two X chromosomes, males and an X and a Y.

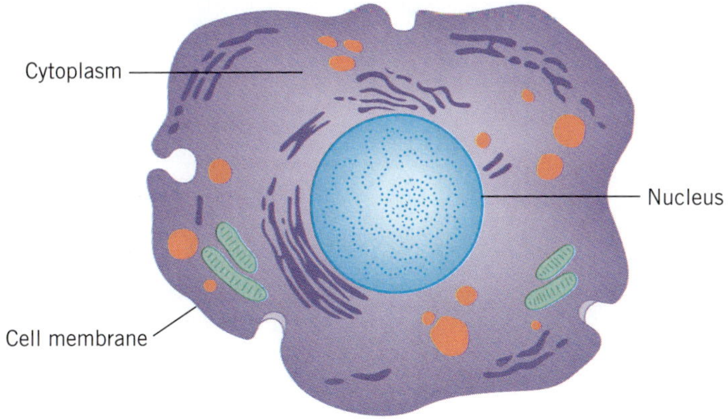

Figure 4.1
Major subdivisions of the cell.

many fewer genes. When the pair consists of two X chromosomes (XX), the person is female; when it comprises one of each type (XY), the person is male. We will discuss the role of the sex chromosomes in more detail in Chapter 15.

Although there are many specialized cells, they can be divided into two broad types—*body cells* and *germ cells*. These cells are distinguished principally by how they reproduce and the roles they play in hereditary transmission.

Cells constantly reproduce; their reproduction is probably the most fundamental genetic process that takes place in our bodies. In the time that it takes you to read this sentence, more than 100 million cells in your body will have reproduced. Body cells, by far the larger category, reproduce by a process called mitosis, whereas germ cells reproduce by a process called meiosis.

Mitosis
The process by which body cells reproduce, resulting in two identical cells.

In **mitosis**, diagramed on the left-hand side of Figure 4.2 (with only two pairs of chromosomes for simplicity), each parent cell produces two identical child cells

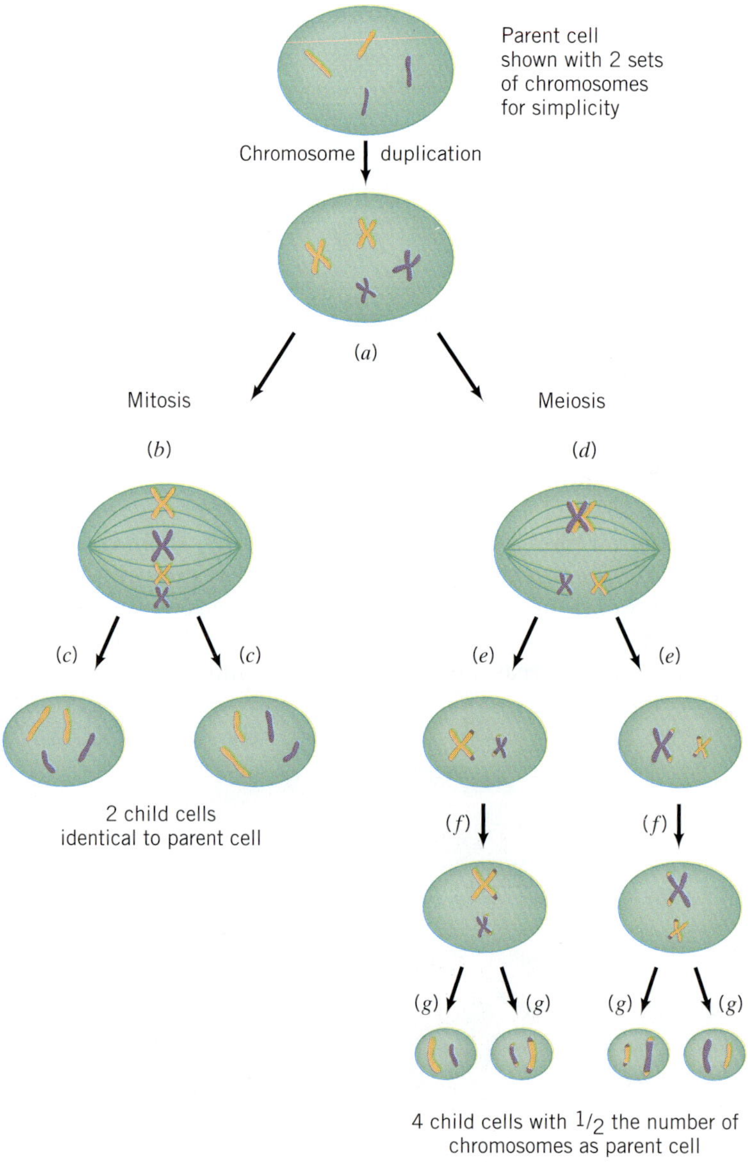

Figure 4.2
Mitosis and meiosis. Mitosis results in two cells identical with the parent cell and with each other. Meiosis results in four cells different from the parent cell and from each other. Adapted from *Biology: Exploring Life* (p. 152) by G. D. Brum & L. K. McKane, 1989, New York: John Wiley & Sons. Copyright © 1989 by John Wiley & Sons, Inc. Adapted by permission of John Wiley & Sons, Inc.

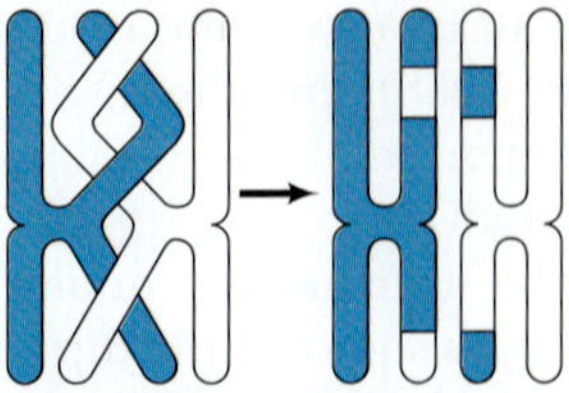

Figure 4.3
Crossing over results in the exchange of genetic material. After the crossover, all four strands are different. Adapted from *Biology: Exploring Life* (p. 44) by G. D. Brum and L .K. McKane, 1989, New York: John Wiley & Sons. Copyright © 1989 by John Wiley & Sons, Inc. Adapted by permission of John Wiley & Sons, Inc.

through a series of three phases. In the first phase (4.2*a*), each of the 46 chromosomes in the cell duplicates itself, producing two identical strands connected near their centers, like an X. Next, these joined strands line up at the cell's midline (4.2*b*). Each X splits and the two identical chromosomal strands move to opposite sides of the cell, a nucleus forms around each set of chromosomes, and the cell itself divides in two (4.2*c*). With mitosis complete, each new cell contains 46 chromosomes and is genetically identical to the parent cell.

In **meiosis**, the process by which germ cells reproduce, four child cells are produced that are all different from one another and that contain only 23 chromosomes each. These child cells, called *gametes*, are the sperm or the ova that will combine at conception to form a new individual with the full complement of 46 chromosomes. Meiosis, diagramed on the right side of Figure 4.2, requires several additional phases. The 46 chromosomes of the cell similarly duplicate themselves into two identical strands that remain attached like an X (4.2*a*). Then an important new process occurs. The X-shaped chromosomes pair up with their partners (remember, the 46 chromosomes are arranged in 23 pairs) and the strands of one X exchange pieces with the strands of the partner X (4.2*d*). This process, called **crossing over**, means that the two strands that form each X are no longer identical. (Figure 4.3 offers a greatly simplified representation of such an exchange). The Xs then line up at the midline of the cell. One X from each pair moves to one end of the cell,a nucleus forms around each half, and the cell divides (4.2*e*). This process is then repeated (4.2*f* and 4.2*g*). Thus, when meiosis is complete, the resulting four gametes possess 23 chromosomes each and are genetically unique. (In males, all four gametes become sperm; in females, three of the gametes disintegrate and only one ovum is produced.)

Meiosis
The process by which germ cells produce four gametes (sperm or ova), each with half the number of chromosomes of the parent cell.

Crossing over
The exchange of genetic material between pairs of chromosomes during meiosis.

If we consider that every one of the 23 chromosomes in a gamete now represents a one-of-a-kind combination of genetic material and that these 23 chromosomes must combine with another set of original chromosomes from a gamete of the other parent, it should become clear why people come in so many sizes, colors, and shapes. Crossing over virtually assures that no two people (except identical twins produced from the same fertilized egg) will ever be exactly the same.

Gene
A segment of DNA on the chromosome. The basic unit of inheritance.

Inside the Chromosome

The idea that inheritance must involve genes on the chromosomes was generally accepted by the early 1940s, although no one had yet seen a **gene** or had any idea how it worked. The big breakthrough came in 1953, when James Watson and Francis Crick reported that they had uncovered the structure of a long and complicated molecule called **deoxyribonucleic acid (DNA)** that was the carrier of genet-

Deoxyribonucleic acid (DNA)
A stairlike, double-helix molecule that carries genetic information on chromosomes.

James Watson received the Nobel Prize with Francis Crick for discovering the structure of the DNA molecule.

ic information (Watson & Crick, 1953). The tale of their discovery is one of the most exciting detective stories in modern science (Watson, 1968), and the discovery itself earned them the Nobel Prize in 1962. Most important, their findings opened the door for an understanding of the basis of life itself.

Watson and Crick found that the DNA molecule has the structure of a double helix, much like the sides of a spiral staircase joined by rungs, as shown at the top of Figure 4.4. These rungs are composed of four bases: adenine (A), thymine (T), guanine (G), and cytosine (C). Each rung, called a *nucleotide*, consists of a pair of these bases linked together. Only two types of pairings occur, A–T and G–C. The *sequence* of these base pairs (rungs) determines the coded information carried by the gene.

Since each nucleotide base can link to only one other base, each half-rung of the DNA molecule can serve as a blueprint for the other half. Thus, during cell division, the chromosome "unzips" down the length of the staircase, breaking the links that connect the bases at the middle of each rung. The half-rungs then pair, base by base, with new material to form two new, identical copies of the original DNA sequence, as shown at the bottom of Figure 4.4.

What, then, is a gene? A gene is just a section of the DNA strand containing some set of these nucleotide rungs. On average, a gene contains about 1,000 nucleotides, although some contain as many as 2 million. Again, when we consider that the chromosomes in a human body cell together contain about 100,000 genes, and that each chromosome underwent the crossing-over process during meiosis, it is easy to understand why each individual person is truly unique.

The precise sequence of the nucleotides in a gene is extremely important. For example, 450 base pairs make up a gene that controls a characteristic of red blood cells. Only one base pair of the 450 differentiates a person who has normal blood from one who suffers from the devastating blood disease, sickle-cell anemia. In some genes, the sequence of nucleotides is so rigidly specified that it is essentially a family fingerprint. So-called DNA fingerprinting is increasingly used as forensic evidence (as in the O. J. Simpson trial) to convict murderers and rapists—or sometimes to free the innocent—and to help determine who may have fathered a child (Jeffreys, Brookfield, & Semeonoff, 1992).

The number and precise sequence of nucleotides in the genes also answers the question posed earlier about how the cell knows to develop into a human rather than a chimpanzee. The sequence is especially critical here because approximately 98% of human DNA is also found in the DNA of the chimpanzee ("Biological Systems," 1988).

Alleles
Genes for the same trait located in the same place on a pair of chromosomes.

The location of genes on the chromosome is likewise very important. For each pair of chromosomes, the genes for the same trait (eye color or nose shape) are in the same locations and are called **alleles**. We will see shortly that both genes are involved in how the trait is expressed, but that because the two alleles are not always the same, many different combinations of characteristics can result. Being located at the same place on the chromosome also makes possible the crossing-over process discussed earlier. In this way, variations of a trait are swapped between chromosomes but the trait itself remains a part of each and so gets passed on during reproduction. Finally, scientists have begun to map the precise locations of various genes on the human chromosomes, which will give them a clearer picture of the human genome (see Box 4.1) as well as make it possible to alter a person's hereditary code through genetic engineering (discussed in Chapter 5).

How do genes affect behavior? The answer to this question is complex and not yet entirely understood. It begins with the fact that there are two kinds of genes—structural genes and regulator genes. The job of the *structural genes* is to guide the

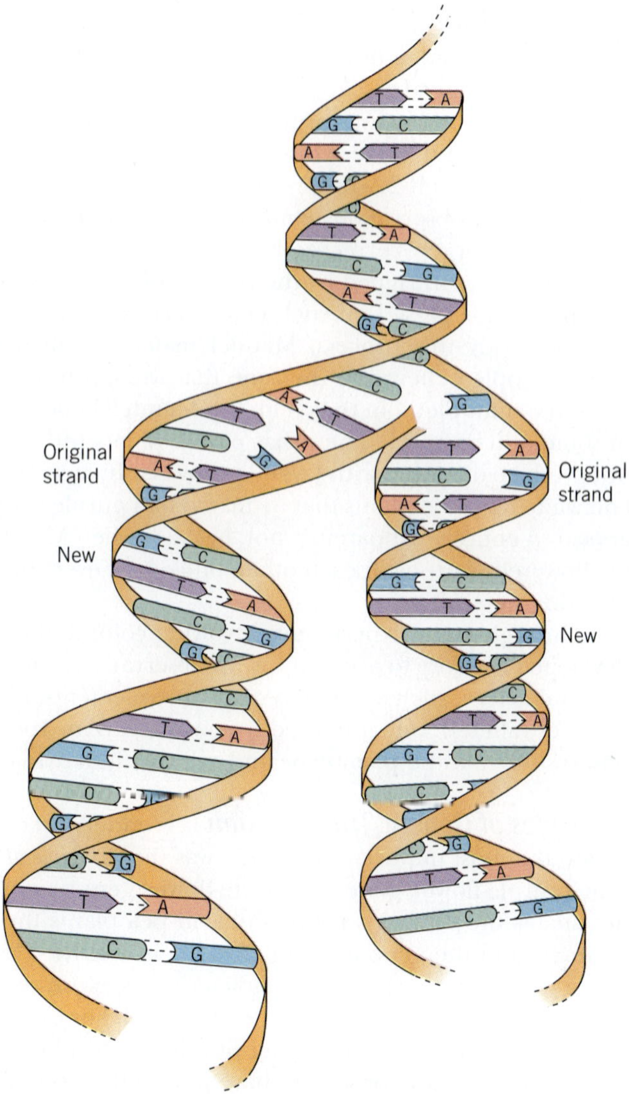

Figure 4.4
Structure and replication of DNA.

production of proteins, which serve many different functions in various parts of the body. The job of the *regulator genes* is to control the activities of the structural genes. The regulator genes thus can selectively suppress the production of protein so that the cells in a particular organ, such as the heart, liver, or brain, produce only proteins that are appropriate for that organ. The regulator genes also turn structural genes on and off at different points in development—for example, initiating and controlling the many changes that take place during puberty. They apparently do this in response to what is going on in their environment—meaning the cells around them—demonstrating that even at this molecular level, nature and nurture always operate together.

Through these as yet poorly understood processes, our genes can affect our sensory abilities, our nervous system, our muscles and bones, and so on, thus influencing our behavior and development in a reasonably direct manner. Later in the chapter, we will see how genes also appear to affect human behavior through more indirect processes.

The pioneering work of Gregor Mendel with pea plants paved the way for the modern science of genetics.

Phenotype
The characteristic of a trait that is expressed or observable.

Genotype
The arrangement of genes underlying a trait.

Mendel's Studies

Scientists' knowledge of genetic processes has relied in recent years on the development of advanced research techniques and powerful laboratory instruments. Yet some of the fundamental principles of heredity have been understood since the mid-1800s, when they were discovered and described by an Austrian monk named Gregor Mendel (1822–1884). Working alone in his garden, Mendel used pea plants, careful observations, and brilliant logic to develop a theory of inheritance that remains largely correct today.

Mendel was intrigued by the process of hereditary transmission. He wondered how pea plants passed on such characteristics as flower color to the next generation. To study this process, Mendel mated purple-flowered and white-flowered plants. People believed at the time that when a mother and father had different traits, the traits blend in the child. But Mendell believed that the process must work in some other way. He knew that parent plants with purple and white flowers did not produce offspring with lavender flowers. In fact, all the offspring of the purple- and white-flowered plants that he mated had purple flowers. Had the white trait disappeared entirely? Apparently not, because when Mendel next mated the new purple-flowered plants with each other, one out of every four of the second-generation offspring were white.

Through many experiments involving color and other characteristics, Mendel developed a theory to account for his observations. He correctly deduced that each observable trait, such as color, requires two elements, which we now know are a pair of genes (alleles), one inherited from each parent. Today, we call the expressed, or observable, trait the **phenotype** and call the underlying genes the **genotype**.

Principles of Genetic Transmission Mendel's theory involved several new principles, the most important of which was the *principle of dominance*: The alleles of a trait (purple-flower gene and white-flower gene) are not equal, and one usually dominates the other. As it turns out, in pea plants the gene for purple flowers is *dominant* and the gene for white flowers is *recessive*. Mendel discovered that when either gene is dominant, that characteristic is expressed; only when both genes are recessive is the other characteristic expressed. For example, if we think of the color trait in the pea plant as involving purple (P) or white (w) genes, then plants with the genotype PP, Pw, or wP will have purple flowers, and only those with the genotype ww will have white flowers. Plants thus can have the same phenotype (purple flowers) with different genotypes (PP, Pw, or wP).

Note how this principle explains what Mendel found when he mated the plants described earlier. As diagramed in Figure 4.5, the genotypes of the original parent plants must have been PP and ww. When mated, each child plant then had one purple-flower gene and one white-flower gene (Pw), having received one from each parent. But because the purple-flower gene is dominant, the phenotype of all the first-generation plants was purple. From the next mating, however, four combinations could occur: purple from both parents; purple from parent 1 and white from parent 2; white from parent 1 and purple from parent 2; and white from both parents. Theoretically, since each of these four combinations has an equal chance of occurring, and since the purple gene dominates whenever it is present, three-fourths of the new plants should be purple, and one-fourth should be white. This is exactly what Mendel observed.

Mendel's theory included several other principles. The *principle of segregation* states that each inheritable trait is passed on to the offspring as a separate unit (the alleles that produce flower color are separate from one another and passed on that

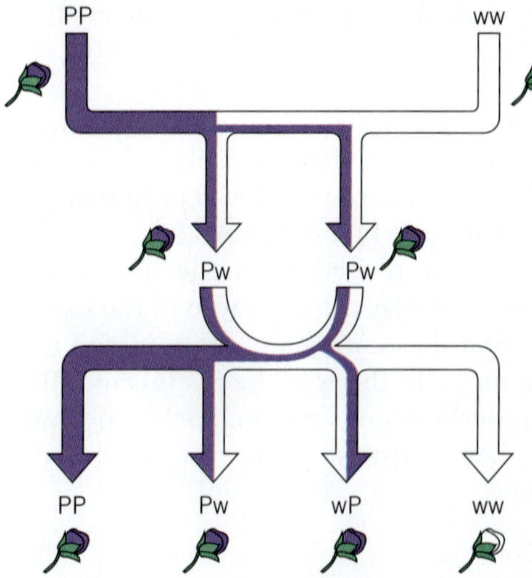

Figure 4.5
The four combinations of genes that can result after two generations when the original mating occurred between a plant with two dominant genes for color and a plant with two recessive genes for color.

way, which is why the blending idea was incorrect). The *principle of independent assortment* asserts that traits are passed on independently of one another (for example, which flower-color trait is passed on has no bearing on which stem-length trait is passed on).

Mendel's principles have proved to be surprisingly accurate, not just for pea plants, but throughout the huge variety of life-forms. Indeed, his discovery of dominant and recessive traits applies to many human characteristics, as shown in Table 4.1. One commonly cited example is eye color, the gene for brown eye color is dominant, while that for blue eye color is recessive. Thus, a mother and father who both possess brown–blue gene combinations for eye color have brown eyes themselves and are three times as likely to produce a brown-eyed child as a blue-eyed child.

Revisions of Mendel's Principles Years of research have supported Mendel's basic ideas, but have also uncovered other processes involved in hereditary transmission. For instance, single traits are sometimes the product of more than one pair of genes—a process known as **polygenic inheritance**. In humans, intelligence and skin color are traits affected by a number of genes. Also, some traits result from genes that display **incomplete dominance**, that is, they are neither entirely dominant nor entirely recessive. For example, sickle-cell anemia is passed on through a recessive gene. However, the blood of people who have this recessive gene along

Polygenic inheritance
The case in which a trait is determined by a number of genes.

Incomplete dominance
The case in which a dominant gene does not completely suppress the effect of a recessive gene, which is then somewhat expressed in the phenotype.

Table 4.1
Some Common Dominant and Recessive Traits

Dominant	*Recessive*
Brown eyes	Blue, gray, or green eyes
Normal hair	Baldness (in men)
Dark hair	Blond hair
Normal color vision	Color blindness
Freckles	No freckles
Dimples	No dimples
Free earlobes	Attached earlobes
Double-jointed thumbs	Tight thumb ligaments

with a dominant normal gene will show some mild characteristics of the disease (this differs from the early idea of blending, however, because the two genes remain separate and are passed on that way to future generations).

Codominance
The case in which both alleles are dominant and each is completely expressed in the phenotype.

A third addition to Mendel's principles involves **codominance**, in which both genes of a trait are dominant and so both characteristics are expressed completely. For example, the genes for A and B blood types are codominant, so a person who inherits one from each parent will have blood type AB.

Mendel's principles must also be revised in another important way. Scientists now know that the environment can play a crucial role in the expression of genes. As just one example, the fur color of the Arctic fox changes with temperature from white in winter to brown in summer. In this way, the fox is camouflaged in both the winter snow and the brown underbrush of summer. Such gene-environment interactions affect the phenotypic characteristics of many species, the scope of which we are just beginning to appreciate.

✓ *To Recap...*

Genes carry hereditary information from one generation to the next and direct and regulate development throughout life.

Cell reproduction occurs by mitosis in body cells and by meiosis in germ cells. Mitosis results in two identical cells with 46 chromosomes apiece, whereas meiosis produces four different gametes, each with 23 chromosomes. Gametes are the sperm and ova that combine to form a new cell with the full 46 chromosomes.

The basis of life is DNA, a double-helix-shaped molecule in the cell nucleus that contains billions of nucleotides. The nucleotides on a chromosome are subdivided into genes. Alleles are pairs of genes on the chromosomes that determine a trait. The precise order of nucleotides is important in the gene's functioning and also can serve as a molecular fingerprint for forensic purposes. The fixed location of genes on the chromosomes permits the crossing-over process and also has prompted scientists' attempts to map the human genome and to alter its structure.

Structural genes direct the production of proteins. Regulator genes control the activity of the structural genes and also turn them on and off as required across development.

Mendel's research with pea plants led to the first scientific theory of inheritance, based on the concept of dominant and recessive genes. His principles of segregation and independent assortment are generally accepted today, although several other processes have been added: single traits may be affected by more than one gene; genes may be neither completely dominant nor completely recessive; the genes for some traits are both dominant; and the environment may influence phenotypic characteristics.

Genetic Disorders

Although in the great majority of cases a person's genetic makeup results in normal development, genes can occasionally be a source of problems. Some human disorders are entirely hereditary and are passed along according to the same principles of inheritance that determine eye color and nose shape. Other genetic disorders are not inherited but may result from errors during cell division in meiosis. Chromosomes and the genes they carry can also be made abnormal by radiation, drugs, viruses, chemicals, and perhaps even the aging process.

In this section, we examine the various kinds of genetic disorders and some common examples of each. We will limit our discussion here to genetic errors in the 22 pairs of autosomes. Problems related to the sex chromosomes will be described in Chapter 15.

Hereditary Disorders

Abnormal genes are typically passed along to offspring according to Mendel's principles as well. Whether defective genes are expressed in the phenotype depends on whether they are dominant or recessive. If a defective gene inherited from one parent is recessive, the dominant (and usually normal) allele from the other parent can prevent the problem. Of course, the problem gene still exists in the genotype and will be passed on to half the person's offspring.

Dominant Traits Dominant genes that cause severe problems typically disappear from the species, because the affected people usually do not live to reproduce. In a few cases, however, severely disabling dominant genes are passed on because they do not become active until relatively late in life. People with these genes may reproduce before they know that they have inherited the disease.

An example is **Huntington's chorea**. The age of onset of this disease varies, but it typically strikes people between about 30 and 40 years of age. Quite suddenly, the nervous system begins to deteriorate, resulting in uncontrollable muscular movements and disordered brain function. In the 17th century, three brothers carrying the abnormal gene for this disorder came to North America from England. By 1965, more than 1,000 affected individuals could be traced directly to this family. The disease became well known to many Americans when it took the life of folksinger Woody Guthrie. Until recently, the children of a person stricken with Huntington's chorea had no way of knowing whether they also carried the gene and could pass it on to their offspring. Late in 1983, scientists discovered which chromosome carries the gene for Huntington's chorea, and 10 years later, they located the exact gene responsible for the disease and learned how to tell whether a person has inherited it (Morell, 1993).

Huntington's chorea
An inherited disease in which the nervous system suddenly deteriorates, resulting in uncontrollable muscular movements and disordered brain function. The disease typically strikes people between about 30 and 40 years of age and ultimately causes death.

Recessive Traits Like Mendel's purple flowers, which did not reveal the white-flower gene they carried, parents can carry problem recessive genes that have no effect on them. If both parents carry such a gene, they can combine in the offspring to produce the disorder (just as two brown-eyed parents can produce a blue-eyed child). It has been estimated that on average, each of us carries four potentially lethal genes as recessive traits (Scarr & Kidd, 1983), but because most of these dangerous genes are rare, it is unlikely that we will mate with someone who has a matching recessive gene. Even then, the probability of a child's receiving both recessive genes is only 1 in 4.

Some diseases carried by recessive genes produce errors of metabolism, which cause the body to mismanage sugars, fats, proteins, or carbohydrates. With **Tay-Sachs disease**, the nervous system disintegrates because of the lack of an enzyme that breaks down fats in brain cells. The fatty deposits swell, and the brain cells die. Tay-Sachs disease is rare in the general population, occurring in only 1 in 300,000 births. However, among Ashkenazic Jews, who account for more than 90% of the Jewish population of the United States, it occurs in 1 in every 3,600 births. Infants afflicted with the disease appear normal at birth and through their first half-year. Then, at about 8 months of age, they usually become extremely listless, and often by the end of their first year, they are blind. Most stricken children die by the age of 6. At present, there is no treatment for the disorder.

Tay-Sachs disease
An inherited disease in which the lack of an enzyme that breaks down fats in brain cells causes progressive brain deterioration. Affected children usually die by the age of 6.

Phenylketonuria (PKU) An inherited metabolic disease caused by a recessive gene. It can produce severe mental retardation if dietary intake of phenylalanine is not controlled for the first several years of life.

A more encouraging story is that of **phenylketonuria (PKU)**, a problem involving the body's management of protein. This disease occurs when the body fails to produce an enzyme that breaks down phenylalanine, an amino acid. As a result, abnormal amounts of the substance accumulate in the blood and harm the developing brain cells. Infants with PKU are typically healthy at birth but, if untreated, begin to deteriorate after a few months of life as the blood's phenylalanine level mounts. Periodic convulsions and seizures may occur, and the victims usually become severely retarded.

Our understanding of how PKU disrupts normal metabolism has resulted in one of the early victories of science over genetic abnormalities. Discovery of the mechanism of the disease led to the development of special diets, which are low in phenylalanine and thus prevent its accumulation in the bloodstream. Children placed on these special diets shortly after birth are able to develop normally. Because of the dramatic results of timely intervention in this disease, newborn babies are now routinely tested for PKU through a simple urine-screening procedure. The lesson in the PKU story is that genes are not necessarily destiny—how or whether a gene's influence is played out can depend on interactions with the environment.

Sickle-cell anemia (SCA) An inherited blood disease caused by a recessive gene. The red blood cells assume a sickle shape and do not distribute oxygen efficiently to the cells of the body.

A recessive genetic abnormality that does not involve metabolism is **sickle-cell anemia (SCA)**. People who have inherited a gene for this recessive trait from both parents have red blood cells that do not contain normal hemoglobin, a protein that carries oxygen throughout the body. Instead, abnormal hemoglobin causes their red blood cells to become sickled, as shown in Figure 4.6. These sickled cells tend to clog small blood vessels instead of easily passing through them as normal cells do, thus preventing blood from reaching parts of the body. An unusual oxygen demand, such as brought on by physical exertion, may cause the sufferer to experience severe pain, tissue damage, and even death because of the inadequate supply of oxygen. As we indicated earlier, the gene for this disease is not entirely recessive (incomplete dominance), and people who have only one gene for SCA may show characteristics of the condition.

About 9% of African-Americans carry the recessive gene for SCA. Among the Bamba, a tribe in Africa, the incidence has been reported to be as high as 39%.

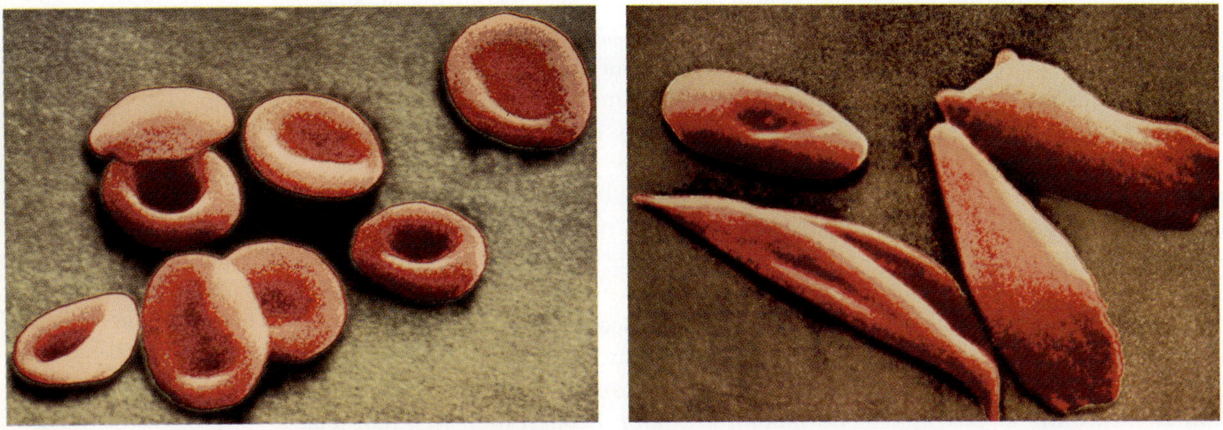

Figure 4.6
Scanning electron micrographs of red blood cells from normal individuals (*left*) and individuals with sickle-cell anemia (*right*).

Such a high rate of occurrence seems surprising from a Darwinian perspective, by which nonadaptive traits are weeded out through natural selection, because individuals who have two genes for SCA frequently die young and produce few children. How, then, could such a characteristic be preserved through evolution? The answer reveals a rare instance in which a gene is maladaptive for one purpose but adaptive for another. Scientists have noted that the Bamba live in areas where the incidence of malaria is high, but Bamba children who carry the SCA gene are about half as likely to have malarial parasites as those who do not. Although it is unclear how this gene offers resistance to malaria, its presence appears to permit more carriers to grow up and have children, even though 1 in 4 will have SCA. Apparently, the negative effects of malarial parasites on reproduction are greater than the effects of carrying the SCA gene.

African children who carry a recessive gene for sickle-cell anemia have a reduced likelihood of contracting malaria.

It is likely that many new findings are on the horizon of genetic research. Within the last few years, investigators have discovered the gene for a type of Alzheimer's disease that runs in families. They also have located the genes for cystic fibrosis and for amytrophic lateral sclerosis (ALS), also known as Lou Gehrig's disease. The genetic locus of many other diseases may soon be discovered as part of the Human Genome Project, discussed in Box 4.1.

The discoveries of precise locations of genes that cause physical disorders has raised hope that we might also be able to find genes that account for behavioral problems. For example, there have been reports in recent years of discoveries of chromosomal locations for alcoholism, aggressiveness, manic-depressive disorder, schizophrenia, and hyperactivity. In addition, scientists have reported identifying a homosexuality gene on the X chromosome (Hamer et al., 1993). But we must be cautious in this area. Many scientists believe that no single gene will ever be found that alone accounts for a complex behavior, and not all early reports have been supported by subsequent research (Horan, 1993; Plomin, 1995b).

Down syndrome A chromosomal disorder caused by an extra chromosome. Its effects include mental retardation and a characteristic physical appearance.

Structural Defects in the Chromosome

The genetic abnormalities we have discussed thus far are all passed along according to the regular principles of inheritance. But genetically based problems may also result from physical changes in chromosomes. These changes often occur during meiosis in one of the parents, and they can involve any of the 22 autosomes or the sex chromosome. As mentioned, environmental hazards can also damage chromosomes.

One of the most frequently observed effects of structural abnormality is **Down syndrome**, named after John Langdon H. Down, the physician who first described it. In Down syndrome, one of the pairs of chromosomes has a third member. Infants afflicted with this disorder are moderately to severely retarded and have a distinctive appearance that includes a flattened face and folded eyelids. They also tend to have poor muscle tone and problems with expressive language. The cause of Down syndrome was identified in 1957, marking the first time a human disease had been directly linked to a chromosomal disorder.

Children with Down syndrome have physical features that include flattened faces and folds on the eyelids.

The likelihood that a couple will produce a child with Down syndrome increases dramatically with the age of the mother. Fewer than 1 in 1,000 babies of mothers under age 30 have Down syndrome, whereas the incidence is 74 times greater for women between the ages of 45 and 49. (Still, only a small proportion of births to these older mothers involve Down syndrome.) The age of the father is not as important, but the father contributes the extra chromosome in 20 to 30% of cases (Behrman & Vaughan, 1987).

Serious problems can also be caused when part of a chromosome is missing. For example, the deletion of a small amount of genetic material from one chro-

BOX 4.1

THE HUMAN GENOME PROJECT

If scientists knew where each of the genes were on the 24 human chromosomes (22 autosomes, plus X and Y), they would be in a better position to learn what each of these genes does. The potential benefits would be enormous. Health scientists, for example, would possess the tools to identify defective genes that produce many inherited diseases. In some cases, these defects could be detected even before people showed their effects, and preventive treatment might be possible. Locating the genes on the chromosomes is referred to as *mapping the genome.*

But such mapping is only one step toward understanding. If scientists knew the exact sequence of nucleotides in each gene, they would be able to specify how the gene is defective. This knowledge might, in turn, make it possible to correct the defective sequence. Identifying the sequence of the 3 billion nucleotides in the DNA molecule is called *sequencing the genome.*

In 1989 the United States launched the Human Genome Project, headed by James Watson, one of the discoverers of the DNA molecule (Cooper, 1994). The purpose of the research is to map and sequence human DNA. This project has been likened to the Manhattan Project, which produced the atomic bomb, or the Apollo program, which placed the first human being on the moon (Watson, 1990). One official exclaimed: "It's going to tell us everything. Evolution, disease, everything will be based on what's in that magnificent tape called DNA" (Jaroff, 1989, p. 63).

The task is not only exciting but overwhelming. At this point, about 2 million of the 3 billion nucleotides have been sequenced, and the capacity for sequencing has reached about 1 million per year. At this rate, it would take 3,000 years to sequence the whole genome (National Institutes of Health, 1993).

But the hope is that new technology will make it possible to complete the job of mapping and sequencing the genome within 15 years at a cost to the U.S. government of $3 billion. Automatic sequencers are being developed that can sequence between 100,000 and 1 million nucleotides per day. Furthermore, scientists in the San Francisco area reported in 1989 that they had taken the first clear photograph of DNA—seen in Figure 4.7—through a revolutionary technique. It may be possible in the future for scientists to read the code of life from photographs of this type (Beebe et al., 1989).

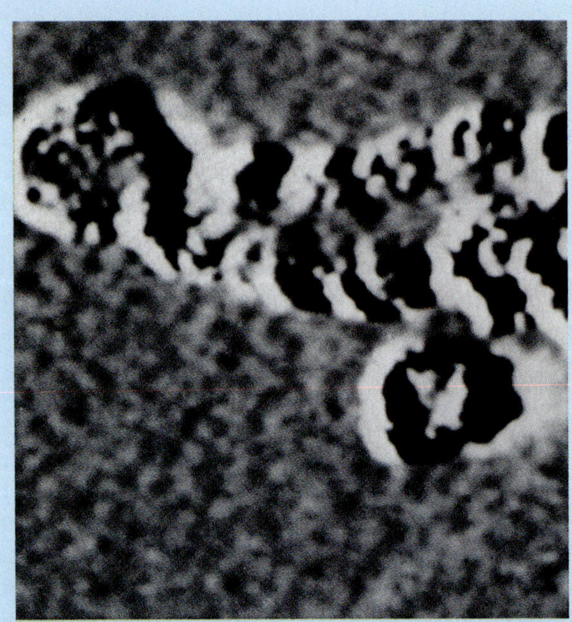

Figure 4.7
The first published high-resolution photograph of a strand of DNA, taken with a scanning tunneling microscope. From "Direct Observation of Native DNA Structures with the Scanning Tunneling Microscope" by T. P. Beebe et al., 1989, *Science, 243,* p. 371. Copyright © 1989 by the AAAS. Reprinted by permission.

mosome produces *cri du chat*, "cry of the cat," syndrome. Affected infants, who have a catlike cry, have mental retardation and neuromuscular problems. Another example is Wilms' tumor. Children who have this disorder have no iris, the colored part of the eye, and are more likely to have cancer of the kidney during infancy or early childhood.

Given the billions of sperm cells generated by the male and the 2 million or so ova generated by the female, we should not be surprised that genetic imperfections sometimes occur. These variations, or *mutations*, are the driving force behind evolution. When the "errors" turn out to be adaptive, they result in improvements in the species or the creation of a new species. The overwhelming majority of mutations, however, are maladaptive. Through a natural screening process in humans, about 90% of all genetic abnormalities result in miscarriage rather than live births. So although more than 5,000 single-gene disorders have been identified in humans (McKusick, 1994), only about 1% of all babies have detectable chromosomal abnormalities.

One important application of our rapidly accumulating knowledge about genetic disorders involves genetic counseling for couples and prospective parents. We discuss this topic in Chapter 5.

✓ To Recap...

Certain disorders are transmitted genetically on the autosomes according to Mendelian principles. Huntington's chorea is caused by a dominant gene that is expressed in all carriers, whereas Tay-Sachs disease, phenylketonuria, and sickle-cell anemia are caused by recessive genes expressed only when the individual inherits the defective gene from both parents. Other genetic diseases, such as Down syndrome, are caused by structural defects in chromosomes, which may occur during meiosis in one of the parents.

Models of Gene-Environment Interaction

We have seen what genes are and how they determine certain physical characteristics, such as eye and hair color. Genes also can cause physical abnormalities and intellectual deficits, as in Down syndrome. But psychologists have been most interested in the questions of how and how much genes typically affect human behavior and development.

When thinking about the role of genes in development, we must keep in mind an important distinction that we first discussed in Chapter 1. Recall that some psychologists focus on normative development—they are concerned with the ways in which humans are alike. Other psychologists are more interested in idiographic processes—they focus on what makes us different from one another. We can look at this issue in another way. Humans are different from other species, which are in turn different from one another. What gives a species its identity are the characteristics that all members *share*, that is, how they are alike. And there is no doubt that genes are responsible for making each species unique. Psychologists who study normative development thus are really trying to learn about humans as a species. But humans (and all other animals) also differ among themselves—not just in physical characteristics, but in behavior and development as well. These are the individual differences of interest to psychologists who take an idiographic approach. How much of a role do genes play in these sorts of differences? This is the main question being asked today by researchers in the field of **behavior genetics** and, in essence, it forms the basis of the modern nature–nurture debate (Scarr, 1992).

Behavior genetics The field of study that explores the role of genes in producing individual differences in behavior and development.

All contemporary psychologists believe that genes (nature) and environment (nurture) interact to determine human behavior, but they differ as to which factor they feel has more influence. A related and perhaps even more useful question concerns *how* genes and environment exert their effects, that is, by what processes do these factors operate and how do they interact with one another?

In this section we examine four theoretical models that attempt to explain how genes and environment work together to determine any child's behavior and development. As the models are complex, we will present only their fundamental ideas. But they illustrate the increasing role that psychologists seem to be ascribing to genetic processes as this area is becoming better understood. In the final section, we examine the methods by which researchers have been testing these models and some of the evidence they have uncovered.

Gottesman's Limit-Setting Model

An early model proposed by Irving Gottesman (1974) suggested that genes interact with the environment by setting the upper and lower limits of our development. Our environment and experiences then presumably determine where in this **reaction range** we end up.

Reaction range
In Gottesman's model, the term for the range of ability or skill that is set by the genes.

Figure 4.8 illustrates this model by showing the ranges of possible basketball skill that might exist for groups of children born with different genotypes, representing different heights. Group A consists of children who carry a gene that makes them unusually short. Groups B and C represent typical girls and boys, respectively, who are of average height for their gender. Group D represents children who have inherited genes that make them unusually tall. Note that the reaction range (RR) of the groups varies, with the tallest individuals having the widest potential range of basketball abilities, and shortest having the narrowest. The graph also includes three

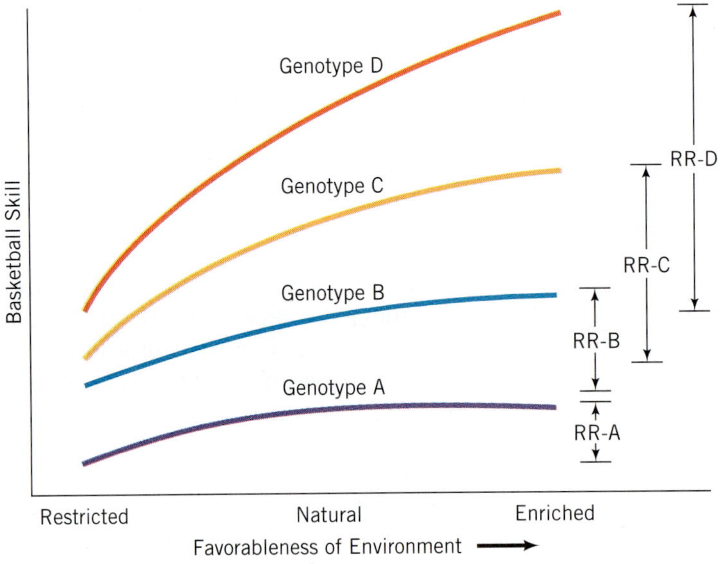

Figure 4.8
The reaction range concept, showing the simultaneous influences of genes and environment. Adapted from "Developmental Genetics and Ontogenetic Psychology: Overdue Détente and Propositions from a Matchmaker" by I. I. Gottesman, 1974. In A. D. Pick (Ed.), *Minnesota Symposia on Child Psychology*, Vol. 8, p. 60. Copyright © 1974 by the University of Minnesota Press. Adapted by permission.

levels of environment: restricted (where perhaps the child has no exposure to basketball at all), natural (the environment of a youngster growing up in a typical U.S. town), and enriched (such as when the child's father is a basketball coach).

Note how genes and environment interact in this model. The genes have set the limits on potential basketball skills such that very short children (Group A) will not become proficient at these skills regardless of their environment, whereas very tall children (Group D) have the greatest opportunity to benefit from a more supportive environment. But it is important to note also that the reaction ranges overlap. This means that either poor genes or a poor environment can be overcome somewhat by strength in the other. This model, of course, could be applied to many other behaviors and abilities, such as mathematics performance, musical ability, or any number of traits or skills.

In Gottesman's model, genes thus play a relatively passive role in human development, establishing our reaction range limits and then having no further influence. Newer models of gene-environment interaction view things very differently.

Scarr's Niche-Picking Model

In the model offered by Sandra Scarr, genes play a much more active role in development than simply setting limits (Scarr, 1992, 1993; Scarr & McCartney, 1983). They could almost be thought of as trying to take complete charge of the child's development—including the kind of environment that the child experiences.

The traditional view in psychology has been that different family environments cause children to develop in different ways. For example, we know that children whose parents provide books, educational activities, and encouragement to succeed tend to perform well in school, and children whose parents are harsh and punitive are more likely to be aggressive and to display various other behavior problems. The child's developmental outcome therefore was assumed to be rather directly determined by the child's family environment.

Scarr disagrees with this view. Her model invokes an important idea discussed in Chapter 2, namely, that children play a role in producing their own environments. This, she proposes, occurs through the genes. Consider the family example again. Although parents do provide children with their family environment, they also provide them with their genes. The child's genes, in turn, operate in three different ways—which Scarr believes change as the child grows from infancy to adolescence—to influence the family environment.

According to Scarr and McCartney's model, niche-picking occurs when children choose environments that reflect and support their genetic predispositions.

During infancy, genes exert their influence principally in a *passive* manner. The baby's environment is almost entirely dictated by the parents, but because the parents and child share so many of the same genes, the environment they create is usually very consistent with, and supportive of, the child's genotype. For example, musically inclined parents are likely both to give birth to musically inclined children and to provide a musical home environment for them.

As children get older, their genes operate through a more *evocative* process. Children now do things that evoke certain responses from the parents and others (recall Bronfenbrenner's notion of developmentally generative and developmentally disruptive behaviors, presented in Chapter 2). For example, a child who speaks and reads early—behaviors that likely have some genetic basis—may prompt parents to provide a rich language environment, including books, storytelling, and educational games. In this way, the child's genes help create an environment with which they are compatible and that serves to further their goals.

Finally, as children gain more independence, their genes can operate in a more *active* manner to produce environments that suit them. Children, on their own, can seek out the particular environments, or *niches*, that best fit their interests and talents—such as the library, the gym, or the rock concert.

Scarr's model of gene-environment interaction does not ignore the importance of the child's family environment, but it views the environment less as a direct cause of the child's development and more as a vehicle that enables the genes to guide the child along a particular developmental path. Scarr contends that genetic influences actually grow stronger with age, as children become better able actively to recruit the environments their genes demand. This prediction runs counter to the traditional view that our genes start us off in a particular direction and then our environment more or less takes over. We will examine the evidence on this and other aspects of the model in the next section.

Plomin's Environmental Genetics Model

A third model of gene-environment interaction has been presented by Robert Plomin (1994, 1995b; Plomin, DeFries, 1997). His approach shares many of the same ideas as Scarr's model. He believes that children's developmental outcomes are related to their family environments for two reasons: (1) children share many genes with their parents who, in turn, provide the environment for their children; and (2) children evoke from their parents the sorts of responses and surroundings that suit their genes.

Plomin has gone so far as to refer to his work as *environmental genetics*, which means the study of how our genes influence our environments in order to get what they want. Further, his model is not limited to parent–child interactions but also extends to other family members (Plomin et al., 1994).

Nonshared environment A concept used in behavior genetics to refer to presumed aspects of the environment that children experience differently.

The most important addition in Plomin's model is the concept of **nonshared environment** (Hetherington, Reiss, & Plomin, 1994). This idea is most easily understood in terms of siblings. We know that children raised in the same family have many similarities. Psychologists have not been surprised to find that intelligence, physical abilities, personality, and other characteristics are generally more similar between brothers and sisters than they are between unrelated children. These similarities have always been assumed to result from siblings' sharing both many of the same genes (50%) and the same family environment. Given these two major sources of similarity, a more interesting question becomes why many siblings behave and develop so differently from one another.

Plomin's answer is that although these children live in the same family, they do not necessarily experience the same environments. Rather, parents often treat children differently from one another, and children frequently react to the same family events and experiences in different ways. Moreover, the source of both these differences, Plomin believes, is genetic. His argument is that although 50% of siblings' genes are the same, 50% are also different. These different genes, Plomin contends, lead siblings to evoke different treatment from their parents and to respond in different ways to the same events. In short, the aspects of the family environment that they experience differently—the nonshared aspects—are what make siblings different from one another.

What about siblings' similarities? Perhaps the most controversial aspect of this model is that, like Scarr and other behavior geneticists, Plomin believes that the similarities we see in siblings result mostly from their genetic similarity (the 50% of the genes they share). Their common family environment, by contrast, is thought to contribute very little to explaining why they are alike. Again, we will examine the research evidence on this idea later in the chapter.

Bronfenbrenner and Ceci's Bioecological Model

The most recent and perhaps most complex of the models we will consider is that of Urie Bronfenbrenner and Stephen Ceci (Bronfenbrenner & Ceci, 1994; Bronfenbrenner & Morris, 1998). This model derives from Bronfenbrenner's ecological approach, described in Chapter 2, and is strongly influenced by the development-in-context concept. We will see shortly why they call it a *bioecological model.*

Bronfenbrenner and Ceci assign much more importance to the environment than do the behavior geneticists. They agree with the idea that children's genes influence their development and that they do so, to some degree, by steering the environment in the right direction. But the bioecological model adds to this picture a more explicit description of how and when this occurs.

According to this analysis, genes can only exert their influence when certain experiences activate them. These experiences, called **proximal processes**, are interactions between the child and the child's direct-contact (microsystem) world—parents, siblings, toys, books, pets, and anything else of significance in the child's immediate environment—that have a positive effect on the child's psychological functioning. Such interactions may involve, for example, play with siblings, social activities with friends, reading and problem solving with parents, and other sorts of stimulating experiences. An additional requirement is that these interactions must take place fairly regularly and must continue for some time. When these requirements hold, the child's genes are able to use the experiences to achieve their ends, and, as a result, the child reaches his or her maximum genetic potential. But if proximal processes are weak or missing in the child's life, the genes cannot fully express themselves and so the child's development will remain below what it could have been.

Proximal processes Bronfenbrenner and Ceci's term for interactions between the child and aspects of the microsystem that have positive effects on psychological functioning and that help maximize expression of the child's genetic potential.

Bronfenbrenner and Ceci also believe that proximal processes are valuable to the child in both high- and lower-quality environments, but in different ways. When the environment is stable and rich with resources—as is the case in many middle-class households—these interactions have the best opportunity to help children develop their fullest abilities (such as the example of musical talent described earlier). When the child's environment is disorganized and disadvantaged—as in many poor neighborhoods—proximal processes can help prevent undesirable genetic outcomes that might otherwise have occurred (such as aggression, violence, or other problem behaviors to which genes may have predisposed the child).

Note how the child's biology (genes) and ecology (immediate environment) contribute more equally and in greater interaction in this model than in either the more strongly genetic or strongly environmental approaches. Perhaps for this reason, Bronfenbrenner and Ceci use the term *bioecological* to describe it.

✓ To Recap...

Four models attempt to explain how genes and environment interact to produce human development. In Gottesman's limit-setting model, genes play a passive role by setting the limits within which environmental effects can be observed. Genes play a more active role in Scarr's niche-picking model, controlling the child's environment through processes that move from passive (infancy) to evocative (early childhood) to active (later childhood). Plomin's model adds the concept of nonshared environment, whereby differences in the behavior of siblings are assumed to result from those aspects of the environment that they experience differently. Bronfenbrenner and Ceci's bioecological model proposes that genes exert their influence on the environment through proximal processes—stimulating interactions between the child and aspects of the microsystem—which must be frequent and continuing in the child's life.

Studying the Effects of Genes on Behavior

How do researchers study the influences of genes on behavior to determine which of these models is most accurate? Not easily. People are not pea plants, and scientists are not free to mate humans of their choice to see how the offspring will turn out. Researchers have to rely solely on observation, experiments of nature, and careful analyses of their data. Fortunately, scientists' statistical methods and their access to large populations of research participants have come a long way since Mendel's time.

The effects of genes on human behavior and development have been studied extensively over the years in three principal areas: intellectual abilities, psychiatric disorders (including children's behavior problems), and aspects of personality (including infant temperament). In this section we present some of what psychologists have learned about genetic contributions to these areas as we examine the four major methods that have been used in their investigation: family studies, adoption studies, twin studies, and combinations of these approaches.

Family Studies

Because children inherit 50% of their genes from each parent, similarities among family members are not surprising. The family-study approach looks for such similarities over generations in traits suspected to have a genetic basis.

One of the earliest reports claiming to demonstrate a genetic basis for intelligence was Henry Goddard's study of the Kallikak family, published in 1912. During the Revolutionary War, a soldier whom Goddard called Martin Kallikak (a pseudonym) had an illegitimate son by a retarded tavern maid. Later, Kallikak married a woman of normal intelligence from a respected family.

Goddard traced five generations of Kallikak's offspring from these two lines. Of the 480 or so descendants of the tavern maid, he identified many as criminal, alcoholic, or "immoral," and 25% as retarded. In contrast, the 496 descendants from Kallikak's marriage were all intellectually normal, according to Goddard, and most occupied respected positions in their communities. Since Kallikak was the father to both family lines, Goddard concluded that the differences between them must be due to the genetic differences between his two mates. Of course, this conclusion ignored the vastly different environments and upbringing of the two lines of descendants. Distinguishing between hereditary and environmental influences is a major limitation of the family-study method. As scientists have pointed out, lots of things run in families—names, religious beliefs, and cake recipes, for example. Not all of these are determined by our genes.

Family studies can be of value, however. Sometimes they point up characteristics that might have a genetic component and so encourage more definitive research using one of the more rigorous methods that we discuss next. For example, family studies have shown that children of mothers who have schizophrenia—a disorder that produces confused thought and language, hallucinations, and unpredictable actions—are about 10 times as likely as children of normal mothers to develop schizophrenia. Also, people who have schizophrenia are 8 times more likely to have a close relative with the disorder than are those who do not have schizophrenia (Gottesman & Shields, 1982). Do these statistics support a nature or nurture interpretation? Research using more sophisticated methods has been providing some answers.

Adoption Studies

Children are usually similar to their parents in a number of important and not-so-important ways. What is the source of these similarities? We have noted that parents share many of the same genes with their children and that they also share a similar environment. But our theoretical models suggest different contributions for nature and nurture. Which, in fact, is more influential? Or do they contribute equally?

The adoption-study method is designed to address this issue. Children who are living in adoptive homes are compared with their biological parents (who share their genes, but not their environments) and with their adoptive parents (who share their environments, but not their genes). If the correlation with one set of parents is stronger than that with the other, we have a good idea of which factor plays the larger role in the behavior or trait we are measuring.

Sometimes the method includes siblings, since many adoptive families go on to adopt a second child. These two children now share the same environment (although perhaps some of it is also nonshared), but none of the same genes. Their similarity on whatever behaviors we choose to study can thus be compared with the similarity of biological siblings in families used for comparison. Again, differences in the correlations between the two sets of siblings could shed light on whether environment or heredity has more influence on the behaviors of interest.

A major study that has employed this approach is the Colorado Adoption Project. This research, begun in 1975, is a longitudinal study of about 250 families with adopted children and, for comparison, 250 families with biological children. The children were first studied when they were infants and preschoolers, and they have been followed and studied since (DeFries, Plomin, & Fulker, 1994; Plomin & DeFries, 1985).

One focus of this project has been intelligence (we discuss methods of studying intelligence again in Chapter 10). The children have been tested using a variety of different instruments and on both general intellectual ability and specific cognitive skills (such as memory, vocabulary, spatial relations, and others). The findings clearly support a role for genetic processes. Stronger correlations have been found between the scores of biological siblings versus adoptive siblings, and between children and their biological parents versus their adoptive parents. These findings indicate that, at least to some degree, children inherit their intellectual abilities (Cardon, 1994; Cherny & Cardon, 1994).

But what about the role of the environment on intelligence? Does it operate completely independently of the child's genetic makeup? An additional question posed by the project has been whether Plomin is correct in his belief that children's genes help shape their environments. One study examined an instrument called the HOME (Home Observation for Measurement of the Environment), designed to assess the quality of children's family environments, including the amount and kinds of stimulation provided by the mother. Scores on this measure have repeatedly been found to correlate well with children's IQ scores, which seems to indicate that the quality of the early environment directly affects the child's intellectual development. Using the sibling-adoption method, however, project researchers found that biological siblings were more similar in their HOME scores than were adopted siblings (Braungart, Fulker, & Plomin, 1992; Saudino & Plomin, 1997). These findings can be interpreted as supporting the idea that children's genes sometimes play a passive role in producing their home and family environments—in this case because the mother's genes influenced both the biological children's intelligence and the environment she provided them. The previously found connections between the HOME and children's intelligence thus may involve more than just an environmental effect.

Adoption studies have also addressed the issue of schizophrenia, described earlier. Children of schizophrenic mothers who are placed in adoptive homes are around 10 times as likely to develop schizophrenia as are either the biological children of the adoptive parents or adopted children of normal mothers (Plomin et al., 1997). This finding suggests a major role for heredity in the development of the disease and is consistent with other research showing that psychological disorders can be inherited (Rutter et al., 1990).

Again we can ask the question, Can genetic processes be involved in what appear to be environmental influences on psychological problems? Evidence from adoption research suggests that they can. One recent study sought to explain the hostile and antisocial behaviors of a group of adolescents who had been adopted at birth. The researchers hypothesized that these behaviors could be connected to both their biological and their adoptive parents but that both connections involved the children's genes. The researchers first showed that these adolescents were more likely to have biological parents with psychiatric disorders than were a comparison group of adopted adolescents who showed no such problems. This finding simply demonstrates that some problem behaviors can be inherited (Rutter & Caesar, 1991). The researchers next showed that the troubled adolescents also were more likely to have adoptive parents who used harsh and inconsistent punishment. This apparent environmental influence also has been found many times before (Patterson, Reid, & Dishion, 1992).

What makes the study important is that, using sophisticated statistical methods, the researchers were able to relate the adoptive parents' disciplinary practices to the biological parents' history of psychiatric problems, but only in those children who displayed the behavior problems. Given that the only connection between the sets of parents was the child, the findings would seem to require a behavior-genetics explanation. Specifically, the researchers speculated that (1) the children initially inherited their behavior problems from their biological parents; (2) these problems then evoked responses (harsh discipline) from their adoptive parents; and (3) the parents' disciplinary practices then served to maintain the children's problem behaviors. In this way, genes connected the children's antisocial behaviors to the biological parents through a passive process and connected them to the adoptive parents through an evocative process (Ge et al., 1996).

Finally, adoption studies have produced two additional findings of importance to behavior geneticists: (1) adoptive (unrelated) siblings are more similar to one another in the early years than in adolescence, and (2) the psychological characteristics of an adopted child, with age, become increasingly similar to those of the biological mother and less similar to those of the adoptive mother. The first of these findings can be explained by the concept of nonshared environment, with family influences serving to separate the siblings rather than make them alike (Dunn & McGuire, 1994). The second finding seems to support the contention that genes play a stronger role in development as children get older. This may be because parents generally control children's environments at younger ages, but as children grow older, they are increasingly able to choose their own environments and experiences, thus permitting their genes to operate in a more active way to influence their behavior (McGue, 1993; Plomin, Fulker, et al., 1997).

Twin Studies

Approximately 1 of every 85 births yields twins, providing investigators with an interesting opportunity to study the role of genetic similarity. Twins come in two varieties. **Identical twins** develop from the same fertilized egg and are called **monozygotic twins (MZ)** (*mono*, "one"; *zygote*, "fertilized egg"). They have exactly the same genes. **Fraternal twins** develop from two different eggs and are called **dizygotic twins (DZ)** (*di*, "two"). Their genetic makeup is no more similar than that of any two children who have the same parents; on average, 50% of the genes of dizygotic twins are the same.

Identical (monozygotic [MZ]) twins
Twins who develop from a single fertilized ovum and thus inherit identical genetic material.

Fraternal (dizygotic [DZ]) twins
Twins who develop from separately fertilized ova and who thus are no more genetically similar than are other siblings.

The logic of the twin-study approach begins with the assumption that fraternal twins share an environment that is as similar as the environment shared by identical twins. Researchers then look at a particular trait or behavior displayed by the sets of twins. If the trait is more similar in the identical twins than in the fraternal twins, we should be able to conclude that the greater similarity must result from the greater similarity of their genes.

Many twin studies have specifically targeted intelligence and its heritability. As shown in Table 4.2, hundreds of studies have been conducted, with virtually every one finding higher correlations between the IQ scores of MZ twins than between those of DZ twins (Bouchard & McGue, 1981; McGue et al., 1993). Clearly, intelli-

Identical twins, whose genetic makeup is precisely the same, are commonly employed in research designs examining the effects of genes on human development.

Table 4.2
Average Correlations of Various Abilities from Several Twin Studies

Trait	Number of Studies	Average Correlation: Identical Twins	Average Correlation: Fraternal Twins
Ability			
General intelligence	30	.82	.59
Verbal comprehension	27	.78	.59
Number and mathematics	27	.78	.59
Spatial visualization	31	.65	.41
Memory	16	.52	.36
Reasoning	16	.74	.50
Clerical speed and accuracy	15	.70	.47
Verbal fluency	12	.67	.52
Divergent thinking	10	.61	.50
Language achievement	28	.81	.58
Social studies achievement	7	.85	.61
Natural science achievement	14	.79	.64
All abilities	211	.74	.54

Source: Adapted from "Heredity and Environment: Major Findings from Twin Studies of Ability, Personality and Interests" by R. C. Nichols, 1978, *Homo, 29,* Table 1, p. 163.

gence—at least when measured by IQ tests—has a genetic component. In recent work with infants, whose intelligence is assessed using instruments that rely less on language and verbal abilities and more on simple motor and perceptual responses (we discuss these differences more fully in Chapter 10), MZ twins also showed higher correlations than did DZ twins (Cherny, Fulker, Emde, et al., 1994).

Twin studies have also been used to address a variety of personality issues. Many such studies have been conducted with adults and have produced some unusual findings. For example, if one identical twin experiences divorce, the chance that the other twin will experience divorce is six times that of the general population; the likelihood falls to two times the population average for a fraternal twin. Of course, there is no such thing as a divorce gene; the increase in risk for divorce is probably related to personality characteristics affected by genetic inheritance (McGue & Lykken, 1992).

An important personality area in children involves their *temperament.* Babies come into the world with a particular style of responding. Some are irritable and cry frequently; some are easygoing and smile a lot; some are active; some are cuddly; and so forth. Aspects of temperament sometimes persist well into the early school years and may eventually form the basis for adult personality. (We take up this subject again in Chapter 12.) Do genes influence temperament? Apparently they do, at least to some extent. As early as 3 months of age, and throughout the first years of life, identical twins are more similar than fraternal twins on a variety of measures, including attention, activity, and involvement in testing (Braungart et al., 1992; Emde et al., 1992). One study looked at the trait of shyness, testing twin babies at 14 and 20 months in both the laboratory and at home. Genes were found to be strongly involved in this aspect of temperament at both ages and in both locations (Cherny, Fulker, Corley, et al., 1994).

Twin studies have also been used to look at developmental issues in older children and adolescents, including parent–child relationships. For example, a recent

Table 4.3
Average Correlations of Children's Ratings of Father–Son Relationships

	11-year-olds		*17-year-olds*	
Relationship factor	***MZ***	***DZ***	***MZ***	***DZ***
Conflict with father	.44	.36	.62	.01
Involvement with father	.46	.28	.64	.39
Son's regard for father	.32	.32	.58	.24
Father's regard for son	.34	.35	.53	.14
Structure provided by father	.27	.46	.43	.35
Support provided by father	.45	.31	.64	.15

Source: Adapted from "Genetic and Environmental Influences on Parent-Son Relationships: Evidence for Increasing Genetic Influence during Adolescence" by I. J. Elkins, M. McGue, and W. G. Iacono, 1997, *Developmental Psychology, 33*, 351–363. Adapted by permission.

study asked MZ and DZ boys, ages 11 and 17 years, to rate the quality of their relationships with their mothers and fathers. Two particularly clear findings were found on the ratings of the fathers, as shown in Table 4.3. The higher correlations between the identical twins demonstrate that genes must have contributed to these father–son relationships. And the higher correlations by the older MZ twins again offer evidence for the idea that gene effects get stronger over the course of development (Elkins et al., 1997).

Finally, behavior geneticists have used twins to examine whether genetic influences underlie certain changes we see in children's development and behavior. Physical development such as height and weight tends to occur in spurts and plateaus. The rhythm of these life events is called **developmental pacing**. Psychologists assume that developmental pacing is guided by the regulator genes, which turn the structural genes on and off at different points in development and thus control protein production. But what about similar sorts of changes in behavioral traits, such as intellectual abilities? Are they also controlled by our genes? One way to address this question is to see whether identical twins show more *concordance* (similarity) in these changes than do fraternal twins. The evidence suggests that they do. Figure 4.9 shows the results of a study comparing the intellectual development of almost 500 pairs of identical and fraternal twins, followed from the ages of 3 months to 15 years. The MZ twins clearly showed greater concordance in their shifts in performance than did the DZ twins, supporting the notion that genes direct the pacing of these abilities (Wilson, 1983, 1986).

Developmental pacing The rate at which spurts and plateaus occur in an individual's physical and mental development.

Combined Twin-Study and Adoption-Study Approaches

There is one major problem with the twin-study approach: How do we know that a family treats a set of fraternal twins as similarly as a set of identical twins? Because identical twins look more alike, and perhaps because they know they are identical, parents and others may expect them to act the same. These expectations may influence how people behave toward the children and, as a result, may affect how the children themselves behave. A method that avoids these problems involves twins who are separated early in life and raised in different adoptive homes. If genes play a role in creating individual differences in behavior, then identical twins raised apart should still be more alike than are fraternal twins raised apart. Although this combined approach is the most desirable, it also is the most difficult to use, because so few twins are raised apart.

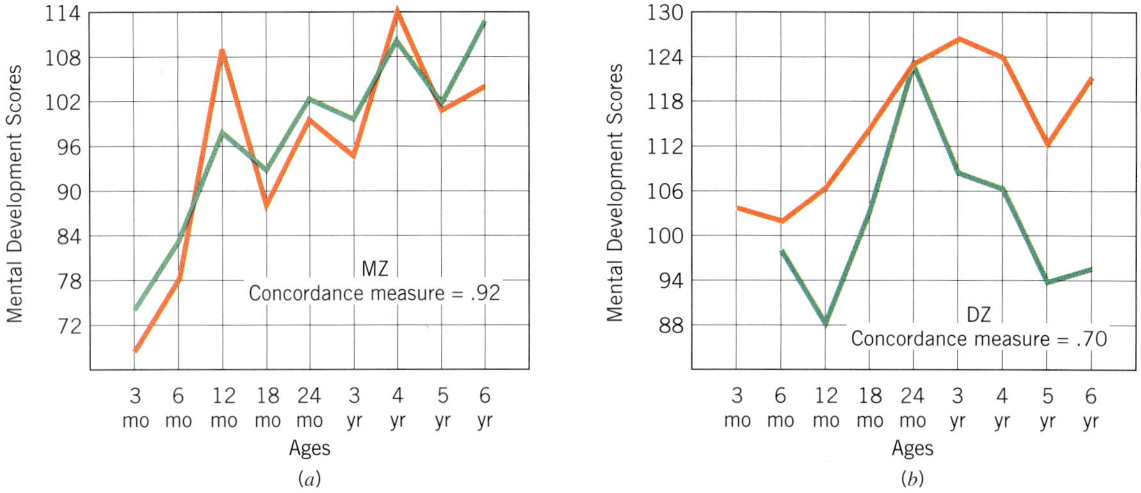

Figure 4.9

Concordance in IQ changes in (*a*) identical, or monozygotic (MZ), twins and (*b*) fraternal, or dizygotic (DZ), twins from 3 months to 6 years of age. The scales are different to accommodate different ranges of scores. The important point is that changes in performance are more similar for monozygotic twins. Adapted from "The Louisville Twin Study: Developmental Synchronies in Behavior" by R. S. Wilson, 1983, *Child Development, 54*, p. 301. Copyright © 1983 by The Society for Research in Child Development, Inc. Adapted by permission.

The best-known research project of this type is the Minnesota Study of Twins Reared Apart (Bouchard et al., 1990). The study involves 58 MZ and 46 DZ twins who are currently in their 40s. Supporting the role of genetics in personality characteristics, the identical twins have been found to be more similar in their religious interests, attitudes, and values than are the fraternal twins (Waller et al., 1990).

To study issues relating to early development the project used a retrospective approach in which twins were asked to recall and describe their family environments when they were children. Identical twins were more similar than fraternal twins in their reporting of family support, which included acceptance or rejection by their mothers and fathers as well as support provided by family members to one another. These results can be taken to mean that the identical twins were treated more similarly because their identical genotypes evoked the same sorts of responses from other family members. But not all the recollections showed this pattern. On questions relating to family organization and activities, the MZ and DZ twins did not differ (Hur & Bouchard, 1995). Once again, it appears that genes and environment probably exert their effects on different aspects of behavior.

✓ *To Recap...*

Psychologists have used four research strategies to study the influence of heredity on behavior: family studies, adoption studies, twin studies, and a combination of the twin study and the adoption study. In three areas in particular—psychiatric disorders, intellectual performance, and personality—genetic processes play a significant role.

Evidence gathered using the different methods supports behavior geneticists' belief that genes not only transmit traits from parents to children in a passive way, but also operate in more evocative and active ways to make children's environments compatible with their genotypes. This research also finds support for the hypothesis that genes exert stronger effects as children get older and for the idea that nonshared environments make adoptive siblings more dissimilar with age.

Conclusion

Much of what we have presented in this chapter is very new. Psychologists are just beginning to understand the various ways in which genes affect development, in part because we have only recently developed effective methods for studying genetic influences. But there can be little doubt that progress in this area will occur rapidly in the coming years. What will that likely mean for developmental psychology?

First, researchers may find that genetic processes reach into more areas of development than we now suspect. As we have seen, genes do more than transmit our ancestors' heritage to our children; they also continue to guide and regulate behavior throughout our lives. It is undoubtedly this second function that promises to bring the most surprises and exciting findings as behavior geneticists probe the limits of genetic forces.

On the other hand, genes will never be the whole story. The sheer volume of material in this chapter on genetic processes may give the false impression that environmental factors eventually will be reduced to minor players in the human drama. We certainly do not believe that. In the chapters that follow, we will see that environmental influences are crucial for understanding how our development unfolds. In fact, these influences likewise are being shown to exert effects in areas that we used to assume were governed exclusively by our biology.

Maybe the most important thing for developmental researchers to keep in mind is that any genetic process occurs within an environmental context. Rather than studying these two sources of influence in isolation, then, it is important to apply the development-in-context idea and focus on how nature and nurture combine to determine human development. This advice also makes sense for students of developmental psychology. If there is one message that you should take away from this course, it is this: At every point in development genes and environment work together to determine each and every aspect of our behavior. With that in mind, we move ahead to begin our look at the basics and the complexities of the growing child.

Visual Summary for Chapter 4:
Genetics: The Biological Context of Development

Mechanisms of Inheritance

Cell Division

Type of cell		Process		Outcome
Body cells	→	Mitosis	→	Two identical cells, each with 46 chromosomes.
Germ cells	→	Meiosis	→	Four different gametes, each with 23 chromosomes.

Inside the Chromosome

DNA	→	A double-helix shaped molecule that contains billions of nucleotides.
Gene	→	A segment of DNA on the chromosome. The basic unit of inheritance.
Alleles	→	Pairs of genes on the chromosomes that determine a trait.
Structural genes	→	Genes that direct the production of proteins.
Regulator genes	→	Genes that control the activity of structural genes, turning them on and off as required across development.

Principles of Genetic Transmission from Mendel's Studies

Principle of dominance	→	When one allele is dominant and the other recessive, only the characteristic associated with the dominant allele is expressed.
Principle of segregation	→	Each inheritable trait is passed on to the offspring as a separate unit.
Principle of independent assortment	→	Traits are passed on to the offspring independently of one another.

Revisions of Mendel's Principles

Polygenic inheritance	→	Single traits are sometimes the products of more than one pair of genes.
Incomplete dominance	→	Some genes are neither entirely dominant nor entirely recessive.
Codominance	→	For some traits, both members of a pair of genes are dominant.

Genetic Disorders

Cause of disorder		Explanation		Examples
Dominant traits	→	Caused by a dominant gene and therefore expressed in all carriers.	→	Huntington's chorea
Recessive traits	→	Caused by a recessive gene and therefore expressed only when the defective gene is inherited from both parents.	→	Tay-Sachs disease, phenylketonuria, sickle-cell anemia
Chromosome defects	→	Caused by a structural defect in the chromosome that may have occurred during meiosis in one of the parents.	→	Down syndrome

Models of Gene-Environment Interaction

Model		Explanation
Gottesman's Limit-Setting Model	→	Genes set the upper and lower limits for development; environmental influences determine development within this reaction range.
Scarr's Niche-Picking Model	→	Genes control the child's environment through processes that move from passive (infancy) to evocative (early childhood) to active (later childhood).
Plomin's Environmental Genetics Model	→	Differences in the behavior of siblings result from those aspects of the environment they experience differently (nonshared environment).
Brofenbrenner's and Ceci's Bioecological Model	→	Genes exert their influence on the environment through proximal processes stimulating interactions between the child and aspects of the microsystem which must be frequent and continuing in the child's life.

Studying Gene Effects on Behavior

Type of Study		Description		Assumption
Family studies	→	Look for similarities over generations of a family in traits suspected to have a genetic basis.	→	Similarities among family members are assumed to be the result of heredity. Limitation: It can be very difficult to distinguish between heredity and environmental influences in family studies.
Adoption studies	→	Adopted children are compared both with their biological parents and with their adoptive parents; they may also be compared with siblings in the adoptive home.	→	If the correlation with biological parents is greater, genetic factors are assumed to play the stronger role; if the correlation with adoptive parents is greater, environmental factors play the stronger role.
Twin studies	→	Monozygotic twins and dizygotic twins are compared in terms of their similarity on traits suspected to have a genetic basis.	→	If the correlation is greater between MZ twins than between DZ twins, genetic factors are assumed to play the stronger role. Limitation: MZ twins may have a more similar environment than DZ twins.
Combined twin and adoption studies	→	Compares twins separated early in life and raised in different adoptive homes.	→	Controls for the similar-environment limitation of twin studies. If MZ twins are more similar than DZ twins, even when raised apart, the greater similarity is assumed to be the result of genetic factors.

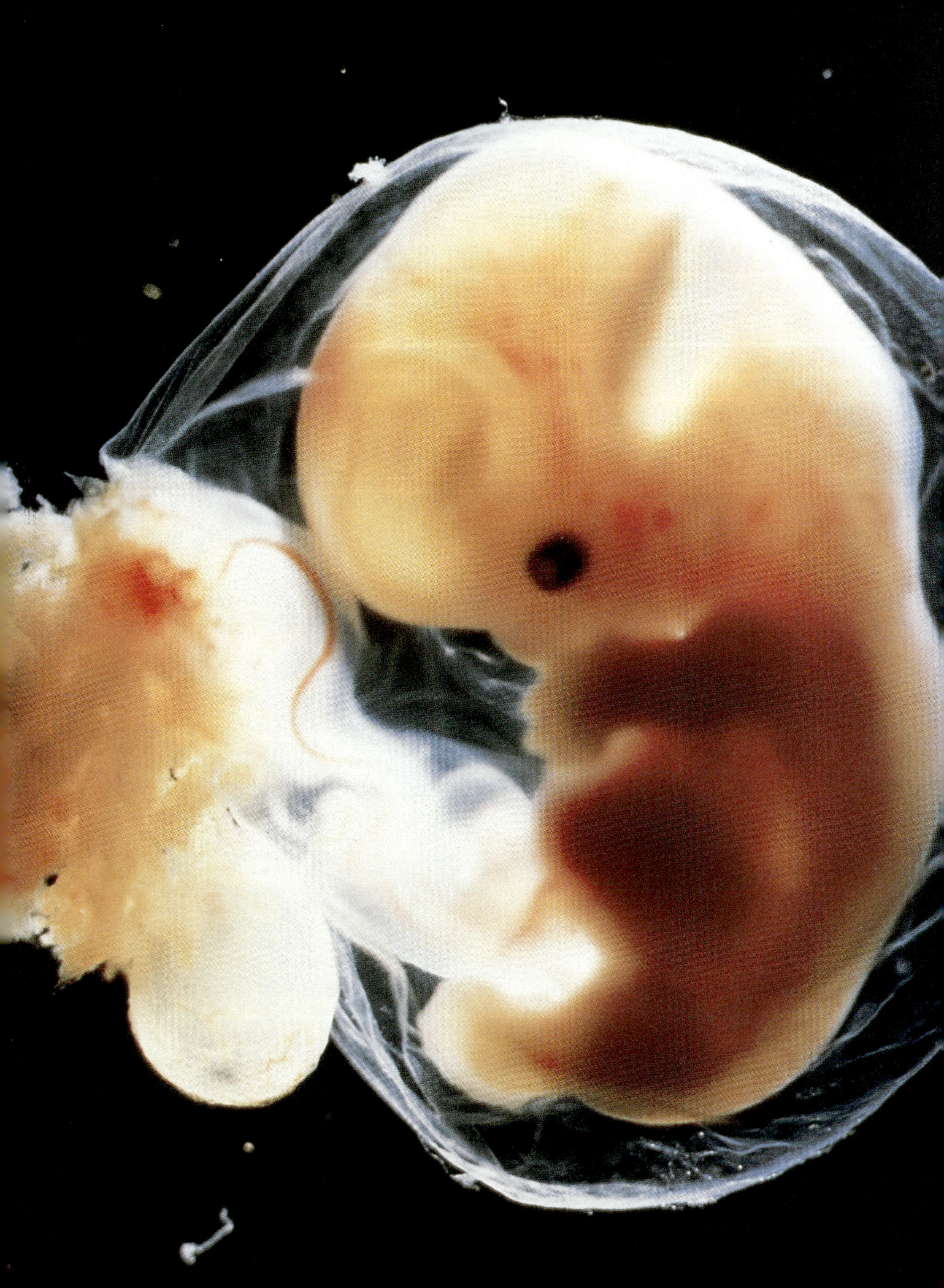

Chapter 5

Prenatal Development

In 1989, Jennifer Johnson of Sanford, Florida, became the first woman to be convicted of dealing cocaine to her newborn baby–through the umbilical cord! The case represented a relatively new trend in the war on drugs. Because no state laws made it illegal for women to pass drugs to fetuses, prosecutors had turned to laws aimed at dealers who sold drugs to minors. The case against Johnson, who had used cocaine during her pregnancy, essentially claimed that she had dealt drugs to her baby. A Florida appeals court upheld Johnson's conviction in 1991.

Law enforcement agencies in Florida and across the nation had good reason for concern about drug use among pregnant women. Experts had estimated that the number of babies born to women who used illegal drugs during their pregnancies had climbed to 375,000 a year. Some of these babies died, and others had various medical and behavioral problems. Many were abandoned, becoming boarder babies in public hospitals. Prosecuting mothers, some said, was one way to get the mothers into treatment and thus to protect their babies.

Many legal and medical professionals disagreed, however, arguing that pregnant women would be less–not more–likely to seek treatment if they feared prosecution. Legal experts also pointed out that drug-trafficking laws were never meant to be used to prosecute pregnant women. In 1992, the Florida Supreme Court struck down Johnson's conviction on precisely those grounds, holding that the Florida legislature had not intended state laws to be used in that way. Similar cases throughout the state were dropped as a result of the ruling.

A decade later, the problem of how fetuses can be legally protected from their mothers' drug use still has not been fully resolved. A central legal issue in this controversial area–and in the abortion controversy as well–is, What are a fetus's rights? However this question is eventually resolved in the U.S. legal system, one thing is certain: women who use drugs during pregnancy place their children at risk.

In this chapter we examine the development of the child during the nine-month prenatal period. Drugs, we will see, are only one of many risk factors a fetus may face while growing in the mother's womb.

When we consider the course of a child's life, the 9 months between conception and birth may be the most unappreciated period of development. This is probably because the events that occur during this time are largely hidden from view. Yet during these 9 months, what begins as a microscopic fertilized egg undergoes a series of dramatic changes and eventually emerges as a living, breathing baby.

You can probably imagine how people from ancient cultures must have struggled to explain how a fully formed creature could appear at birth. As late as the 18th century, some believed that people were completely formed even before conception. One theory, *homunculism,* proposed that each sperm cell contained a tiny individual, like the one shown in Figure 5.1, who would grow when deposited in a woman's womb. Another theory held that the fully formed baby resided instead in the ovum (Needham, 1959).

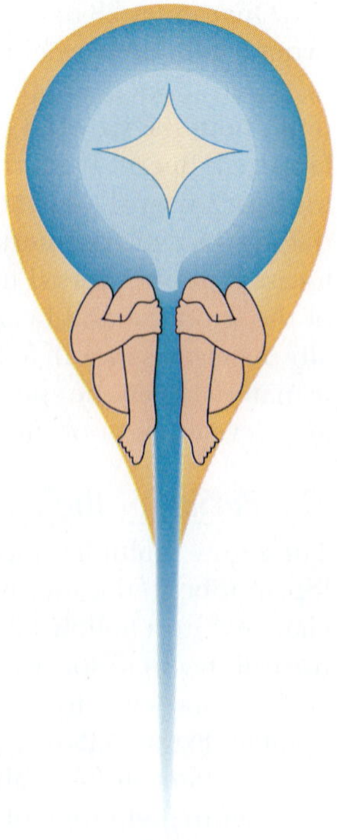

Figure 5.1
Copy of a seventeenth-century drawing of a sperm. The miniature human was thought to enlarge after entering the ovum.

Just a bit more than 100 years ago, a Swiss zoologist, peering through a microscope, became the first person to see a sperm enter an egg, fertilize it, and produce the cell for a new embryo. Such discoveries led to our current understanding of fertilization and prenatal development (Touchette, 1990; Wasserman, 1988). This understanding also includes knowledge about factors that impair development, such as genetic defects, infections, drugs, and environmental poisons.

Stages of Prenatal Development

Even though it is the largest cell in the body, the ovum is no larger than the period at the end of this sentence, and the sperm cell that fertilizes it weighs less than 1/30,000 as much. This tiny genetic package nevertheless grows into a baby billions of times larger in only 9 months.

Every stage of development along the journey from conception to birth represents a mix of the influences of nature and nurture. Even the genetic material that the mother and father contribute to the offspring can be affected by environmental factors, such as radiation. And other environmental factors, such as nutrition, infections, and drugs, can also influence development. In this section, we follow the baby's prenatal development through three stages, or periods—the period of the zygote, the period of the embryo, and the period of the fetus. First we consider the starting point of development—conception.

Conception

Prenatal development begins at **conception**, or fertilization, when a sperm unites with an ovum (egg) to form a single cell, called a **zygote**. The zygote receives 23 chromosomes from the mother and 23 from the father, to form a new and genetically unique person.

Conception
The combining of the genetic material from a male gamete (sperm) and a female gamete (ovum); fertilization.

Zygote
A fertilized ovum.

Millions of sperm from the father enter the vagina of the mother, but only several hundred reach the ovum and only one actually fertilizes it.

Once every 28 or so days, about halfway through a woman's menstrual cycle, an ovum is produced by either her left or right ovary (they alternate each month) and begins to travel through the fallopian tube toward the uterus, which at this point is only about the size of a plum. For the next 24 hours, the ovum is capable of being fertilized. Sperm from the male, which are deposited in the vagina, remain viable for 2 to 3 days. This time is crucial since their longer journey takes them through the cervix and the uterus before entering the fallopian tube where the ovum is located. Of the several million sperm that are typically deposited, only 100 to 200 of the strongest and healthiest make it all the way to the ovum, and only one actually penetrates its wall to fertilize it. Within about an hour of penetration, the genetic material from the sperm and the ovum have completely merged to form a zygote, and development of the baby begins.

The Period of the Zygote (Conception to Second Week)

The zygote multiplies rapidly as it continues its 4-day, 4-inch journey through the fallopian tube to the uterus. At first the zygote is a solid mass of cells, but it gradually changes into a hollow sphere as it prepares to implant into the wall of the uterus. Now the cells begin to specialize, some forming an inner cell mass, which will become the embryo, and some forming important structures that will support the embryo's development. Figure 5.2 diagrams the events of the first week of human development.

Implantation takes about a week. During this time, the zygote settles into the blood-enriched lining of the uterus, where it will remain attached for the duration of the pregnancy. The period of the zygote ends about 2 weeks after fertilization, which corresponds to the first missed menstrual period. By the time a woman suspects she may be pregnant, then, prenatal development is well under way.

Embryo
The developing organism from the third week, when implantation is complete, through the eighth week after conception.

The Period of the Embryo (Third to Eighth Week)

The period of the **embryo** begins when implantation is complete and lasts for around 6 weeks. Although the embryo at first is only the size of an apple seed, all major internal and external structures form during this period. For that reason, these weeks are the most delicate of the pregnancy and the time when the growing

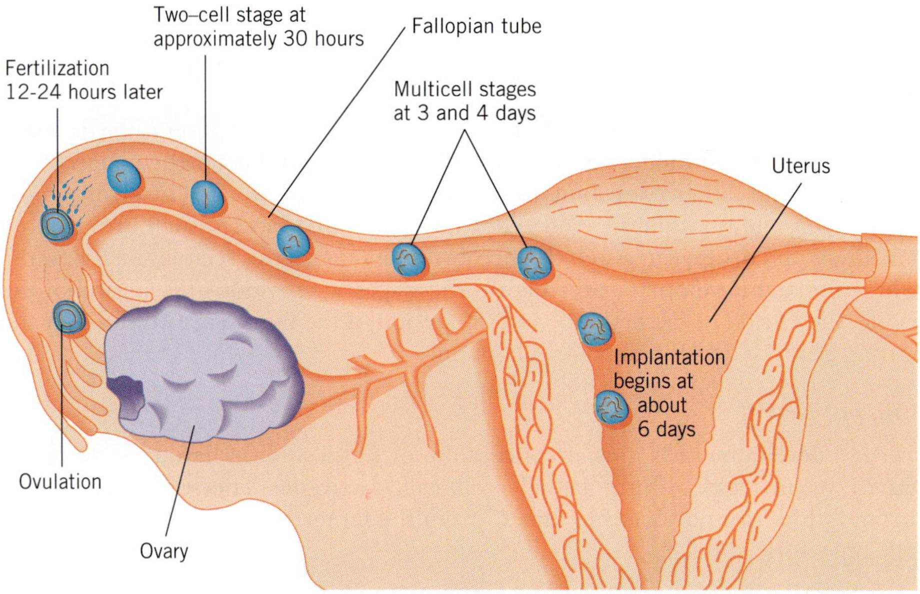

Figure 5.2
Schematic representation of the events of the first week of human development.

embryo is most vulnerable to threats from the internal and external environments (discussed shortly).

In the third week, the inner cell mass differentiates into three layers, from which all body structures will emerge. Two layers form first—the *endodermal* layer and the *ectodermal* layer. The endodermal cells will develop into some internal organs and glands. The ectodermal cells become the parts of the body that maintain contact with the outside world—the nervous system; the sensory parts of the eyes, nose, and ears; skin; and hair. The third cell layer then appears between the endodermal and ectodermal layers. This is the *mesodermal* layer, which will give rise to muscles, cartilage, bone, sex organs, and the heart. The heart is beating by the end of the third week.

Around the beginning of the fourth week, the embryo looks something like a tiny tube. The shape of the embryo gradually changes, however, because cell multiplication is more rapid in some locations than in others. By the end of the fourth week, the embryo assumes a curved form, as shown in Figure 5.3. We can distinguish a bump below the head, which is the primitive heart, and the upper and lower limbs, which have just begun to form as tiny buds.

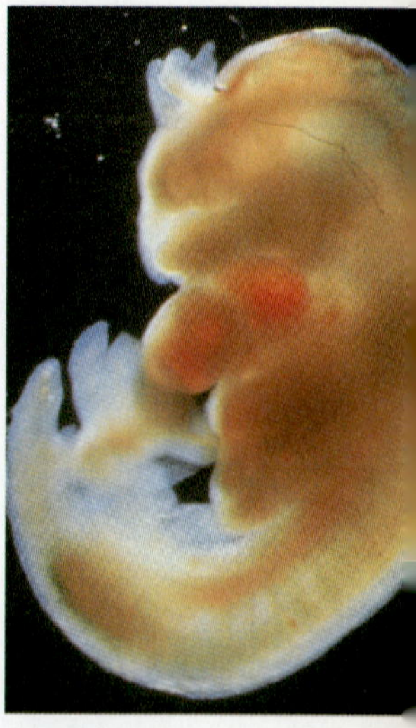

Figure 5.3
An embryo at 4 weeks.

The embryo's body changes less in the fifth week, but the head and brain develop rapidly. The upper limbs form, and the lower limbs appear and look like small paddles. In the sixth week, the head continues to grow rapidly, and differentiation of the limbs occurs as elbows, fingers, and wrists become recognizable. It is now possible to discern the ears and eyes. The limbs develop rapidly in the seventh week, and stumps appear that will form fingers and toes.

By the end of the eighth week, the embryo has distinctly human features. Almost half of the embryo consists of the head. The eyes, ears, toes, and fingers are easily distinguishable. All internal and external structures have formed. Thus, in 8 weeks, a single, tiny, undifferentiated cell has proliferated into a remarkably complex organism consisting of millions of cells differentiated into heart, kidneys, eyes, ears, nervous system, brain, and other structures. Its mass has increased a staggering 2 million percent. Figure 5.4 gives some indication of the magnitude of this change.

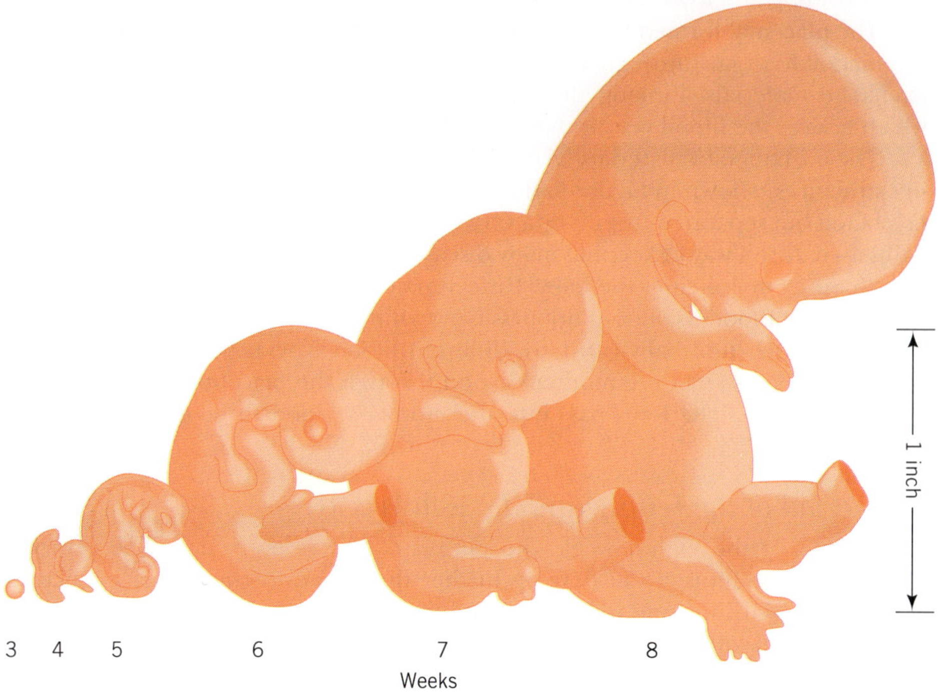

Figure 5.4
Human ova and embryos showing growth and body form from 3 to 8 weeks. Adapted from *Textbook of Embryology*, 5th ed. (p. 87), by H. E. Jordan and J. E. Kindred, 1948, New York: Appleton-Century-Crofts. Copyright © 1948 by Appleton-Century-Crofts. Adapted by permission.

Figure 5.5
Maternal structures that support the embryo and fetus include the placental villi, amniotic sac, placenta, and umbilical cord.

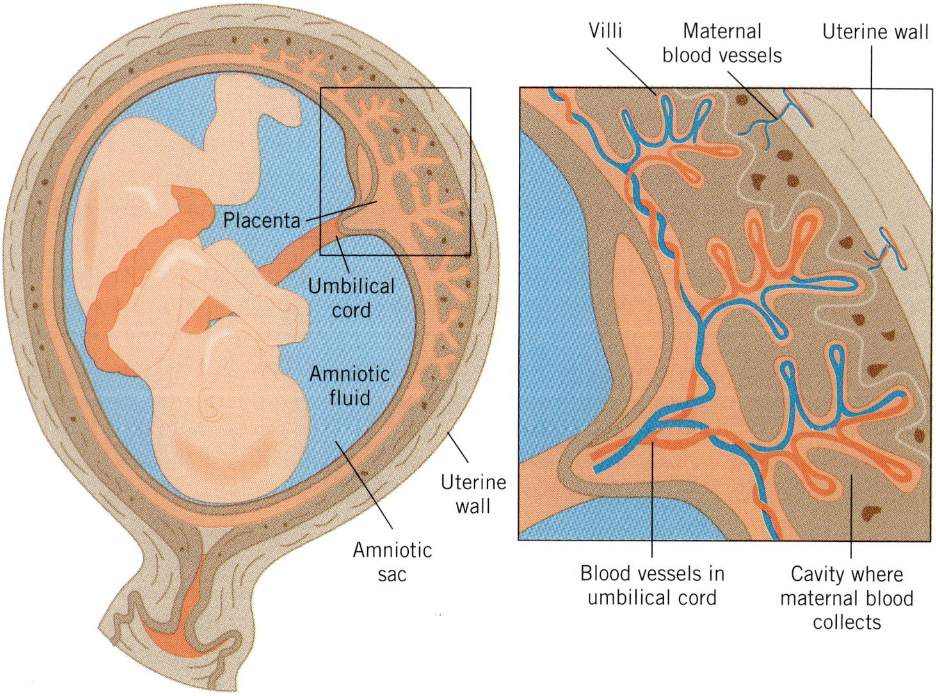

Amniotic sac
A fluid-containing watertight membrane that surrounds and protects the embryo and fetus.

Placenta
An organ that forms where the embryo attaches to the uterus. This organ exchanges nutrients, oxygen, and wastes between the embryo or fetus and the mother through a very thin membrane that does not allow the passage of blood.

Umbilical cord
A soft cable of tissue and blood vessels that connects the fetus to the placenta.

Fetus
The developing organism from the ninth week to the 38th week after conception.

The Prenatal Environment Just as the embryo's inner cell mass changes rapidly in the early weeks of development, so do its other cells. Three major structures arising from these cells develop by the end of the embryonic period: the amniotic sac, the placenta, and the umbilical cord, illustrated in Figure 5.5.

The **amniotic sac** is a watertight membrane filled with fluid. As the embryo grows, the amniotic sac surrounds it, cushioning and supporting it within the uterus and providing an environment with a constant temperature.

The **placenta**, formed from both the mother's tissue and the embryo's tissue, is a remarkable organ through which the mother and the embryo (later the fetus) exchange materials. Linking the embryo to the placenta is the **umbilical cord**, which houses the blood vessels that carry these materials.

The exchange of materials takes place in the placental villi. These ornate-looking structures (shown in Figure 5.5) are small blood vessels immersed in the mother's blood but separated from it by a very thin membrane. The membrane serves as a filter—nature's way of keeping many diseases, germs, and impurities in the mother's blood from reaching the baby. Unfortunately, as we will see shortly, it is not a perfect filter. Blood itself does not pass between the mother and the fetus (which is why the mother and baby can have different blood types); however, oxygen and nutrients do pass from the mother's blood through the placenta to the fetus, and waste products of the fetus pass into the mother's blood to be carried away and excreted.

The Period of the Fetus (Ninth to 38th Week)

At the end of the eighth week, the period of the **fetus** begins. The principal changes for the fetus are to develop further the already formed organ structures and to increase in size and weight. Beginning its third month weighing less than an ounce and measuring 2 inches in length, the average fetus will be born 266 days after conception weighing about 7 to 8 lb and measuring about 20 inches in length. Fetal growth begins to slow around the eighth month—which is good for both the mother and the fetus because if it did not, the fetus would weigh 200 lb at birth!

External Changes During this period, the fetus's appearance changes drastically. The head grows less than do other parts of the body, so that its ratio decreases from 50% percent of the body mass at 12 weeks toward 25% at birth. The skin, which has been transparent, begins to thicken during the third month. Facial features, which appeared almost extraterrestrial at 6 weeks, become more human looking as the eyes move from the sides of the head to the front.

The eyelids seal shut near the beginning of the third month and remain that way for the next 3 months. Nails appear on fingers and toes by the fourth month, and pads appear at the ends of the fingers that will uniquely identify the individual for life. Head hair also begins to grow. A bone structure begins to support a more erect posture by 6 months.

Growth of Internal Organs Changes in external appearance are accompanied by equally striking internal changes. By 3 months, the brain has organized into functional subdivisions—seeing, hearing, thinking, and so on. The 100 billion cells of the adult brain are already present in the fetus by the fifth month, but the 14 trillion connections they will make between themselves and incoming and outgoing nerve cells will not be completed until well after birth. Other nerve cells grow and establish connections throughout fetal development.

A major mystery facing scientists is how the single, undifferentiated zygote cell can give rise to billions of fibers that properly connect eyes, ears, touch sensors, muscles, and the parts of the brain. Although an inborn plan of some sort must guide how this wiring proceeds, it is clear that environmental factors and interactions between nerve cells also play a role, as no two brains are wired identically, not even those of identical twins, who have exactly the same genetic material (Edelman, 1993; Rakic, 1988).

Other internal organs continue to develop. Sexual development becomes apparent in males by the end of the third month with the appearance of external sexual organs. In females, the precursors of ova, or *oocytes*, form on the outer covering of the ovaries; all the oocytes the female will ever possess will be present at birth. The fallopian tubes, uterus, and vagina develop, and the external labia become discernible.

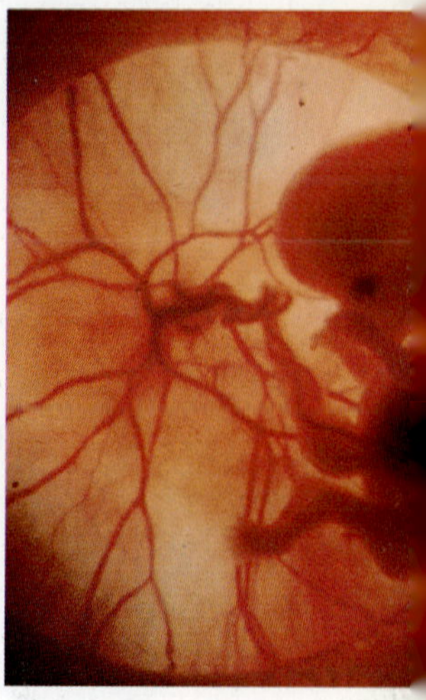

Until birth, the fetus remains immersed in fluid within the amniotic sac, receiving oxygen and nourishment through the umbilical cord. The fetus in the photo is 12 weeks into gestation.

Early Signs of Behavior Fetal activity begins in the third month, when the fetus is capable of forming a fist and wiggling the toes; the mother, however, feels none of this. The fetus also appears to become sensitive to environmental stimulation, moving its whole body in response to a touch stimulus.

By the fourth month the eyes are sensitive to light through the lids, and by the fifth month a loud noise may activate the fetus. During this same month, the fetus swims effortlessly, a luxury gradually lost later as quarters become increasingly cramped. The fetus is now capable of kicking and turning and may begin to display rhythms of sleep and activity. By the seventh month, brain connections are sufficient for the fetus to exhibit a sucking reflex when the lips are touched.

Toward Independence The later stages of prenatal development ready the fetus to live outside the mother's body. Although separate from the mother in many ways during development, the fetus is nevertheless completely dependent on her for survival during most of the prenatal period. Recall that the support system in the uterus provides oxygen, nutrients, waste disposal, and a constant temperature for the fetus. Although physicians have made marked progress in saving premature babies, they have been unable to lower the age of viability under around 23 to 24 weeks of fetal age.

The major obstacle to independent life for a fetus born prematurely is the immaturity of the air sacs of the lungs, which have to exchange carbon dioxide for oxygen. The fetus's inability to digest food or control body temperature is also a problem, and fat has not yet formed under the skin to assist in temperature regulation.

By 6 to 7 months of age, the fetus has a chance of survival outside the mother's body. The brain is sufficiently developed to provide at least partial regulation of breathing, swallowing, and body temperature. However, a baby born after only 7 months of development will need to be provided with extra oxygen, will have to take food in very small amounts, and will have to live for several weeks in an incubator for temperature control.

In the eighth month, fat appears under the skin, and although the digestive system is still too immature to extract nutrients from food adequately, the fetus begins to store maternal nutrients in its body. Even a baby born at 8 months, however, is susceptible to infection. Beginning in the eighth month, the mother's body contributes disease-fighting antibodies, which she has developed through her own exposure to foreign bodies, to the fetus. This process is not complete until 9 months of fetal age. It is an important process, because the antibodies help protect babies from infection until they are around 6 months of age when they can produce their own antibodies in substantial amounts.

Development in Family Context

Families Created by Alternative Methods of Conception

Infertility can be a frustrating problem for couples hoping to start a family. Sometimes the difficulty involves the woman's eggs (or lack of them); other times the problem lies in the quantity or quality of the male sperm. Fortunately, medical science today offers couples several alternative methods for conceiving a child.

When the problem involves the male, the most common solution is *donor insemination,* in which sperm donated from another male is injected into the female, where it initiates a pregnancy. Another popular method is *in vitro fertilization.* In this process, an egg and sperm (donated from either a third party or from one or both members of the couple) are combined in a laboratory procedure; then the fertilized egg is implanted in the female's uterus where, if all goes well, it begins to develop.

These new reproductive technologies have effectively solved a long-standing problem of biology. But what are the psychological implications of these procedures? What impact do they have on the children who are products of this technology and on their parents?

One study investigated this issue by comparing families with a child conceived by each of these two methods with both families whose children were conceived naturally and families whose children were adopted (Golombok et al., 1995). The focus of the study was social-emotional development and family functioning. Parents and children were interviewed, observed interacting with one another, and given a battery of tests.

The researchers wondered whether families formed with the help of new technologies might experience more difficulties than the natural-conception families, for several possible reasons. For one, the child in most cases was genetically unrelated to one or both of the parents, but in only one family was the child informed of this. Would the nongenetic parent have difficulty relating to the child? Would the child feel deceived when eventually made aware of the situation? Would the absence of a biological connection among all family members interfere with the establishment of the normal social and emotional bonds? Among the other concerns were whether the parents would feel unduly stressed by the unusual situation and whether the parents' relationship with one another would suffer if only one parent were genetically related to the child.

The results of the study are perhaps a little surprising. Parents of children conceived by the two alternative reproductive methods were found to be similar to the adoptive parents and superior to parents in the natural-conception families in a number of areas. Mothers in these families were rated as warmer and more emotionally involved with their children, and both mothers and fathers were found to interact more with their children. These parents also reported less stress than those in families with naturally conceived children. The children showed no ill effects of their unusual beginnings. Their feelings about themselves, their relations with their parents and with other children, and their overall psychological adjustment were no different from those of the children in the two comparison groups.

One conclusion drawn by the researchers was that genetic ties between parents and children may not be as important as the parents' strong commitment to parenthood. This seems reasonable, since parents who must seek special methods of conception would likely be heavily invested in the job of parenting. Their other major conclusion was that the new reproductive technologies appear to pose no serious threat to family functioning or harmony. Nevertheless, this area is still very new and will warrant continued evaluation as more children are conceived by these new techniques.

✓ *To Recap...*

Prenatal development begins with conception and proceeds through the period of the zygote, the period of the embryo, and the period of the fetus. At conception, a sperm cell penetrates an egg cell to form a zygote. The zygote multiplies rapidly as it migrates toward the uterus, where it becomes fully implanted by the end of the second week.

Now an embryo, the cell mass rapidly differentiates into organs (a heart, kidneys, eyes, ears, a nervous system, and a brain) and support structures (the amniotic sac, the placenta, and the umbilical cord). In the 6 weeks that make up the period of the embryo, a cluster of cells is transformed into a complex and differentiated organism.

At the end of the eighth week, the fetal period begins. The primary task for the fetus is growth and further development of organ systems. Behavior begins in the third month. The fetus grows toward increasing independence, but is unable to survive before about 23 to 24 weeks of fetal age. By 9 months following conception, the normal fetus is ready to face the external world.

Teratology: History, Principles, and Natural Events

It is natural to think that prenatal development depends only on genes and that the environment begins to affect the baby only after birth. Yet, although the uterus may not seem like an environment in the usual sense, it is the only home the embryo and fetus know. We will see that a number of factors affect the quality of this home and determine whether development is normal or abnormal—indeed, whether development can occur at all.

Approximately 3 to 5% of all live-born babies are identified as malformed at birth. Some malformations are difficult to detect at first, but become apparent with age. Thus, by the early school years, approximately 6 to 7% of children are identified as having *congenital malformations*—malformations that existed at birth. Many more babies would be born with malformations were it not for a natural prenatal process that results in miscarriage or spontaneous abortion. It is estimated that 90% of some kinds of malformations end in spontaneous abortions and that without this natural screening process, the observed incidence of congenital malformation would be 12% or more (Shepard, 1986).

We have already seen that some abnormalities are caused by genetic defects. Malformations may also be caused by infectious diseases, poor nutrition, age, and perhaps even the mother's emotional state, as well as by drugs and other environmental hazards. Nongenetic agents that can cause malformation in the embryo and fetus are referred to as **teratogens** (*tera* is a Latin base meaning "monster"). The term *teratology* refers to the study of the effect of teratogens on prenatal development.

Teratogen
An agent that can cause abnormal development in the fetus.

Much of our discussion of teratogens will focus on their physical effects. Indeed, teratogens are defined in terms of their creation of physical malformations. However, psychologists have noted increasingly that teratogens can have psychological and behavioral effects as well. This realization has given rise to a new field, called **psychoteratology**. Researchers in this field use behavior rather than physical outcomes to study the potentially damaging effects of teratogens and have found that behavioral effects may show up even when physical effects do not. Thus in many cases, behavioral measures may be more sensitive than physical measures (Fein et al., 1983; Voorhees & Mollnow, 1987).

Psychoteratology
The study of the harmful effects of teratogens through the use of behavioral measures, such as learning ability.

Historical Ideas

The field of teratology achieved scientific status only recently, but it has had an interesting history. The birth of malformed babies probably gave rise to at least some of the creatures of Greek mythology, such as the one-eyed cyclops and various creatures that are part human and part beast (Warkany, 1977). But although monsters were sometimes idolized in ancient times, people in the medieval period believed that the birth of malformed babies portended catastrophe, and malformed infants and children were often put to death. Some believed that these babies were produced through the mating of humans with animals, and it was not unusual for mothers and midwives who delivered malformed babies to be put on trial for witchcraft.

Such practices gradually gave way to the more benign belief that maternal fright, thoughts, and impressions could create a monster birth (Warkany, 1981). Running parallel to these theories were ancient beliefs that the food and drink a pregnant woman ingested could affect the fetus. In the Bible, an angel admonishes a man named Manoah that when his wife conceives a son, she should "drink no wine nor strong drink, and eat not any unclean thing" (Judges 13:4).

Despite the apparent fact that people of biblical times believed that maternal nourishment could affect the development of the fetus, a great deal of time elapsed before people fully realized the potential effects of the external world on the fetus. People generally believed that the embryo and fetus lived in a privileged environment, protected against harm by the placenta and its amniotic world.

By 1930, however, there was general recognition that X rays could produce intrauterine growth retardation, microcephaly (an abnormally small head and brain), and small eyes. By the mid-1940s, it had become obvious that a pregnant mother who contracted rubella (German measles) during the early months of pregnancy had a relatively high chance of producing a baby with congenital abnormalities of the eye, ear, heart, and brain.

Still, these events were seen as exceptional. A major disaster finally shook people's faith in the privileged-environment belief, but only as recently as the early 1960s. A mild and seemingly harmless sedative, thalidomide, was marketed in the late 1950s, and many pregnant women took it. Physicians soon noticed a sharp increase in the number of babies born with defective limbs. Careful questioning of mothers, analysis of doctors' prescriptions, and epidemiological research implicated thalidomide as the culprit. The field of teratology experienced a dramatic surge as a result of this event and has been expanding rapidly ever since.

General Principles

Many teratogens have been identified as causing defects in humans. Evaluating an agent for teratogenic effects, however, is fraught with problems. For obvious reasons, animals must be the "guinea pigs" for substance testing, but the potential teratogen may not have the same effect on animal and human fetuses. Furthermore, people often take more than one drug, and a particular drug may do damage only in combination with another drug, with a disease, or with stress. Some common teratogens and their effects are listed in Table 5.1.

Six principles capture important features of how teratogens act (Hogge, 1990).

1. *A teratogen's effect depends on the genetic makeup of the organism exposed to it.* A prime example is thalidomide. The human fetus is extremely sensitive to this substance, but rabbits and rats are not. One reason thalidomide was not initially suspected to be a teratogen was that testing on these animals revealed no ill effects. The principle of genetic differences in sensitivity also applies to individuals within a species. Some babies are malformed because their mothers drank alcohol during pregnancy, but others are apparently not affected by this practice.

2. *The effect of a teratogen on development depends partly on timing.* Even before conception, teratogens can affect the formation of the parents' germ cells. Formation of female germ cells begins during fetal life, and formation of sperm can occur up to 64 days before the sperm are expelled. Thus, a fetus can be affected by drugs that the pregnant grandmother took decades earlier or by X-ray exposure that the father experienced many weeks before conception.

For 2 to 3 weeks after conception, the zygote's fluids do not mix with those of the mother, so the zygote is relatively impervious to some teratogens. After the zygote has attached to the uterus, however, substances in the mother's bloodstream can pass through the placental barrier and mix with the blood of the embryo, and the embryo enters a particularly sensitive period. Teratogens can produce organ malformation from 2 to 8 weeks because this is a time when organs are forming. After the organs have formed, teratogens primarily produce growth retardation or tissue damage (Goldman, 1980).

Which organ is affected by a teratogen depends in part on which organ is forming. Rubella is an example of how crucial timing can be. Rubella affects only 2 to 3% of the offspring of mothers infected within 2 weeks after their last period, whereas it affects 50% of offspring when infection occurs during the first month following conception, 22% when it occurs during the second month, and 6 to 8% when it occurs during the third month. The incidence falls to very low levels thereafter. Whether ear, eye, heart, or brain damage occurs depends on the stage of the

Table 5.1
Some Teratogens and Conditions That May Harm the Fetus

Teratogen	*Potential Effect*
Therapeutic Drugs	
Aspirin	In large quantities, miscarriage, bleeding, newborn respiratory problems
Barbiturates	Newborn respiratory problems
Diethylstilbestrol (DES) (a drug to prevent miscarriage)	Genital abnormalities in both sexes, vaginal and cervical cancer in adolescent females
Isoretinoin (a vitamin A derivative for treating acne)	Malformations of the head and ears, heart and central nervous system defects, behavior problems
Phenytoin (an anticonvulsant drug)	Threefold increase in likelihood of heart defects and growth retardation
Streptomycin	Hearing loss
Tetracycline	Most commonly, staining of teeth; can also affect bone growth
Thalidomide	Deformed limbs, sensory deficits, defects in internal organs, death
Street Drugs	
Cocaine and crack	Growth retardation, premature birth, irritableness in the newborn, withdrawal symptoms
Heroin and methadone	Growth retardation, premature birth, irritableness in the newborn, withdrawal symptoms, sudden infant death syndrome
LSD and marijuana	Probable cause of premature birth and growth retardation when used heavily; originally implicated in chromosomal breakage, but this effect is uncertain
Maternal Condition	
Age	For teenage women and women over 35, lighter-weight babies than for women in the optimal childbearing years; likelihood of Down syndrome birth increases with advancing age
Alcohol use	Brain and heart damage, growth retardation, mental retardation, fetal alcohol syndrome
Diabetes	A threefold increase in all types of birth defects, including babies born without a brain, with spina bifida, and with heart defects
Malnutrition	Increased likelihood of growth retardation, prematurity, inattention; poor social interactive ability, especially when mother also has a history of malnutrition before pregnancy
Phenylketonuria (PKU)	Growth retardation of brain and head, mental retardation, heart defects
Smoking	Growth retardation, prematurity
Infections	
AIDS (acquired immunodeficiency syndrome)	Congenital malformations; leaves infant vulnerable to infections of all types
Cytomegalovirus	Deafness, blindness, abnormal head and brain growth, mental retardation
Herpes	Mental retardation, eye damage, death
Rubella	Mental retardation, eye damage, deafness, heart defects
Syphilis	Mental retardation, miscarriage, blindness, deafness, death
Toxoplasmosis	Abnormalities in brain and head growth, mental retardation
Environmental Hazards	
Lead	Miscarriage, anemia, mental retardation
Mercury	Abnormal head and brain growth, motor incoordination, mental retardation
PCBs	Growth retardation
Radiation	Leukemia, abnormal brain and body growth, cancer, genetic alterations, miscarriage, stillbirth

formation of each organ when the mother is infected (Murata et al., 1992; Whitley & Goldenberg, 1990).

3. *The effect of a teratogen may be unique.* For example, thalidomide produces gross limb defects, whereas rubella primarily affects sensory and internal organs.

4. *The abnormal development caused by teratogens may be severe.* Teratogenic effects may include malformation of limbs or other parts of the body, growth retardation, functional and behavioral disorders, or even death.

5. *Teratogens differ in how they gain access to the fetus.* Radiation passes to the fetus directly through the mother's body, for example, whereas chemicals usually travel to the fetus through the blood and across the placental membrane. Physical blows are partially cushioned by the mother's body and the amniotic fluid. The mother's blood may be able to filter some potentially harmful chemicals to protect the fetus. The placenta, too, serves as a filter, but not as a complete barrier; materials may be slowed by this filter, but will not necessarily be stopped. Some teratogens move past this filter faster than others.

6. *The likelihood and degree of abnormal development increase with the fetus's dosage of the harmful agent.* Depending on the amount of the teratogen to which the fetus is exposed, the outcome can range from no effect at all to death.

Natural Challenges

Much current media attention focuses on potential teratogens that mothers voluntarily consume or to which mothers are exposed in the modern industrial environment. Yet, the mothers and fetuses have always faced natural challenges from the environment. Infectious diseases can harm the fetus, and the quality of the mother's nutrition affects how the fetus develops. Parental age and even maternal experiences and stress may also have an effect.

Maternal Infectious Diseases

Several viral and bacterial infections in the mother can damage the fetus. We discuss some of the more common ones here.

Rubella. Rubella virus can damage the central nervous system of the fetus, resulting in blindness, deafness, and mental retardation. The heart, liver, and bone structure may also be damaged, depending on the timing of infection.

Herpes. Two viruses in the herpes group can produce central nervous system damage. *Cytomegalovirus (CMV),* the most common intrauterine viral infection, may cause abnormal brain and head growth, encephalitis, blindness, and mental retardation. An estimated 33,000 infants are born with CMV each year, but only 10% of them are seriously affected.

Because pregnant mothers are often unaware that they have been infected by CMV, doctors have made little progress in discovering the specific effects of fetal exposure at particular ages. CMV can be transmitted by sexual contact, blood transfusions, or mixing of body fluids (Behrman & Vaughan, 1987).

Another herpes virus, *herpes virus type 2,* infects the genitals of adults. This virus had reached epidemic levels in the United States by the early 1980s. In the infant, herpes 2 can cause encephalitis, central nervous system damage, and blood-clotting problems. Most herpes 2 infections of infants occur following direct contamination by the mother's infected birth canal (Murata et al., 1992; Whitley & Goldenberg, 1990).

HIV. Another virus that reached epidemic levels in the 1980s is the human immunodeficiency virus (HIV), which causes acquired immunodeficiency syndrome, or AIDS. The virus is transmitted from one person to another exclusively through body fluids.

There are three major avenues for transmission. The first is through sexual intercourse by way of male semen or female vaginal fluids. The second is through blood exchange. Many people have been infected with the virus through transfusions of blood donated by infected individuals, but improved blood screening has reduced this threat dramatically. HIV-infected blood is exchanged most commonly through intravenous drug injection by addicts who share the same needle (Palca, 1990). The third means of transmission is from mother to infant through breast milk (European Collaborative Study, 1991).

In addition to causing AIDS, the human immunodeficiency virus can act as a teratogen. Some infected babies are born with facial deformities—larger-than-normal eye separation, boxlike foreheads, flattened nose bridges, and misshapen eye openings.

Syphilis and Gonorrhea. Syphilis and gonorrhea are sexually transmitted diseases. After declining for several years, the incidence of syphilis began to increase in the late 1980s. This disease is caused by a spirochete, a type of bacteria, which can infect the fetus and cause central nervous system damage, deformities of the teeth and skeleton, and even death. The fetus is relatively resistant to infection from the syphilis spirochete until the fourth or fifth month.

Gonorrhea is also caused by a bacterial agent. Its incidence has been reported to be as high as 30% in some populations. Premature birth, premature rupture of membranes, and spontaneous abortion are associated with gonorrhea. The fetus is affected in about 30% of cases. The most common problem is eye infection, which can lead to blindness if untreated. Fortunately, almost all newborns are treated with silver nitrate eyedrops at birth to prevent this problem (Murata et al., 1992; Whitley & Goldenberg, 1990).

Nutrition The original fertilized egg must multiply into trillions of cells to form the fully developed fetus. During prenatal development, cells increase not only in number but also in size. As Table 5.2 illustrates, the baby and its accompanying support system will weigh 25 to 30 lb by the ninth month of pregnancy, billions of times the weight of the fertilized egg.

Where does all of this mass come from? The answer is obvious—from the mother. Thinking about the issue this way brings home the importance of maternal nutrition. The quality of the fetus's cells can be no better than that of the nutrients the mother supplies through the placental circulation system. Oddly, this simple fact is often not fully appreciated. Earlier we said that, at least in the early stages of development, the functioning of cells depends on the environment they are in. The quality of the mother's nutrition is probably the most important environmental influence on the fetus and newborn baby (Morgane et al., 1993).

The prospective mother, then, must supply nutrients for the fetus and its support system. In part, her ability to do this depends on her nutrition during pregnancy. But it also depends to a great extent on her nutritional status *before* pregnancy. Both the mothers and their fetuses fare more poorly when the mother has had long-term malnutrition than when the mother has good prepregnancy nutrition (Rosso, 1990). Additionally, how well the placenta passes nutrients to the fetus, maternal disease, and genetic factors can affect fetal nutrition.

Maternal malnutrition can have devastating effects on the fetus. Autopsies of severely malnourished stillborn infants from third-world countries reveal that their

Table 5.2
Weight Gain during Pregnancy

Development	*Weight Gain (lb)*
Infant at birth	7 1/2
Placenta	1
Increase in mother's blood volume to supply placenta	4
Increase in size of mother's uterus and muscles to support it	2 1/2
Increase in size of mother's breasts	3
Fluid to surround infant in amniotic sac	2
Mother's fat stores	5–10
Total	25–30

Source: Reprinted by permission from page 495 of *Understanding Nutrition*, Fourth Edition, by E. N. Whitney and E. M. N. Hamilton; Copyright © 1987 by Wadsworth Publishing Co.

brains weighed up to one-third less than expected. Deficits in the size of major internal organs of between 6 and 25% have been found in the United States in infants born to urban poor families (Naeye, Diener, & Dellinger, 1969; Parekh et al., 1970). Malnutrition is associated with increased rates of spontaneous abortion, infant death, and congenital defects. Pregnant women who have inadequate diets are also more likely to have small and premature babies (Bauerfeld & Lachenmeyer, 1992). (Problems associated with low birth weight are discussed in Chapter 6.)

As is sometimes the case with teratogens, however, it can be difficult to isolate the effects of malnourishment from other factors. Malnutrition is often accompanied by inadequate housing and health care and inferior education and sanitation, as well as the daily stress of poverty. Catastrophes sometimes provide a means for separating out the influences of at least some of these factors. During World War II, for example, the entire populations of many countries had severely limited food supplies not associated with the other factors. Food supplies in the Netherlands were especially scarce, and, in addition to a decline in conceptions, there was a substantial increase in miscarriages, stillbirths, and congenital malformations.

Food quantity is not the only issue in maternal nutrition. The pregnant woman and her fetus have special dietary needs. Proteins, vitamins, and minerals are especially important. Animal studies reveal that protein deficits produce damage to the kidneys, intestines, and skeletal growth in the fetus. Low intake of certain vitamins can affect the eyes and internal organs and increase the number of malformations (Rosso, 1990).

Trace elements in the diet are also important. An absence of iron in the mother's blood can produce anemia in her baby. Diets lacking iodine are associated with an increased likelihood of cretinism, a severe thyroid deficiency that causes physical stunting and mental deficiency. Deficits of copper, manganese, and zinc produce central nervous system damage and other negative effects in rats, and zinc deficiency has been implicated in the occurrence of anencephaly (absence of the cortex of the brain) in people in Turkey and other Eastern countries. Vegetarians are vulnerable to deficiencies of vitamins, especially B12, iron, and zinc, as well as to inadequate caloric intake (Rosso, 1990).

Convincing evidence of the importance of one B vitamin, folic acid, has recently become available. Deficits of folic acid in pregnant mothers had been associated with neural tube defects—anencephaly and nonclosure of the spinal cord (spina bifida)—in babies.

What are the intellectual abilities of babies who are malnourished during fetal life? The outcome depends, to a large extent, on their childhood environments. Children who were malnourished as fetuses because of World War II but had adequate diet and stimulation as infants and children showed no long-term intellectual deficit. Many Korean children suffered malnutrition during the Korean War but were later adopted by families who provided them with good nutrition and education. These children later performed as well on intellectual and achievement tests as children who had not suffered early malnutrition. The general conclusion is that an enriched home environment may compensate for many of the effects of early malnutrition, but the outcome also depends on when during pregnancy the malnutrition occurred and how severe it was (Morgane et al., 1993; Vietze & Vaughan, 1988; Zeskind & Ramey, 1981).

On the other hand, babies who are malnourished both as fetuses and after birth are more likely to show delayed motor and social development. They become relatively inattentive, unresponsive, and apathetic (Bauerfeld & Lachenmeyer, 1992). Health organizations worldwide have recognized the lasting consequences of early nutritional deficits and have initiated attempts to supplement the diets of pregnant women and infants. Babies with supplemented diets are more advanced in motor development and more socially interactive and energetic, an encouraging sign that the consequences of bad nutrition may be avoided (Joos et al., 1983).

Excesses of nutrients can also be damaging. For example, recall from Chapter 4 that people with the disease phenylketonuria (PKU) are unable to break down the amino acid phenylalanine. Mothers who have phenylketonuria, even though they have protected themselves through early dietary restrictions, still have excesses of phenylalanine circulating in their blood. The fetus, though genetically normal, may suffer brain damage from intrauterine exposure to this excess product. Pregnant women can protect the fetus by maintaining a restricted diet during pregnancy (Koch & Dela Cruz, 1991).

Excesses of the sugar galactose in diabetic mothers may cause cataracts and other physical problems, even death, in fetuses; the babies at birth are more likely to have passive muscle tone and to be less attentive (Langer, 1990). Just as deficits in iodine can cause problems, excess iodine can have a detrimental affect on thyroid function in the fetus. Excess vitamin supplementation has been implicated in birth defects in both humans and animals (Rosso, 1990).

Maternal Experiences and Stress Of all the factors that might influence the fetus, none has generated more speculation than that of the mother's own experiences. The belief that the mother's mental impressions could affect the fetus is quite old. We may chuckle when we hear that a pregnant woman's child will favor classical music if the mother listens to Beethoven. Yet surveys in modern times in the United States and Europe reveal that many people still believe that birthmarks are caused by maternal frights or unsatisfied food cravings; for example, an unsatisfied craving for strawberries may produce a strawberry-colored birthmark (Ferriera, 1969).

Modern investigators have dismissed beliefs in magical influences on the fetus and have focused on psychological factors that have fairly well documented influences on the body. For example, psychological stress increases the activity of the adrenal glands. The secretions from these glands enter the mother's blood and can be transmitted to the fetus through the placenta. Additionally, hormones released during stress can reduce the blood flow and oxygen available to the fetus. Thus, identifiable physical pathways exist by which maternal emotional states could affect the fetus.

Investigators have used various methods to assess the effects of stress in pregnant women and have examined the relation between the stress and abnormalities in the newborn. High levels of reported anxiety were related to such problems as increases in fetal activity, congenital malformations, irritability, and feeding and digestive difficulties in the baby (Ferriera, 1969; Sontag, 1944, 1966; Stott, 1969).

Again, there are problems in interpreting these relations because of limitations in researchers' ability to control all the factors that might be related to anxiety. Often mothers' reports of anxiety were obtained after their babies were born. These reports of anxiety might have been influenced by the babies' malformation or irritability rather than the other way around—the cause-and-effect problem mentioned in Chapter 3. Further, there is often no way to separate prenatal and postnatal influences on the infant. A mother who has reported a great deal of prenatal anxiety may handle her infant differently, for example, and it may be this handling that makes her baby irritable.

One study showed that women who reported marital difficulties and ambivalence about their pregnancies later reported more problems, including depression, when their babies were 5 months of age (Field et al., 1985). But depressed mothers' interactions with their babies are less optimal, and it appears that their negative judgments about their babies reflected their own states and their impact on the infants rather than their anxiety during pregnancy (Cohn et al., 1990; Vaughn et al., 1987).

Finally, the genetic relation between the mother and her baby, rather than the prenatal experience, may be the operative factor. A mother who is genetically predisposed to anxiety, which might reflect abnormal hormonal activity, could pass this genetic predisposition on to her fetus.

A recent study avoided some of the problems of prior studies by using low birth weight and early delivery as measures of the effects of stress on babies. These measures do not depend on the babies' postnatal interactions with their mothers or on the mothers' judgments of the babies. A group of women completed anxiety questionnaires during their pregnancies. Independent of other medical risk factors, there was a relation between a woman's reported anxiety and the likelihood that she would give birth early or have a baby with low birth weight. The physical pathways already described could have been responsible for these outcomes. It is also possible that women under stress do not look after their health—failing, for example, to get adequate rest or nutrition—which, in turn, might be responsible for the outcomes (Lobel, Dunkel-Schetter, & Scrimshaw, 1992).

The question of whether maternal experiences affect the fetus is a difficult one to answer. There seems little doubt that a relation exists between maternal stress and the likelihood of problems in the offspring, but we know neither why the relation exists nor how strong it is (Istvan, 1986).

Parental Age The typical age at which a woman gives birth to her first child has risen dramatically in the United States since the 1970s. Between 1970 and 1986, the rate of first births to mothers between the ages of 30 and 39 rose 136%. Although the optimal childbearing years generally have been thought to be between ages 25 and 29, age has become less important in mothers who have chosen to delay their first birth past these years. These women today are better educated than were their counterparts decades ago, and they are more likely to seek early prenatal care and to be in good health. Babies born to mothers between 30 and 34 years of age are now almost as heavy as those born to mothers in the optimal range (Ventura, 1989). (Birth weight is a widely used indicator of newborn status.)

As we saw in Chapter 4, increased maternal age is associated with an increased likelihood of giving birth to a baby with Down syndrome. A mother's chances of giving birth to a Down syndrome infant are almost 74 times greater at age 49 than at age 30.

The father's age also carries a risk for the fetus, because the relative frequency of mutation in the father's sperm increases with age. Down syndrome is attributable to the father rather than the mother in 20 to 30% of cases (Behrman & Vaughan, 1987). Another genetic disorder related to the father's age is *achondroplasia,* a mutation that becomes dominant in the child who inherits it and causes bone deformities. The most obvious characteristics are dwarfism and a large head with a prominent forehead and a depressed bridge of the nose. As shown in Figure 5.6, the relative likelihood that a child will inherit achondroplasia increases with the father's age much as the relative likelihood of Down syndrome increases with the mother's age (Friedman, 1981).

In general, babies who are born to mothers in their teens are also at greater risk. Around 500,000 babies a year are born to teenage mothers in the United States, (Brooks-Gunn & Chase-Lansdale, 1995). There is some disagreement about whether the negative effect of early motherhood is due mostly to poorer prenatal care for teenage mothers or to their biological immaturity. One study showed that even when teenage mothers received the same prenatal care as older mothers, they were more likely to give birth to premature or underweight babies (Leppert, Namerow, & Barker, 1986). Other evidence, however, suggests that the less advan-

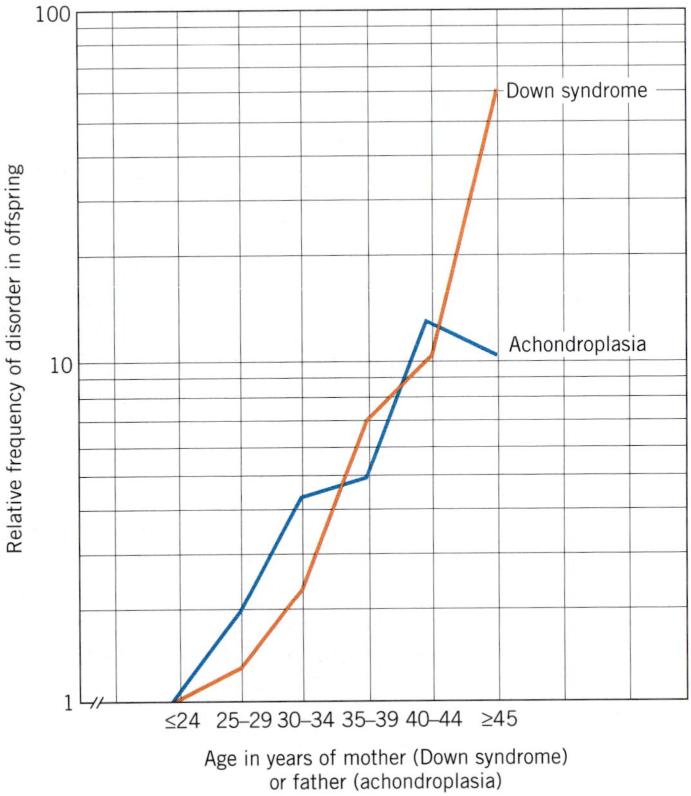

Figure 5.6
Relative frequency of Down syndrome and achondropiasia in the offspring of mothers (Down syndrome) and fathers (achondroplasia) of various ages. From "Paternal Age Effect" by J. M. Friedman. Reprinted with permission from The American College of Obstetricians and Gynecologists (*Obstetrics and Gynecology*, Vol. 57, 1981, p. 746).

taged socioeconomic status of teenage mothers is responsible for the negative effect on their babies (Murata et al., 1992).

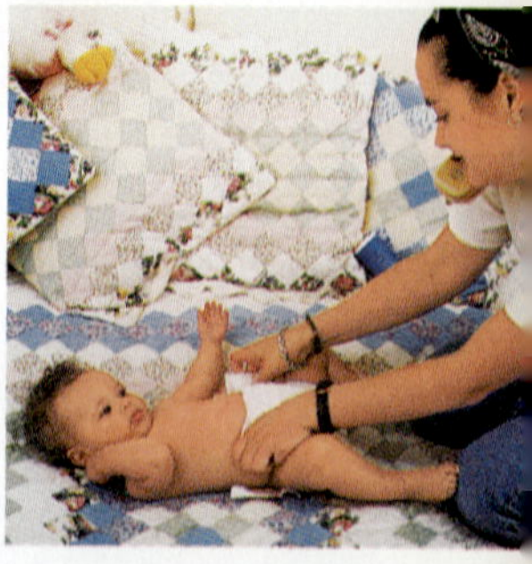

Teenage pregnancy has skyrocketed in recent years. Babies of teenage mothers generally do less well than average. It is unclear what roles biological, social, and economic factors play in this outcome.

✓ To Recap...

Teratology is the study of agents that interfere with normal prenatal development. The emerging field of psychoteratology focuses on the behavioral effects of teratogens. These effects may not always be obvious at birth and do not always include physical problems.

Six principles describe how teratogens act: (1) the effect depends on the genetic makeup of the organism; (2) the effect depends on timing; (3) the effect may be unique to the teratogen; (4) the effect may include serious disorders or death; (5) teratogens gain access to the fetus in different ways; and (6) the effect increases with the level of exposure.

There are a number of natural challenges to the health of the embryo and the fetus. Infectious diseases, such as rubella and AIDS, can cause severe damage. Nutritional factors are important for normal fetal growth, so poor nutrition is also harmful. The ultimate effect of fetal malnutrition depends in part on postnatal nutrition and on the level of stimulation in the environment. Although there is strong suspicion that maternal stress and experiences during pregnancy can affect the fetus, more research is needed. Parental age is another risk factor for the fetus. As the age of the parents increases, there is increased risk of Down syndrome and achondroplasia. On average, teenage women are more likely to have premature or underweight babies than are women in the optimal childbearing age range, but the reasons might involve socioeconomic factors primarily.

Teratology: Drugs and Environmental Chemicals

To this point we have considered natural challenges to the health of the fetus. There are also chemical hazards created by people. Such chemicals include those that people ingest—intentionally and accidentally—as well as substances released into the environment.

Drugs

"The desire to take medicine is, perhaps, the greatest feature which distinguishes us from animals." So said Sir William Osler, a medical historian (Finnegan & Fehr, 1980). People in our culture today consume chemicals not only as medicines to treat specific conditions but as means to induce various mental states. Many such substances—alcohol, caffeine, and nicotine—have become so much a part of daily life that we often do not think of them as drugs. A drug, however, can be defined as any substance other than food intended to affect the body. The average pregnant woman takes 4 to 10 drugs of some sort during pregnancy, and up to 80% of the drugs are not prescribed by a doctor.

We mentioned earlier that the effects of thalidomide dramatically increased awareness of the potential damage that chemicals can do to the fetus. The tragic consequences of the sedative became apparent in the early 1960s, soon after the drug appeared on the market. Depending on when a mother took the drug, her baby was born with malformations of the eyes and ears, deformation of the internal organs, or fused fingers and toes. Some babies were born with a rare defect called *phocomelia,* a condition in which the limbs are drastically shortened and the hands and feet are connected to the torso like flippers.

The teratogenic effects of thalidomide were especially surprising because doctors considered it a mild drug. The women who took it experienced no apparent side effects, and the drug produced no harmful effects in the offspring of pregnant animals on which it was tested. Clearly, we had a lot to learn about how chemicals affect the fetus, and we still do. This incomplete knowledge makes it all the more unwise for pregnant women to ingest drugs that they can avoid.

Street Drugs The increasing availability of powerful mood- and mind-altering illegal drugs since the 1960s has been a major health concern in the United States and, unfortunately, has provided substantial evidence about the dangers of drug intake by pregnant women, both to themselves and to their fetuses. Addictive drugs have attracted the most attention.

Heroin addicts, for example, are more likely to have medical complications during pregnancy and labor, and their newborn babies are more likely to undergo drug-withdrawal symptoms. Frequently, addiction to heroin is compounded by poor nutrition and inadequate health care; almost 75% of addicts do not see a physician during pregnancy. Medical complications, including anemia, cardiac disease, hepatitis, tuberculosis, hypertension, and urinary infections, occur in 40 to 50% of heroin-dependent women who are observed during the prenatal period. These women are more likely to miscarry or to give birth prematurely. Their babies are usually lighter than normal and are more likely to have brain bleeding, low blood sugar, and jaundice.

Heroin-dependent expectant mothers may use methadone, a synthetic drug designed to help break the heroin habit, but methadone is also addictive and is associated with sudden infant death syndrome, or SIDS (in which the baby unexpectedly stops breathing and dies). Infants withdrawing from methadone may experience withdrawal symptoms even more severe than those associated with withdrawal from heroin (Chasnoff et al., 1984; Finnegan & Fehr, 1980). Offspring of heroin-addicted mothers are less well coordinated at 4 months of age and are less attentive at 1 year than are their agemates (Voorhees & Mollnow, 1987).

Applications

Beginning Life with Two Strikes: Cocaine-Exposed Babies

The story at the beginning of the chapter described the case of a pregnant woman passing cocaine to her fetus. Unfortunately, that case was not especially unusual. A conservative estimate is that at least 100,000 fetuses a year are exposed to cocaine (Hawley & Disney, 1992). The ready availability of cocaine, especially in the much cheaper form of hard crack, has increased use of the drug to epidemic proportions.

Cocaine affects the fetus indirectly through reduced maternal blood flow to the uterus, limiting the fetus's supply of nutrients and oxygen. Additionally, cocaine passes through the placenta and enters the fetus's bloodstream, where it gains direct access to the brain in as little as 3 minutes. In the brain, cocaine affects chemical nerve transmitters in addition to increasing heart rate and blood pressure.

Cocaine-exposed babies are more likely to be miscarried or born dead. If they are born alive, they are more likely to be premature or to suffer retarded growth. They also are more likely to be difficult to arouse and irritable, and they may frequently be jittery and shaky. They may have difficulty regulating their level of alertness and with their sleep patterns and they may be hard to handle (DiPietro et al., 1995; Phillips et al., 1996; Regalado et al., 1995).

Despite these problems, studies have turned up conflicting findings as to how babies exposed to cocaine turn out. Some studies have reported that exposed

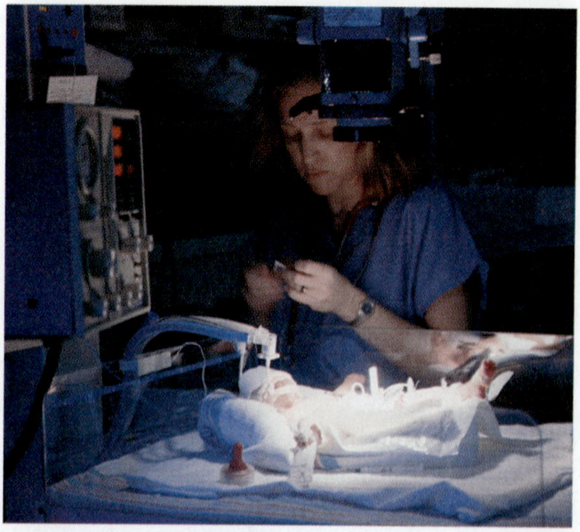

Newborn babies who have been exposed to cocaine as fetuses are more likely to be premature, jittery, and irritable and to have disrupted sleep patterns.

babies later are more impulsive than nonexposed babies and less able to function in unstructured settings. Other studies report few or no long-term effects that can be attributed to cocaine exposure alone. Cocaine research shares the same difficulties as research on many other teratogens. Mothers who use cocaine are more likely to use other drugs and to smoke and drink. They are also more likely to live in poverty and chaos, to be undernourished and in poor health, and to be depressed. Given this complex of factors, which often exist both before and after a child is born, it is difficult to pinpoint the role of prenatal cocaine exposure on the child's development (Barone, 1993; DiPietro et al., 1995; Hawley & Disney, 1992).

Investigators are becoming more sensitive to the effects of the postnatal environment on the cocaine-exposed child. Given an irritable baby who has difficulty falling into regular sleep patterns and a mother who is depressed, has few resources, and continues her drug habit, there is little likelihood that a healthy mother–infant interaction will develop. Many investigators believe that the quality of this relationship and the postnatal environment are the major determinants of the child's outcome (Mayes, 1992).

Some legal authorities believe that pregnant mothers who use drugs should be prosecuted, as was Jennifer Johnson. They believe that such mothers are unfit to care for their children. Others argue that it would be counterproductive, that a child's future prospects would worsen if the child were removed from his or her mother. They make the case that resources should be committed to helping these mothers kick the drug habit and providing them with education and support to enable them to provide a stable home for their children.

The use of marijuana and hallucinogens accelerated rapidly in the 1960s and 1970s, creating concern about their teratogenic potential. Early research suggested that chromosome breakage was more frequent in users of these drugs and that the users were more likely to experience miscarriages or to have babies with limb malformations. As with heroin and cocaine, however, the effects of the drugs are difficult to separate from other environmental and health-care practices.

Research suggests that the heavy use of marijuana may cause newborns to be jittery and to habituate poorly to visual stimuli (Jones & Lopez, 1990). However, other recent studies have found that moderate use of marijuana has much less extreme effects if the users otherwise engage in good health practices. A study in Ottawa, Canada, in which mothers had good prenatal care, found no effect on the offspring of maternal marijuana users at 2, 3, 5, or 6 years of age, although the exposed children did have lower verbal and memory scores when they were 4 years old (Fried, O'Connell, & Watkinson, 1992).

Development in Cultural Context

Ganja Use in Jamaica

A study in Jamaica underlines the importance of considering cultural context in health-care practices. As we have noted, one of the most difficult tasks that scientists face in evaluating effects on the fetus is separating these effects from other factors. In the U.S., marijuana consumption may be associated with alcohol consumption, smoking, poor nutrition and health care, antisocial behavior, and economic level. It is hard to separate these factors from the influence of marijuana alone.

In Jamaica, marijuana is referred to as ganja. Ganja use is very common among pregnant women in Jamaica and is not associated with the use of other drugs, smoking, or alcohol consumption. Furthermore, social disapproval is not a factor in ganja use in Jamaica. Smoking ganja is seen as a sign of independence from men, both economical and social. Often, women of lower economic status who smoke ganja sell it to earn money to provide food and housing—an option that is not available to nonsmokers.

An extensive study of offspring of ganja-using mothers found that they performed as well on assessments at 1 month and 5 years of age as did children of nonusers; in fact, on a few measures, they did better (although the differences were small and may have reflected the better access to resources of the ganja-using mothers). These data should *not* be taken to mean that marijuana use by pregnant women is safe—clearly, much more research needs to be done—but it does illustrate how studying the practices of different cultures can help us better evaluate the effects of drug use (Dreher & Hayes, 1993; Dreher, Nugent, & Hudgins, 1994; Hayes et al., 1991).

Therapeutic Drugs Many pregnant women take prescribed drugs as part of a continuing regimen of health care—for example, to treat diabetes or blood-clotting tendencies—or as treatments for health problems brought on by the pregnancy. Some of these drugs may increase the risk of fetal problems, creating the need to weigh the risk to the fetus from taking the drug against the risk to the mother from not taking it.

Anticoagulants, anticonvulsants (for epileptics), antibiotics, and even heavy use of aspirin have been implicated in increased likelihood of fetal growth retardation, fetal malformations, and fetal and newborn death, especially when taken during the first 3 months of pregnancy. The action of these drugs is often not straightforward. For example, aspirin, which is harmless at a particular dosage in rats, can be teratogenic if administered with benzoic acid, a widely used food preservative. However, it is important to keep in mind that the danger from these drugs is fairly low and that by far the majority of mothers taking them have healthy infants. Indeed, there is still considerable controversy over whether some of these drugs are teratogenic at all (Hopkins, 1987; Jones et al., 1988).

The effects of sex hormones are more clear. These hormones are sometimes used to treat breast cancer in women and to reduce the likelihood of miscarriage. The use of sex hormones in early pregnancy has been associated with central nervous system malformations in offspring and, more frequently, with masculinization of the external genitalia of females.

Some pregnant women took a particularly damaging synthetic hormone, diethylstilbestrol (DES), in the 1950s and early 1960s to reduce the likelihood of miscarriage. Much later, physicians discovered that a high percentage of the female children of these women developed vaginal and cervical problems when they reached adolescence, and some of these offspring developed cancer of the cervix (Harper, 1981). Recently, evidence has accumulated that the male offspring of mothers who took DES are more likely to develop testicular cancer and to have a lowered sperm count (Sharpe & Skakkebaek, 1993). The studies of sex hormones illustrate yet another problem in detecting teratogenic agents—the possible delay by many years of any observable effect.

Some drugs offer unique benefits but are also powerful teratogens and thus considerably controversial. Accutane, a medication for the treatment of serious acne, came on the market in the early 1980s. Within a year, there were reports of birth defects associated with its use. By 1988, at least 62 deformed babies had been born to Accutane-using mothers, and the figure is now in the hundreds. Many people argue that the drug should be taken off the market, especially because young women who use it may become pregnant unknowingly or be unaware of its effects. Others argue that it is unfair to deprive people who are not at risk (e.g., males) of the unique therapeutic benefits of Accutane. The manufacturer of the drug has compromised by adding strong warning statements to the label and urging dermatologists to have women screened for pregnancy before they write a prescription for its use (Sun, 1988).

The effects of one prescription sedative, thalidomide, have already been described. Research on barbiturates and tranquilizers—both depressants—has turned up mixed results. Although some investigators have found associations between congenital defects and sedatives, others have not. Phenobarbital, however, has been associated with congenital defects and blood coagulation problems in newborns (Jones, Johnson, & Chambers, 1992). Tranquilizers such as diazepam (Valium) and chlordiazepoxide (Librium) are taken by millions of people each year. These tranquilizers they can produce a cleft palate in mice, and cleft palates in humans have been reported to be four times as frequent when these tranquilizers were taken in the first 3 months of pregnancy (Goldman, 1980; Voorhees & Mollnow, 1987).

Caffeine Caffeine, a substance present in coffee, tea, chocolate, and some soft drinks, is the drug most commonly consumed during pregnancy. Strangely, the possible effect of caffeine on the fetus has received relatively little attention. As is often the case, one of the difficulties in determining the effect of caffeine is separating its effects from the effects of other drugs, such as nicotine and alcohol. Some studies have associated caffeine use with miscarriage, premature birth, lower birth weight, irritability, and poorer muscular development and reflexes in the newborn (Dlugosz & Bracken, 1992; Eskanazi, 1993; Heller, 1987). The potential problems seem to become more likely as the amount of caffeine increases (Infante-Rivard et al., 1993).

Nicotine Between one-fourth and one-third of the women of childbearing age in North America smoke. The effects of nicotine and cigarette smoke on the fetus have been well investigated. Smoking is known to impair the functioning of the placenta, especially oxygen exchange. The following are some risks to women who smoke while they are pregnant:

- On average, their babies are smaller.
- The likelihood of premature delivery and complications increases with the number of cigarettes they smoke per day (Cornelius et al., 1995).
- Their babies are 25 to 56% more likely to die at birth or soon thereafter (Murata et al., 1992).
- Their babies are as much as 50% more likely to develop cancer (Stjernfeldt et al., 1986).

According to longitudinal studies, detrimental effects on their children's height and reading ability may last into early adolescence (Fogelman, 1980). Other studies have found an association between a poorer performance on language and cognitive tasks and how much the mothers smoked while pregnant (Fried, O'Connell, & Watkinson, 1992). Impulsivity and attentional deficits have recently been found in 6-year-olds whose mothers smoked while pregnant (Fried, Watkinson, & Gray, 1992). Even passive exposure of pregnant, nonsmoking women to others' smoke apparently affects the growth of the fetus (Martin & Bracken, 1986).

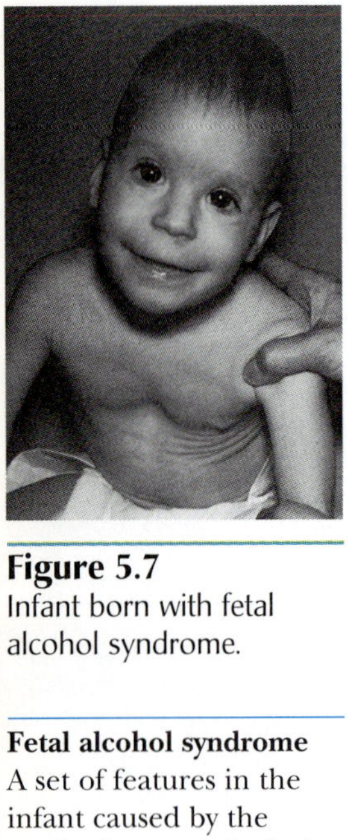

Figure 5.7
Infant born with fetal alcohol syndrome.

Fetal alcohol syndrome
A set of features in the infant caused by the mother's use of alcohol during pregnancy; typically includes facial malformations and other physical and mental disabilities.

Alcohol In the United States, alcohol is the most widely used drug that is known to harm the fetus (Olson, 1994). It poses a major preventable health problem. Among the causes of birth defects in the United States, alcohol ranks third, just behind Down syndrome and spina bifida. It is the leading cause of congenital mental retardation in the Western world (Murata et al., 1992; Warren & Bast, 1988). Withdrawal effects in newborns of mothers who drink heavily can mimic those of drug addiction (Abel, 1980, 1981).

Although the effects of alcohol on the fetus were suspected in the 18th century, a clear picture of the consequences of chronic maternal alcoholism on the fetus did not emerge until 1973, when investigators described **fetal alcohol syndrome**, a unique set of features in the fetus caused by the mother's alcohol consumption (Jones et al., 1973). A photo of a child with this syndrome appears in Figure 5.7.

Limb and facial malformations, congenital heart disease, failure to thrive, anomalies of the external genitalia, growth retardation, mental retardation, and learning disabilities are associated with fetal alcohol syndrome. Behavior problems compound these difficulties, as infants with fetal alcohol syndrome are irritable, sleep less well, and are difficult to feed (Wekselman et al., 1995). By school age, these children are more likely to have difficulty sustaining effort and attention and to have language problems and motor-performance deficits (Larsson, Bohlin, & Tunell, 1985; Streissguth et al., 1985).

Research indicates that chronic alcohol use by the mother increases the risk to the fetus by almost 50%. Some of the effects just described, however, have been observed in infants whose mothers were not chronic alcohol users but who drank sporadically and heavily. Furthermore, the effects of alcohol can be increased by smoking and other drugs. What level of alcohol use during pregnancy is safe? One expert has cautioned against chronic use exceeding 45 drinks per month or 6 drinks at any one time; these levels double or triple the risk of congenital malformations, growth retardation, and functional abnormalities in the fetus.

The effects of relatively low levels of alcohol consumption are less clear. In one study, even alcohol consumption within the limits of what could be defined as social drinking reduced alertness in newborns and their ability to habituate to a repeated stimulus, and some effects have been shown to be evident even in the teen years (Hunt et al., 1995; Streissguth et al., 1989). However, in two studies, children of low-risk women with good prenatal care who consumed less than one drink per day performed as well as the offspring of nondrinkers on tests of cognition and language and measures of attention and impulsivity (Fried, O'Connell, & Watkinson, 1992; Fried, Watkinson, & Gray, 1992).

Environmental Chemicals

The number and amount of chemicals in our environment have increased explosively since the beginning of the Industrial Revolution. Insecticides, herbicides, fungicides, solvents, detergents, food additives, and miscellaneous other chemicals have become common in our daily existence. Each year, thousands of new compounds are synthesized by industry or created as a result of reactions in the environment. It has been estimated that humans are exposed to significant amounts of approximately 5 million of these environmental chemicals. Only a small fraction of them are tested as potential teratogens in pregnant laboratory animals.

Researchers often find that chemicals are potentially teratogenic in animals, but the doses that they use are typically quite large. People generally experience comparable doses only in rare instances, such as industrial accidents or concentrated dumping (for example, in Love Canal, a former chemical dumping ground near Niagara Falls). The rates of defective births and spontaneous abortions are monitored routinely in many hospitals in the United States, providing a measure of protection against long-term chronic exposure of undiscovered teratogens. However, as we have seen, complex interactions among chemicals and delayed effects can often make detection difficult.

A clear example of the effects of environmental chemicals comes from Cubatão, a small town in an industrial valley in Brazil. Cubatão was slowly choking through pollution of its streams, air, and countryside. Thousands of tons of particulate matter were being discharged into the air from smokestacks, and huge amounts of organic matter and heavy metals were being dumped into the streams. Through an ambitious cleanup program the town reduced discharges of particulate matter by 72%, organic waste into rivers by 93%, and heavy metals by 97%. The infant mortality rate in Cubatão dropped to one-half the 1984 rate (Brooke, 1991).

Of the various chemicals present in the environment, metals have come under special scrutiny. Mercury and lead have been suspected teratogens for many years. A disaster comparable to that caused by thalidomide occurred in Japan between 1954 and 1960, when people ate fish from a bay that had been contaminated with mercury from industrial dumping. Many mothers who ate the fish gave birth to infants with severe neurological symptoms resembling cerebral palsy. Prenatal exposure to lead from automobile exhausts and lead-base paints has been implicated in miscarriages, neuromuscular problems, and mental retardation (Bellinger et al., 1986). Follow-ups of children who experienced high lead exposure as babies reveal negative effects even after 11 years on vocabulary, motor coordination, reading ability, and higher-level thinking (Needleman et al., 1990).

Another group of environmental chemicals that can harm fetuses consists of polychlorinated biphenyls (PCBs), widely used as lubricants, insulators, and ingredients in paints, varnishes, and waxes. Cooking oil used in Japan in 1968 and in Taiwan in 1979 was accidentally contaminated by PCBs, and pregnant women who used the oil were more likely to have stillborn infants and infants with darkly pigmented skin.

In the United States, PCB levels are relatively high in fish taken from Lake Michigan. Offspring of mothers who ate these fish were smaller at birth, had somewhat smaller heads, and were more likely to startle and be irritable. Babies who had detectable PCB levels in their blood at birth performed more poorly on various visual measures at both 7 months and 4 years of age (Jacobson & Jacobson, 1988; Jacobson et al., 1985; Jacobson et al., 1992). PCBs are widely distributed and appear to be well established in the food chain, though not at levels that are typically detrimental to fetuses (Rogan, 1982).

✓ To Recap...

Not only natural challenges, but also exposure to drugs and chemicals may pose risks to the developing embryo and fetus. Street drugs, although illegal, have become increasingly available over the past four decades and can have highly negative effects on the fetus. Babies of drug-addicted mothers may be born addicted, and they are likely to have many developmental problems. Therapeutic drugs may also be harmful, as was the case with thalidomide.

Some substances are so common in our daily lives that we may fail to think of them as drugs. Caffeine, nicotine, and alcohol are examples. No firm conclusions have been drawn regarding the effects of caffeine consumption during pregnancy, but smoking has consistently been shown to affect growth and to increase the risk of premature delivery and birth complications, and alcohol consumption can produce a range of physical malformations and intellectual consequences, including fetal alcohol syndrome.

Exposure to harmful chemicals can also occur when we take in the chemical by-products of industry through the food we eat and the air we breathe. Mercury and lead have been documented as particularly teratogenic, and PCBs also appear harmful.

Preventing, Detecting, and Treating Birth Defects

We noted earlier that spontaneous abortion ends fetal development in most cases in which the fetus has genetic abnormalities or a problem exists in the uterine environment. Although there are thousands of genetic abnormalities and challenges to the fetus, it is important to view these risks in perspective. More than 90% of infants are born healthy and normal, and the large majority of the remaining infants have minor problems that can be corrected or will be outgrown. Still, small percentages can translate to large numbers of people, and statistics provide little comfort to those affected. In a single year, as many as 200,000 babies may be born with birth defects in the United States, and 15 million Americans have some kind of handicap caused by a birth defect.

Can anything be done to prevent birth defects? How can a mother be sure the baby she is carrying is healthy? And how can birth defects be treated?

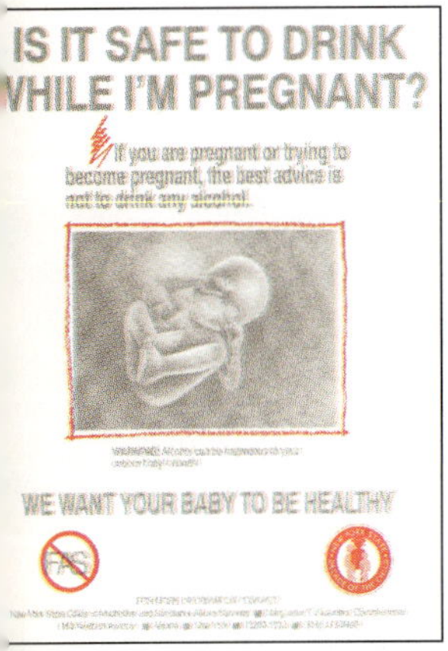

As research has furthered our knowledge of factors that can harm the fetus, agencies have become increasingly effective in alerting expectant mothers.

Prevention

At present, not all birth defects can be prevented. The causes of some are not controllable; the causes of others are not even known. Certain steps, however, can significantly lower the risk from teratogens. For example, a woman planning to become pregnant can avoid drinking alcohol, smoking, and taking unnecessary drugs, and she can eat prudently. Prenatal care is very important both for assessing risk and for monitoring the woman's progress and the fetus's development. Some experts advise women to see a physician even before they conceive (Murata et al., 1992).

Rapid progress in the area of genetics has made it possible for people to exert some control over the incidence of genetic problems. **Genetic counseling** involves a range of activities focused on determining the likelihood that a couple will conceive a child with a genetic disorder. Couples who are contemplating pregnancy often want to know the chances that their baby will be normal. DNA analysis of their blood may determine whether they are carriers of a defective dominant or recessive gene, as in the case of Tay-Sachs disease or cystic fibrosis. If one parent is a carrier of a defective dominant gene that is autosomal, the chances are 1 in 2 that their baby will be normal. If both parents are carriers of the same defective recessive gene, the chances are 3 in 4 that their baby will be healthy.

Defective genes on the sex chromosome affect the chances differently, depending on whether the fetus is a male or female and whether the mother or father is the carrier. When couples are at risk and the woman has become pregnant, parents often consider procedures for assessing whether the fetus is normal.

Genetic counseling The practice of advising prospective parents about genetic diseases and the likelihood that they might pass on defective genetic traits to their offspring.

Screening for Abnormalities

Significant progress has been made in detecting problems in newborn infants, which opens up the possibility for early treatment. Phenylketonuria (PKU) again serves as an example. Although scientists understood at the beginning of the 1960s what caused PKU and how to treat it through diet, they had no method for determining which newborn infants had PKU. By the time they discovered the defect in a child, irreversible damage had occurred. Then, in 1961, a blood test was developed to detect excess phenylalanine in the blood. Infants with PKU were put on a special diet until they were around 7 years of age to prevent the severe retardation, seizures, and skin lesions characteristic of untreated PKU. By the late 1960s, approximately 90% of all babies in the United States were being screened at birth. Today, PKU is no longer a major health problem.

Even more dramatic advances permit parents to learn about the status of the fetus as early as 9 to 11 weeks into a pregnancy and, as we shall see, sometimes in the first days following conception.

Ultrasound Imaging

Ultrasound imaging uses soundlike waves to provide a continuous picture of the fetus and its environment. The level of detail in this image permits identification of the sex of the fetus by 16 to 20 weeks and reveals abnormal head growth; defects of the heart, bladder, and kidneys; some chromosomal anomalies; and neural-tube defects (Anderson & Allison, 1990; Nakahara et al., 1993; Stoll et al., 1993). Ultrasound imaging is also helpful for diagnostic procedures that require collection of amniotic fluid or tissue, such as amniocentesis and chorionic villus sampling. Finally, ultrasound can determine whether there is more than one fetus.

As with many technological advances, concerns have arisen about how ultrasound imaging is used. Because China has developed a one-child policy and its citizens favor males, ultrasound imaging is being used there to determine the sex of the fetus in order to identify female fetuses for abortion. The practice is spreading in Asia, upsetting the ratio of male to female births. The ratio has reached 118.5 male per 100.0 female births in China (Kristof, 1993).

Ultrasound imaging A noninvasive procedure for detecting physical defects in the fetus. A device that produces soundlike waves of energy is moved over the pregnant woman's abdomen, and reflections of these waves form an image of the fetus.

Amniocentesis A procedure for collecting cells that lie in the amniotic fluid surrounding the fetus. A needle is passed through the mother's abdominal wall into the amniotic sac to gather discarded fetal cells. These cells can be examined for chromosomal and genetic defects.

Amniocentesis

An especially important tool for assessment is **amniocentesis**, because it provides samples of both the amniotic fluid and the fetal cells in it. A nee-

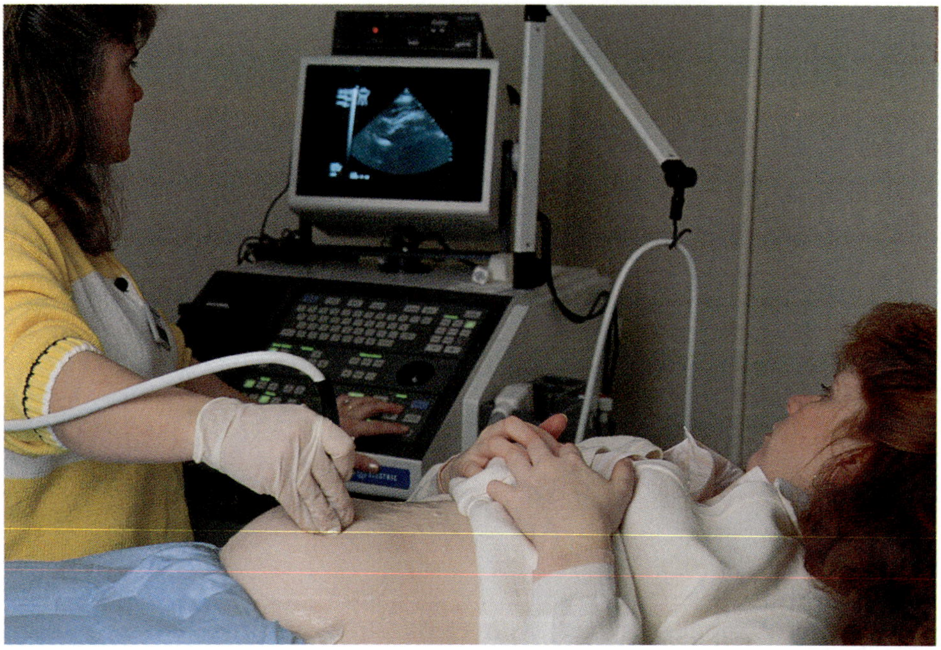

Ultrasound imaging permits identification of abnormalities in the developing fetus, as well as of other characteristics, such as gender, size, and position.

dle is passed through the mother's abdomen and into the amniotic cavity to collect the fluid. Analysis of the fluid can reveal abnormalities. For example, alpha-feto protein (FEP), a substance the fetus produces, circulates in the amniotic fluid. Abnormally high levels of FEP occur when the fetus has certain types of damage to the brain, the central nervous system, or the liver and kidneys. Chromosomal analysis of the fetal cells can also detect problems.

Women over the age of 35 frequently opt to have amniocentesis because of their heightened risk of having babies with Down syndrome, a defect that shows up in a chromosomal cell analysis. Interestingly, awareness of the risk associated with maternal age, coupled with the availability of amniocentesis and the option of terminating pregnancy, has completely changed the maternal age distribution of Down syndrome births. Now, 80% of babies with Down syndrome are delivered to mothers under age 35, because amniocentesis is not a routine procedure for these women (Behrman & Vaughan, 1987). Fetal cells can also be tested for genetic defects such as sickle-cell anemia, cystic fibrosis, and Duchenne muscular dystrophy (Winston & Handyside, 1993). The list of detectable diseases lengthens almost daily with increasing knowledge of which genes produce particular diseases.

The amniocentesis procedure does have its drawbacks. It increases the risk of miscarriage by around 0.5 percent (Cunningham, MacDonald, & Gant, 1989). Also, amniocentesis is most effective after the period during which abortion is safest for the mother. Chorionic villus sampling, a relatively new procedure, can make information about the fetus available much earlier.

Chorionic villus sampling (CVS)
A procedure for gathering fetal cells earlier in pregnancy than is possible through amniocentesis. A tube is passed through the vagina and cervix so that fetal cells can be gathered at the site of the developing placenta.

Chorionic Villus Sampling In a procedure called **chorionic villus sampling (CVS)**, cells are collected from the chorion, a part of the placenta. A small tube is inserted through the cervix and into the fetal placenta to collect a sample of fetal cells. These cells reveal large-scale defects of the chromosomes or more minute defects in the DNA. CVS is possible as early as 9 to 11 weeks, but carries a slightly higher risk of miscarriage than amniocentesis, around 2% (Cunningham et al., 1989).

Test-Tube Screening Scientists have succeeded in screening embryos in the test tube before they are implanted in the mother's uterus. Egg cells are collected from the mother and then fertilized in a petri dish through in vitro fertilization. One cell is removed from each embryo when it reaches the eight-cell stage. From this one cell, the sex of the embryo can be determined, and, within a few hours, the DNA of the cell can be checked for suspected anomalies.

Chloe O'Brien, born in the United Kingdom in April 1992, was the first baby to be born after in vitro fertilization following DNA analysis before implantation. The parents were carriers of the cystic fibrosis gene. If they had conceived in the normal fashion and had discovered that their fetus had cystic fibrosis by the other techniques described, they would have faced a decision on abortion. By this technique, they were assured that the embryo that was implanted was free of this disease. Chloe is doing fine (Fogle, 1992; Handyside et al., 1992).

It is possible to detect almost 200 disorders through various screening techniques. However, only around 10% of women who have at-risk pregnancies participate in prenatal screening. The risk of problem pregnancy is higher for a woman who (1) has had miscarriages or has had children with congenital disorders, (2) is outside the optimal childbearing age range, (3) has relatives (or is carrying a child whose biological father has relatives) with genetic abnormalities, (4) is poor and has inadequate medical supervision and nutrition, or (5) takes drugs during pregnancy.

Applications
A Population Approach to Genetic Screening

A highly successful program of genetic population screening has demonstrated the value of a well-publicized effort to inform parents of reproductive risks. The program, the first of its kind, was initiated in 1970 to identify carriers of Tay-Sachs disease. This disorder is carried as a recessive gene in about 1 of 29 American Jews. If two carriers mate, 1 of 4 of their children, on average, will have Tay-Sachs disease.

The effort to identify carriers, begun through a community education and neighborhood-based screening campaign in the Baltimore, Maryland–Washington, D.C., area, had tested more than 354,000 Jewish adults by 1981. Virtually all couples identified as carriers elected to have amniocentesis during their pregnancies, which numbered 912 by 1981, and 202 fetuses were diagnosed as having Tay-Sachs. All but 13 of these pregnancies were voluntarily terminated by the parents; the babies born to the remaining 13 were afflicted with Tay-Sachs, as predicted. The incidence of this fatal disease was thus reduced by 65 to 75% over the prior decade (Kaback, 1982).

In 1990, a similar program on a much larger scale was contemplated to screen parents for cystic fibrosis. The Tay-Sachs program had targeted 1 to 2 million people, but geneticists were considering screening the entire U.S. population of reproductive age—perhaps 100 to 200 million people. One in 25 Caucasians is a carrier of cystic fibrosis, which puts the level of risk in the general population near the level of risk for Tay-Sachs in American Jews. Current tests can identify about 70% of cystic fibrosis carriers, and efforts are under way to develop techniques for identifying the remaining 30% (Roberts, 1990).

Many ethical issues arise from our increasing skill in fetal screening. Should damaged fetuses be aborted? If so, how disabling must the genetic defect be? If a child is diagnosed as genetically damaged as a fetus, should insurance companies be able to deny the child insurance, given that the companies know that health expenses will be exorbitant compared with those of other children?

Treatment

The growing sophistication of diagnostic procedures has made early detection of developmental abnormalities more likely. But what happens when a fetus is found to be developing abnormally? The parents may decide to terminate the pregnancy, but there may be treatment alternatives. Developments in the medical treatment of fetuses parallel the rapid advances in early diagnosis. Current approaches to prenatal treatment fall into three categories: medical therapy, surgery, and genetic manipulation.

Medical Therapy Medical therapy is currently the most widely available of the three methods. An example is providing extra vitamins to the mother when enzyme deficiencies are discovered in the blood of the fetus.

An exciting first in medical therapy was reported in mid-1989. Parents in Lyons, France, whose first child had died in infancy of a hereditary disorder, learned that the fetus the mother was carrying had the same disorder, involving an immune deficiency that leaves the infant open to almost any infection. Doctors decided to try to treat the fetus in the womb. They injected immune cells from the thymus and liver of two aborted fetuses into the umbilical cord, the first time this had been done. After the baby was born, the injected cells multiplied, as the doctors had hoped (Elmer-DeWitt, 1994).

Researchers recently discovered that women who have AIDS are less likely to pass the disease on to their fetuses if they have certain antibodies in their blood. It may be possible to immunize AIDS-carrying pregnant mothers to increase the number of these antibodies (Stephens, 1990).

Surgery The use of fetal surgery is illustrated by the experience of a pregnant woman who had earlier given birth to an infant with hydrocephaly, an abnormal accumulation of fluid inside the skull that results in brain damage. An ultrasound diagnosis indicated that the fetus was accumulating fluid on the brain and would likely suffer brain damage if treatment was delayed until birth. Surgeons at the University of Colorado Medical School, working through a long, hollow tube inserted through the mother's abdomen and the amniotic sac, inserted a small valve in the back of the fetus's head to permit the excess fluid to drain, thereby relieving pressure on the brain. The fetus survived the surgery and, at 16 months of age, appeared to be normal (Clewell et al., 1982; Fadiman, 1983).

Physicians are now able to carry out surgery on fetuses to avoid the damage caused by blockage of the urinary tract and a small number of other problems (Ohlendorf-Moffat, 1991). In the near future, fetuses who have a neural-tube defect may also be treatable. Neural-tube defects often result in infants' being born with an opening in the back of the head through which part of the brain protrudes. The current treatment involves removing the external brain tissue and closing the skull after birth, which often leaves the infant blind and mentally retarded.

Working with monkeys, researchers at the National Institute of Child Health and Human Development have operated on fetuses by removing them from the uterus and conducting a similar operation, as shown in Figure 5.8. Apparently, the brain tissue at least partially regenerates, because the monkey fetuses, carried to term, are able to see. This treatment may someday be available for human fetuses.

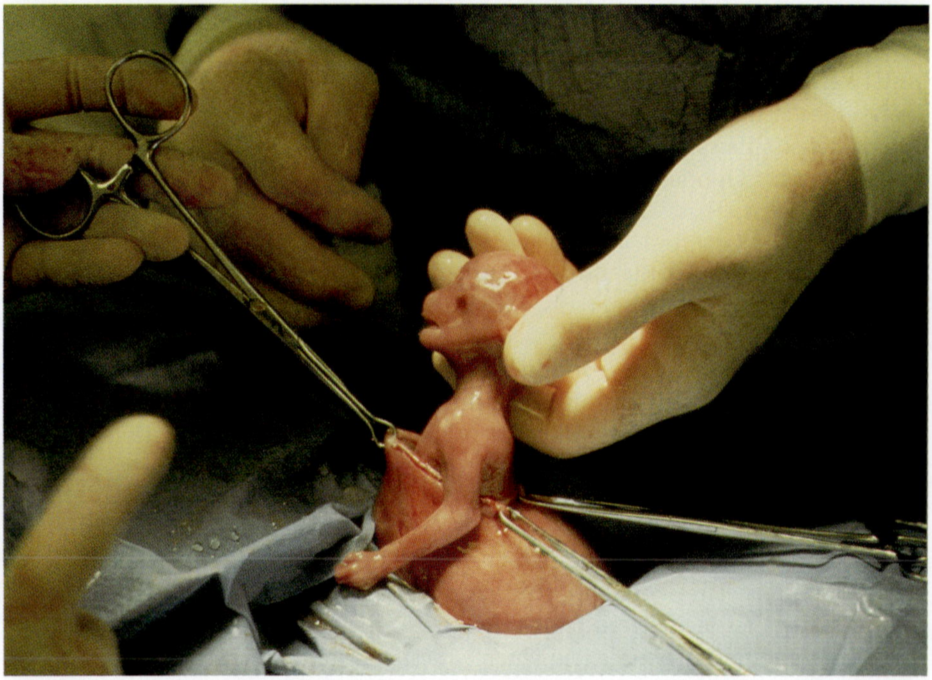

Figure 5.8
Brain surgery on a monkey fetus. The fetus was taken halfway out of the uterus for the procedure and then replaced to continue development inside the mother.

Genetic Engineering Probably the greatest promise for prenatal treatment lies in the field of genetic engineering. Suppose we could detect, say, the lack of an enzyme in a fetus's blood and could identify the specific gene that caused the defect. Working in the laboratory with a blood sample from the fetus, we would clip out the defective gene and insert a synthetic gene. After producing many copies of the blood cells containing the repaired chromosome, we would inject them into the fetus, where they would survive and replicate and provide sufficient amounts of the enzyme for normal development.

In September 1990, scientists undertook the first federally approved attempt at human gene therapy of this kind. It involved a 4-year-old girl who suffered from ADA deficiency, a severe and incurable disease of the immune system. Cells were extracted from the girl, and harmless viruses were used to carry the needed ADA gene into the cells. The cells—a billion or so—were then reinjected into the child's bloodstream. The cells are producing the needed ADA, but the child will need repeated treatments. Scientists are working on techniques to make repeated treatments unnecessary by carrying out similar procedures during the fetal stage. They will try to replace the cells in the fetus that give rise to all the ADA-producing cells; thus these cells will not die during the lifetime of the patient (Capecchi, 1994; Karson, Polvino, & Anderson, 1992).

Ethical Considerations

The ability to diagnose abnormal development raises innumerable ethical questions—questions that people may find difficult to answer. Today's fetal-screening techniques can detect the presence of sickle-cell anemia, Huntington's chorea, Down syndrome, cystic fibrosis, and numerous other maladies. What are the consequences of this knowledge? If no treatment is possible, the options are to terminate the pregnancy or to bring a child with a serious disorder into the world.

Increasingly, special-interest groups and the federal government have become involved in this decision process. Movements to prevent the use of federal or state funds for abortions, and some that would make any abortion illegal, are underway. Proponents of these movements argue from a moral and ethical pro-life perspective. Opponents emphasize the individual mother's right to make a personal, moral, and ethical choice. Opponents also point out that prohibitions would discriminate against poorer citizens, who may not have personal funds to pay for abortion.

In a related area, two successive U.S. presidents have made different decisions regarding research on the use of aborted fetal tissue to treat various illnesses. President George Bush banned research with fetal tissue, and President Bill Clinton lifted this ban soon after he took office. Those who oppose such research argue that women might seek more abortions in order to sell their fetuses for research. Others claim that this is extremely unlikely and that the research could lead to humanitarian treatments for those who have debilitating diseases, such as Parkinson's, for whom fetal tissue provides the best hope.

The treatment of newborn infants with severe disorders is a controversial issue as well, as in the case of Baby Jane Doe. On October 11, 1983, on Long Island, Baby Jane Doe was born with hydrocephalus, spina bifida, and microcephaly. Her parents had two options. They could approve two operations, after which it was likely that she would live past age 20 but be paralyzed, severely retarded, and in pain; or they could refuse to permit surgery, in which case she would likely die before the age of 3. They chose not to allow surgery. But others felt it was not the parents' choice to make alone. Most significantly, the U.S. Justice Department, for the first time, sued on behalf of the medical rights of an infant with a disability. Ultimately, the U.S. Supreme Court ruled against the government and with the parents' right to choose (Holden, 1986).

Decisions regarding the health and life of a fetus or infant are intensely emotional and deeply embedded in social, ethical, and moral convictions. They are also very personal. As new technologies are developed, the fine line that separates these personal beliefs and feelings on the one side, and the government's role in protecting the rights of fetuses and infants on the other, may become increasingly blurred.

✓ To Recap...

We have progressed dramatically in our understanding of prenatal diseases and in our ability to diagnose and treat them. In some cases, the most useful approach is prevention, perhaps through genetic counseling.

During pregnancy, diagnostic procedures provide a window on prenatal development that was unknown only a few decades ago. Ultrasound imaging can detect growth anomalies, such as abnormal head growth. Amniocentesis and chorionic villus sampling provide fetal cells that can be analyzed for chromosomal defects and several genetic problems, as well as some other disorders. Screening has even been carried out on embryos in test tubes. When problems are detected, treatment can sometimes proceed even while the fetus is still in the uterus. Medical therapy is one possibility, as when there are chemical imbalances. Surgery is a second possibility. On the horizon is the possibility of gene therapy.

As we become more skilled at understanding genetics, screening for and diagnosing problems, and developing treatment alternatives, however, individuals and society at large face a new array of ethical dilemmas.

Conclusion

We live at a time when knowledge and technology in many fields are expanding at a dizzying pace. Nowhere are the effects of progress more dramatic than in biology and health-related fields. The field of prenatal development has benefited enormously from these advances.

Only relatively recently have we developed an understanding of the processes of conception and embryological development. It has been especially important for us to learn that differentiation of body parts and limbs occurs in the first 8 weeks or so after conception. With this knowledge, we have been better able to understand why infections and certain drugs have more devastating effects on the organism during the early prenatal period than later.

Our awareness that the placenta does not always filter out chemicals and toxins from the mother's blood and that these substances thus enter the bloodstream of the fetus has had profound effects. Scientists actively look for causes of abnormal development that were previously ignored. Environmental pollutants, drugs, and other chemicals are suspect, and it is now routine to test new chemicals for toxic effects on the fetus. The new field of psychoteratology may provide even more sensitive indicators of harmful substances. Although we may not always know how or why these substances affect the fetus, at least we are learning when they do. Partly because of this knowledge, the ratio of birth deaths to live births in the United States has reached an all-time low.

An important message from this information is that the baby is in an environment from the moment of conception. By the time of birth, interactions between genes and the environment have been at play during the full 9 months of development.

One might come away from this chapter fearful about all the things that threaten a baby's prenatal development. Keep in mind, though, that the very large majority of babies are born healthy and intact. Fortunately, as we have learned about the dangers that the fetus faces, we have been increasingly able to take precautions that will increase the likelihood that the newborn will get a healthy start.

Visual Summary for Chapter 5: Prenatal Development

Stages of Prenatal Development

Period	Duration	Major Events of the Period
Zygote	Conception to 2nd week	At conception a zygote is formed, combining the 23 chromosomes from the father with the 23 chromosomes from the mother. The zygote becomes fully implanted in the uterus by the end of the second week.
Embryo	3rd to 8th week	All major internal and external structures, as well as support structures needed for protection and growth, form during this period.
Fetus	9th to 38th week	Development of the organ structures formed in the embryonic period continues, and the fetus increases in size and weight. The age of viability is considered to be 23 to 24 weeks of age.

Teratology: History, Principles, and Natural Events

Six Principles of How Teratogens Act

1. A teratogen's effect depends on the genetic makeup of the organism.
2. A teratogen's effect depends partly on timing.
3. The effect may be unique to the teratogen.
4. The effect may include death or serious disorders.
5. Teratogens gain access to the fetus in different ways.
6. The effect of a teratogen increases with the level of exposure to it.

Natural Challenges to the Health of the Embryo and Fetus

Challenge	Effect
Infectious Diseases	Diseases such as rubella, herpes, HIV, syphilis, and gonorrhea have the potential to harm a developing embryo or fetus.
Malnutrition	Maternal malnutrition may be associated with deficits in size of the brain and major internal organs in the fetus, small and premature babies, and increased rates of spontaneous abortion, infant death, and congenital defects.
Maternal Experiences and Stress	Maternal stress may be associated with abnormalities in the newborn, although more research is needed in this area.
Parental Age	Both the mother's and father's age are associated with increased risk for certain chromosomal or genetic abnormalities. Teenage mothers are also at higher risk for having premature or underweight babies, although the reasons may primarily involve socioeconomic factors.

Teratology: Drugs and Environmental Chemicals

Teratogen		Consequence
Street Drugs	→	Babies of drug-addicted mothers may be born addicted and are likely to have many developmental problems.
Therapeutic Drugs	→	Therapeutic drugs may also be harmful to the fetus, as was the case with thalidomide.
Caffeine	→	Some studies suggest risk associated with caffeine.
Nicotine	→	Can affect growth and can increase the risk of premature delivery and birth complications.
Alcohol	→	Can produce physical malformations and intellectual deficits, including fetal alcohol syndrome.
Environmental Chemicals	→	Mercury, lead, and PCBs appear to be harmful to the fetus.

Preventing, Detecting, and Treating Birth Defects

Methods of Screening for Abnormalities in the Fetus

Method		Description
Ultrasound Imaging	→	Uses soundlike waves to provide a continuous picture of the fetus and its environment. Can detect certain growth abnormalities.
Amniocentesis	→	Examines a sample of the amniotic fluid and the fetal cells contained in it. Can identify chromosomal defects and several genetic problems.
Chorionic Villus Sampling	→	Examines fetal cells collected from a sample of the chorion, a part of the placenta. Can identify chromosomal defects and several genetic problems.
Test-tube Screening	→	Embryos that are the result of in vitro fertilization can be screened for DNA abnormalities before being implanted into the mother's uterus.

Treatment of Abnormalities in the Fetus

Treatment of abnormalities in the fetus can involve in utero *medical therapy or surgery. Genetic engineering holds promise as a treatment in the future.*

Chapter 6

Physical Development: Birth, Motor Skills, and Growth

So-called miracles of medical science seem almost commonplace today. Even so, the birth of septuplets to an Iowa woman on November 19, 1997, took the world by surprise. The babies, four boys and three girls, were the first set of septuplets born alive in the United States.

The more fetuses a woman is carrying, the greater the risk to each one; so the risk with seven is extremely high. The only other known set of septuplets born alive in the world were born in Saudi Arabia earlier in 1997, and three of those babies died within a month of their birth. In the United States, no septuplets had been born since 1985. Of those septuplets, one was stillborn, three died within weeks, and the remaining three had medical and developmental problems. In contrast, the Iowa septuplets, born about 2 months prematurely, seemed surprisingly healthy. One doctor who helped deliver the babies said that they were "so well grown, so well developed, it just strikes me as a miracle."

But this miracle didn't happen without help. Advances not only in fertility treatments but also in prenatal and neonatal care made the pregnancy and the successful delivery possible. Bobbi McCaughey, the babies' mother, had been taking a fertility drug when the septuplets were conceived, and her pregnancy was carefully monitored by specialists. After the ninth week, she remained in bed. For a month before the babies' delivery, she was confined to a hospital.

At the 31st week—9 weeks short of the 40 weeks for a full-term pregnancy—doctors decided to deliver the babies when Mrs. McCaughey began having contractions. A team of more than 40 specialists were on hand for the delivery, which was performed by cesarean section. The babies ranged in size from 2.5 to 3.4 lb—normal for their gestational age, which is unusual in multiple pregnancies, but still small enough to require a long hospital stay and special treatment. In all, experts estimated that the cost of medical attention for mother and babies would reach $1 million.

Although septuplets are extremely rare, multiple births in general have become much more common as more and more women are using fertility drugs that increase the number of eggs produced in a single cycle. In the United States, the number of multiple births involving three or more babies has quadrupled since the 1970s. The high cost of medical care in many of these cases—and, more important, the high cost in terms of risk to the health of both the mother and the fetuses—has raised serious ethical questions. Is the promise of a medical miracle worth the cost and the risk? Should controls be placed on technology in this area? Debate on such questions is sure to continue as more multiple births occur.

We begin this chapter by examining the birth process, including the problems some newborns face, and how medical science has learned to deal with them.

This chapter focuses on the child's physical development, beginning at birth and continuing through adolescence. Physical development involves more than just growth, although that is certainly an important part of it. We will also see how a baby acquires the motor skills to manipulate objects and to explore the environment, skills that have enormous psychological impact on development.

Psychological and physical growth depend crucially on the maturation of the brain, so we devote part of our discussion to how the brain develops and operates. Finally, we examine the physical changes during adolescence that prepare the body for reproduction but that also can affect the individual's self-image and identity.

Birth and the Perinatal Period

Perinatal period
The events and environment surrounding the birth process.

Our story starts with birth and its surrounding events—the **perinatal period**. Birth is truly a momentous event, as the child moves from a relatively sheltered and protected environment to the busy and much-less-predictable outside world, where the remainder of development will occur.

Typically, the birth process proceeds smoothly. In this technological age, we sometimes forget that humans have accomplished this feat over millions of years without hospitals, doctors, or elaborate equipment. Occasionally, however, modern technology is crucial for making the process work and even for saving the baby's life. After briefly describing the physical aspects of birth, we consider problems that can arise and the notion of infants at risk.

Labor and Delivery

Typically around 38 weeks after fertilization, a pregnant woman will go into labor, the first step in the birth process. Labor appears to be initiated by changes in the fetal brain (Nathanielsz, 1995). Chemicals are released that signal the muscles of the mother's uterus to start contracting rhythmically, initially every 15 to 20 minutes and then at shorter and shorter intervals. The complete birth process requires about 8 to 16 hours for the first baby and about half as much for later babies.

Labor consists of three stages, shown in Figure 6.1. The first and longest stage begins when the early contractions start to narrow the uterus and dilate (widen) the cervical opening through which the baby will pass. This stage ends when the cervix is fully dilated, usually about 10 cm. By the end of this stage, the contractions are very intense, occurring every 2–3 minutes. The second stage begins when the fetus starts to pass through the cervix and ends when the baby has been completely delivered into the world. During this stage, the contractions are long and closely spaced and the mother is encouraged to assist the process by pushing with each contrac-

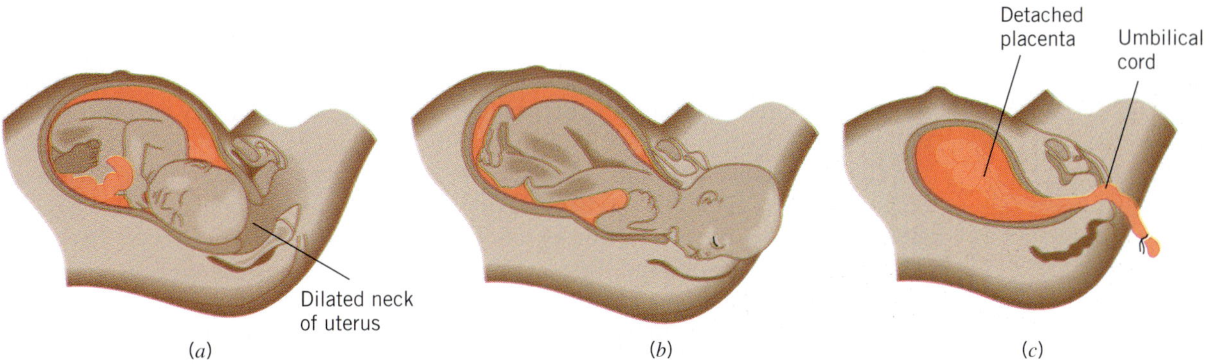

Figure 6.1
The three stages of labor: (*a*) the neck of the uterus dilates; (*b*) the baby is delivered; and (*c*) the placenta is expelled.

tion. The third stage, which often lasts only minutes, involves the delivery of the placenta and related other membranes, referred to as the *afterbirth*.

Technological advances permit the monitoring of the fetus's state during birth. Physicians can visualize the fetus, the umbilical cord, and the placenta by ultrasound to determine, for example, whether there is a danger that the umbilical cord will wrap around the fetus's neck (which can cause strangulation). They also can record electronically the heart rate and activity of the fetus through the mother's abdomen to determine whether there are signs of **fetal distress**, which would be indicated by an abnormally high or low heart rate (Anderson & Allison, 1990).

Fetal distress
A condition of abnormal stress in the fetus, reflected during the birth process in an abnormal fetal heart rate.

Cesarean section
Surgical delivery of the fetus directly from the uterus; performed when normal delivery is prohibited.

Sometimes birth cannot proceed according to nature's plan because, for example, the baby is lying in an unusual position in the uterus (such as sideways or buttocks down), delivery is proceeding too slowly, or the baby's head is too large to pass through the cervical opening. In such cases, the doctor often elects to perform a **cesarean section**, in which the baby is surgically removed directly from the uterus. The rate of cesarean deliveries skyrocketed from 5% in 1969 to 25% in 1990. Some critics charged that many of these procedures were performed for unjustifiable reasons, such as greater convenience for doctors or reduced risk of malpractice suits (Guillemin, 1993; Van Tuinen & Wolfe, 1993). Perhaps because of such criticism the rate fell back to 22% in 1993, and many public health officials are working toward having it decrease to about 15% by the year 2000 (Clarke & Taffel, 1995; Paul & Miller, 1995).

Although the stages of birth are the same in all cultures, there are many variations in how cultures think about and deal with birth. Practices have changed fairly rapidly in the United States. For instance, as recently as 1972, only 27% of U.S. hospitals permitted fathers or other family members in the delivery room. By 1980, 80% of U.S. hospitals had an open policy, and today very few do not.

Applications

Cultural Attitudes toward Birth

It has been said that in most Western countries, pregnancy, labor, and delivery are treated as if they were the symptoms of an illness. Pregnant women are encouraged to visit the doctor regularly. Most give birth in a hospital, lying down (some say for the convenience of the doctor), and having been given drugs to block pain. Often, after the baby is born doctors and nurses, not the baby's mother, take over the baby's care, at least for a while. Fortunately, this view of pregnancy and birth has begun to give way to a more realistic understanding that these processes are both normal and healthy.

Has Western civilization been unique in looking at pregnancy as a sort of disability and birth as a process requiring medical intervention? Not entirely. Among the Cuna Indians of Panama, for example, a pregnant woman must visit the medicine man daily for herbal medicines and women are given medication throughout labor. Various interventions during labor are practiced in many cultures: The pregnant woman's abdomen may be massaged, perhaps with masticated roots or melted butter, or even constricted to help push the baby out. For difficult cases, midwives of Myanmar (formerly Burma) tread on the woman's abdomen with their feet.

Nevertheless, the attitude of the West is often contrasted with that of cultures in which birth is seen as an everyday occurrence. Among the Jarara of South America, for example, labor and birth are so much a part of daily life that a woman may give birth in a passageway or shelter in view of everyone. In many cultures,

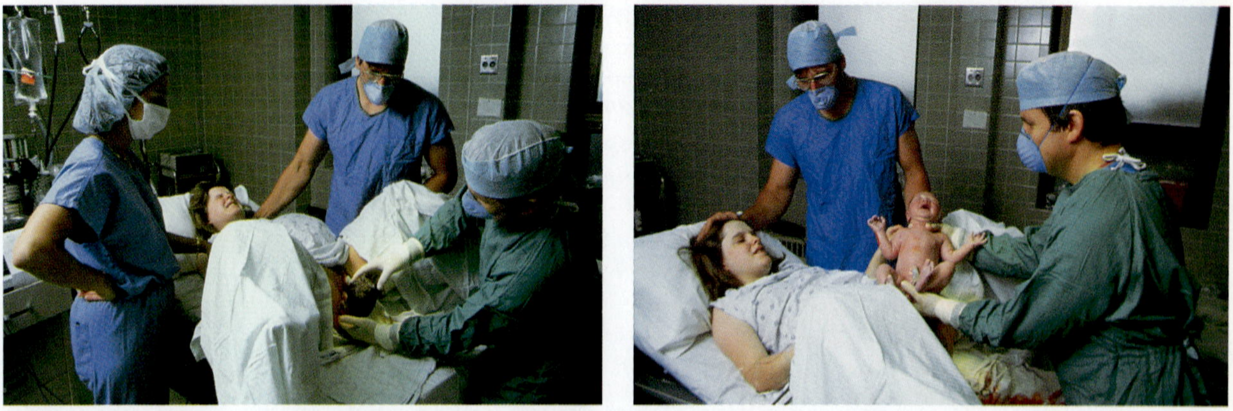

In Western society, birth typically takes place in a hospital with the mother lying on her back. Medication for pain, once administered routinely, has given way to more natural methods of dealing with the physical discomfort.

women give birth alone. And non-Western women commonly deliver in an upright position—kneeling, sitting, squatting, and even standing—rather than lying down (Mead & Newton, 1967).

There has been a trend in the West toward making birth more "natural." An English obstetrician, Grantly Dick-Read, wrote a book called *Natural Childbirth* in 1933 and a second, called *Childbirth without Fear*, in 1944 to put forth the view that Western societies had created an association between childbirth and pain. Fear of pain, he said, actually created tension and muscle cramping that produced pain unnecessarily. These ideas were reinforced by Dr. F. Lamaze in *Painless Childbirth* (1970). Lamaze's popular method of preparation for childbirth is based on conditioning through breathing and muscle exercises and on educating the mother about pregnancy and labor.

A parallel movement has emphasized the baby's experience of birth. In *Birth without Violence* (1975), Dr. F. Leboyer argued that the infant's transition into the outside world—already stressful because of the birth process itself—should not be made more difficult by bright lights, noise, and insensitive handling. Leboyer introduced a more gentle approach to limit the assault on the baby's senses—a darkened and quiet room, gentle massage, and a warm bath.

Other, related obstetric practices have emerged in recent years. One involves having the father present during the birth process, sometimes serving as the mother's breathing coach. Another is a return to giving birth at home, often with the assistance of a trained midwife rather than a doctor (O'Connor, 1993; Vedam & Kolodjii, 1995).

Is the naturalist trend right? Research in this field is inadequate at this point to allow us to draw any firm conclusions about what might be best for the mother or the baby. Maybe the truly remarkable fact is that mothers and newborns usually survive the birth process just fine, whatever the rituals with which their cultures surround them.

Culture also affects the likelihood that the mother will survive pregnancy and childbirth. In the United States, because of improved health care, maternal deaths per 100,000 pregnant women fell from approximately 660 in 1931 to 7.4 in 1986.

Table 6.1
U.S. Infant Mortality Rates 1915–1995 (deaths in the first year per 1,000 live births)

Year	*African-Americans*	*Whites*	*All Races*
1915	150.4	92.8	95.7
1925	105.3	65.0	69.0
1935	80.1	49.2	53.2
1945	56.2	35.6	38.3
1955	43.1	23.6	26.4
1965	41.7	21.5	24.7
1975	26.2	14.2	16.1
1985	18.2	9.3	10.6
1995	15.1	6.3	7.6

Source: Based on information from U.S. Department of Health and Human Services, National Center for Health Statistics, Vital Statistics of the United States, 1995, and Monthly Vital Statistics Reports from 1996.

But around the world even today, 500,000 women each year lose their lives from complications of pregnancy and labor. In Nigeria, for example, the death rate is still 800 per 100,000.

Often, health-care facilities simply are not available to pregnant women, or transportation to health facilities is a problem. But sometimes a cultural clash is the issue. A dramatic example comes from an area in Ghana that has a large population of Muslim refugees from Mali. It is the Muslim women's custom to wear long black dresses. For native Ghanans, however, the color black symbolizes evil and death. As a result, the local hospitals do not admit women dressed in black and try to get them to change their dress. The Muslim women resist these attempts and simply refuse to go to the hospitals, thus they often do not receive necessary care.

Babies face hazards during the birth process as well, and some do not survive. Scientists and physicians have devoted enormous efforts to addressing these problems and are making good progress. As shown in Table 6.1, infant mortality rates in the United States have dropped markedly in recent years, although less so for African-Americans than for whites. Still, in 1993, 21 countries had newborn mortality rates lower than that of the United States (Wegman, 1994).

The Concept of Risk

Parents worry about whether their baby will be normal. In more than 9 of 10 cases, the baby is born on time and healthy. But some parents and their babies are not so fortunate. Approximately 3% of all babies born in the United States each year—120,000 or so infants—are born with major physical malformations.

Whereas some babies have immediately obvious physical problems, other babies are considered **at risk** for developmental delays and cognitive and social problems. Psychologists believe that the earlier they can identify these babies, the earlier they can intervene to help. Thus, over the past few decades, hundreds of studies have attempted to discover what factors put infants in the highest category of risk. Three indicators seem to be most important: maternal and family characteristics, the physical compromise of the newborn, and the performance of the newborn on behavioral assessments.

At risk
Describes babies who have a higher likelihood than other babies of experiencing developmental problems.

Maternal and Family Characteristics A baby's chances of developing problems can be predicted in part from the family context in which the child is born.

Around 85% of the risk of severe developmental problems can be attributed to what happens in the prenatal period. As mentioned in the preceding chapter, several maternal factors increase risk for the fetus, including the mother's use of drugs or alcohol, exposure to viral infections during pregnancy, smoking, and poor nutrition (Chomitz, Cheung, & Lieberman, 1995). A major factor in the United States is the failure of the mother to seek prenatal care from a physician. Of mothers who saw a doctor at any time during pregnancy, only 6% had babies with low birth weights, whereas the figure was 3.5 times greater for mothers who did not see a doctor (Bronfenbrenner, 1989).

Low birth weight is an important indicator of risk. We have already seen that the incidence of infant mortality is higher among African-Americans than among whites. So, too, is the incidence of low birth weight. This situation may reflect the fact that whereas only about 20% of pregnant white women fail to see a doctor in the first 3 months of pregnancy, the comparable figure for African-American women is 38% (Halpern, 1993; Kopp & Kaler, 1989).

Failure to see a doctor is in part attributable to lack of financial resources available to the mother. Financial problems increase the likelihood of low birth weight sixfold (Binsacca et al., 1987). Babies born to families who have strained financial resources, poor social support, and little education are more at risk than are those born to more advantaged families. One set of experts recently made the following projection of the percent of newborn babies that will face various risk factors by the year 2000 (Barnard, Morisset, & Spieker, 1993, p. 386):

Not wanted (12%)

Born at low birth weight and/or premature (7%)

Mothers are substance abusers (11%)

Parents are alcoholics (10%)

Mothers are teenagers (10%)

Mothers are not married (30%)

Mothers have not completed high school (20%)

Family income is below the federal poverty line (23%)

Physical Compromise of the Newborn A second general indicator of risk is evidence of physical problems in the newborn, most frequently, low birth weight. Around 6 to 7% of the babies born in the United States each year (around 250,000) have a low birth weight, below 2,500 gr (about 5.5 lb). And low-birth-weight babies are about 40 times more likely to die in the first month of life than are babies with normal birth weight (Freda et al., 1990; Paneth, 1995). They also are at greater risk for many problems, large and small (Hack, Klein, & Taylor, 1995). Why is this so?

The newborn must make a number of adaptations to the outside world. Temperature control and nutrition are no longer provided by the mother's body, but these needs are rather easily met by the parents or other providers. Breathing, however, is a different story. After living in a water world for almost 9 months, the baby must draw the first breath of air within seconds after birth. Babies with low birth weight are more likely to have difficulty initiating or maintaining breathing. Failure to breathe prevents the delivery of oxygen to cells—a condition called **anoxia**—which can cause the cells to die. The brain cells are especially sensitive to oxygen deficits. Severe anoxia, for example, may damage the brain area that controls movement of the limbs, resulting in a spastic-type movement referred to as cerebral palsy (Vaughn, McKay, & Behrman, 1984).

Anoxia
A deficit of oxygen to the cells, which can produce brain or other tissue damage.

Preterm
Describes babies born before the end of the normal gestation period.

Low-birth-weight babies may be placed in two groups. One comprises babies whose birth weights are low because they were born **preterm**, meaning before the end of the normal 38 weeks of pregnancy. Preterm babies often have the breathing problems just described. In many, tiny blood vessels in the brain burst, causing bleeding and contributing to the infant's risk.

Even disregarding these physical challenges, development in the preterm baby may lag behind that in a full-term baby, at least for a time. Although we would expect the preterm infant, who is comparable to a fetus still in the womb, to be less advanced than the full-term baby, even when matched for the number of days following fertilization, the preterm infant usually has less mature brain patterns and is more disorganized and difficult to soothe (Als, Duffy, & McAnulty, 1988; Duffy, Als, & McAnulty, 1990). Longer term, these babies can be expected to have more frequent problems with growth and overall health issues. Studies indicate that by the elementary school years, preterm infants, especially boys, are at greater risk for both behavior and academic problems (Hack et al., 1995).

Small for gestational age (SGA)
Describes babies born at a weight in the bottom 10% of babies of a particular gestational age.

The other group of babies born with a low birth weight are those whose fetal growth was retarded. These babies are considered **small for gestational age (SGA)**. They may be born at the expected gestational age of 9 months, or they may be born earlier (and so be both SGA *and* preterm), but they are in this category because their weight places them among the bottom 10% of babies born at that particular gestational age. Although the cause is frequently unknown, several factors appear to increase the likelihood that a baby's prenatal growth will be delayed, including chromosomal abnormalities, infections, poor maternal nutrition, and maternal substance abuse.

SGA babies generally face fewer developmental risks than do preterm babies (Wilcox & Skjoerven, 1992), but some problems can be expected. For example, these infants do not arouse easily, and they tend to have poor muscle tone, appearing limp when held. They also are disadvantaged beyond the newborn period; for example, they show poorer recognition memory than do babies born at normal weight (Gotlieb, Baisini, & Bray, 1988). SGA babies who are preterm perform more poorly on verbal tests of IQ as preschoolers than do preterm babies whose weights were appropriate for their ages, although their eventual developmental course depends heavily on the quality of their postbirth environment (Dowling & Bendell, 1988; Gorman & Pollitt, 1992).

Steady improvement in technology has produced a dramatic decline in deaths resulting from low birth weight. Although a birth weight below 2,500 g (5.5 lb) is classified as low, babies weighing only 500 g (a little more than 1 lb) have at least a 25% chance of living, and the odds rise to more than 90% for babies who weigh at least 1,000 g (about 2.2 lb) (Minde, 1993).

Much of this progress can be attributed to the development of neonatal intensive care units (NICUs). In these facilities, low-birth-weight babies receive various forms of stimulation—rocking, sound recordings of the mother's heartbeat, high-contrast mobiles, gentle massage, and the like—which appear to assist their early development (Field, 1995; Mueller, 1996; Thoman, 1993). One consequence of these interventions is that very tiny babies who would once have died at birth are now kept alive. These babies, however, face strong challenges to life and well-being; the lighter the baby, the higher these risks.

Physical and Behavioral Assessment A third indicator of risk is poor performance on standard assessments. Perhaps as a sign of things to come, almost all babies born in the United States begin life with a test. Tests are used to screen babies for disorders, to determine whether a baby's nervous system is intact, and to characterize how a newborn responds to social and physical stimuli. Even though newborns are new to the external world, they possess a surprising range of behaviors and functions. Newborn tests can assess more than 85% of such behaviors and functions (Francis, Self, & Horowitz, 1987). Here we consider the most often used tests: the Apgar exam, the Prechtl test, and the Brazelton Neonatal Behavioral Assessment Scale.

In 1953, Dr. Virginia Apgar introduced a test that permitted obstetricians to record objectively the status of the newborn. This test has become the standard for the baby's first assessment. The *Apgar exam* focuses on five of the newborn's vital functions, which are measured by heart rate, respiration, muscle tone, response to a mildly painful stimulus, and skin color. The newborn receives a score from 0 to 2 on each of these items. For example, the baby earns a 2 for the heart-rate category if the heart beats 100–140 times per minute; a 1 if the rate is less than 100; and a 0 if no beat is detectable. Babies are typically assessed on the five categories almost immediately after birth and then again 5 minutes later. The highest possible score is 10. On average, about 77% of newborns receive a score of 8–10, 17% a score of 3–7, and 6% a score of 0–2 (Apgar, 1953).

Investigators use the Apgar to identify babies who may need special monitoring and attention through early infancy. Several factors tend to lower the Apgar score, including maternal depression, anxiety, smoking, drinking, and labor medication. Psychologists have examined the relation between a newborn's Apgar score and intellectual functioning later in infancy and early childhood. The results have been mixed. Some investigators have reported a positive relation, but others report no relation when socioeconomic status, race, and gender are taken into consideration (Francis et al., 1987).

Low Apgar scores have also been related to sudden infant death syndrome (SIDS), defined as the sudden death of any infant under 1 year of age that cannot be explained by any physical or medical cause (Willinger, James, & Catz, 1991). SIDS is the leading cause of death among infants younger than 12 months, peaking between 2 and 4 months of age (Dwyer & Ponsonby, 1995; Guntheroth, 1995). Although the definitive cause of the disorder is unknown, effective preventive measures include placing babies on their backs to sleep; keeping them away from pillows, stuffed toys, or bedding; and maintaining a smoke-free environment (Fleming et al., 1996; Willinger, 1995).

The Apgar exam assesses vital life processes and can be quickly administered, but the results provide only limited information. An extensive assessment of neurological functioning, the *Prechtl test*, is much more informative (Prechtl, 1977; Prechtl & Beintema, 1964). This examination includes items similar to those in the Apgar but also assesses alertness, spontaneous movements and tremors, facial expressions, reactions to placement in various postures, and around 15 reflexes. Babies who show fetal distress during birth or who need assistance with instruments to pass through the birth canal earn lower scores on the Prechtl test (Leijon, 1980; Prechtl, 1968). Labor medication and premature birth also tend to depress Prechtl scores (Belsey et al., 1981; Forslund & Bjerre, 1983).

The questions addressed by the Apgar and Prechtl tests, such as how well the newborn is managing such functions as breathing, independent blood circulation, and certain reflexes, are obviously important. But such measurements may tempt us to think of the newborn as something of a machine whose vital functions operate at a certain level of efficiency and who responds in a fixed way to stimuli. The newborn is a much more complex creature, with a wealth of behavioral tools. Moreover, new-

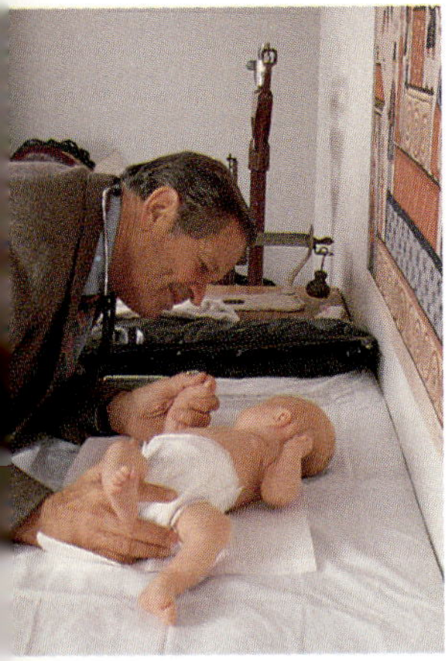

T. Berry Brazelton developed a widely used scale for assessing the newborn.

born babies differ substantially in how they behave, and these differences may affect how parents and others treat them. For these reasons, investigators have focused increasingly on tests of how well the newborn's behavior is *organized.*

The *Brazelton Neonatal Behavioral Assessment Scale* is the most comprehensive of the newborn tests. The main idea underlying this scale is that the seemingly helpless newborn actually possesses organized behaviors for dealing with both attractive stimuli—such as pleasant sights, sounds, and tastes—and offensive stimuli—such as loud noises and pinpricks (Brazelton, Nugent, & Lester, 1987). Assessors observe the baby in a number of states, or levels of alertness, to obtain a sense of the baby's style and temperament. An important feature of the exam is that it evaluates the newborn's ability to habituate. Recall from Chapter 2 that habituation is a simple form of learning in which a reflex response to a stimulus declines or disappears when the stimulus repeatedly occurs.

The exam includes items in four categories: attention and social responsiveness; muscle tone and physical movement; control of alertness (habituation, irritability, and excitability); and physiological response to stress. The baby's performance on these measures provides indicators of well-being and risk. For example, a baby who is unable to habituate to a repeated stimulus or to remain alert may fall into a higher risk category.

All the newborn assessments discussed here do a fairly good job of characterizing how a baby is doing in the early period. However, they are poor predictors of ultimate intelligence and personality, and none of the risk factors we have discussed is very dependable when considered in isolation. This fact may seem surprising to anyone who has seen a very low-weight baby in the newborn intensive-care nursery. A 2-lb baby, who is little more than tubes, able to breathe only with a respirator, and perhaps suffering internal brain bleeding, may seem to be on the verge of death. Amazingly, this baby is more than likely to turn out fine (Sostek et al., 1987). The best predictor of developmental difficulties is the *number* of risk factors to which an infant is subjected. The greater the number, the more likely that the infant will have problems (Sameroff et al., 1993).

Development in Family Context

Infants at Risk: Environment Holds the Key

Some babies who are born at risk have suffered brain or central nervous system damage that affects their functioning throughout life. However, in many cases, whether babies born at risk achieve normal development appears to depend largely on the context in which they are reared. Because most of the research supporting this finding has been carried out with preterm infants, we will focus on that work, but many of these factors play a role in determining the outcome of any baby at risk.

One factor in a baby's development progress is the quality of the relationship that forms between the parents and the baby (Mangelsdorf et al., 1996). At-risk babies often pose special challenges to this relationship. For example, the preterm baby may spend weeks in a plastic enclosure in a special-care hospital nursery that affords the parents little opportunity to hold and cuddle the baby. When finally at home, the baby is likely to have an irritating cry, be difficult to soothe, and have irregular patterns of sleep and wakefulness (Frodi et al., 1978; Parmelee & Garbanati, 1987).

These real problems are aggravated by people's reactions to preterm babies. In one study, several sets of parents were shown a film of a 5-month-old baby after they had been told that the baby was either normal, difficult, or premature (a term the researchers used for both SGA and preterm babies). Those who were told that the baby was premature judged crying segments of the film as more negative than did other parents, and physiological measures indicated that they experienced the baby's cries as more stressful (Frodi et al., 1978).

Other investigators have observed that parents treat their premature children differently even after apparent differences between them and full-term babies have disappeared (Barnard, Bee, & Hammond, 1984a; Beckwith & Parmelee, 1986). The tendency to expect negative behavior from premature infants has been referred to as "prematurity stereotyping" (Stern & Karraker, 1992). Such stereotypes increase the possibility that a negative cycle between parent and infant will be set in motion. Of course, the degree to which this occurs depends in part on the tolerance and flexibility of the caregivers, which is often related to their accurate understanding of the infant's needs (Benasich & Brooks-Gunn, 1996).

A contributor to disruption of the parent–infant relationship in the past was the policy of hospitals not to permit the parents to hold or touch their infant in the special-care nursery because of the fear of infection. We can easily imagine how a mother's confidence in caring for her newborn might be jeopardized after being limited for 6 to 8 weeks to watching the baby through a transparent incubator shield. As investigators began to recognize the importance of the very earliest social interactions between mother and infant, the situation changed. A group at Stanford University took the daring step of permitting parents to handle their infants in the special-care nursery and demonstrated that no increased danger of infection resulted (Barnett et al., 1970). Subsequent work demonstrated that handling enhanced mothers' self-confidence in responding to their babies (Leiderman & Seashore, 1975; Seashore et al., 1973).

A related factor is the lack of stimulation that infants often experience when they must spend time in the hospital. The temperature-controlled, patternless plastic chambers in which they are placed deprive them not only of human physical contact but of sensory input as well. As we have seen, intervention procedures introduced by NICUs have begun to address this problem.

There is concern, however, that, for some premature babies, added stimulation becomes overstimulation and has a negative rather than a positive effect. Investigators now tend to suggest that each baby must be considered individually. One creative idea is to provide stimulation that the babies themselves can decide to experience or avoid. For example, one investigator placed a "breathing" teddy bear in the baby's bed, which the baby could either contact or avoid. Premature babies who had the breathing bear tended to stay near it more than those who had a non-breathing bear, and they spent a longer amount of time in quiet sleep (Thoman, 1993; Thoman, Ingersoll, & Acebo, 1991).

Another factor that may affect the development of the preterm infant is the family's socioeconomic status. By 2 to 3 years of age, children born preterm into families that have strong financial resources seem indistinguishable from children born at term. These more positive outcomes for infants of more advantaged parents might be related to the reduction of other stresses in the parents' lives—fewer financial problems and lower incidence of sickness, for example—and to their better access to and use of health and psychological professionals. Family stresses tend to reduce the emotional availability of parents for their infants, their tolerance for negative behavior, and their ability to organize family tasks (Hoy, Bill, & Sykes, 1988). Enrichment pro-

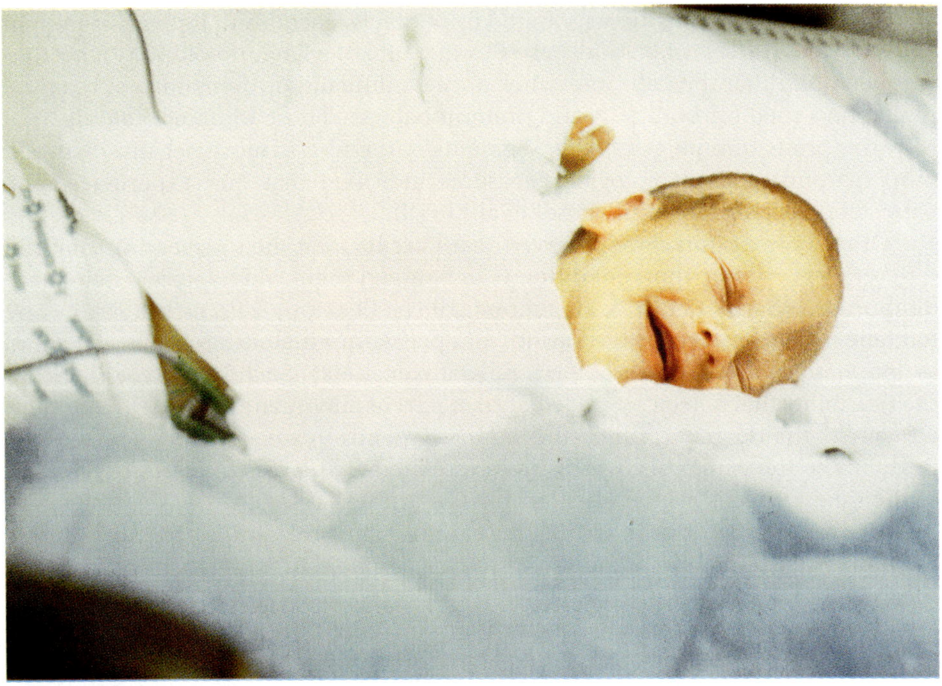

Premature babies benefit from opportunities to control their exposure to a mild stimulus that changes, such as the "breathing bear" discussed in the text.

grams have been shown to be effective for families with low-birth-weight infants both for increasing the child's cognitive capabilities and for reducing behavior problems at 2 and 3 years of age (Brooks-Gunn et al., 1993; Dudley et al., 1993).

The contextual factors we have considered here affect the development of all babies. What recent research has told us is that these factors are especially important for babies born at risk (Hack et al., 1995).

✓ To Recap...

Labor begins with regular contractions of the uterus and passes through three stages. Most births proceed normally, and technological advances have helped improve the outcomes of those that do not. Cultures vary considerably in their attitudes and practices regarding birth.

Psychologists have been particularly interested in identifying babies born at risk for developmental problems. One indicator of risk is maternal and family characteristics. Whether the mother receives prenatal care from a physician seems especially important. A second indicator of risk is physical compromise of the newborn, most frequently identified by low birth weight. Low-birth-weight babies have more difficulties with breathing, which may lead to anoxia.

Babies have low birth weights for two reasons: preterm babies were born before the end of the normal gestation period; SGA babies are small for their gestational age because of growth retardation in the womb. Whatever the cause of low birth weight, these babies show differences from normal-weight infants, and these differences may persist for several years. However, at least for preterm babies, the differences may disappear by the early school years.

A third indicator of risk is provided by newborn assessments. These tests include the Apgar exam, the most common and easiest to use; the Prechtl test, which adds more neurological functions; and the Brazelton Neonatal Behavioral Assessment Scale, the most comprehensive test. No single risk indicator predicts intelligence or personality especially well, but the number of risk factors seems to be a good predictor of developmental problems.

The Organized Newborn

Look at a newborn baby and you will see that the baby's face, if he is awake, changes expression rapidly for no apparent reason and his legs and arms often flail around with no seeming purpose or pattern. A sleeping baby is less active, but her sleep is punctuated by twists, turns, startles, and grunts—a fairly unorganized picture. Seeing these behaviors, you can understand why, during most of the history of child psychology, people considered the newborn a passive and helpless creature whose activity was essentially random. Any organized behavior depended on external stimulation. Is it true that the newborn comes into the world with no organized patterns of behavior for sleeping, eating, getting the caregiver's attention, or even moving? Must caregivers teach the baby all these things?

Research on newborn behavior since the 1960s has drastically changed our views. Certainly the newborn is not as coordinated or predictable as the 2-year-old, but the behavior of the newborn is neither random nor disorganized. The newborn possesses natural rhythms of activity that generate patterns of sleeping and wakefulness, eating, and motion. Moreover, the newborn is equipped with many reflexive responses to external stimulation and a few organized behavioral patterns for investigating and controlling the environment through looking, sucking, and crying.

States of Alertness

Often the first question grandparents and friends ask the nurse about the new baby is, "Is the baby asleep or awake?" But there are other possibilities. Forty years ago, Peter Wolff, at the Harvard Medical School, carefully watched several newborn babies for many hours and was struck by how much their levels of alertness varied, yet how similar these levels were from one baby to another (Wolff, 1959, 1966). He captured these observations by defining six states of infant alertness: (1) quiet, or deep, sleep; (2) active, or light, sleep; (3) drowsiness; (4) alert inactivity; (5) alert activity; and (6) crying. These states are described in Table 6.2.

Table 6.2
States of the Infant

State	*Characteristics*
Deep Sleep	Regular breathing; eyes closed with no eye movements; no activity except for occasional jerky movements
Light sleep	Eyes closed but rapid eye movements can be observed; activity level low; movements are smoother than in deep sleep; breathing may be irregular
Drowsiness	Eyes may open and close but look dull when open; responses to stimulation are delayed, but stimulation may cause state to change; activity level varies
Alert inactivity	Eyes open and bright; attention focused on stimuli; activity level relatively low
Alert activity	Eyes open; activity level high; may show brief fussiness; reacts to stimulation with increases in startles and motor activity
Crying	Intense crying that is difficult to stop; high level of motor activity

Electroencephalograph (EEG)
An instrument that measures brain activity by sensing minute electrical changes at the top of the skull.

Rapid eye movement (REM) sleep
A stage of light sleep in which the eyes move rapidly while the eyelids are closed.

Several aspects of these states and how they change with age make them useful for understanding early development, for assessing the effects of various factors—such as teratogens—on development, and for comparing one infant with another. Recordings of brain activity by an **electroencephalograph (EEG)** reveal that states become increasingly distinct with age. Investigators believe this change reflects how the baby's brain matures (Sadeh & Anders, 1993). Similar information can also be obtained by examining the ease with which babies move from one state to the next (Halpern, MacLean, & Baumeister, 1995).

The time distribution of sleep states changes rapidly with age, as shown in Figure 6.2 (Groome et al., 1997). Whereas the fetus of 25 weeks gestational age engages almost exclusively in active sleep, the newborn spends only about half the time in active sleep and half in quiet sleep. By 3 months, quiet sleep occurs twice as much as active sleep (Berg & Berg, 1987; Gardner, Karmel, & Magnano, 1992). In active sleep, babies periodically move and breathe irregularly, but the most notable feature is that they frequently move their eyes back and forth with their eyelids closed (as do adults), so this sleep state is often called **rapid eye movement**, or **REM, sleep**.

The shift from dominantly active, or REM, sleep to dominantly quiet sleep has aroused considerable speculation about the function of REM sleep. In the adult, REM sleep constitutes only about 20% of total sleep time and is associated with

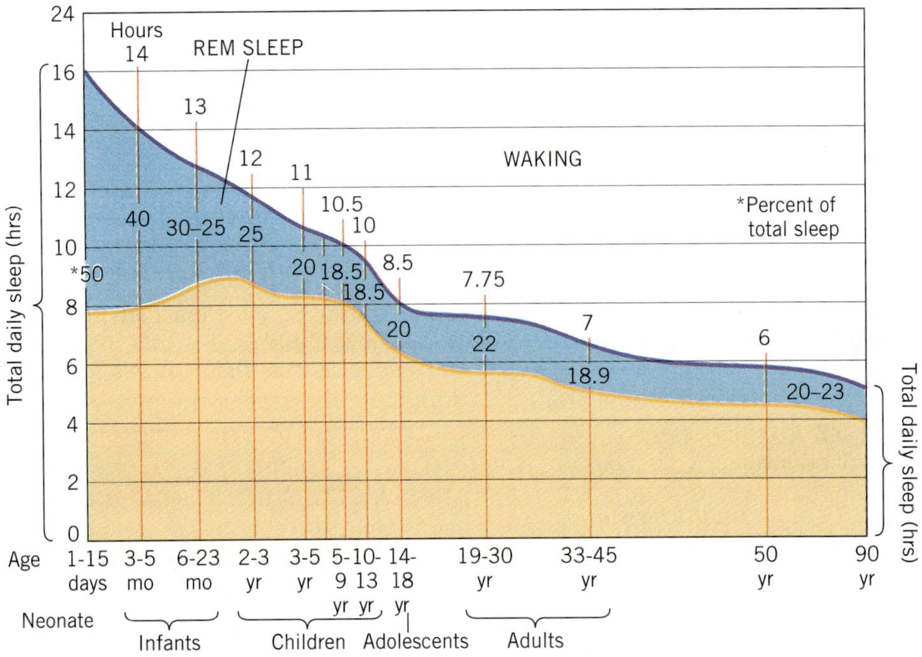

Figure 6.2
Although the total amount of sleep time declines with age, the drop is most noticeable for REM sleep during the first 2 to 3 years of life. The amount of quiet sleep is about the same for newborns and 3-year-olds, but the percentage of sleep time spent in the REM state declines from around 50% to around 25% over this time span. From "Ontogenic Development of the Human Sleep–Dream Cycle" by H. P. Roffwarg, J. N. Muzio, and W. C. Dement, 1966, *Science, 152* p. 608. Copyright © 1966 by the AAAS. Reprinted by permission. The figure reproduced here contains revisions made by Roffwarg et al. since the original publication in 1966.

dreaming. Research suggests that the high rate of REM activity in early development reflects a kind of internal motor that keeps nerve pathways active until the baby receives enough stimulation from the external world (Kandel & O'Dell, 1992). Consistent with this idea is the finding that babies who have longer awake periods, which presumably provide needed stimulation, have shorter REM periods during sleep (Boismer, 1977; Denenberg & Thoman, 1981).

Since the organization of sleep states—how well they are differentiated and their time distribution—reflects brain maturation, we might expect babies at risk to be less organized than other infants. Indeed, state organization is affected in babies of alcoholic and drug-addicted mothers, and babies who are unstable in their time distribution across various states between 2 and 5 weeks of life are more likely than are relatively stable babies to have later medical and behavioral problems (Halpern et al., 1995).

To this point, we have talked about infant states in terms of the internal processes they reflect. But states also play an important role in infants' interactions with the environment. When babies are in states of alertness—rather than crying, asleep, or drowsy—they are more receptive to stimuli and learn more readily (Berg & Berg, 1987; Thoman, 1990). Thus, states affect the impact of external events. External events, in turn, can affect an infant's state. For example, a crying baby will often shift to a quiet, alert state if picked up by an adult and gently rocked up and down on the adult's shoulder (Korner & Thoman, 1970; Pederson & Ter Vrugt, 1973).

Another external factor is where the baby sleeps. Although sleep and its various states have a strong biological basis, it is not clear where nature intended babies to sleep. In the United States, most middle-class families have babies sleep by themselves in their own beds. Among many lower-class families and some ethnic groups—such as African-Americans—babies are more likely to sleep with their parents. The most common reason given by middle-class mothers for the separate sleeping arrangements is the desire to build the infant's independence. The most common reasons given by mothers who prefer sharing a bed are the desire to develop a closeness with the infant as well as the ease of feeding and caregiving (Kawasaki et al., 1994; Lozoff, Wolff, & Davis, et al., 1984; Morelli et al., 1992). Not enough research has been directed toward this question to provide a good scientific answer as to what is best.

Rhythms

Most children and adults have regular patterns of daily activity. For the most part, they sleep at night, are awake during the day, and eat at fairly predictable times. We can say that their daily patterns obey a repeating rhythm. On the other hand, one need only look at the red, tired eyes of a new parent to know that the newborn baby's habits are not so regular. Can we conclude, then, that the baby enters the world with no rhythms at all and must be taught by the parents when to eat, when to sleep, and when to wake? Not at all. Newborn babies are rhythmic creatures. The newborn's biological clock just seems to tick at a different rate than ours, and it gradually shifts into synchrony with ours as the baby develops.

The newborn's states, like the adult's, occur as rhythms cycling within other rhythms. The baby engages in a cycle of active and quiet sleep that repeats each 50 to 60 minutes. This cycle is coordinated with a cycle of wakefulness that occurs once every 3 to 4 hours (Parmelee & Sigman, 1983). What produces this behavior? We might suspect that the sleep–wake cycle reflects a cycle of hunger or of external disruption by caregivers. However, the cycle seems to be internally controlled. Even before the first feeding and with external distractions held to a minimum, newborns still display roughly these same sleep–wake cycles (Emde, Swedberg, & Suzuki, 1975).

Much to the relief of their parents, infants gradually adapt to the 24-hour light–dark cycle. Sleep periods become longer at night, usually around 5 or 6 weeks of age, as awake periods lengthen during the day. By 12 to 16 weeks, the pattern of sleeping at night and being awake during the day is fairly well established, even though the baby still sleeps about the same amount as the newborn (Berg & Berg, 1987).

Although the rhythms of the newborn seem to be biologically programmed, they are not free from environmental influences. For example, newborn babies who stay in their mothers' rooms in the hospital begin to display day–night differences in their sleep cycles earlier than babies who stay in the hospital nursery. These rooming-in babies also spend more time in quiet sleep and less time crying than do babies in nursery groups (Keefe, 1987). Apparently, prenatal experience can also affect rhythmic activity. Newborns who have alcoholic or drug-dependent mothers have more difficulty synchronizing their various sleep–wake rhythms and adapting to the night–day cycle than do other babies (Parmelee & Sigman, 1983; Sander et al., 1977).

Reflexes

We have seen that the newborn baby has identifiable states of alertness and that these states fit into overall rhythms. Newborns are also equipped with a number of behaviors and behavior patterns. Some of these, called **reflexes**, are highly stereotyped and occur as brief responses to specific stimuli. As we discussed in Chapter 2, reflexes have evolved in humans over millions of years because they serve (or served at one time) an important survival function.

Reflex
An automatic and stereotyped response to a specific stimulus.

Reflexes are not of interest only to psychologists trying to understand early development; they can have applied value as well because their presence or absence provides information about the baby's brain and nervous system. For example, an infant should reflexively bend to the left side when the doctor runs a thumb along the left side of the baby's spinal column. If this reflex occurs on the left side but not on the right side, it may indicate damage to the nerves on the right side.

Some reflexes last throughout life, but the reflexes of most interest here are those that disappear in the first year of life, because their disappearance indicates the development of more advanced brain functions. Table 6.3 lists some of the more common reflexes as well as the stimuli that produce them and their developmental course. We discuss only a few of these reflexes here.

Rooting reflex
The turning of the infant's head toward the cheek at which touch stimulation is applied, followed by opening of the mouth.

The **rooting reflex** is the first to appear. If we stroke a newborn's cheek next to the mouth, the baby will turn the head to that side and search with the mouth. This reflex is adaptive in an evolutionary sense because it helps the baby find the nipple of the mother's breast for feeding. This reflex appears as early as 2 to 3 months gestational age and represents the first indication that the fetus can respond to touch. Rooting generally disappears in infants around 3 to 4 months of age (Peiper, 1963).

Palmar reflex
The infant's finger grasp of an object that stimulates the palm of the hand.

The **palmar reflex** is elicited by pressure against the palm of a newborn's hand, such as with a finger, as shown in Figure 6.3*a*. The baby responds by grasping the finger tightly. Newborns are capable of supporting their own weight in this manner—a potentially important ability for babies of our evolutionary ancestors, who needed to cling tightly to the fur of their mothers as they moved along through the jungle. This reflex disappears at 3 to 4 months of age, and children will not again be able to support their own weight until around 4 or 5 years of age (McGraw, 1940).

Moro reflex
The infant's response to loss of head support or to a loud sound, consisting of thrusting the arms and fingers outward, followed by clenching the fists and making a grasping motion of the arms across the chest.

The **Moro reflex** consists of a series of reactions to sudden sound or the loss of head support. The infant first thrusts her arms outward, opens her hands, arches

(a) (b) (c)

Figure 6.3
Some newborn reflexes: (a) palmar, (b) stepping, and (c) tonic neck.

her back, and stretches her legs outward, then she brings her arms inward in an embracing motion with fingers formed into fists. The absence of a Moro reflex is a sign of brain damage, and its failure to disappear after 6 or 7 months of age is also cause for concern. Moro, who first described the reflex (Moro, 1918), argued that it was a relic of an adaptive reaction by primates to grab for support while falling, but others have disputed this argument (e.g., Peiper, 1963). As with many newborn reflexes, the evolutionary roots of the Moro reflex are not certain.

Stepping reflex
The infant's response to pressure on the soles of the feet, consisting of stepping (flexing) movements.

When pressure is applied to the soles of the feet, the baby will flex her legs up and down in the **stepping reflex**, shown in Figure 6.3b. This reflex usually disappears by around 3 months of age. The disappearance of the reflex at this time

Table 6.3
Newborn Reflexes

Name	*Testing Method*	*Response*	*Developmental Course*	*Significance*
Blink	Flash a light in infant's eyes	Closes both eyes	Permanent	Protects eyes from strong stimuli
Biceps reflex	Tap on the tendon of the biceps muscle	Contracts the biceps muscle	Brisker in the first few days than later	Absent in depressed infants or those with congenital muscular disease
Knee jerk or patellar tendon reflex	Tap on the tendon below the patella or kneecap	Quickly extends or kicks the knee	More pronounced in the first 2 days than later	Absent or difficult to obtain in depressed infants or infants with muscular disease; exaggerated in hyperexcitable infants
Babinski	Gently stroke the side of the infant's foot from heel to toes	Flexes the big toe dorsally; fans out the other toes; twists foot inward	Usually disappears near the end of the 1st year; replaced by plantar flexion of big toe in the normal adult	Absent in infants with defects of the lower spine; retention important in diagnosing poor myelination of motor tracts of the brainstem in older children and adults
Withdrawal reflex	Prick the sole of the infant's foot with a pin	Flexes leg	Constantly present during the first 10 days; present but less intense later	Absent with sciatic nerve damage
Plantar or toe grasp	Press finger against the ball of the infant's foot	Curls all toes under	Disappears between 8 and 12 months	Absent in infants with defects of the lower spinal cord
Tonic neck reflex	Lay baby down on back	Turns head to one side; baby assumes fencing position, extending arm and leg on this side, bending opposite limbs, and arching body away from direction faced	Found as early as 28th prenatal week; frequently present in first weeks, disappears by 3 or 4 months	Paves way for eye-hand coordination

seems to result from the increasing weight of the baby's legs. Research has shown that if the legs are supported in water, the reflex can be demonstrated in older infants (Thelen & Fisher, 1982, 1983). Similarly, if the reflex is practiced, it can become stronger (Zelazo, Zelazo, & Kolb, 1972; Zelazo et al., 1993).

Tonic neck reflex
The infant's postural change when the head is turned to the side, consisting of extension of the arm on that side and clenching of the other arm in what looks like a fencer's position.

A few reflexes of the newborn occur in the absence of any obvious external stimulation. The **tonic neck reflex**, or fencer's position, is an example. When the head turns to one side, the newborn tends to extend the arm on that side while flexing the arm on the opposite side, as shown in Figure 6.3*c*.

Although there is an automatic quality to reflexes, environmental factors do affect them. For example, a baby who has just nursed may not show a rooting

Table 6.3
Newborn Reflexes

Name	*Testing Method*	*Response*	*Developmental Course*	*Significance*
Palmar or hand grasp	Press rod or finger against the infant's palm	Grasps the object with fingers; can suspend own weight for brief period of time	Increases during the 1st month and then gradually declines and is gone by 3 or 4 months	Weak or absent in depressed babies
Moro reflex (embracing reflex)	Make a sudden loud sound; let the baby's head drop back a few inches; or suspend baby horizontally, then lower hands rapidly about six inches and stop abruptly	Extends arms and legs and then brings arms toward each other in a convulsive manner; fans hands out at first, clenches them slightly	Begins to decline in third month, generally gone by fifth month	Absent or constantly weak Moro indicates serious disturbance of the central nervous system; may have originated with primate clinging
Stepping or automatic walking reflex	Support baby in upright position with bare feet on flat surface; move the infant forward and tilt him slightly from side to side	Makes rhythmic stepping movements	Disappears in 2 to 3 months	Absent in depressed infants
Swimming reflex	Hold baby horizontally on stomach in water	Alternates arm and leg movements, exhaling through the mouth	Disappears at 6 months	Demonstrates coordination of arms and legs
Rooting reflex	Stroke cheek of infant lightly with finger or nipple	Turns head toward finger, opens mouth, and tries to suck finger	Disappears at approximately 3 to 4 months	Absent in depressed infants; appears in adults with severe cerebral palsy
Babkin or palmarmental reflex	Apply pressure on both of baby's palms when lying on back	Opens mouth, closes eyes, and turns head to midline	Disappears in 3 to 4 months	Inhibited by general depression of central nervous system

Source: Excerpted from *Child Psychology: A Contemporary Viewpoint*, 2nd ed. (Table 4.1), by E. M. Hetherington and R. D. Parke, 1979, New York: McGraw-Hill. Copyright © 1979 by McGraw-Hill, Inc. Excerpted by permission of the McGraw-Hill Company.

response, and most other reflexes are also somewhat sensitive to the baby's biological state. Still, reflexes are generally tied to specific stimuli and are rarely seen in their absence. This is not the case for the behaviors we refer to as congenitally organized behaviors.

Congenitally Organized Behaviors

Not all early behaviors are responses to stimulation. The newborn also initiates activities and is capable of sustaining them over considerable periods of time. Such activities are called **congenitally organized behaviors**. Specifically, looking, sucking, and crying are three well-organized behaviors that, unlike reflexes, are often not elicited by a discrete, identifiable stimulus. These behaviors provide infants with means to get nourishment and to control and explore their environments.

Congenitally organized behavior
Early behaviors of newborns that do not require specific external stimulation and that show more adaptability than simple reflexes.

Looking The newborn's looking behavior is often unexpected (Crouchman, 1985). New parents may be amazed when their baby, even in the first moments of life, will lie with eyes wide open, seemingly examining them and other objects in the room. In a room that is dimly lit, the light coming through the window may be an especially attractive target. And babies do not simply respond reflexively to light when they look. As early as 8 hours after birth, and in complete darkness, babies open their eyes wide and engage in frequent eye movements, as though they were searching for something to explore (Haith, 1991). We will have more to say about early perception in the next chapter. Our point now is that looking behavior shows that newborns possess tools for acting on their world, not just for reacting to it.

Sucking In some respects, sucking seems to fit the definition of a reflex, since it is easily elicited by oral stimulation, at least when the newborn is hungry. In other respects, though, it is not reflexlike. Babies may suck spontaneously, even during sleep. The sucking act also is not stereotyped, but adapts to a variety of conditions, such as how much fluid can be obtained with each suck. In addition, sucking is sensitive to sensory events. Babies who are sucking tend to stop when they see something start to move or when they hear a voice (Haith, 1966). These characteristics set sucking apart from simpler reflexes.

Sucking is a marvelously coordinated act. Babies suck one to two times each second, and each suck requires an orchestration of actions. Milk is extracted from the nipple both by suction (as with a straw) and by a squeezing action, and these actions must be coordinated with both breathing and swallowing. Some babies show excellent sucking coordination from birth, whereas others may require a week or so of practice (Peiper, 1963).

No other newborn behavior seems to serve quite as many purposes as sucking. It is, of course, a way to get nourishment, but it is also a primary means by which babies begin to explore the world. Even at birth, many babies suck their fingers and thumbs, and it appears that some newborns have even practiced this as fetuses. Later, they will continue to explore with their mouths as they become better able to grasp and find new objects (Rochat, 1989).

Sucking also seems to buffer the infant against pain and overstimulation. Agitated babies quiet when they suck on a pacifier, especially when it contains a sweet substance (Smith & Blass, 1996). One study found that crying during circumcision was reduced by about 40% when babies were permitted to suck on a pacifier (Gunnar, Fisch, & Malone, 1984). This finding confirms experimentally what civilizations have known for some time; for thousands of years, Jewish babies have been encouraged to suck on wine-soaked cotton during circumcision. Finally, sucking plays a social role in the process of emotional attachment between infant and mother (Bowlby, 1969; Crook, 1979).

Crying A third organized behavior of the newborn is crying. Like sucking, crying coordinates various components of behavior, such as breathing, vocalizing, and muscular tensing, in a rhythmic pattern. Psychologists have been interested in crying both as a diagnostic tool and for its social role.

Wolff (1969) distinguished three types of cries in the very young infant: a hungry, or basic, cry; a mad, or angry, cry; and a pain cry. The first two are similar in pitch but different in that the mad cry forces more air through the vocal cords, producing more variation. The pain cry has a more sudden onset with a much longer initial burst and a longer period of breath holding between cries. Other researchers have identified the types as expressing hunger, fear, or pain (Wasz-Hockert, Michelsson,

& Lind, 1985). Adults have little difficulty in distinguishing various cries based on their timing and patterning (Zeskind, Klein, & Marshall, 1992). We will discuss the role of crying as an early form of communication again in Chapter 11.

The crying of healthy, newborn infants is fairly characteristic in both pitch and rhythm. An unusual cry, therefore, can signal problems. Babies who are immature or brain damaged produce higher-frequency cries with abnormal timing patterns (Lester, 1976, 1984). Babies who show evidence of malnutrition at birth or who are preterm often also have higher-pitched cries with abnormal timing patterns (Zeskind, 1983). Infants who have genetic anomalies, such as the *cri du chat* syndrome (in which the infant's cry sounds like that of a cat) and Down syndrome, have atypical cries as well.

Some investigators have speculated that babies influence early social relationships with their caregivers by the nature of their cries (Lester, 1984). Cries of babies at risk are perceived as more grating, piercing, and aversive than the cries of other babies, and "difficult" babies seem to have more aversive cries than "easy" babies (Lounsbury & Bates, 1982). As noted earlier, cries experienced as aversive may set in motion a negative cycle between baby and caregiver.

More broadly, crying is a major factor in early social interaction because it is one of the infant's basic tools for getting the caregiver to come closer. Because adults dislike hearing babies cry, they typically do something to quiet the crying baby. Parents may try various techniques for soothing a baby who fusses for no apparent reason (Emde, Gaensbauer, & Harmon, 1976). Picking the baby up is an effective quieter, swaddling, or wrapping a baby snugly in a blanket, and pacifiers are also sometimes effective, as is continuous or rhythmic sound (Brackbill et al., 1966; Campos, 1989). Even in the first month of life, crying may be controlled by events other than food or pain relief; infants often stop crying if they have interesting things to watch or sounds to listen to (Wolff, 1969). Babies learn very early to use crying to control the social environment, sometimes producing what Wolff has called the fake cry, to get the caregiver's attention, as early as 3 weeks of age.

The three congenitally organized behaviors of looking, sucking, and crying are gradually fine-tuned by the infant to explore and control the physical and social world more effectively. Other skills, such as reaching, grasping, and walking, also play a role, and elaborate emotional behaviors, such as smiling and laughing, will enrich the social interactions of the developing infant. We will leave the more social components of early development to Chapter 12 and consider next some other physical accomplishments of the infant.

✓ *To Recap...*

The activity of newborns is not random, but is organized into states, rhythms, reflexes, and congenitally organized behaviors. The newborn's level of alertness is typically categorized according to six states, varying from quiet sleep to crying. Several aspects of these states change with age, providing information about early development. Although state organization is controlled primarily by internal factors, state can be affected by external stimulation. Conversely, the baby's response to stimulation is affected by the state the baby is in.

The newborn's states occur in rhythmic cycles. A basic rest–activity cycle is coordinated with a longer sleep–wake cycle. With age, the baby gradually adapts to the 24-hour, light–dark cycle.

Other evidence for behavioral organization is found in reflexes. Although some reflexes last through life, others, such as the rooting, palmar, Moro, and tonic neck reflexes, disappear during the first year. These reflexes and their developmental courses provide important information about the baby's central nervous system.

Congenitally organized behaviors such as looking, crying, and sucking are available at birth but, unlike reflexes, are not easily attributable to a particular stimulus. These are examples of inborn behaviors that the infant possesses for exploring and controlling the physical and social aspects of the world.

Motor Development

Looking, crying, and sucking are limited in their ability to control the environment. Imagine for a moment that you cannot move around or grasp and manipulate objects so that you must depend on others to provide interesting things for you to inspect. This is the state of the newborn baby. Before long, however, these limitations disappear and the infant is a go-for-everything, grab-anything 9-month-old.

The acquisition of motor skills is a key feature of development in human infancy, in effect giving the baby power tools for acquiring knowledge and gaining a sense of competence and self-control. These skills continue to development well into the childhood years, when they play important roles in other aspects of development.

Motor development can be divided into two general categories. The first comprises **postural development** and **locomotion**, which involve control of the trunk of the body and coordination of the arms and legs for moving around. The second category is **prehension**, the ability to use the hands as tools for such purposes as eating, building, and exploring.

Postural development
The increasing ability of the baby to control parts of their body, especially the head and the trunk.

Locomotion
The movement of a person through space, such as walking and crawling.

Prehension
The ability to grasp and manipulate objects with the hands.

Proximodistal
Literally, near to far. This principle of development refers to the tendency of body parts to develop in a trunk-to-extremities direction.

Cephalocaudal
Literally, head to tail. This principle of development refers to the tendency of body parts to mature in a head-to-foot progression.

Principles and Sequences

The progression of motor skills tends to follow two general principles. The first principle is that development proceeds in a **proximodistal** direction—that is, body parts closest to the center of the body come under control before parts farther out.

The acquisition of early prehensile skills provides a good example. In the first weeks, the newborn can position himself toward an object, but cannot reach it. Although his arm movements seem random, the infant does direct some movements toward the object. In the second month of life, the baby sweeps his hand more deliberately near the object and begins to contact it more consistently. By 4 months of age, the infant can often grab at objects in a way that looks convincingly deliberate, but he uses the whole hand, with as yet little individual finger control. Gradually, the baby coordinates his fingers, so that at 6 months of age, he may reach with one hand for a cube with all fingers extended. Once the object is in hand, the baby may transfer the cube from hand to hand and rotate his wrist so as to see it from various perspectives. By 9 months, the baby can grasp a small pellet neatly between forefinger and thumb, and the 1-year-old can hold a crayon to make marks on paper.

The second principle is that control over the body develops in a **cephalocaudal**, or head-to-foot, direction. The progression of early postural and locomotor skills illustrates this principle.

The newborn who is placed on her stomach can move her head from side to side, although her head must be supported when she is lifted to someone's shoulder. The 3-month-old infant first holds her head erect and steady in the vertical position, and then pushes off the mattress with her hands to lift her head and shoulders and look. At 6 months, the baby can pull herself to a sitting position and may even be able to drag herself around a bit by her arms (crawling). But only at around 8 months can the baby use her legs to move herself forward with her belly off the floor (creeping). By the time the infant is 1 year old, the parents are likely to find her standing in the crib, rattling the side bars and perhaps distressed by being unable to figure out how to sit down again! Typically, soon after her first birthday, the baby is able to control the legs sufficiently to begin walking without support.

The top portion of Figure 6.4 shows a typical baby's stages of progression toward self-produced locomotion. The cephalocaudal progression just described is clearly evident, with the hands most active early on and responsibility for movement gradually transferring down to the legs. The lower portion of Figure 6.4 illustrates how babies can reach the same goal by following different routes (Largo et al., 1985). Some babies, for example, never crawl before walking. Psychologists now know that infants do not all develop a given motor skill (such as walking or standing) in the same way—a point to which we will return in a moment.

Table 6.4 presents some of the milestones of motor-skill acquisition, and, again, the proximodistal and cephalocaudal principles described earlier are apparent. The majority of babies follow these general sequences. It is important to note, however, that the ages given in the table are only approximate; some infants master these skills earlier, and others master them later. This variation in *when* motor skills are developed has taken on new significance since the recent discovery that infants also vary in *how* they develop specific skills. The result is that psychologists are now thinking about motor development very differently.

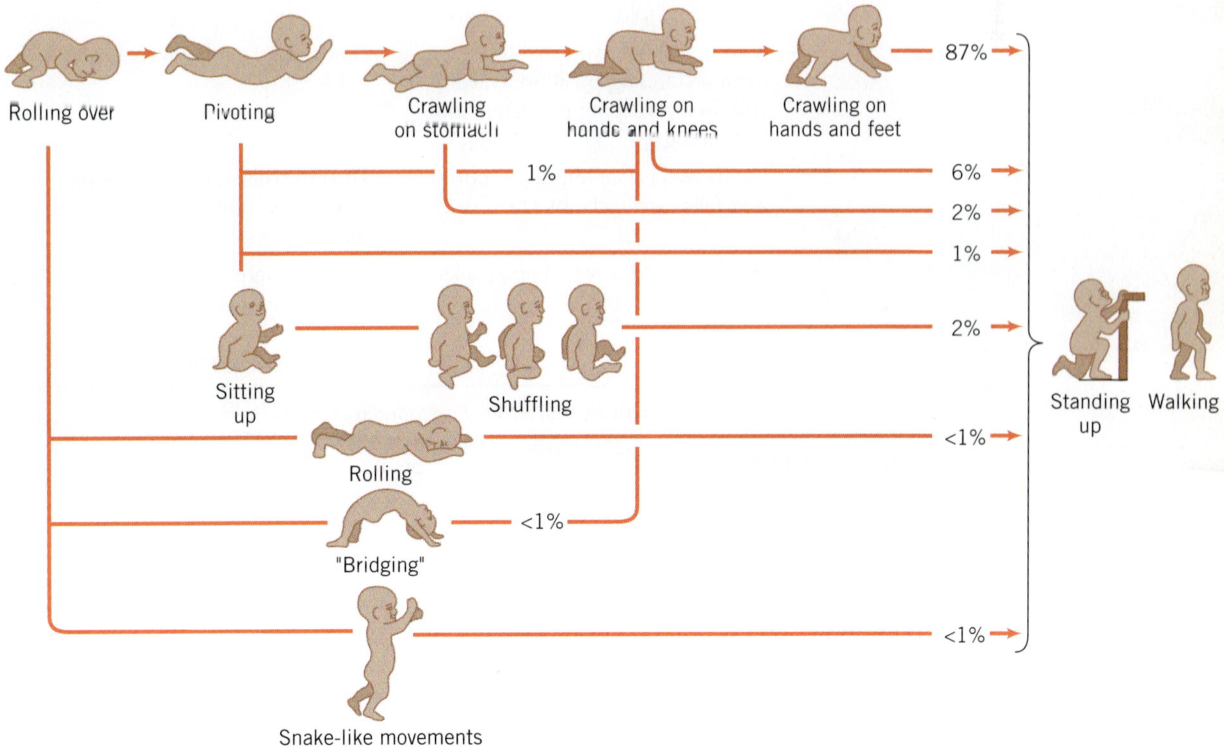

Figure 6.4
Most babies follow a fairly regular sequence in learning to walk, gradually transferring responsibility for movement from the arms to the feet. But some skip certain stages of crawling, and others never crawl at all. Adapted from "Early Development of Locomotion: Significance of Prematurity, Cerebral Palsy and Sex" by R. H. Largo, L. Molinari, M. Weber, L. C. Pinto, and G. Duc, 1985, *Developmental Medicine and Child Neurology, 27*, pp. 183–191, Figure 2. Copyright © 1985 by MacKeith Press. Adapted by permission.

Table 6.4
Motor Milestones

Age in Months	*Locomotion and Postural Development*	*Prehension and Manipulative Skills*
0	Turns head to side when lying on stomach; poor head control when lifted; alternating movements of legs when on stomach as if to crawl	Reflex grasp–retains hold on ring
3	Head erect and steady when held vertically; when on stomach, elevates head and shoulders by arms or hands or elbows; sits with support; anticipates adjustment of lifting	Grasps rattle; reaches for objects with two hands
6	Sits alone momentarily; pulls self to sitting position with adult's hand as puller; rolls from back to stomach	Grasps cube with simultaneous flexion of fingers; reaches with one hand and rotates the wrist; transfers cube between hands
9	Sits alone; pulls self to sitting position in crib; makes forward progress in prone position toward toy; walks holding on to furniture	Opposes thumb and finger in seizing cube; picks up pellet with forefinger and thumb
12	Stands alone; lowers self to sitting from a standing position; walks with help; creeping perfected; into everything	Holds crayon adaptively to make a mark
18	Walks well (since about 15 months) and falls rarely; climbs stairs or chair	Throws balls into box; scribbles vigorously; builds tower of three or more blocks
24	Walks up and down stairs; walks backward; runs	Places square in form board; imitates folding of paper; piles tower of six blocks; puts blocks in a row to form a train

Source: Based on information from *Manual for the Bayley Scales of Infant Development* by N. Bayley, 1969, New York: Psychological Corporation; and "The Denver Developmental Screening Test" by W. K. Frankenburg and J. Dodds, 1967, *Journal of Pediatrics, 71*, pp. 181–191.

The Nature and Nurture of Motor-Skills Development

Motor skills appear in a fairly predictable sequence and at similar times from one infant to another. Does this mean that sitting, crawling, reaching, and so forth are genetically programmed and simply emerge according to a biological set of instructions within the child? More and more, psychologists are answering this question no.

For one thing, different child-rearing experiences—often associated with different cultural practices—can clearly affect the timing of motor-skill development. For example, African infants generally sit, stand, and walk from one to several months earlier than do American infants (Konner, 1976; Super, 1981). But how the infants are dealt with, not heredity, seems to account for much of the difference.

One investigator reported that the Kipsigis in western Kenya believe their infants will not sit, stand, or walk without practice. Thus they energetically provide practice for their infants in these skills. For example, they dig a special hole in the ground using sand to reinforce their infants' sitting skills. In the development of skills that are not encouraged in this way, such as crawling and rolling over, Kenyan babies do not differ from American babies (Super, 1981). Mothers in Jamaica provide their babies with similar types of early physical stimulation, and these babies, too, develop motor skills earlier than do white infants in other cultures (Hopkins, 1991).

A glance back at Figure 6.4 shows a second reason that genetics cannot rigidly control motor development: Not all babies get to the same place by following the same path. Using the microgenetic method described in Chapter 3, researchers have carefully charted the development of motor skills in many individual infants. One study examined the development of reaching and grasping in four infants from ages 3 weeks to 1 year. Although all four eventually were able to reach out and grasp a toy, the manner in which they achieved this goal varied considerably from one child to the next (Thelen, Corbetta, & Spencer, 1996).

Kipsigis (in Kenya, Africa), believe that their infants need practice to learn certain postural skills, such as sitting. Photo used by permission of Dr. Charles Super, Pennsylvania State University.

A Dynamic Systems Approach These sorts of findings have prompted researchers to think about motor development in a new way. The **dynamic systems** approach was developed within the science of physics, but in developmental psychology it has been applied to children's motor development most extensively by Esther Thelen (Thelen, 1995; Thelen & Smith, 1994, 1998).

Dynamic systems Thelen's model of the development of motor skills, in which infants who are motivated to accomplish a task create a new motor behavior from their available physical abilities.

Thelen proposes that both nature and nurture contribute to the development of motor skills. Given that the emergence of these skills follows a predictable sequence for most babies, biological factors would seem to be strongly involved. Because practice and experience can affect motor-skills development and because children seem to acquire specific skills somewhat differently, environmental factors must be involved as well. Thelen argues that developmentalists need a model to help them understand the combined contributions of these two factors.

According to her dynamic systems analysis, the crucial element that unites the nature and nurture contributions and, more important, that stimulates the development of any particular skill, is the infant's "task." As babies mature biologically and cognitively, they become motivated to accomplish more and more things in the world around them. They seek to reach things, to grasp things, to move or shake things, to move themselves closer to things, and so on. These are the tasks of infancy. In order to accomplish such tasks, babies learn that various motor behaviors—such as those involving the arms, fingers, head, shoulders, and so on—can be useful.

Sometimes, though, the task requires a behavior that the child does not possess, so the infant must create such a behavior. To do this, the infant draws on the physical responses and abilities already available to her—what the baby can already do with arms, legs, hands, and fingers; muscle strength; balance and coordination; and so on. These abilities, of course, depend largely on age and biological maturation, but they also depend on the abilities the baby has created up to that point. A 9-month-old, therefore, should have many more physical responses and abilities on which to draw on than would, say, a 4-month-old. As a result, even when faced with the same task, the two children will likely create different new motor behaviors and so accomplish the task in different ways. Note that this is true not only for babies of different ages; *any* two children, even of the same age, will have different physical resources available to them as a result of both their genetic differences and their different experiences up to that point.

Thelen has found that as infants try to assemble a new motor behavior from the abilities currently available to them, they go through two stages. The first stage involves *exploration*, as the baby tries many different responses in a relatively random and uncoordinated fashion. In the second stage, *selection*, the baby learns exactly

Classics of Research

BOX 6.1

DOES MOTOR DEVELOPMENT DEPEND ON PRACTICE OR ON MATURATION

The nature–nurture debate regarding motor development is very old. During the 1920s and 1930s, the Zeitgeist in developmental psychology leaned heavily toward biological explanations of children's development. We saw in Chapter 1 that G. Stanley Hall's early evolutionary views were revised and resurrected during this period by his student Arnold Gesell at Yale University.

One major theoretical issue of the time concerned children's motor-skills acquisition. Learning-oriented psychologists, such as John B. Watson, argued that the crawling, climbing, and walking displayed by all normal infants represented reflexes conditioned through experience and practice. But Gesell and other biologically oriented theorists believed that these behaviors emerged according to a genetic timetable. Simple biological maturation, not conditioning and learning principles, guide their appearance.

To compare these two theories, Gesell developed a research method called the *co-twin control*, which used identical twins so that biological factors would be the same for the two infants. Gesell then selected one infant, whom he termed twin T, to receive training and extra practice each day at climbing stairs and related motor skills. The control infant, twin C, received no extra practice. After 6 weeks of training, twin T had become a very accomplished climber—but so had twin C. Gesell interpreted these findings to mean that the climbing skill must have been a result only of the children's biological development and not of their practice or experience (Gesell & Thompson, 1929). Studies of the same sort by other researchers appeared to confirm this conclusion (McGraw, 1935).

Later research, however, demonstrated that Gesell's conclusions had been a bit simplistic. Whereas extra training may not accelerate children's motor development, some amount of experience appears necessary for development to occur normally. Infants deprived of physical stimulation or the opportunity to move about were found to have delayed motor development (Dennis, 1960; Dennis & Najarian, 1957). When such infants were then given extra stimulation, their motor skills improved rapidly (Sayegh & Dennis, 1965).

The method of the co-twin control was a useful technique for comparing the effects of maturation and learning (which is, of course, a specific case of nature versus nurture). But as psychologists now agree, both of these processes are essential for normal motor development.

what works and what doesn't work and fine-tunes the many responses into an efficient package.

In short, the dynamic systems approach predicts that the motor skill a particular child develops at any given time will depend on (a) the task at hand, including how difficult it is and how motivated the child is to accomplish it, and (b) the physical abilities the child already possesses that form the starting point for creating the new behavior. The first of these (the task) is obviously very much influenced by the baby's environment and experiences; the second (the infant's physical abilities) is strongly influenced by the baby's biological maturation, but also by prior experiences.

Research Examples Thelen demonstrated these principles in a clever laboratory study. Three-month-old infants were placed in cribs on their backs, where they could see a mobile suspended above them. The babies' feet were individually attached with cords to the mobile in such a way that either single kicks or alternating kicking movements were effective in making the mobile move. At first the babies explored different leg movements, but after a short while they learned to produce the necessary kicking behaviors, presumably because they were motivated to accomplish the task of moving the mobile. Thelen next tied each baby's feet loosely together, so that the motor behavior that would best move the mobile was a combined two-foot kick. Again the infants explored various leg movements before finally selecting a coordinated leg action that was effective in achieving their purpose (Thelen, 1994).

Another example involves locomotion. Researchers at the University of Denver videotaped the motions of babies' body parts as they learned to creep across the floor to reach an object. As shown in Figure 6.5, the babies wore black bodysuits that had small reflective markers (the kind bicyclists wear at night) at the shoulder, elbow, and other joints. Reflections from these markers were read by a computer and analyzed to determine the path, velocity, and timing of the children's movements.

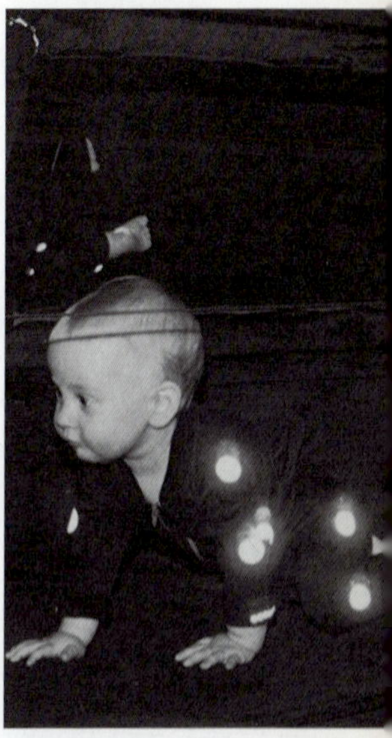

Figure 6.5
Scientists use computerized techniques to track light reflections on babies' joints to study how babies acquire skill in crawling. (Photo by permission of Dr. Janette Benson, University of Denver.)

The researchers found that once babies have the physical strength to move along with their bodies held above the floor, they begin to explore different patterns of arm-and-leg coordination and eventually settle on a diagonal pattern (right hand and left leg, then left hand and right leg) as the most efficient and stable way of locomotoring along, and thus reaching the object (Benson, 1990; Freedland & Bertenthal, 1994).

The essence of the dynamic systems approach, then, is that an infant does not simply wake up one morning with a new motor skill that has emerged spontaneously from her genetic code. Instead, a new skill is developed only when the infant is motivated to accomplish a task and has sufficient physical abilities to assemble into the necessary motor behavior.

Why, then, do most babies follow the same general sequence of motor development? The answer is probably simply that the physical resources of infants at the same points in development are reasonably similar and infants' tasks in any given culture tend also to be reasonably similar. On the other hand, Thelen's dynamic systems analysis shows why it also shouldn't be surprising that babies differ in the timing of their motor-skill development and in the manner in which they acquire these skills. Nature provides most of the raw material of motor development, but nurture determines the timing and direction development will take.

The Psychological Implications of Motor Development

Learning to move around is not only a motor accomplishment for babies; it also helps them organize their world (Bertenthal, Campos, & Kermoian, 1994). For example, babies' self-produced locomotion seems to contribute to their spatial understanding (discussed in more detail in Chapter 7). In one study, a toy was hidden in one of two colored containers placed in front of an infant. Infants with crawling experience were better able to find the toy under a variety of conditions—such as when the babies were placed on the opposite side of the table (thereby reversing the left or right location of the toy from the baby's perspective)—than were babies of the same age who had not yet mastered crawling (Benson & Uzgiris, 1985).

A baby's control over body movement also helps her understand the meaning of distance and heights. Crawling seems to be related to infants' learning to fear heights (Campos, Bertenthal, & Kermoian, 1992). Later, when babies can control their distance from their mothers or other caregivers, they use their motor skills to venture off (when they feel safe) or to return for comfort (when they feel insecure), as we will see again in Chapter 12 (Ainsworth, 1983).

Motor Development in Childhood

Motor development has attracted the most attention from infant researchers, but motor skills continue to develop during the childhood years (Gallahue, 1989).

An infant's first steps are a major milestone of development.

By the second birthday, most children have overcome their battle with gravity and balance and are able to move about and handle objects fairly efficiently. Their early abilities form the basis for skills that appear between 2 and 7 years of age. Three sets of fundamental movement skills emerge: locomotor movements, manipulative movements, and stability movements.

Locomotor movements include walking, running, jumping, hopping, skipping, and climbing. Manipulative movements include throwing, catching, kicking, striking, and dribbling. Stability movements involve body control relative to gravity and include bending, turning, swinging, rolling, head standing, and beam walking. These fundamental skills typically appear in all children and can be further refined by adolescents, who may develop exceptional skills as skaters, dancers, and gymnasts.

The refinement of motor skills depends a great deal on the development of the muscles and the nerve pathways that control them, but other factors are important as well. Motor skills depend in part on sensory and perceptual skills, for example, and children acquire many of their motor skills in play, which involves social and physical interaction.

One important aspect of motor skills is reaction time—the time required for the external stimulus to trigger the ingoing nerve pathways, for the individual to make a decision, and for the brain to activate the muscles through the outgoing nerve pathways. Reaction time improves substantially through the preschool and elementary school years, even for simple motor movements (Bard, Hay, & Fleury, 1990; Dougherty & Haith, 1993).

✓ *To Recap...*

Motor development can be categorized as (1) locomotion and postural development or (2) prehension. In both, control over the body develops in a cephalocaudal and a proximodistal direction.

Infants' motor-skills development follows a reasonably predictable sequence, but differences in the timing and manner in which skills are acquired have led psychologists to doubt that motor development is rigidly genetically programmed.

Thelen's dynamic systems approach incorporates the contributions of both nature and nurture to motor development. The infant's task is viewed as the element that stimulates the development of new motor behaviors, as the baby attempts to accomplish the desired task by creating the necessary motor skill from the available physical resources. This process involves two stages: exploration and selection.

The infant's growing ability to act on the world has major psychological consequences. The infant gains knowledge of the environment, including spatial relations, height, and distance.

Motor development beyond infancy consists of increasing coordination of fundamental movement skills, including locomotor, manipulative, and stability movements.

The Human Brain

It is hardly necessary to say that the brain is central to every aspect of development and every sort of human function. Already we have mentioned connections between behavior and neurological maturity in newborns. In this section, we look more directly at the structure and development of the brain.

Neuron
A nerve cell, consisting of a cell body, axon, and dendrites. Neurons transmit activity from one part of the nervous system to another.

Structure of the Brain

The brain contains approximately 100 billion nerve cells, or **neurons**; each of these cells has around 3,000 connections with other cells, which adds up to several quadrillion message paths. No one completely understands how all these communication paths work, but we do know quite a bit.

Like every other cell, each neuron has a nucleus and a cell body. But neurons are unique among cells in that they develop extensions on opposite sides, as shown in Figure 6.6. On the incoming side, the extensions, called **dendrites**, often form a tangle of strands that look like the roots of plants. The outgoing extension, called

Dendrite
One of a net of short fibers extending out from the cell body in a neuron; receives activity from nearby cells and conducts that activity to the cell body.

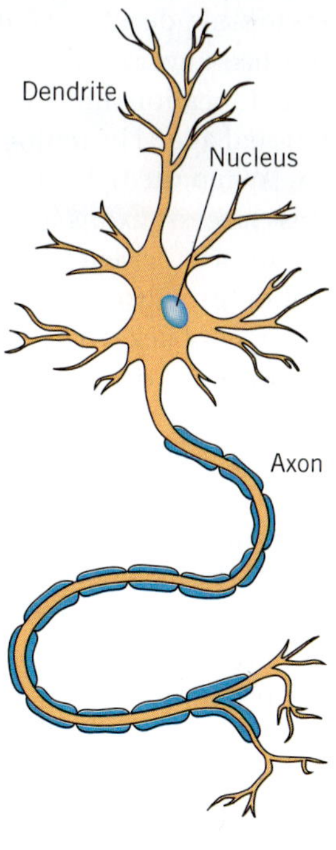

Figure 6.6
A nerve cell, or neuron.

Axon
A long fiber extending from the cell body in a neuron; conducts activity from the cell.

Myelin
A sheath of fatty material that surrounds and insulates the axon, resulting in speedier transmission of neural activity.

Synapse
The small space between neurons across which neural activity is communicated from one cell to another.

Neurotransmitter
A chemical that transmits electrical activity from one neuron across the synapse to another neuron.

Brain stem
The lower part of the brain, closest to the spinal cord; includes the cerebellum, which is important for maintaining balance and coordination.

Midbrain
A part of the brain that lies above the brain stem; serves as a relay station and as a control area for breathing and swallowing and houses part of the auditory and visual systems.

Cerebrum
The highest brain center; includes both hemispheres of the brain and the interconnections between them.

Cerebral cortex
The thin sheet of gray matter that covers the brain.

an **axon**, is more like a single strand. Axons usually extend farther from the cell than do dendrites and may be quite long. They are often covered by a sheath of a fatty substance, **myelin**, which insulates them and speeds message transmission. Cells do not quite touch one another, but are separated by fluid-filled gaps called **synapses**. Information is passed along a neuron as an electrical signal and crosses the synapse by the flow of chemicals called **neurotransmitters**.

The brain has three major parts. The **brain stem** includes the cerebellum, which controls balance and coordination. The **midbrain** serves as a relay station and controls breathing and swallowing. The **cerebrum**, the highest brain center, includes the left and right hemispheres and the bundle of nerves that connect them.

Of most interest to psychologists is the relatively thin shell of gray matter that covers the brain, called the **cerebral cortex**. This structure appears to be the most recently evolved part of the brain and is crucial for the functioning of the senses, language, memory, thought, and decision making, and the control of voluntary actions. Particular areas of the cerebral cortex have specific responsibilities, although some areas are more specialized than others. The cortex has more than 40 different functional areas. Some specialized tasks are identified in Figure 6.7.

Development of the Brain

Scientists only partially understand how the brain, in its amazing complexity, develops. It begins as a hollow tube. The neurons are generated along the outer walls of this tube and then travel to their proper locations (Kolb, 1989).

Scientists have identified three stages in this process. The first is *cell production.* Most neurons are produced between 10 and 26 weeks following conception, which means that the fetal brain generates these cells at a rate of 250,000 per minute. Cell production occurs from about 10 to 26 weeks, and then no more cells are produced for the rest of the person's life. The brain actually overproduces neurons and then trims them back by as much as 50% (Barinaga, 1993; Raff et al., 1993).

Once the cells have been produced near the center of the brain, they must migrate outward to their proper locations. This *cell migration* is the second stage of early brain development. How do the neurons know where to go? That question has not been answered. It seems likely that there is a chemical attraction between the target location and the migrating neuron. Migration is complete by 7 months gestational age (Huttenlocher, 1990).

When the neuron has found its home, the third stage, *cell elaboration,* begins. In this process, axons and dendrites form synapses with other cells. Cell elaboration continues for years after birth and produces as many as 100% more synapses than will eventually exist in the adult. Thus, as they are being formed, synapses are also being cut back. Experience plays an important role in the eventual sculpting of the connections of the brain through this process. Neurons and their connections compete for survival, and the ones that are used appear to survive, whereas those that are not used disappear (Diamond, 1991).

The fetus's brain grows faster than any other organ (except, perhaps, the eye), and this pace continues in infancy. At birth, the baby's body weight is only 5% of adult weight, whereas the brain weighs 25% of its adult value. By three years of age, the brain has attained 80% of its ultimate weight, compared with 20% for body weight (Morgan & Gibson, 1991; Tanner, 1990). However, the brain does not mature uniformly.

The first area to mature is the primary motor area. It may not be surprising to learn that within this area, the locations that control activity near the head mature first and maturation proceeds downward. This is the cephalocaudal direction in

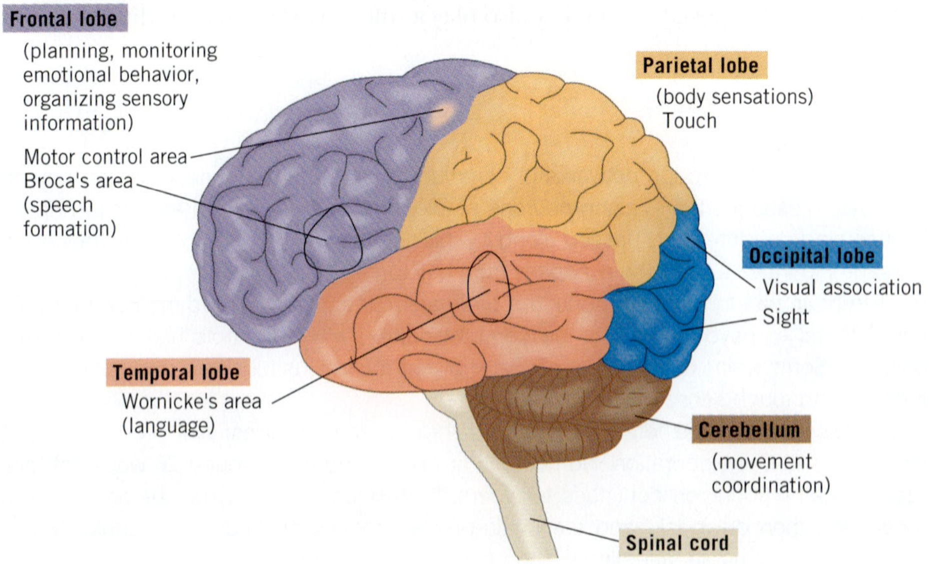

Figure 6.7
Some areas of the cerebral cortex are specialized for particular functions; this diagram shows only a few.

which motor control proceeds. Similarly, the areas that correspond to the arms mature earlier than those that control the fingers, which corresponds to the proximodistal principle.

Not far behind the motor area in maturity are the major sensory areas—touch, vision, and hearing, in that order. Myelin formation, or *myelination,* indicates how mature an area is. For example, the tracts that control fine-motor movement continue to myelinate until about age 4, whereas the areas concerned with attention and consciousness continue to myelinate up to puberty (Tanner, 1990).

Hemispheric Specialization

The two hemispheres of the brain are not perfectly symmetrical, but are *lateralized*—meaning that the left brain and the right brain are somewhat specialized. The left side of the brain is usually more specialized for language performance and the right side for spatial and mathematical tasks. Another way to think about this distinction is that the left side is more oriented to words and concepts, and the right side is more oriented to images. Pictures of the brain produced by a technique called *positron emission tomography (PET)* have confirmed that the left side of the brain is typically more active during language tasks and the right side more active during mathematical tasks. At the same time, however, these pictures show that most tasks, such as reading and listening, involve many areas of the brain (Corina, Vaid, & Bellugi, 1992; Posner et al., 1988).

Also, in some people, the right rather than the left side of the brain appears to be dominant for language, or there is mixed dominance. Left-handers more frequently fall into these categories than do right-handers. Problems with reading performance are sometimes associated with mixed or right-side dominance for language. Children who have *dyslexia* (reading difficulties), but who have otherwise normal or superior intelligence, are more likely to lack strong left-brain dominance than are normal readers.

Hemispheric specialization appears quite early. For example, electrical brain recordings in newborn infants reveal more activity in response to speech sounds on the left than on the right side (Molfese & Molfese, 1979). In Chapter 15, we will see that hemispheric specialization may also play a role in certain gender differences in development.

✓ To Recap...

The brain operates through networks of communication that involve neurons and neuron pathways. Messages travel along neurons as electrical signals, which are picked up by the incoming dendrites and passed along by the outgoing axons. Neurotransmitters allow messages to travel across the synapses from cell to cell.

The brain has three major parts: the brain stem, the midbrain, and the cerebrum. Of most interest to psychologists is the cerebral cortex, which controls higher-level brain functions. Some areas of the cortex are specialized for various functions, including visual, auditory, and touch sensation.

Development of the fetal brain passes through three stages: cell production, cell migration, and cell elaboration. No neurons are produced after around 26 weeks of fetal age, but cell elaboration continues for years. Both neurons and synapses are overproduced and then cut back, and the cutting-back process continues into adolescence. Experience plays a role, affecting which neurons and synapses will die.

The left and right hemispheres of the brain are specialized to some extent. Evidence suggests that even at birth, the left side of the brain is usually prepared to control language functioning and the right side to control spatial and mathematical functioning.

Physical Growth

Physical growth does not proceed at a steady rate, but slows and speeds up throughout childhood.

Growth is perhaps the most fundamental aspect of child development. It is continuous throughout childhood, but it does not happen uniformly. Arnold Gesell once commented that growth does not proceed as a balloon inflates, with each part expanding equally fast (Gesell, 1954). Rather, the overall rate of growth fluctuates during the growth years, with different body parts growing at different rates. In this section, we discuss the unfolding of whole-body growth, adolescent sex differentiation, and factors that affect physical growth and development.

Growth in Size

We saw in Chapter 5 that the fetus's growth rate is dramatically high, although it necessarily slows as birth approaches. This general slowing trend characterizes growth up to adolescence.

Figure 6.8 shows an average growth curve for males and females. Boys and girls are approximately the same height until around 10 years of age. A growth spurt typically occurs between 10 and 12 years of age for girls and between 12 and 14 years of age for boys. This age difference accounts for the common observation that girls, on average, are taller than boys in grades 7 and 8, a relation that permanently reverses a few years later. In North America and northern and western Europe, where good records have been kept, we know that height increases are just about completed by 15.5 years of age in girls and 17.5 years in boys; less than 2% of growth is added afterwards (Malina, 1990; Tanner, 1990).

Charts like that in Figure 6.8 may give the impression that there is, or should be, a normal growth rate. But few children exactly fit the averages on these charts. Although it is obvious that individuals reach different ultimate heights and weights, it may be less apparent that their *rates* of growth may also differ. To illustrate, Figure 6.9 shows a growth curve for three girls. Girl B reached menarche, the onset of menstruation, before girls A and C. She was taller than both at age 12, but was ulti-

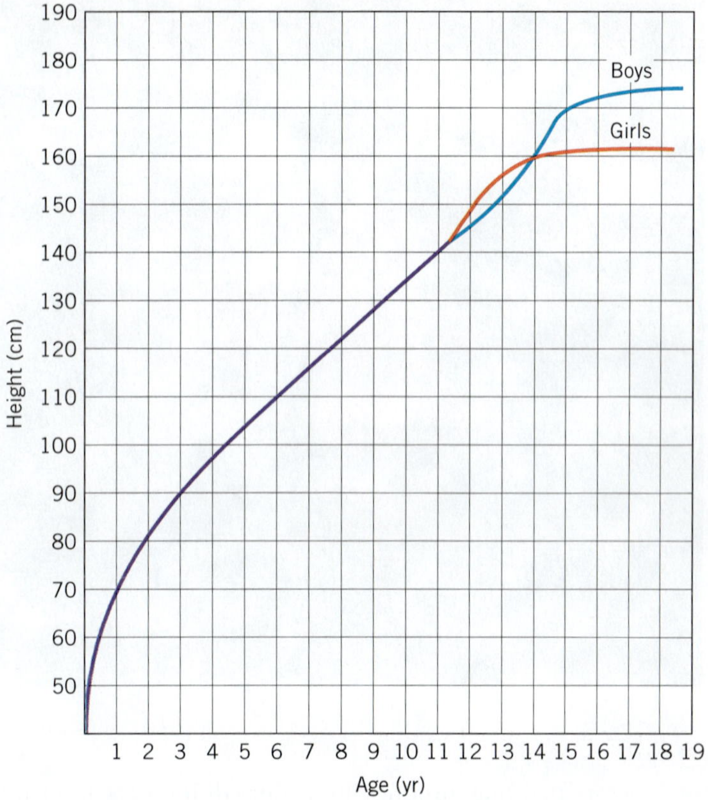

Figure 6.8
Typical male and female growth curves. Birth length doubles by around the 4th year, but growth slows, and length doubles again only around the 13th year. Adult height can be estimated by doubling the height of males at 24 months and of females at 18 months (Lowrey, 1978; Tanner, 1990). From "Standards for Growth and Growth Velocities" by J. M. Tanner, R. H. Whitehouse, and M. Takaishi, 1966, *Archives of Disease in Childhood, 41*, p. 467. Copyright © 1966 by *Archives of Disease in Childhood*. Reprinted by permission.

mately shorter than girl A. Such differences in age of onset of the growth spurt are likely to accompany differences in age of puberty. They may also have long-term implications for personality development, a topic to which we return later.

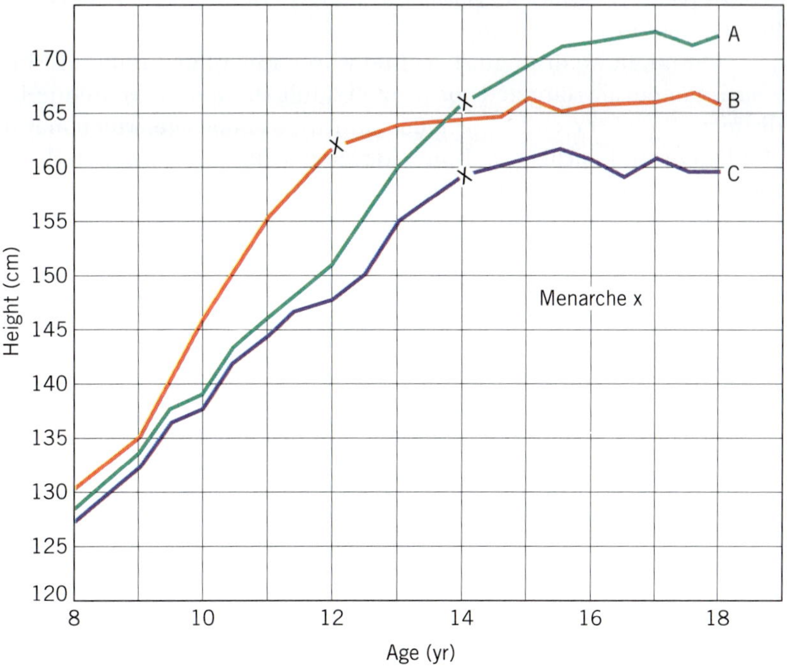

Figure 6.9
Curves showing the heights of three girls over time. Age of menarche is indicated by an *x*. Adapted from "Individual Patterns of Development" by N. Bayley, 1956, *Child Development, 27*, p. 52. Copyright © 1956 by The Society for Research in Child Development, Inc. Adapted by permission.

The pace of growth during childhood and adolescence is influenced by both nature and nurture factors.

Factors that may produce individual differences in growth rates include malnutrition and disease. For example, researchers recorded the growth rate of a child who suffered from two episodes of inadequate nutrition (Prader, Tanner, & von Harnack, 1963). The child's growth was severely affected. After the episodes were over, the child did not simply return to his normal rate of growth. Rather, he experienced a remarkable acceleration in growth, which returned him to his expected growth path. This *catch-up growth* is relatively common as an aftermath of disease or limited malnutrition (Tanner, 1963).

How might we distinguish a child whose rate of maturation is slow from a child who is genetically targeted for a small adult stature? A technique for making this distinction uses the child's skeletal maturity, or **bone age**, which may differ from the child's chronological age. Bones develop from the center and extend outward toward the bone ends, called the *epiphyses.* As a bone reaches its ultimate length, the epiphyses close and no further growth is possible. Scientists can use X-rays to determine how a child's bone development compares with that of his or her peers and approximately how much more growth remains to occur (Tanner, 1990).

Bone age
The degree of maturation of an individual as indicated by the extent of hardening of the bones.

Changes in Body Proportion and Composition

Another aspect of growth rate concerns the rates at which different parts of the body develop. Figure 6.10 shows a graph of proportional growth of the body. Most noticeably, the relative size of the head changes from 50% of total body length at 2 months fetal age, to 25% at birth, and to only about 10% by adulthood. This shift reflects the cephalocaudal, or top-down, sequence of development described earlier.

We have seen that a spurt in height accompanies adolescence. More of this height comes from trunk growth than from leg growth. However, in one of the few violations of the cephalocaudal and proximodistal principles, leg growth occurs

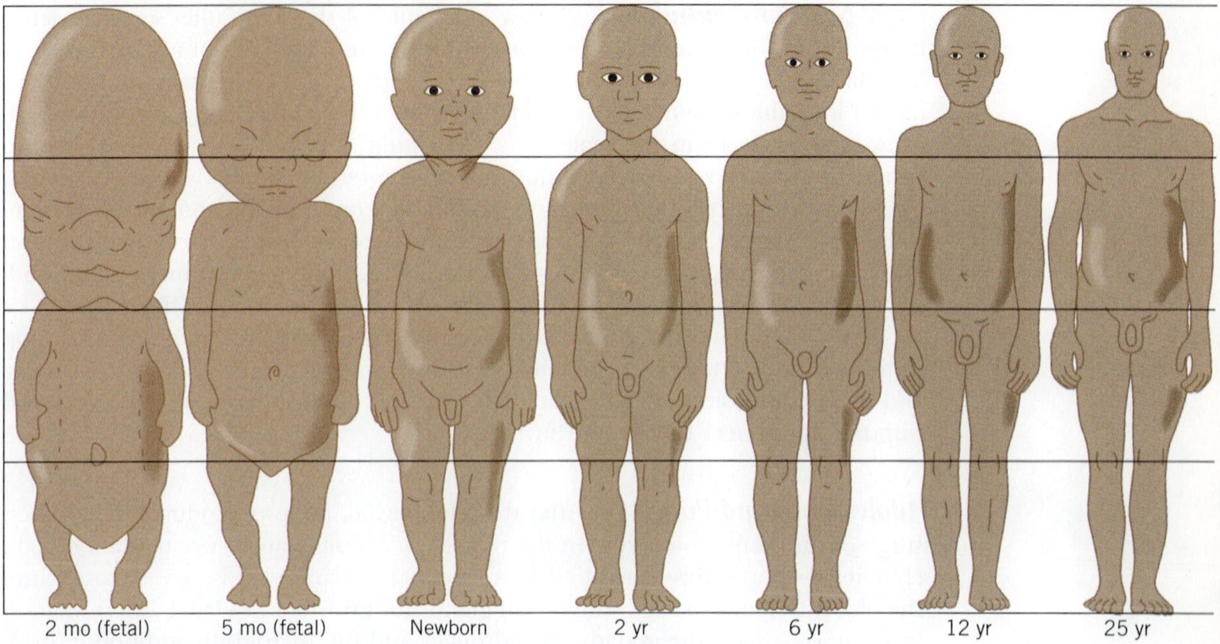

Figure 6.10
Body proportions at several ages. From *Growth* by W. J. Robbins, S. Brady, A. G. Hogan, C. M. Jackson, and C. W. Greene, 1928, New Haven: Yale University Press, p. 118.

earlier than trunk growth by 6 to 9 months. Parents often wonder whether children at this stage will always be all hands and feet (Tanner, 1990).

Internal organs also follow individual paths of growth. Up to about 6 to 8 years of age, the brain grows much faster than the body in general and the reproductive organs grow much slower. Then the rate of brain growth slows to a gradual halt, whereas the reproductive system reaches a plateau between 5 and 12 years of age and surges at around 14 years of age.

The proportion of fat to muscle also changes with age and differs for boys and girls. The fetus begins to accumulate fat in the weeks before birth. This process continues until around 9 months after birth. After that, fat gradually declines until around 6 to 8 years of age. Girls have a bit more fat than boys at birth. This difference increases gradually through childhood until about 8 years of age and then increases more rapidly.

During the adolescent growth spurt, girls continue to gain fat faster than males. Muscle growth also occurs during adolescence, more strikingly for boys than for girls (Malina, 1990). However, because girls reach their growth spurt before males, there is a 2-year period in which girls, on average, have more muscle than boys. Changes in body proportions that occur in adolescence result in greater shoulder width and muscular development in males and broader hips and more fat in females.

Sex Differentiation and Puberty

We have seen that gender affects body size and composition. Now we look more closely at the physical aspects of gender in the growth years and especially in adolescence.

Early Sex Differentiation We saw in Chapter 4 that the father's sperm determines the sex of the fetus by contributing either an X (female) or a Y (male) chromosome to the 23rd pair. In the fetus, the gonads (ovaries in females and testes in males) look the same for males and females when they first appear, but they develop somewhat faster in the male. It is interesting to note that every fetus is on a course to be female unless male hormones, secreted by the newly formed gonads, interrupt this process. Fetal hormones also affect brain wiring and appear responsible, for example, for the eventual sex differences in hemispheric specialization and for cyclic (menstruation) versus noncyclic hormone production in adulthood. We will have much more to say about early sex differentiation in Chapter 15.

Sex differentiation continues from birth until puberty. Although girls develop somewhat faster than boys, they share relatively similar heights, body proportions, and body composition in the years between birth and puberty, at least compared with the differences that occur during puberty.

Adolescence and Puberty After the fetal period, puberty produces the greatest surge of differentiation between the two sexes. These changes occur when certain chemicals—hormones—provided by various endocrine glands, are released into the bloodstream. Especially important glands for growth and sexual differentiation in adolescence are the gonads, the adrenals, and the thyroid. In addition, growth hormone, secreted by the pituitary gland, helps stimulate bone growth (Kulin, 1991; Paikoff & Brooks-Gunn, 1990; Stanhope, 1989).

Puberty
The period in which chemical and physical changes in the body occur that enable sexual reproduction.

The most significant aspect of development during adolescence is **puberty**, the series of changes that culminate in sexual maturity and the ability to reproduce. Puberty usually begins between the ages of 10 and 14, typically earlier for girls than for boys.

In males, the first sign of puberty, which occurs at around age 11 on average, is an enlargement of the testes and a change in the texture and color of the scrotum. Later, the penis enlarges, pubic hair appears, and sperm production begins, followed by the appearance of hair under the arms and on the face. Near the end of puberty, the larynx lengthens, causing the male voice to become deeper. This lengthening is sometimes evident in a breaking of the voice.

For females, the first sign of puberty is breast budding, which may occur as early as 8 years of age and as late as 13 years, followed by the appearance of pubic hair. Menarche occurs relatively late in puberty. In northern and central Europe and North America, 95 percent of girls begin menarche between 11 and 15 years of age. Usually, ovulation follows the onset of menarche by 1 or 2 years.

How fast adolescents move through puberty varies as widely as when they start. For example, it may take a girl as few as 1.5 years or as many as 5 years to complete puberty. If we were to study a single class of boys and girls in elementary school, beginning when the first student began puberty and following the group until the last student finished puberty, chances are we would have to follow the group for a full 10 years (Petersen, 1987). We can imagine how much variation in maturation there would be in the middle years and how it might play out in social relations, self-image, and confidence.

Attitudes toward Puberty Psychologists studying adolescence used to focus on physical changes. As investigators have learned more about the dynamics of adolescent change, however, they have increasingly emphasized social and cultural factors. More and more, investigators talk about biosocial or psychobiological factors in adolescence rather than only about biological factors (Lerner, Lerner, & Tubman, 1989; Smith, 1989).

Consider, for example, how girls react to the onset of menarche. This event usually heightens a girl's self-esteem and her prestige among peers. However, girls who are psychologically unprepared for menarche, perhaps because they lack information about it, have more negative feelings about its onset. Later in life, these girls are also more negative about menstruation, report more severe symptoms, and are more self-conscious about it than are other girls (Brooks-Gunn, 1987, 1991).

Social factors also influence how adolescents feel about the changes in their bodies and when they occur. At least in the United States, the ideal female is thin. But as we have seen, females add fat during puberty, and their hips broaden. In contrast, males add muscle and shoulder width, characteristics that better fit the preferred cultural image of males. Not surprisingly, then, early-maturing females tend to be more dissatisfied with their bodies during puberty than late-maturing females, whereas the opposite is true for males (Crockett & Petersen, 1987; Graber et al., 1994).

Only limited research exists on how early and late maturers succeed later in life. When studied as young adults, adolescent boys who had been early maturers had more stable careers than late maturers. They scored higher on tests of sociability, dominance, self-control, and responsibility. Late maturers had more negative self-concepts and more feelings of rejection by others and were more likely to have suffered maladjustment in late adolescence. On the positive side, late-maturing boys were more nurturant and seemed better able than earlier maturers to face their emotions and feelings (Brooks-Gunn & Reiter, 1990).

Factors That Affect Growth and Maturation

Our genes play a major part in our growth and physical maturation. Thus children tend to resemble their parents—tall parents, for example, usually have taller children than do short parents. But like every other aspect of human development, growth and maturation are also influenced by the context of development.

Heredity Recall from Chapter 4 that investigators sometimes compare similarities in identical twins with similarities in fraternal twins to determine how much genetic factors influence particular behaviors. A similar strategy yields information about the role of heredity in the onset and pace of puberty and body structure.

One study of twins has been under way in Louisville, Kentucky, for over 30 years, and more than 500 twins have been studied. Identical twins have been found to become increasingly close in height up to around 4 years of age and to stabilize at a very high correlation of around .94. Fraternal twins of the same sex do the opposite. At birth, their correlation in height is about .77, but it drops to .59 at 2 years and to .49 at 9 years, at which point it stabilizes. A similar pattern exists for weight (Wilson, 1986b). Identical twins are also more similar than fraternal twins in their spurts and lags in growth (Mueller, 1986).

Several other measures support the role of heredity in the rate of maturation. Identical twins display much higher similarity in the age of eruption of their teeth than do fraternal twins, and they are more similar in the pace of bone development, as well as in breast development in girls and testicular development in boys. The age of onset of menarche differs by less than 4 months in identical twins. One study revealed that even when identical twins were raised apart, the onset of menarche differed by an average of only 2.8 months. In contrast, fraternal twins raised together typically differ by 6 to 12 months in the age of onset of menarche. These two studies imply that genes play a substantial role in maturation, a conclusion also supported by similarities in the age of onset of menarche between mothers and daughters (Bailey & Garn, 1986).

If genetic factors influence maturation and eventual stature, we might expect to find maturational differences among genetic groups. In fact, we do. Asians reach puberty faster than do Europeans and move through it more quickly (but achieve a smaller stature). Africans proceed through adolescence at about the same pace as Europeans and Americans, but when they have equivalent quality of life, they reach a taller stature (Evelyth, 1986).

Exercise Physical activity generally has beneficial effects on development, but there is some evidence of negative effects if exercise is taken to extremes. Very strenuous exercise in highly intensive training programs (for example, training for wrestling) may reduce the rate of growth (Gallahue, 1989). Ballet dancers exercise strenuously and strive to keep their bodies slim, factors that seem to be related to their tendency to reach menarche at a later age than nondancers (Brooks-Gunn, 1987). Once menarche has begun, exercise affects the regularity of the menstrual cycle. Female athletes who train intensively often experience irregular menstrual periods during their training regime (Firsch, 1984).

Nutrition It should come as no surprise that relations have been found between the adequacy of a child's nutrition and various measures of that child's growth and development. Considering that about 40% of the world's children below age 5 are underweight, this is not a minor issue (Pollitt et al., 1996).

Poor nutrition is thought to be especially damaging during gestation and the early years of life, because brain growth is so rapid during this period. For example, children in Chile who died from malnutrition in their first or second year showed lower brain weight, less brain protein, fewer brain cells, and less myelin than expected (Bálazs et al., 1986). Growth occurs in two ways: by increases in the number of cells and by increases in cell size. Increases in cell number usually characterize early growth, whereas increases in cell size are responsible for all growth after about 18 months. Thus the impact of malnutrition may be different at different ages.

Zinc deficiency can produce abnormal metabolism and growth failure (child on left).

Even mild-to-moderate malnutrition can cause problems in children (Ricciutti, 1993). A major research project investigated the diets of children in Kenya, Egypt, and Mexico. The report concluded that even when children were consuming ample quantities of food, the quality of their diets affected their scores on various tests of cognitive and intellectual development. Deficiencies in certain vitamins (principally, vitamins A, B12, and D) and minerals (especially calcium, iron, and zinc) seemed to be most clearly involved (Sigman, 1995).

Recent studies indicate, however, that the effects of early malnutrition are not as irreversible as was once thought. Dietary correction and stimulating environments can have remarkable recuperative effects, although prevention is clearly better than treatment. Research in Brazil and Colombia documents the effects of preventive measures. When food supplements were provided from midpregnancy to the time the child was 3 years of age, benefits for both growth and weight could be observed even 3 years after the intervention (Paine et al., 1992; Super, Herrera, & Mora, 1990).

Why does undernutrition affect intellectual development? Although direct biological effects on the brain seem to be involved, social and psychological factors may also play a role. For example, because poor nutrition reduces children's energy levels, it may limit their active exploration and learning. One theory also suggests

Eating disorders during adolescence often result from a preoccupation with weight and from distorted concepts of body image.

that babies who are smaller in size and delayed in motor abilities—two common effects of early undernutrition—tend to be treated and cared for more like younger infants, thereby receiving less verbal and cognitive stimulation (Pollitt et al., 1993).

Eating disorders represent an area of nutrition that has received increasing attention in recent years. With one such disorder, **anorexia nervosa**, the individual, most often a young female, voluntarily engages in severe dietary restriction in order to maintain a body physique that is extremely thin. The damaging effects of this self-starvation include muscle wasting, dry skin and hair, constipation, dehydration, and sleep disturbance. Sometimes growth and development are impaired, menstruation ceases, and breast development is permanently affected. Adolescent anorexics often have a distorted concept of nourishment and body image.

Anorexia nervosa
A severe eating disorder, usually involving excessive weight loss through self-starvation, most often found in teenage girls.

Another eating disorder is **bulimia**, which involves binging on large quantities of food and then self-induced vomiting to purge the excess calories and maintain a normal weight level. This disorder often results in damage to teeth and gums, cracked and damaged lips, and serious imbalances in body fluids. Bulimics, like anorexics, also frequently have distorted concepts of food and body image, and they often have guilt, anxiety, and depression (Hsu, 1990; Leon, 1991; Rees & Trahms, 1989).

Bulimia
A disorder of food binging and sometimes purging by self-induced vomiting, typically observed in teenage girls.

Obesity, or excess fat storage, is one of the most common disorders in the United States today. Obesity is usually defined as weight 20% or more over a standard weight for height. Obesity appears to be a particular problem among Hispanic Americans (Olvera-Ezzell, Power, & Cousins, 1990). It may result from genetic predisposition, overeating, or a combination of both, and it frequently has an early onset, by 4 or 5 years of age (Eichorn, 1970, 1979).

Obesity
A condition of excess fat storage; often defined as weight more than 20% over a standardized, ideal weight.

Obesity has several effects on development. Obese females tend to begin puberty earlier than do nonobese females, for example, and obese males hit their growth spurt earlier than do their counterparts. Obesity has psychological consequences as well. Many obese children feel insecure and are overprotected by their parents. They frequently experience school difficulties, neuroses, and social problems. A vicious cycle may become established in which social and psychological problems induce eating, and weight gain further contributes to the problems.

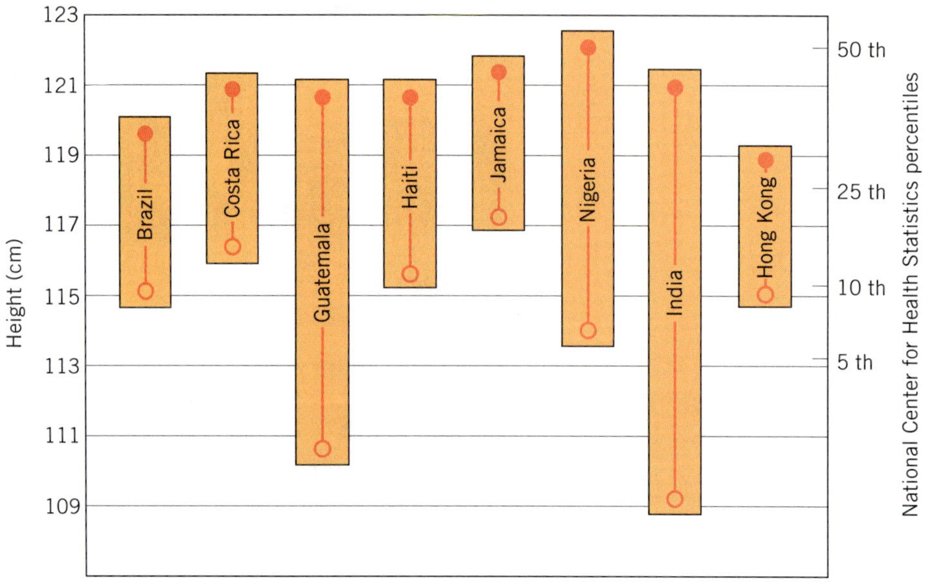

Figure 6.11
Average heights of 7-year-old boys in several countries. The solid circles at the top indicate the heights of boys from higher socioeconomic classes, and the open circles at the bottom indicate the heights of boys from lower socioeconomic classes. Adapted from "Genetics, Environment, and Growth: Issues in the Assessment of Nutritional Status" by R. Martorell, 1984. In A. Velasquez and H. Bourges (Eds.), *Genetic Factors in Nutrition* (p. 382), Orlando, FL: Academic Press. Copyright © 1984 by Academic Press. Adapted by permission.

Development in Cultural Context

Social Class and Poverty

The quality of life varies dramatically between rich and poor countries. The childhood death rate is 10 times higher in developing than in developed countries. One estimate is that 11 million fewer children would die each year if the poor countries of the world had the same death rates as the wealthy countries (Altman, 1993). However, even in the wealthiest countries, all citizens do not have equal access to resources.

In virtually every country in the world, there are differences in social classes, and these differences determine access to nutrition and health care. Differences in physical development between social classes are consistently found. As Figure 6.11 shows, for example, there is much less difference in height among young boys of the higher socioeconomic class across several countries than there is between higher and lower socioeconomic classes within a country. Social class itself is not the cause of such physical variations; rather, they result from the many differences in nutrition, health care, disease, environmental enrichment, and opportunity.

The United States is not immune to these problems. Some 14.3 million children under 18 years of age live in poverty, about one in every five U.S. children. And the likelihood of being poor is not evenly distributed among racial groups. Whereas approximately 40% of African-American families and 35% of Hispanic-American families with children are poor, only 13% of non-Hispanic white families live in poverty (Brooks-Gunn et al., 1995). Furthermore, poverty is a growing problem. In 1990, the poverty rate was one-third higher than what it was in the two preceding decades (Duncan, Brooks-Gunn, & Klebanov, 1994; Halpern, 1993).

Behind these grim statistics are children and parents who have inadequate access to health care, housing, and nutrition. The gravest consequence of these conditions is death. A recent study found that death rates among children were seven times higher in the poorest counties than in the richest counties (Halpern, 1993).

A child's well-being may be affected even before conception. Poor women are more likely to have inferior health before pregnancy and inadequate health care during pregnancy. They are also more likely to experience high levels of stress during pregnancy and to engage in behavior that is harmful to their health. Consequently, the fetus is more likely to experience intrauterine stress, a contributor to premature labor and delivery and to low birth weight (Chomitz et al., 1995).

The daily grind of poverty and typically overcrowded living conditions following birth can compound a baby's risk of problems. Poverty can drain parents' energy and undermine their self-confidence and feeling of control over their lives. Exhaustion, irritability, anger, and a feeling of futility are often the result, with consequences for the parent–child relationship. Parents may not have the psychological resources to share their infant's joy and pleasure, which would provide them positive feedback for meeting the infant's needs.

Not all poor families are the same, of course. Some children grow up poor in extended families where neighborhood and social support is ample and the social network pulls together to help them rise to the challenge of limited resources and excel. Still, these children and families face formidable odds.

The Clinton presidential administration has made several proposals to address some of the problems of the poor, including one that would make health care more accessible. But some people argue that caring for the poor is not the government's responsibility. Clearly, the problems of poverty and adequate health care for all will be with us for years to come.

Physical Abnormality Growth depends crucially on normal functioning of the pituitary and thyroid glands. In adolescence, sex-gland secretions play an important role in the growth spurt. Abnormalities in the functioning of any of these glands can produce dwarfism or giantism. If diagnosed in time, glandular abnormalities can be corrected. For example, some children fail to grow because of a deficit in growth hormone, perhaps as a result of a tumor of the hypothalamus in the brain. If this problem is discovered early enough, substances can be administered to stimulate the pituitary to produce growth hormone, often substantially speeding growth.

Growth problems can also be caused by diseases of organs such as the heart, liver, and kidneys and by various bone diseases (Kreipe & Strauss, 1989; Lowrey, 1978).

Abuse and Psychological Trauma We have focused up to now on physical aspects of the context of growth and development, but psychological trauma can also impair growth. A *failure-to-thrive* syndrome has been described in infants who fail to gain weight for no obvious reasons other than psychological disturbances or maltreatment and abuse by parents. Frequently, these babies gain weight readily when their care is transferred to hospital personnel (Benoit, 1993; Drotar et al., 1990).

A report on 13 children between the ages of 3 and 11 years provides an example of how psychological trauma can affect growth. These children lived in homes

Child abuse has reached alarming levels in the United States. Abuse can limit growth and can cause permanent brain and other physical damage.

that were unusually stressful as a result of marital problems or alcohol abuse, and there were several cases of child abuse. The children appeared to have abnormally low pituitary gland activity, and their growth rates were substantially impaired. Shortly after they were removed from their homes, the circulation of growth hormone from the pituitary increased, and the growth of most of the children accelerated (Powell, Brasel, & Blizzard, 1967). Thus, there is at least some environmental control over a characteristic that was once thought to be controlled almost exclusively by genetics.

This relationship between psychological environment and growth is of special concern in the United States, where child abuse is reaching alarming levels. The National Center on Child Abuse and Neglect reported 160,932 cases of confirmed abuse of children under age 3 in the United States in 1990, and a majority of the 1,200 children who died from abuse that year were under 3 (Mrazek, 1993). Because most cases are not reported, it is difficult to know how much abuse occurs, but it is estimated that 2.2 million children a year are abused, 25% of them under 2 years of age (Zigler, Hopper, & Hall, 1993).

Historical Trends There is evidence that growth rates have changed over recent history in some parts of the world. In Europe and North America after about 1900 the average height of 5- to 7-year-olds increased 1 to 2 centimeters per decade and the average height of 10- to 14-year-olds increased 2 to 3 centimeters per decade. Adult height, however, increased only 0.6 cm per decade between 1880 and 1960. Thus the increase in children's heights apparently reflected a trend toward faster maturation more than a trend toward greater ultimate stature. Before this century it was fairly typical for people to grow until age 25 or so, whereas today growth usually continues only until about age 18 or 19.

The trend toward faster maturation has also been reflected in the age of menarche, which has decreased over the last century (Meredith, 1963; Tanner, 1987). Earlier maturation can be explained by better living conditions—better nourishment, better health care, and lowered incidence of disease. The trend began to level off in the 1970s.

✓ *To Recap...*

Growth is continuous through childhood but does not proceed uniformly. The rate of growth gradually slows, then experiences a spurt at adolescence, and stops soon afterward. Growth rates vary widely among children, as do the heights ultimately reached. Bone age is one way to distinguish a child who will be a short adult from one who is maturing slowly. Different parts of the body develop at different rates, following a cephalocaudal progression. Body organs also vary in rates of maturation; the brain, for example, develops very early.

Boys and girls grow fairly similarly until adolescence. Girls typically experience the adolescent growth spurt and puberty earlier than do boys. Boys add more height once their growth spurt has begun, as well as more muscle mass and shoulder width. Girls add relatively more fat and hip width. The adolescent's attitude toward these changes may reflect social and cultural factors, such as the amount of information he or she has about the changes and the body image that society holds up as ideal.

Many factors influence growth and maturation. Genetic processes are clearly important, but such environmental factors as exercise, nutrition, social class, disease, abuse, and psychological trauma also come into play. Some of these environmental variables, such as better nutrition, have accelerated growth rates in many developed countries during the 20th century.

Conclusion

This chapter concludes a set of three chapters that concern the more biological aspects of human development. In Chapters 4 and 5, we focused on genetics and prenatal development. In the present chapter, we discussed the behaviors and physical equipment the baby brings to the world and how this basic equipment develops through infancy, childhood, and adolescence.

Until recently, psychologists have not been very open to considering the physical and biological bases of behavior. Rather, a tension existed between the more physically based and the more psychologically based disciplines, with psychologists more focused on demonstrating that social and environmental factors influence behavior. However, the mood seems to be changing. As we have seen, biological influences that we might at first imagine would act on their own are found, on closer examination, to cooperate with environmental factors to produce their ultimate effect. We have seen many examples of this interdependence—for instance, in the effects of health care on birth mortality, of the family setting on the outcome of infants at risk, of prenatal exposure to cocaine on the newborn's state organization and rhythms, of practice on motor development, and of psychological trauma on growth. For this reason, many of the tensions that once existed between psychologists and biologists have largely disappeared, and the search is on to understand how biological factors and experience collaborate to influence human development.

No better evidence of this collaboration exists than in the successful efforts of psychologists, biologists, and neuroscientists to have the decade of the 1990s declared the decade of the brain. President George Bush signed a resolution to this effect in October 1989, committing the United States to the expenditure of significant research dollars and effort aimed at understanding both the psychological and the biological mysteries of this most important organ. Perhaps by the turn of the 21st century, exciting advances in our understanding of human development will reflect the wisdom of this national commitment to better understanding.

Visual Summary for Chapter 6:

Physical Development: Birth, Motor Development, and Growth

Birth and the Perinatal Period

Indicators of Risk for Developmental Problems

Maternal and Family Characteristics →	*A number of maternal and family factors, especially whether the mother receives prenatal care, are important in identifying babies at risk for developmental problems.*
Physical Compromise of the Newborn →	*Low birthweight is an important indicator of risk. Low birthweight babies may be preterm, or they may be small for gestational age (SGA).*
Physical and Behavioral Assessment →	*Newborn assessments, such as the Apgar exam, the Prechtl test, and the Brazelton Neonatal Behavioral Assessment Scale are also used to assess risk.*

The Organized Newborn

Activity of Newborns

States →	*The newborn's level of alertness can be categorized according to six states varying from quiet sleep to crying.*
Rhythms →	*The newborn's states occur in rhythmic cycles. A basic rest-activity cycle is coordinated with a longer sleep-wake cycle.*
Reflexes →	*Newborns possess a number of reflexes, some that last through life, and others that disappear during the first year.*
Congenitally Organized Behaviors →	*Congenitally organized behaviors are present in the newborn and differ from reflexes in that they are not easily attributable to a particular stimulus and are more adaptable.*

Motor Development

Categories

Locomotion/Postural →	*Control of trunk of the body and arms and legs for moving around.*
Prehension →	*Ability to use hands as tools.*

Motor Development

Principles

Proximodistal	Motor skills develop from center of the body to parts farther out.
Cephalocaudal	Motor skills develop from head to feet.
Dynamic Systems Approach	Individual motor skills develop when infants are motivated to accomplish a task and when they possess the sufficient physical resources.
Stages	During exploration, many different responses are tried somewhat randomly; during selection, responses are fine-tuned and coordinated.

Motor Development in Childhood

Fundamental Movement Skills	Locomotor, manipulative, and stability.
Reaction Time	Improves through preschool and elementary years.

The Human Brain

Three Stages in the Development of the Fetal Brain

Cell Production	Most neurons are produced between 10 and 26 weeks after conception.
Cell Migration	Following production, cells migrate to their proper locations, a process that is completed by 7 months gestational age.
Cell Elaboration	Axons and dendrites form synapses with other cells, a process that continues for years.

Hemispheric Specialization

Left Hemisphere	Prepared at birth to control language function in most people.
Right Hemisphere	Prepared at birth to control spatial and mathematical functioning in most people.

Human Growth

Growth in Size, Proportion, and Composition	Growth is continuous, but not uniform, throughout childhood. The rate of growth gradually slows, then spurts at adolescence and stops soon afterwards. Different parts of the body, as well as body organs, develop at different rates.
Sex Differentiation and Puberty	Boys and girls grow fairly similarly until puberty. Girls tend to experience the adolescence growth spurt and puberty earlier than boys. Once their growth spurt has begun, boys add more height, muscle mass, and shoulder width; girls add relatively more fat and hip width.
Factors Affecting Growth	Human growth is influenced not only by heredity, but also by environmental factors such as nutrition, exercise, poverty, disease, and even abuse and psychological trauma.

A$\bar{B}$ error Infants' tendency to search in the original location in which an object was found rather than in its most recent hiding place. A characteristic of stage 4 of object permanence.

Academic self-concept The part of self-esteem involving children's perceptions of their academic abilities.

Accommodation Changing existing cognitive structures to fit with new experiences. One of the two components of adaptation in Piaget's theory.

Adaptation The tendency to fit with the environment in ways that promote survival. One of the two biologically based functions stressed in Piaget's theory.

Adult Attachment Interview (AAI) An instrument used to assess an adult's childhood recollections of the attachment relationship with the primary caregiver.

Affect The outward expression of emotions through facial expressions, gestures, intonation, and the like.

Aggression Behavior that is intended to cause harm to persons or property and that is not socially justifiable.

Alleles Genes for the same trait located in the same place on a pair of chromosomes.

Amniocentesis A procedure for collecting cells that lie in the amniotic fluid surrounding the fetus. A needle is passed through the mother's abdominal wall into the amniotic sac to gather discarded fetal cells. These cells can be examined for chromosomal and genetic defects.

Amniotic sac A fluid-containing watertight membrane that surrounds and protects the embryo and fetus.

Androgen insensitivity A genetic disorder in which the fetus does not respond to masculinizing hormones. Affected individuals (XX or XY) usually are feminine in appearance and interests.

Androgens Hormones that have masculinizing effects and are more abundant in males.

Androgyny A personality type composed of desirable characteristics of the masculine and feminine personality types.

Anorexia nervosa A severe eating disorder, usually involving excessive weight loss through self-starvation, most often found in teenage girls.

Anoxia A deficit of oxygen to the cells, which can produce brain or other tissue damage.

Appearance–reality distinction Distinction between how objects appear and what they really are. Understanding the distinction implies an ability to judge both appearance and reality correctly when the two diverge.

Assimilation Interpreting new experiences in terms of existing cognitive structures. One of the two components of adaptation in Piaget's theory.

At risk Describes babies who have a higher likelihood than other babies of experiencing developmental problems.

Attachment Q-Set A method of assessing attachment in which cards bearing descriptions of the child's interactions with the caregiver are sorted into categories to create a profile of the child.

Attention-deficit hyperactivity disorder (ADHD) A developmental disorder characterized by difficulty in sustaining attention, hyperactivity, and impulsive and uncontrolled behavior.

Attention The selection of particular sensory input for perceptual and cognitive processing and the exclusion of competing input.

Autobiographical memory Specific, personal, and long-lasting memory regarding the self.

Automatization An increase in the efficiency with which cognitive operations are executed as a result of practice. A mechanism of change in information-processing theories.

Autosomes The 22 pairs of human chromosomes, other than the sex chromosomes

Axon A long fiber extending from the cell body in a neuron; conducts activity from the cell.

Babbling drift A hypothesis that infants' babbling gradually gravitates toward the language they are hearing and soon will speak.

Behavior analysis B. F. Skinner's environmental/learning theory, which emphasizes the role of operant learning in changing observable behaviors.

Behavior genetics The field of study that explores the role of genes in producing individual differences in behavior and development.

Behavioral homophyly Similarity between peers in behaviors and interests. Such similarity is one determinant of friendship selection.

Behaviorism A theory of psychology, first advanced by John B. Watson, that human development results primarily from conditioning and learning processes.

Bioecological theory Theory of intelligence that emphasizes the interplay of domain-specific knowledge and basic cognitive processes in the generation of intelligent behavior.

Bone age The degree of maturation of an individual as indicated by the extent of hardening of the bones.

Brain lateralization The organization of the human brain into left and right hemispheres that perform different functions.

Brain stem The lower part of the brain, closest to the spinal cord; includes the cerebellum, which is important for maintaining balance and coordination.

Brightness constancy The experience that the brightness of an object remains the same even though the amount of light it reflects back to the eye changes (because of shadows or changes in the illuminating light).

Bulimia A disorder of food binging and sometimes purging by self-induced vomiting, typically observed in teenage girls.

Cartesian dualism René Descartes's idea that the mind and body are separate, which helped clear the way for the scientific study of human development.

Case study A research method that involves only a single individual, often with a focus on a clinical issue.

Categorical perception The ability to detect differences in speech sounds that correspond to differences in meaning; the ability to discriminate phonemic boundaries.

Categorical self The "Me" component of the self, which involves one's objective personal characteristics.

Catharsis The psychoanalytic belief that the likelihood of aggression can be reduced by viewing aggression or by engaging in high-energy behavior.

Centration Piaget's term for the young child's tendency to focus on only one aspect of a problem at a time, a perceptually biased form of responding that often results in incorrect judgments.

Cephalocaudal Literally, head to tail. This principle of development refers to the tendency of body parts to mature in a head-to-foot progression.

Cerebral cortex The thin sheet of gray matter that covers the brain.

Cerebrum The highest brain center; includes both hemispheres of the brain and the interconnections between them.

Cesarean section Surgical delivery of the fetus directly from the uterus; performed when normal delivery is prohibited.

Chorionic villus sampling (CVS) A procedure for gathering fetal cells earlier in pregnancy than is possible through amniocentesis. A tube is passed through the vagina and cervix so that fetal cells can be gathered at the site of the developing placenta.

Chromosomes Chemical strands in the cell nucleus that contain the genes. The nucleus of each human cell has 46 chromosomes, with the exception of the gametes, which have 23.

Chronosystem Bronfenbrenner's term for the passage of time as a context for studying human development.

Clarification question A response that indicates that a listener did not understand a statement.

Class inclusion The knowledge that a subclass cannot be larger than the superordinate class that includes it. In Piaget's theory, a concrete operational achievement.

Clinical method Piaget's principal research method, which involved a semistructured interview with questions designed to probe children's understanding of various concepts.

Clique A kind of group typical in adolescence, consisting usually of 5 to 10 members whose shared interests and behavior patterns set them apart from their peers.

Codominance The case in which alleles are both dominant and each is completely expressed in the phenotype.

Coercive family process Gerald Patterson's term for the method by which some families control one another through aggression and other coercive means.

Cognition Higher-order mental processes, such as reasoning and problem solving, through which humans attempt to understand the world.

Cohort effect A problem sometimes found in cross-sectional research in which people of a given age are affected by factors unique to their generation.

Coining Children's creation of new words to label objects or events for which the correct label is not known.

Color constancy The experience that the color of an object remains the same even though the wavelengths it reflects back to the eye change (because of changes in the color of the illuminating light).

Comparative research Research conducted with nonhuman species to provide information relevant to human development.

Competence Self-evaluation that includes both what one would like to achieve and one's confidence in being able to achieve it.

Competition model A proposed strategy children use for learning grammar in which they weight possible cues in terms of availability and reliability.

Computer simulation Programming a computer to perform a cognitive task in the same way that humans are thought to perform it. An information-processing method for testing theories of underlying process.

Concept A mental grouping of different items into a single category on the basis of some unifying similarity or set of similarities.

Conception The combining of the genetic material from a male gamete (sperm) and a female gamete (ovum); fertilization.

Concrete operations Form of intelligence in which mental operations make logical problem solving with concrete objects possible. The third of Piaget's periods, extending from about 6 to 11 years of age.

Conditioned reflex method John B. Watson's name for the Pavlovian conditioning process in which reflexive responses can be conditioned to stimuli in the environment.

Conditioned stimulus (CS) A neutral stimulus that comes to elicit a response (UCR) through a conditioning process in which it is consistently paired with another stimulus (UCS) that naturally evokes the response.

Congenital adrenal hyperplasia (CAH) A hormonal disorder caused by an overproduction of androgens during pregnancy. Afflicted females have large genitals and display male personality characteristics; afflicted males tend to be slightly more masculine in their interests and interactions.

Congenitally organized behavior Early behaviors of newborns that do not require specific external stimulation and that show more adaptability than simple reflexes.

Conservation The knowledge that the quantitative properties of an object or collection of objects are not changed by a change in appearance. In Piaget's theory, a concrete operational achievement.

Constraints Implicit assumptions about word meanings that are hypothesized to narrow down the possibilities children must consider and hence to facilitate the task of word learning.

Constructive memory Effects of the general knowledge system on how information is interpreted and thus remembered.

Constructivism Piaget's belief that children actively create knowledge rather than passively receive it from the environment.

Continuity versus discontinuity debate The scientific controversy regarding whether development is constant and connected (continuous) or uneven and disconnected (discontinuous).

Controversial child A child who receives both many positive and many negative nominations in sociometric assessments by peers.

Conventional level Kohlberg's third and fourth stages of moral development. Moral reasoning is based on the view that a social system must be based on laws and regulations.

Cooing A stage in the preverbal period, beginning at about 2 months, when babies primarily produce one-syllable vowel sounds.

Correlation The relation between two variables, described in terms of direction and strength.

Correlation coefficient (r) A number between +1.00 and −1.00 that indicates the direction and strength of a correlation between two variables.

Cross-cultural studies Research designed to determine the influence of culture on some aspect of development and in which culture typically serves as an independent variable.

Crossing over The exchange of genetic material between pairs of chromosomes during meiosis.

Cross-sectional design A research method in which people of different ages are studied simultaneously to examine the effects of age on some aspect of behavior.

Cross-sequential design A research method combining longitudinal and cross-sectional designs.

Cultural compatibility hypothesis The hypothesis that schooling will be most effective when methods of instruction are compatible with the child's cultural background.

Cultural relativism The idea that certain behaviors or patterns of development vary from one culture to another.

Deep structure Chomsky's term for the inborn knowledge humans possess about the properties of language.

Defensive reflex A natural reaction to novel stimuli that tends to protect the organism from further stimulation and that may include orientation of the stimulus receptors away from the stimulus source and a variety of physiological changes.

Deferred imitation Imitation of a model observed some time in the past.

Delay-of-gratification technique An experimental procedure for studying children's ability to postpone a smaller, immediate reward in order to obtain a larger, delayed one.

Dendrite One of a net of short fibers extending out from the cell body in a neuron; receives activity from nearby cells and conducts that activity to the cell body.

Deoxyribonucleic acid (DNA) A stairlike, double-helix molecule that carries genetic information on chromosomes.

Dependent variable The variable that is predicted to be affected by an experimental manipulation. In psychology, usually some aspect of behavior.

Descriptive research Research based solely on observations, with no attempt to determine systematic relations among the variables.

Developmental pacing The rate at which spurts and plateaus occur in an individual's physical and mental development.

Developmental psychology The branch of psychology devoted to the study of changes in behavior and abilities over the course of development.

Dialectical process The process in Vygotsky's theory whereby children learn through problem-solving experiences shared with others.

Dialogic reading Form of joint picture-book reading in which the adult uses open-ended questions and other prompts to encourage the child to tell the story, with the goal of promoting linguistic skills.

Discourse Language used in social interactions; conversation.

Dishabituation The recovery of a habituated response that results from a change in the eliciting stimulus.

Displaced aggression Retaliatory aggression directed at a person or object other than the one against whom retaliation is desired.

Display rules The expectations and attitudes a society holds toward the expression of affect.

Dominance hierarchy A structured social group in which members higher on the dominance ladder control those who are lower, initially through aggression and conflict, but eventually simply through threats.

Down syndrome A chromosomal disorder caused by an extra chromosome. Its effects include mental retardation and a characteristic physical appearance.

Dynamic assessment Method of assessing children's abilities derived from Vygotsky's concept of the zone of proximal development. Measures the child's ability to benefit from adult-provided assistance, typically in a test-train-retest design.

Dynamic systems Thelen's model of the development of motor skills, in which infants who are motivated to accomplish a task create a new motor behavior from their available physical abilities

EAS model Plomin and Buss's theory of temperament, which holds that temperament can be measured along the dimensions of emotionality, activity, and sociability.

Ecological approach An approach to studying development that focuses on individuals within their environmental contexts.

Egocentrism In infancy, an inability to distinguish the self (e.g., one's actions or perceptions) from the outer world. In later childhood, an inability to distinguish one's own perspective (e.g., visual experience, thoughts, feelings) from that of others.

Electroencephalograph (EEG) An instrument that measures brain activity by sensing minute electrical changes at the top of the skull.

Embryo The developing organism from the third week, when implantation is complete, through the eighth week after conception.

Emotion An internal reaction or feeling, which may be either positive (such as joy) or negative (such as anger), and may reflect a readiness for action.

Encoding Attending to and forming internal representations of certain features of the environment. A mechanism of change in information-processing theories.

Epigenetic principle According to Erikson, the genetic process that guides personality formation through its stages of development.

Equilibration Piaget's term for the biological process of self-regulation that propels the cognitive system to higher and higher forms of equilibrium.

Equilibrium A characteristic of a cognitive system in which assimilation and accommodation are in balance, thus permitting adaptive, nondistorted responses to the world.

Erogenous zones According to Freud's theory of psychosexual development, the areas of the body where the libido resides during successive stages of development. The child seeks physical pleasure in the erogenous zone at which the libido is located.

Estrogens and progesterone Hormones that have feminizing effects and are more abundant in females.

Ethology The study of development from an evolutionary perspective.

Evaluative self-reactions Bandura's term for consequences people apply to themselves as a result of meeting or failing to meet their personal standards.

Existential self The "I" component

of the self, which is concerned with the subjective experience of existing.

Exosystem Social systems that can affect children but in which they do not participate directly. Bronfenbrenner's third layer of context.

Expansion A repetition of speech in which errors are corrected and statements are elaborated.

Expertise Organized factual knowledge with respect to some content domain.

Expressive style Vocabulary acquired during the naming explosion that emphasizes the pragmatic functions of language.

False belief The realization that people can hold beliefs that are not true. Such understanding, which is typically acquired during the preoperational period, provides evidence of the ability to distinguish the mental from the nonmental.

False self behavior Behaving in a way that is knowingly different from how one's true self would behave.

Fast-mapping A process in which children acquire the meaning of a word after a brief exposure.

Fetal alcohol syndrome A set of features in the infant caused by the mother's use of alcohol during pregnancy; typically includes facial malformations and other physical and mental disabilities.

Fetal distress A condition of abnormal stress in the fetus, reflected during the birth process in an abnormal fetal heart rate.

Fetus The developing organism from the ninth week to the thirty-eighth week after conception.

Forbidden-toy technique An experimental procedure for studying children's resistance to temptation in which the child is left alone with an attractive toy and instructed not to play with it.

Formal operations Form of intelligence in which higher-level mental operations make possible logical reasoning with respect to abstract and hypothetical events and not merely concrete objects. The fourth of Piaget's periods, beginning at about 11 years of age.

Fragile X syndrome An X-linked genetic disorder, most often expressed in males, producing retarded intellectual development, language and behavior problems, and identifiable physical characteristics.

Fraternal (dizygotic [DZ]) twins Twins who develop from separately fertilized ova and who thus are no more genetically similar than are other siblings.

Friendship An enduring relationship between two individuals, characterized by loyalty, intimacy, and mutual affection.

Functionalist model A theory of language development that stresses the uses of language and the context in which it develops.

g General intelligence; g is assumed to determine performance on a wide range of intellectual measures.

Gender consistency Understanding that one's gender cannot be changed by superficial changes in clothing, occupation, etc.

Gender constancy Understanding that one's gender is a fixed part of the self; it includes gender identity, gender stability, and gender consistency.

Gender identity disorder (GID) A disorder in which children, most often males, appear uncomfortable with their biological sex and display behavior more typical of the opposite sex.

Gender identity Knowledge of one's own gender.

Gender role (sex-role stereotype) A pattern of behaviors that is considered appropriate for males or females by the culture in which they live.

Gender schema A cognitive structure used to organize information regarding one's gender.

Gender script A familiar routine or sequence of events that is typically associated with only one gender.

Gender segregation (sex cleavage) The tendency for male and female children to play in same-sex groups.

Gender stability Understanding that one's gender will remain the same throughout life.

Gender-role knowledge Understanding that a certain toy, activity, or personal characteristic is considered more appropriate for one sex than the other.

Gene A segment of DNA on the chromosome. The basic unit of inheritance.

Genetic counseling The practice of advising prospective parents about genetic diseases and the likelihood that they might pass on defective genetic traits to their offspring.

Genetic epistemology Jean Piaget's term for the study of children's knowledge and how it changes with development.

Genotype The arrangement of genes underlying a trait.

Goodness of fit A concept describing the relation between a baby's temperament and her social and environmental surroundings.

Grammar The study of the structural properties of language, including syntax, inflection, and intonation.

Group A collection of individuals who interact regularly in a consistent, structured fashion and who share values and a sense of belonging to the group.

Habituation The decline or disappearance of a reflex response as a result of repeated elicitation. The simplest type of learning.

Haptic perception The perceptual experience that results from active exploration of objects by touch.

Heritability The proportion of variance in a trait (such as IQ) that can be attributed to genetic variance in the sample being studied.

Hierarchical model of intelligence A model of the structure of intelligence in which intellectual abilities are seen as being organized hierarchically, with broad, general abilities at the top of the hierarchy and more specific skills nested underneath.

Holophrase A single word used to express a larger idea; common during the second year of life.

HOME (Home Observation for Measurement of the Environment) An instrument for assessing the quality of the early home environment. Included are dimensions such as maternal involvement and variety of play materials.

Hostile (retaliatory) aggression Aggression whose purpose is to cause pain or injury.

Huntington's chorea An inherited disease in which the nervous system suddenly deteriorates, resulting in uncontrollable muscular movements and disordered brain function. The disease typically strikes people between about 30 and 40 years of age and ultimately causes death.

Hypothesis A predicted relation between a phenomenon and a factor assumed to affect it that is not yet supported by a great deal of evidence. Hypotheses are tested in experimental investigations.

Hypothetical-deductive reasoning A form

of problem solving characterized by the ability to generate and test hypotheses and draw logical conclusions from the results of the tests. In Piaget's theory, a formal operational achievement.

Identical (monozygotic [MZ]) twins Twins who develop from a single fertilized ovum and thus inherit identical genetic material.

Identification The Freudian process through which the child adopts the characteristics of the same-sex parent during the phallic stage.

Identity In Erikson's theory, the component of personality that develops across the eight stages of life and that motivates progress through the stages.

Imitation Behavior of an observer that results from and is similar to the behavior of a model.

Immanent justice Literally, inherent justice; refers to the expectation of children in Piaget's stage of moral realism that punishment must follow any rule violation, including those that appear to go undetected.

Imprinting A biological process in some species in which the young acquire an emotional attachment to the mother through following.

Incomplete dominance The case in which a dominant gene does not completely suppress the effect of a recessive gene, which is then somewhat expressed in the phenotype.

Independent variable The variable in an experiment that is systematically manipulated.

Infantile amnesia The inability to remember experiences from the first 2 or 3 years of life.

Inflections The aspect of grammar that involves adding endings to words to modify their meaning.

Inhibition Kagan's proposed temperamental response style characterizing infants who react to unfamiliar events and people with timidity and avoidance.

Innate releasing mechanism A stimulus that triggers an innate sequence or pattern of behaviors.

Institutionalization studies Examinations of the effects of naturally occurring deprivation (such as in certain kinds of orphanage rearing) on children's development.

Instrumental aggression Aggression whose purpose is to obtain something desired.

Intentional behavior In Piaget's theory, behavior in which the goal exists prior to the action selected to achieve it; made possible by the ability to separate means and end.

Interactional synchrony The smooth intermeshing of behaviors between mother and baby.

Interactionist perspective The theory that human development results from the combination of nature and nurture factors.

Internal working model An infant's and a caregiver's cognitive conception of each other, which they use to form expectations and predictions.

Internalization Vygotsky's term for the child's incorporation, primarily through language, of bodies of knowledge and tools of thought from the culture.

Invariants Aspects of the world that remain the same even though other aspects have changed. In Piaget's theory, different forms of invariants are understood at different stages of development.

Joint attention Using cues (such as direction of gaze) to identify and share the attentional focus of another.

Kin selection A proposed mechanism by which an individual's altruistic behavior toward a kin member increases the likelihood of the survival of genes similar to those of the individual.

Kinetic cues Visual cues that indicate the relative distances of objects through movement either of the objects or of the observer.

Klinefelter's syndrome (XXY) A chromosomal disorder of males in which an extra X chromosome is present; men with the syndrome have long arms, little body hair, an underdeveloped penis, and somewhat feminine personality characteristics.

Language acquisition device (LAD) Chomsky's proposed brain mechanism for analyzing speech input; the mechanism that allows young children to acquire quickly the language to which they are exposed.

Language acquisition support system (LASS) Bruner's proposed process by which parents provide children assistance in learning language.

Law (principle) A predicted relation between a phenomenon and a factor assumed to affect it that is supported by a good deal of scientific evidence.

Learnability theory A nativistic theory of language acquisition that uses mathematical models to determine the kinds of evidence necessary to learn grammatical rules.

Learning A relatively permanent change in behavior that results from practice or experience.

Lexical contrast theory A theory of semantic development holding that (1) children automatically assume that a new word has a meaning different from that of any other word they know and (2) children always choose word meanings that are generally accepted over more individualized meanings.

Lexicon A vocabulary, or repertoire of words.

Libido Sigmund Freud's term for the sexual energy that he believed is possessed by all children from birth and then moves to different locations on the body over the course of development.

Locomotion The movement of a person through space. Psychologists have been most interested in movements that individuals control themselves, such as walking and crawling.

Longitudinal design A research method in which the same individuals are studied repeatedly over time.

Looking-glass self The conception of the self based on how one thinks others see him or her.

Macrosystem The culture or subculture in which the child lives. Bronfenbrenner's fourth layer of context.

Mastery motivation An inborn desire to affect or control one's environment.

Maternal bonding The mother's emotional attachment to the child, which appears shortly after birth and which some theorists believe develops through early contact during a sensitive period.

Maternal separation anxiety Strong negative emotional reactions experienced by some mothers when separated from their children.

Maturation The biological processes assumed by some theorists to be primarily responsible for human development.

Meiosis The process by which germ cells produce four gametes (sperm or ovum), each with half the number of chromosomes of the parent cell.

Mesosystem The interrelationships among the child's microsystems. The second of Bronfenbrenner's layers of context.

Metamemory Knowledge about memory.

Microanalysis A research technique for studying dyadic interactions, in which two individuals are simultaneously videotaped with different cameras, and then the tapes are examined side by side.

Microgenetic method A research method in which a small number of individuals are observed repeatedly in order to study an expected change in a developmental process.

Microsystem The environmental system closest to the child, such as the family or school. The first of Bronfenbrenner's layers of context.

Midbrain A part of the brain that lies above the brain stem; serves as a relay station and as a control area for breathing and swallowing and houses part of the auditory and visual systems.

Mitosis The process by which body cells reproduce, resulting in two identical cells.

Mnemonic strategies Techniques (such as rehearsal or organization) that people use in an attempt to remember something.

Modal action pattern A sequence of behaviors elicited by a specific stimulus.

Moral conduct The aspect of children's moral development concerned with behavior.

Moral dilemmas Stories used by Piaget and others to assess children's levels of moral reasoning.

Moral realism Piaget's second stage of moral development, in which children's reasoning is based on objective and physical aspects of a situation and is often inflexible.

Moral reasoning The aspect of children's moral development concerned with knowledge and understanding of moral issues and principles.

Moral relativism Piaget's third stage of moral development, in which children view rules as agreements that can be altered and consider people's motives or intentions when evaluating their moral conduct.

Moral rules Rules used by a society to protect individuals and to guarantee their rights.

Moro reflex The infant's response to loss of head support or to a loud sound, consisting of thrusting the arms and fingers outward, followed by clenching the fists and making a grasping motion of the arms across the chest.

Motherese Simplified speech directed at very young children by adults and older children.

Motion parallax An observer's experience that a closer object moves across the field of view faster than a more distant object when both objects are moving at the same speed or when the objects are stationary and the observer moves.

Myelin A sheath of fatty material that surrounds and insulates the axon, resulting in speedier transmission of neural activity.

Naming explosion A period of language development, beginning at about 18 months, when children suddenly begin to acquire words (especially labels) at a high rate.

Nativism The theory that human development results principally from inborn processes that guide the emergence of behaviors in a predictable manner.

Nativistic theory A theory of language development, originated by Chomsky, that stresses innate mechanisms separate from cognitive processes.

Natural selection An evolutionary process proposed by Charles Darwin in which characteristics of an individual that increase its chances of survival are more likely to be passed along to future generations.

Nature versus nurture debate The scientific controversy regarding whether the primary source of developmental change rests in biological (nature) factors or in environmental and experiential (nurture) factors.

Negative correlation A correlation in which two variables change in opposite directions.

Negative reinforcer A consequence that makes the behavior it follows more likely through the removal of something unpleasant.

Neglected child A child who receives few nominations of any sort, positive or negative, in sociometric assessments by peers. Such children seem to be ignored by the peer group.

Neuron A nerve cell, consisting of a cell body, axon, and dendrites. Neurons transmit activity from one part of the nervous system to another.

Neurotransmitter A chemical that transmits electrical activity from one neuron across the synapse to another neuron.

New York Longitudinal Study (NYLS) A well-known longitudinal project conducted by Thomas and Chess to study infant temperament and its implications for later psychological adjustment.

Nonshared environment A concept used in behavior genetics to refer to presumed aspects of the environment that children experience differently.

Normative versus idiographic development The question of whether research should focus on identifying commonalities in human development (normative development) or on the causes of individual differences (idiographic development).

Norms A timetable of age ranges indicating when normal growth and developmental milestones are typically reached.

Obesity A condition of excess fat storage; often defined as weight more than 20% over a standardized, ideal weight.

Object permanence The knowledge that objects have a permanent existence that is independent of our perceptual contact with them. In Piaget's theory, a major achievement of the sensorimotor period.

Objective responsibility Responsibility assigned solely in terms of an action's objective and physical consequences. Children in Piaget's stage of moral realism evaluate situations using this concept.

Objectivity A characteristic of scientific research; it requires that the procedures and subject matter of investigations should be formulated so that they could, in principle, be agreed on by everyone.

Observational learning A form of learning in which an observer's behavior changes as a result of observing a model.

Operant behaviors Voluntary behaviors controlled by their consequences. The larger category of human behaviors.

Operant learning A form of learning in which the likelihood of an operant behavior changes as a result of its reinforcing or punishing consequences.

Operating principle A hypothetical innate strategy for analyzing language input and discovering grammatical structure.

Operating space In Case's theory, the resources necessary to carry out cognitive operations.

Operations Piaget's term for the various forms of mental action through which older children solve problems and reason logically.

Organization The tendency to integrate knowledge into interrelated cognitive structures. One of the two biologically based functions stressed in Piaget's theory.

Orienting reflex A natural reaction to novel stimuli that enhances stimulus processing and includes orientation of the eyes and ears to optimize stimulus reception, inhibition of ongoing activity, and a variety of physiological changes.

Ovaries The female gonadal structure that produces the ovum.

Overextension An early language error in which children use labels they already know for things whose names they do not yet know.

Overregularization An early structural language error in which children apply inflectional rules to irregular forms (e.g., adding *-ed* to *say*).

Palmar reflex The infant's finger grasp of an object that stimulates the palm of the hand.

Paradox of altruism The logical dilemma faced by ethological theorists who try to reconcile self-sacrificial behavior with the concepts of natural selection and survival of the fittest.

Parallel play A form of play in which children play next to each other and with similar materials but with no real interaction or cooperation.

Peer-mediated intervention Form of intervention for children with sociometric problems in which responses of the peer group are utilized to elicit more effective social behaviors from the target children.

Perception The interpretation of sensory stimulation based on experience.

Perinatal period The events and environment surrounding the birth process.

Periods Piaget's term for the four general stages into which his theory divides development. Each period is a qualitatively distinct form of functioning that characterizes a wide range of cognitive activities.

Peripheral vision The perception of visual input outside the area on which the individual is fixating.

Personal agency The understanding that one can be the cause of events.

Phenotype The characteristic of a trait that is expressed or observable.

Phenylketonuria (PKU) An inherited metabolic disease caused by a recessive gene. It can produce severe mental retardation if dietary intake of phenylalanine is not controlled for the first several years of life.

Phoneme A sound contrast that changes meaning.

Phonemics The branch of phonology that deals with the relation between speech sounds and meaning.

Phonetics The branch of phonology that deals with articulation skills.

Phonics An approach to reading instruction that stresses letter–sound correspondences and the build-up of words from individual units.

Phonological awareness The realization that letters correspond to sounds and the ability to perform specific letter-to-sound translations.

Phonology The study of speech sounds.

Pictorial cues Visual cues that indicate the relative distances of objects through static, picturelike information—for example, interposition of one object in front of another.

Placenta An organ that forms where the embryo attaches to the uterus. This organ exchanges nutrients, oxygen, and wastes between the embryo or fetus and the mother through a very thin membrane that does not allow the passage of blood.

Polygenic inheritance The case in which a trait is determined by a number of genes.

Positive correlation A correlation in which two variables change in the same direction.

Positive reinforcer A consequence that makes the behavior it follows more likely through the presentation of something pleasant.

Postconventional level Kohlberg's final stages of moral development. Moral reasoning is based on the assumption that the value, dignity, and rights of each individual person must be maintained.

Postural development The increasing ability of the baby to control parts of the body, especially the head and the trunk.

Pragmatics The study of the social uses of language.

Preconventional level Kohlberg's first two stages of moral development. Moral reasoning is based on the assumption that individuals must serve their own needs.

Prehension The ability to grasp and manipulate objects with the hands.

Preoperational Form of intelligence in which symbols and mental actions begin to replace objects and overt behaviors. The second of Piaget's periods, extending from about 2 to about 6 years old.

Pretend play A form of play in which children use an object or person as a symbol to stand for something else.

Preterm Describes babies born before the end of the normal gestation period.

Primary caregiver The person, usually the mother, with whom the infant develops the major attachment relationship.

Principle of mutual exclusivity A proposed principle of semantic development stating that children assume that an object can have only one name.

Private speech Speech children produce and direct toward themselves during a problem-solving activity.

Production deficiency The failure to generate a mnemonic strategy spontaneously.

Productivity The property of language that permits humans to produce and comprehend an infinite number of statements.

Progressive decentering Piaget's term for the gradual decline in egocentrism that occurs across development.

Prosocial behavior The aspect of moral conduct that includes socially desirable behaviors such as sharing, helping, and cooperating; often used interchangeably with *altruism* by modern researchers.

Proximal processes Bronfenbrenner and Ceci's term for interactions between the child and aspects of the microsystem that have positive effects on psychological functioning and that help to maximize expression of the child's genetic potential.

Proximodistal Literally, near to far. This principle of development refers to the tendency of body parts to develop in a trunk-to-extremities direction.

Psychometric An approach to the study of intelligence that emphasizes the use of standardized tests to identify individual differences among people.

Psychoteratology The study of the harmful effects of teratogens through the use of behavioral measures, such as learning ability.

Puberty The period in which chemical and physical changes in the body occur that enable sexual reproduction.

Punisher A consequence that makes the behavior it follows less likely, either through the presentation of something unpleasant or the removal of something desirable.

Qualitative identity The knowledge that the qualitative nature of something is not changed by a change in its appearance. In Piaget's theory, a preoperational achievement.

Rapid eye movement (REM) sleep A stage of irregular sleep in which the eyes move rapidly while the eyelids are closed.

Reaction range In Gottesman's model, the term for the range of ability or skill that is set by the genes.

Reactivation The preservation of the memory for an event through reencounter with at least some portion of the event in the interval between initial experience and memory test.

Recall memory The retrieval of some past stimulus or event that is not perceptually present.

Recapitulation theory An early biological notion, later adopted by psychologist G. Stanley Hall, that the development of the individual repeats the development of the species.

Recast A response to speech that restates it using a different structure.

Reciprocal altruism A proposed mechanism by which an individual's altruistic behavior toward members of the social group may promote the survival of the individual's genes through reciprocation by others or may ensure the survival of similar genes.

Reciprocal determinism Albert Bandura's proposed process describing the interaction of a person's characteristics and abilities (P), behavior (B), and environment (E).

Recognition memory The realization that some perceptually present stimulus or event has been encountered before.

Reduplicated babbling A stage in the preverbal period, beginning at about 6 months, when infants produce strings of identical sounds, such as *dadada.*

Referential style Vocabulary acquired during the naming explosion that involves a large proportion of nouns and object labels.

Reflex A biological relation in which a specific stimulus reliably elicits a specific response.

Rejected child A child who receives few positive and many negative nominations in sociometric assessments by peers. Such children seem to be disliked by the peer group.

Relational aggression Aggression designed to damage or disrupt social relationships.

Reliability The consistency or repeatability of a measuring instrument. A necessary property of a standardized test.

Representation The use of symbols to picture and act on the world internally.

Repression Freud's term for the process through which desires or motivations are driven into the unconscious, as typically occurs during the phallic stage.

Respondent behaviors Responses based on reflexes, which are controlled by specific eliciting stimuli. The smaller category of human behaviors.

Respondent (classical) conditioning A form of learning, involving reflexes, in which a neutral stimulus acquires the power to elicit a reflexive response (UCR) as a result of being associated (paired) with the naturally eliciting stimulus (UCS). The neutral stimulus then becomes a conditioned stimulus (CS).

Respondent extinction A process related to respondent conditioning in which the conditioned stimulus (CS) gradually loses its power to elicit the response as a result of no longer being paired with the unconditioned stimulus (UCS).

Response inhibition The absence of a particular response that has just been modeled; often the result of vicarious punishment.

Reversal-replication (ABAB) design An experimental design in which the independent variable is systematically presented and removed several times. Can be used in studies involving very few research participants.

Reversibility Piaget's term for the power of operations to correct for potential disturbances and thus arrive at correct solutions to problems.

Rooting reflex The turning of the infant's head toward the cheek at which touch stimulation is applied, followed by opening of the mouth.

Rules Procedures for acting on the environment and solving problems.

Scaffolding A method of teaching in which the adult adjusts the level of help provided in relation to the child's level of performance, the goal being to encourage independent performance.

Scatter diagram A graphic illustration of a correlation between two variables.

Schemes Piaget's term for the cognitive structures of infancy. A scheme consists of a set of skilled, flexible action patterns through which the child understands the world.

Scientific method The system of rules used by scientists to conduct and evaluate their research.

Script A representation of the typical sequence of actions and events in some familiar context.

Selective attention Concentration on a stimulus or event with attendant disregard for other stimuli or events.

Self-consciousness A concern about the opinions others hold about one.

Self-efficacy Bandura's term for people's ability to succeed at various tasks, as judged by the people themselves.

Self-esteem (self-worth) A person's evaluation of the self, and the affective reactions to that evaluation.

Self-evaluation The part of the self-system concerned with children's opinions of themselves and their abilities.

Self-knowledge (self-awareness) The part of the self-system concerned with children's knowledge about themselves.

Self-regulation The part of the self-system concerned with self-control.

Self-schema An internal cognitive portrait of the self used to organize information about the self.

Self-system The set of interrelated processes—self-knowledge, self-evaluation, and self-regulation—that make up the self.

Semantic bootstrapping A proposed mechanism of grammatical development in which children use semantic cues to infer aspects of grammar.

Semantics The study of how children acquire words and their meanings.

Sensation The experience resulting from the stimulation of a sense organ.

Sensitive period A period of development during which certain behaviors are more easily learned.

Sensorimotor schemes Skilled and generalizable action patterns by which infants act on and understand the world. In Piaget's theory, the cognitive structures of infancy.

Sensorimotor Form of intelligence in which knowledge is based on physical interactions with people and objects. The first of Piaget's periods, extending from birth to about 2 years.

Separation protest Crying and searching by infants separated from their mothers; an indication of the formation of the attachment bond.

Seriation The ability to order stimuli along some quantitative dimension, such as length. In Piaget's theory, a concrete operational achievement.

Sex chromosomes The pair of human chromosomes that determines one's sex. Females have two X chromosomes, males have an X and a Y.

Sex difference A behavior or characteristic in which males and females usually differ as a result of biological or environmental factors.

Sex differentiation The process through which biological sex differences emerge.

Sex (gender) An individual's biological maleness or femaleness.

Sex typing The process by which children develop the sex role considered by their culture to be appropriate for their gender.

Sex-limited traits Genes that affect males and females differently but that are not carried on the sex chromosomes.

Sex-linked (X-linked) genes Genes found only on the sex chromosomes, most often the X chromosome.

Sexual dimorphism The existence in most species of biological differences between males and females for the purpose of reproduction.

Sexual orientation A person's sexual preference. Heterosexuals are attracted to members of the opposite sex and homosexuals are attracted to members of the same sex.

Shape constancy The experience that the physical shape of an object remains the same even though the shape of its projected image on the eye varies.

Short-term storage space In Case's theory, the resources necessary to store results from previous cognitive operations while carrying out new ones.

Sickle-cell anemia (SCA) An inherited blood disease caused by a recessive gene. The red blood cells assume a sickle shape and do not distribute oxygen efficiently to the cells of the body.

Size constancy The experience that the physical size of an object remains the same even though the size of its projected image on the eye varies.

Small for gestational age (SGA) Describes babies born at a weight in the bottom 10% of babies of a particular gestational age.

Social cognition Knowledge of the social world and interpersonal relationships.

Social comparison Comparing one's abilities to those of others.

Social conventions Rules used by a society to govern everyday behavior and to maintain order.

Social problem-solving skills Skills needed to resolve social dilemmas.

Social referencing Using information gained from other people to regulate one's own behavior.

Social referential communication A form of communication in which a speaker sends a message that is comprehended by a listener.

Social support Resources (both tangible and intangible) provided by other people in times of uncertainty or stress.

Social withdrawal Self-imposed isolation from the peer group.

Socialization The process through which society molds the child's beliefs, expectations, and behavior.

Social-learning theory A form of environmental/learning theory that adds observational learning to respondent and operant learning as a process through which children's behavior changes.

Sociobiology A branch of biology that attempts to discover the evolutionary origins of social behavior.

Sociogenesis The process of acquiring knowledge or skills through social interactions.

Sociometric techniques Procedures for assessing children's social status based on evaluations by the peer group. Sociometric techniques may involve ratings of degree of liking, nominations of liked or disliked peers, or forced-choice judgments between pairs of peers.

Speech act An instance of speech used to perform pragmatic functions, such as requesting or complaining.

+1 stage technique A method of investigating the hierarchical organization of moral stages; children are exposed to reasoning one stage above their own in order to maximize cognitive conflict and thus induce movement to the higher stage.

Stepping reflex The infant's response to pressure on the soles of the feet, consisting of stepping (flexing) movements.

Stimulus generalization A process related to respondent conditioning in which stimuli that are similar to the conditioned stimulus (CS) also acquire the power to elicit the response.

Strange Situation procedure Ains-worth's laboratory procedure for assessing the strength of the attachment relationship by observing the infant's reactions to a series of structured episodes involving the mother and a stranger.

Strategy construction The creation of strategies for processing and remembering information. A mechanism of change in information-processing theories.

Strategy selection Progressively greater use of relatively effective strategies in comparison to relatively ineffective ones. A mechanism of change in information-processing theories.

Study strategies Mnemonic strategies (such as outlining and note taking) that students use in an attempt to remember school material.

Surface structure Chomsky's term for the way words and phrases are arranged in spoken languages.

Symbolic function The ability to use one thing (such as a mental image or word) as a symbol to represent something else.

Symbolic play Form of play in which the child uses one thing in deliberate pretense to stand for something else.

Synapse The small space between neurons across which neural activity is communicated from one cell to another.

Syntactic bootstrapping A proposed mechanism of semantic development in which children use syntactic cues to infer the meanings of words.

Syntax The aspect of grammar that involves word order.

Tabula rasa Latin phrase, meaning "blank slate," used to describe the newborn's mind as entirely empty of inborn abilities, interests, or ideas.

Tay-Sachs disease An inherited disease in which the lack of an enzyme that breaks down fats in brain cells causes progressive brain deterioration. Affected children usually die by the age of 6.

Telegraphic speech Speech from which unnecessary function words (e.g., *in, the, with*) are omitted; common during early language learning.

Temperament The aspect of personality studied in infants, which includes their emotional expres-siveness and responsiveness to stimulation.

Teratogen An agent that can cause abnormal development in the fetus.

Testes The male gonadal structure that produces the sperm.

Theory of mind Thoughts and beliefs concerning the mental world.

Theory A broad set of statements describing the relation between a phenomenon and the factors assumed to affect it.

Tonic neck reflex The infant's postural change when the head is turned to the side, consisting of extension of the arm on that side and clenching of the other arm in what looks like a fencer's position.

Tools of intellectual adaptation Vygotsky's term for the techniques of thinking and problem solving that children internalize from their culture.

Transactional influence A bidirectional, or reciprocal, relationship in which individuals influence one another's behaviors.

Transformational grammar A set of rules developed by the LAD to translate a language's surface structure to a deep structure that the child can innately understand.

Transitivity The ability to combine relations logically to deduce necessary conclusions—for example, if $A > B$ and $B > C$, then $A > C$. In Piaget's theory, a concrete operational achievement.

Turner's syndrome A chromosomal disorder of females in which one X chromosome is absent; women with the syndrome have no ovaries, do not menstruate, are short in stature, and display ultrafeminine personality characteristics.

Ultrasound imaging A noninvasive procedure for detecting physical defects in the fetus. A device that produces sound-like waves of energy is moved over the pregnant woman's abdomen, and reflections of these waves form an image of the fetus.

Umbilical cord A soft cable of tissue and blood vessels that connects the fetus to the placenta.

Unconditioned response (UCR) The response portion of a reflex, which is reliably elicited by a stimulus (UCS).

Unconditioned stimulus (UCS) The stimulus portion of a reflex, which reliably elicits a respondent behavior (UCR).

Underextension A language error in which children fail to apply labels they know to things for which the labels are appropriate.

Universals of development Aspects of development or behavior that are common to children everywhere.

Utilization deficiency The failure of a recently developed mnemonic strategy to facilitate recall.

Validity The accuracy with which a measuring instrument assesses the attribute that it is designed to measure. A necessary property of a standardized test.

Variable Any factor that can take on different values along a dimension.

Vestibular sensitivity The perceptual experience that results from motion of the body and the pull of gravity.

Vicarious punishment Punishing consequences experienced when viewing a model that affect an observer similarly.

Vicarious reinforcement Reinforcing consequences experienced when viewing a model that affect an observer similarly.

Visual accommodation The automatic adjustment of the lens of the eye to produce a focused image of an object on the light-sensitive tissue at the back of the eye.

Visual acuity The clarity with which visual images can be perceived.

Visual self-recognition The ability to recognize oneself; often studied in babies by having them look into mirrors.

Wariness of strangers A general fear of unfamiliar people that appears in many infants at around 8 months of age and indicates the formation of the attachment bond.

Whole-word An approach to reading instruction that stresses learning and visual retrieval of entire words.

47,XYY syndrome A chromosomal disorder of males in which an extra Y chromosome is present; men with the syndrome have large body builds and very masculine personality characteristics.

Zeitgeist The spirit of the times, or the ideas shared by most scientists during a given period.

Zone of proximal development Vygotsky's term for the difference between what children can do by themselves and what they can do with help from an adult.

Zygote A fertilized ovum.

References

ABBEDUTO, L., DAVIES, B., & FURMAN, L. (1998). The development of speech act comprehension in mentally retarded individuals and nonretarded children. *Child Development, 59,* 1460–1472.

ABEL, E. L. (1980). Fetal alcohol syndrome: Behavioral teratology. *Psychological Bulletin, 87,* 29–50.

ABEL, E. L. (1981). Behavioral teratology of alcohol. *Psychological Bulletin, 90,* 564–581.

ABOUD, F. E. (1985). Children's application of attribution principles to social comparisons. *Child Development, 56,* 682–688.

ABOUD, F. E., & MENDELSON, M. J. (1996). Determinants of friendship selection and quality: Links to child-mother attachment. In W. M. Bukowski, A. F. Newcomb, & W. W. Hartup (Eds.), *The company they keep: Friendship in childhood and adolescence.* New York: Cambridge University Press.

ABRAMOVITCH, R., & GRUSEC, J. E. (1978). Peer imitation in a natural setting. *Child Development, 49,* 60–65.

ABRAMOVITCH, R., CORTER, C., PEPLER, D. J., & STANHOPE, L. (1986). Sibling and peer interaction: A final follow-up and a comparison. *Child Development, 57,* 217–229.

ACKERMAN, B. P. (1993). Children's understanding of the speaker's meaning in referential communication. *Journal of Experimental Child Psychology, 55,* 56–86.

ACKERMAN, B. P., & SILVER, S. (1990). Children's understanding of private keys in referential communication. *Journal of Experimental Child Psychology, 50,* 217–242.

ACKERMAN, B. P., SZYMANSKI, J., & SILVER, D. (1990). Children's use of common ground in interpreting ambiguous referential utterances. *Developmental Psychology, 26,* 234–245.

ACREDOLO, L. P. (1978). Development of spatial orientation in infancy. *Developmental Psychology, 14,* 224–234.

ACREDOLO, L. P. (1985). Coordinating perspectives on infant spatial orientation. In R. Cohen (Ed.), *The development of spatial cognition.* Hillsdale, NJ: Erlbaum.

ACREDOLO, L. P., & GOODWYN, S. W. (1988). Symbolic gesturing in normal infants. *Child Development, 59,* 450–466.

ACREDOLO, L. P., & GOODWYN, S. W. (1990). Development of communicative gesturing. In R. Vasta (Ed.), *Annals of child development* (Vol. 7). Greenwich, CT: JAI Press.

ADAMS, G. R., ABRAHAM, K. G., & MARKSTROM, C. A. (1987). The relations among identity development, self-consciousness, and self-focusing during middle and late adolescence. *Developmental Psychology, 23,* 292–297.

ADAMS, M. J. (1990). *Beginning to read: Thinking and learning about print.* Cambridge: MIT Press.

ADAMS, M. J., TREIMAN, R., & PRESSLEY, M. (1998). Reading, writing, and literacy. In W. Damon (Series Ed.) & I. E. Sigel & K. A. Renninger (Vol. Eds.), *Handbook of child psychology: Vol. 4. Child psychology in practice* (5th ed.). New York: Wiley.

ADAMS, P. L., MILNER, J. R., & SCHREPF, N. A. (1984). *Fatherless children.* New York: Wiley.

ADAMS, R. J. (1989). Newborns' discrimination among mid- and long-wavelength stimuli. *Journal of Experimental Child Psychology, 47,* 30–141.

ADAMS, R. J. (1995). Further exploration of human neonatal chromatic-achromatic distinction. *Journal of Experimental Child Psychology, 60,* 344–360.

ADAMSON, L. B. (1995). *Communication development during infancy.* Madison, WI: Brown & Benchmark.

ADAMSON, L. B., & BAKEMAN, R. (1991). The development of shared attention during infancy. In R. Vasta (Ed.), *Annals of child development* (Vol. 8). London: Kingsley.

AIELLO, J. R., NICOSIA, G., & THOMPSON, D. E. (1979). Physiological, social, and behavioral consequences of crowding on children and adolescents. *Child Development, 50,* 195–202.

AINSWORTH, M. D. S. (1983). Patterns of infant–mother attachment as related to maternal care: Their early history and their contribution to continuity. In D. Magnusson & V. Allen (Eds.), *Human development: An interactional perspective.* New York: Academic Press.

AINSWORTH, M. D. S. (1992). A consideration of social referencing in the context of attachment theory and research. In S. Feinman (Ed.), *Social referencing and the social construction of reality in infancy.* New York: Plenum.

AINSWORTH, M. D. S., BLEHAR, M. C., WATERS, E., & WALL, S. (1978). *Patterns of attachment: A psychological study of the strange situation.* Hillsdale, NJ: Erlbaum.

AINSWORTH, M. D. S., & BOWLBY, J. (1991). An ethological approach to personality development. *American Psychologist, 46,* 331–341.

AINSWORTH, M. D. S., & WITTIG, B. A. (1969). Attachment and exploratory behavior of one-year-olds in a strange situation. In B. M. Foss (Ed.), *Determinants of infant behavior* (Vol. 4). London: Methuen.

ALESSANDRI, S. M. (1992). Effects of maternal work status in single-parent families on children's perception of self and family and school achievement. *Journal of Experimental Child Psychology, 54,* 417–433.

ALFIERI, T., RUBLE, D. N., & HIGGINS, E. T. (1996). Gender stereotypes during adolescence: Developmental changes and the transition to junior high school. *Developmental Psychology, 32,* 1129–1137.

ALIBALI, M. W., FLEVARES, L. M., & GOLDIN-MEADOW, S. (1997). Assessing knowledge conveyed in gesture: Do teachers have the upper hand? *Journal of Educational Psychology, 89,* 183–193.

ALLEN, L. S., & GORSKI, R. A. (1992). Sexual orientation and the size of the anterior commissure in the human brain. *Proceedings of the National Academy of Sciences, USA, 89,* 7199–7202.

ALLEY, T. R. (1983). Infantile head shape as an elicitor of adult protection. *Merrill-Palmer Quarterly, 29,* 411–427.

ALS, H., DUFFY, F. H., & McANULTY, G. B. (1988). Behavioral differences between preterm and full-term newborns as measured with the APIB System Scores: I. *Infant Behavior and Development, 11,* 305–318.

ALTMAN, L. (1993, July 7). World Bank reports health gains for poor. *New York Times,* p. A6.

AMERICAN ASSOCIATION OF UNIVERSITY WOMEN. (1992). *How schools shortchange women.* Wellesley, MA: American Association of University Women and National Education Association.

AMERICAN PSYCHIATRIC ASSOCIATION. (1994). *Diagnostic and statistical manual of mental disorders* (4th ed.). Washington, DC: Author.

ANDERSON, D. R., LORCH, E. P., FIELD, D. E., COLLINS, P. A., & NATHAN, J. G. (1986). Television viewing at home: Age trends in visual attention and time with T.V. *Child Development, 57,* 1024–1033.

ANDERSON, E., HETHERINGTON, E. M., CLINGEMPEEL, W. G. (1989). Transformations in family relations at puberty: Effects of family context. *Journal of Early Adolescence, 9,* 310–334.

ANDERSON, G. M., & ALLISON, D. J. (1990). Intrauterine growth retardation and the routine use of ultrasound. In R. B. Goldbloom & R. S. Lawrence (Eds.), *Preventing disease: Beyond the rhetoric.* New York: Springer-Verlag.

ANDERSSON, B.-E. (1992). Effects of day-care on cognitive and socio-emotional competence of thirteen-year-old Swedish schoolchildren. *Child Development, 63,* 20–36.

ANGLIN, J. M. (1993). Vocabulary development: A morphological analysis. *Monographs of the Society for Research in Child Development, 58*(10, Serial No. 238).

ANGOFF, W. H. (1988). The nature–nurture debate, aptitudes, and group differences. *American Psychologist, 43,* 713–720.

ANISFELD, E., CASPER, V., NOZYCE, M., & CUNNINGHAM, N. (1990). Does infant carrying promote attachment? An experimental study of the effects of increased physical contact on the development of attachment. *Child Development, 61,* 1617–1627.

ANISFELD, M. (1991). Neonatal imitation. *Developmental Review, 11,* 60–97.

ANISFELD, M. (1996). Only tongue protrusion modeling is matched by neonates. *Developmental Review, 16,* 149–161.

ANTELL, S. E., & KEATING, D. P. (1983). Perception of numerical invariance in neonates. *Child Development, 54,* 695–701.

ANTONINI, A., & STRYKER, M. P. (1993). Rapid remodeling of axonal arbors in the visual cortex. *Science, 260,* 1819–1821.

APGAR, V. (1953). A proposal for a new method of evaluation of the newborn infant. *Current Researches in Anesthesia and Analgesia, 32,* 260–267.

APPEL, L. F., COOPER, R. G., McCARRELL, N., SIMS-KNIGHT, J., YUSSEN, S. R., & FLAVELL, J. H. (1972). The development of the distinction between perceiving and memorizing. *Child Development, 43,* 1365–1381.

APPLEY, M. (1986). G. Stanley Hall: Vow on Mount Owen. In S. H. Hulse & B. F. Green (Eds.), *One hundred years of psychological research in America.* Baltimore: Johns Hopkins University Press.

ARBUTHNOT, J., SPARLING, Y., FAUST, D., & KEE, W. (1983). Logical and moral development in preadolescent children. *Psychological Reports, 52,* 209–210.

ARCHER, J. (1991). The influence of testosterone on human aggression. *British Journal of Psychology, 82,* 1–28.

ARCHER, J. (1992). *Ethology and human development.* London: Harvester Wheatsheaf and Barnes & Noble.

ARCHER, J. (1994). Testosterone and aggression: A theoretical review. *Journal of Offender Rehabilitation, 21,* 3–39.

ARCHER, J. (1996). Sex differences in social behavior: Are the social role and evolutionary explanations compatible? *American Psychologist, 51,* 909–917.

ARIES, P. (1962). *Centuries of childhood: A social history of family life.* New York: Knopf.

ASENDORPF, J. B. (1990a). Beyond social withdrawal: Shyness, unsociability, and peer avoidance. *Human Development, 33,* 250–259.

ASENDORPF, J. B. (1990b). Development of inhibition during childhood: Evidence for situational specificity and a two-factor model. *Developmental Psychology, 26,* 721–730.

ASENDORPF, J. B. (1994). The malleability of behavioral inhibition: A study of individual developmental functions. *Developmental Psychology, 30,* 912–919.

ASENDORPF, J. B., & BAUDONNIERE, P. (1993). Self-awareness and other-awareness: Mirror self-recognition and synchronic imitation among unfamiliar peers. *Developmental Psychology, 29,* 88–95.

ASENDORPF, J. B., WARKENTIN, V., & BAUDONNIERE, P. (1996). Self-awareness and other-awareness II: Mirror-self recognition, social contingency awareness, and synchronic imitation. *Developmental Psychology, 32,* 313–321.

ASHCRAFT, M. H. (1990). Strategic processing in children's mental arithmetic: A review and proposal. In D. F. Bjorklund (Ed.), *Children's strategies: Contemporary views of cognitive development.* Hillsdale, NJ: Erlbaum.

ASHER, S. R. (1985). An evolving paradigm in social skill training research with children. In B. H. Schneider, K. H. Rubin, & J. E. Ledingham (Eds.), *Children's peer relations: Issues in assessment and intervention.* New York: Springer-Verlag.

ASHER, S. R., & COIE, J. D. (Eds.). (1990). *Peer rejection in childhood.* New York: Cambridge University Press.

ASHER, S. R., & HYMEL, S. (1981). Children's social competence in peer relations: Sociometric and behavioral assessment. In J. D. Wine & M. D. Smye (Eds.), *Social competence.* New York: Guilford.

ASHER, S. R., PARKER, J. G., & WALKER, D. L. (1996). Distinguishing friendship from acceptance: Implications for intervention and assessment. In W. M. Bukowski, A. F. Newcomb, & W. W. Hartup (Eds.), *The company they keep: Friendship in childhood and adolescence.* New York: Cambridge University Press.

ASHER, S. R., RENSHAW, P. D., & HYMEL, S. (1982). Peer relations and the development of social skills. In S. G. Moore (Ed.), *The young child: Reviews of research* (Vol. 3). Washington, DC: National Association for the Education of Young Children.

ASHMEAD, D. H., DAVIS, D. L., WHALEN, T., & ODOM, R. D. (1991). Sound localization and sensitivity to interaural time differences in human infants. *Child Development, 62,* 1211–1226.

ASHMEAD, D. H., & PERLMUTTER, M. (1980). Infant memory in everyday life. In M. Perlmutter (Ed.), *New directions for child development: No. 10. Children's memory.* San Francisco: Jossey-Bass.

ASLIN, R. N., & SHEA, S. L. (1990). Velocity thresholds in human infants: Implications for the perception of motion. *Developmental Psychology, 26,* 589–598.

ASLIN, R. N., JUSCZYK, P. W., & PISONI, D. B. (1998). Speech and auditory processing during infancy: Constraints on and precursors to language. In W. Damon (Series Ed.) & D. Kuhn & R. S. Siegler (Vol. Eds.), *Handbook of child psychology: Vol. 2. Cognition, perception, and language* (5th ed.). New York: Wiley.

ASLIN, R. N., PISONI, D. B., & JUSCZYK, P. W. (1983). Auditory development and speech perception in infancy. In P. H. Mussen (Series Ed.) & M. M. Haith & J. J. Campos (Vol. Eds.), *Handbook of child psychology: Vol. 2. Infancy and developmental psychobiology.* New York: Wiley.

ASTINGSON, J. W. (1988). Children's production of commissive speech acts. *Journal of Child Language, 15,* 411–423.

ASTINGTON, J. W. (1993). *The child's discovery of the mind.* Cambridge, MA: Harvard University Press.

ATTILI, G. (1990). Successful and disconfirmed children in the peer group: Indices of social competence within an evolutionary perspective. *Human Development, 33,* 238–249.

ATTILI, G., VERMIGLI, P., & SCHNEIDER, B. H. (1997). Peer acceptance and friendship patterns within a cross-cultural perspective. *International Journal of Behavioral Development, 21,* 277–288.

AZMITIA, M., & MONTGOMERY, R. (1993). Friendship, transactive dialogues, and the development of scientific reasoning. *Social Development, 2,* 202–221.

BACHU, A. (1995). *Fertility of American women: June, 1994* (U.S. Bureau of the Census Current Population Report No. P20–482). Washington, DC: U.S. Government Printing Office.

BAENNINGER, M., & NEWCOMBE, N. (1989). The role of experience in spatial test performance: A meta-analysis. *Sex Roles, 20,* 327–344.

BAHRICK, L. E. (1983). Infants' perception of substance and temporal synchrony in multimodal events. *Infant Behavior and Development, 6,* 429–451.

BAHRICK, L. E. (1992). Infants' perceptual differentiation of amodal and modality-specific audio-visual relations. *Journal of Experimental Child Psychology, 53,* 180–199.

BAHRICK, L. E. (1995). Intermodal origins of self-perception. In P. Rochat (Ed.), *The self in infancy: Theory and research.* Amsterdam: Elsevier.

BAHRICK, L. E., & PICKENS, J. N. (1994). Amodal relations: The basis for intermodal perception and learning in infancy. In D. J. Lewkowicz & R. Lickliter (Eds.), *The development of intersensory perception: Comparative perspectives.* Hillsdale, NJ: Erlbaum.

BAHRICK, L. E., & PICKENS, J. N. (1995). Infant memory for object motion across a period of three months: Implications for a four-phase attention function. *Journal of Experimental Child Psychology, 59,* 343–371.

BAILEY, J. M., BOBROW, D., WOLFE, M., & MIKACH, S. (1995). Sexual orientation of adult sons of gay fathers. *Developmental Psychology, 31,* 124–129.

BAILEY, J. M., MILLER, J. S., & WILLERMAN, L. (1993). Maternally rated childhood gender nonconformity in homosexuals and heterosexuals. *Archives of Sexual Behavior, 22,* 461–469.

BAILEY, J. M., & PILLARD, R. C. (1991). A genetic study of male sexual orientation. *Archives of General Psychiatry, 48,* 1089–1096.

BAILEY, J. M., WILLERMAN, L., & PARKS, C. (1991). A test of the maternal stress theory of human male homosexuality. *Archives of Sexual Behavior, 20,* 277–293.

BAILEY, J. M., & ZUCKER, K. J. (1995). Childhood sex-typed behavior and sexual orientation: A conceptual analysis and quantitative review. *Developmental Psychology, 31,* 43–55.

BAILEY, S. M., & GARN, S. M. (1986). The genetics of maturation. In F. Falkner & J. M.

Tanner (Eds.), *Human growth: A comprehensive treatise.* New York: Plenum.

BAILLARGEON, R. (1986). Representing the existence and the location of hidden objects: Object permanence in 6- and 8-month-old infants. *Cognition, 23,* 21–41.

BAILLARGEON, R. (1987a). Object permanence in $3\frac{1}{2}$- and $4\frac{1}{2}$-month-old infants. *Developmental Psychology, 23,* 655–664.

BAILLARGEON, R. (1987b). Young infants' reasoning about the physical and spatial properties of a hidden object. *Cognitive Development, 2,* 179–200.

BAILLARGEON, R. (1993). The object concept revisited: New directions in the investigation of infants' physical knowledge. In H. W. Reese (Ed.), *Advances in child development and behavior* (Vol. 23). New York: Academic Press.

BAILLARGEON, R. (1994). How do infants learn about the physical world? *Current Directions in Psychological Science, 3,* 133–140.

BAILLARGEON, R. (1995). A model of physical reasoning in infancy. In C. K. Rovee-Collier & L. P. Lipsitt (Eds.), *Advances in infancy research* (Vol. 9). Norwood, NJ: Ablex.

BAILLARGEON, R., KOTOVSKY, L., & NEEDHAM, A. (1995). The acquisition of physical knowledge in infancy. In D. Sperber, D. Premack, & A. J. Premack (Eds.), *Causal cognition: A multidisciplinary debate.* New York: Clarendon Press.

BAKER, L., SONNENSCHEIN, S., SERPELL, R., FERNANDEZ-FEIN, S., & SCHER, D. (1994). *Contexts of emergent literacy: Everyday home experiences of urban pre-kindergarten children.* (Reading Research Report No. 24). National Reading Research Center, University of Georgia and University of Maryland.

BAKER-WARD, L., ORNSTEIN, P. A., & HOLDEN, D. J. (1984). The expression of memorization in early childhood. *Journal of Experimental Child Psychology, 37,* 555–575.

BALABAN, M. T. (1995). Affective influences on startle in five-month-old infants: Reactions to facial expressions of emotion. *Child Development, 66,* 28–36.

BALDWIN D. A. (1991). Infants' contributions to the achievement of joint reference. *Child Development, 63,* 875–890.

BALDWIN, D. A. (1995). Understanding the link between joint attention and language. In C. Moore & P. J. Dunham (Eds.), *Joint attention: Its origins and role in development.* Hillsdale, NJ: Erlbaum.

BALDWIN, D. A., & MOSES, L. J. (1994). Early understanding of referential intent and attentional focus: Evidence from language and emotion. In C. Lewis & P. Mitchell (Eds.), *Children's early understanding of mind.* Hillsdale, NJ: Erlbaum.

BALDWIN, D. A., & MOSES, L. J. (1996). The ontogeny of social information gathering. *Child Development, 67,* 1915–1939.

BALÁZS, R., JORDAN, T., LEWIS, P. D., & PATEL, A. J. (1986). Undernutrition and brain development. In F. Falkner & J. M. Tanner (Eds.), *Human growth: A comprehensive treatise.* New York: Plenum.

BANDURA, A. (1965). Influence of models' reinforcement contingencies on the acquisition of imitative responses. *Journal of Personality and Social Psychology, 1,* 589–595.

BANDURA, A. (1973). *Aggression: A social learning analysis.* Englewood Cliffs, NJ: Prentice-Hall.

BANDURA, A. (1977). *Social learning theory.* Englewood Cliffs, NJ: Prentice Hall.

BANDURA, A. (1978). The self system in reciprocal determinism. *American Psychologist, 33,* 344–358.

BANDURA, A. (1983). Psychological mechanisms of aggression. In R. G. Geen & E. I. Donnerstein (Eds.), *Aggression: Theoretical and empirical reviews* (Vol. 1). New York: Academic Press.

BANDURA, A. (1986). *Social foundations of thought and action: A social cognitive theory.* Englewood Cliffs, NJ: Prentice-Hall.

BANDURA, A. (1989). Social cognitive theory. In R. Vasta (Ed.), *Annals of child development* (Vol. 6). Greenwich, CT: JAI Press.

BANDURA, A. (1991a). Self-regulation of motivation through anticipatory and self-regulatory mechanisms. In R. A. Dienstbier (Ed.), *Perspectives on motivation: Nebraska symposium on motivation* (Vol. 38). Lincoln: University of Nebraska Press.

BANDURA, A. (1991b). Social cognitive theory of moral thought and action. In W. M. Kurtines & J. L. Gewirtz (Eds.), *Handbook of moral behavior and development: Vol. 1. Theory.* Hillsdale, NJ: Erlbaum.

BANDURA, A. (1992). Social cognitive theory. In R. Vasta (Ed.), *Six theories of child development: Revised formulations and current issues.* London: Kingsley.

BANDURA, A. (1994). Social cognitive theory of mass communication. In J. Bryant & D. Zillman (Eds.), *Media effects: Advances in theory and research.* Hillsdale, NJ: Erlbaum.

BANDURA, A. (1997). *Self-efficacy: The exercise of control.* New York: W. H. Freeman.

BANDURA, A., & SCHUNK, D. H. (1981). Cultivating competence, self-efficacy, and intrinsic interest through proximal self-motivation. *Journal of Personality and Social Psychology, 41,* 586–598.

BANKS, M. S., & GINSBURG, A. P. (1985). Infant visual preferences: A review and new theoretical treatment. In H. W. Reese (Ed.), *Advances in child development and behavior* (Vol. 19). Orlando, FL: Academic Press.

BANKS, M. S., & SALAPATEK, P. (1983). Infant visual perception. In P. H. Mussen (Series Ed.) & M. M. Haith & J. J. Campos (Vol. Eds.), *Handbook of child psychology: Vol. 2. Infancy and developmental psychobiology.* New York: Wiley.

BARD, C., HAY, L., & FLEURY, M. (1990). Timing and accuracy of visually directed movements in children: Control of direction and amplitude components. *Journal of Experimental Child Psychology, 50,* 102–118.

BARGLOW, P., VAUGHN, B. E., & MOLITOR, N. (1987). Effects of maternal absence due to employment on the quality of infant-mother attachment. *Child Development, 58,* 45–954.

BARINGA, M. (1993). Death gives birth to the nervous system. But how? *Science, 259,* 762–763.

BARKER, R. G., & WRIGHT, H. F. (1951). *One boy's day: A specimen record of behavior.* New York: Harper & Row.

BARKER, R. G., & WRIGHT, H. F. (1955). *Midwest and its children.* New York: Harper & Row.

BARKLEY, R. A. (1990). *Attention-deficit hyperactivity disorder: A handbook for diagnosis and treatment.* New York: Guilford.

BARNARD, K. E., BEE, H. L., & HAMMOND, M. A. (1984a). Developmental changes in maternal interactions with term and preterm infants. *International Journal of Behavior and Development, 7,* 101–113.

BARNARD, K. E., BEE, H. L., & HAMMOND, M. A. (1984b). Home environment and cognitive development in a healthy, low-risk sample: The Seattle study. In A. W. Gottfried (Ed.), *Home environment and early cognitive development.* New York: Academic Press.

BARNARD, K. E., MORISSET, C. E., & SPIEKER, S. (1993). Preventive interventions: Enhancing parent–infant relationships. In C. H. Zeanah, Jr. (Ed.), *Handbook of infant mental development.* New York: Guilford.

BARNETT, C. R., LEIDERMAN, P. H., GROBSTEIN, R., & KLAUS, M. H. (1970). Neonatal separation: The maternal side of interactional deprivation. *Pediatrics, 45,* 197–205.

BARNETT, M. A. (1987). Empathy and related responses in children. In N. Eisenberg & J. Strayer (Eds.), *Empathy and its development.* New York: Cambridge University Press.

BARNETT, W. S. (1995). Long-term effects of early childhood programs on cognitive and school outcomes. In The Center for the Future of Children (Ed.), *The future of children.* Los Altos, CA: The David and Lucile Packard Foundation.

BARON, R. A. (1983). The control of human aggression: A strategy based on incompatible responses. In R. G. Geen & E. I. Donnerstein (Eds.), *Aggression: Theoretical and empirical reviews* (Vol. 2). New York: Academic Press.

BARON-COHEN, S. (1995). *Mindblindness: An essay on autism and theory of mind.* Cambridge: MIT Press.

BARONE, D. (1993). Wednesday's child: Literacy development of children prenatally exposed to crack or cocaine. *Research in the Teaching of English, 27,* 7–45.

BARRERA, M., & MAURER, D. (1981). The perception of facial expressions by the three-month-old. *Child Development, 52,* 203–206.

BARTON, E. J. (1981). Developing sharing: An analysis of modeling and other behavioral techniques. *Behavior Modification, 5,* 386–398.

BASH, M. A. S., & CAMP, B. W. (1985). *Think aloud: Classroom program.* Champaign, IL: Research Press.

BATES, E. (1990). Language about me and you: Pronominal reference and the emerging concept of self. In D. Cicchetti & M. Beeghly (Eds.), *The self in transition: Infancy to childhood.* Chicago: University of Chicago Press.

BATES, E., CAMAIONI, L., & VOLTERRA, V. (1975). The acquisition of performatives prior to speech. *Merrill-Palmer Quarterly, 21,* 205–226.

BATES, E., & CARNEVALE, G. F. (1993). New directions in research on language development. *Developmental Review, 13,* 436–470.

BATES, E., & MacWHINNEY, B. (1982). Functionalist approaches to grammar. In E. Wanner & L. Gleitman (Eds.), *Language acquisition: The state of the art.* New York: Cambridge University Press.

BATES, E., & MacWHINNEY, B. (1987). Competition, variation, language learning. In B. MacWhinney (Ed.), *Mechanisms of language acquisition.* Hillsdale, NJ: Erlbaum.

BATES, E., O'CONNELL, B., & SHORE, C. (1987). Language and communication in infancy. In J. D. Osofsky (Ed.), *Handbook of infant development* (2nd ed.). New York: Wiley.

BATES, J. E. (1987). Temperament in infancy. In J. D. Osofsky (Ed.), *Handbook of infant development* (2nd ed.). New York: Wiley.

BATES, J. E. (1990). Conceptual and empirical linkages between temperament and behavior problems: A commentary on the Sanson, Prior, and Kyrios study. *Merrill-Palmer Quarterly, 36,* 193–199.

BATES, J. E., & BAYLES, K. (1984). Objective and subjective components in mothers' perceptions of their children from age 6 months to 3 years. *Merrill-Palmer Quarterly, 30,* 111–130.

BATES, J. E., BAYLES, K., BENNETT, D. S., RIDGE, B., & BROWN, M. M. (1991). Origins of externalizing behavior problems at eight years of age. In D. Pepler & K. Rubin (Eds.), *Development and treatment of childhood aggression.* Hillsdale, NJ: Erlbaum.

BATES, J. E., & WACHS, T. D. (1994). *Temperament: Individual differences at the interface of biology and behavior.* Washington, DC: American Psychological Association.

BATES, J. E., WACHS, T. D., & EMDE R. N. (1994). Toward practical uses for biological concepts of temperament. In J. E. Bates & T. D. Wachs (Eds.), *Temperament: Individual differences at the interface of biology and behavior.* Washington, DC: American Psychological Association.

BATSON, C. D., & OLESON, K. C. (1991). Current status of the empathy-altruism hypothesis. In M. S. Clark (Ed.), *Review of personality and social psychology: Prosocial behavior.* Newbury Park, CA: Sage.

BAUER, P. J. (1992). Holding it all together: How enabling relations facilitate young children's event recall. *Cognitive Development, 7,* 1–28.

BAUER, P. J. (1993a). Identifying subsystems of autobiographical memory: Commentary on Nelson. In C. A. Nelson (Ed.), *Minnesota symposia on child psychology: Vol. 26. Memory and affect in development.* Hillsdale, NJ: Erlbaum.

BAUER, P. J. (1993b). Memory for gender-consistent and gender-inconsistent event sequences by twenty-five-month-old children. *Child Development, 64,* 285–297.

BAUER, P. J., & FIVUSH, R. (1992). Constructing event representations: Building on a foundation of variation and enabling relations. *Cognitive Development, 2,* 381–401.

BAUER, P. J., HERTSGAARD, L. A., & DOW, G. A. (1994). After 8 months have passed: Long-term recall of events by 1- to 2-year-old children. *Memory, 2,* 353–382.

BAUER, P. J., & MANDLER, J. M. (1992). Putting the horse before the cart: The use of temporal order in recall of events by one-year-old children. *Developmental Psychology, 28,* 441–452.

BAUER, P. J., & TRAVIS, L. L. (1993). The fabric of an event: Different sources of temporal invariance differentially affect 24-month-olds' recall. *Cognitive Development, 8,* 319–341.

BAUERFELD, S. L., & LACHENMEYER, J. R. (1992). Prenatal nutritional status and intellectual development: Critical review and evaluation. In B. B. Lahey & A. E. Kazdin (Eds.), *Advances in clinical child psychology* (Vol. 14). New York: Plenum.

BAUMRIND, D. (1971). Current patterns of parental authority. *Developmental Psychology Monograph, 4,* 1–103.

BAUMRIND, D. (1989). Rearing competent children. In W. Damon (Ed.), *Child development today and tomorrow.* San Francisco: Jossey-Bass.

BAUMRIND, D. (1991). The influence of parenting style on adolescent competence and substance abuse. *Journal of Early Adolescence, 11,* 56–95.

BAYLEY, N. (1970). Development of mental abilities. In P. H. Mussen (Ed.), *Carmichael's manual of child psychology* (3rd ed., Vol. 1). New York: Wiley.

BAYLEY, N. (1993). *Bayley Scales of Infant Development: Birth to Two Years* (2nd ed.). New York: The Psychological Corporation.

BEAR, G. G. (1989). Sociomoral reasoning and antisocial behaviors among normal sixth graders. *Merrill-Palmer Quarterly, 35,* 181–196.

BEAUCHAMP, D. K., COWART, B. J., MENNELLA, J. A., & MARSH, R. R. (1994). Infant salt taste: Developmental, methodological, and contextual factors. *Developmental Psychobiology, 27,* 353–365.

BECKER, J. (1993). Young children's numerical use of number words: Counting in many-to-one situations. *Developmental Psychology, 29,* 458–465.

BECKER, J. (1994). "Sneak-shoes," "sworders," and "nose-beards": A case study of lexical innovation. *First Language, 14,* 195–211.

BECKER, J. M. F. (1977). A learning analysis of the development of peer-oriented behavior in nine-month-old infants. *Developmental Psychology, 13,* 481–491.

BECKWITH, L., & PARMELEE, A. (1986). EEG patterns of preterm infants, home environment, and later IQ. *Child Development, 57,* 777–789.

BEDARD, J., & CHI, M. T. H. (1992). Expertise. *Current Directions in Psychological Science, 1,* 135–139.

BEEBE, B., ALSON, D., JAFFE, J., FELDSTEIN, S., & CROWN, C. (1988). Vocal congruence in mother–infant play. *Journal of Psycholinguistic Research, 17,* 245–259.

BEEBE, T. P., JR., WILSON, T. E., OGLETREE, D. F., KATZ, J. E., BALHORN, R., SALMERON, M. D., & SIERHAUS, W. J. (1989). Direct observation of native DNA structures with the scanning tun-neling microscope. *Science, 243,* 370–372.

BEHREND, D. A. (1988). Overextensions in early language comprehension: Evidence from a signal detection approach. *Journal of Child Language, 15,* 63–75.

BEHREND, D. A., ROSENGREN, K. S., & PERLMUTTER, M. (1992). The relation between private speech and parental interactive style. In R. M. Diaz & L. E. Berk (Eds.), *Private speech: From social interaction to self-regulation.* Hillsdale, NJ: Erlbaum.

BEHRMAN, R. E., & VAUGHAN, V. C., III. (1987). *Nelson textbook of pediatrics* (3rd ed.). Philadelphia: Saunders.

BEIER, E. G. (1991). Freud: Three contributions. In G. A. Kimble, M. Wertheimer, & C. L. White (Eds.), *Portraits of pioneers in psychology.* Hillsdale, NJ: Erlbaum.

BEILIN, H. (1978). Inducing conservation through training. In G. Steiner (Ed.), *Psychology of the 20th century: Vol. 7. Piaget and beyond.* Zurich: Kindler.

BEILIN, H. (1989). Piagetian theory. In R. Vasta (Ed.), *Annals of child development* (Vol. 6). Greenwich, CT: JAI Press.

BEILIN, H. (1992a). Piaget's enduring contribution to developmental psychology. *Developmental Psychology, 28,* 191–204.

BEILIN, H. (1992b). Piaget's new theory. In H. Beilin & P. B. Pufall (Eds.), *Piaget's theory: Prospects and possibilities.* Hillsdale, NJ: Erlbaum.

BELLINGER, D., LEVITON, A., NEEDLEMAN, H. L., WATERNAUX, C., & RABINOWITZ, M. (1986). Low-level lead exposure and infant development in the first year. *Neurobehavioral Toxicology and Teratology, 8,* 151–161.

BELSEY, E. M., ROSENBLATT, D. B., LIEBERMAN, B. A., REDSHAW, M., CALDWELL, J., NOTARIANNI, L., SMITH, R. L., & BEARD, R. W. (1981). The influence of maternal analgesia on neonatal behavior: I. Pethidine. *British Journal of Obstetrics and Gynecology, 887,* 398–406.

BELSKY, J. (1988). The "effects" of infant day care reconsidered. *Early Childhood Research Quarterly, 3,* 235–272.

BELSKY, J. (1996). Parent, infant, and social-contextual antecedents of father–son attachment security. *Developmental Psychology, 32,* 905–913.

BELSKY, J., FISH, M., & ISABELLA, R. (1991). Continuity and discontinuity in infant negative and positive emotionality: Family antecedents and attachment consequences. *Developmental Psychology, 27,* 421–431.

BELSKY, J., GILSTRAP, B., & ROVINE, M. (1984). The Pennsylvania Infant and Family Development Project: I. Stability and change in mother–infant and father–infant interaction in a family setting at one, three, and nine months. *Child Development, 55,* 692–705.

BELSKY, J., ROSENBERGER, K., & CRNIC, K. (1995). The origins of attachment security: "Classical" and contextual determinants. In S. Goldberg, R. Muir, & J. Kerr (Eds.), *Attachment theory: Social, developmental, and clinical perspectives.* Hillsdale, NJ: The Analytic Press.

BELSKY, J., & ROVINE, M. (1988). Nonmaternal care in the first year of life and infant–parent attachment security. *Child Development, 59,* 157–167.

BELSKY, J., ROVINE, M., & TAYLOR, D. G. (1984). The Pennsylvania Infant and Family Development Project; III. The origins of individual differences in infant–mother attachment: Maternal and infant contributions. *Child Development, 55,* 718–728.

BELSKY, J., STEINBERG, L., & DRAPER, P. (1991). Childhood experience, interpersonal development, and reproductive strategy: An evolutionary theory of socialization. *Child Development, 62,* 647–670.

BEM, D. J. (1996). Exotic becomes erotic: A developmental theory of sexual orientation. *Psychological Review, 103,* 320–335.

BEM, S. L. (1974). The measurement of psychological androgyny. *Journal of Consulting and Clinical Psychology, 42,* 155–162.

BEM, S. L. (1975). Sex role adaptability: One consequence of psychological androgyny. *Journal of Personality and Social Psychology, 31,* 634–643.

BEM, S. L. (1979). Theory and measurement of androgyny: A reply to the Pedhazur-Tetenbaum and Locksley-Colten critiques. *Journal of Personality and Social Psychology, 37,* 1047–1054.

BEM, S. L. (1981). Gender schema theory: A cognitive account of sex-typing. *Psychological Review, 88,* 354–364.

BEM, S. L. (1985). Androgyny and gender schema theory. In T. B. Sonderegger (Ed.), *Nebraska symposium on motivation: Psychology and gender* (Vol. 32). Lincoln: University of Nebraska Press.

BEM, S. L. (1987). Masculinity and femininity exist only in the mind of the perceiver. In J. M. Reinisch, L. A. Rosenblum, & S. A. Sanders (Eds.), *Masculinity/femininity: Basic perspectives.* New York: Oxford University Press.

BEM, S. L. (1989). Genital knowledge and gender constancy in preschool children. *Child Development, 60,* 649–662.

BEM, S. L. (1993). *The lenses of gender: Transforming the debate on sexual inequality.* New Haven, CT: Yale University Press.

BENASICH, A. A., & BROOKS-GUNN, J. (1996). Maternal attitudes and knowledge of child-rearing: Associations with family and child outcomes. *Child Development, 67,* 1186–1205.

BENASICH, A. A., BROOKS-GUNN, J., & CLEWELL, B. C. (1992). How do mothers benefit from early intervention programs? *Journal of Applied Developmental Psychology, 13,* 311–362.

BENBOW, C. (1992). Academic achievement in mathematics and science of students between ages 13 and 23: Are there differences among students in the top one percent of mathematics ability? *Journal of Educational Psychology, 84,* 51–61.

BENEDICT, H. (1979). Early lexical development: Comprehension and production. *Journal of Child Language, 6,* 183–200.

BENENSON, J. F. (1993). Greater preference among females than males for dyadic interaction in early childhood. *Child Development, 64,* 544–555.

BENENSON, J. F., APOSTOLERIS, N. H., & PARNASS, J. (1997). Age and sex differences in dyadic and group interaction. *Developmental Psychology, 33,* 538–543.

BENENSON, J. F., & DWECK, C. S. (1986). The development of trait explanations and self-evaluations in the academic and social domains. *Child Development, 57,* 1179–1187.

BENOIT, D. (1993). Failure to thrive and feeding disorders. In C. H. Zeanah, Jr. (Ed.), *Handbook of infant mental development.* New York: Guilford.

BENSON, J. B. (1990). The significance and development of crawling in human infancy. In J. E. Clark & J. H. Humphrey (Eds.), *Advances in motor development research* (Vol. 3). New York: AMS Press.

BENSON, J. B., & UZGIRIS, I. C. (1985). Effects of self-initiated locomotion on infant search activity. *Developmental Psychology, 21,* 923–931.

BERENBAUM, S. A. (1990). Congenital adrenal hyperplasia: Intellectual and psychosexual functioning. In C. Holmes (Ed.), *Psychoneuroendocrinology: Brain, behavior, and hormonal interactions.* New York: Springer-Verlag.

BERENBAUM, S. A., & HINES, M. (1992). Early androgens are related to sex-typed toy preferences. *Psychological Science, 3,* 203–206.

BERENBAUM, S. A., & SNYDER, E. (1995). Early hormonal influences on childhood sex-typed activity and playmate preferences: Implications for the development of sexual orientation. *Developmental Psychology, 31,* 31–42.

BERG, W. K., & BERG, K. M. (1987). Psychophysiological development in infancy. In J. Osofsky (Ed.), *Handbook of infant development* (2nd ed.). New York: Wiley.

BERK, L. E. (1994). Why children talk to themselves. *Scientific American, 271,* 78–83.

BERK, L. E., & SPUHL, S. T. (1995). Maternal interaction, private speech, and task performance in preschool children. *Early Childhood Research Quarterly, 10,* 145–169.

BERKO, J. (1958). The child's learning of English morphology. *Word, 14,* 150–177.

BERKOWITZ, L. (1993). *Aggression: Its causes, consequences, and control.* New York: Academic Press.

BERKOWITZ, M. W., GIBBS, J. C., & BROUGHTON, J. M. (1980). The relation of moral judgment stage disparity to developmental effects of peer dialogues. *Merrill-Palmer Quarterly, 26,* 341–357.

BERNDT, T. J. (1979). Developmental changes in conformity to peers and parents. *Developmental Psychology, 15,* 608–616.

BERNDT, T. J. (1981). Age changes and changes over time in prosocial intentions and behavior between friends. *Developmental Psychology, 17,* 408–416.

BERNDT, T. J. (1986a). Children's comments about their friendships. In M. Perlmutter (Ed.), *Minnesota symposia on child psychology: Vol. 18. Cognitive perspectives on children's social and behavioral development.* Hillsdale, NJ: Erlbaum.

BERNDT, T. J. (1986b). Sharing between friends: Contexts and consequences. In E. C. Mueller & C. R. Cooper (Eds.), *Process and outcome in peer relationships.* New York: Academic Press.

BERNDT, T. J. (1988). The nature and significance of children's friendships. In R. Vasta (Ed.), *Annals of child development* (Vol. 5). Greenwich, CT: JAI Press.

BERNDT, T. J. (1989a). Friendships in childhood and adolescence. In W. Damon (Ed.), *Child development today and tomorrow.* San Francisco: Jossey-Bass.

BERNDT, T. J. (1989b). Obtaining support from friends during childhood and adolescence. In D. Belle (Ed.), *Children's social networks and social supports.* New York: Wiley.

BERNDT, T. J. (1996a). Exploring the effects of friendship quality. In W. M. Bukowski, A. F. Newcomb, & W. W. Hartup (Eds.), *The company they keep: Friendship in childhood and adolescence.* New York: Cambridge University Press.

BERNDT, T. J. (1996b). Transitions in friendship and friends' influence. In J. A. Graber, J. Brooks-Gunn, & A. C. Petersen (Eds.), *Transi-*

tions through adolescence: Interpersonal domains and context. Mahwah, NJ: Erlbaum

BERNDT, T. J., & HANNA, N. A. (1995). Intimacy and self-disclosure in friendships. In K. J. Rotenberg (Ed.), *Disclosure processes in children and adolescents.* New York: Cambridge University Press.

BERNDT, T. J., & KEEFE, K. (1995). Friends' influence on adolescents' adjustment to school. *Child Development, 66,* 1312–1329.

BERNDT, T. J., MILLER, K. E., & PARK, K. (1989). Adolescents' perceptions of friends' and parents' influence on aspects of their school adjustment. *Journal of Early Adolescence, 9,* 419–435.

BERNDT, T. J., & PERRY, T. B. (1990). Distinctive features and effects of adolescent friendships. In R. Montemayor, G. R. Adams, & T. P. Gullotta (Eds.), *From childhood to adolescence: A transitional period?* London: Sage.

BERNIER, J. G., & SIEGEL, D. H. (1994). Attention-deficit hyperactivity disorder: A family ecological systems perspective. *Families in Society, 75,* 142–150.

BERRY, G., & ASAMEN, J. K. (Eds.). (1993). *Children and television: Images in a changing sociocultural world.* Newbury Park, CA: Sage.

BERSOFF, D. M., & MILLER, J. G. (1993). Culture, context, and the development of moral accountability judgments. *Developmental Psychology, 29,* 664–676.

BERTENTHAL, B. I. (1996). Origins and early development of perception, action, and representation. *Annual Review of Psychology, 47,* 431–459.

BERTENTHAL, B. I., & BAI, D. L. (1989). Infants' sensitivity to optical flow for controlling posture. *Developmental Psychology, 25,* 936–945.

BERTENTHAL, B. I., CAMPOS, J. J., & BARRETT, K. (1984). Self-produced locomotion: An organizer of emotional, cognitive, and social development in infancy. In R. Emde & R. Harmon (Eds.), *Continuities and discontinuities in development.* New York: Plenum.

BERTENTHAL, B. I., CAMPOS, J. J., & HAITH, M. M. (1980). Development of visual organization: The perception of subjective contours. *Child Development, 51,* 1072–1080.

BERTENTHAL, B. I., CAMPOS, J. J., & KERMOIAN, R. (1994). An epigenetic perspective on the development of self-produced locomotion and its consequences. *Current Directions in Psychological Science, 3,* 140–145.

BERTENTHAL, B. I., & CLIFTON, R. K. (1998). Perception and action. In W. Damon (Series Ed.) & D. Kuhn & R. S. Siegler (Vol. Eds.), *Handbook of child psychology: Vol. 2. Cognition, perception, and language* (5th ed.). New York: Wiley.

BERTENTHAL, B. I., & FISCHER, K. W. (1978). Development of self-recognition in the infant. *Developmental Psychology, 11,* 44–50.

BEST, C. T. (1995). Learning to perceive the sound pattern of English. In C. Rovee-Collier & L. P. Lipsitt (Eds.), *Advances in infancy research* (Vol. 9). Norwood, NJ: Ablex.

BEST, D. L., & WILLIAMS, J. E. (1993). A cross-cultural viewpoint. In A. E. Beall & R. J. Sternberg (Eds.), *The psychology of gender.* New York: Guilford.

BHAVNAGRI, N., & PARKE, R. D. (1991). Parents as direct facilitators of children's peer relationships: Effects of age of child and sex of parent. *Journal of Social and Personal Relationships, 8,* 423–440.

BIALYSTOK, E., & CUMMINS, J. (1991). Language, cognition, and education of bilingual children. In E. Bialystok (Ed.), *Language processing in bilingual children.* Cambridge: Cambridge University Press.

BICKERTON, D. (1984). The language bioprogram hypothesis. *Behavioral and Brain Sciences, 7,* 173–187.

BIERNAT, M., & WORTMAN, C. (1991). Sharing of home responsibilities between professionally employed women and their husbands. *Journal of Personality and Social Psychology, 60,* 844–860.

BIGELOW, A. E. (1981). The correspondence between self- and image movement as a cue to self-recognition for young children. *Journal of Genetic Psychology, 139,* 11–26.

BIGLER, R. S. (1997). Conceptual and methodological issues in the measurement of children's sex typing. *Psychology of Women Quarterly, 21,* 53–69.

BIGLER, R. S., & LIBEN, L. S. (1990). The role of attitudes and interventions in gender-schematic processing. *Child Development, 61,* 1440–1452.

BIGLER, R. S., & LIBEN, L. S. (1993). A cognitive-developmental approach to social stereotyping and reconstructive memory in Euro-American children. *Child Development, 64,* 1507–1518.

BIJOU, S. W. (1995). *Behavior analysis of child development.* Reno, NV: Context Press.

BILLY, J. O. G., TANFER, K., GRADY, W. R., & KLEPINGER, D. H. (1993). The sexual behavior of men in the United States. *Family Planning Perspectives, 25,* 52–60.

BINSACCA, D. B., ELLIS, J., MARTIN, D. G., & PETITTI, D. B. (1987). Factors associated with low birthweight in an inner-city population: The role of financial problems. *American Journal of Public Health, 77,* 505–506.

BIOLOGICAL SYSTEMS. (1988, June 10). *Science,* p. 1383.

BIRCH, L. L., & BILLMAN, J. (1986). Preschool children's food sharing with friends and acquaintances. *Child Development, 57,* 387–395.

BIRNHOLZ, J. C., & BENACERRAF, B. R. (1983). The development of human fetal hearing. *Science, 222,* 516–518.

BISANZ, J., & LeFEVRE, J. (1990). Strategic and nonstrategic processing in the development of mathematical cognition. In D. F. Bjorklund (Ed.), *Children's strategies: Contemporary views of cognitive development.* Hillsdale, NJ: Erlbaum.

BIVENS, J. A., & BERK, L. E. (1990). A longitudinal study of the development of elementary school children's private speech. *Merrill-Palmer Quarterly, 36,* 443–463.

BJORKLUND, D. F. (1987). How age changes in knowledge base contri-bute to the development of children's memory: An interpretive review. *Developmental Review, 7,* 93–130.

BJORKLUND, D. F. (Ed.). (1990). *Children's strategies: Contemporary views of cognitive development.* Hillsdale, NJ: Erlbaum.

BJORKLUND, D. F. (1995). *Children's thinking* (2nd ed.). Pacific Grove, CA: Brooks/Cole.

BJORKLUND, D. F. (1997). In search of a metatheory for cognitive development (or, Piaget is dead and I don't feel so good myself). *Child Development, 68,* 144–148.

BJORKLUND, D. F., & COYLE, T. R. (1995). Utilization deficiencies in the development of memory strategies. In F. E. Weinert & W. Schneider (Eds.), *Memory performance and competencies: Issues in growth and development.* Mahwah, NJ: Erlbaum.

BJORKLUND, D. F., & KIPP, K. (1996). Parental investment theory and gender differences in the evolution of inhibition mechanisms. *Psychological Bulletin, 120,* 163–188.

BJORKLUND, D. F., MUIR-BROADDUS, J. E., & SCHNEIDER, W. (1990). The role of knowledge in the development of strategies. In D. F. Bjorklund (Ed.), *Children's strategies: Contemporary views of cognitive development.* Hillsdale, NJ: Erlbaum.

BJORKLUND, D. F., & SCHNEIDER, W. (1996). The interaction of knowledge, aptitude, and strategies in children's memory performance. In H. W. Reese (Ed.), *Advances in child development and behavior* (Vol. 26). San Diego: Academic Press.

BLACKBURN, R. (1993). *The psychology of criminal conduct.* Chichester, England: Wiley.

BLAKE, J., & BOYSSON-BARDIES, B. (1992). Patterns in babbling: A cross-linguistic study. *Journal of Child Language, 19,* 51–74.

BLAKEMORE, J. E. O., LaRUE, A. A., & OLEJNIK, A. B. (1979). Sex-appropriate toy preferences and the ability to conceptualize toys as sex-role related. *Developmental Psychology, 15,* 339–340.

BLANCHARD, R., & BOGAERT, A. F. (1996). Homosexuality in men and number of older brothers. *American Journal of Psychiatry, 153,* 27–31.

BLANCHARD, R., & ZUCKER, K. J. (1994). Reanalysis of Bell, Weinberg, and Hammersmith's data on birth order, sibling sex ratio, and parental age in homosexual men. *American Journal of Psychiatry, 151,* 1375–1376.

BLANCARD, R., ZUCKER, K. J., BRADLEY, S. J., & HUME, C. S. (1995). Birth order and sibling sex ratio in homosexual male adolescents and probably prehomosexual feminine boys. *Developmental Psychology, 31,* 22–30.

BLASI, A. (1980). Bridging moral cognition and moral action: A critical review of the literature. *Psychological Bulletin, 88,*1–45.

BLASI, A. (1983). Moral cognition and moral action: A theoretical perspective. *Developmental Review, 3,* 178–210.

BLASI, A., & GLODIS, K. (1995). The development of identity: A critical analysis from the perspective of the self as subject. *Developmental Review, 15,* 404–433.

BLASS, E. M., & SMITH, B. A. (1992). Differential effects of sucrose, fructose, glucose, and lactose. *Developmental Psychology, 28,* 804–810.

BLASS, E. M., GANCHROW, J. R., & STEINER, J. E. (1984). Classical conditioning in newborn humans 2–48 hours of age. *Infant Behavior and Development, 7,* 223–235.

BLOCK, J., & ROBINS, R. W. (1993). A longitudinal study of consistency and change in self-esteem from early adolescence to early adulthood. *Child Development, 64,* 909–923.

BLOCK, J. H. (1983). Differential premises arising from differential socialization of the sexes: Some conjectures. *Child Development, 54,* 1335–1354.

BLOOM, L. (1973). *One word at a time.* The Hague, Netherlands: Mouton.

BLOOM, L. (1993, Winter). Word learning. *SRCD Newsletter,* pp. 1–13.

BLOOM, L. (1998). Language acquisition in developmental contexts. In W. Damon (Series Ed.) & D. Kuhn & R. S. Siegler (Vol. Eds.), *Handbook of child psychology: Vol. 2. Cognition, perception, and language* (5th ed.). New York: Wiley.

BLOOM, L., HOOD, L., & LIGHTBROWN, P. (1974). Imitation in language development: If, when, and why. *Cognitive Psychology, 6,* 380–420.

BLOOM, L., LIGHTBROWN, P., & HOOD, L. (1975). Structure and variation in child language. *Monographs of the Society for Research in Child Development, 40* (2, Serial No. 160).

BLOOM, L., MARGULIS, C., TINKER, E., & FUJITA, N. (1996). Early conversations and word learning: Contributions from child and adult. *Child Development, 67,* 3154–3175.

BLOOM, P. (1996). Controversies in language acquisition: Word learning and the part of speech. In R. Gelman & T. Au (Eds.), *Perceptual and cognitive development.* San Diego: Academic Press.

BLOUNT, B. G. (1982). The ontogeny of emotions and their vocal expression in infants. In S. A. Kuczaj (Ed.), *Language development* (Vol. 2). Hillsdale, NJ: Erlbaum.

BLURTON-JONES, N. (1972). *Ethological studies of child behavior.* Cambridge: Cambridge University Press.

BLYTH, D. A., SIMMONS, R. G., & CARLTON-FORD, S. (1983). The adjustment of early adolescents to school transitions. *Journal of Early Adolescence, 3,* 105–120.

BOCCIA, M., & CAMPOS, J. J. (1989). Maternal emotional signals, social referencing, and infants' reactions to strangers. In N. Eisenberg (Ed.), *New directions for child development* (Vol. 44). San Francisco: Jossey-Bass.

BODROVA, E., & LEONG, D. J. (1996). *Tools of the mind: The Vygotskian approach to early childhood education.* Englewood Cliffs, NJ: Merrill.

BOGGIANO, A. K., MAIN, D. S., & KATZ, P. A. (1988). Children's preference for challenge: The role of perceived competence and control. *Journal of Personality and Social Psychology, 54,* 134–141.

BOHANNON, J. N., III, PADGETT, R. J., NELSON, K. E., & MARK, M. (1996). Useful evidence on negative evidence. *Developmental Psychology, 32,* 551–555.

BOHANNON, J. N., III, & STANOWICZ, L. (1988). The issue of negative evidence: Adult responses to children's language errors. *Developmental Psychology, 24,* 684–689.

BOISMER, J. D. (1977). Visual stimulation and wake–sleep behavior in human neonates. *Developmental Psychology, 10,* 219–227.

BOLDIZAR, J. P., PERRY, D. G., & PERRY, L. C. (1989). Outcome values and aggression. *Child Development, 60,* 571–579.

BOLES, D. B. (1980). X-linkage of spatial ability: A critical review. *Child Development, 51,* 625–635.

BOLLES, R. C., & BEECHER, M. D. (Eds.). (1988). *Evolution and learning.* Hillsdale, NJ: Erlbaum.

BOOM, J., & MOLENAAR, P. C. M. (1989). A developmental model of hierarchical stage structure in objective moral judgments. *Developmental Review, 9,* 133–145.

BOONE, S. L. (1991). Aggression in African-American boys: A discriminant analysis. *Genetic, Social, and General Psychology Monographs, 117,* 205–228.

BORKE, H. (1975). Piaget's mountains revisited: Changes in the egocentric landscape. *Developmental Psychology, 11,* 240–243.

BORNSTEIN, M. H. (Ed.). (1987). *Sensitive periods in development: Interdisciplinary perspectives.* Hillsdale, NJ: Erlbaum.

BORNSTEIN, M. H. (Ed.). (1991). *Cultural approaches to parenting.* Hillsdale, NJ: Erlbaum.

BORNSTEIN, M. H, & SIGMAN, M. D. (1986). Continuity in mental development from infancy. *Child Development, 57,* 251–274.

BORNSTEIN, M. H., & TAMIS-LeMONDA, C. S. (1990). Activities and interactions of mothers and their firstborn infants in the first six months of life: Covariation, stability, continuity, correspondence, and prediction. *Child Development, 61,* 1206–1217.

BORSTELMANN, L. J. (1983). Children before psychology: Ideas about children from antiquity to the later 1800s. In W. Kessen (Ed.), *Handbook of child psychology: Vol. 1. History, theory, and methods.* New York: Wiley.

BOSTON, M. B., & LEVY, G. D. (1991). Changes and differences in preschoolers' understanding of gender scripts. *Cognitive Psychology, 6,* 417–432.

BOTTOMS, B. L., & GOODMAN, G. S. (Eds.). (1996). *International perspectives on child abuse and children's testimony: Psychological research and law.* Thousand Oaks, CA: Sage.

BOTTOMS, B. L., GOODMAN, G. S., SCHWARTZ-KENNEY, B. M., SACHSENMAIER, T., & THOMAS, S. (1990, March). *Keeping secrets: Implications for children's testimony.* Paper presented at the American Psychology and Law Society Meeting, Williamsburg, VA.

BOUCHARD, T. J., JR. (1997). IQ similarity in twins reared apart: Findings and responses to critics. In R. J. Sternberg & E. L. Grigorenko (Eds.), *Intelligence, heredity, and environment.* New York: Cambridge University Press.

BOUCHARD, T. J., JR., LYKKEN, D. T., McGUE, M., SEGAL, N. L., & TELLEGEN, A. (1990). Sources of human psychological differences: The Minnesota Study of Twins Reared Apart. *Science, 250,* 223–228.

BOUCHARD, T. J., JR., LYKKEN, D. T., TELLEGEN, A., & MCGUE, M. (1996). Genes, drives, environment and experience: EPD theory—revised. In C. Benbow & D. Lubinski (Eds.), *From psychometrics to giftedness: Essays in honor of Julian Stanley.* Baltimore: Johns Hopkins University Press.

BOUCHARD, T. J., JR., & McGUE, M. (1981). Familial studies of in-telligence: A review. *Science, 212,* 1055–1059.

BOWERMAN, M. (1975). Cross-linguistic similarities at two stages of syntactic development. In E. H. Lenneberg & E. E. Lenneberg (Eds.), *Foundations of language: A multidisciplinary approach.* New York: Academic Press.

BOWERMAN, M. (1976). Semantic factors in the acquisition of rules for word use and sentence construction. In D. M. Morehead & A. E. Morehead (Eds.), *Normal and deficient child language.* Baltimore: University Park Press.

BOWERMAN, M. (1981). Language development. In H. C. Triandis & A. Heron (Eds.), *Handbook of cross-cultural psychology: Vol. 4. Developmental psychology.* Boston: Allyn & Bacon.

BOWERMAN, M. (1982). Reorganizational processes in lexical and syntactic development. In E. Wanner & L. R. Gleitman (Eds.), *Language acquisition: The state of the art.* New York: Cambridge University Press.

BOWERMAN M. (1988). Inducing the latent structure of language. In F. S. Kessel (Ed.), *The development of language and language researchers: Essays in honor of Roger Brown.* Hillsdale, NJ: Erlbaum.

BOWLBY, J. (1969). *Attachment and loss: Vol. 1. Attachment.* New York: Basic Books.

BOWLBY, J. (1973). *Attachment and loss: Vol. 2. Separation.* New York: Basic Books.

BOWLBY, J. (1980). *Attachment and loss: Vol. 3. Loss.* New York: Basic Books.

BOWLBY, J. (1982). *Attachment and loss: Vol. 1. Attachment* (2nd ed.). New York: Basic Books. (Original work published 1969).

BOWLBY, J. (1988). *A secure base: Parent–child attachment and healthy human development.* New York: Basic Books.

BOYES, M. C., & ALLEN, S. G. (1993). Styles of parent–child interaction and moral reasoning in adolescence. *Merrill-Palmer Quarterly, 39,* 551–570.

BRABANT, S., & MOONEY, L. (1986). Sex role stereotyping in the Sunday comics: Ten years later. *Sex Roles, 14,* 141–148.

BRABANT, S., & MOONEY, L. A. (1997). Sex role stereotyping in the Sunday comics: A twenty year update. *Sex Roles, 37,* 269–281.

BRACKBILL, Y., ADAMS, G., CROWELL, D. H., & GRAY, M. L. (1966). Arousal level in neonates and preschool children under continuous auditory stimulation. *Journal of Experimental Child Psychology, 4,* 178–188.

BRACKEN, B. A. (Ed.). (1996). *Handbook of self-concept: Developmental, social, and clinical considerations.* New York: Wiley.

BRADBARD, M. R., MARTIN, C. L., ENDSLEY, R. C., & HALVERSON, C. F. (1986). Influence of sex stereotypes on children's exploration and memory: A competence versus performance distinction. *Developmental Psychology, 22,* 481–486.

BRADDICK, O., & ATKINSON, J. (1988). Sensory selectivity, attentional control, and cross-channel integration in early visual development. In A. Yonas (Ed.), *Minnesota symposia on child psychology: Vol. 20. Perceptual development in infancy.* Hillsdale, NJ: Erlbaum.

BRADLEY, R. H. (1994). The HOME Inventory: Review and reflections. In H. W. Reese (Ed.), *Advances in child development and behavior* (Vol. 25). San Diego: Academic Press.

BRADLEY, R. H., & CALDWELL, B. M. (1984a). 174 children: A study of the relationship between home environment and cognitive development during the first 5 years. In A. W. Gottfried (Ed.), *Home environment and early cognitive development.* New York: Academic Press.

BRADLEY, R. H., & CALDWELL, B. M. (1984b). The relation of infants' home environments to achievement test performance in first grade: A follow-up study. *Child Development, 55,* 803–809.

BRAINE, M. D. S. (1976). Children's first word combinations. *Monographs of the Society for Research in Child Development, 41* (1, Serial No. 164).

BRAINE, M. D. S., & RUMAINE, B. (1983). Logical reasoning. In P. H. Mussen (Series Ed.) & J. H. Flavell & E. M. Markman (Vol. Eds.), *Handbook of child psychology: Vol. 3. Cognitive development.* New York: Wiley.

BRANDT, M. M., & STRATTNER-GREGORY, M. J. (1980). Effect of highlighting intention on intentionality and restitutive justice. *Developmental Psychology, 16,* 147–148.

BRANIGAN, G. (1979). Some reasons why successive single word utterances are not. *Journal of Child Language, 6,* 411–421.

BRAUNGART, J. M., FULKER, D. W., & PLOMIN, R. (1992). Genetic mediation of the home environment during infancy: A sibling adoption study of the HOME. *Developmental Psychology, 28,* 1048–1055.

BRAUNGART, J. M., PLOMIN, R., DeFRIES, J. C., & FULKER, D. W. (1992). Genetic influence on tester-rated infant temperament as assessed by Bayley's Infant Behavior Record: Non-adoptive and adoptive siblings and twins. *Developmental Psychology, 28,* 40–47.

BRAZELTON, T. B. (1982). Joint regulation of neonate-parent behavior. In E. Z. Tronick (Ed.), *Social interchange in infancy: Affect, cognition, and communication.* Baltimore: University Park Press.

BRAZELTON, T. B., & YOGMAN, M. W. (Eds.). (1986). *Affective development in infancy.* Norwood, NJ: Ablex.

BRAZELTON, T. B., NUGENT, J. K., & LESTER, B. M. (1987). Neonatal Behavioral Assessment Scale. In J. D. Osofsky (Ed.), *Handbook of infant development* (2nd ed.). New York: Wiley.

BREINER, S. J. (1990). *Slaughter of the innocents: Child abuse through the ages.* New York: Plenum.

BREMNER, J. G. (1996). *Infancy.* Cambridge, MA: Blackwell.

BRETHERTON, I. (1987). New perspectives on attachment relations: Security, communication, and internal working models. In J. D. Osofsky (Ed.), *Handbook of infant development* (2nd ed.). New York: Wiley.

BRETHERTON, I. (1988). How to do things with one word: The ontogenesis of intentional message making in infancy. In M. D. Smith & J. L. Locke (Eds.), *The emergent lexicon.* San Diego: Academic Press.

BRETHERTON, I. (1993). From dialogue to internal working models: The co-construction of self in relationships. In C. A. Nelson (Ed.), *Minnesota symposium on child development: Vol. 26. Memory and affect in development.* Hillsdale, NJ: Erlbaum.

BRETHERTON, I. (1995). The origins of attachment theory: John Bowlby and Mary Ainsworth. In S. Goldberg, R. Muir, & J. Kerr (Eds.), *Attachment theory: Social, developmental, and clinical perspectives.* Hillsdale, NJ: The Analytic Press.

BRETHERTON, I., & BEEGHLY, M. (1982). Talking about internal states: The acquisition of an explicit theory of mind. *Developmental Psychology, 18,* 906–921.

BRETHERTON, I., & WATSON, M. W. (Eds.). (1990). *New directions for child development: No. 48. Children's perspectives on the family.* San Francisco: Jossey-Bass.

BREWER, W. F., HERDRICH, D. J., & VOSNIADOU, S. (1987, January). *A cross-cultural study of children's development of cosmological models: Samoan and American data.* Paper presented at the Third International Conference on Thinking, Honolulu.

BRIDGES, A. (1986). Actions and things: What adults talk about to 1-year-olds. In S. A. Kuczaj & M. D. Barrett (Eds.), *The development of word meaning.* New York: Springer-Verlag.

BRIDGES, L. J., CONNELL, J. P., & BELSKY, J. (1988). Similarities and differences in infant–mother and infant–father interaction in the Strange Situation: A component process analysis. *Developmental Psychology, 24,* 92–100.

BROBERG, A. G., LAMB, M. E., & HWANG, P. (1990). Inhibition: Its stability and correlates in sixteen- to forty-month-old children. *Child Development, 61,* 1153–1163.

BROBERG, A. G., WESSELS, H., LAMB, M. E., & HWANG, C. P. (1997). Effects of day care on the development of cognitive abilities in 8-year-olds: A longitudinal study. *Developmental Psychology, 33,* 62–69.

BRODY, G. H. (Ed.). (1996). *Sibling relationships: Their causes and consequences.* Norwood, NJ: Ablex.

BRODY, G. H. (1998). Sibling relationship quality: Its causes and consequences. *Annual Review of Psychology, 49,* 1–24.

BRODY, G. H., GRAZIANO, W. G., & MUSSER, L. M. (1983). Familiarity and children's behavior in same-age and mixed-age peer groups. *Developmental Psychology, 19,* 568–576.

BRODY, G. H., & HENDERSON, R. W. (1977). Effects of multiple model variations and rationale provision on the moral judgments and explanations of young children. *Child Development, 48,* 1117–1120.

BRODY, G. H., & SHAFFER, D. R. (1982). Contributions of parents and peers to children's moral socialization. *Developmental Review, 2,* 31–75.

BRODY, G. H., & STONEMAN, Z. (1995). Sibling relationships in middle childhood. In R. Vasta (Ed.), *Annals of child development* (Vol. 11). London: Kingsley.

BRODY, N. (1997). Intelligence, schooling, and society. *American Psychologist, 52,* 1046–1050.

BRODZINSKY, D. M., LANG, R., & SMITH, D. W. (1995). Parenting adopted children. In M. H. Bornstein (Ed.), *Handbook of parenting: Vol. 3. Status and social conditions of parenting.* Mahwah, NJ: Erlbaum.

BRONFENBRENNER, U. (1962). Soviet methods of character education: Some implications for research. *Religious Education, 57,* 545–561.

BRONFENBRENNER, U. (1970). *Two worlds of childhood: U.S. and U.S.S.R.* New York: Russell Sage Foundation.

BRONFENBRENNER, U. (1979). *The ecology of human development: Experiments by nature and design.* Cambridge: Harvard University Press.

BRONFENBRENNER, U. (1989). Ecological systems theory. In R. Vasta (Ed.), *Annals of child development* (Vol. 6). Greenwich, CT: JAI Press.

BRONFENBRENNER, U. (1992). Ecological

systems theory. In R. Vasta (Ed.), *Six theories of child development: Revised formulations and current issues.* London: Kingsley.

BRONFENBRENNER, U., & CECI, S. J. (1994). Nature–nurture reconceptualized in developmental perspective: A bioecological model. *Psychological Review, 101,* 568–586.

BRONFENBRENNER, U., & MORRIS, P. A. (1998). The ecology of developmental processes. In W. Damon (Ed.), *Handbook of child psychology: Vol. 1. Theoretical models of human development.* New York: Wiley.

BRONSON, W. C. (1981). *Toddlers' behaviors with agemates: Issues of interaction, cognition, and affect.* Norwood, NJ: Ablex.

BRONSTEIN, P. (1994). Differences in mothers' and fathers' behaviors toward children: A cross-cultural comparison. *Developmental Psychology, 20,* 995–1003.

BROOKE, J. (1991, June 15). Signs of life in Brazil's industrial valley of death. *New York Times International,* p. 2.

BROOKS-GUNN, J. (1987). Pubertal processes and girls' psychological adaptation. In R. M. Lerner & T. L. Foch (Eds.), *Biological psychosocial interactions in early adolescence.* Hillsdale, NJ: Erlbaum.

BROOKS-GUNN, J. (1991). Maturational timing variations in adolescent girls, consequences of. In R. M. Lerner, A. C. Petersen, & J. Brooks-Gunn (Eds.), *Encyclopedia of adolescence* (Vol. 2). New York: Garland.

BROOKS-GUNN, J., & CHASE-LANSDALE, P. L. (1995). Adolescent parenthood. In M. H. Bornstein (Ed.), *Handbook of parenting: Vol. 3. Status and social conditions of parenting.* Mahwah, NJ: Erlbaum.

BROOKS-GUNN, J., KLEBANOV, P., LIAW, F., & DUNCAN, G. (1995). Toward an understanding of the effects of poverty upon children. In H. E. Fitzgerald, B. M. Lester, & B. Zuckerman (Eds.), *Children of pov-erty: Research, health, and policy issues.* New York: Garland.

BROOKS-GUNN, J., KLEBANOV, P. K., LIAW, F., & SPIKER, D. (1993). Enhancing the development of low-birthweight premature infants: Changes in cognition and behavior over the first three years. *Child Development, 64,* 736–753.

BROOKS-GUNN, J., & LEWIS, M. (1984). The development of early visual self-recognition. *Developmental Review, 4,* 215–239.

BROOKS-GUNN, J., & REITER, E. O. (1990). The role of pubertal processes. In S. S. Feldman & G. R. Elliott (Eds.), *At the threshold: The developing adolescent.* Cambridge: Harvard University Press.

BROWN, A. L., & CAMPIONE, J. C. (1990). Communities of learning and thinking, or a context by any other name. In D. Kuhn (Ed.), *Developmental perspectives on teaching and learning thinking skills.* Basel, Switzerland: Karger.

BROWN, A. L., & FERRARA, R. A. (1985). Diagnosing zones of proximal development. In J. V. Wertsch (Ed.), *Culture, communication, and cognition: Vygotskian perspectives.* Cambridge: Cambridge University Press.

BROWN, A. L., PALINCSAR, A. S., & ARMBRUSTER, B. B. (1984). Instructing comprehension-fostering activities in interactive learning situations. In H. Mandl, N. L. Stein, & T. Trabasso (Eds.), *Learning and comprehension of text.* Hillsdale, NJ: Erlbaum.

BROWN, B. B. (1990). Peer groups and peer cultures. In S. S. Feldman & G. R. Elliott (Eds.), *At the threshold: The developing adolescent.* Cambridge: Harvard University Press.

BROWN, K. W., & GOTTFRIED, A. W. (1986). Development of cross-modal transfer in early infancy. In L. P. Lipsitt & C. K. Rovee-Collier (Eds.), *Advances in infancy research* (Vol. 4). Norwood, NJ: Ablex.

BROWN, R. (1958a). How shall a thing be called? *Psychological Review, 65,* 14–21.

BROWN, R. (1958b). *Words and things.* Glencoe, IL: Free Press.

BROWN, R. (1973). *A first language: The early stages.* Cambridge: Harvard University Press.

BROWN, R., & HANLON, C. (1970). Derivational complexity and order of acquisition in child speech. In J. R. Hayes (Ed.), *Cognition and the development of language.* New York: Wiley.

BROWNELL, C. A. (1990). Peer social skills in toddlers: Competencies and constraints illustrated by same-age and mixed-age interaction. *Child Development, 61,* 838–848.

BROWNELL, C. A., & BROWN, E. (1992). Peers and play in infants and toddlers. In V. B. Van Hasselt & M. Hersen (Eds.), *Handbook of social development.* New York: Plenum.

BROWNELL, C. A., & CARRIGER, M. S. (1990). Changes in cooperation and self-other differentiation during the second year. *Child Development, 61,* 1164–1174.

BROWNELL, C. A., & STRAUSS, M. A. (1984). Infant stimulation and development: Conceptual and empirical considerations. *Journal of Children in Contemporary Society, 6,* 109–130.

BRUNER, J. (1979). Learning how to do things with words. In D. Aaronson & R. W. Rieber (Eds.), *Psycholinguistic research: Implications and applications.* Hillsdale, NJ: Erlbaum.

BRUNER, J. (1983). *Child's talk: Learning to use language.* New York: Norton.

BRUNER, J., & GOODMAN, C. C. (1947). Value and need as organizing factors in perception. *Journal of Abnormal and Social Psychology, 42,* 33–44.

BRUNER, J., GOODNOW, J. J., & AUSTIN, G. A. (1956). *A study of thinking.* New York: Wiley.

BRUNER, J., ROY, C., & RATNER, N. (1982). The beginnings of request. In K. E. Nelson (Ed.), *Children's language* (Vol. 3). Hillsdale, NJ: Erlbaum.

BRYANT, B. K. (1985). The Neighborhood Walk: Sources of support in middle childhood. *Monographs of the Society for Research in Child Development, 50* (3, Serial No. 210).

BRYDEN, M. P. (1982). *Laterality: Functional asymmetry in the intact brain.* New York: Academic Press.

BUCHER, B., & SCHNEIDER, R. E. (1973). Acquisition and generalization of conservation by pre-schoolers, using operant training. *Journal of Experimental Child Psychology, 16,* 187–204.

BUDWIG, N. (1995). *A developmental-functionalist approach to child language.* Mahwah, NJ: Erlbaum.

BUGENTAL, D. B., & GOODNOW, J. J. (1998). Socialization processes. In W. Damon (Ed.), *Handbook of child psychology: Vol. 3. Social, emotional, and personality development.* New York: Wiley.

BUHRMESTER, D. (1990). Intimacy of friendship, interpersonal competence, and adjustment during preadolescence and adolescence. *Child Development, 61,* 1101–1111.

BUHRMESTER, D. (1992). The developmental courses of sibling and peer relationships. In F. Boer & J. Dunn (Eds.), *Children's sibling relationships: Developmental and clinical issues.* Hillsdale, NJ: Erlbaum.

BUHRMESTER, D. (1996). Need fulfillment, interpersonal competence, and the developmental contexts of early adolescent friendship. In W. M. Bukowski, A. F. Newcomb, & W. W. Hartup (Eds.), *The company they keep: Friendship in childhood and adolescence.* New York: Cambridge University Press.

BUHRMESTER, D., & FURMAN, W. (1990). Perceptions of sibling relationships during middle childhood and adolescence. *Child Development, 61,* 1387–1398.

BUHRMESTER, D., & PRAGER, K. (1995). Patterns and functions of self-disclosure during childhood and adolescence. In K. J. Rotenberg (Ed.), *Disclosure processes in children and adolescents.* New York: Cambridge University Press.

BUKOWSKI, W. M., & HOZA, B. (1989). Popularity and friendship: Issues in theory, measurement, and outcome. In T. J. Berndt & G. W. Ladd (Eds.), *Peer relationships in child development.* New York: Wiley.

BULLOCK, M., & LUTKENHAUS, P. (1988). The development of volitional behavior in the toddler years. *Child Development, 59,* 664–674.

BULLOCK, M., & LUTKENHAUS, P. (1990). Who am I? Self-understanding in toddlers. *Merrill-Palmer Quarterly, 36,* 217–238.

BURHANS, K. K., & DWECK, C. S. (1995). Helplessness in early childhood: The role of contingent worth. *Child Development, 66,* 1719–1738.

BURTON, R. V. (1963). The generality of honesty reconsidered. *Psychological Review, 70,* 481–499.

BURTON, R. V. (1984). A paradox in theories and research in moral development. In W. M. Kurtines & J. L. Gewirtz (Eds.), *Morality, moral behavior, and moral development.* New York: Wiley.

BUSHNELL, E. W. (1982). Visual-tactual knowledge in 8-, 9-, and 11-month-old infants. *Infant Behavior and Development, 5,* 63–75.

BUSHNELL, E. W. (1994). A dual-processing approach to cross-modal matching: Implications for development. In D. J. Lewkowicz & R. Lickliter (Eds.), *The development of intersensory perception: Comparative perspectives.* Hillsdale, NJ: Erlbaum.

BUSHNELL, I. W. R., SAI, F., & MULLIN, J. T. (1989). Neonatal recognition of the mother's face. *British Journal of Developmental Psychology, 7,* 3–15.

BUSS, A. H., & PLOMIN, R. (1984). *Temperament: Early developing personality traits.* Hillsdale, NJ: Erlbaum.

BUSS, A. H., & PLOMIN, R. (1986). The EAS approach to temperament. In R. Plomin & J. Dunn (Eds.), *The study of temperament: Changes, continuities and challenges.* Hillsdale, NJ: Erlbaum.

BUSS, D. M. (1995). Psychological sex differences: Origins through sexual selection. *American Psychologist, 50,* 164–168.

BUSSEY, K., & BANDURA, A. (1984). Gender constancy, social power, and sex-linked modeling. *Journal of Personality and Social Psychology, 47,* 1292–1302.

BUSSEY, K., & BANDURA, A. (1992). Self-regulatory mechanisms governing gender development. *Child Development, 63,* 1236–1250.

BUSSEY, K., & PERRY, D. G. (1982). Same-sex imitation: The avoidance of cross-sex models or the acceptance of same-sex models? *Sex Roles, 8,* 773–784.

BUTLER, R. (1990). The effects of mastery and competitive conditions on self-assessment at different ages. *Child Development, 61,* 201–210.

BUTLER, R. (1992). What young people want to know when: The effects of mastery and ability on social information seeking. *Journal of Social and Personality Psychology, 62,* 934–943.

BUTLER, R., & RUZANY, N. (1993). Age and socialization effects on the development of social comparison motives and normative ability assessment in kibbutz and urban children. *Child Development, 64,* 532–543.

BUTTERWORTH, G. (1990). Self-perception in infancy. In D. Cicchetti & M. Beeghly (Eds.), *The self in transition: Infancy to childhood.* Chicago: University of Chicago Press.

BUTTERWORTH, G. (1995a). Origins of mind in perception and action. In C. Moore & P. J. Dunham (Eds.), *Joint attention: Its origins and role in development.* Hillsdale, NJ: Erlbaum.

BUTTERWORTH, G. (1995b). The self as an object of consciousness in infancy. In P. Rochat (Ed.), *The self in infancy: Theory and research.* Amsterdam: Elsevier.

BUZZELLI, C. A. (1995). Teacher-child discourse in the early childhood classroom: A dialogic model of self-regulation and moral development. In S. Reifel (Ed.), *Advances in early education and day care.* (Vol. 7). Greenwich, CT: JAI Press.

BYNE, W., & PARSONS, B. (1993). Human sexual orientation: The biologic theories reappraised. *Archives of General Psychiatry, 50,* 228–239.

BYRNE, B. M. (1996). Academic self-concept: Its structure, measurement, and relation to academic achievement. In B. A. Bracken (Ed.), *Handbook of self-concept: Developmental, social, and clinical considerations.* New York: Wiley.

BYRNES, J. B., & TAKAHIRA, S. (1993). Explaining gender differences on SAT-math items. *Developmental Psychology, 29,* 805–810.

BYRNES, J. P. (1988). Formal operations: A systematic reformulation. *Developmental Review, 8,* 66–87.

CAIN, K. M., & DWECK, C. S. (1995). The relation between motivational patterns and achievement cognitions through the elementary years. *Merrill-Palmer Quarterly, 41,* 25–52.

CAIRNS, E. (1987). *Caught in crossfire: Children and the Northern Ireland conflict.* Belfast, Northern Ireland: Appletree Press.

CAIRNS, E. (1996). *Children and political violence.* Oxford, England: Blackwell.

CAIRNS, R. B. (1986). An evolutionary and developmental perspective on aggressive patterns. In C. Zahn-Waxler, E. M. Cummings, & R. Iannotti (Eds.), *Altruism and aggression: Biological and social origins.* Cambridge: Cambridge University Press.

CAIRNS, R. B. (1998). The making of developmental psychology. In W. Damon (Ed.), *Handbook of child psychology: Vol. 1. Theoretical models of human development.* New York: Wiley.

CAIRNS, R. B., & CAIRNS, B. D. (1988). The sociogenesis of self concepts. In N. Bolger, A. Caspi, G. Downey, & M. Moorehouse (Eds.), *Persons in context: Developmental processes.* New York: Cambridge University Press.

CAIRNS, R. B., CAIRNS, B. D., NECKERMAN, H. J., FERGUSON, L. L., & GARIEPY, J. (1989). Growth and aggression: I. Childhood to early adolescence. *Developmental Psychology, 25,* 320–330.

CAIRNS, R. B., CAIRNS, B. D., NECKERMAN, H. J., GEST, S. D., & GARIEPY, J. (1988). Social networks and aggressive behavior: Peer support or peer rejection? *Developmental Psychology, 24,* 815–823.

CALDERA, Y. M., HUSTON, A. C., & O'BRIEN, M. (1989). Social interactions and play patterns of parents and toddlers with feminine, masculine, and neutral toys. *Child Development, 60,* 70–76.

CALDWELL, B. M. (1964). The effects of infant care. In M. L. Hoffman & L. W. Hoffman (Eds.), *Review of child development research* (Vol. 1). New York: Russell Sage Foundation.

CALDWELL, B. M., & BRADLEY, R. (1979). *Home Observation for Measurement of the Environment.* Unpublished manuscript, University of Arkansas.

CALHOUN, J. B. (1962). Population density and social pathology.*Scientific American, 206,* 139–148.

CALKINS, S. D., & FOX, N. A. (1992). The relations among infant temperament, security of attachment, and behavioral inhibition at twenty-four months. *Child Development, 63,* 1456–1472.

CALLANAN, M. A. (1985). How parents label objects for young children: The role of input in the acquisition of category hierarchies. *Child Development, 56,* 508–523.

CAMARATA, S., & LEONARD, L. B. (1986). Young children pronounce object words more accurately than action words. *Journal of Child Language, 13,* 51–65.

CAMPBELL, R. L., & CHRISTOPHER, J. C. (1996). Moral development theory: A critique of its Kantian presuppositions. *Developmental Review, 16,* 1–47.

CAMPOS, J. J., BERTENTHAL, B. I., & KERMOIAN, R. (1992). Early experience and emotional development: The emergence of wariness of heights. *Psychological Science, 3,* 61–64.

CAMPOS, J. J., HIATT, S., RAMSAY, D., HENDERSON, C., & SVEJDA, M. (1978). The emergence of fear on the visual cliff. In M. Lewis & L. Rosenblum (Eds.), *The origins of affect.* New York: Plenum

CAMPOS, J., MUMME, D., KERMOIAN, R., & CAMPOS, R. (1994). A functionalist perspective on the nature of emotion. In N. Fox (Ed.), The development of emotion regulation: Biological and behavioral considerations. *Monographs of the Society for Research in Child Development, 59*(2–3, Serial No. 240).

CAMPOS, R. G. (1989). Soothing pain-elicited distress in infants with swaddling and pacifiers. *Child Development, 60,* 781–792.

CAMRAS, L. A., MALATESTA, C. Z., & IZARD, C. E. (1991). The development of facial expressions in infancy. In R. Felman & B. Rime (Eds.), *Fundamentals of nonverbal behavior.* Cambridge: Cambridge University Press.

CAMRAS, L., OSTER, L. A., CAMPOS, J. J., MIYAKE, K., & BRADSHAW, D. (1992). Japanese and American infants' responses to arm restraint. *Developmental Psychology, 28,* 578–583.

CANTER, R. J., & AGETON, S. S. (1984). The epidemiology of adolescent sex-role attitudes. *Sex Roles, 11,* 657–676.

CAPECCHI, M. R. (1994, March). Targeted gene replacement. *Scientific American,* pp. 52–59.

CAPLAN, M., VESPO, J. E., PEDERSEN, J., & HAY, D. F. (1991). Conflict and its resolution in small groups of one- and two-year-olds. *Child Development, 62,* 1513–1524.

CAPLAN, P. J., MacPHERSON, G. M., & TOBIN, P. (1985). Do sex-related differences in spatial abilities exist? A multilevel critique with new data. *American Psychologist, 40,* 786–799.

CAPRON, C., & DUYME, M. (1989). Assessment of effects of socio-economic status on IQ in a full cross-fostering study. *Nature, 340,* 552–554.

CARDON, L. R. (1994). Specific cognitive abilities. In J. C. DeFries, R. Plomin, & D. W. Fulker (Eds.), *Nature and nurture during middle childhood.* Oxford, England: Blackwell.

CAREY, S. (1977). The child as word learner. In M. Halle, J. Bresnan, & G. A. Miller (Eds.), *Linguistic theory and psychological reality.* Cambridge: MIT Press.

CAREY, S. (1985). *Conceptual change in childhood.* Cambridge: MIT Press.

CAREY, W. B., & McDEVITT, S. C. (1978). Revision of the Infant Temperament Questionnaire. *Pediatrics, 61,* 735–739.

CARLSON, M., & EARLS, F. (1997). Psychological and neuroendocrinological sequelae of early social deprivation in institutionalized children in Romania. In C. S. Carter, I. I. Lederhendler, & B. Kirkpatrick (Eds.), *The integrative neurobiology of affiliation.* New York: New York Academy of Sciences.

CARLSON, V., CICCHETTI, D., BARNETT, D., & BRAUNWALD, K. G. (1989). Finding order in disorganization: Lessons from research on maltreated infants' attachments to their caregivers. In D. Cicchetti & V. Carlson (Eds.), *Child maltreatment: Theory and research on the causes and consequences of child abuse and neglect.* New York: Cambridge University Press.

CARNEGIE TASK FORCE. (1994). *Starting points: Meeting the needs of our youngest children.* New York: Carnegie Corporation of New York.

CARON, A. J., CARON, R. F., & MacLEAN, D. J. (1988). Infant discrimination of naturalistic emotional expressions: The role of face and voice. *Child Development, 59,* 604–616.

CARPENDALE, J. I. M., & KREBS, D. L. (1995). Variations in moral judgment as a function of type of dilemma and moral choice. *Journal of Personality, 63,* 289–313.

CARR, M., KURTZ, B. E., SCHNEIDER, W., TURNER, L. A., & BORKOWSKI, J. G. (1989). Strategy acquisition and transfer among American and German children: Environmental influences on meta-cognitive development. *Developmental Psychology, 25,* 765–771.

CARRAHER, T. N., CARRAHER, D. W., & SCHLIEMANN, A. D. (1985). Mathematics in the streets and schools. *British Journal of Developmental Psychology, 3,* 21–29.

CARROLL, J. L., & REST, J. R. (1981). Development in moral judgment as indicated by rejection of lower-style statements. *Journal of Research in Personality, 15,* 538–544.

CARTER, D. B., & LEVY, G. D. (1988). Cognitive aspects of early sex-role development: The influence of gender schemas on preschoolers' memories and preferences for sex-typed toys and activities. *Child Development, 59,* 782–792.

CARTER, D. B., & McCLOSKEY, L. A. (1984). Peers and maintenance of sex-typed behavior: The development of children's conceptions of cross-gender behavior in their peers. *Social Cognition, 2,* 294–314.

CASE, R. (1985). *Intellectual development.* New York. Academic Press.

CASE, R. (1991). Stages in the development of the young child's first sense of self. *Developmental Review, 11,* 210–230.

CASE, R. (1992). *The mind's staircase: Exploring the conceptual underpinnings of children's thought and knowledge.* Hillsdale, NJ: Erlbaum.

CASE, R., & OKAMOTO, Y. (1996). The role of central conceptual structures in the development of children's thought. *Monographs of the Society for Research in Child Development, 61* (1–2, Serial No. 246).

CASEY, M. B., NUTTAL, R., PEZARIS, E., & BENBOW, C. P. (1995). The influence of spatial ability on gender differences in mathematics college entrance test scores across diverse samples. *Developmental Psychology, 31,* 697–705.

CASPI, A. (1998). Personality development across the life span. In W. Damon (Ed.), *Handbook of child psychology: Vol. 3. Social, emotional, and personality development.* New York: Wiley.

CASPI, A., & ELDER, G. H., JR. (1988). Childhood precursors of the life course: Early personality and life disadvantage. In E. M. Hetherington, R. M. Lerner, & M. Perlmutter (Eds.), *Child development in a life-span perspective.* Hillsdale, NJ: Erlbaum.

CASPI, A., ELDER, G. H., JR., & BEM, D. J. (1987). Moving against the world: Life-course patterns of explosive children. *Developmental Psychology, 23,* 308–313.

CASPI, A., ELDER, G. H., JR., & BEM, D. J. (1988). Moving away from the world: Life-course patterns of shy children. *Developmental Psychology, 24,* 824–831.

CASPI, A., HENRY, B., McGEE, R. O., MOFFITT, T. E., & SILVA, P. A. (1995). Temperamental origins of child and adolescent behavior problems: From age 3 to age 15. *Child Development, 66,* 55–68.

CASPI, A., MOFFITT, T. E., NEWMAN, D. L., & SILVA, P. A. (1996). Behavioral observations at age 3 predict adult psychiatric disorders: Longitudinal evidence from a birth cohort. *Archives of General Psychiatry, 53,* 1033–1039.

CASSIDY, J. (1988). Child–mother attachment and the self in six-year-olds. *Child Development, 59,* 121–134.

CASSIDY, J., KIRSH, S. J., SCOLTON, K. L., & PARKE, R. D. (1996). Attachment and representations of peer relationships. *Developmental Psychology, 32,* 892–904.

CASSIDY, J., PARKE, R. D., BUTKOVSKY, L., & BRAUNGART, J. M. (1992). Family-peer connections: The roles of emotional expressiveness within the family and children's understanding of emotions. *Child Development, 63,* 603–618.

CATON, H. (1990). *The Samoa reader.* Lanham, MD: University Press of America.

CATRON, T. F., & MASTERS, J. C. (1993). Mothers' and children's conceptualizations of corporal punishment. *Child Development, 64,* 1815–1828.

CATSAMBIS, S. (1994). The path to math: Gender and racial-ethnic differences in mathematics participation from middle school to high school. *Sociology of Education, 67,* 199–215.

CAUGHY, M. O. (1996). Health and environmental effects on the academic readiness of school-age children. *Developmental Psychology, 32,* 515–522.

CAVANAUGH, J. C., & PERLMUTTER, M. (1982). Metamemory: A critical examination. *Child Development, 53,* 11–28.

CECI, S. J. (1990). *On intelligence . . . more or less: A bioecological theory.* Englewood Cliffs, NJ: Prentice Hall.

CECI, S. J. (1991). How much does schooling influence general intelligence and its cognitive components? A reassessment of the evidence. *Developmental Psychology, 27,* 703–722.

CECI, S. J. (1992, September/October). Schooling and intelligence. *Psychological Science Agenda,* pp. 7–9.

CECI, S. J. (1993). Contextual trends in intellectual development. *Developmental Review, 13,* 403–435.

CECI, S. J. (1996). *On intelligence: A bioecological treatise on intellectual development* (expanded ed.). Cambridge: Harvard University Press.

CECI, S. J., & BRUCK, M. (1993). Suggestibility of the child witness: A historical review and synthesis. *Psychological Bulletin, 113,* 403–439.

CECI, S. J., & BRUCK, M. (1995). *Jeopardy in the courtroom: A scientific analysis of children's testimony.* Washington, DC: American Psychological Association.

CECI, S. J., & BRUCK, M. (1998). Children's testimony. In W. Damon (Series Ed.) & I. E. Sigel & K. A. Renninger (Vol. Eds.), *Handbook of child psychology: Vol. 4. Child psychology in practice* (5th ed.). New York: Wiley.

CECI, S. J., & LIKER, L. K. (1986). A day at the races: A study of IQ, expertise, and cognitive complexity. *Journal of Experimental Psychology: General, 115,* 255–266.

CECI, S. J., & WILLIAMS, W. M. (1997). Schooling, intelligence, and income. *American Psychologist, 52,* 1051–1058.

CECI, S. J., LEICHTMAN, M., & WHITE, T. (in press). Interviewing preschoolers: Remembrance of things planted. In D. P. Peters (Ed.), *The child witness in context: Cognitive, social, and legal perspectives.* Dordrecht, Holland: Kluwer.

CHALL, J. S. (1983). *Learning to read: The great debate* (updated ed.). New York: McGraw-Hill.

CHALMERS, J. B., & TOWNSEND, M. A. R. (1990). The effects of training in social perspective taking on socially maladjusted girls. *Child Development, 61,* 178–190.

CHAMBERLAIN, P., & PATTERSON, G. R. (1995). Discipline and child compliance in parenting. In M. H. Bornstein (Ed.), *Handbook of parenting: Vol. 4. Applied and practical parenting.* Mahwah, NJ: Erlbaum.

CHANDLER, M. J. (1973). Egocentrism and antisocial behavior: The assessment and training of social perspective-taking skills. *Developmental Psychology, 9,* 326–332.

CHANDLER, M. J., & LALONDE, C. (1996). Shifting to an interpretive theory of mind: 5-to-7-year-olds' changing conceptions of mental life. In A. J. Sameroff & M. M. Haith (Eds.), *The five to seven year shift: The age of reason and responsibility.* Chicago: University of Chicago Press.

CHANDLER, M. J., GREENSPAN, S., & BARENBOIM, C. (1973). Judgments of intentionality in response to videotaped and verbally presented moral dilemmas: The medium is the message. *Child Development, 44,* 315–320.

CHAPMAN, M. (1988). *Constructive evolution: Origins and development of Piaget's thought.* Cambridge: Cambridge University Press.

CHAPMAN, M. (1992). Equilibration and the dialectics of organization. In H. Beilin & P. B. Pufall (Eds.), *Piaget's theory: Prospects and possibilities.* Hillsdale, NJ: Erlbaum.

CHARLESWORTH, R., & HARTUP, W. W. (1967). Positive social reinforcement in the nursery school peer group. *Child Development, 38,* 993–1002.

CHARLESWORTH, W. R. (1978). Ethology: Its relevance for observational studies of human adaptation. In G. P. Sackett (Ed.), *Observing behavior* (Vol. 1). Baltimore: University Park Press.

CHARLESWORTH, W. R. (1983). An ethological approach to cognitive development. In C. J. Brainerd (Ed.), *Recent advances in cognitive-developmental theory: Progress in cognitive development research.* New York: Springer-Verlag.

CHARLESWORTH, W. R. (1992). Darwin and developmental psychology: Past and present. *Developmental Psychology, 28,* 5–16.

CHARLESWORTH, W. R. (1995). An evolutionary approach to cognition and learning. In C. A. Nelson (Ed.), *Minnesota symposia on child psychology: Vol. 28. Basic and applied perspectives on learning, cognition, and development.* Mahwah, NJ: Erlbaum.

CHASNOFF, I. J., SCHNOLL, S. H., BURNS, W. J., & BURNS, K. (1984). Maternal narcotic substance abuse during pregnancy: Effects on infant development. *Neurobehavioral Toxicology and Teratology, 6,* 277–280.

CHAVEZ, D. (1985). Perpetuation of gender inequality: A content analysis of comic strips. *Sex Roles, 13,* 93–102.

CHEN, C., & STEVENSON, H. W. (1995). Motivation and mathematics achievement: A comparative study of Asian-American, Caucasian-American, and East Asian high school students. *Child Development, 66,* 1215–1234.

CHEN, M. (1985). Gender differences in adolescents' use of and attitudes toward computers. In M. McLaughlin (Ed.), *Communication yearbook* (Vol. 10). Beverly Hills, CA: Sage.

CHEN, X., & RUBIN, K. H. (1994). Family conditions, parental acceptance, and social competence and aggression in Chinese children. *Social Development, 3,* 269–290.

CHEN, X., RUBIN, K. H., & LI, Z. (1995). Social functioning and adjustment in Chinese children: A longitudinal study. *Developmental Psychology, 31,* 531–539.

CHEN, X., RUBIN, K. H., & SUN, Y. (1992). Social reputation and peer relationships in Chinese and Canadian children: A cross-cultural study. *Child Development, 63,* 1336–1343.

CHERNY, S. S. (1994). Home environmental influences on general cognitive ability. In J. C. DeFries, R. Plomin, & D. W. Fulker (Eds.), *Nature and nurture during middle childhood.* Cambridge, MA: Blackwell.

CHERNY, S. S., & CARDON, L. R. (1994). General cognitive ability. In J. C. DeFries, R. Plomin, & D. W. Fulker (Eds.), *Nature and nurture during middle childhood.* Oxford, England: Blackwell.

CHERNY, S. S., FULKER, D. W., CORLEY, R. P., PLOMIN, R., & DeFRIES, J. C. (1994). Continuity and change in infant shyness from 14 to 20 months. *Behavior Genetics, 24,* 365–379.

CHERNY, S. S., FULKER, D. W., EMDE, R. N., ROBINSON, J., CORLEY, R. P., REZNICK, J. S., PLOMIN, R., & DeFRIES, J. C. (1994). A developmental-genetic analysis of continuity and change in the Bayley mental development index from 14 to 24 months: The MacArthur Longitudinal Twin Study. *Psychological Science, 5,* 354–360.

CHERRY, L., & LEWIS, M. (1976). Mothers and two-year-olds. A study of sex differentiated aspects of verbal interaction. *Developmental Psychology, 12,* 278–282.

CHESS, S., & THOMAS, A. (1987). *Origins and evolution of behavior disorders: From infancy to early adult life.* Cambridge: Harvard University Press.

CHI, M. T. H. (1978). Knowledge structures and memory development. In R. S. Siegler (Ed.), *Children's thinking: What develops?* Hillsdale, NJ: Erlbaum.

CHI, M. T. H., GLASER, R., & FARR, M. J. (Eds.). (1988). *The nature of expertise.* Hillsdale, NJ: Erlbaum.

CHI, M. T. H., & KOESKE, R. D. (1983). Network representation of a child's dinosaur knowledge. *Developmental Psychology, 19,* 29–39.

CHIPMAN, S. F., BRUSH, L., & WILSON, D. (Eds.). (1985). *Women and mathematics: Balancing the equation.* Hillsdale, NJ: Erlbaum.

CHOI, S. (1997). Language-specific input and early semantic development: Evidence from children learning Korean. In D. I. Slobin (Ed.), *The crosslinguisitic study of language acquisition: Vol. 5. Expanding the contexts.* Mahwah, NJ: Erlbaum.

CHOI, S., & GOPNIK, A. (1995). Early acquisition of verbs in Korean: A cross-linguistic study. *Journal of Child Language, 22,* 497–530.

CHOMITZ, V. R., CHEUNG, L., & LIEBERMAN, E. (1995). The role of lifestyle in preventing low birth weight. *The future of children* (Vol. 5, No. 1). Los Angeles: Packard Foundation.

CHOMSKY, N. (1959). A review of B. F. Skinner's *Verbal Behavior. Language, 35,* 26–58.

CHOMSKY, N. (1965). *Aspects of the theory of syntax.* Cambridge: MIT Press.

CHOMSKY, N. (1995). *The minimalist program.* Cambridge: MIT Press.

CHURCH, R. B., & GOLDIN-MEADOW, S. (1986). The mismatch between gesture and speech as an index of transitional knowledge. *Cognition, 23,* 43–71.

CICCHETTI, D. (1991). Fractures in the crystal: Developmental psychopathology and the emergence of self. *Developmental Review, 11,* 271–287.

CICCHETTI, D., BEEGHLY, M., CARLSON, V., & TOTH, S. (1990). The emergence of self in atypical populations. In D. Cicchetti & M. Beegly (Eds.), *The self in transition: Infancy to childhood.* Chicago: University of Chicago Press.

CICCHETTI, D., & CARLSON, V. (Eds.). (1989). *Child maltreatment: Theory and research on the causes and consequences of child abuse and neglect.* New York: Cambridge University Press.

CICCHETTI, D., LYNCH, M., SHONK, S., & MANLY, J. T. (1992). An organizational perspective on peer relations in maltreated children. In R. D. Parke & G. W. Ladd (Eds.), *Family-peer relationships: Modes of linkage.* Hillsdale, NJ: Erlbaum.

CILLESSEN, A. H. N., VAN IJZENDOORN, H. W., VAN LIESHOUT, C. F. M., & HARTUP, W. W. (1992). Heterogeneity among peer-rejected boys: Subtypes and stabilities. *Child Development, 63,* 893–905.

CLARKE, A. M., & CLARKE, A. D. B. (1976). *Early experience: Myth and evidence.* New York: Free Press.

CLARK, E. V. (1982). The young word-maker: A case study of innovation in the child's lexicon. In E. Wanner & L. R. Gleitman (Eds.), *Language acquisition: The state of the art.* Cambridge: Cambridge University Press.

CLARK, E. V. (1983). Meanings and concepts. In P. H. Mussen (Series Ed.) & J. H. Flavell & E. M. Markman (Vol. Eds.), *Handbook of child psychology: Vol. 3. Cognitive development.* New York: Wiley.

CLARK, E. V. (1987). The principle of contrast: A constraint on language acquisition. In B. MacWhinney (Ed.), *Mechanisms of language acquisition.* Hillsdale, NJ: Erlbaum.

CLARK, E. V. (1993). *The lexicon in acquisition.* New York: Cambridge University Press.

CLARK, R. (1977). What's the use of imitation? *Journal of Child Language, 4,* 341–358.

CLARK, R., HYDE, J. S., ESSEX, M. J., & KLEIN, M. H. (1997). Length of maternity leave and quality of mother-infant interactions. *Child Development, 68,* 364–383.

CLARKE, S., & TAFFEL, S. (1995). Changes in

cesarean delivery in the United States, 1988 and 1993. *Birth, 22,* 63–67.

CLARKE-STEWART, K. A. (1989). Infant day care: Maligned or malignant? *American Psychologist, 44,* 266–273.

CLARKE-STEWART, K. A., GRUBER, C. P., & FITZGERALD, L. M. (1994). *Children at home and in day care.* Hillsdale, NJ: Erlbaum.

CLEWELL, W. H., JOHNSON, M. L., MEIER, P. R., NEWKIRK, J. B., ZIDE, S. L., HENDEE, R. W., BOWES, W. A., JR., HECHT, F., O'KEEFE, D., HENRY, G. P., & SHIKES, R. H. (1982). A surgical approach to the treatment of fetal hydrocephalus. *New England Journal of Medicine, 306,* 1320–1325.

CLIFTON, R. K., GWIAZDA, J., BAUER, J. A., CLARKSON, M. G., & HELD, R. M. (1988). Growth in head size during infancy: Implications for sound localization. *Developmental Psychology, 24,* 477–483.

CLINGEMPEEL, W. G., COLYAR, J. J., BRAND, E., & HETHERINGTON, E. M. (1992). Children's relations with maternal grandparents: A longitudinal study of family structure and pubertal status effects. *Child Development, 63,* 1404–1422.

CLOPTON, N. A., & SORELL, G. T. (1997). Gender differences in moral reasoning: Stable or situational? *Psychology of Women Quarterly, 17,* 85–101.

CLUMECK, H. V. (1980). The acquisition of tone. In G. H. Yeni-Komshian, J. Kavanagh, & C. A. Ferguson (Eds.), *Child phonology: Vol. 1. Production.* New York: Academic Press.

COHEN, D. (1979). *J. B. Watson: The founder of behaviorism.* London: Routledge & Kegan Paul.

COHEN, D., & STRAYER, J. (1996). Empathy in conduct-disordered and comparison youth. *Developmental Psychology, 32,* 988–998.

COHEN, S., & WILLS, T. A. (1985). Stress, social support, and the buffering hypothesis. *Psychological Bulletin, 98,* 310–357.

COHEN, S. E. (1974). Developmental differences in infants' attentional responses to face–voice incongruity of mother and stranger. *Child Development, 45,* 1155–1158.

COHN, D. A., COWAN, P. A., COWAN, C. P., & PEARSON, J. (1992). Mothers' and fathers' working models of childhood attachment relationships, parenting styles, and child behavior. *Development and Psychopathology, 4,* 417–431.

COHN, J. F., CAMPBELL, S. B., MATIAS, R., & HOPKINS, J. (1990). Face-to-face interactions of postpartum depressed and nondepressed mother–infant pairs at 2 months. *Developmental Psychology, 26,* 15–23.

COHN, J. F., & TRONICK, E. Z. (1983). Three-month-old infants' reaction to simulated maternal depression. *Child Development, 54,* 185–193.

COIE, J. D., & CILLESSEN, A. H. N. (1993). Peer rejection: Origins and effects on children's development. *Current Directions in Psychological Science, 2,* 89–92.

COIE, J. D., & DODGE, K. A. (1998). Aggression and antisocial behavior. In W. Damon (Ed.), *Handbook of child psychology: Vol. 3. Social, emotional, and personality development.* New York: Wiley.

COIE, J. D., DODGE, K. A., & KUPERSMIDT, J. B. (1990). Peer group behavior and social status. In S. R. Asher & J. D. Coie (Eds.), *Peer rejection in childhood.* New York: Cambridge University Press.

COIE, J. D., & KREHBIEL, G. (1984). Effects of academic tutoring on the social status of low-achieving, socially rejected children. *Child Development, 55,* 1465–1478.

COIE, J. D., & KUPERSMIDT, J. (1983). A behavioral analysis of emerging social status in boys' groups. *Child Development, 54,* 1400–1416.

COIE, J. D., LOCHMAN, J. E., TERRY, R., & HYMAN, C. (1992). Predicting early adolescent disorder from childhood aggression and peer rejection. *Journal of Consulting and Clinical Psychology, 60,* 783–792.

COLBY, A., & KOHLBERG, L. (1987). *The measurement of moral judgment* (Vols. 1–2). New York: Cambridge University Press.

COLE, M. (1998). Culture and schooling. In W. Damon (Series Ed.) & I. E. Sigel & K. A. Renninger (Vol. Eds.), *Handbook of child psychology: Vol. 4. Child psychology in practice* (5th ed.). New York: Wiley.

COLE, P. M. (1986). Children's spontaneous control of facial expression. *Child Development, 57,* 1309–1321.

COLEMAN, W. (1971). *Biology in the nineteenth century: Problems of form, function, and transformation.* New York: Wiley.

COLLAER, M. L., & HINES, M. (1995). Human behavioral sex differences: A role for gonadal hormones during early development? *Psychological Bulletin, 118,* 55–107.

COLLIS, G. M. (1985). On the origins of turn-taking: Alternation and meaning. In M. D. Barrett (Ed.), *Children's single-word speech.* New York: Wiley.

COLOMBO, J. (1993). *Infant cognition: Predicting later intellectual functioning.* Thousand Oaks, CA: Sage.

COLOMBO, J., & BUNDY, R. S. (1981). A method for the measurement of infant auditory selectivity. *Infant Behavior and Development, 4,* 219–223.

COMMONS, M. L., MILLER, P. M., & KUHN, D. (1982). The relation between formal operational reasoning and academic course selection and performance among college freshmen and sophomores. *Journal of Applied Developmental Psychology, 3,* 1–10.

CONDRY, J. C., & ROSS, D. F. (1985). Sex and aggression: The influence of gender label on the perception of aggression in children. *Child Development, 56,* 225–233.

CONGER, D., & ELDER, G. H., JR. (1994). *Families in troubled times.* Hawthorne, NY: Aldine de Gruyter.

CONGER, R. D., GE, X., ELDER, LORENZ, F. O., & SIMONS, R. L. (1 Economic stress, coercive family process, developmental problems of adolescents. *Chi Development, 65,* 541–561.

CONNELL, J. P., & ILARDI, B. C. (1987.) Self-system concomitants of discrepancies between children's and teachers' evaluations of academic competence. *Child Development, 58,* 1297–1307.

CONNELL, J. P., & WELLBORN, J. G. (1991). Competence, autonomy, and relatedness: A motivational analysis of self-system processes. In M. R. Gunnar & L. A. Sroufe (Eds.), *Minnesota symposium on child development: Vol. 23. Self processes and development.* Hillsdale, NJ: Erlbaum.

CONSORTIUM FOR LONGITUDINAL STUDIES. (1983). *As the twig is bent . . .* lasting effects of preschool programs. Hillsdale, NJ: Erlbaum.

CONSTANZO, P. R. (1970). Conformity development as a function of self-blame. *Journal of Personality and Social Psychology, 14,* 366–374.

CONTI, D. J., & CAMRAS, L. A. (1984). Children's understanding of conversational principles. *Journal of Experimental Child Psychology, 38,* 456–463.

COOK, E. P. (1985). *Psychological androgyny.* New York: Pergamon.

COOK, E. P. (1987). Psychological androgyny: A review of the research. *The Counseling Psychologist, 15,* 471–513.

COOLEY, C. H. (1902). *Human nature and the social order.* New York: Charles Scribner's Sons.

COOPER, C. R. (1980). Development of collaborative problem solving among preschool children. *Developmental Psychology, 16,* 433–440.

COOPER, N. G. (Ed.). (1994). *The human genome project: Deciphering the blueprint of heredity.* Mill Valley, CA: University Science Books.

COOPER, R. G. (1984). Early number development: Discovering number space with addition and subtraction. In C. Sophian (Ed.), *Origins of cognitive skills.* Hillsdale, NJ: Erlbaum.

COOPER, R. P., & ASLIN, R. N. (1989). The language environment of the young infant: Implications for early perceptual development. *Canadian Journal of Psychology, 43,* 247–265.

COOPER, R. P., & ASLIN, R. N. (1990). Preference for infant-directed speech in the first month after birth. *Child Development, 61,* 1584–1595.

COOPER, R. P., & ASLIN, R. N. (1994). Developmental differences in infant attention to the spectral properties of infant-directed speech. *Child Development, 65,* 1663–1677.

CORINA, D. P., VAID, J., & BELLUGI, U. (1992). The linguistic basis of left hemisphere specialization. *Science, 255,* 1258–1260.

CORNELIUS, M., TAYLOR, P., GEVA, D., & DAY, N. (1995). Prenatal tobacco exposure and marijuana use among adolescents: Effects on offspring gestational age, growth, and morphology. *Pediatrics, 95,* 738–743.

COSTER, W. J., GERSTEN, M. S., BEEGHLY, M., & CICCHETTI, D. (1989). Communicative functioning in maltreated toddlers. *Developmental Psychology, 25,* 1020–1029.

COSTIN, S. E., & JONES, D. C. (1992). Friendship as a facilitator of emotional responsiveness and prosocial interventions among young children. *Developmental Psychology, 28,* 941–947.

COVEY, H. C., MENARD, S., & FRANZESE, R. J. (1997). *Juvenile gangs* (2nd ed.). Springfield, IL: Charles C. Thomas.

COWAN, C. P., & COWAN, P. A. (1992). *When partners become parents.* New York: Basic Books.

COWAN, P. A. (1978). *Piaget: With feeling.* New York: Holt, Rinehart & Winston.

COWAN, P. A., & McHALE, J. P. (1997). *New directions for child psychology: Family-level dynamics and children's development.* San Francisco: Jossey-Bass.

COWAN, P. A., POWELL, D., & COWAN, C. P. (1998). Parenting interventions: A family systems perspective. In W. Damon (Ed.), *Handbook of child psychology: Vol 4. Child psychology in practice.* New York: Wiley.

COX, B. D., & LIGHTFOOT, C. (Eds.). (1997). *Sociogenetic perspectives on internalization.* Mahwah, NJ: Erlbaum.

COX, D., & WATERS, H. S. (1986). Sex differences in the use of organization strategies: A developmental analysis. *Journal of Experimental Child Psychology, 41,* 18–37.

COX, M. J., OWEN, M. T., HENDERSON, V. K., & MARGAND, N. A. (1992). Prediction of infant–father and infant–mother attachment. *Developmental Psychology, 28,* 474–483.

COYLE, T. R., & BJORKLUND, D. F. (1997). Age differences in, and consequences of, multiple- and variable-strategy use on a multitrial sort-recall task. *Developmental Psychology, 33,* 372–380.

COZBY, P. C., BROWN, K. W., WORDEN, P. E., & KEE, D. W. (1998). *Research methods in human development* (2nd ed.). Mountain View, CA: Mayfield.

CRAIG, R. S. (1992). The effect of television's daily part in gender portrayals in television commercials: A continuing analysis. *Sex Roles, 26,* 197–211.

CRAIN-THORESON, C., & DALE, P. S. (1992). Do early talkers become early readers? Linguistic precocity, preschool language, and emergent literacy. *Developmental Psychology, 28,* 421–429.

CRAVENS, H. (1992). A scientific project locked in time: The Terman genetic studies of genius, 1920s–1950s. *American Psychologist, 47,* 183–189.

CRICK, N. R. (1995). Relational aggression: The role of intent attributions, feelings of distress, and provocation type. *Development and Psychopathology, 7,* 313–322.

CRICK, N. R., BIGBEE, M. A., & HOWES, C. (1996). Gender differences in children's normative beliefs about aggression: How do I hurt thee? Let me count the ways. *Child Development, 67,* 1003–1014.

CRICK, N. R., CASAS, J. F., & MOSHER, M. (1997). Relational and overt aggression in preschool. *Developmental Psychology, 33,* 579–588.

CRICK, N. R., & DODGE, K. A. (1994). A review and reformulation of social information-processing mechanisms in children's social adjustment. *Psychological Bulletin, 115,* 74–101.

CRICK, N. R., & DODGE, K. A. (1996). Social information-processing mechanisms in reactive and proactive aggression. *Child Development, 67,* 993–1002.

CRICK, N. R., & GROTPETER, J. K. (1995). Relational aggression, gender, and social-psychological adjustment. *Child-Development, 66,* 710–722.

CRITTENDEN, P. M., & AINSWORTH, M. D. S. (1989). Child maltreatment and attachment theory. In D. Cicchetti & V. Carlson (Eds.), *Child maltreatment: Theory and research on the causes and consequences of child abuse and neglect.* New York: Cambridge University Press.

CROCKETT, L. J., & PETERSEN, A. C. (1987). Pubertal status and psychosocial development: Findings from the early adolescence study. In R. M. Lerner & T. L. Foch (Eds.), *Biological psychosocial interactions in early adolescence.* Hillsdale, NJ: Erlbaum.

CROOK, C. K. (1979). The organization and control of infant sucking. In H. W. Reese & L. P. Lipsitt (Eds.), *Advances in child development and behavior* (Vol. 14). New York: Academic Press.

CROSS, S. E., & MARKUS, H. R. (1993). Gender in thought, belief, and action: A cognitive approach. In A. E. Beall & R. J. Sternberg (Eds.), *The psychology of gender.* New York: Guilford.

CROUCHMAN, M. (1985). What mothers know about their newborns' visual skills. *Developmental Medicine and Child Neurology, 27,* 455–460.

CROUTER, A. C., MANKE, B. A., & MCHALE, S. M. (1995). The family context of gender intensification in early adolescence. *Child Development, 66,* 317–329.

CROWELL, D. H. (1987). Childhood aggression and violence: Contemporary issues. In D. H. Crowell, I. M. Evans, & C. R. O'Donnell (Eds.), *Childhood aggression and violence: Sources of influence, prevention, and control.* New York: Plenum.

CROWELL, J. A., & FELDMAN, S. S. (1991). Mothers' working models of attachment relationships and mother and child behavior during separation and reunion. *Developmental Psychology, 27,* 597–605.

CUMMINGS, E. M., HOLLENBECK, B., IANNOTTI, R., RADKE-YARROW, M., & ZAHN-WAXLER, C. (1986). Early organization of altruism and aggression: Developmental patterns and individual differences. In C. Zahn-Waxler, E. M. Cummings, & R. Iannotti (Eds.), *Altruism and aggression: Biological and social origins.* New York: Cambridge University Press.

CUMMINGS, S., & TAEBEL, D. (1980). Sex inequality and the reproduction consciousness: An analysis of sex-role stereotyping among children. *Sex Roles, 6,* 631–644.

CUMMINS, J. (1991). Interdependence of first- and second-language proficiency in bilingual children. In E. Bialystok (Ed.), *Language processing in bilingual children.* Cambridge: Cambridge University Press.

CUNNINGHAM, F. G., MacDONALD, P. C., & GANT, N. F. (1989). *Williams obstetrics* (18th ed.). London: Appleton & Lange.

CURTISS, S. (1977). *Genie: A psycholinguistic study of a modern day "wild child."* New York: Academic Press.

CZESCHLIK, T., & ROST, D. H. (1995). Sociometric types and children's intelligence. *British Journal of Developmental Psychology, 13,* 177–189.

DABBS, J. M., JR. (1992). Testosterone measurements in social and clinical psychology. *Journal of Social and Clinical Psychology, 11,* 302–321.

DABBS, J. M., JR., & MORRIS, R. (1990). Testosterone, social class, and antisocial behavior in a sample of 4,462 men. *Psychological Science, 1,* 209–211.

DALY, M., & WILSON, M. (1983). *Sex, evolution, and behavior* (2nd ed.). Boston: PWS.

DAMON, W. (1977). *The social world of the child.* San Francisco: Jossey-Bass.

DAMON, W. (1980). Patterns of change in children's social reasoning: A two-year longitudinal study. *Child Development, 51,* 1010–1017.

DAMON, W. (1981). Exploring children's social cognition on two fronts. In J. H. Flavell & L. Ross (Eds.), *Social cognitive development.* Cambridge: Cambridge University Press.

DAMON, W. (1983). *Social and personality development.* New York: Norton.

DAMON, W., & COLBY, A. (1987). Social influence and moral change. In W. M. Kurtines & J. L. Gewirtz (Eds.), *Moral development through social interaction.* New York: Wiley.

DAMON, W., & HART, D. (1988). *Self-understanding in childhood and adolescence.* New York: Cambridge University Press.

DAMON, W., & HART, D. (1992). Self-understanding and its role in social and moral development. In M. H. Bornstein & M. E. Lamb (Eds.), *Developmental psychology: An advanced textbook* (3rd ed.). Hillsdale, NJ: Erlbaum.

DAMON, W., & KILLEN, M. (1982). Peer interaction and the process of change in children's moral reasoning. *Merrill-Palmer Quarterly, 28,* 347–367.

DANDY, E. B. (1991). *Black communications: Breaking down the barriers.* Chicago: African American Images.

DANEMAN, M., & CASE, R. (1981). Syntactic form, semantic complexity, and short-term memory: Influences on children's acquisition of new linguistic structures. *Developmental Psychology, 17,* 367–378.

DANNEMILLER, J. L. (1985). The early phase of dark adaptation in human infants. *Vision Research, 25,* 207–212.

DANNEMILLER, J. L., & HANKO, S. A. (1987). A test of color constancy in 4-month-old infants. *Journal of Experimental Child Psychology, 44,* 255–267.

DANNER, F. W., & DAY, M. C. (1977). Eliciting formal operations. *Child Development, 48,* 1600–1606.

DARWIN, C. (1872). *The expression of emotions in man and animals.* London: Murray.

DARWIN, C. (1877). A biographical sketch of an infant. *Mind, 2,* 285–294.

DASEN, P. R. (1975). Concrete operational development in three cultures. *Journal of Cross-Cultural Psychology, 6,* 156–172.

D'AUGELLI, A. R., & PATTERSON, C. J. (Eds.). (1995). *Lesbian, gay, and bisexual identities over the lifespan: Psychological perspectives.* New York: Oxford University Press.

DAVIDSON, D. (1996). The role of schemata in children's memory. In H. W. Reese (Ed.), *Advances in child development and behavior* (Vol. 26). San Diego: Academic Press.

DAVIDSON, D., & HOE, S. (1993). Children's recall and recognition memory for typical and atypical actions in script-based stories. *Journal of Experimental Child Psychology, 55,* 104–126.

DAVIDSON, D., CAMERON, P., & JERGOVIC, D. (1995). The effects of children's stereotypes on their memory for elderly individuals. *Merrill-Palmer Quarterly, 41,* 70–90.

DAVIS, K. (1947). Final note on a case of extreme isolation. *American Journal of Sociology, 45,* 554–565.

DAVIS, M., & EMORY, E. (1995). Sex differences in neonatal stress reactivity. *Child Development, 66,* 14–27.

DAVIS, T. L. (1995). Gender differences in masking negative emotions: Ability or motivation? *Developmental Psychology, 31,* 660–667.

DAWKINS, R. (1976). *The selfish gene.* New York: Oxford University Press.

DAY, M. C. (1975). Developmental trends in visual scanning. In H. W. Reese (Ed.), *Advances in child development and behavior* (Vol. 10). New York: Academic Press.

DAY, R. H. (1987). Visual size constancy in infancy. In B. E. McKenzie & R. H. Day (Eds.), *Perceptual development in early infancy: Problems and issues.* Hillsdale, NJ: Erlbaum.

DEARY, I. J. (1995). Auditory inspection time and intelligence: What is the causal direction? *Developmental Psychology, 31,* 237–250.

DEATER-DECKARD, K., SCARR, S., McCARTNEY, K., & EISENBERG, M. (1994). Paternal separation anxiety: Relationships with parenting stress, child-rearing attitudes, and maternal anxieties. *Psychological Science, 5,* 341–346.

DEAUX, K. (1993). Sorry, wrong number—A reply to Gentile's call. Sex or gender? *Psychological Science, 4,* 125–126.

DEBARYSHE, B. D., PATTERSON, G. R., & CAPALDI, D. M. (1993). Performance model for academic achievement in early adolescent boys. *Developmental Psychology, 29,* 795–804.

DeCASPER, A. J., & FIFER, W. P. (1980). Of human bonding: Newborns prefer their mothers' voices. *Science, 208,* 1174–1176.

DeCASPER, A. J., LECANUET, J.-P., BUSNEL, M.-C., GRANIER-DEFERRE, C., & MAUGEAIS, R. (1994). Fetal reactions to recurrent maternal speech. *Infant Behavior and Development, 17,* 159–164.

DeCASPER, A. J., & PRESCOTT, P. A. (1984). Human newborns' perception of male voices: Preference, discrimination, and reinforcing value. *Developmental Psychobiology, 17,* 481–491.

DeCASPER, A. J., & SPENCE, M. J. (1986). Newborns prefer a familiar story over an unfamiliar one. *Infant Behavior and Development, 9,* 133–150.

DeCASPER, A. J., & SPENCE, M. J. (1991). Auditory mediated behavior during the perinatal period: A cognitive view. In M. J. S. Weiss & P. R. Zelazo (Eds.), *Newborn attention: Biological constraints and the influence of experience.* Norwood, NJ: Ablex.

DE COOKE, P. A., & BROWNELL, C. A. (1995). Young children's help-seeking in mastery-oriented contexts. *Merrill-Palmer Quarterly, 41,* 229–246.

DeFRIES, J. C., PLOMIN, R., & FULKER, D. W. (Eds.). (1994). *Nature and nurture during middle childhood* (Chapter 2). Cambridge, MA: Blackwell.

DEL CARMEN, R., PEDERSEN, F. A., HUFFMAN, L. C., & BRYAN, Y. E. (1993). Dyadic distress management predicts subsequent security of attachment. *Infant Behavior and Development, 16,* 131–147.

DEKAY, W. T., & BUSS, D. M. (1992). Human nature, individual differences, and the importance of context: Perspectives from an evolutionary psychology. *Current Directions in Psychological Science, 1,* 184–189.

DEKOVIC, M., & JANSSENS, J. M. A. M. (1992). Parents' childrearing style and child's sociometric status. *Developmental Psychology, 28,* 925–932.

DE LISI, R., & STAUDT, J. (1980). Individual differences in college students' performance on formal operations tasks. *Journal of Applied Developmental Psychology, 1,* 201–208.

DeLOACHE, J. S., CASSIDY, D. J., & CARPENTER, C. J. (1987). The three bears are all boys: Mothers' gender labeling of neutral picture book characters. *Sex Roles, 17,* 163–178.

DeLOACHE, J. S., MILLER, K. F., & PIERROUTSAKSOS, S. L. (1998). Reasoning and problem solving. In W. Damon (Series Ed.) & D. Kuhn & R. S. Siegler (Vol. Eds.), *Handbook of child psychology: Vol. 2. Cognition, perception, and language* (5th ed.). New York: Wiley.

DELOZIER, C. D., & ENGEL, E. (1982). Sexual differentiation as a model for genetic and environmental interaction affecting physical and psychological development. In W. R. Gove & G. R. Carpenter (Eds.), *The fundamental connection between nature and nurture: A review of the evidence.* Lexington, MA: Lexington.

DEMETRAS, M. J., POST, K. N., & SNOW, C. E. (1986). Feedback to first language learners: The role of repetitions and clarification questions. *Journal of Child Language, 13,* 275–292.

DEMETRIOU, A., SHAYER, M., & EFKLIDES, A. (Eds.). (1993). *Neo-Piagetian theories of cognitive development.* New York: Routledge.

D'EMILIO, J. (1983). *Sexual politics, sexual communities: The making of a homosexual minority in the United States, 1940–1970.* Chicago: University of Chicago Press.

DEMOS, V. (1986). Crying in early infancy: An illustration of the motivational function of affect. In T. B. Brazelton & M. Yogman (Eds.), *Affect and early infancy.* Norwood, NJ: Ablex.

DENENBERG, V., & THOMAN, E. (1981). Evidence for a functional role for active (REM) sleep in infancy. *Sleep, 4,* 185–191.

DENHAM, S. A., & McKINLEY, M. (1993). Sociometric nominations of preschoolers: A psychometric analysis. *Early Education and Development, 4,* 109–122.

DENHAM, S. A., ZOLLER, D., & COUCHOUD, E. A. (1994). Socialization of preschoolers' emotion understanding. *Developmental Psychology, 30,* 928–936.

DENNEY, N. W., & DUFFY, D. M. (1974). Possible environmental causes of stages in moral reasoning. *Journal of Genetic Psychology, 125,* 277–284.

DENNIS, W. (1960). Causes of retardation among institutional children: Iran. *Journal of Genetic Psychology, 96,* 47–59.

DENNIS, W. (1973). *Children of the creche.* New York: Appleton-Century-Crofts.

DENNIS, W., & NAJARIAN, P. (1957). Infant development under environmental handicap. *Psychological Monographs, 71* (7, Whole No. 436).

DENTON, K., & ZARBATANY, L. (1996). Age differences in support processes in conversations between friends. *Child Development, 67,* 1360–1373.

DE RIBAUPIERRE, A., RIEBEN, L., & LAUTREY, J. (1991). Developmental change and individual differences: A longitudinal study using Piagetian tasks. *Genetic, Social, and General Psychology Monographs, 117,* 285–311.

DeROSIER, M., KUPERSMIDT, J., & PATTERSON, C. (1994). Children's academic and behavioral adjustment as a function of the chronicity and proximity of peer rejection. *Child Development, 65,* 1799–1813.

DeVILLIERS, J. G. (1980). The process of rule learning in child speech: A new look. In K. E. Nelson (Ed.), *Children's language* (Vol. 2). New York: Gardner.

DeVRIES, M. W., & SAMEROFF, A. J. (1984). Culture and temperament: Influences on infant temperament in three East African societies. *American Journal of Orthopsychiatry, 54,* 83–96.

DEVRIES, R. (1969). Constancy of generic identity in the years three to six. *Monographs of the Society for Research in Child Development, 34,* (3, Serial No. 127).

DeVRIES, R. (1991). The cognitive-developmental paradigm. In W. M. Kurtines & J. L. Gewirtz (Eds.), *Handbook of moral behavior and development: Vol. 1. Theory.* Hillsdale, NJ: Erlbaum.

DEVRIES, R., & ZAN, B. (1994). *Moral classrooms, moral children: Creating a constructivist atmosphere in early education.* New York: Teachers College Press.

De WAAL, F. (1996). *Good natured: The origins of right and wrong in humans and other animals.* Cambridge: Harvard University Press.

De WOLFF, M. S., & VAN IJZENDOORN, M. H. (1997). Sensitivity and attachment: A meta-analysis on parental antecedents of infant attachment. *Child Development, 68,* 571–591.

DIAMOND, A. (1991). Frontal lobe involvement in cognitive changes during the first year of life. In K. Gibson, M. Konner, & A. Petersen (Eds.), *Brain and behavioral development.* New York: Aldine de Gruyter.

DIAMOND, M., & SIGMUNDSON, K. (1997). Sex reassignment at birth: Long-term review and clinical implications. *Archives of Pediatric Adolescent Medicine, 151,* 298–304.

DIAZ, R. M. (1983). Thought and two languages: The impact of bilingualism on cognitive development. *Review of Research in Education, 10,* 23–54.

DIAZ, R. M. (1985). Bilingual cognitive development: Addressing three gaps in current research. *Child Development, 56,* 1376–1388.

DIAZ, R. M., & BERK, L. E. (Eds). (1992). *Private speech: From social interaction to self-regulation.* Hillsdale, NJ: Erlbaum.

DIAZ, R. M., NEAL, C. J., & VACHIO, A. (1991). Maternal teaching in the zone of proximal development: A comparison of low- and high-risk dyads. *Merrill-Palmer Quarterly, 37,* 83–108.

DICK-READ, G. (1933). *Natural childbirth.* New York: Dell.

DICK-READ, G. (1944). *Childbirth without fear.* New York: Dell.

DIEN, D. S. F. (1982). A Chinese perspective on Kohlberg's theory of moral development. *Developmental Review, 2,* 331–341.

DIENER, C. I., & DWECK, C. S. (1978). An analysis of learned helplessness: Continuous changes in performance, strategy, and achievement cognitions following failure. *Journal of Personality and Social Psychology, 36,* 451–462.

DIENER, C. I., & DWECK, C. S. (1980). An analysis of learned helplessness: II. The processing of success. *Journal of Personality and Social Psychology, 39,* 940–952.

DIENER, M. L., GOLDSTEIN, L. H., & MANGELSDORF, S. C. (1995). The role of prenatal expectations in parents' reports of infant temperament. *Merrill-Palmer Quarterly, 41,* 172–190.

DINGES, M. M., & OETTING, E. R. (1993). Similarity in drug use patterns between adolescents and their friends. *Adolescence, 28,* 253–266.

DION, K. K., & BERSCHEID, E. (1974). Physical attractiveness and peer perception among children. *Sociometry, 37,* 1–12.

DiPIETRO, J. A. (1981). Rough and tumble play: A function of gender. *Developmental Psychology, 17,* 50–58.

DiPIETRO, J. A., HODGSON, D. M., COSTIGAN, K. A., HILTON, S. C., & JOHNSON, T. R. B. (1996). Fetal neurobehavioral development. *Child Development, 67,* 2553–2567.

DIPIETRO, J. A., HODGSON, D. M., COSTIGAN, K. A., & JOHNSON, T. R. B. (1996). Fetal antecedent of infant temperament. *Child Development, 67,* 2568–2583.

DIPIETRO, J. A., SUESS, P. E., WHEELER, J. S., SMOUSE, P. H., & NEWLIN, D. B. (1995). Reactivity and regulation in cocaine-exposed neonates. *Infant Behavior and Development, 18,* 407–414.

DISHION, T. J. (1990). The family ecology of boys' peer relations in middle childhood. *Child Development, 61,* 874–892.

DITTMANN, R. W., KAPPES, M. H., KAPPES, M. E., BORGER, D., MEYER-BAHLBERG, H. F. L., STEGNER, H., WILLIG, R. H., & WALLIS, H. (1990). Congenital adrenal hyperplasia: II. Gender-related behavior and attitudes in female patients and sisters. *Psychoneuroendocrinology, 15,* 410–420.

DLUGOSZ, L., & BRACKEN, M. B. (1992). Reproductive effects of caffeine: A review and theoretical analysis. *Epidemiological Review, 14,* 83–100.

DODGE, K. A. (1986). A social information processing model of social competence in children. In M. Perlmutter (Ed.), *Minnesota symposia on child psychology: Vol. 18. Cognitive perspectives on children's social and behavioral development.* Hillsdale, NJ: Erlbaum.

DODGE, K. A., & CRICK, N. R. (1990). Social-information processing bases of aggressive behavior in children. *Personality and Social Psychology Bulletin, 16,* 8–22.

DODGE, K. A., & FELDMAN, E. (1990). Issues in social cognition and sociometric status. In S. R. Asher & J. D. Coie (Eds.), *Peer rejection in childhood.* Cambridge: Cambridge University Press.

DODGE, K. A., MURPHY, R. R., & BUCHSBAUM, K. (1984). The assessment of intention-cue detection skills in children: Implications for developmental psychopathology. *Child Development, 55,* 163–173.

DODGE, K. A., & SOMBERG, D. R. (1987). Hostile attributional biases among aggressive boys are exacerbated under conditions of threats to the self. *Child Development, 58,* 213–224.

DONALDSON, M. (1982). Conservation: What is the question? *British Journal of Psychology, 73,* 199–207.

DORE, J. (1976). Children's illocutionary acts. In R. Freedle (Ed.), *Comprehension and production.* Hillsdale, NJ: Erlbaum.

DORE, J. (1985). Holophrases revisited: Their "logical" development during dialog. In M. D. Barrett (Ed.), *Children's single-word speech.* New York: Wiley.

DORNBUSCH, S. M., GLASGOW, K. L., & LIN, I.-C. (1996). The social structure of schooling. *Annual Review of Psychology, 47,* 401–429.

DORNBUSCH, S. M., RITTER, P. L., LEIDERMAN, P. H., ROBERTS, D. F., & FRALEIGH, M. J. (1985). The relation of parenting style to adolescent school performance. *Child Development, 58,* 1244–1257.

DOUGHERTY, T., & HAITH, M. M. (1993, March). *Processing speed in infants and children: A component of IQ?* Paper presented at the meeting of the Society for Research in Child Development, New Orleans.

DOUGHERTY, T. M., & HAITH, M. M. (1997). Infant expectations and reaction time as predictors of childhood speed of processing and IQ. *Developmental Psychology, 33,* 146–155.

DOWLING, M., & BENDELL, D. (1988). Characteristics of small-for-gestational-age infants. *Infant Behavior and Development, 11,* 77.

DOYLE, A., CONNOLLY, J., & RIVEST, L. (1980). The effect of playmate familiarity on the social interactions of young children. *Child Development, 51,* 217–223.

DRAPER, P., & HARPENDING, H. (1988). A sociobiological perspective on the development of human reproductive strategies. In K. B. MacDonald (Ed.), *Sociobiological perspectives on human development.* New York: Springer-Verlag.

DREHER, M. C., & HAYES, J. S. (1993). Triangulation in cross-cultural research of child development in Jamaica. *Western Journal of Nursing Research, 15,* 216–229.

DREHER, M. C., NUGENT, K., & HUDGINS, R. (1994). Prenatal marijuana exposure and neonatal outcomes in Jamaica: An ethnographic study. *Pediatrics, 93,* 254–260.

DROTAR, D. K., ECKERLE, D., SATOLA, J., PALLOTTA, J., & WYATT, B. (1990). Maternal interactional behavior with nonorganic failure-to-thrive infants: A case comparison study. *Child Abuse and Neglect, 14,* 41–51.

DuBOIS, D. L., & HIRSCH, B. J. (1990). School and neighborhood friendship patterns of blacks and whites in early adolescence. *Child Development, 61,* 524–536.

DUBOW, E. F., TISAK, J., CAUSEY, D., HRYSHKO, A., & REID, G. (1991). A two-year longitudinal study of stressful life events, social support, and social problem-solving skills: Contributions to children's behavioral and academic adjustment. *Child Development, 62,* 583–599.

DUCKWORTH, E. (1987). *The having of wonderful ideas and other essays on teaching and learning.* New York: Teachers College Press.

DUDLEY, M., GYLER, L., BLINK-HORN, S., & BARNETT, B. (1993). Psychosocial interventions for very low birthweight infants: Their scope and efficacy. *Australian and New Zealand Journal of Psychiatry, 27,* 74–83.

DUFFY, F. H., ALS, H., & McANULTY, G. B. (1990). Behavioral and electrophysiological evidence for gestational age effects in healthy preterm and full-term infants studied two weeks after expected due date. *Child Development, 61,* 1271–1286.

DUFFY, J., GUNTHER, G., & WALTERS, L. (1997). Gender and mathematical problem solving. *Sex Roles, 37,* 477–494.

DUFRESNE, A., & KOBASIGAWA, A. (1989). Children's spontaneous allocation of study time: Differential and sufficient aspects. *Journal of Experimental Child Psychology, 47,* 274–296.

DUNCAN, G. J., BROOKS-GUNN, J., & KLEBANOV, P. K. (1994). Economic deprivation and early childhood development. *Child Development, 65,* 296–318.

DUNHAM, P., & DUNHAM, F. (1992). Lexical development during middle infancy: A mutually driven infant-caregiver process. *Developmental Psychology, 28,* 414–420.

DUNN, J. (1992). Sisters and brothers: Current issues in developmental research. In F. Boer & J. Dunn (Eds.), *Children's sibling relationships: Developmental and clinical issues.* Hillsdale, NJ: Erlbaum.

DUNN, J. (1993). *Young children's close relationships.* Newbury Park, CA: Sage.

DUNN, J. (1994). Sibling relationships and perceived self-competence: Patterns of stability between childhood and early adolescence. In A. Sameroff & M. M. Haith (Eds.), *Reason and responsibility: The passage through childhood.* Chicago: University of Chicago Press.

DUNN, J. (1996). Sibling relationships and perceived self-competence: Patterns of stability between childhood and early adolescence. In A. J. Sameroff & M. M. Haith (Eds.), *The five to seven year shift: The age of reason and responsibility.* Chicago: University of Chicago Press.

DUNN, J., & KENDRICK, C. (1982). The speech of two- and three-year-olds to infant siblings: "Baby talk" and the context of communication. *Journal of Child Language, 9,* 579–595.

DUNN, J., & McGUIRE, S. (1992). Sibling and peer relationships in childhood. *Journal of Child Psychology and Psychiatry and Allied Disciplines, 33,* 67–105.

DUNN, J., & McGUIRE, S. (1994). Young children's nonshared experiences: A summary of studies in Cambridge and Colorado. In E. M. Hetherington, D. Reiss, & R. Plo-min (Eds.), *Separate social worlds of siblings: The impact of nonshared environment on development.* Hillsdale, NJ: Erlbaum.

DUNN, J., & MUNN, P. (1986). Siblings and the development of prosocial behaviors. *International Journal of Behavioral Development, 9,* 265–284.

DUSEK, J. B., & JOSEPH, G. (1983). The bases of teacher expectancies: A meta-analysis. *Journal of Educational Psychology, 75,* 327–346.

DWECK, C. S. (1975). The role of expectations and attributions in the alleviation of learned helplessness. *Journal of Personality and Social Psychology, 31,* 674–685.

DWECK, C. S. (1986). Motivational processes affecting learning. *American Psychologist, 41,* 1040–1048.

DWECK, C. S. (1991). Self-theories and goals: Their role in motivation, personality, and development. In R. A. Dienstbier (Ed.), *Nebraska Symposia on Motivation* (Vol. 38). Lincoln: University of Nebraska Press.

DWECK, C. S., DAVIDSON, W., NELSON, S., & ENNA, B. (1978). Sex differences in learned helplessness: II. The contingencies of evaluative feedback in the classroom, and III. An experimental analysis. *Developmental Psychology, 14,* 268–276.

DWECK, C. S., & GILLIARD, D. (1975). Expectancy statements as determinants of reaction to failure: Sex differences in persistence and expectancy change. *Journal of Personality and Social Psychology, 32,* 1077–1084.

DWECK, C. S., & GOETZ, T. E. (1980). Attributions and learned helplessness. In J. H. Harvey, W. Ickles, & R. F. Kidd (Eds.), *New directions in attribution research* (Vol. 2). Hillsdale, NJ: Erlbaum.

DWECK, C. S., & LEGGETT, E. L. (1988). A social-cognitive approach to motivation and personality. *Psychological Review, 95,* 256–273.

DWECK, C. S., & REPPUCCI, N. D. (1973). Learned helplessness and reinforcement responsibility in children. *Journal of Personality and Social Psychology, 25,* 109–116.

DWYER, T., & PONSONBY, A. (1995). SIDS epidemiology and incidence. *Pediatric Annals, 24,* 350–356.

DYKENS, E. M., HODAPP, R. M., & LECKMAN, J. F. (1994). *Behavior and development in fragile X syndrome.* London: Sage.

EAGLY, A. H. (1987). *Sex differences: A social-role interpretation.* Hillsdale, NJ: Erlbaum.

EAGLY, A. H. (1995). The science and politics of comparing women and men. *American Psychologist, 50,* 145–158.

EAGLY, A. H., & CROWLEY, M. (1987). Gender and helping behavior: A meta-analytic review of the social psychological literature. *Psychological Bulletin, 100,* 283–308.

EAGLY, A. H., & STEFFEN, V. J. (1986). Gender and aggressive behavior: A meta-analytic review of the social psychological literature. *Psychological Bulletin, 100,* 309–330.

EAST, P. L., & ROOK, K. S. (1992). Compensatory patterns of support among children's peer relationships: A test using school friends, nonschool friends, and siblings. *Developmental Psychology, 28,* 163–172.

EASTERBROOKS, M. A., & GOLDBERG, W. A. (1984). Toddler development in the family: Impact of father involvement and parenting characteristics. *Child Development, 55,* 740–752.

EATON, W. O. (1994). Temperament, development, and the Five-Factor Model: Lessons from activity level. In C. F. Halverson, Jr., G. A. Kohnstamm, & R. P. Martin (Eds.), *The developed structure of temperament and personality from infancy to adulthood.* Hillsdale, NJ: Erlbaum.

EATON, W. O., & ENNS, L. R. (1986). Sex differences in human motor activity level. *Psychological Bulletin, 100,* 19–28.

EATON, W. O., & SAUDINO, K. J. (1992). Prenatal activity level as a temperament dimension? Individual differences and the developmental functions in fetal movement. *Infant Behavior and Development, 15,* 57–70.

EATON, W. O., & YU, A. P. (1989). Are sex differences in child motor activity level a function of sex differences in maturational status? *Child Development, 60,* 1005–1011.

ECCLES, J. S., & MIDGLEY, C. (1990). Changes in academic motivation and self-perception during early adolescence. In R. Montemayor, G. R. Adams, & T. P. Gullotta (Eds.), *From childhood to adolescence: A transitional period?* Newbury Park, CA: Sage.

ECCLES, J. S., MIDGLEY, C., & ADLER, T. (1984). Grade-related changes in the school environment: Effects on achievement motivation. In J. G. Nicholls (Ed.), *The development of achievement motivation.* Greenwich, CT: JAI Press.

ECCLES, J. S., MIDGLEY, C., WIGFIELD, A., BUCHANAN, C. M., REUMAN, D., FLANAGAN, C., & MACIVER, D. (1993). Development during adolescence: The impact of stage-environment fit on young adolescents' experiences in schools and in families. *American Psychologist, 48,* 90–101.

ECCLES, J., WIGFIELD, A., HAROLD, R. D., & BLUMENFELD, P. (1993). Age and gender differences in children's self- and task perceptions during elementary school. *Child Development, 64,* 830–847.

ECKERMAN, C. O. (1993). Imitation and toddlers' achievement of co-ordinated action with others. In J. Nadel & L. Camaioni (Eds.), *New perspectives in early communicative development.* New York: Routledge.

ECKERMAN, C. O., DAVIS, C. C., & DIDOW, S. (1989). Toddlers' emerging ways of achieving social coordinations with a peer. *Child Development, 60,* 440–453.

ECKERMAN, C. O., & STEIN, M. R. (1990). How imitation begets imitation and toddlers' generation of games. *Developmental Psychology, 26,* 370–378.

ECKSTEIN, S., & SHEMESH, M. (1992). The rate of acquisition of formal operational schemata in adolescence: A secondary analysis. *Journal of Research in Science Teaching, 29,* 441–451.

EDELMAN, G. M. (1993). Neural Darwinism: Selection and reentrant signaling in higher brain function. *Neuron, 10,* 115–125.

EDER, R. A. (1989). The emergent personologist: The structure and content of 3 1/2-, 5 1/2-, and 7 1/2-year-olds' concepts of themselves and others. *Child Development, 60,* 1218–1228.

EDER, R. A. (1990). Uncovering young children's psychological selves: Individual and developmental differences. *Child Development, 61,* 849–863.

EDWARDS, C. P. (1986). Cross-cultural research on Kohlberg's stages: The basis for consensus. In S. Modgil & C. Modgil (Eds.), *Lawrence Kohlberg: Consensus and controversy.* Philadelphia: Falmer.

EGELAND, B., & FARBER, E. (1984). Infant–mother attachment: Factors related to its development and changes over time. *Child Development, 55,* 753–771.

EGELAND, B., & HEISTER, M. (1995). The long-term consequences of infant day-care and mother–infant attachment. *Child Development, 66,* 474–485.

EHRHARDT, A. A. (1985). The psychobiology of gender. In A. S. Rossi (Ed.), *Gender and the life course.* New York: Aldine.

EHRHARDT, A. A., & MEYER-BAHLBURG, H. F. L. (1981). Effects of prenatal sex hormones on gender-related behavior. *Science, 211,* 1312–1318.

EIBL-EIBESFELDT, I. (1989). *Human ethology.* Hawthorne, NY: Aldine de Gruyter.

EICHORN, D. (1970). Physiological development. In P. H. Mussen (Ed.), *Carmichael's Manual of Child Psychology* (3rd ed.). New York: Wiley.

EICHORN, D. (1979). Physical development: Current foci of research. In J. D. Osofsky (Ed.), *Handbook of infant development.* New York: Wiley.

EIDUSON, B. T. (1980). Changing sex roles in alternative family styles: Implications for young children. In E. J. Anthony & C. Chiland (Eds.), *The child in his family: Preventive child psychiatry in an age of transition* (Vol. 6). New York: Wiley.

EIDUSON, B. T., KORNFEIN, M., ZIMMERMAN, I. L., & WEISNER, T. S. (1982). Comparative socialization practices in alternative family settings. In M. E. Lamb (Ed.), *Nontraditional families.* New York: Plenum.

EIFERMANN, R. R. (1971). Social play in childhood. In R. E. Herron & B. Sutton-Smith (Eds.), *Child's play.* New York: Wiley.

EILERS, R. E., & OLLER, D. K. (1988). Precursors to speech: What is innate and what is acquired? In R. Vasta (Ed.), *Annals of child development* (Vol. 5). Greenwich, CT: JAI Press.

EIMAS, P. D. (1975). Auditory and phonetic coding of the cues for speech: Discrimination of the [r-l] distinction by young infants. *Perception and Psychophysics, 18,* 341–347.

EISENBERG, N. (1982). The development of reasoning regarding prosocial behavior. In N. Eisenberg (Ed.), *The development of prosocial behavior.* New York: Academic Press.

EISENBERG, N. (1986). *Altruistic emotion, cognition, and behavior.* Hillsdale, NJ: Erlbaum.

EISENBERG, N. (1987). The relation of altruism and other moral behaviors to moral cognition: Methodological and conceptual issues. In N. Eisenberg & J. Strayer (Eds.), *Empathy and its development.* New York: Cambridge University Press.

EISENBERG, N. (1989). Empathy and sympathy. In W. Damon (Ed.), *Child development today and tomorrow.* San Francisco: Jossey-Bass.

EISENBERG, N. (1990). Prosocial development in early and mid-adolescence. In R. Montemayor, G. R. Adams, & T. P. Gullotta (Eds.), *From childhood to adolescence: A transitional period?* Newbury Park, CA: Sage.

EISENBERG, N., CAMERSON, E., TRYON, K., & DODEZ, R. (1981). Socialization of prosocial behavior in the preschool classroom. *Developmental Psychology, 17,* 773–782.

EISENBERG, N., CARLO, G., MURPHY, B., & VAN COURT, P. (1995). Prosocial development in late adolescence: A longitudinal study. *Child Development, 66,* 1179–1197.

EISENBERG, N., & FABES, R. A. (1991). Prosocial behavior and empathy: A multimethod, developmental perspective. In P. Clark (Ed.), *Review of personality and social psychology.* Newbury Park, CA: Sage.

EISENBERG, N., & FABES, R. A. (1998). Prosocial development. In W. Damon (Ed.), *Handbook of child psychology: Vol. 3. Social, emotional, and personality development.* New York: Wiley.

EISENBERG, N., FABES, R. A., CARLO, G., SPEER, A. L., SWITZER, G., KARBON, M., & TROYER, D. (1993). The relations of empathy-related and maternal practices to children's comforting behavior. *Journal of Experimental Child Psychology, 55,* 131–150.

EISENBERG, N., MARTIN, C. L., & FABES, R. A. (1996). Gender development and gender effects. In D. C. Berliner & R. C. Calfee (Eds.), *The handbook of educational psychology.* New York: Simon & Schuster.

EISENBERG, N., & MURPHY, B. (1995). Parenting and children's moral development. In M. H. Bornstein (Ed.), *Handbook of parenting: Vol. 4. Applied and practical parenting.* Mahwah, NJ: Erlbaum.

EISENBERG, N., TRYON, K., & CAMERON, E. (1984). The relation of preschoolers' peer interaction to their sex-typed toy choices. *Child Development, 55,* 1044–1050.

EISENBERG, N., WOLCHIK, S. A., HERNANDEZ, R., & PASTERNACK, J. F. (1985). Parental socialization of young children's play: A short-term longitudinal study. *Child Development, 56,* 1506–1513.

EISENBERG, R. B. (1976). *Auditory competence in early life.* Baltimore: University Park Press.

EISIKOVITS, Z., & SAGI, A. (1982). Moral development and discipline encountered in delinquent and nondelinquent adolescents. *Journal of Youth and Adolescence, 11,* 217–246.

EKMAN, P. (1993). Facial expression and emotion. *American Psychologist, 48,* 384–392.

EL ABD, S., TURK, J., & HILL, P. (1995). Annotation: Psychological characteristics of Turner syndrome. *Journal of Child Psychology and Psychiatry, 36,* 1109–1125.

ELARDO, R., & BRADLEY, R. H. (1981). The Home Observation for Measurement of the Environment (HOME) scale: A review of research. *Developmental Review, 1,* 113–145.

ELDER, G. H., JR. (1998). The life course and human development. In W. Damon (Ed.), *Handbook of child psychology: Vol. 1. Theoretical models of human development.* New York: Wiley.

ELDER, G. H., JR., & CASPI, A. (1988). Human development and social change: An emerging perspective on the life course. In N. Bolger, A. Caspi, G. Downey, & M. Moorehouse (Eds.), *Persons in context: Developmental processes.* New York: Cambridge University Press.

ELDER, G. H., JR., CASPI, A., & DOWNEY, G. (1986). Problem behavior and family relationships: Life course and intergenerational themes. In A. B. Sorensen, F. E. Weinert, & L. R. Sherrod (Eds.), *Human development and the life course: Multidisciplinary perspectives.* Hillsdale, NJ: Erlbaum.

ELDER, G. H., JR., SHANAHAN, M., & CLIPP, E. C. (1994). When war comes to men's lives: Life course patterns in family, work, and health. *Psychology and Aging, 9,* 5–16.

ELICKER, J., ENGLUND, M., & SROUFE, L. A. (1992). Predicting peer competence and peer relationships in childhood from early parent–child relationships. In R. D. Parke & G. W. Ladd (Eds.), *Family-peer relationships: Modes of linkage.* Hillsdale, NJ: Erlbaum.

ELKIND, D. (1980). Strategic interactions in early adolescence. In J. Adelson (Ed.), *Handbook of adolescent psychology.* New York: Wiley.

ELKINS, I. J., McGUE, M., & IACONO, W. G. (1997). Genetic and environmental influences on parent-son relationships: Evidence for increasing genetic influence during adolescence. *Developmental Psychology, 33,* 351–363.

ELLIOTT, R., & VASTA, R. (1970). The modeling of sharing: Effects associated with vicarious reinforcement, symbolization, age, and generalization. *Journal of Experimental Child Psychology, 10,* 8–15.

ELLIS, L., & AMES, M. A. (1987). Neurohormonal functioning and sexual orientation: A theory of homosexuality-heterosexuality. *Psychological Bulletin, 101,* 233–258.

ELLIS, S. (1997). Strategy choice in sociocultural context. *Developmental Review, 17,* 490–524.

ELLIS, S., ROGOFF, B., & CROMER, C. C. (1981). Age segregation in children's social interactions. *Developmental Psychology, 17,* 399–407.

ELLSWORTH, C. P., MUIR, D. W., & HAINS, S. M. J. (1993). Social competence and person-object differentiation: An analysis of the still-face effect. *Developmental Psychology, 29,* 63–73.

ELMER-DeWITT, P. (1994, January 17). The genetic revolution. *Time,* pp. 46–53.

EMDE, R. N. (1992). Individual meaning and increasing complexity: Contributions of Sigmund Freud and René Spitz to developmental psychology. *American Psychologist, 28,* 347–359.

EMDE, R. N., BIRINGEN, Z., CLYMAN, R. B., & OPPENHEIM, D. (1991). The moral sense of infancy: Affective core and procedural knowledge. *Developmental Review, 11,* 251–270.

EMDE, R. N., GAENSBAUER, T. J., & HARMON, R. J. (1976). Emotional expression in infancy: A biobehavioral study. *Psychological Issues Monograph Series, 10* (Whole No. 37). New York: International Universities Press.

EMDE, R. N., & HARMON, R. J. (Eds.). (1984). *Continuities and discontinuities in development.* New York: Plenum.

EMDE, R. N., PLOMIN, R., ROBINSON, J., CORLEY, R., DeFRIES, J., FULKER, D. W., REZNICK, J. S., CAMPOS, J., KAGAN, J., & ZAHN-WAXLER, C. (1992). Temperament, emotion, and cognition at fourteen months: The MacArthur Longitudinal Twin Study. *Child Development, 63,* 1437–1455.

EMDE, R. N., SWEDBERG, J., & SUZUKI, B. (1975). Human wakefulness and biological rhythms after birth. *Archives of General Psychiatry, 32,* 780–783.

EMERY, R. E., & LAUMANN-BILLINGS, L. (1998). An overview of the nature, causes, and consequences of abusive family relationships: Toward differentiating maltreatment and violence. *American Psychologist, 53,* 121–135.

EMMERICH, W., & SHEPARD, K. (1982). Development of sex-differentiated preferences during late childhood and adolescence. *Developmental Psychology, 18,* 406–417.

ENGLUND, M. M., REED, T., & SROUFE, L. A. (March, 1993). *Continuity of social competence from infancy to adolescence.* Paper presented at the meeting of the Society for Research in Child Development, New Orleans.

ENNIS, R. H. (1976). An alternative to Piaget's conceptualization of logical competence. *Child Development, 47,* 903–919.

ENNOURI, K., & BLOCH, H. (1996). Visual control of hand approach movements in newborns. *British Journal of Developmental Psychology, 14,* 327–338.

ENRIGHT, R. D., BJERSTEDT, A., ENRIGHT, W. F., LEVY, V. M., LAPSLEY, D. K., BUSS, R. R., HARWELL, M., & ZINDLER, M. (1984). Distributive justice development: Cross-cultural, contextual, and longitudinal evaluations. *Child Development, 55,* 1737–1751.

ENRIGHT, R. D., & SATTERFIELD, S. J. (1980). An ecological validation of social cognitive development. *Child Development, 51,* 156–161.

ENTWISTLE, D. R., ALEXANDER, K. L., PALLAS, A. M., & CADIGAN, D. (1987). The emergent academic self-image of first-graders: Its response to social structure. *Child Development, 58,* 1190–1206.

EPSTEIN, J. L. (1983). Selections of friends in differently organized schools and classrooms. In J. L. Epstein & M. Karweit (Eds.), *Friends in school.* New York: Academic Press.

EPSTEIN, J. L. (1986). Friendship selection: Developmental and environmental influences. In E. C. Mueller & C. R. Cooper (Eds.), *Process and outcome in peer relationships.* New York: Academic Press.

EPSTEIN, J. L. (1989). The selection of friends: Changes across the grades and in different school environments. In T. J. Berndt & G. W. Ladd (Eds.), *Peer relationships in child development.* New York: Wiley.

EPSTEIN, Y. M. (1981). Crowding stress and human behavior. *Journal of Social Issues, 37,* 126–144.

ERICKSON, M. F., SROUFE, L. A., & EGELAND, B. (1985). The relationship between quality of attachment and behavior problems in pre-school in a high-risk sample. In I. Bretherton & E. Waters (Eds.), Growing points of attachment theory and research. *Monographs of the Society for Research in Child Development, 50* (1–2, Serial No. 209).

ERON, L. D. (1987). The development of aggressive behavior from the perspective of a developing behaviorism. *American Psychologist, 42,* 435–442.

ERON, L. D., & HUESMANN, L. R. (1986). The role of television in the development of prosocial and antisocial behavior. In D. Olweus, J. Block, & M. Radke-Yarrow (Eds.), *Development of antisocial and prosocial behavior.* Orlando, FL: Academic Press.

ERON, L. D., HUESMANN, L. R., BRICE, P., FISCHER, P., & MERMELSTEIN, R. (1983). Age trends in the development of aggression, sex typing, and related television habits. *Developmental Psychology, 19,* 71–77.

ERON, L. D., HUESMANN, L. R., DUBOW, E., ROMANOFF, R., & YARMEL, R. W. (1987). Aggression and its correlates over 22 years. In D. H. Crowell, I. M. Evans, & C. R. O'Donnell (Eds.), *Childhood aggression and violence: Sources of influence, prevention, and control.* New York: Plenum.

ERVIN, S. M. (1964). Imitation and structural change in children's language. In E. H. Lenneberg (Ed.), *New directions in the study of language.* Cambridge: MIT Press.

ERWIN, P. (1993). *Friendship and peer relations in children.* Chichester, England: Wiley.

ESKANAZI, B. (1993). Caffeine during pregnancy: Grounds for concern? *Journal of the American Medical Association, 270,* 2973–2974.

ETAUGH, C., COLLINS, G., & GERSON, A. (1975). Reinforcement of sex-typed behaviors of two-year-old children in a nursery school setting. *Developmental Psychology, 11,* 255.

ETZEL, B. C., & GEWIRTZ, J. L. (1967). Experimental modification of caretaker-maintained high rate operant crying in a 6- and a 20-week old infant (*Infans tyrannotearus*): Extinction of crying with reinforcement of eye contact and smiling *Journal of Experimental Child Psychology, 5,* 303–317.

EUROPEAN COLLABORATIVE STUDY. (1991). Children born to women with HIV-1 infection: Natural history and risk of transmission. *Lancet, 337,* 253–260.

EVELYTH, P. B. (1986). Population differences in growth. In F. Falkner & J. M. Tanner (Eds.), *Human growth: A comprehensive treatise.* New York: Plenum.

EYER, D. E. (1992). *Mother–infant bonding: A scientific fiction.* New Haven, CT: Yale University Press.

FABES, R. A., EISENBERG, N., KARBON, M., TROYER, D., & SWITZER, G. (1994). The relations of children's emotion regulation to their vicarious emotional responses and comforting behavior. *Child Development, 65,* 1678–1693.

FABES, R. A., EISENBERG, N., & MILLER, P. A. (1990). Maternal correlates of children's vicarious emotional responsiveness. *Developmental Psychology, 26,* 639–648.

FABRICIUS, W. V., & CAVALIER, L. (1989). The role of causal theories about memory in young children's memory strategy choice. *Child Development, 60,* 298–308.

FABRICIUS, W. V., & STEFFE, L. (1989, April). *Considering all possible combinations: The early beginnings of a formal operational skill.* Paper presented at the meeting of the Society for Research in Child Development, Kansas City, MO.

FADERMAN, L. (1991). *Odd girls and twilight lovers: A history of lesbian life in twentieth-century America.* New York: Columbia University Press.

FADIMAN, A. (1983, April). The unborn patient. *Life,* pp. 38–44.

FAGAN, J. F., III. (1973). Infants' delayed recognition memory and forgetting. *Journal of Experimental Child Psychology, 16,* 424–450.

FAGAN, J. F., III. (1992). Intelligence: A theoretical viewpoint. *Current Directions in Psychological Science, 1,* 82–86.

FAGAN, J. F., III, & DETTERMAN, D. H. (1992). The Fagan Test of Infant Intelligence: A technical summary. *Journal of Applied Developmental Psychology, 13,* 173–193.

FAGAN, J. F., III, & SHEPHERD, P. A. (1986). *The Fagan Test of Infant Intelligence: Training manual.* Cleveland, OH: Infantest Corporation.

FAGOT, B. I. (1977). Consequences of moderate cross-gender behavior in preschool children. *Child Development, 48,* 902–907.

FAGOT, B. I. (1982). Sex role development. In R. Vasta (Ed.), *Strategies and techniques of child study.* New York: Academic Press.

FAGOT, B. I. (1985). Stages in thinking about early sex role development. *Developmental Review, 5,* 83–98.

FAGOT, B. I. (1997), Attachment, parenting, and peer interactions of toddler children. *Developmental Psychology, 33,* 489–499.

FAGOT, B. I., & GAUVAIN, M. (1997). Mother-child problem solving: Continuity through the early childhood years. *Developmental Psychology, 33,* 480–488.

FAGOT, B. I., & HAGAN, R. (1991). Observations of parent reactions to sex-stereotyped behaviors: Age and sex effects. *Child Development, 62,* 617–628.

FAGOT, B. I., HAGAN, R., LEINBACH, M. D., & KRONSBERG, S. (1985). Differential reactions to assertive and communicative acts of toddler boys and girls. *Child Development, 56,* 1499–1505.

FAGOT, B. I., & LEINBACH, M. D. (1987). Socialization of sex roles within the family. In D. B. Carter (Ed.),*Current conceptions of sex roles and sex typing: Theory and research.* New York: Praeger.

FAGOT, B. I., & LEINBACH, M. D. (1993). Gender-role development in young children: From discrimination to labeling. *Developmental Review, 13,* 205–224.

FAGOT, B. I., LEINBACH, M. D., & HAGAN, R. (1986). Gender labeling and the adoption of sex-typed behaviors. *Developmental Psychology, 22,* 440–443.

FAGOT, B. I., LEINBACH, M. D., & O'BOYLE, C. (1992). Gender labeling, gender stereotyping, and parenting behaviors. *Developmental Psychology, 28,* 225–230.

FALBO, T., & POSTON, D. L., JR. (1993). The academic, personality, and physical outcomes of only children in China. *Child Development, 64,* 18–35.

FANTUZZO, J. W., MCDERMOTT, P. A., MANZ, P. H., HAMPTON, V. R., & BURDICK, N. A. (1996). The Pictorial Scale of Perceived Competence and Social Acceptance: Does it work with low-income urban children? *Child Development, 67,* 1071–1084.

FANTZ, R. L. (1961). The origin of form perception. *Scientific American, 204,* 66–72.

FANTZ, R. L. (1963). Pattern vision in newborn infants. *Science, 140,* 296–297.

FARBER, S. L. (1981). *Identical twins reared apart: A reanalysis.* New York: Basic Books.

FARRAR M. J. (1990). Discourse and the acquisition of grammatical morphemes. *Journal of Child Language, 17,* 607–624.

FARRAR, M. J. (1992). Negative evidence and grammatical morpheme acquisition. *Developmental Psychology, 28,* 90–98.

FARRAR, M. J., & GOODMAN, G. S. (1990). Developmental differences in the relation between scripts and episodic memory: Do they exist? In R. Fivush & J. Hudson (Eds.), *Knowing and remembering in young children.* New York: Cambridge University Press.

FARRAR, M. J., & GOODMAN, G. S. (1992). Developmental changes in event memory. *Child Development, 63,* 173–187.

FARRINGTON, D. P. (1994). Childhood, adolescent, and adult features of violent males. In L. R. Huesmann (Ed.), *Aggressive behavior: Current perspectives.* New York: Plenum.

FARVER, J. M., & BRANSTETTER, W. H. (1994). Preschoolers' prosocial responses to their peers' distress. *Developmental Psychology, 30,* 334–341.

FARVER, J. M., & FROSCH, D. L. (1996). L.A. stories: Aggression in preschoolers' spontaneous narratives after the riots of 1992. *Child Development, 67,* 19–32.

FARVER, J. M., & SHIN, Y. L. (1997). Social pretend play in Korean- and Anglo-American pre-schoolers. *Child Development, 68,* 544–556.

FAY, R. E., TURNER, C. F., KLASSEN, A. D., & GAGNON, J. H. (1989). Prevalence and patterns of same-gender contact among men. *Science, 243,* 338–348.

FEIN, G. G., SCHWARTZ, P. M., JACOBSON, S. W., & JACOBSON, J. L. (1983). Environmental toxin and behavioral development: A new role for psychological research. *American Psychologist, 38,* 1198–1205.

FEINGOLD, A. (1992). Sex differences in variability in intellectual abilities: A new look at an old controversy. *Review of Educational Research, 62,* 61–84.

FEINGOLD, A. (1993). Cognitive gender differences: A developmental perspective. *Sex Roles, 29,* 91–112.

FEINMAN, S. (1981). Why is cross-sex role behavior more approved for girls than for boys? *Sex Roles, 7,* 289–300.

FEINMAN, S., ROBERTS, D., HSIEH, K., SAWYER, D., & SWANSON, D. (1992). A critical review of social referencing in infancy. In S. Feinman (Ed.), *Social referencing and the social construction of reality in infancy.* New York: Plenum.

FEIRING, C., & LEWIS, M. (1987). The child's social network: Sex differences from three to six years. *Sex Roles, 17,* 621–636.

FELDLAUFER, H., MIDGLEY, C., & ECCLES, J. S. (1988). Student, teacher, and observer perceptions of the classroom environment before and after the transition to junior high school. *Journal of Early Adolescence, 8,* 133–156.

FELDMAN, J. F., BRODY, N., & MILLER, S. (1980). Sex differences in non-elicited neonatal behaviors. *Merrill-Palmer Quarterly, 26,* 63–73.

FENNEMA, E., & TARTRE, L. A. (1985). The use of spatial visualization in mathematics by girls and boys. *Journal for Research in Mathematics Education, 16,* 184–206.

FENSON, L., DALE, P. S., REZNICK, J. S., BATES E., THAL, D. J., & PETHICK, S. J. (1994). Variability in early communicative development. *Monographs of the Society for Research in Child Development, 59* (5, Serial No. 242).

FERGUSON, C. A. (1983). Reduplication in child phonology. *Journal of Child Language, 10,* 239–243.

FERGUSON, L. R. (1970). Dependency motivation in socialization. In R. A. Hoppe, G. A. Milton, & E. C. Simmel (Eds.), *Early experience and the process of socialization.* New York: Academic Press.

FERGUSON, T. J., & RULE, B. G. (1988). Children's evaluations of retaliatory aggression. *Child Development, 59,* 961–968.

FERNALD, A. (1991). Prosody in speech to children: Prelinguistic and linguistic functions. In R. Vasta (Ed.), *Annals of child development* (Vol. 8). London: Kingsley.

FERNALD, A. (1993). Approval and disapproval: Infant responsiveness to vocal affect in familiar and unfamiliar languages. *Child Development, 64,* 657–674.

FERNALD, A., & MORIKAWA, H. (1993). Common themes and cultural variations in Japanese and American mothers' speech to infants. *Child Development, 64,* 637–656.

FERNALD, A., & O'NEILL, D. K. (1993). Peekaboo across cultures: How mothers and infants play with voices, faces, and expectations. In K. MacDonald (Ed.), *Parent-child play.* Albany: State University of New York Press.

FERRIERA, A. J. (1969). *Prenatal environment.* Springfield, IL: Charles C. Thomas.

FESHBACH, N. D., & FESHBACH, S. (1982). Empathy training and the regulation of aggression: Potentialities and limitations. *Academic Psychology Bulletin, 4,* 399–413.

FESHBACH, S., & SINGER, R. D. (1971). *Television and aggression: An experimental field study.* San Francisco: Jossey-Bass.

FEUERSTEIN, R. (1979). *The dynamic assessment of retarded performers.* Baltimore: University Park Press.

FIELD, D. (1987). A review of preschool conservation training: An analysis of analyses. *Developmental Review, 7,* 210–251.

FIELD, T. M. (1987). Affective and interactive disturbances in infants. In J. D. Osofsky (Ed.), *Handbook of infant development* (2nd ed.). New York: Wiley.

FIELD, T. M. (1995). Massage therapy for infants and children. *Developmental and Behavioral Pediatrics, 16,* 105–111.

FIELD, T. M., & ROOPNARINE, J. L. (1982). Infant-peer interactions. In T. M. Field, A. Huston, H. C. Quay, L. Troll, & G. E. Finley (Eds.), *Review of human development.* New York: Wiley.

FIELD, T. M., & WALDEN, T. A. (1982). Production and perception of facial expressions in infancy and early childhood. In H. W. Reese & L. P. Lipsitt (Eds.), *Advances in child development and behavior* (Vol. 16). New York: Academic Press.

FIELD, T. M., COHEN, D., GARCIA, R., & GREENBERG, R. (1985). Mother–stranger face discrimination by the newborn. *Infant Behavior and Development, 7,* 19–25.

FIELD, T. M., HEALY, B., GOLDSTEIN, S., & GUTHERTZ, M. (1990). Behavior-state matching and synchrony in mother–infant interactions of nondepressed versus depressed dyads. *Developmental Psychology, 26,* 7–14.

FIFER, W. P., & MOON, C. M. (1995). The effects of fetal experience with sound. In J.-P. Lecanuet, W. P. Fifer, N. A. Krasnegor, & W. P. Smotherman (Eds.), *Fetal development: A psychobiological perspective.* Hillsdale, NJ: Erlbaum.

FINE, G. A. (1987). *With the boys: Little League baseball and preadolescent culture.* Chicago: University of Chicago Press.

FINEGAN, J. K., NICCOLS, G. A., & SITARENIOS, G. (1992). Relations between prenatal testosterone levels and cognitive abilities at 4 years. *Developmental Psychology, 28,* 1075–1089.

FINLAY, D., & IVINSKIS, A. (1987). Cardiac change responses and attentional mechanisms in infants. In B. E. McKenzie & R. H. Day (Eds.), *Perceptual development in early infancy: Problems and issues.* Hillsdale, NJ: Erlbaum.

FINNEGAN, L. P., & FEHR, K. O. (1980). The effects of opiates, sedative-hypnotics, amphetamines, cannabis, and other psychoactive drugs on the fetus and newborn. In O. J. Kalant (Ed.), *Research advances in alcohol and drug problems: Vol. 5. Alcohol and drug problems in women.* New York: Plenum.

FIREMAN, G., & BEILIN, H. (1990, May). *Preformationism and Piaget's stage concept.* Paper presented at the meeting of the Jean Piaget Society, Philadelphia.

FIRSCH, R. E. (1984). Fatness, puberty, and fertility. In J. Brooks-Gunn & A. C. Petersen (Eds.), *Girls at puberty: Biological, psychological, and social perspectives.* New York: Plenum.

FISCHER, K. W. (1980). A theory of cognitive development: The control and construction of hierarchies of skills. *Psychological Review, 87,* 477–531.

FISCHER, M., & LEITENBERG, H. (1986). Optimism and pessimism in elementary school-aged children. *Child Development, 57,* 241–248.

FISHBEIN, H. D. (1984). *The psychology of infancy and childhood: Evolutionary and cross-cultural perspectives.* Hillsdale, NJ: Erlbaum.

FISHBEIN, H. D., & IMAI, S. (1993). Preschoolers select playmates on the basis of gender and race. *Journal of Applied Developmental Psychology, 14,* 303–316.

FISHER, C. B., & LERNER, R. M. (Eds.). (1994). *Applied developmental psychology.* New York: McGraw-Hill.

FISHER, C. B., & TRYON, W. W. (1990). *Ethics in applied developmental psychology: Emerging issues in an emerging field.* Norwood, NJ: Ablex.

FISHER, E. P. (1992). The impact of play on development: A meta-analysis. *Play and Culture, 5,* 159–181.

FISHER-THOMPSON, D. (1990). Adult gender typing of children's toys. *Sex Roles, 23,* 291–303.

FIVUSH, R. (1991). The social construction of personal narratives. *Merrill-Palmer Quarterly, 37,* 59–82.

FIVUSH, R. (1993). Emotional content of parent–child conversations about the past. In C. A. Nelson (Ed.), *Minnesota symposia on child psychology: Vol. 26. Memory and affect in development.* Hillsdale, NJ: Erlbaum.

FIVUSH, R. (1994). Constructing narrative, emotion, and self in parent-child conversations about the past. In U. Neisser & R. Fivush (Eds.), *The remembering self: Construction and accuracy in the self-narrative.* New York: Cambridge University Press.

FIVUSH, R., HADEN, C., & REESE, E. (1996). Remembering, recounting, and reminiscing: The development of autobiographical memory in social context. In D. C. Rubin (Ed.), *Remembering our past: Studies in autobiographical memory.* New York: Cambridge University Press.

FIVUSH, R., & KUEBLI, J. (1997). Making everyday events emotional: The construal of emotion in parent–child conversations about the past. In N. L. Stein, P. A. Ornstein, B. Tversky, & C. J. Brainerd (Eds.), *Memory for everyday and emotional events.* Mahwah, NJ: Erlbaum.

FIVUSH, R., KUEBLI, J., & CLUBB, P. A. (1992). The structure of events and event representations: A developmental analysis. *Child Development, 63,* 188–201.

FLAKS, D. K., FICHER, I., MASTERPASQUA, F., & JOSEPH, G. (1995). Lesbians choosing motherhood: A comparative study of lesbian and heterosexual parents and their children. *Developmental Psychology, 31,* 105–114.

FLAVELL, J. H. (1963). *The developmental psychology of Jean Piaget.* Princeton, NJ: Van Nostrand.

FLAVELL, J. H. (1970). Developmental studies of mediated memory. In H. W. Reese & L. P. Lipsitt (Eds.), *Advances in child development and behavior* (Vol. 5). New York: Academic Press.

FLAVELL, J. H. (1971). First discussant's comments: What is memory development the development of? *Human Development, 14,* 272–278.

FLAVELL, J. H. (1985). *Cognitive development* (2nd ed.). Englewood Cliffs, NJ: Prentice Hall.

FLAVELL, J. H. (1986). The development of children's knowledge about the appearance–reality distinction. *American Psychologist, 41,* 418–425.

FLAVELL, J. H. (1992a). Cognitive development: Past, present, and future. *Developmental Psychology, 28,* 998–1005.

FLAVELL, J. H. (1992b). Perspectives on perspective taking. In H. Beilin & P. B. Pufall (Eds.), *Piaget's theory: Prospects and possibilities.* Hillsdale, NJ: Erlbaum.

FLAVELL, J. H., BEACH, D. H., & CHINSKY, J. M. (1966). Spontaneous verbal rehearsal in a memory task as a function of age. *Child Development, 37,* 283–299.

FLAVELL, J. H., FLAVELL, E. R., & GREEN, F. L. (1983). Development of the appearance–reality distinction. *Cognitive Psychology 15,* 95–120.

FLAVELL, J. H., FRIEDRICHS, A., & HOYT, J. (1970). Developmental changes in memorization processes. *Cognitive Psychology, 1,* 324–340.

FLAVELL, J. H., GREEN, F. L., & FLAVELL, E. R. (1989). Young children's ability to differentiate appearance–reality and Level 2 perspectives in the tactile modality. *Child Development, 60,* 201–213.

FLAVELL, J. H., LINDBERG, N. A., GREEN, F. L., & FLAVELL, E. R. (1992). The development of children's understanding of the appearance–reality distinction between how people look and what they are really like. *Merrill-Palmer Quarterly, 38,* 513–524.

FLAVELL, J. H., & MILLER, P. H. (1998). Social cognition. In W. Damon (Series Ed.) & D. Kuhn & R. S. Siegler (Vol. Eds.), *Handbook of child psychology: Vol. 2. Cognition, perception, and language* (5th ed.). New York: Wiley.

FLAVELL, J. H., MILLER, P. H., & MILLER, S. A. (1993). *Cognitive development* (3rd ed.). Englewood Cliffs, NJ: Prentice Hall.

FLAVELL, J. H., SHIPSTEAD, S. G., & CROFT, K. (1980). What young children think you see when their eyes are closed. *Cognition, 8,* 369–387.

FLAVELL, J. H., ZHANG, H.-D., ZOU, H., DONG, Q., & QI, S. (1983). A comparison between the development of the appearance–reality distinction in the People's Republic of China and the United States. *Cognitive Psychology, 15,* 459–466.

FLEMING, P., BLAIR, P., BACON, C., BENSLEY, D., SMITH, I., TAYLOR, E., BERRY, J., GOLDING, J., & TRIPP, J. (1996). Environments of infants during sleep andrisk of the sudden infant death syndrome: Results of 1993–5 case-control study for confidential inquiry into still-births and deaths in infancy. *British Medical Journal, 313,* 191–195.

FLETCHER, A. C., DARLING, N. E., STEINBERG, L., & DORNBUSCH, S. M. (1995). The company they keep: Relation of adolescents' adjustment and behavior to their friends' perceptions of authoritative parenting in the social network. *Developmental Psychology, 31,* 300–310.

FLYNN, J. R. (1987). Massive IQ gains in 14 nations: What IQ tests really measure. *Psychological Bulletin, 101,* 171–191.

FOGEL, A., & THELEN, E. (1987). Development of early expressive and communicative action: Reinterpreting the evidence from a dynamic systems perspective. *Developmental Psychology, 23,* 747–761.

FOGELMAN, K. (1980). Smoking in pregnancy and subsequent development of the child. *Child Care, Health and Development, 6,* 233–249.

FOGLE, S. (1992). Pretty BABI: Blastomere screen detects CF gene. *Journal of NIH Research, 4,* 46.

FORMAN, E. A. (1992). Discourse, intersubjectivity, and the development of peer collaboration: A Vygotskian approach. In L. T. Winegar & J. Valsiner (Eds.), *Children's development within social context: Vol. 1. Metatheory and theory.* Hillsdale, NJ: Erlbaum.

FORSLUND, M., & BJERRE, I. (1983). Neurological assessment of preterm infants at term conceptional age in comparison with normal full-term infants. *Early Human Development, 8,* 195–208.

FOX, N. A. (Ed.) (1994). The development of emotion regulation: Biological and behavioral considerations. *Monographs of the Society for Research in Child Development, 59*(2–3, Serial No. 240).

FOX, N. A., KIMMERLY, N. L., & SCHAFER, W. D. (1991). Attachment to mother/attachment to father: A meta-analysis. *Child Development, 62,* 210–225.

FRANCIS, P. L., SELF, P. A., & HOROWITZ, F. D. (1987). The behavioral assessment of the neonate: An overview. In J. D. Osofsky (Ed.), *Handbook of infant development* (2nd ed.). New York: Wiley.

FRANKEL, K. A., & BATES, J. E. (1990). Mother–toddler problem solving: Antecedents of attachment, home behavior, and temperament. *Child Development, 61,* 810–819.

FRASER, S. (Ed.). (1995). *The Bell Curve wars: Race, intelligence, and the future of America.* New York: Basic Books.

FRAUENGLASS, M. H., & DIAZ, R. M. (1985). Self-regulatory functions of children's speech: A critical analysis of recent challenges to Vygotsky's theory. *Developmental Psychology, 21,* 357–364.

FREDA, M. C., ANDERSON, F. H., DAMUS, K., PROUST, D., BRUSTMAN, L., & MERKATZ, I. R. (1990). Lifestyle for inner city women at high risk for preterm birth. *Journal of Advanced Nursing, 15,* 364–372.

FREEBURG, T. J., & LIPPMAN, M. Z. (1986). Factors influencing discrimination of infant cries. *Journal of Child Language, 13,*3–13.

FREEDLAND, R. L., & BERTENTHAL, B. I. (1994). Developmental stages in interlimb coordination: Transition to hands-and-knees crawling. *Psychological Science, 5,* 26–32.

FRENCH, D. C. (1988). Heterogeneity of peer-rejected boys: Aggressive and nonaggressive subtypes. *Child Development, 59,* 976–985.

FRENCH, D. C. (1990). Heterogeneity of peer rejected girls. *Child Development, 61,* 2028–2031.

FREUND, L. S. (1990). Maternal regulation of children's problem-solving behavior and its impact on children's performance. *Child Development, 61,* 113–126.

FREY, K. S., & RUBLE, D. N. (1987). What children say about classroom performance: Sex and grade differences in perceived competence. *Child Development, 58,* 1066–1078.

FREY, K. S., & RUBLE, D. N. (1992). Gender constancy and the "cost" of sex-typed behavior: A test of the conflict hypothesis. *Developmental Psychology, 28,* 714–721.

FRIED, P. A., O'CONNELL, C. M., & WATKINSON, M. A. (1992). Sixty- and 72-month follow-up of children prenatally exposed to marijuana, cigarettes, and alcohol: Cognitive and language assessment. *Developmental and Behavioral Pediatrics, 13,* 383–391.

FRIED, P. A., WATKINSON, B., & GRAY, R. (1992). A follow-up study of attentional behavior in 6-year-old children exposed prenatally to marijuana, cigarettes, and alcohol. *Neuro-toxicology and Teratology, 14,* 299–311.

FRIEDMAN, H. S., TUCKER, J. S., SCHWARTZ, J. E., TOMLINSON-KEASEY, C., MARTIN, L. R., WINGARD, D. L., & CRIQUI, M. H. (1995). Psychosocial and behavioral predictors of longevity: The aging and death of the "Termites." *American Psychologist, 50,* 69–78.

FRIEDMAN, J. M. (1981). Genetic disease in the offspring of older fathers. *Obstetrics and Gynecology, 57,* 745–749.

FRIEDRICH-COFER, L. K., & HUSTON, A. C. (1986). Television violence and aggression: The debate continues. *Psychological Bulletin, 100,* 364–371.

FRIEDRICH-COFER, L. K., HUSTON-STEIN, A., KIPNIS, D. M., SUSMAN, E. J., & CLEWETT, A. S. (1979). Environmental enhancement of prosocial television content: Effects on interpersonal behavior, imaginative play, and self-regulation in a natural setting. *Developmental Psychology, 15,* 637–646.

FRISCH, H. L. (1977). Sex stereotypes in adult–infant play. *Child Development, 48,* 1671–1675.

FRITH, U. (1989). *Autism: Explaining the enigma.* Oxford, England: Basil Blackwell.

FRODI, A. M., LAMB, M. E., LEAVITT, L. A., & DONOVAN, W. L. (1978). Fathers' and mothers' responses to infant smiles and cries. *Infant Behavior and Development, 1,* 187–198.

FROMING, W. J., ALLEN, L., & JENSEN, R. (1985). Altruism, role-taking, and self-awareness: The acquisition of norms governing altruistic behavior. *Child Development, 56,* 1223–1228.

FROMKIN, V., & RODMAN, R. (1988). *An introduction to language* (4th ed.). New York: Holt, Rinehart, and Winston.

FRY, D. P. (1988). Intercommunity differences in aggression among Zapotec children. *Child Development, 59,* 1008–1019.

FUKAHARA, H., SHIMURA, Y., & YAMANOUCHI, I. (1988, November). *The transmission of ambient noise and self-produced sound into the human body.* Poster presented at the second joint meeting of the Acoustical Society of America and the Acoustical Society of Japan, Honolulu.

FULLARD, W., & REILING, A. M. (1976). An investigation of Lorenz's "babyness." *Child Development, 47,* 1191–1193.

FULLARD, W., MCDEVITT, S. C., & CAREY, W. B. (1984). Assessing temperament in one to three year old children. *Journal of Pediatric Psychology, 9,* 205–217.

FULLER, B. (1987). Defining school quality. In J. Hannway & M. Lockhead (Eds.), *The contribution of social sciences to educational policy and practice: 1965–1985.* Berkeley, CA: McCuthan.

FURMAN, W. (1987). Acquaintanceship in middle childhood. *Developmental Psychology, 23,* 563–570.

FURMAN, W., & GAVIN, L. A. (1989). Peers' influence on adjustment and development. In T. J. Berndt & G. W. Ladd (Eds.), *Peer relationships in child development.* New York: Wiley.

FURMAN, W., & MASTERS, J. C. (1980). Affective consequences of social reinforcement, punishment, and neutral behavior. *Developmental Psychology, 16,* 100–104.

FURNAM, A., ABRAMSKY, S., & GUNTER, B. (1997). A cross-cultural content analysis of children's television advertisements. *Sex Roles, 37,* 91–99.

FURNAM, A., & BITAR, N. (1993). The stereotyped portrayal of men and women in British television advertisements. *Sex Roles, 29,* 297–310.

FURROW, D., BAILLIE, C., McCLAREN, J., & MOORE, C. (1993). A further look at the motherese hypothesis: A reply to Gleitman, Newport, and Gleitman. *Journal of Child Language, 20,* 363–375.

FURROW, D., NELSON, K., & BENEDICT, H. (1979). Mothers' speech to children and syntactic development: Some simple relationships. *Journal of Child Language, 6,* 423–442.

FURSTENBERG, F. F., JR., & CHERLIN, A. J. (1991). *Divided families.* Cambridge: Harvard University Press.

GALAMBOS, N. L., ALMEIDA, D. M., & PETERSEN, A. C. (1990). Masculinity, femininity, and sex role attitudes in early adolescence: Exploring gender intensification. *Child Development, 61,* 1905–1914.

GALEN, B. R., & UNDERWOOD, M. K. (1997). A developmental investigation of social aggression among children. *Developmental Psychology, 33,* 589–600.

GALLAGHER, A. M., & DE LISI, R. (1994). Gender differences in Scholastic Aptitude Test—mathematics problem solving among high-ability students. *Journal of Educational Psychology, 86,* 204–211.

GALLAHUE, D. L. (1989). *Understanding motor development* (2nd ed.). Carmel, IN: Benchmark Press.

GALPERT, L., & DOCKRELL, J. (1995). Is understanding the experimenter's intention the clue to conservation ability? *International Journal of Behavioral Development, 18,* 505–517.

GARAI, J. E., & SCHEINFELD, A. (1968). Sex differences in mental and behavioral traits. *Genetic Psychology Monographs, 77,* 169–299.

GARBARINO, J., & ABRAMOWITZ, R. H. (1992). The family as a social system. In J. Garbarino (Ed.), *Children and families in the social environment* (2nd ed.). New York: Aldine de Gruyter.

GARBARINO, J., DUBROW, N., KOSTELNY, K., & PARDO, C. (1992). *Children in danger: Coping with the consequences of community violence.* San Francisco: Jossey-Bass.

GARBARINO, J., GABOURY, M. T., & PLANTZ, M. C. (1992). Social policy, children, and their families. In J. Garbarino (Ed.), *Children and families in the social environment* (2nd ed.). New York: Aldine de Gruyter.

GARBARINO, J., & KOSTELNY, K. (1995). Parenting and public policy. In M. H. Bornstein (Ed.), *Handbook of parenting: Vol. 3. Status and social conditions of parenting.* Mahwah, NJ: Erlbaum.

GARBARINO, J., & KOSTELNY, K. (1996). The effects of political violence on Palestinian children's behavior problems: A risk accumulation model. *Child Development, 67,* 33–45.

GARDEN, R. A. (1987). The second IEA mathematics study. *Comparative Education Review, 31,* 47–68.

GARDNER, H. (1983). *Frames of mind: The theory of multiple intelligences.* New York: Basic Books.

GARDNER, H. (1993). *Multiple intelligences.* New York: Basic Books.

GARDNER, H. (1995). Reflections on multiple intelligences: Myths and messages. *Phi Delta Kappan, 77*(2).

GARDNER, J. M., KARMEL, B. Z., & MAGNANO, C. L. (1992). Arousal/visual preference interactions in high-risk neonates. *Developmental Psychology, 28,* 821–830.

GARMEZY, N., & RUTTER, M. (Eds.). (1983). *Stress, coping, and development in children.* New York: McGraw-Hill.

GARMON, L. C., BASINGER, K. S., GREGG, V. R., & GIBBS, J. C. (1996). Gender differences in stage and expression of moral judgment. *Merrill-Palmer Quarterly, 42,* 418–437.

GARNER, P. W., JONES, D. C., & MINER, J. L. (1994). Social competence among low-income pre-schoolers: Emotion socialization practices and social cognitive correlates. *Child Development, 65,* 622–637.

GARNER, R. (1990). Children's use of strategies in reading. In D. F. Bjorklund (Ed.), *Children's strategies: Contemporary views of cognitive development.* Hillsdale, NJ: Erlbaum.

GARRISON, W. T., & EARLS, F. J. (1987). *Temperament and child psychopathology.* Newbury Park, CA: Sage.

GARROD, A., BEAL, C., & SHIN, P. (1990). The development of moral orientation in elementary school children. *Sex Roles, 22,* 13–26.

GARVEY, C. (1986). Peer relations and the growth of communication. In E. C. Mueller & C. R. Cooper (Eds.), *Process and outcome in peer relationships.* New York: Academic Press.

GAUVAIN, M., & FAGOT, B. I. (1995). Child temperament as a mediator of mother-toddler problem solving. *Social Development, 4,* 257–278.

GE, X., CONGER, R. D., CADORET, R. J., NEIDERHISER, J. M., YATES, W., TROUGHTON, E., & STEWART, M. A. (1996). The developmental interface between nature and nurture: A mutual in-fluence model of child antisocial behavior and parents' behaviors. *Developmental Psychology, 32,* 574–589.

GEARY, D. C. (1995a). *Children's mathematical development.* Washington, DC: American Psychological Association.

GEARY, D. C. (1995b). Reflections of evolution and culture in children's cognition. *American Psychologist, 50,* 24–37.

GEARY, D. C. (1996a). International differences in mathematical achievement: Their nature, courses, and consequences. *Current Directions in Psychological Science, 5,* 133–137.

GEARY, D. C. (1996b). Sexual selection and sex differences in mathematical abilities. *Behavioral and Brain Sciences, 19,* 229–284.

GEARY, D. C., FAN, L., & BOW-THOMAS, C. C. (1992). Numerical cognition: Loci of ability differences comparing children from China and the United States. *Psychological Science, 3,* 180–185.

GEEN, R. G. (1983). Aggression and television violence. In R. G. Geen & E. I. Donnerstein (Eds.), *Aggression: Theoretical and empirical reviews* (Vol. 2). New York: Academic Press.

GELFAND, D. M., & HARTMANN, D. P. (1982). Response consequences and attributions: Two contributors to prosocial behavior. In N. Eisenberg (Ed.), *The development of prosocial behavior.* New York: Academic Press.

GELMAN, R. (1982). Basic numerical abilities. In R. J. Sternberg (Ed.), *Advances in the psychology of human intelligence* (Vol. 1). Hillsdale, NJ: Erlbaum.

GELMAN, R. (1991). Epigenetic foundations of knowledge structures: Initial and transcendent constructions. In S. Carey & R. Gelman (Eds.), *The epigenesis of mind.* Hillsdale, NJ: Erlbaum.

GELMAN, R., & BAILLARGEON, R. (1983). A review of some Piagetian concepts. In P. H. Mussen (Series Ed.) & J. H. Flavell & E. M. Markman (Vol. Eds.), *Handbook of child psychology: Vol. 3. Cognitive development.* New York: Wiley.

GELMAN, R., & GALLISTEL, C. R. (1978). *The child's understanding of number.* Cambridge: Harvard University Press.

GELMAN, S. A. (1996). Concepts and theories. In R. Gelman & T. Au (Eds.), *Perceptual and cognitive development.* San Diego: Academic Press.

GELMAN, S. A., & COLEY, J. D. (1990). The importance of knowing a dodo is a bird: Categories and inferences in 2-year-old children. *Developmental Psychology, 26,* 796–804.

GELMAN, S. A., & MARKMAN, E. M. (1986). Categories and induction in young children. *Cognition, 23,* 183–209.

GELMAN, S. A., & MARKMAN, E. M. (1987). Young children's inductions from natural kinds: The role of categories and appearances. *Child Development, 58,* 1532–1541.

GELMAN, S. A., WILCOX, S. A., & CLARK, E. V. (1989). Conceptual and lexical hierarchies in young children. *Cognitive Development, 4,* 309–326.

GENESEE, F. (1989). Early bilingual development: One language or two? *Journal of Child Language, 16,* 161–179.

GENESEE, F. (Ed.). (1994). *Educating second language children.* New York: Cambridge University Press.

GENTILE, D. A. (1993). Just what are sex and gender anyway? *Psychological Science, 4,* 120–124.

GENTNER, D. (1982). Why nouns are learned before verbs: Linguistic relativity versus natural partitioning. In S. A. Kuczaj (Ed.), *Language development* (Vol. 2). Hillsdale, NJ: Erlbaum.

GEORGE, C., & SOLOMON, J. (1989). Internal working models of parenting and security of attachment at age six. *Infant Mental Health Journal, 10,* 222–237.

GEORGE, C., KAPLAN, N., & MAIN, M. (1985). *The Adult Attachment Interview.* Unpublished manuscript, University of California, Department of Psychology, Berkeley.

GERBNER, G., GROSS, L., MORGAN, M., & SIGNORELLI, N. (1994). Growing up with television: The cultivation perspective. In J. Bryant & D. Zillman (Eds.), *Media effects: Advances in theory and research.* Hillsdale, NJ: Erlbaum.

GERGEN, K. J. (1994). Mind, text, and society: Self-memory in social context. In U. Neisser & R. Fivush (Eds.), *The remembering self: Construction and accuracy in the self-narrative.* New York: Cambridge University Press.

GERSHKOFF-STOWE, L., & SMITH, L. B. (1991, April). *Changes in pointing and labeling during the naming explosion.* Poster session presented at the Meeting of the Society for Research in Child Development, Seattle, WA.

GESELL, A. (1954). The ontogeneses of infant behavior. In L. Carmichael (Ed.), *Manual of child psychology* (2nd ed.). New York: Wiley.

GESELL, A., & ILG, F. L. (1943). *Infant and child in the culture of today.* New York: Harper.

GESELL, A., & THOMPSON, H. (1929). Learning and growth in identical infant twins: An experimental study by the method of co-twin control. *Genetic Psychological Monographs, 6,* 1–24.

GESELL, A., & THOMPSON, H. (1938). *The psychology of early growth.* New York: Macmillan.

GEWIRTZ, J. L. (1991). Social influence on child and parent via stimulation and operant learning mechanisms. In M. Lewis & S. Feinman (Eds.), *Social influences and socialization in infancy.* New York: Plenum.

GEWIRTZ, J. L., & BOYD, E. F. (1976). Mother–infant interaction and its study. In H. W. Reese (Ed.), *Advances in child development and behaviors* (Vol. 11). New York: Academic Press.

GEWIRTZ, J. L., & BOYD, E. F. (1977). Experiments on mother–infant interaction underlying mutual attachment acquisition: The infant conditions the mother. In T. Alloway, P. Pliner, & L. Kramer (Eds.), *Advances in the study of communication and affect: Vol. 3. Attachment behavior.* New York: Plenum.

GEWIRTZ, J. L., & PELAEZ-NOGUERAS, M. (1991a). The attachment metaphor and the conditioning of infant separation protests. In J. L. Gewirtz & W. M. Kurtines (Eds.), *Intersections with attachment.* Hillsdale, NJ: Erlbaum.

GEWIRTZ, J. L., & PELAEZ-NOGUERAS, M. (1991b). Proximal mechanisms underlying the acquisition of moral behavior patterns. In W. M. Kurtines & J. L. Gewirtz (Eds.), *Handbook of moral behavior and development: Vol. 1. Theory.* Hillsdale, NJ: Erlbaum.

GEWIRTZ, J. L., & PELAEZ-NOGUERAS, M. (1992a). B. F. Skinner's legacy to human infant behavior and development. *American Psychologist, 47,* 1411–1422.

GEWIRTZ, J. L., & PELAEZ-NOGUERAS, M. (1992b). Social referencing as a learned process. In S. Feinman (Ed.), *Social referencing and the social construction of reality in infancy.* New York: Plenum.

GHATALA, E. S., LEVIN, J. R., PRESSLEY, M., & LODICO, M. G. (1985). Training cognitive strategy monitoring in children. *American Educational Research Journal, 22,* 199–216.

GIANINO, A., & TRONICK, E. Z. (1988). The mutual regulation model: The infant's self and interactive regulation coping and defense. In T. Field, P. McCabe, & N. Schneiderman (Eds.), *Stress and coping.* Hillsdale, NJ: Erlbaum.

GIBBS, J. C. (1987). Social processes in delinquency: The need to facilitate empathy as well as sociomoral reasoning. In W. M. Kurtines & J. L. Gewirtz (Eds.), *Moral development through social interaction.* New York: Wiley.

GIBBS, J. C. (1991). Sociomoral developmental delay and cognitive distortion: Implications for the treatment of antisocial youth. In W. M. Kurtines & J. L. Gewirtz (Eds.), *Handbook of moral behavior and development: Vol. 3. Application.* Hillsdale, NJ: Erlbaum.

GIBBS, J. C., & SCHNELL, S. V. (1985). Moral judgment "versus" socialization: A critique. *American Psychologist, 40,* 1071–1080.

GIBBS, J. T. (Ed.). (1988). *Young, black, and male in America: An endangered species.* Dover, MA: Auburn House.

GIBSON, E. J. (1969). *Principles of perceptual learning and development.* New York: Appleton-Century-Crofts.

GIBSON, E. J. (1988). Exploratory behavior in the development of perceiving, acting, and the acquiring of knowledge. *Annual Review of Psychology, 39,* 1–41.

GIBSON, E. J. (1993). Ontogenesis of the perceived self. In U. Neisser (Ed.), *The perceived self: Ecological and interpersonal sources of self-knowledge.* Cambridge, MA: Cambridge University Press.

GIBSON, E. J., & WALK, R. D. (1960). The "visual cliff." *Scientific American, 202,* 64–71.

GIBSON, E. J., & WALKER, A. (1984). Development of knowledge of visual-tactual affordances of substance. *Child Development, 55,* 453–460.

GIBSON, J. J. (1966). *The senses considered as perceptual systems.* Boston: Houghton Mifflin.

GILLIGAN, C. (1982). *In a different voice: Psychological theory and women's development.* Cambridge: Harvard University Press.

GILLIGAN, C., & ATTANUCCI, J. (1988). Two moral orientations: Gender differences and similarities. *Merrill-Palmer Quarterly, 34,* 223–237.

GILLY, M. (1988). Gender roles in advertising: A comparison of television advertisements in Australia, Mexico, and the United States. *Journal of Marketing, 52,* 75–85.

GINSBURG, H. J. (1975, April). *Variations of aggressive interaction among male elementary school children as a function of spatial density.* Paper presented at the meeting of the Society for Research in Child Development, Denver, CO.

GINSBURG, H. J. (1980). Playground as laboratory: Naturalistic studies of appeasement, altruism, and the Omega child. In D. R. Omark, F. F. Strayer, & D. G. Freedman (Eds.), *Dominance relations: An ethological view of human conflict and social interaction.* New York: Garland.

GINSBURG, H., & OPPER, S. (1988). *Piaget's theory of intellectual development* (3rd ed.). Englewood Cliffs, NJ: Prentice Hall.

GINSBURG, H. P., KLEIN, A., & STARKEY, P. (1998). The development of children's mathematical thinking: Theory, research, and practice. In W. Damon (Series Ed.) & I. E. Sigel, & K. A. Renninger (Vol. Eds.), *Handbook of child psychology: Vol. 4. Child psychology in practice* (5th ed.). New York: Wiley.

GLADUE, B. A. (1994). The biopsychology of sexual orientation.*Current Directions in Psychological Science, 3,* 150–154.

GLADUE, B. A., BEATTY, W. W., LARSON, J., & STATON, R. D. (1990). Sexual orientation and spatial ability in men and women. *Psychobiology, 18,* 101–108.

GLASSMAN, M. (1994). All things being equal: The two roads of Piaget and Vygotsky. *Developmental Review, 114,* 186–214.

GLASSMAN, M., & ZAN, B. (1995). Moral activity and domain theory: An alternative interpretation of research with young children. *Developmental Review, 15,* 434–457.

GLEASON, J. B., & WEINTRAUB, S. (1978). Input and the acquisition of communicative competence. In K. E. Nelson (Ed.), *Children's language* (Vol. 1). New York: Gardner.

GLEITMAN, L. R. (1990). The structural sources of word meaning. *Language Acquisition, 1,* 3–55.

GLEITMAN, L. R., NEWPORT, E. L., & GLEITMAN, H. (1984). The current status of the motherese hypothesis. *Journal of Child Language, 11,* 43–79.

GLENN, S. M., CUNNINGHAM, C. C., & JOYCE P. F. (1981). A study of auditory preferences in nonhandicapped infants and infants with Down's syndrome. *Child Development, 52,* 1303–1307.

GODDARD, M., DURKIN, K., & RUTTER, D. R. (1985). The semantic focus of maternal speech: A comment on Ninio and Bruner (1978). *Journal of Child Language, 12,* 209–213.

GOLD, D., & BERGER, C. (1978). Problem-solving performance of young boys and girls as a function of task appropriateness and sex identity. *Sex Roles, 4,* 183–193.

GOLDBERG, S. (1983). Parent–infant bonding: Another look. *Child Development, 54,* 1355–1382.

GOLDFIELD, B. A. (1993). Noun bias in maternal speech to one-year-olds. *Journal of Child Language, 20,* 85–99.

GOLDFIELD, B. A., & REZNICK, J. S. (1990). Early lexical acquisition: Rate, content, and the vocabulary spurt. *Journal of Child Language, 17,* 171–183.

GOLDIN-MEADOW, S., ALIBALI, M. W., & CHURCH, R. B. (1993). Transitions in concept acquisition: Using the hand to read the mind. *Psychological Review, 100,* 279–297.

GOLDIN-MEADOW, S., & MYLANDER, C. (1984). Gestural communication in deaf children: The effects and noneffects of parental input on early language development. *Monographs of the Society for Research in Child Development, 49* (3–4, Serial No. 207).

GOLDIN-MEADOW, S., WEIN, D., & CHANG, C. (1992). Assessing knowledge through gesture: Using children's hands to read their minds. *Cognition and Instruction, 9,* 201–219.

GOLDMAN, A. S. (1980). Critical periods of prenatal toxic insults. In R. H. Schwartz & S. J. Yaffe (Eds.), *Drug and chemical risks to the fetus and newborn.* New York: Alan R. Liss.

GOLDSMITH, H. H., BUSS, K. A., & LEMERY, K. S. (1997). Toddler and childhood temperament: Expanded content, stronger genetic evidence, new evidence for the importance of environment. *Developmental Psychology, 33,* 891–905.

GOLDSMITH, H. H., BUSS, A. H., PLOMIN, R., ROTHBART, M. K., THOMAS, A., CHESS, S., HINDE, R. A., & MCCALL, R. B. (1987). Roundtable: What is temperament. Four approaches. *Child Development, 58,* 505–529.

GOLDSMITH, H. H., & HARMAN, C. (1994). Temperament and attachment: Individuals and relationships. *Current Directions in Psychological Science, 3,* 53–57.

GOLDSMITH, H. H., & ROTHBART, M. K. (1991) Contemporary instruments for assessing early temperament by questionnaire and in the laboratory. In J. Strelau & A. Angleitner

(Eds.), *Explorations in temperament: International perspectives on theory and measurement.* New York: Plenum.

GOLDSTEIN, A. P., & GLICK, B. (1987). *Aggression replacement training: A comprehensive intervention for aggressive youth.* Champaign, IL: Research Press.

GOLDSTEIN, A. P., & GLICK, B. (1994). Aggression replacement training: Curriculum and evaluation. *Simulation and Gaming, 25,* 9–26.

GOLINKOFF, R. M., HIRSH-PASEK, K., CAULEY, K., & GORDON, L. (1987). The eyes have it: Lexical and syntactic comprehension in a new paradigm. *Journal of Child Language, 14,* 23–45.

GOLOMBOK, S., COOK, R., BISH, A., & MURRAY, C. (1995). Families created by the new reproductive technologies: Quality of parenting and social and emotional development of the children. *Child Development, 66,* 285–298.

GOOD, T. L. (1993). Teacher expectations. In L. Anderson (Ed.), *International encyclopedia of education* (2nd ed.). Oxford, England: Pergamon.

GOOD, T. L., & BROPHY, J. E. (1997). *Looking in classrooms* (7th ed.). New York: Longman.

GOODMAN, G. S., HIRSCHMANN, J. E., HEPPS, D., & RUDY, L. (1991). Children's memory for stressful events. *Merrill-Palmer Quarterly, 37,* 109–158.

GOODMAN, G. S., PYLE TAUB, E., JONES, D. P. H., ENGLAND, P., PORT, L. K., RUDY, L., & PRADO, L. (1992). Testifying in criminal court. *Monographs of the Society for Research in Child Development, 57* (5, Serial No. 229).

GOODMAN, G. S., & QUAS, J. A. (1997). Trauma and memory: Individual differences in children's recounting of a stressful experience. In N. L. Stein, P. A. Ornstein, B. Tversky, & C. Brainerd (Eds.), *Memory for everyday and emotional events.* Mahwah, NJ: Erlbaum.

GOODMAN, G. S., & TOBEY, A. E. (1994). Memory development within the context of child sexual abuse investigations. In C. B. Fisher & R. M. Lerner (Eds.), *Applied developmental psychology.* New York: McGraw-Hill.

GOODMAN, R., & STEVENSON, J. (1989). A twin study of hyperactivity: II. The aetiological role of genes, family relationships, and perinatal adversity. *Journal of Child Psychology and Psychiatry, 30,* 691–709.

GOODNOW, J. J. (1988). Children, families, and communities: Ways of viewing their relationships to each other. In N. Bolger, A. Caspi, G. Downey, & M. Moorehouse (Eds.), *Persons in context.* New York: Cambridge University Press.

GOODNOW, J. J., & COLLINS, W. A. (1990). *Development according to parents: The nature, sources, and consequences of parents' ideas.* Hillsdale, NJ: Erlbaum.

GOODZ, N. S. (1989). Parental language mixing in bilingual families. *Journal of Infant Mental Health, 10,* 25–34.

GOOSENS, F. A., & VAN IJZENDOORN, M. H. (1990). Quality of infants' attachments to professional caregivers: Relation to infant–parent attachment and day-care characteristics. *Child Development, 61,* 832–837.

GOPNIK, A., & MELTZOFF, A. N. (1987). Early semantic developments and their relationship to object permanence, means–ends understanding and categorization. In K. Nelson & A. VanKleek (Eds.), *Children's language* (Vol. 6). Hillsdale, NJ: Erlbaum.

GOPNIK, A., & MELTZOFF, A. N. (1992). Categorization and mapping: Basic-level sorting in eighteen-month-olds and its relation to language. *Child Development, 63,* 1091–1103.

GOPNIK, A., & MELTZOFF, A. N. (1997). *Words, thoughts, and theories.* Cambridge: MIT Press.

GORMAN, K. S., & POLLITT, E. (1992). Relationship between weight and body proportionality at birth, growth during the first year of life, and cognitive development at 36, 48, and 60 months. *Infant Behavior and Development, 15,* 279–296.

GOSWAMI, U. (1995). Transitive relational mappings in three- and four-year-olds: The analogy of Goldilocks and the three bears. *Child Development, 66,* 877–892.

GOSWAMI, U., & BRYANT, P. (1990). *Phonological skills and learning to read.* Hove, England: Erlbaum.

GOTLIB, I. H., & HAMMEN, C. L. (1992). *Psychological aspects of depression: Toward a cognitive-interpersonal integration.* New York: Wiley.

GOTLIEB, S. J., BAISINI, F. J., & BRAY, N. W. (1988). Visual recognition memory in IVGR and normal birthweight infants. *Infant Behavior and Development, 11,* 223–228.

GOTTESMAN, I. I. (1974). Developmental genetics and ontogenetic psychology: Overdue detente and propositions from a matchmaker. In A. Pick (Ed.), *Minnesota symposium on child psychology.* Minneapolis: University of Minnesota Press.

GOTTESMAN, I. I., & SHIELDS, J. (1982). *Schizophrenia.* Cambridge: Cambridge University Press.

GOTTFRIED, A. W. (Ed.). (1984a). *Home environment and early cognitive development.* New York: Academic Press.

GOTTFRIED, A. W. (1984b). Home environment and early cognitive development: Integration, meta-analyses, and conclusions. In A. W. Gottfried (Ed.), *Home environment and early cognitive development.* New York: Academic Press.

GOTTMAN, J. M. (1983). How children become friends. *Monographs of the Society for Research in Child Development, 48* (3, Serial No. 201).

GOTTMAN, J. M., GONSO, J., & RASMUSSEN, B. (1975). Social interaction, social competence, and friendship in children. *Child Development, 46,* 709–718.

GOTTMAN, J. S. (1990). Children of gay and lesbian parents. In F. W. Bozett & M. B. Sussman (Eds.), *Homosexuality and family relations.* New York: Harrington Park Press.

GRABER, J. A., BROOKS-GUNN, J., PAIKOFF, R. L., & WARREN, M. P. (1994). Prediction of eating problems: An 8-year study of adolescent girls. *Developmental Psychology, 30,* 823–834.

GRAHAM, F. K., & CLIFTON, R. K. (1966). Heart-rate change as a component of the orienting response. *Psychological Bulletin, 65,* 305–320.

GRAHAM, S., & HOCHN, S. (1995). Children's understanding of aggression and withdrawal as social stigmas: An attributional analysis. *Child Development, 66,* 1143–1161.

GRAHAM, S., & HUDLEY, C. (1994). Attributions of aggressive and nonaggressive African-American male early adolescents: A study of construct accessibility. *Developmental Psychology, 30,* 365–373.

GRAHAM, S., HUDLEY, C., & WILLIAMS, E. (1992). Attributional and emotional determinants of aggression among African-American and Latino young adolescents. *Developmental Psychology, 28,* 731–740.

GRAHAM, S., & JUVONEN, J. (1998). A social cognitive perspective on peer aggression and victimization. In R. Vasta (Ed.), *Annals of child development.* (Vol. 13). London: Kingsley.

GRALINSKI, J. H., & KOPP, C. B. (1993). Everyday rules for behavior: Mothers' requests to young children. *Developmental Psychology, 29,* 573–584.

GRATTAN, M. P., De VOS, E., LEVY, J., & McCLINTOCK, M. K. (1992). Asymmetric action in the human newborn: Sex differences in patterns of organization. *Child Development, 62,* 273–289.

GRAY, S. W., & RAMSEY, B. K. (1982). The Early Training Project: A life-span view. *Human Development, 25,* 48–57.

GRAY, S. W., RAMSEY, B. K., & KLAUS, R. A. (1982). *From 3 to 20: The early training project.* Baltimore: University Park Press.

GRAY, W. M. (1990). Formal operational thought. In W. F. Overton (Ed.), *Reasoning, necessity, and logic: Developmental perspectives.* Hillsdale, NJ: Erlbaum.

GRAY, W. M., & HUDSON, L. M. (1984). Formal operations and the imaginary audience. *Developmental Psychology, 20,* 619–627.

GRAZIANO, W. G. (1987). Lost in thought at the choice point: Cognition, context, and equity. In J. C. Masters & W. P. Smith (Eds.), *Social comparison, social justice, and relative deprivation.* Hillsdale, NJ: Erlbaum.

GREEN, J. A., JONES, L. E., & GUSTAFSON, G. E. (1987). Perception of cries by parents and nonparents: Relation to cry acoustics. *Developmental Psychology, 23,* 370–382.

GREEN, K. D., FOREHAND, R., BECK, S. J., & VOSK, B. (1980). An assessment of the relationship among measures of children's social competence and children's academic achievement. *Child Development, 51,* 1149–1156.

GREEN, R. (1974). *Sexual identity conflict in children and adults.* New York: Basic Books.

GREEN, R. (1987). *The "sissy boy syndrome" and the development of homosexuality.* New Haven, CT: Yale University Press.

GREENFIELD, P. M. (1966). On culture and conservation. In J. S. Bruner, R. R. Olver, & P. M. Greenfield (Eds.), *Studies in cognitive growth.* New York: Wiley.

GREENLEAF, B. K. (1978). *Children through the ages: A history of childhood.* New York: McGraw-Hill.

GREENOUGH, W. T., & BLACK, J. E. (1992). Induction of brain structure by experience: Substrates for cognitive development. In M. R. Gunnar & C. A. Nelson (Eds.), *Minnesota symposia on child psychology: Vol. 24. Developmental behavioral neuroscience.* Hillsdale, NJ: Erlbaum.

GREENOUGH, W. T., BLACK, J. E., & WALLACE, C. S. (1987). Experience and brain development. *Child Development, 58,* 539–559.

GREENWALD, A., & PRATKANIS, A. (1984). The self. In R. Wyer & T. Srull (Eds.), *Handbook of social cognition* (Vol. 3). Hillsdale, NJ: Erlbaum.

GREGORY, R. (1978). *Eye and brain: The psychology of seeing* (3rd ed.). New York: McGraw Hill.

GRIFFITHS, P. (1985). The communicative functions of children's single-word speech. In M. D. Barrett (Ed.), *Children's single-word speech.* New York: Wiley.

GRIMSHAW, J. (1981). Form, function, and the language-acquisition device. In C. L. Baker & J. J. McCarthy (Eds.), *The logical problem of language acquisition.* Cambridge: MIT Press.

GRINDER, R. E. (1967). *A history of genetic psychology: The first science of human development.* New York: Wiley.

GROLNICK, W., BRIDGES, L. J., & CONNELL, J. P. (1996). Emotion regulation in two-year-olds: Strategies and emotional expression in four contexts. *Child Development, 67,* 928–941.

GRONAU, R. C., & WAAS, G. A. (1997). Delay of gratification and cue utilization: An examination of children's social information processing. *Merrill-Palmer Quarterly, 43,* 305–322.

GRONLUND, N. (1959). *Sociometry in the classroom.* New York: Harper.

GROOME, L. J., SWIBER, M. J., ATTERBURY, J. L., BENTZ, L. S., & HOLLAND, S. B. (1997). Similarities and differences in behavioral state organization during sleep periods in the perinatal infant before and after birth. *Child Development, 68,* 1–11.

GROSSMANN, K., GROSSMANN, K. E., SPANGLER, G., SUESS, G., & UNZNER, L. (1985). Maternal sensitivity and newborns' orientation responses as related to quality of attachment in northern Germany. In I. Bretherton & E. Waters (Eds.), Growing points of attachment theory and research. *Monographs of the Society for Research in Child Development, 50*(1–2, Serial No. 209).

GROSSMAN, K. E. (1995). The evolution and history of attachment research and theory. In S. Goldberg, R. Muir, & J. Kerr (Eds.), *Attachment theory: Social, developmental, and clinical perspectives.* Hillsdale, NJ: The Analytic Press.

GROSSMANN, K. E., & GROSSMANN, K. (1990). The wider concept of attachment in cross-cultural research. *Human Development, 33,* 31–47.

GROTEVANT, H. D. (1989). Child development within the family context. In W. Damon (Ed.), *Child development today and tomorrow.* San Francisco: Jossey-Bass.

GROVES, B., ZUCKERMAN, B., MARANS, S., & COHEN, D. (1993). Silent victims: Children who witness violence. *Journal of the American Medical Association, 269,* 262–264.

GRUENEICH, R. (1982). Issues in the developmental study of how children use intention and consequence information to make moral evaluations. *Child Development, 53,* 29–43.

GRUSEC, J. E. (1992). Social learning theory and developmental psychology: The legacy of Robert Sears and Albert Bandura. *Developmental Psychology, 28,* 776–786.

GRUSEC, J. E., & ABRAMOVITCH, R. (1982). Imitation of peers and adults in a natural setting: A functional analysis. *Child Development, 53,* 636–642.

GRUSEC, J. E., & GOODNOW, J. J. (1994). Impact of parental discipline methods on the child's internalization of values: A reconceptualization of current points of view. *Developmental Psychology, 30,* 4–19.

GRUSEC, J. E., KUCZYNSKI, L., RUSHTON, J. P., & SIMUTIS, Z. M. (1979). Learning resistance to temptation through observation. *Developmental Psychology, 15,* 233–240.

GRUSEC, J. E., & LYTTON, H. (1988). *Social development: History, theory, and research.* New York: Springer-Verlag.

GUERIN, D. W., & GOTTFRIED, A. W. (1994). Developmental stability and change in parent reports of temperament: A ten-year longitudinal investigation from infancy through preadolescence. *Merrill-Palmer Quarterly, 40,* 334–355.

GUERRA, N. G., & SLABY, R. G. (1990). Cognitive mediators of aggression in adolescent offenders: 2. Intervention. *Developmental Psychology, 26,* 269–277.

GUILFORD, J. P. (1988). Some changes in the structure-of-the-intellect model. *Educational and Psychological Measurement, 48,* 1–4.

GUILLEMIN, J. (1993). Cesarean birth: Social and political aspects. In B. K. Rothman (Ed.), *Encyclopedia of childbearing.* Phoenix, AZ: Oryx Press.

GUISINGER, S., & BLATT, S. J. (1994). Individuality and relatedness. *American Psychologist, 49,* 104–111.

GUNNAR, M. R., FISCH, R. O., & MALONE, S. (1984). The effects of a pacifying stimulus on behavioral and adrenocortical responses to circumcision in the newborn. *Journal of the American Academy of Child Psychiatry, 23,* 34–38.

GUNNAR, M. R., MALONE, S., VANCE, G., & FISCH, R. O. (1985). Coping with aversive stimulation in the neonatal period: Quiet sleep and plasma cortisol levels during recovery from circumcision. *Child Development, 56,* 824–834.

GUNTER, B. (1995). *Television and gender representation.* London: John Libbey.

GUNTHEROTH, W. (1995). *Crib death: The sudden infant death syndrome* (3rd ed.). Armonk, NY: Futura.

GURMAN BARD, E., & ANDERSON, A. (1983). The unintelligibility of speech to children. *Journal of Child Language, 10,* 265–292.

GURUCHARRI, C., & SELMAN, R. L. (1982). The development of interpersonal understanding during childhood, preadolescence, and adolescence: A longitudinal follow-up study. *Child Development, 53,* 924–927.

GUSTAFSON, G. E., & HARRIS, K. L. (1990). Women's responses to young infants' cries. *Developmental Psychology, 26,* 144–152.

HAAPASALO, J., & TREMBLAY, R. E. (1994). Physically aggressive boys from age 6 to 12: Family background, parenting behavior, and prediction of delinquency. *Journal of Consulting and Clinical Psychology, 62,* 1044–1052.

HACK, M., KLEIN, N. K., & TAYLOR, H. G. (1995). Long-term developmental outcomes of low birth weight infants. *The future of children* (Vol. 5, No. 1). Los Angeles: Packard Foundation.

HADJISTAVROPOULOS, H. D., CRAIG, K. D., GRUNAU, R. V. E., & JOHNSTON, C. C. (1994). Judging pain in newborns: Facial and cry determinants. *Journal of Pediatric Psychology, 19,* 485–491.

HAECKEL, E. (1977). Last words on evolution. In D. N. Robinson (Ed.), *Significant contributions to the history of psychology: 1750–1920.* Washington, DC: University Publications of America. (Original work published 1906).

HAGEN, J.W., & HALE, G. A. (1973). The development of attention in children. In A. D. Pick (Ed.), *Minnesota symposia on child psychology* (Vol. 7). Minneapolis: University of Minnesota Press.

HAGERMAN, R. J. (1996). Biomedical advances in developmental psychology: The case of Fragile X syndrome. *Developmental Psychology, 32,* 416–424.

HAGGERTY, R., GARMEZY, N., RUTTER, M., & SHERROD, L. R. (Eds.). (1994). *Stress, risk and resilience in children and adolescents: Processes, mechanisms, and interventions.* New York: Cambridge University Press.

HAIGHT, W., & MILLER, P. J. (1993). *Pretending at home.* Albany, NY: SUNY Press.

HAINLINE, L., & ABRAMOV, I. (1992). Assessing visual development: Is infant vision good enough? In C. Rovee-Collier & L. P. Lipsitt (Eds.), *Advances in infancy research* (Vol. 7). Norwood, NJ: Ablex.

HAITH, M. M. (1966). The response of the human newborn to visual movement. *Journal of Experimental Child Psychology, 3,* 235–243.

HAITH, M. M. (1980). *Rules that babies look by.* Hillsdale, NJ: Erlbaum.

HAITH, M. M. (1986). Sensory and perceptual processes in early infancy. *Journal of Pediatrics, 109,* 158–171.

HAITH, M. M. (1991). Gratuity, perception-action integration and future orientation in infant vision. In F. Kessel, A. Sameroff, & M. Bornstein (Eds.), *The past as prologue in developmental psychology: Essays in honor of William Kessen.* Hillsdale, NJ: Erlbaum.

HAITH, M. M. (1993). Preparing for the 21st century: Some goals and challenges for studies of infant sensory and perceptual development. *Developmental Review, 13,* 354–371.

HAITH, M. M. (1994). Visual expectations as the first step toward the development of future-oriented processes. In M. M. Haith, J. B. Benson, R. J. Roberts, Jr., & B. F. Pennington (Eds.), *The development of future-oriented processes.* Chicago: University of Chicago Press.

HAITH, M. M., & BENSON, J. B. (1998). Infant cognition. In W. Damon (Series Ed.) & D. Kuhn & R. S. Siegler (Vol. Eds.), *Handbook of child psychology: Vol. 2. Cognition, perception, and language* (5th ed.). New York: Wiley.

HAITH, M. M., BENSON, J. B., ROBERTS, R. J., JR., & PENNINGTON, B. F. (Eds.). (1994). *The development of future-oriented processes.* Chicago: University of Chicago Press.

HAITH, M. M., BERGMAN, T., & MOORE, M. J. (1977). Eye contact and face scanning in early infancy. *Science, 198,* 853–855.

HAITH, M. M., WENTWORTH, N., & CANFIELD, R. L. (1993). The formation of expectations in early infancy. In C. Rovee-Collier & L. P. Lipsitt (Eds.), *Advances in infancy research* (Vol. 8). Norwood, NJ: Ablex.

HALFORD, G. S. (1989). Reflections on 25 years of Piagetian cognitive developmental psychology, 1963–1988. *Human Development, 32,* 325–357.

HALFORD, G. S. (1993). *Children's understanding: The development of mental models.* Hillsdale, NJ: Erlbaum.

HALL, G. S. (1904). *Adolescence: Its psychology and its relations to physiology, anthropology, sociology, sex, crime, religion, and education* (2 vols.). New York: Appleton.

HALPERN, D. F. (1992). *Sex differences in cognitive abilities* (2nd ed.). Hillsdale, NJ: Erlbaum.

HALPERN, L. F., MacLEAN, JR., W. E., & BAUMEISTER, A. A. (1995). Infant sleep–wake characteristics: Relation to neurological status and the prediction of developmental outcome. *Developmental Review, 15,* 255–291.

HALPERN, R. (1993). Poverty and infant development. In C. H. Zeanah, Jr. (Ed.), *Handbook of infant mental development.* New York: Guilford.

HAMER, D. H., HU, S., MAGNUSON, V. L., HU, N., & PATTATUCCI, A. M. L. (1993). A linkage between DNA markers on the X chromosome and male sexual orientations. *Science, 261,* 321–327.

HAMMEN, C., & ZUPAN, B. A. (1984). Self-schemas, depression, and the processing of personal information in children. *Journal of Experimental Child Psychology, 37,* 598–608.

HAMPSON, J., & NELSON, K. (1993). The relation of maternal language to variation in rate and style of language acquisition. *Journal of Child Language, 20,* 313–342.

HANDYSIDE, A. H., LESKO, J. G., TARÍN, J. J., WINSTON, R. M. L., & HUGHES, M. R. (1992). Birth of a normal girl after in vitro fertilization and preimplantation diagnostic testing for cystic fibrosis. *New England Journal of Medicine, 327,* 905–909.

HANNA, E., & MELTZOFF, A. N. (1993). Peer imitation by toddlers in laboratory, home, and day-care contexts: Implications for social learning and memory. *Developmental Psychology, 29,* 701–710.

HANSON, S. M. H. (1988). Divorced fathers with custody. In P. Bronstein & C. P. Cowan (Eds.), *Fatherhood today: Men's changing role in the family.* New York: Wiley.

HARDING, C. G. (1983). Setting the stage for language acquisition: Communication development in the first year. In R. M. Golinkoff (Ed.), *The transition from prelinguistic to linguistic communication.* Hillsdale, NJ: Erlbaum.

HARKNESS, S., & SUPER, C. M. (1987). The use of cross-cultural research in child development. In R. Vasta (Ed.), *Annals of child development* (Vol. 4). Greenwich, CT: JAI Press.

HARLOW, H. F., & HARLOW, M. K. (1966). Learning to love. *American Scientist, 54,* 244–272.

HARPER, L., & KRAFT, R. H. (1986). Lateralization of receptive language in pre-schoolers: Test–retest reliability in a dichotic listening task. *Developmental Psychology, 22,* 553–556.

HARPER, P. S. (1981). *Practical genetic counseling.* Baltimore: University Park Press.

HARRIS, L. J. (1977). Sex differences in the growth and use of language. In E. Donelson & J. E. Gullahorn (Eds.), *Women: A psychological perspective.* New York: Wiley.

HARRIS, M., BARRETT, M., JONES, D., & BROOKES, S. (1988). Linguistic input and early word meaning. *Journal of Child Language, 15,* 77–94.

HARRIS, M., JONES, D., & GRANT, J. (1983). The nonverbal context of mothers' speech to infants. *First Language, 4,* 21–30.

HARRIS, P. L. (1983). Infant cognition. In P. H. Mussen (Series Ed.) & M. M. Haith & J. J. Campos (Vol. Eds.), *Handbook of child psychology: Vol. 2. Infancy and developmental psychobiology.* New York: Wiley.

HARRIS, P. L. (1989). Object permanence in infancy. In A. Slater & G. Bremner (Eds.), *Infant development.* Hillsdale, NJ: Erlbaum.

HART, C. H., DeWOLF, D. M., WOZNIAK, P., & BURTS, D. C. (1992). Maternal and paternal disciplinary styles: Relations with preschoolers' playground behavioral orientations and peer status. *Child Development, 63,* 879–892.

HART, D. (1988a). The development of personal identity in adolescence: A philosophical dilemma approach. *Merrill-Palmer Quarterly, 34,* 105–114.

HART, D. (1988b). A longitudinal study of adolescents' socialization and identification as predictors of adult moral judgment development. *Merrill-Palmer Quarterly, 34,* 245–260.

HART, D., & DAMON, W. (1985). Contrasts between understanding self and understanding others. In R. L. Leahy (Ed.), *The development of the self.* Orlando, FL: Academic Press.

HART, D., & FEGLEY, S. (1995). Prosocial behavior and caring in adolescence: Relations to self-understanding and social judgment. *Child Development, 66,* 1346–1359.

HART, D., & FEGLEY, S. (1997). Children's self-awareness and self-understanding in cultural context. In U. Neisser & D. A. Jopling (Ed.), *The conceptual self in context: Culture, experience, and self-understanding.* New York: Cambridge University Press.

HART, D., & YATES, M. (1996). The interrelation of self and identity in adolescence: A developmental account. In R. Vasta (Ed.), *Annals of child development* (Vol. 12). London: Kingsley.

HART, D., YATES, M., FEGLEY, S., & WILSON, G. (1995). Moral commitment among inner-city adolescents. In M. Killen & D. Hart (Eds.), *Morality in everyday life: Developmental perspectives.* New York: Cambridge University Press.

HART, S. N. (1991). From property to person status: Historical perspective on children's rights. *American Psychologist, 46,* 53–59.

HARTER, S. (1981). A new self-report scale of intrinsic versus extrinsic orientation in the classroom: Motivational and informational components. *Developmental Psychology, 17,* 300–312.

HARTER, S. (1982). A developmental perspective on some parameters of self-regulation in children. In P. Karoly & F. H. Kanfer (Eds.), *Self-management and behavior change: From theory to practice.* New York: Pergamon.

HARTER, S. (1983). Developmental perspectives on the self-system. In E. M. Hetherington (Ed.), *Handbook of child psychology: Vol. 4. Socialization, personality, and social development.* New York: Wiley.

HARTER, S. (1985). Competence as a dimension of self-evaluation: Toward a comprehensive model of self-worth. In R. L. Leahy (Ed.), *The development of the self.* Orlando, FL: Academic Press.

HARTER, S. (1986). Processes underlying the construction, maintenance, and enhancement of the self-concept in children. In J. Suls &

A. Greenwald (Eds.), *Psychological perspectives on the self* (Vol. 3). Hillsdale, NJ: Erlbaum.

HARTER, S. (1987). The determinants and mediational role of global self-worth in children. In N. Eisenberg (Ed.), *Contemporary topics in developmental psychology.* New York: Wiley.

HARTER, S. (1988). Developmental processes in the construction of the self. In T. D. Yawkey & J. E. Johnson (Eds.), *Integrative processes and socialization: Early to middle childhood.* Hillsdale, NJ: Erlbaum.

HARTER, S. (1990). Causes, correlates and the functional role of self-worth: A life-span perspective. In R. J. Sternberg & J. Kolligian (Eds.), *Competence considered.* New Haven, CT: Yale University Press.

HARTER, S. (1994). Developmental changes in self-understanding across the 5 to 7 shift. In A. Sameroff & M. M. Haith (Eds.), *Reason and responsibility: The passage through childhoood.* Chicago: University of Chicago Press.

HARTER, S. (1998). The development of self-representations. In W. Damon (Ed.), *Handbook of child psychology: Vol. 3. Social, emotional, & personality development.* New York: Wiley.

HARTER, S., & CONNELL, J. P. (1984). A model of the relationship among children's academic achievement and their self-perceptions of competence, control, and motivational orientation. In J. Nicholls (Ed.), *The development of achievement motivation.* Greenwich, CT: JAI Press.

HARTER, S., MAROLD, D. B., WHITESELL, N. R., & COBBS, G. (1996). A model of the effects of perceived parent and peer support on adolescent false self behavior. *Child Development, 67,* 360–374.

HARTER, S., & MONSOUR, A. (1992). Developmental analysis of conflict caused by opposing attributes in the adolescent self-portrait. *Developmental Psychology, 28,* 251–260.

HARTER, S., & PIKE, R. (1984). The Pictorial Scale of Perceived Competence and Social Acceptance for Young Children. *Child Development, 55,* 1969–1982.

HARTIG, M., & KANFER, F. H. (1973). The role of verbal self-instructions in children's resistance to temptation. *Journal of Personality and Social Psychology, 25,* 259–267.

HARTSHORNE, H., & MAY, M. S. (1928–1930). *Studies in the nature of character* (3 vols.). New York: Macmillan.

HARTUP, W. W. (1983). Peer relations. In P. H. Mussen (Series Ed.) & E. M. Hetherington (Vol. Ed.), *Handbook of child psychology: Vol. 4. Socialization, personality, and social development.* New York: Wiley.

HARTUP, W. W. (1992a). Conflict and friendship relations. In C. U. Shantz & W. W. Hartup (Eds.), *Conflict in child and adolescent development.* Cambridge: Cambridge University Press.

HARTUP, W. W. (1992b). Friendships and their developmental significance. In H. McGurk (Ed.), *Childhood social development: Contemporary perspectives.* Hillsdale, NJ: Erlbaum.

HARTUP, W. W. (1992c). Peer relations in early and middle childhood. In V. B. Van Hasselt & M. Hersen (Eds.), *Handbook of social development.* New York: Plenum.

HARTUP, W. W. (1993). Adolescents and their friends. In B. Laursen (Ed.), *New directions for child development: No. 60. Close friendships in adolescence.* San Francisco: Jossey-Bass.

HARTUP, W. W. (1996a). The company they keep: Friendships and their developmental significance. *Child Development, 67,* 1–13.

HARTUP, W. W. (1996b). Cooperation, close relationships, and cognitive development. In W. M. Bukowski, A. F. Newcomb, & W. W. Hartup (Eds.), *The company they keep: Friendship in childhood and adolescence.* New York: Cambridge University Press.

HARTUP, W. W., DAIUTE, C., ZAJAC, R., & SHALL, W. (1995). *Collaboration in creative writing by friends and nonfriends.* Unpublished manuscript, University of Minnesota, Minneapolis.

HARTUP, W. W., FRENCH, D. C., LAURSEN, B., JOHNSON, M. K., & OGAWA, J. R. (1993). Conflict and friendship relations in middle childhood: Behavior in a closed-field situation. *Child Development, 64,* 445–454.

HARTUP, W. W., & STEVENS, N. (1997). Friendships and adaptation in the life course. *Psychological Bulletin, 121,* 355–370.

HARVARD LAW REVIEW. (1989). *Sexual orientation and the law.* Cambridge: Harvard University Press.

HARVEY, S. E., & LIEBERT, R. M. (1979). Abstraction, inference, and acceptance in children's processing of an adult model's moral judgments. *Developmental Psychology, 15,* 552–558.

HARWOOD, R. L. (1992). The influence of culturally derived values on Anglo and Puerto Rican mothers' perceptions of attachment behavior. *Child Development, 63,* 822–839.

HARWOOD, R. L., & MILLER, J. G. (1991). Perceptions of attachment behavior: A comparison of Anglo and Puerto Rican mothers. *Merrill-Palmer Quarterly, 37,* 583–599.

HARWOOD, R. L., MILLER, J. G., & IRIZARRY, N. L. (1995). *Culture and attachment.* New York: Guilford.

HASSELHORN, M. (1992). Task dependency and the role of category typicality and metamemory in the development of an organizational strategy. *Child Development, 63,* 202–214.

HATANO, G. (1990). Commentary: Toward the cultural psychology of mathematical cognition. *Monographs of the Society for Research in Child Development, 55* (1–2, Serial No. 221).

HATTIE, J., & MARSH, H. W. (1996). Future directions in self-concept research. In B. A. Bracken (Ed.), *Handbook of self-concept: Developmental, social, and clinical considerations.* New York: Wiley.

HAVILAND, J. M., & LELWICA, M. (1987). The induced affect response: 10-week-old infants' response to three emotion expressions. *Developmental Psychology, 23,* 97–104.

HAWKINS, J., PEA, R. D., GLICK, J., & SCRIBNER, S. (1984). "Merds that laugh don't like mushrooms": Evidence for deductive reasoning in preschoolers. *Developmental Psychology, 20,* 584–594.

HAWLEY, T. L., & DISNEY, E. R. (1992). Crack's children: The consequences of maternal cocaine abuse. Social Policy Report. *Society for Research in Child Development, 6,* 1–23.

HAY, D. F. (1984). Social conflict in early childhood. In G. J. Whitehurst (Ed.), *Annals of child development* (Vol. 1). Greenwich, CT: JAI Press.

HAY, D. F. (1985). Learning to form relationships in infancy: Parallel attainments with parents and peers. *Developmental Review, 5,* 122–161.

HAY, D. F. (1986). Learning to be social: Some comments on Schaffer's *The child's entry into a social world. Developmental Review, 6,* 107–114.

HAY, D. F. (1994). Prosocial development. *Journal of Child Psychology and Psychiatry, 35,* 29–71.

HAY, D. F., CASTLE, J., STIMSOM, C., & DAVIES, L. (1995). The social construction of character in toddlerhood. In M. Killen & D. Hart (Eds.), *Morality in everyday life.* New York: Cambridge University Press.

HAY, D. F., & MURRAY, P. (1982). Giving and requesting: Social facilitation of infants' offers to adults. *Infant Behavior and Development, 5,* 301–310.

HAY, D. F., MURRAY, P., CECIRE, S., & NASH, A. (1985). Social learning of social behavior in early life. *Child Development, 56,* 43–57.

HAY, D. F., NASH, A., & PEDERSEN, J. (1983). Interaction between six-month-old peers. *Child Development, 54,* 557–562.

HAY, L. (1984). Discontinuity in the development of motor control in children. In W. Prinz & A. F. Sanders (Eds.), *Cognition and motor processes.* Berlin: Springer-Verlag.

HAYDEN-THOMSON, L., RUBIN, K. H., & HYMEL, S. (1987). Sex preferences in sociometric choices. *Developmental Psychology, 23,* 558–562.

HAYES, D. S., GERSHMAN, E., & BOLIN, L. J. (1980). Friends and enemies: Cognitive bases for preschool children's unilateral and reciprocal relationships. *Child Development, 51,* 1276–1279.

HAYES, J. S., LAMPART, R., DREHER, M. C., & MORGAN, L. (1991). Five-year follow-up of rural Jamaican children whose mothers used marijuana during pregnancy. *W. I. Medical Journal, 40,* 120–123.

HAYNE, H. (1996). Categorization in infancy. In C. Rovee-Collier & L. P. Lipsitt (Eds.), *Advances in infancy research* (Vol. 10). Norwood, NJ: Ablex.

HAYNES, H., WHITE, B. L., & HELD, R. (1965). Visual accommodation in human infants. *Science, 148,* 528–530.

HAZEN, N. L., & DURRETT, M. E. (1982). Relationship of security of attachment to exploration and cognitive mapping abilities in 2-year-olds. *Developmental Psychology, 18,* 751–759.

HEAROLD, S. (1986). A synthesis of 1043 effects of television on social behavior. In G. Comstock (Ed.), *Public communication and behavior* (Vol. 1). Orlando, FL: Academic Press.

HEATH, S. B. (1983). *Ways with words: Language, life, and work in communities and classrooms.* New York: Cambridge University Press.

HEBB, D. O. (1949). *The organization of behavior.* New York: Wiley.

HEDGES, L. V., & NOWELL, A. (1995). Sex differences in mental test scores, variability, and numbers of high-scoring individuals. *Science, 269,* 41–45.

HEIBECK, T., & MARKMAN, E. M. (1987). Word learning in children: An examination of fast mapping. *Child Development, 58,* 1021–1034.

HEIMANN, M., NELSON, K. E., & SCHALLER, J. (1989). Neonatal imitation of tongue protrusion and mouth opening: Methodological aspects and evidence of early individual differences. *Scandinavian Journal of Psychology, 30,* 90–101.

HEKMAN, S. J. (1995). *Moral voices, moral selves: Carol Gilligan and feminist moral theory.* University Park: The University of Pennsylvania Press.

HELLER, J. (1987). What do we know about the risk of caffeine consumption in pregnancy? *British Journal of Addiction, 82,* 885–889.

HELWIG, C. C., HILDEBRANDT, C., & TURIEL, E. (1995). Children's judgments about psychological harm in social context. *Child Development, 66,* 1680–1693.

HENRY, B., CASPI, A., MOFFITT, T. E., & SILVA, P. A. (1996). Temperamental and familial predictors of violent and nonviolent criminal convictions: Age 3 to age 18. *Developmental Psychology, 32,* 614–623.

HEPBURN, M. A. (1995). TV violence: Myth and reality. *Social Education, 59,* 309–311.

HERMAN, J. F., & SIEGEL, A. W. (1978). The development of cognitive mapping of the large-scale environment. *Journal of Experimental Child Psychology, 26,* 389–406.

HERRNSTEIN, R. J. (1971, September). I.Q. *Atlantic Monthly,* pp. 43–64.

HERRNSTEIN, R. J. (1973). *IQ in the meritocracy.* Boston: Little, Brown.

HERRNSTEIN, R. J., & MURRAY, C. (1994). *The bell curve: Intelligence and class structure in American life.* New York: Free Press.

HERSHENSON, M. (1964). Visual discrimination in the human newborn. *Journal of Comparative and Physiological Psychology, 58,* 270–276.

HESS, E. K., & PETROVICH. S. (1991). Ethology and attachment: A historical perspective. In J. L. Gewirtz & W. M. Kurtines (Eds.), *Intersections with attachment.* Hillsdale, NJ: Erlbaum.

HESS, R. D., & MIURA, I. T. (1985). Gender differences in enrollment in computer-camps and classes. *Sex Roles, 13,* 193–203.

HETHERINGTON, E. M. (1993). An overview of the Virginia Longitudinal Study of Divorce and Remarriage: A focus on early adolescence. *Journal of Family Psychology, 7,* 39–56.

HETHERINGTON, E. M., BRIDGES, M., & INSABELLA, G. M. (1998). What matters? What does not? Five perspectives on the association between marital transitions and children's adjustment. *American Psychologist, 53,* 167–184.

HETHERINGTON, E. M., CLING-EMPEEL, W. G., ANDERSON, E. R., DEAL, J. E., STANLEY-HAGAN, M., HOLLIER, E. A., & LINDNER, M. S. (1992). Coping with marital transitions: A family perspective. *Monographs of the Society for Research in Child Development, 57* (2–3, Serial No. 227).

HETHERINGTON, E. M., & JODL, K. M. (1994). Stepfamilies as settings for child development. In A. Booth & J. Dunn (Eds.), *Stepfamilies: Who benefits? Who does not?* Hillsdale, NJ: Erlbaum.

HETHERINGTON, E. M., REISS, D., & PLOMIN, R. (Eds.). (1994). *Separate social worlds of siblings: The impact of nonshared environment on development.* Hillsdale, NJ: Erlbaum.

HETHERINGTON, E. M., & STANLEY-HAGAN, M. M. (1995). Parenting in divorced and remarried families. In M. H. Bornstein (Ed.), *Handbook of parenting: Vol. 3. Status and social conditions of parenting.* Mahwah, NJ: Erlbaum.

HEWLETT, B. S. (Ed.). (1992). *Father–child relations: Cultural and biosocial contexts.* New York: Aldine de Gruyter.

HICKMANN, M. (1986). Psychosocial aspects of language acquisition. In P. Fletcher & M. Garman (Eds.), *Language acquisition: Studies in first language acquisition* (2nd ed.). New York: Cambridge University Press.

HICKS, D. (1996). *Discourse, learning, and schooling.* New York: Cambridge University Press.

HIGGINS, A., POWER, C., & KOHLBERG, L. (1984). The relationship of moral atmosphere to judgments of responsibility. In W. M. Kurtines & J. L. Gewirtz (Eds.), *Morality, moral behavior, and moral development.* New York: Wiley.

HIGGINS, E. T. (1991). Development of self-regulatory and self-evaluative processes: Costs, benefits, and tradeoffs. In M. R. Gunnar & L. A. Sroufe (Eds.), *Minnesota symposia on child development:* Vol. 23. *Self processes and development.* Hillsdale, NJ: Erlbaum.

HILGARD, E. R. (1987). *Psychology in America: A historical survey.* San Diego: Harcourt Brace Jovanovich.

HILL, J. P., & LYNCH, M. E. (1983). The intensification of gender-related role expectations during early adolescence. In J. Brooks-Gunn & A. C. Petersen (Eds.), *Girls at puberty: Biological and psychological perspectives.* New York: Plenum.

HINDE, R. A. (1983). Ethology and child development. In P. H. Mussen (Series Ed.) & M. M. Haith & J. J. Campos (Vol. Eds.), *Handbook of child psychology: Vol. 2. Infancy and developmental psychobiology.* New York: Wiley.

HINDE, R. A. (1986). Some implications of evolutionary theory and comparative data for the study of human prosocial and aggressive behavior. In D. Olweus, J. Block, & M. Radke-Yarrow (Eds.), *Development of antisocial and prosocial behavior.* New York: Academic Press.

HINES, M. (1982). Prenatal gonad hormones and sex differences in human behavior. *Psychological Bulletin, 92,* 56–80.

HINES, M., & GREEN, R. (1991). Human hormonal and neural correlates of sex-typed behaviors. *Review of Psychiatry, 10,* 536–555.

HINES, M., & KAUFMAN, F. R. (1994). Androgen and the development of human sex-typical behavior: Rough-and-tumble and sex of preferred playmates in children with congenital adrenal hyperplasia (CAH). *Child Development, 65,* 1042–1053.

HIRSCH, B. J., & RENDERS, R. J. (1986). The challenge of adolescent friendships: A study of Lisa and her friends. In S. E. Hobfolk (Ed.), *Stress, social support, and women.* Washington, DC: Hemisphere.

HIRSH-PASEK, K., & GOLINKOFF, R. M. (1996). *The origins of grammar: Evidence from early language comprehension.* Cambridge: MIT Press.

HIRSH-PASEK, K., TREIMAN, R., & SCHNEIDERMAN, M. (1984). Brown and Hanlon revisited: Mothers' sensitivity to ungrammatical forms. *Journal of Child Language, 11,* 81–88.

HITTLEMAN, J. H., & DICKES, R. (1979). Sex differences in neonatal eye contact time. *Merrill-Palmer Quarterly, 25,* 171–184.

HO, D. Y. F. (1986). Chinese patterns of socialization: A critical review. In M. H. Bond (Ed.), *The psychology of Chinese people.* New York: Oxford University Press.

HO, D. Y. F. (1987). Fatherhood in Chinese culture. In M. E. Lamb (Ed.), *The father's role: Cross-cultural perspectives.* Hillsdale, NJ: Erlbaum.

HOCK, E., & DEMEIS, D. K. (1990). Depression in mothers of infants: The role of maternal employment. *Developmental Psychology, 26,* 285–291.

HOCK, E., & SCHIRTZINGER, M. B. (1992). Maternal separation anxiety: Its developmental course and relation to maternal mental health. *Developmental Psychology, 63,* 93–102.

HODAPP, R. M., & GOLDFIELD, E. C. (1985). Self- and other regulation during the infancy period. *Developmental Review, 5,* 274–288.

HOEK, D., INGRAM, D., & GIBSON, D. (1986). Some possible causes of children's early word overextensions. *Journal of Child Language, 13,* 477–494.

HOFF-GINSBERG, E. (1990). Maternal speech and the child's development of syntax: A further look. *Journal of Child Language, 17,* 85–99.

HOFF-GINSBERG, E., & SHATZ, M. (1982). Linguistic input and the child's acquisition of language. *Psychological Bulletin, 92,* 3–26.

HOFFMAN, L. W. (1984). Work, family, and the socialization of the child. In R. D. Parke (Ed.), *The family: Review of child development research* (Vol. 7). Chicago: University of Chicago Press.

HOFFMAN, L. W. (1989). Effects of maternal employment in the two-parent family. *American Psychologist, 44,* 283–292.

HOFFMAN, M. L. (1970). Moral development. In P. H. Mussen (Ed.), *Carmichael's manual of child psychology* (3rd ed., Vol. 2). New York: Wiley.

HOFFMAN, M. L. (1981). Perspectives on the difference between understanding people and understanding things: The role of affect. In J. H. Flavell & L. Ross (Eds.), *Social cognitive development.* New York: Cambridge University Press.

HOFFMAN, M. L. (1982). Development of prosocial motivation: Empathy and guilt. In N. Eisenberg-Berg (Ed.), *Development of prosocial behavior.* New York: Academic Press.

HOFFMAN, M. L. (1984a). Empathy, its limitations, and its role in a comprehensive moral theory. In W. M. Kurtines & J. L. Gewirtz (Eds.), *Morality, moral behavior, and moral development.* New York: Wiley.

HOFFMAN, M. L. (1984b). Parent discipline, moral internalization, and development of prosocial motivation. In E. Staub, D. Bar-Tal, J. Karylowski, & J. Reykowski (Eds.), *Development and maintenance of prosocial behavior.* New York: Plenum.

HOFFMAN, M. L. (1987). The contribution of empathy to justice and moral judgment. In N. Eisenberg & J. Strayer (Eds.), *Empathy and its development.* New York: Cambridge University Press.

HOFFMAN, M. L. (1991). Empathy, social cognition, and moral action. In W. M. Kurtines & J. L. Gewirtz (Eds.), *Handbook of moral behavior and development: Vol. 1. Theory.* Hillsdale, NJ: Erlbaum.

HOFFMAN, M. L. (1994). Discipline and internalization. *Developmental Psychology, 30,* 26–28.

HOGGE, W. A. (1990). Teratology. In I. R. Merkatz & J. E. Thompson (Eds.), *New perspectives on prenatal care.* New York: Elsevier.

HOLDEN, C. (1986). High court says no to administration's Baby Doe rules. *Science, 232,* 1595–1596.

HOLMES, J. (1995). "Something there is that doesn't love a wall": John Bowlby, attachment theory, and psychoanalysis. In S. Goldberg, R. Muir, & J. Kerr (Eds.), *Attachment theory: Social, developmental, and clinical perspectives.* Hillsdale, NJ: The Analytic Press.

HOLSTEIN, C. (1976). Irreversible, stepwise sequence in the development of moral judgment: A longitudinal study of males and females. *Child Development, 47,* 51–61.

HOOD, K. E., DRAPER, P., CROCKETT, L. J., & PETERSEN, A. C. (1987). The ontogeny and phylogeny of sex differences in development: A biosocial synthesis. In D. B. Carter (Ed.), *Current conceptions of sex roles and sex-typing: Theory and research.* New York: Praeger.

HOOK, J. (1982). Development of equity and altruism in judgments of reward and damage allocation. *Developmental Psychology, 18,* 825–834.

HOOK, J. (1983). The development of children's equity judgments. In R. L. Leahy (Ed.), *The child's construction of social equality.* New York: Academic Press.

HOOKER, K., NESSELROADE, D. W., NESSELROADE, J. R., & LERNER, R. M. (1987). The structure of intraindividual temperament in the context of mother–child dyads: P-technique factor analyses of short-term change. *Developmental Psychology, 23,* 332–346.

HOPKINS, A. (1987). Prescribing in pregnancy: Epilepsy and anticonvulsant drugs. *British Medical Journal, 294,* 497–501.

HOPKINS, B. (1991). Facilitating early motor development: An intracultural study of West Indian mothers and their infants living in Britain. In J. K. Nugent, B. M. Lester, & T. B. Brazelton (Eds.), *The cultural context of infancy: Vol. 2. Multicultural and interdisciplinary approaches to parent–infant relations.* Norwood, NJ: Ablex.

HORAN, J. (1993, June). Eugenics revisited. *Scientific American,* pp. 122–131.

HORAN, R. F., & ROSSER, R. A. (1984). Multivariable analysis of spatial abilities by sex. *Developmental Review, 4,* 381–411.

HORN, J. M. (1983). The Texas Adoption Project: Adopted children and their intellectual resemblance to biological and adoptive parents. *Child Development, 54,* 268–275.

HORNE, A. M., & SAYGER, T. V. (1990). *Treating conduct and oppositional defiant disorders in children.* New York: Pergamon.

HORNIK, R., & GUNNAR, M. R. (1988). A descriptive analysis of infant social referencing. *Child Development, 59,* 626–634.

HOROWITZ, F. D. (1992). John B. Watson's legacy: Learning and environment. *Developmental Psychology, 28,* 360–367.

HORT, B. E., LEINBACH, M. D., & FAGOT, B. I. (1991). Is there coherence among the cognitive components of gender acquisition? *Sex Roles, 24,* 195–207.

HOWE, C. (1981). *Acquiring language in a conversational context.* Orlando, FL: Academic Press.

HOWE, M. L., & COURAGE, M. L. (1993). On resolving the enigma of infantile amnesia. *Psychological Bulletin, 113,* 305–326.

HOWE, M. L., & RABINOWITZ, F. M. (1990). Resource panacea? Or just another day in the developmental forest? *Developmental Review, 10,* 125–154.

HOWES, C. (1983). Patterns of friendship. *Child Development, 54,* 1041–1053.

HOWES, C. (1987). Social competence with peers in young children: Developmental sequences. *Developmental Review, 7,* 252–272.

HOWES, C. (1992). *The collaborative construction of pretend.* New York: SUNY Press.

HOWES, C. (1997). Children's experiences in center-based child care as a function of teacher background and adult:child ratio. *Merrill-Palmer Quarterly, 43,* 404–425.

HOWES, C., & HAMILTON, C. E. (1992). Children's relationships with caregivers: Mothers and child care teachers. *Child Development, 63,* 859–866.

HOWES, C., & MATHESON, C. C. (1992). Sequences in the development of competent play with peers: Social and social pretend play. *Developmental Psychology, 28,* 961–974.

HOWES, C., PHILLIPS, D. A., & WHITEBOOK, M. (1992). Thresholds of quality: Implications for the social development of children in center-based child care. *Child Development, 63,* 449–460.

HOWES, C., & RUBENSTEIN, J. L. (1979). *Influences on toddler peer behavior in two types of daycare.* Unpublished manuscript, Harvard University, Cambridge.

HOWES, C., UNGER, O., & SEIDNER, L. B. (1989). Social pretend play in toddlers. Parallels with social play and with solitary pretend. *Child Development, 60,* 77–84.

HOY, E. A., BILL, J. M., & SYKES, D. H. (1988). Very low birthweight: A long-term developmental impairment? *International Journal of Behavioral Development, 11,* 37–67.

HSU, L. K. G. (1990). *Eating disorders.* New York: Guilford.

HUDLEY, C., & GRAHAM, S. (1993). An attributional intervention to reduce peer-directed aggression among African-American boys. *Child Development, 64,* 124–138.

HUDSON, J. A. (1990). The emergence of autobiographical memory in mother–child conversation. In R. Fivush & J. A. Hudson (Eds.), *Knowing and remembering in young children.* Hillsdale, NJ: Erlbaum.

HUDSON, J. A., & NELSON, K. (1983). Effects of script structure on children's story recall. *Developmental Psychology, 19,* 625–635.

HUESMANN, L. R., & ERON, L. D. (1986). *Television and the aggressive child: A cross-national perspective.* Hillsdale, NJ: Erlbaum.

HUESMANN, L. R., LAGERSPETZ, K., & ERON, L. D. (1984). Intervening variables in the television violence–aggression relation: Evidence from two countries. *Developmental Psychology, 20,* 746–775.

HUESMANN, L. R., & MILLER, L. S. (1994). Long-term effects of repeated exposure to media violence in childhood. In L. R. Huesmann (Ed.), *Aggressive behavior: Current perspectives.* New York: Plenum.

HUMPHREY, D. E., & HUMPHREY, G. K. (1987). Sex differences in infant reaching. *Neurophysiologia, 25,* 971–975.

HUNT, E., STREISSGUTH, A. P., KERR, B., & OLSON, H. C. (1995). Mother's alcohol consumption during pregnancy: Effects on spatial-visual reasoning in 14-year-old children. *Psychological Science, 6,* 339–342.

HUNT, J. McV. (1961). *Intelligence and experience.* New York: Ronald Press.

HUNTER, J. E., & HUNTER, R. F. (1984). Validity and utility of alternative predictors of job performance. *Psychological Bulletin, 96,* 72–98.

HUR, Y., & BOUCHARD, T. J., JR. (1995). Genetic influences on perceptions of family environment: A reared apart twin study. *Child Development, 66,* 330–345.

HUSTON, A. C. (1983). Sex-typing. In E. M. Hetherington (Ed.), *Handbook of child psychology: Vol. 4. Socialization, personality, and social development.* New York: Wiley.

HUSTON, A. C. (1985). The development of sex typing: Themes from recent research. *Developmental Review, 5,* 1–17.

HUSTON, A. C., & ALVAREZ, M. M. (1990). The socialization context of gender role development in early adolescence. In R. Montemayor, G. R. Adams, & T. P. Gullotta (Eds.), *From childhood to adolescence: A transitional period?* Newbury Park, CA: Sage.

HUSTON, A. C., CARPENTER, J. C., ATWATER, J. B., & JOHNSON, L. M. (1986). Gender, adult structuring of activities, and social behavior in middle childhood. *Child Development, 57,* 1200–1209.

HUSTON, A. C., & WRIGHT, J. C. (1998). Mass media and children's development. In W. Damon (Ed.), *Handbook of child psychology: Vol. 4. Child psychology in practice.* New York: Wiley.

HUSTON, A. C., WRIGHT, J. C., RICE, M. L., KERKMAN, D., & St. PETERS, H. (1990). Development of television viewing patterns in early childhood: A longitudinal analysis. *Developmental Psychology, 26,* 409–420.

HUTCHINS, E. (1983). Understanding Micronesian navigation. In D. Gentner & A. Stevens (Eds.), *Mental models.* Hillsdale, NJ: Erlbaum.

HUTTENLOCHER, J., HAIGHT, W., BRYK, A., SELTZER, M., & LYONS, T. (1991). Early vocabulary growth: Relation to language input and gender. *Developmental Psychology, 27,* 236–248.

HUTTENLOCHER, J., SMILEY, P., & CHARNEY, R. (1983). Emergence of action categories in the child: Evidence from verb meanings. *Psychological Review, 90,* 72–93.

HUTTENLOCHER, P. R. (1990). Morphometric study of human cerebral cortex development. *Neuropsychologia, 28,* 517–527.

HYDE, J. S. (1984). How large are gender differences in aggression? A developmental meta-analysis. *Developmental Psychology, 20,* 722–736.

HYDE, J. S. (1986). Gender differences in aggression. In J. S. Hyde & M. C. Linn (Eds.), *The psychology of gender differences: Advances through meta-analysis.* Baltimore: Johns Hopkins University Press.

HYDE, J. S., & LINN, M. C. (1988). Gender differences in verbal ability: A meta-analysis. *Psychological Bulletin, 104,* 53–69.

HYLTENSTAM, K., & OBLER, L. (Eds.). (1989). *Bilingualism across the lifespan: Aspects of acquisition, maturity, and loss.* Cambridge: Cambridge University Press.

HYMEL, S. (1983). Preschool children's peer relations: Issues in sociometric assessment. *Merrill-Palmer Quarterly, 29,* 237–260.

HYMEL, S., WAGNER, E., & BUTLER, L. J. (1990). Reputational bias: View from the peer group. In S. R. Asher & J. D. Coie (Eds.), *Peer rejection in childhood.* New York: Cambridge University Press.

IANNOTTI, R. (1978). Effect of role-taking experiences on role taking, empathy, altruism, and aggression. *Developmental Psychology, 14,* 119–124.

IDE, J. K., PARKERSON, J., HAERTEL, G. D., & WALBERG, H. J. (1981). Peer group influence on educational outcomes: A quantitative synthesis. *Journal of Educational Psychology, 73,* 472–484.

INAGAKI, K., & HATANO, G. (1987). Young children's spontaneous personification as analogy. *Child Development, 58,* 1013–1020.

INAGAKI, K., & SUGIYAMA, K. (1988). Attributing human characteristics: Developmental changes in over- and underattribution. *Cognitive Development, 3,* 55–70.

INFANTE-RIVARD, C., FERNANDEZ, A., GAUTHIER, R., & RIVARD, C. (1993). Fetal loss associated with caffeine intake before and during pregnancy. *Journal of the American Medical Association, 270,* 2940–2943.

INHELDER, B., & PIAGET, J. (1958). *The growth of logical thinking from childhood to adolescence.* New York: Basic Books.

INHELDER, B., & PIAGET, J. (1964). *The early growth of logic in the child.* New York: Norton.

ISABELLA, R. A. (1993). Origins of attachment: Maternal interactive behavior across the first year. *Child Development, 64,* 605–621.

ISABELLA, R. A. (1994). The origins of infant–mother attachment: Maternal behavior and infant development. In R. Vasta (Ed.), *Annals of child development* (Vol. 10). London: Kingsley.

ISABELLA, R. A., & BELSKY, J. (1991). Interactional synchrony and the origins of infant–mother attachment: A replication study. *Child Development, 62,* 373–384.

ISABELLA, R. A., BELSKY, J., & VON EYE, A. (1989). Origins of infant–mother attachment. An examination of interactional synchrony during the infant's first year. *Developmental Psychology, 25,* 12–21.

ISTVAN, J. (1986). Stress, anxiety, and birth outcomes: A critical review of the evidence. *Psychological Bulletin, 100,* 331–348.

IZARD, C. (1989). *The maximally discriminative facial movement coding system (MAX)* (rev. ed.). Newark: University of Delaware, Information Technologies and University Media Services.

IZARD, C. (1993). Organizational and motivational functions of discrete emotions. In M. Lewis & J. Haviland (Eds.), *Handbook of emotions.* New York: Guilford.

IZARD, C. (1995). Innate and universal facial expressions: Evidence from developmental and cross-cultural research. *Psychological Bulletin, 115,* 288–299.

IZARD, C. E., FANTAUZZO, C. A., CASTLE, J. M., HAYNES, O. M., RAYIAS, M. F., & PUTNAM, P. H. (1995). The ontogeny and significance of infants' facial expressions in the first 9 months of life. *Developmental Psychology, 31,* 997–1013.

JACKLIN, C. N. (1981). Methodological issues in the study of sex-related differences. *Developmental Review, 1,* 266–273.

JACKLIN, C. N., DiPIETRO, J. A., & MacCOBY, E. E. (1984). Sex-typing behavior and sex-typing pressure in child/parent interactions. *Archives of Sexual Behavior, 13,* 413–425.

JACKLIN, C. N., & REYNOLDS, C. (1993). Gender and childhood socialization. In A. E. Beall & R. J. Sternberg (Eds.), *The psychology of gender.* New York: Guilford.

JACKLIN, C. N., WILCOX, K. T., & MacCOBY, E. E. (1988). Neonatal sex steroid hormones and intellectual abilities of six year old boys and girls. *Developmental Psychobiology, 21,* 567–574.

JACKSON, J. F. (1993). Multiple caregiving among African Americans and infant attachment. The need for an emic approach. *Human Development, 36,* 87–102.

JACOBS, J. E. (1991). Influence of gender stereotypes on parent and child mathematics attitudes. *Journal of Educational Psychology, 83,* 518–527.

JACOBSEN, T., EDELSTEIN, W., & HOFMANN, V. (1994). A longitudinal study of the relation between representations of attachment in childhood and cognitive functioning in childhood and adolescence. *Developmental Psychology, 30,* 112–124.

JACOBSON, J. L., & JACOBSON, S. W. (1988). New methodologies for assessing the effects of prenatal toxic exposure on cognitive functioning in humans. In M. Evans (Ed.), *Toxic contaminants and ecosystem health: A Great Lakes focus.* New York: Wiley.

JACOBSON, J. L., JACOBSON, S. W., PADGETT, R. J., BRUMITT, G. A., & BILLINGS, R. L. (1992). Effects of prenatal PCB exposure on cognitive processing efficiency and sustained attention. *Developmental Psychology, 28,* 297–306.

JACOBSON, S., FEIN, G. G., JACOBSON, J. L., SCHWARTZ, P. M., & DOWLER, J. K. (1985). The effect of intrauterine PCB exposure on visual recognition memory. *Child Development, 56,* 853–860.

JACOBVITZ, D., & SROUFE, L. A. (1987). The early caregiver-child relationship and attention-deficit disorder with hyperactivity in kindergarten: A prospective study. *Child Development, 58,* 1496–1504.

JADACK, R. A., HYDE, J. S., MOORE, C. F., & KELLER, M. L. (1995). Moral reasoning about sexually transmitted diseases. *Child Development, 66,* 167–177.

JAEGER, E., & WEINRAUB, M. (1990). Early nonmaternal care and infant attachment: In search of process. In K. McCartney (Ed.), *New directions for child development: No. 49. Child care and maternal employment: A social ecology approach.* San Francisco: Jossey-Bass.

JAMES, W. (1890). *Principles of psychology.* New York: Holt.

JAMES, W. (1892). *Psychology: The briefer course.* New York: Holt.

JAMISON, W. (1977). Developmental inter-relationships among concrete operational tasks: An investigation of Piaget's stage concept. *Journal of Experimental Child Psychology, 24,* 235–253.

JANKOWIAK, W. (1992). Father–child relations in urban China. In B. S. Hewlett (Ed.), *Father–child relations: Cultural and biosocial contexts.* New York: Aldine de Gruyter.

JANSSENS, J. M. A. M., & GERRIS, J. R. M. (1992). Child rearing, empathy, and prosocial development. In J. M. A. M. Janssens & J. R. M. Gerris (Eds.), *Child rearing: Influence on prosocial and moral development.* Amsterdam: Swets & Zeitlinger.

JAROFF, L. (1989, March 20). The gene hunt. *Time,* pp. 62–67.

JEFFERS, V. W., & LORE, R. K. (1979). Let's play at my house: Effects of the home environment on the social behavior of children. *Child Development, 50,* 837–841.

JEFFREYS, A. J., BROOKFIELD, J. F. Y., & SEMEONOFF, R. (1992). Positive identification of an immigration test-case using human DNA fingerprints. *Journal of NIH Research, 4,* 81–87.

JENCKS, C. (1972). *Inequality.* New York: Basic Books.

JENKINS, J. M., & ASTINGTON, J. W. (1996). Cognitive factors and family structure associated with theory of mind development in young children. *Developmental Psychology, 32,* 70–78.

JENNINGS, K. D. (1975). People versus object orientation, social behavior, and intellectual abilities in preschool children. *Developmental Psychology, 11,* 511–519.

JENNINGS, K. D. (1991). Early development of mastery motivation and its relation to the self-concept. In M. Bullock (Ed.), *The development of intentional action: Cognitive, motivational, and interactive-process.* Basel, Switzerland: Karger.

JENSEN, A. R. (1969). How much can we boost IQ and scholastic achievement? *Harvard Educational Review, 39,* 1–123.

JENSEN, A. R. (1972). *Genetics and education.* New York: Harper & Row.

JENSEN, A. R. (1973). *Educability and group differences.* New York: Harper & Row.

JENSEN, A. R. (1980). *Bias in mental testing.* New York: Free Press.

JENSEN, A. R. (1981). *Straight talk about mental tests.* New York: Free Press.

JERISON, H. J. (1982). The evolution of biological intelligence. In R. J. Sternberg (Ed.), *Handbook of human intelligence.* New York: Cambridge University Press.

JESSOR, R., & JESSOR, S. L. (1977). *Problem behavior and psychosocial development.* New York: Academic Press.

JOHNSON, D. B. (1983). Self-recognition in infants. *Infant Behavior and Development, 6,* 211–222.

JOHNSON, E. S., & MEADE, A. C. (1987). Developmental patterns of spatial ability: An early sex difference. *Child Development, 58,* 725–740.

JOHNSON, J. (1991). Constructive processes in bilingualism and their cognitive growth effects. In E. Bialystok (Ed.), *Language processing in bilingual children.* Cambridge: Cambridge University Press.

JOHNSON, M. H., DZIURAWIEC, S., ELLIS, H., & MORTON, J. (1991). Newborns' preferential tracking of facelike stimuli and its subsequent decline. *Cognition, 40,* 1–19.

JOHNSON, M. H., & MORTON, J. (1991). *Biology and cognitive development: The case of face recognition.* Cambridge, MA: Blackwell.

JOHNSON, S. P. (1997). Young infants' perception of object unity: Implications for development of attentional and cognitive skills. *Current Directions in Psychological Science, 6,* 5–11.

JOHNSON, S. P., & ASLIN, R. N. (1995). Perception of object unity in 2-month-old infants. *Developmental Psychology, 31,* 739–745.

JOHNSTON, J. R. (1986). Cognitive prerequisites: The evidence from children learning English. In D. I. Slobin (Ed.), *The crosslinguistic study of language acquisition: Vol. 2. Theoretical issues.* Hillsdale, NJ: Erlbaum.

JONES, C., & ADAMSON, L. B. (1987). Language use in mother–child and mother–child–sibling interactions. *Child Development, 58,* 356–366.

JONES, C., & LOPEZ, R. (1990). Drug abuse and pregnancy. In I. R. Merkatz & J. E. Thompson (Eds.), *New perspectives on prenatal care.* New York: Elsevier.

JONES, D. C. (1985). Persuasive appeals and responses to appeals among friends and acquaintances. *Child Development, 56,* 757–763.

JONES, E. F., & NELSON-LE GALL, S. (1995). The influence of personal effort cues on children's judgments of morality and disposition. *Merrill-Palmer Quarterly, 41,* 53–69.

JONES, G. E., & DEMBO, M. H. (1989). Age and sex role differences in intimate friendships during childhood and adolescence. *Merrill-Palmer Quarterly, 35,* 445–462.

JONES, K. L., JOHNSON, K. A., & CHAMBERS, C. C. (1992). Pregnancy outcome in women treated with phenobarbital monotherapy. *Teratology, 45,* 452–453.

JONES, K. L., LACRO, R. V., JOHNSON, K. A., & ADAMS, J. (1988). Pregnancy outcome in women treated with Tegretol. *Teratology, 37,* 468–469.

JONES, K. L., SMITH, D. W., ULLELAND, C. N., & STREISSGUTH, A. P. (1973). Pattern of malformation in offspring of chronic alcoholic mothers. *Lancet, 1,* 1267–1271.

JONES, M. C. (1924). A laboratory study of fear: The case of Peter. *Pedagogical Seminary, 31,* 308–315.

JONES, S. S. (1996). Imitation or exploration? Young infants' matching of adults' oral gestures. *Child Development, 67,* 1952–1969.

JONES, S. S., COLLINS, K., & HONG, H. (1991). An audience effect on smile production in 10-month-old infants. *Psychological Science, 2,* 45–49.

JOOS, S. K., POLLITT, E., MUELLER, W. H., & ALBRIGHT, D. L. (1983). The Bacon Chow study: Maternal nutritional supplementation and infant behavioral development. *Child Development, 54,* 669–676.

JUSCZYK, P. W. (1997). *The discovery of spoken language.* Cambridge: MIT Press.

JUSCZYK, P. W., CUTLER, A., & REDANZ, N. J. (1993). Infants' preference for the predominant stress patterns of English words. *Child Development, 64,* 675–687.

JUSCZYK, P. W., PISONI, D. B., & MULLENIX, J. (1992). Some consequences of stimulus variability on speech processing by two-month-old infants. *Cognition, 43,* 253–291.

KABACK, M. M. (1982). Screening for reproductive counseling: Social, ethical, and medicolegal issues in the Tay-Sachs disease experience. In *Human genetics: Part B. Medical aspects.* New York: Alan R. Liss.

KAGAN, J. (1970). Attention and psychological change in the young child. *Science, 170,* 826–832.

KAGAN, J. (1991). The theoretical utility of constructs for self. *Developmental Review, 11,* 244–250.

KAGAN, J. (1994). *Galen's prophecy.* New York: Basic Books.

KAGAN, J. (1997). Temperament and the reactions to unfamiliarity. *Child Development, 68,* 139–143.

KAGAN, J., ARCUS, D., SNIDMAN, N., YUFENG, W., HENDLER, J., & GREENE, S. (1994). Reactivity in infants: A cross-national comparison. *Developmental Psychology, 30,* 342–345.

KAGAN, J., KEARSLEY, R., & ZELAZO, P. (1978). *Infancy.* Cambridge: Harvard University Press.

KAGAN, J., REZNICK, J. S., & GIBBONS, J. (1989). Inhibited and uninhibited types of children. *Child Development, 60,* 838–845.

KAGAN, J., REZNICK, J. S., & SNIDMAN, N. (1987). The physiology and psychology of behavioral inhibition. *Child Development, 58,* 1459–1473.

KAGAN, J., REZNICK, J. S., & SNIDMAN, N. (1988). Biological bases of childhood shyness. *Science, 240,* 167–171.

KAGAN, J., REZNICK, J. S., SNIDMAN, N., GIBBONS, J., & JOHNSON, M. O. (1988). Childhood derivatives of inhibition and lack of inhibition to the unfamiliar. *Child Development, 59,* 1580–1589.

KAGAN, J., SNIDMAN, N., & ARCUS, D. M. (1992). Initial reactions to unfamiliarity. *Current Directions in Psychological Science, 1,* 171–174.

KAGAN, J., SNIDMAN, N., & ARCUS, D. (1993). On the temperamental categories of inhibited and uninhibited children. In H. Rubin & J. B. Asendorpf (Eds.), *Social withdrawal, inhibition, and shyness.* Hillsdale, NJ: Erlbaum.

KAIL, R. (1991). Developmental change in speed of processing during childhood and adolescence. *Psychological Bulletin, 109,* 490–501.

KAIL, R. (1995). Processing speed, memory, and cognition. In F. E. Weinert & W. Schneider (Eds.), *Memory performance and competencies: Issues in growth and development.* Mahwah, NJ: Erlbaum.

KAIL, R., & BISANZ, J. (1982). Cognitive development: An information-processing perspective. In R. Vasta (Ed.), *Strategies and techniques of child study.* New York: Academic Press.

KAIL, R., & BISANZ, J. (1992). The information-processing perspective on cognitive development in childhood and adolscence. In R. J. Sternberg & C. A. Berg (Eds.), *Intellectual development.* New York: Cambridge University Press.

KAIL, R., & PELLEGRINO, J. W. (1985). *Human intelligence: Perspectives and prospects.* New York: W. H. Freeman.

KAIL, R., & SIEGEL, A. W. (1977). Sex differences in retention of verbal and spatial characteristics of stimuli. *Journal of Experimental Child Psychology, 23,* 341–347.

KAITZ, M., GOOD, A., ROKEM, A. M., & EIDELMAN, A. I. (1987). Mothers' recognition of their newborns by olfactory cues. *Developmental Psychology, 20,* 587–591.

KAITZ, M., LAPIDOT, P., BRONNER, R., & EIDELMAN, A. I. (1992). Parturient women can recognize their infants by touch. *Developmental Psychology, 28,* 35–39.

KAITZ, M., MEIROV, H., LANDMAN, I., & EIDELMAN, A. I. (1993). Infant recognition by tactile cues. *Infant Behavior and Development, 16,* 333–341.

KAITZ, M., SHIRI, S., DANZIGER, S., HERSHKO, Z., & EIDELMAN, A. I. (1993). Fathers can also recognize their newborns by touch. *Infant Behavior and Development, 17,* 205–207.

KAMII, C., & DEVRIES, R. (1993). *Physical knowledge in preschool education: Implications of Piaget's theory* (rev. ed.). New York: Teachers College Press.

KAMIN, L. (1974). *The science and politics of IQ.* Hillsdale, NJ: Erlbaum.

KAMPTNER, L., KRAFT, R. H., & HARPER, L. V. (1984). Lateral specialization and social-verbal development in preschool children. *Brain and Cognition, 3,* 42–50.

KANDEL, E. R., & O'DELL, T. J. (1992). Are adult mechanisms also used for development? *Science, 258,* 243–245.

KARMEL, B. Z., & MAISEL, E. B. (1975). A neuronal activity model for infant visual attention. In L. B. Cohen & P. Salapatek (Eds.), *Infant perception: From sensation to cognition: Vol. 1. Basic visual processes.* New York: Academic Press.

KARMILOFF-SMITH, A. (1995). Annotation: The extraordinary cognitive journey from foetus through infancy. *Journal of Child Psychology and Psychiatry and Allied Disciplines, 36,* 1293–1313.

KARNIOL, R. (1978). Children's use of intention cues in evaluating behavior. *Psychological Bulletin, 85,* 76–85.

KARNIOL, R., & MILLER, D. T. (1981). The development of self-control in children. In S. S. Brehm, S. M. Kassin, & F. X. Gibbons (Eds.), *Developmental social psychology: Theory and research.* New York: Oxford University Press.

KARSON, E. M., POLVINO, W., & ANDERSON, W. F. (1992). Pros-pects for human gene therapy. *Journal of Reproductive Medicine, 37,* 508–514.

KASHANI, J., DANIEL, A. E., DANDOY, A. C., & HOLCOMB, W. R. (1992). Family violence: Impact on children. *Journal of the American Academy of Child and Adolescent Psychiatry, 31,* 181–182.

KATZ, P. A. (1986). Modification of children's gender stereotyped behavior: General issues and research considerations. *Sex Roles, 14,* 591–602.

KATZ, P. A. (1987). Variations in family constellation: Effects of gender schemata. In L. S. Liben & M. L. Signorella (Eds.), *New directions for child development: Vol. 38. Children's gender schemata.* San Francisco: Jossey-Bass.

KATZ, P. A., & BOSWELL, S. L. (1986). Flexibility and traditionality in children's gender roles. *Genetic, Social, and General Psychology Monographs, 112,* 105–147.

KATZ, P. A., & KSANSNAK, K. R. (1994). Developmental aspects of gender role flexibility and traditionality in middle childhood and adolescence. *Developmental Psychology, 30,* 272–282.

KAUFMAN, A. S., & KAUFMAN, N. L. (1983). *Kaufman Assessment Battery for Children.* Circle Pines, MN: American Guidance Service.

KAWASAKI, C., NUGENT, J. K., MIYASHITA, H., MIYAHARA, H., & BRAZELTON, T. B. (1994). The cultural organization of infants' sleep. *Children's Environments, 11,* 135–141.

KAY, D. A., & ANGLIN, J. M. (1982). Overextension and underextension in the child's expressive and receptive speech. *Journal of Child Language, 9,* 83–98.

KAYE, K. (1982). *The mental and social life of babies.* Chicago: University of Chicago Press.

KAYE, K. L., & BOWER, T. G. R. (1994). Learning and intermodal transfer of information in newborns. *Psychological Science, 5,* 286–288.

KAZDIN, A. E. (1987). *Conduct disorders in childhood and adolescence.* Newbury Park, CA: Sage.

KEARSLEY, R. B. (1973). The newborn's response to auditory stimulation: A demonstration of orienting and defensive behavior. *Child Development, 44,* 582–590.

KEATING, D. P. (1988). Byrnes' reformulation of Piaget's formal operations: Is what's left what's right? Commentary. *Developmental Review, 8,* 376–384.

KEATING, D. P. (1996). Central conceptual structures: Seeking developmental integration. *Monographs of the Society for Research in Child Development, 61* (1–2, Serial No. 246).

KEE, D. W., & GUTTENTAG, R. (1994). Resource requirements of knowledge access and recall benefits of associative strategies. *Journal of Experimental Child Psychology, 57,* 211–223.

KEEFE, K., & BERNDT, T. J. (1996). Relations of friendship quality to self-esteem in early adolescence. *Journal of Early Adolescence, 16,* 110–129.

KEEFE, M. R. (1987). Comparison of neonatal nighttime sleep–wake patterns in nursery versus rooming-in environments. *Nursing Research, 36,* 140–144.

KEENAN, K., & SHAW, D. (1997). Developmental and social influences on young girls' early problem behavior. *Psychological Bulletin, 121,* 95–113.

KEIL, F. C. (1998). Cognitive science and the origins of thought and knowledge. In W. Damon (Ed.), *Handbook of child psychology: Vol. 1. Theoretical models of human development.* New York: Wiley.

KEITH, L. K., & BRACKEN, B. A. (1996). Self-concept instrumentation: A historical and evaluative review. In B. A. Bracken (Ed.), *Handbook of self-concept: Developmental, social, and clinical considerations.* New York: Wiley.

KELLER, H., & SCHOLMERICH, A. (1987). Infant vocalizations and parental reactions during the first four months of life. *Developmental Psychology, 23,* 62–67.

KELLER, M., & WOOD, P. (1989). Development of friendship reasoning: A study of interindividual differences in intraindividual change. *Developmental Psychology, 25,* 820–826.

KELLMAN, P. J. (1996). The origins of object perception. In R. Gelman & T. Au (Eds.), *Perceptual and cognitive development.* San Diego: Academic Press.

KELLMAN, P. J., & BANKS, M. S. (1998). Infant visual perception. In W. Damon (Series Ed.) & D. Kuhn & R. S. Siegler (Vol. Eds.), *Handbook of child psychology: Vol. 2. Cognition, perception, and language* (5th ed.). New York: Wiley.

KELLMAN, P. J., & SPELKE, E. S. (1983). Perception of partly occluded objects in infancy. *Cognitive Psychology, 15,* 483–524.

KEMLER NELSON, D. G., HIRSH-PASEK, K., JUSCZYK, P., & CASSIDY, K. W. (1989). How the prosodic cues in motherese might assist language learning. *Journal of Child Language, 16,* 55–68.

KENDALL, P. C., & BRASWELL, L. (1985). *Cognitive-behavioral therapy for impulsive children.* New York: Guilford.

KENDRICK, D. T., & TROST, M. R. (1993). The evolutionary perspective. In A. E. Beall & R. J. Sternberg (Eds.), *The psychology of gender.* New York: Guilford.

KENT, R. D., & BAUER, H. R. (1985). Vocalizations of one-year-olds. *Journal of Child Language, 12,* 491–526.

KERNS, K. A. (1994). A longitudinal examination of links between mother-child attachment and children's friendships in early childhood. *Journal of Social and Personal Relationships, 11,* 379–381.

KERNS, K. A. (1996). Individual differences in friendship quality: Links to child-mother attachment. In W. M. Bukowski, A. F. Newcomb, & W. W. Hartup (Eds.), *The company they keep: Friendship in childhood and adolescence.* New York: Cambridge University Press.

KERR, M., LAMBERT, W. W., & BEM, D. J. (1996). Life course sequelae of childhood shyness in Sweden: Comparison with the United States. *Developmental Psychology, 32,* 1100–1105.

KERR, M., LAMBERT, W. W., STATTIN, H., & KLACKENBERG-LARSSON, I. (1994). Stability of inhibition in a Swedish longitudinal sample. *Child Development, 65,* 138–146.

KIMBALL, M. M. (1989). A new perspective on women's math achievement. *Psychological Bulletin, 105,* 198–214.

KIMURA, D., & HAMPSON, E. (1993). Neural and hormonal mechanisms mediating sex differences in cognition. In P. A. Vernon (Ed.), *Biological approaches to the study of human intelligence.* Norwood, NJ: Ablex.

KIMURA, D., & HAMPSON, E. (1994). Cognitive pattern in men and women is influenced by fluctuations in sex hormones. *Current Directions in Psychological Science, 3,* 57–61.

KISER, L. J., BATES, J. E., MASLIN, C. A., & BAYLES, K. (1986). Mother–infant play at six months as a predictor of attachment security at thirteen months. *Journal of the American Academy of Child Psychiatry, 25,* 68–75.

KISILEVSKY, B. S., & MUIR, D. W. (1984). Neonatal habituation and dishabituation to tactile stimulation during sleep. *Developmental Psychology, 20,* 367–373.

KLAHR, D., & MacWHINNEY, B. (1998). Information processing. In W. Damon (Series Ed.) & D. Kuhn & R. S. Siegler (Vol. Eds.), *Handbook of child psychology: Vol. 2. Cognition, perception, and language* (5th ed.). New York: Wiley.

KLAHR, D., & ROBINSON, M. (1981). Formal assessment of problem solving and planning processes in preschool children. *Cognitive Psychology, 13,* 113–148.

KLAUS, M. H., & KENNELL, J. H. (1976). *Maternal–infant bonding.* St. Louis: Mosby.

KLAUS, M. H., KENNELL, J. H., & KLAUS, P. H. (1995). *Bonding: Building the foundations of secure attachment and independence.* Reading, MA: Addison-Wesley.

KLEIN, M. W. (1995). Street gang cycles. In J. Q. Wilson & J. Petersilia (Eds.), *Crime.* San Francisco: Institute for Contemporary Studies.

KLEMCHUK, H. P., BOND, L. A., & HOWELL, D. C. (1990). Coherence and correlates of level 1 perspective taking in young children. *Merrill-Palmer Quarterly, 36,* 369–387.

KLIMES-DOUGAN, B., & KISTNER, J. (1990). Physically abused pre-schoolers' responses to peers' distress. *Developmental Psychology, 26,* 599–602.

KLINNERT, M. D., CAMPOS, J. J., SORCE, J. F., EMDE, R. N., & SVEJDA, M. (1983). Emotions as behavior regulators: Social referencing in infancy. In R. Plutchik & H. Kellerman (Eds.), *Emotions in early development: Vol. 2. The emotions.* New York: Academic Press.

KLINNERT, M. D., SORCE, J. F., EMDE, R. N., STENBERG, C., & GAENSBAURER, T. (1984). Continuities and change in early emotional life: Maternal perceptions of surprise, fear, and anger. In R. N. Emde & R. J. Harmon (Eds.), *Continuities and discontinuities in development.* New York: Plenum.

KNIGHT, G. P., BERNING, A. L., WILSON, S. L., & CHAO, C. (1987). The effects of information-processing demands and social-situational factors on the social decision making of children. *Journal of Experimental Child Psychology, 43,* 244–259.

KOCH, R., & De La CRUZ, F. (1991). The danger of birth defects in the children of women with phenylketonuria. *Journal of NIH Research, 3,* 61–63.

KOCHANSKA, G. (1993). Toward a synthesis of parental socialization and child temperament in early development of conscience. *Child Development, 64,* 325–347.

KOCHANSKA, G. (1995). Children's temperament, mothers' discipline, and security of attachment: Multiple pathways to emerging internalization. *Child Development, 66,* 597–615.

KOCHANSKA, G. (1997). Multiple pathways to conscience for children with different temperaments: From toddlerhood to age 5. *Developmental Psychology, 33,* 228–240.

KOCHANSKA, G., MURRAY, K., & COY, K. C. (1997). Inhibitory control as a contributor to conscience in childhood: From toddler to early school age. *Child Development, 68,* 263–277.

KOCHANSKA, G., & THOMPSON, R. A. (1997). The emergence and development of conscience in toddlerhood and early childhood. In J. E. Grusec & L. Kuczynski (Eds.), *Handbook of parenting and the transmission of values.* New York: Wiley.

KOENIGSKNECHT, R. A., & FRIEDMAN, P. (1976). Syntax development in boys and girls. *Child Development, 47,* 1109–1115.

KOHLBERG, L. (1969). Stage and sequence: The cognitive-developmental approach to socialization. In D. A. Goslin (Ed.), *Handbook of socialization theory and research.* Chicago: Rand McNally.

KOHLBERG, L. (1984). *The psychology of moral development: The nature and validity of moral stages.* San Francisco: Harper & Row.

KOHLBERG, L. (1986). A current statement on some theoretical issues. In S. Modgil & C. Modgil (Eds.), *Lawrence Kohlberg: Consensus and controversy.* Philadelphia: Falmer.

KOHLBERG, L. (1987). The development of moral judgment and moral action. In L. Kohlberg (Ed.), *Child psychology and childhood education: A cognitive-developmental view.* New York: Longman.

KOHLBERG, L., & CANDEE, D. (1984). The relationship of moral judgment to moral action. In W. M. Kurtines & J. L. Gewirtz (Eds.), *Morality, moral behavior, and moral development.* New York: Wiley.

KOHLBERG, L., & KRAMER, R. (1969). Continuities and discontinuities in childhood and adult moral development. *Human Development, 12,* 93–120.

KOHLBERG, L., & ULLIAN, D. Z. (1974). Stages in the development of psychosexual concepts and attitudes. In R. C. Friedman, R. M. Richart, & R. L. VandeWiele (Eds.), *Sex differences in behavior.* New York: Wiley.

KOHLBERG, L., LEVINE, C., & HEWER, A. (1983). *Moral stages: A current formulation and a response to critics.* Basel, Switzerland: Karger.

KOHLBERG, L., YAEGER, J., & HJERTHOLM, E. (1968). Private speech: Four studies and a review of theories. *Child Development, 39,* 817–826.

KOHLER, F. W., & FOWLER, S. A. (1985). Training prosocial behaviors to young children: An analysis of reciprocity with untrained peers. *Journal of Applied Behavior Analysis, 18,* 187–200.

KOLB, B. (1989). Brain development, plasticity, and behavior. *American Psychologist, 44,* 1203–1212.

KONNER, M. J. (1976). Maternal care, infant behavior and development among the Kung. In R. B. Lee & I. DeVore (Eds.), *Kalahari hunter-gatherers.* Cambridge: Harvard University Press.

KOPP, C. B. (1991). Young children's progression to self-regulation: In M. Bullock (Ed.), *The development of intentional action: Cognitive, motivational, and interactive process.* Basel, Switzerland: Karger.

KOPP, C. B., & KALER, S. R. (1989). Risk in infancy: Origins and implications. *American Psychologist, 44,* 224–230.

KORN, S. J. (1984). Continuities and discontinuities in difficult/easy temperament: Infancy to young adulthood. *Merrill-Palmer Quarterly, 30,* 189–199.

KORNER, A. F., & THOMAN, E. (1970). Visual alertness in neonates as evoked by maternal care. *Journal of Experimental Child Psychology, 10,* 67–78.

KORNHABER, M. (1994). *The theory of multiple intelligences: Why and how schools use it.* Cambridge: Harvard Graduate School of Education.

KORNHABER, M., KRECHEVSKY, M., & GARDNER, H. (1990). Engaging intelligence. *Educational Psychologist, 25,* 177–199.

KOSTELNY, K., & GARBARINO, J. (1994). Coping with the consequences of living in danger: The case of Palestinian children and youth. *International Journal of Behavioral Development, 17,* 595–611.

KOURILSKY, M., & KEHRET-WARD, T. (1984). Kindergartners' attitudes toward distributive justice: Experiential mediators. *Merrill-Palmer Quarterly, 30,* 49–64.

KOZOL, J. (1991). *Savage inequalities: Children in America's schools.* New York: Crown.

KOZULIN, A. (1990). *Vygotsky's psychology.* Cambridge: Harvard University Press.

KRAFT, R. H. (1984). Lateral specialization and verbal/spatial ability in preschool children: Age, sex, and familial handedness differences. *Neuropsychologia, 22,* 319–335.

KREBS, D. (1987). The challenge of altruism in biology and psychology. In C. Crawford, M. Smith, & D. Krebs (Eds.), *Sociobiology and psychology: Ideas, issues, and applications.* Hillsdale, NJ: Erlbaum.

KREBS, D., DENTON, K., & HIGGINS, N. C. (1987). On the evolution of self-knowledge and self-deception. In K. B. MacDonald (Ed.), *Sociobiological perspectives on human development.* New York: Springer-Verlag.

KREBS, D. L., & GILLMORE, J. (1982). The relationship and the first stages of cognitive development, role-taking abilities, and moral development. *Child Development, 53,* 877–886.

KREBS, D. L., & VAN HESTEREN, F. (1994). The development of altruism: Toward an integrative model. *Developmental Review, 14,* 103–158.

KREIPE, R. E., & STRAUSS, J. (1989). Adolescent medical disorders, behavior and development. In G. R. Adams, R. Montemayor, & T. P. Gullotta (Eds.), *Biology of adolescent behavior and development.* Newbury Park, CA: Sage.

KREITLER, S., & KREITLER, H. (1989). Horizontal decalage: A problem and its solution. *Cognitive Development, 4,* 89–119.

KREUTZER, M. A., LEONARD, C., & FLAVELL, J. H. (1975). An interview study of children's knowledge about memory. *Monographs of the Society for Research in Child Development, 40* (1, Serial No. 159).

KREVANS, J., & GIBBS, J. C. (1996). Parents' use of inductive discipline: Relations to children's empathy and prosocial behavior. *Child Development, 67,* 3263–3277.

KRISTOF, N. D. (1993, July 21). Ultrasound undertaker: China's peasants find new way to avoid unwanted daughters. *The Denver Post,* p. 2A.

KROLL, J. (1977). The concept of childhood in the middle ages. *Journal of the History of Behavioral Sciences, 13,* 384–393.

KROPP, J. P., & HAYNES, O. M. (1987). Abusive and nonabusive mothers' ability to identify general and specific emotion signals of infants. *Child Development, 58,* 187–190.

KRUGER, A. C. (1992). The effect of peer and adult-child transactive discussions on moral reasoning. *Merrill-Palmer Quarterly, 38,* 191–211.

KUCHUK, A., VIBBERT, M., & BORNSTEIN, M. H. (1986). The perception of smiling and its experiential correlates in three-month-old infants. *Child Development, 57,* 1054–1061.

KUCZAJ, S. A. (1977). The acquisition of regular and irregular past tense forms. *Journal of Verbal Learning and Verbal Behavior, 16,* 589–600.

KUCZAJ, S. A. (1982). Language play and language acquisition. In H. W. Reese (Ed.), *Advances in child development and behavior* (Vol. 17). New York: Academic Press.

KUHL, P. K. (1991). Perception, cognition, and the ontogenetic and phylogenetic emergence of human speech. In S. Brauth, W. Hall, & R. Dooling (Eds.), *Plasticity of development.* Cambridge: MIT Press/Bradford Books.

KUHL, P. K. (1993). Early linguistic experience and phonetic perception: Implications for theories of developmental speech perception. *Journal of Phonetics, 21,* 125–139.

KUHL, P. K., & MELTZOFF, A. N. (1988). Speech as an intermodal object of perception. In A. Yonas (Ed.), *Minnesota symposia on child psychology: Vol. 20. Perceptual development in infancy.* Hillsdale, NJ: Erlbaum.

KUHN, D. (1991). *The skills of argument.* New York: Cambridge University Press.

KUHN, D. (1992a). Cognitive development. In M. H. Bornstein & M. E. Lamb (Eds.), *Developmental psychology: An advanced textbook* (3rd ed.). Hillsdale, NJ: Erlbaum.

KUHN, D. (1992b). Piaget's child as scientist. In H. Beilin & P. B. Pufall (Eds.), *Piaget's theory: Prospects and possibilities.* Hillsdale, NJ: Erlbaum.

KUHN, D. (1995). Microgenetic study of change: What has it told us? *Psychological Science, 6,* 133–139.

KUHN, D., HO, V., & ADAMS, C. (1979). Formal reasoning among pre- and late-adolescents. *Child Development, 50,* 1128–1135.

KUHN, D., LANGER, J., KOHLBERG, L., & HAAN, N. S. (1977). The development of formal operations in logical and moral judgment. *Genetic Psychology Monographs, 95,* 97–188.

KULIN, H. E. (1991). Puberty, hypothalamic-pituitary changes of. In R. M. Lerner, A. C. Peterson, & J. Brooks-Gunn (Eds.), *Encyclopedia of adolescence* (Vol. 2). New York: Garland.

KUPERSMIDT J. B., DeROSIER, M. E., & PATTERSON, C. P. (1995). Similarity as the basis for children's friendships: The roles of sociometric status, aggressive and withdrawn behavior, academic achievement, and demographic characteristics. *Journal of Social and Personal Relationships, 12,* 439–452.

KUPERSMIDT, J. B., & TREJOS, L. (1987, April). *Behavioral correlates of sociometric status among Costa Rican children.* Paper presented at the meeting of the Society for Research in Child Development, Baltimore.

KURDEK, L. A. (1978). Perspective taking as the cognitive basis of children's moral development: A review of the literature. *Merrill-Palmer Quarterly, 34,* 3–28.

KURTINES, W. M., & GRIEF, E. B. (1974). The development of moral thought: Review and evaluation of Kohlberg's approach. *Psychological Bulletin, 81,* 453–470.

KURTINES, W. M., ALVAREZ, M., & AZMITIA, M. (1990). Science and morality: The role of values in science and the study of moral phenomena. *Psychological Bulletin, 107,* 283–295.

KURTZ, B. E., & BORKOWSKI, J. G. (1987). Development of strategic skills in impulsive and reflective children: A longitudinal study of metacognition. *Journal of Experimental Child Psychology, 43,* 129–148.

KURTZ, B. E., SCHNEIDER, W., CARR, M., & RELLINGER, E. (1990). Strategy instruction and attributional beliefs in West Germany and the United States: Do teachers foster metacognitive development? *Contemporary Educational Psychology, 15,* 268–283.

KUTNICK, P. (1986). The relationship of moral judgment and moral action: Kohlberg's theory, criticism and revision. In S. Modgil & C. Modgil (Eds.), *Lawrence Kohlberg: Consensus and controversy.* Philadelphia: Falmer.

LABORATORY OF COMPARATIVE HUMAN COGNITION. (1983). Culture and cognitive development. In P. H. Mussen (Series Ed.) & W. Kessen (Vol. Ed.), *Handbook of child psychology: Vol. 1. History, theory, and methods.* New York: Wiley.

LABOV, W. (1997). Testimony before the United States Senate Subcommittee on Appropriations.

LADD, G. W. (1990). Having friends, keeping friends, making friends, and being liked by peers in the classroom: Predictors of children's early school adjustment? *Child Development, 61,* 1081–1100.

LADD, G. W. (1992). Themes and theories: Perspectives on processes in family-peer relationships. In R. D. Parke & G. W. Ladd (Eds.), *Family-peer relationships: Modes of linkage.* Hillsdale, NJ: Erlbaum.

LADD, G. W., & COLEMAN, C. C. (1997). Children's classroom peer relationships and early school attitudes: Concurrent and longitudinal associations. *Early Education and Development, 8,* 51–66.

LADD, G. W., & COLEMAN, C. (1993). Young children's peer relationships: Forms, features, and functions. In B. Spodek (Ed.), *Handbook of research on the education of young children* (2nd ed.). New York: Macmillan.

LADD, G. W., & HART, C. H. (1992). Creating informal play opportunities: Are parents' and pre-schoolers' initiations related to children's competence with peers? *Developmental Psychology, 28,* 1179–1187.

LADD, G. W., KOCHENDERFER, B. J., & COLEMAN, C. C. (1996). Friendship quality as a predictor of young children's early school adjustment. *Child Development, 67,* 1103–1118.

LADD, G. W., & LESIEUR, K. D. (1995). Parents and children's peer relationships. In M. H. Bornstein (Ed.), *Handbook of parenting: Vol. 4. Applied and practical parenting.* Mahwah, NJ: Erlbaum.

LADD, G. W., PROFILET, S. M., & HART, C. H. (1992). Parents' management of children's peer relations: Facilitating and supervising children's activities in the peer culture. In R. D. Parke & G. W. Ladd (Eds.), *Family-peer relationships: Modes of linkage.* Hillsdale, NJ: Erlbaum.

LaFRENIERE, P., & CHARLESWORTH, W. R. (1983). Dominance, attention, and affiliation in a preschool group: A nine-month longitudinal study. *Ethology and Sociobiology, 4,* 55–67.

LaFRENIERE, P., & SROUFE, L. A. (1985). Profiles of peer competence in the preschool: Interrelations between measures, influence of social ecology, and relation to attachment history. *Developmental Psychology, 21,* 56–69.

LaFRENIERE, P., STRAYER, F. F., & GAUTHIER, R. (1984). The emergence of same-sex affiliative preferences among preschool peers: A developmental/ethological perspective. *Child Development, 55,* 1958–1965.

LAGASSE, L. L., GRUBER, C. P., & LIPSITT, L. P. (1989). The infantile expression of avidity in relation to later assessments of inhibition and attachment. In J. S. Reznick (Ed.), *Perspectives on behavioral inhibition.* Chicago: University of Chicago Press.

LaGRECA, A. M. (1993). Social skills training with children: Where do we go from here? *Journal of Clinical Child Psychology, 22,* 288–298.

LAHEY, B. B., HAMMER, D., CRUMRINE, P. L., & FOREHAND, R. L. (1980). Birth order X sex interactions in child behavior problems. *Developmental Psychology, 16,* 608–615.

LAKIN, M., LAKIN, M. G., & CONSTANZO, P. R. (1979). Group processes in early childhood: A dimension of human development. *International Journal of Behavioral Development, 2,* 171–183.

LAMAZE, F. (1970). *Painless childbirth: Psychoprophylactic method.* Chicago: Henry Regnery.

LAMB, M. E. (1986). The changing roles of fathers. In M. E. Lamb (Ed.), *The father's role: Applied perspectives.* New York: Wiley.

LAMB, M. E. (1998). Nonparental child care: Context, quality, correlates, and consequences. In I. E. Sigel & K. A. Renninger (Eds.), *Handbook of child psychology: Vol. 4. Child psychology in practice.* New York: Wiley.

LAMB, M. E., EASTERBROOKS, M. A., & HOLDEN, G. W. (1980). Reinforcement and punishment among preschoolers: Characteristics, effects, and correlates. *Child Development, 51,* 1230–1236.

LAMB, M. E., & HWANG, C. (1982). Maternal attachment and mother–neonate bonding: A critical review. In M. E. Lamb & A. L. Brown (Eds.), *Advances in developmental psychology* (Vol. 2). Hillsdale, NJ: Erlbaum.

LAMB, M. E., KETTERLINUS, R. D., & FRACASSO, M. P. (1992). Parent–child relationships. In M. H. Bornstein & M. E. Lamb (Eds.), *Developmental psychology: An advanced textbook* (3rd ed.). Hillsdale, NJ: Erlbaum.

LAMB, M. E., MORRISON, D. C., & MALKIN, C. M. (1987). The development of infant social expectations in face-to-face interaction: A longitudinal study. *Merrill-Palmer Quarterly, 33,* 241–254.

LAMB, M. E., & ROOPNARINE, J. L. (1979). Peer influences on sex-role development in preschoolers. *Child Development, 50,* 1219–1222.

LAMB, M. E., & STERNBERG, K. J. (1998). Child care in context: The role and impact of early nonparental child care. In W. Damon (Ed.), *Handbook of child psychology: Vol. 4. Child psychology in practice.* New York: Wiley.

LAMB, M. E., STERNBERG, K., & PRODROMIDIS, M. (1992). Nonmaternal care and the security of infant–mother attachment: A reanalysis of the data. *Infant Behavior and Development, 15,* 71–83.

LAMB, M. E., THOMPSON, R. A., & FRODI, A. M. (1982). Early social development. In R. Vasta (Ed.), *Strategies and techniques of child study.* New York: Academic Press.

LAMBORN, S. D., MOUNTS, N. S., STEINBERG, L., & DORNBUSCH, S. M. (1991). Patterns of competence and adjustment among adolescents from authoritative, authoritarian, indulgent, and neglectful families. *Child Development, 62,* 1049–1065.

LANDAU, B. (1991). Spatial representation of objects in the young blind child. *Cognition, 38,* 145–178.

LANE, I. M., & COON, R. C. (1972). Reward allocation in preschool children. *Child Development, 43,* 1382–1389.

LANGER, O. (1990). Critical issues in diabetes and pregnancy. In I. R. Merkatz & J. E. Thompson (Eds.), *New perspectives on prenatal care.* New York: Elsevier.

LANGER, W. L. (1974). Infanticide: A historical survey. *History of Childhood Quarterly, 1,* 53–365.

LANGLOIS, J. H. (1986). From the eye of the beholder to behavioral reality: Development of social behaviors and social relations as a function of physical attractiveness. In C. P. Herman, M. P. Zanna, & E. T. Higgins (Eds.), *Physical appearance, stigma, and social behavior.* Hillsdale, NJ: Erlbaum.

LANGLOIS, J. H., & DOWNS, A. C. (1979). Peer relations as a function of physical attractiveness: The eye of the beholder or behavioral reality? *Child Development, 50,* 409–418.

LANGLOIS, J. H., RITTER, J. M., CASEY, R. J., & SAWIN, D. B. (1995). Infant attractiveness predicts maternal behaviors and attitudes. *Developmental Psychology, 31,* 464–472.

LANZA, E. (1992). Can bilingual two-year-olds code-switch? *Journal of Child Language, 19,* 633–658.

LAPSLEY, D. K., & QUINTANA, S. M. (1985). Integrative themes in social and developmental theories of self. In J. B. Pryor & J. D. Day (Eds.), *The development of social cognition.* New York: Springer-Verlag.

LARGO, R. H., MOLINARI, L., WEBER, M., PINTO, L. C., & DUC, G. (1985). Early development of locomotion: Significance of prematurity, cerebral palsy and sex. *Developmental Medicine and Child Neurology, 27,* 183–191.

LARNER, M., HALPERN, R., & HARKAVY, O. (Eds.). (1992). *Fair start for children: Lessons learned from seven demonstration projects.* New Haven, CT: Yale University Press.

LARRABEE, M. J. (Ed.). (1993). *An ethic of care: Feminist and interdisciplinary perspectives.* New York: Routledge.

LARSEN, S. F. (1992). Potential flashbulbs: Memories of ordinary news as the baseline. In E. Winograd and U. Neisser (Eds.), *Affect and accuracy in recall: Studies of flashbulb memories.* New York: Cambridge University Press.

LARSSON, G., BOHLIN, A. B., & TUNELL, R. (1985). Prospective study of children exposed to variable amounts of alcohol in utero. *Archives of Disease in Childhood, 60,* 316–321.

LATORRE, R. A., YU, L., FORTIN, L., & MARRACHE, M. (1983). Gender-role adoption and sex as academic and psychological risk factors. *Sex Roles, 9,* 1127–1136.

LAURSEN, B. (1993). Conflict management among close peers. In B. Laursen (Ed.), *New directions for child development: No. 60. Close friendships in adolescence.* San Francisco: Jossey-Bass.

LAURSEN, B., HARTUP, W. W., & KOPLAS, A. L. (1996). Towards understanding peer conflict. *Merrill-Palmer Quarterly, 42,* 76–102.

LAZAR, I., & DARLINGTON, R. (1982). Lasting effects of early education: A report from the Consortium for Longitudinal Studies. *Monographs of the Society for Research in Child Development, 47* (2–3, Serial No. 195).

LEADBEATER, B. J., & BISHOP, S. J. (1994). Predictors of behavior problems in preschool children of inner-city Afro-American and Puerto Rican adolescent mothers. *Child Development, 65,* 638–648.

LEAPER, C. (Ed.). (1994). *Childhood gender segregation: Causes and consequences.* San Francisco: Jossey-Bass.

LEAPER, C., ANDERSON, K. J., & SANDERS, P. (1998). Moderators of gender effects on parents' talk to their children: A meta-analysis. *Developmental Psychology, 34,* 3–27.

LEAVITT, L., & FOX, N. (Eds.). (1993). *Psychological effects of war and violence on children.* Hillsdale, NJ: Erlbaum.

LEBOYER, F. (1975). *Birth without violence.* New York: Knopf.

LEE, C., & BATES, J. E. (1985). Mother–child interaction at the age of two years and perceived difficult temperament. *Child Development, 56,* 1314–1325.

LEE, D. N., & ARONSON, E. (1974). Visual proprioceptive control of standing in human infants. *Perception and Psychophysics, 15,* 529–532.

LEE, V. E., BROOKS-GUNN, J., SCHNUR, E., & LIAW, F.-R. (1990). Are Head Start effects sustained? A longitudinal follow-up comparison of disadvantaged children attending Head Start, no preschool, and other preschool programs. *Child Development, 61,* 495–507.

LEE, V. E., BURKHAM, D. T., ZIMILES, H., & LADEWSKI, J. (1994). Family structure and its effect on behavioral and emotional problems in young adolescents. *Journal of Research on Adolescence, 4,* 405–437.

LEGER, D. W., THOMPSON, R. A., MERRITT, J. A., & BENZ, J. J. (1996). Adult perception of emotion intensity in human infant cries: Effects of infant age and cry acoustics. *Child Development, 67,* 3238–3249.

LEGERSTEE, M., ANDERSON, D., & SCHAFFER, A. (1998). Five- and eight-month-old infants recognize their faces and voices as familiar and social stimuli. *Child Development, 69,* 37–50.

LEI, T., & CHENG, S. (1989). A little but special light on the universality of moral judgment development. In L. Kohlberg, D. Candee, & A. Colby (Eds.), *Rethinking moral development.* Cambridge: Harvard University Press.

LEIDERMAN, P. H., & SEASHORE, M. J. (1975). Mother–infant separation: Some delayed consequences. In *Parent-infant interaction* (CIBA Foundation Symposium No. 33). New York: Elsevier.

LEIJON, I. (1980). Neurology and behavior of newborn infants delivered by vacuum extraction of maternal indication. *Acta Paediatrica Scandinavica, 69,* 626–631.

LEINBACH, M. D., & FAGOT, B. I. (1993). Categorical habituation to male and female faces: Gender schematic processing in infancy. *Infant Behavior and Development, 16,* 317–332.

LEITER, M. P. (1977). A study of reciprocity in preschool play groups. *Child Development, 48,* 1288–1295.

LEMPERS, J. D., FLAVELL, E. R., & FLAVELL, J. H. (1977). The development in very young children of tacit knowledge concerning visual perception. *Genetic Psychology Monographs, 95,* 3–53.

LEMPERT, H. (1984). Topic as starting point for syntax. *Monographs of the Society for Research in Child Development, 49* (5, Serial No. 208).

LENNEBERG, E. H. (1967). *Biological foundations of language.* New York: Wiley.

LENNON, R., & EISENBERG, N. (1987). Gender and age differences in empathy and sympathy. In N. Eisenberg & J. Strayer (Eds.), *Empathy and its determinants.* New York: Cambridge University Press.

LEON, G. R. (1991). Bulimia nervosa in adolescence. In R. M. Lerner, A. C. Petersen, & J. Brooks-Gunn (Eds.), *Encyclopedia of adolescence.* New York: Garland.

LEON, M. (1982). Rules in children's moral judgments: Integration of intent, damage, and rationale information. *Developmental Psychology, 18,* 835–842.

LEPPERT, P. C., NAMEROW, P. B., & BARKER, D. (1986). Pregnancy outcomes among adolescent and older women receiving comprehensive prenatal care. *Journal of Adolescent Health Care, 7,* 112–117.

LERNER, R. M. (1982). Children and adolescents as producers of their own development. *Developmental Review, 2,* 342–370.

LERNER, R. M., CASTELLINO, D. R., TERRY, P. A., VILLARRUEL, F. A., & McKINNEY, M. H. (1995). Developmental contextual perspective on parenting. In M. H. Bornstein (Ed.), *Handbook of parenting: Vol. 2. Biology and ecology of parenting.* Mahwah, NJ: Erlbaum.

LERNER, R. M., LERNER, J. V., & TUBMAN, J. (1989). Organismic and contextual bases of development in adolescence: A developmental contextual view. In G. R. Adams, R. Montemayor, & T. P. Gullotta (Eds.), *Biology of adolescent behavior and development.* Newbury Park, CA: Sage.

LERNER, R. M., & VON EYE, A. (1992). Sociobiology and human development: Arguments and evidence. *Human Development, 35,* 12–33.

LESLIE, A. M., & KEEBLE, S. (1987). Do six-month-olds perceive causality? *Cognition, 25,* 265–288.

LESTER, B. M. (1976). Spectrum analysis of the cry sounds of well-nourished and malnourished infants. *Child Development, 47,* 237–241.

LESTER, B. M. (1984). A biosocial model of infant crying. In L. P. Lipsitt (Ed.), *Advances in infancy research* (Vol. 3). Norwood, NJ: Ablex.

LESTER, B. M., HOFFMAN, J., & BRAZELTON, T. B. (1985). The rhythmic structure of mother–infant interaction in term and preterm infants. *Child Development, 56,* 15–27.

LEUNG, E. H. L., & RHEINGOLD, H. L. (1981). Development of pointing as a social gesture. *Developmental Psychology, 17,* 215–220.

LEVAY, S. (1991). A difference in hypothalamic structure between heterosexual and homosexual men. *Science, 253,* 1034–1037.

LEVAY, S. (1993). *The sexual brain.* Cambridge: MIT Press.

LEVIN, M. (1994). Comment on the Minnesota Transracial Adoption Study. *Intelligence, 19,* 13–20.

LEVIT, A. G., & UTMAN, J. G. A. (1992). From babbling towards the sound systems of English and French: A longitudinal two-case study. *Journal of Child Language, 19,* 19–49.

LEVITT, M. J., GUACCI-FRANCO, N., & LEVITT, J. L. (1993). Convoys of social support in childhood and early adolescence: Structure and function. *Developmental Psychology, 29,* 811–818.

LEVITT, M. J., WEBER, R. A., CLARK, M. C., & MCDONNELL, P. (1985). Reciprocity of exchange in toddler sharing behavior. *Developmental Psychology, 21,* 122–123.

LEVY, G. D. (1989). Developmental and individual differences in preschoolers' recognition memories: The influences of gender schematization and verbal labeling of information. *Sex Roles, 21,* 305–324.

LEVY, G. D., & CARTER, D. B. (1989). Gender schema, gender constancy, and gender-role knowledge: The roles of cognitive factors in preschoolers' gender-role stereotype attributions. *Developmental Psychology, 25,* 444–449.

LEVY, G. D., & FIVUSH, R. (1993). Scripts and gender: A new approach for examining gender-role development. *Developmental Psychology, 13,* 126–146.

LEVY, G. D., TAYLOR, M. G., & GELMAN, S. A. (1995). Traditional and evaluative aspects of flexibility in gender roles, social conventions, moral rules, and physical laws. *Child Development, 66,* 515–531.

LEVY, J. (1981). Lateralization and its implications for variation in development. In E. S. Gollin (Ed.), *Developmental plasticity.* New York: Academic Press.

LEWIS, M. (1981). Self-knowledge: A social cognitive perspective on gender identity and sex-role development. In M. E. Lamb & L. R. Sherrod (Eds.), *Infant social cognition: Empirical and theoretical considerations.* Hillsdale, NJ: Erlbaum.

LEWIS, M. (1987a). Early sex role behavior and school age adjustment. In J. M. Reinisch, L. A. Rosenblum, & S. A. Sanders (Eds.), *Masculinity/femininity: Basic perspectives.* New York: Oxford University Press.

LEWIS, M. (1987b). Social development in infancy and early childhood. In J. D. Osofsky (Ed.), *Handbook of infant development* (2nd ed.). New York: Wiley.

LEWIS, M. (1993a). Early socioemotional predictors of cognitive competence at 4 years. *Developmental Psychology, 29,* 1036–1045.

LEWIS, M. (1993b). Self-conscious emotions: Embarrassment, pride, shame, and guilt. In M. Lewis & J. Haviland (Eds.), *The handbook of emotions.* New York: Guilford.

LEWIS, M. (1994). Myself and me. In S. T. Parker, R. W. Mitchell, & M. L. Boccia (Eds.), *Self-awareness in animals and humans: Developmental perspectives.* New York: Cambridge University Press.

LEWIS, M. (1995a). Aspects of the self: From systems to ideas. In P. Rochat (Ed.), *The self in early infancy: Theory and research.* North Holland, Netherlands: Elsevier.

LEWIS, M. (1995b). Embarrassment: The emotion of self-exposure and evaluation. In J. Tangney & K. Fischer (Eds.), *Self-conscious emotions: The psychology of shame, guilt, embarassment, and pride.* New York: Guilford.

LEWIS, M., & BROOKS-GUNN, J. (1979). *Social cognition and the acquisition of self.* New York: Plenum.

LEWIS, M., ALESSANDRI, S. M., & SULLIVAN, M. W. (1990). Violation of expectancy, loss of control, and anger expression in young infants. *Developmental Psychology, 26,* 745–751.

LEWIS, M., FEIRING, C., McGUFFOG, C., & JASKIR, J. (1984). Predicting psychopathology in six-year-olds from early social relations. *Child Development, 55,* 123–136.

LEWIS, M., & RAMSEY, D. S. (1997). Stress reactivity and self-recognition. *Child Development, 68,* 621–629.

LEWIS, M., RAMSEY, D. S., & KAWAKAMI, K. (1993). Differences between Japanese infants and Caucasian-American infants in behavioral and cortisol response to inoculation. *Child Development, 64,* 1722–1731.

LEWKOWICZ, D. J., & LICKLITER, R. (Eds.) (1994). *The development of intersensory perception: Comparative perspectives.* Hillsdale, NJ: Erlbaum.

LEYENDECKER, B., & SCHOLMERICH, A. (1991). An ecological perspective on infant development. In M. E. Lamb & H. Keller (Eds.), *Infant development: Perspectives from German-speaking countries.* Hillsdale, NJ: Erlbaum.

LIBEN, L. S., & SIGNORELLA, M. L. (Eds.). (1987). *New directions for child development: No. 38. Children's gender schemata.* San Francisco: Jossey-Bass.

LIDDELL, C., & KRUGER, P. (1987). Activity and social behavior in a South African township nursery: Some effects of crowding. *Merrill-Palmer Quarterly, 33,* 195–211.

LIDDELL, C., & KRUGER, P. (1989). Activity and social behavior in a crowded South African nursery: A follow-up study on the effects of crowding at home. *Merrill-Palmer Quarterly, 35,* 209–226.

LIDZ, C. S. (1992). Dynamic assessment: Some thoughts on the model, the medium, and the message. *Learning and Individual Differences, 4,* 125–136.

LIEBERT, R. M. (1984). What develops in moral development? In W. M. Kurtines & J. L. Gewirtz (Eds.), *Morality, moral behavior, and moral development.* New York: Wiley.

LIEBERT, R. M., & SPRAFKIN, J. (1988). *The early window: Effects of television on children and youth* (3rd ed.). New York: Pergamon.

LINDBERG, M. A. (1980). Is knowledge base development a necessary and sufficient condition for memory development? *Journal of Experimental Child Psychology, 30,* 401–410.

LINDSEY, E. W., MIZE, J., & PETTIT, G. S. (1997). Differential play patterns of mothers and fathers of sons and daughters: Implications for children's gender role development. *Sex Roles, 17,* 643–661.

LINN, M. C., & PETERSEN, A. C. (1985). Emergence and characterization of sex differences in spatial ability: A meta-analysis. *Child Development, 56,* 1479–1498.

LIPSCOMB, T. J., MCALLISTER, H. A., & BREGMAN, N. J. (1985). A developmental inquiry into the effects of multiple models on children's generosity. *Merrill-Palmer Quarterly, 31,* 335–344.

LIPSITT, L. P. (1977). Taste in human neonates: Its effect on sucking and heart rate. In J. M. Weiffenbach (Ed.), *Taste and development: The genesis of sweet preference.* Washington, DC: U.S. Government Printing Office.

LIPSITT, L. P. (1990). Learning and memory in infants. *Merrill-Palmer Quarterly, 36,* 53–66.

LIPSITT, L. P. (1992). Discussion: The Bayley Scales of Infant Development: Issues of prediction and outcome revisited. In C. Rovee-Collier & L. P. Lipsitt (Eds.), *Advances in infancy research* (Vol. 7). Norwood, NJ: Ablex.

LIPSITT, L. P., ENGEN, T., & KAYE, H. (1963). Developmental changes in the olfactory threshold of the neonate. *Child Development, 34,* 371–376.

LIST, J. A., COLLINS, W. A., & WESTBY, S. D. (1983). Comprehension and inferences from traditional and nontraditional sex-role portrayals on television. *Child Development, 54,* 1579–1587.

LOBEL, M., DUNKEL-SCHETTER, C., & SCRIMSHAW, S. C. M. (1992). Prenatal maternal stress and prematurity: A prospective study of socioeconomically disadvantaged women. *Health Psychology, 11*(1), 32–40.

LOBEL, T. E., & MENASHRI, J. (1993). Relations of conceptions of gender-role transgressions and gender constancy to gender-typed toy preferences. *Developmental Psychology, 29,* 150–155.

LOCHMAN, J. E., BURCH, P. P., CURRY, J. F., & LAMPRON, L. B. (1984). Treatment and generalization effects of cognitive-behavioral and goal-setting interventions with aggressive boys. *Journal of Consulting and Clinical Psychology, 52,* 915–916.

LOCHMAN, J. E., & WAYLAND, K. (1994). Aggression, social acceptance and race as predictors of negative adolescent outcomes. *Journal of the American Academy of Child and Adolescent Psychiatry, 33,* 1026–1035.

LOCKE, J. (1824). *An essay concerning human understanding.* New York: Seaman. (Original work published 1694).

LOCKE, J. L. (1989). Babbling and early speech: Continuity and individual differences. *First Language, 9,* 191–206.

LOCKE, J. L. (1993). *The child's path to spoken language.* Cambridge: Harvard University Press.

LOCKE, J. L., & PEARSON, D. M. (1990). Linguistic significance of babbling: Evidence from a tracheostomized infant. *Journal of Child Language, 17,* 1–16.

LOCKHEED, M. (1985). Women, girls, and computers: A first look at the evidence. *Sex Roles, 13,* 115–122.

LOCKMAN, J. J. (1984). The development of detour ability during infancy. *Child Development, 55,* 482–491.

LOEBER, R., & FARRINGTON, D. P. (Eds.). (1998). *Serious and violent juvenile offenders: Risk factors and successful interventions.* Thousand Oaks, CA: Sage.

LOEBER, R., & HAY, D. F. (1997). Key issues in the development of aggression and violence from childhood to early adulthood. *Annual Review of Psychology, 48,* 371–410.

LOEBER, R., & STOUTHAMER-LOEBER, M. (1998). Development of juvenile aggression and violence: Some common misconceptions and controversies. *American Psychologist, 53,* 242–259.

LOEHLIN, J. C., LINDZEY, G., & SPUHLER, J. N. (1975). *Race differences in intelligence.* San Francisco: W. H. Freeman.

LOLLIS, S. P., ROSS, H. S., & TATE, E. (1992). Parents' regulation of children's peer interactions: Direct influences. In R. D. Parke & G. W. Ladd (Eds.), *Family-peer relationships: Modes of linkage.* Hillsdale, NJ: Erlbaum.

LONG, B. C. (1989). Sex-role orientation, coping strategies, and self-efficacy of women in traditional and nontraditional occupations. *Psychology of Women Quarterly, 13,* 307–324.

LONIGAN, C. J., & WHITEHURST, G. J. (in press). Examination of the relative influence of parent and teacher involvement in a shared-reading intervention for preschool children from low-income backgrounds. *Early Childhood Research Quarterly.*

LORE, R. K., & SCHULTZ, L. A. (1993). Control of human aggression: A comparative perspective. *American Psychologist, 48,* 16–25.

LORENZ, K. Z. (1937). The companion in the bird's world. *Auk, 54,* 245–273.

LORENZ, K. Z. (1950). Innate behaviour patterns. *Symposia for the Society of Experimental Biology, 4,* 211–268.

LORENZ, K. Z. (1981). *The foundations of ethology.* New York: Springer-Verlag.

LOTT, B., & MALUSO, D. (1993). The social learning of gender. In A. E. Beall & R. J. Sternberg (Eds.), *The psychology of gender.* New York: Guilford.

LOUDAL, L. T. (1989). Sex role messages in television commercials: An update. *Sex Roles, 21,* 715–724.

LOUNSBURY, M. L., & BATES, J. E. (1982). The cries of infants of differing levels of perceived temperamental difficultness: Acoustic properties and effects on listeners. *Child Development, 53,* 677–686.

LOURENCO, O., & MACHADO, A. (1996). In defense of Piaget's theory: A reply to 10 common criticisms. *Psychological Review, 103,* 143–164.

LOVELAND, K. A. (1986). Discovering the affordances of a reflecting surface. *Developmental Review, 6,* 1–24.

LOWREY, G. H. (1978). *Growth and development of children* (7th ed.). Chicago: Year Book Medical Publishers.

LOZOFF, B., WOLFF, A., & DAVIS, N. (1984). Cosleeping in urban families with young children in the United States. *Pediatrics, 74,* 171–182.

LUDEMANN, P. M. (1991). Generalized discrimination of positive facial expressions by seven- and ten-month-old infants. *Child Development, 62,* 55–67.

LUECKE-ALEKSA, D., ANDERSON, D. R., COLLINS, P. A., & SCHMITT, K. L. (1995). Gender constancy and television viewing. *Developmental Psychology, 31,* 773–780.

LUMMIS, M., & STEVENSON, H. W. (1990). Gender differences in beliefs and achievement: A cross-cultural study. *Developmental Psychology, 26,* 254–263.

LUNDMAN, R. J. (1984). *Prevention and control of juvenile delinquency.* New York: Oxford University Press.

LURIA, A. R. (1961). *The role of speech in the regulation of normal and abnormal behavior.* New York: Liveright.

LURIA, A. R. (1982). *Language and cognition.* New York: Wiley.

LUSTER, T., & DENBOW, E. (1992). Home environment and maternal intelligence as predictors of verbal intelligence: A comparison of preschool and school-age children. *Merrill-Palmer Quarterly, 38,* 151–175.

LYNCH, M. P., & EILERS, R. E. (1992). A study of perceptual development for musical tuning. *Perception and Psychophysics, 52,* 599–608.

LYNCH, M. P., EILERS, R. E., OLLER, K. D., & URBANO, R. C. (1990). Innateness, experience, and music perception. *Psychological Science, 1,* 272–276.

LYNCH, M. P., SHORT, L. B., & CHUA, R. (1995). Contributions of experience to the development of musical processing in infancy. *Developmental Psychobiology, 28,* 377–398.

LYON, T. D., & FLAVELL, J. H. (1993). Young children's understanding of forgetting over time. *Child Development, 64,* 789–800.

LYONS, J. A., & SERBIN, L. A. (1986). Observer bias in scoring boys' and girls' aggression. *Sex Roles, 14,* 301–313.

LYONS-RUTH, K., ALPERN, L., & REPACHOLI, B. (1993). Disorganized infant attachment classification and maternal psychosocial problems as predictors of hostile-aggressive behavior in the pre-school classroom. *Child Development, 64,* 572–585.

LYONS-RUTH, K., CONNELL, D. B., & ZOLL, D. (1989). Patterns of maternal behavior among infants at risk for abuse: Relations with infant attachment behavior and infant development at 12 months of age. In D. Cicchetti & V. Carlson (Eds.), *Child maltreatment: Theory and research on the causes and consequences of child abuse and neglect.* New York: Cambridge University Press.

LYTTON, H. (1977). Do parents create, or respond to, differences in twins? *Developmental Psychology, 13,* 456–459.

LYTTON, H. (1980). *Parent–child interaction: The socialization process observed in twin and singleton families.* New York: Plenum.

LYTTON, H., & ROMNEY, D. M. (1991). Parents' sex-related differential socialization of boys and girls: A meta-analysis. *Psychological Bulletin, 109,* 267–296.

MACCOBY, E. E. (1978). *The two sexes: Growing up apart, coming together.* Cambridge, MA: Harvard University Press.

MACCOBY, E. E. (1990). Gender and relationships: A developmental account. *American Psychologist, 45,* 513–521.

MACCOBY, E. E. (1992). The role of parents in the socialization of children: An historical overview. *Developmental Psychology, 28,* 1006–1017.

MACCOBY, E. E. (1995). The two sexes and their social systems. In P. Moen, G. H. Elder, Jr., & K. Luscher (Eds.), *Examining lives in context: Perspectives on the ecology of human development.* Washington, DC: American Psychological Association.

MACCOBY, E. E. (1998). *The two sexes: Growing up apart, coming together.* Cambridge, MA: Harvard University Press.

MACCOBY, E. E., & JACKLIN, C. N. (1974). *The psychology of sex differences.* Stanford, CA: Stanford University Press.

MACCOBY, E. E., & JACKLIN, C. N. (1987). Gender segregation. In H. W. Reese (Ed.), *Advances in child development and behavior* (Vol. 20). Orlando, FL: Academic Press.

MACCOBY, E. E., & MARTIN, J. A. (1983). Socialization in the context of the family: Parent–child interaction. In E. M. Hetherington (Ed.), *Handbook of child psychology: Vol. 4. Socialization, personality, and social development.* New York: Wiley.

MACCOBY, E. E., BUCHANAN, C. M., MNOOKIN, R. H., & DORNBUSCH, S. M. (1993). Post-divorce roles of mothers and fathers in the lives of their children. *Journal of Family Psychology, 7,* 1–15.

MacDONALD, K. B. (1988a). The interfaces between sociobiology and developmental psychology. In K. B. MacDonald (Ed.), *Sociobiological perspectives on human development.* New York: Springer-Verlag.

MacDONALD, K. B. (1988b). *Social and personality development: An evolutionary synthesis.* New York: Plenum.

MacDONALD, K. B. (1988c). Sociobiology and the cognitive-developmental tradition in moral development research. In K. B. MacDonald (Ed.), *Sociobiological perspectives on human development.* New York: Springer-Verlag.

MacDONALD, K. B. (1992). Warmth as a developmental construct: An evolutionary analysis. *Child Development, 63,* 753–773.

MacDONALD, K., & PARKE, R. D. (1986). Parent-child physical play: The effects of sex and age of children and parents. *Sex Roles, 15,* 367–378.

MacFARLANE, A. (1975). Olfaction in the development of social preferences in the human neonate. In *Parent–infant interaction* (CIBA Foundation Symposium No. 33). Amsterdam: Elsevier.

MacFARLANE, A. (1987). *The culture of capitalism.* Oxford, England: Basil Blackwell.

MacKENZIE, B. (1984). Explaining race differences in IQ: The logic, the methodology, and the evidence. *American Psychologist, 39,* 1214–1233.

MacKINNON, C. E., STONEMAN, Z., & BRODY, G. H. (1984). The impact of maternal employment and family form on children's sex-role stereotypes and mothers' traditional attitudes. *Journal of Divorce, 8,* 51–60.

MacWHINNEY, B. (1987). The competition model. In B. MacWhinney (Ed.), *Mechanisms of language acquisition.* Hillsdale, NJ: Erlbaum.

MacWHINNEY, B. (1991). *The CHILDES project: Tools for analyzing talk.* Hillsdale, NJ: Erlbaum.

MacWHINNEY, B. (1998). Models of the emergence of language. *Annual Review of Psychology, 49,* 199–227.

MacWHINNEY, B., & BATES, E. (1993). *The crosslinguistic study of sentence processing.* Cambridge: Cambridge University Press.

MacWHINNEY, B., & CHANG, F. (1995). Connectionism and language learning. In C. A. Nelson (Ed.), *Minnesota symposia on child psychology: Vol. 28. Basic and applied perspectives on learning, cognition, and development.* Mahwah, NJ: Erlbaum.

MacWHINNEY, B., & LEINBACH, J. (1991). Implementations are not conceptualizations: Revising the verb learning model. *Cognition, 40,* 121–157.

MAGNUSSON, D., BERGMAN, L. R., RUDIGER, G., & TORESTAD, B. (Eds.). (1991). *Problems and methods in longitudinal research: Stability and change.* Cambridge: Cambridge University Press.

MAIN, M. (1990). Cross-cultural studies of attachment organization: Recent studies, changing methodologies, and the concept of conditional strategies. *Human Development, 33,* 48–61.

MAIN M., & GOLDWYN, R. (1998). Adult attachment rating and classification systems. In M. Main (Ed.), *Assessing attachment through discourse, drawings, and reunion situations.* New York: Cambridge University Press.

MAIN, M., & SOLOMON, J. (1986). Discovery of a disorganized/disoriented attachment pattern. In T. B. Brazelton & M. W. Yogman

(Eds.), *Affective development in infancy.* Norwood, NJ: Ablex.

MAIN M., & SOLOMON, J. (1990). Procedures for identifying infants as disorganized/disoriented during the Ainsworth Strange Situation. In M. Greenberg, D. Cicchetti, & M. Cummings (Eds.), *Attachment during the preschool years.* Chicago: University of Chicago Press.

MAIN M., KAPLAN, N., & CASSIDY, J. (1985). Security in infancy, childhood and adulthood: A move to the level of representation. In I. Bretherton & E. Waters (Eds.), Growing points of attachment theory and research. *Monographs of the Society for Research in Child Development, 50*(1–2, Serial No. 209).

MALATESTA, C. Z., CULVER, C., TESMAN, J. R., & SHEPARD, B. (1989). The development of emotion expression during the first two years of life. *Monographs of the Society for Research in Child Development, 54*(1–2, Serial No. 219).

MALATESTA, C. Z., GRIGORYEV, P., LAMB, C., ALBIN, M., & CULVER, C. (1986). Emotion socialization and expressive development in preterm and full term infants. *Child Development, 57,* 316–330.

MALATESTA, C. Z., & HAVILAND, J. M. (1982). Learning display rules: The socialization of emotion expression in infancy. *Child Development, 53,* 991–1003.

MALATESTA, C. Z., IZARD, C. E., & CAMRAS, L. (1991). Conceptualizing early infant affect: Emotions as fact, fiction, or artifact? In K. Strongman (Ed.), *International review of studies on emotion.* New York: Wiley.

MALINA, R. M. (1990). Physical growth and performance during the transitional years (9–16). In R. Montemayor, G. R. Adams, & T. Gullotta (Eds.), *From childhood to adolescence: Vol. 2. Advances in adolescent development.* London: Sage.

MANDEL, D., KEMLER NELSON, D. G., & JUSCZYK, P. W. (1996). Infants remember the order of words in a spoken sentence. *Cognitive Development, 11,* 181–196.

MANDLER, J. M. (1983). Representation. In P. H. Mussen (Series Ed.) & J. H. Flavell & E. M. Markman (Vol. Eds.), *Handbook of child psychology: Vol. 3. Cognitive development.* New York: Wiley.

MANDLER, J. M. (1990). Recall of events by preverbal children. In A. Diamond (Ed.), *The development and neural bases of higher cognitive functions.* New York: New York Academy of Sciences.

MANDLER, J. M. (1998). Representation. In W. Damon (Series Ed.) & D. Kuhn & R. S. Siegler (Vol. Eds.), *Handbook of child psychology: Vol. 2. Cognition, perception, and language* (5th ed.). New York: Wiley.

MANDOKI, M. W., SUMMER, G. S., HOFFMAN, R. P., & RICONDA, D. L. (1991). A review of Klinefelter's syndrome in children and adolescents. *Journal of the American Academy of Child and Adolescent Psychiatry, 30,* 167–172.

MANGELSDORF, S. C., PLUNKETT, J. W., DEDRICK, C. F., BERLIN, M., MEISELS, S. J., McHALE, J. L., & DICHTELLMILLER, M. (1996). Attachment security in very low birth weight infants. *Developmental Psychology, 32,* 914–920.

MANNLE, S., & TOMASELLO, M. (1987). Fathers, siblings, and the Bridge Hypothesis. In K. E. Nelson & A. VanKleeck (Eds.), *Children's language* (Vol. 6). Hillsdale, NJ: Erlbaum.

MARANTZ, S., & COATES, S. (1991). Mothers of boys with gender identity disorder: A comparison of matched controls. *Journal of the American Academy of Child and Adolescent Psychiatry, 30,* 310–315.

MARATSOS, M. (1976). *Language development: The acquisition of language structure.* Morristown, NJ: General Learning Press.

MARATSOS, M. (1983). Some current issues in the study of the acquisition of grammar. In P. H. Mussen (Series Ed.) & J. H. Flavell & E. M. Markman (Vol. Eds.), *Handbook of child psychology: Vol. 3. Cognitive development.* New York: Wiley.

MARATSOS, M. (1988). The acquisition of formal word classes. In Y. Levy, I. M. Schlesinger, & M. D. S. Braine (Eds.), *Categories and processes in language acquisition.* Hillsdale, NJ: Erlbaum.

MARATSOS, M. (1998). The acquisition of grammar. In W. Damon (Series Ed.) & D. Kuhn & R. S. Siegler (Vol. Eds.), *Handbook of child psychology: Vol. 2. Cognition, perception, and language* (5th ed.). New York: Wiley.

MARCOVITCH, S., GOLDBERG, S., GOLD, A., & WASHINGTON, J. (1997). Determinants of behavioural problems in Romanian children adopted in Ontario. *International Journal of Behavioral Development, 20,* 17–31.

MARCUS, G. F. (1996). Why do children say "breaked"? *Current Directions in Psychological Science, 5,* 81–85.

MARCUS, G. F., PINKER, S., ULLMAN, M., HOLLANDER, M., ROSEN, T. J., & XU, F. (1992). Overregularization in language acquisition. *Monographs of the Society for Research in Child Development, 57* (4, Serial No. 228).

MARINI, Z., & CASE, R. (1989). Parallels in the development of preschoolers' knowledge about their physical and social worlds. *Merrill-Palmer Quarterly, 35,* 63–87.

MARINI, Z., & CASE, R. (1994). The development of abstract reasoning about the physical and social world. *Child Development, 65,* 147–159.

MARKMAN, E. M. (1989). *Categorization and naming in children: Problems of induction.* Cambridge: MIT Press.

MARKMAN, E. M. (1991). The whole object, taxonomic, and mutual exclusivity assumptions as initial constraints on word meanings. In S. A. Gelman & J. P. Byrnes (Eds.), *Perspectives on language and thought: Interrelations in development.* Cambridge: Cambridge University Press.

MARKSTROM-ADAMS, C. (1989). Androgyny and its relation to adolescent psychosocial well-being: A review of the literature. *Sex Roles, 21,* 325–340.

MARKUS, H. R., CROSS, S., & WURF, E. (1990). The role of the self-system in competence. In R. J. Sternberg & J. Kolligan, Jr. (Eds.), *Competence considered.* New Haven: Yale University Press.

MARKUS, H. R., & KITAYAMA, S. (1991). Culture and self: Implications for cognition, emotion, and motivation. *Psychological Review, 98,* 224–253.

MARKUS, H. R., & NURIUS, P. S. (1984). Self-understanding and self-regulation in middle childhood. In W. A. Collins (Ed.), *Development during middle childhood: The years from six to twelve.* Washington, DC: National Academy Press.

MARSH, H. W. (1993). Academic self-concept: Theory, measurement, and research. In J. Suls (Ed.), *Psychological perspectives on the self* (Vol. 4). Hillsdale, NJ: Erlbaum.

MARSHALL, S. P. (1984). Sex differences in children's mathematics achievement: Solving computations and story problems. *Journal of Educational Psychology, 76,* 194–204.

MARTIN, C. L. (1990). Attitudes and expectations about children with nontraditional and traditional gender roles. *Sex Roles, 22,* 151–165.

MARTIN, C. L. (1993). New directions for investigating children's gender knowledge. *Developmental Review, 13,* 184–204.

MARTIN, C. L. (1994). Cognitive influences on the development and maintenance of gender segregation. In C. Leaper (Ed.). *New directions for child development: The development of gender relationships.* San Francisco: Jossey-Bass.

MARTIN, C. L., EISENBUD, L., & ROSE, H. (1995). Children's gender-based reasoning about toys. *Child Development, 66,* 1453–1471.

MARTIN, C. L., & HALVERSON, C. F. (1981). A schematic-processing model of sex typing and stereotyping in children. *Child Development, 52,* 1119–1134.

MARTIN, C. L., & HALVERSON, C. F. (1983). The effects of sex-typing schemas on young children's memory. *Child Development, 54,* 563–574.

MARTIN, C. L., & HALVERSON, C. F. (1987). The roles of cognition in sex role acquisition. In D. B. Carter (Ed.), *Current conceptions of sex roles and sex typing.* New York: Praeger.

MARTIN, C. L., & LITTLE, J. K. (1990). The relation of gender understanding to children's sex-typed preferences and gender stereotypes. *Child Development, 61,* 1427–1439.

MARTIN, C. L., WOOD, C. H., & LITTLE, J. K. (1990). The development of gender stereotype components. *Child Development, 61,* 1891–1904.

MARTIN, G. B., & CLARK, R. D. (1982). Distress crying in neonates: Species and peer specificity. *Developmental Psychology, 18,* 3–9.

MARTIN, J. A. (1981). A longitudinal study of the consequences of early mother-infant interaction: A microanalytic approach. *Monographs of the Society for Research in Child Development, 46*(3, Serial No. 190).

MARTIN, J. A., MACCOBY, E. E., & JACKLIN, C. N. (1981). Mothers' responsiveness to interactive bidding and nonbidding in boys and girls. *Child Development, 52,* 1064–1067.

MARTIN, T. R., & BRACKEN, M. B. (1986). Association of low birth weight with passive smoke exposure in pregnancy. *American Journal of Epidemiology, 124,* 633–642.

MARTINI, M. (1994). Peer interactions in Polynesia: A view from the Marquesas. In J. L. Roopnarine, J. E. Johnson, & F. H. Hooper (Eds.), *Children's play in diverse cultures.* Albany, NY: SUNY Press.

MARTORANO, S. C. (1977). A developmental analysis of performance on Piaget's formal operational tasks. *Developmental Psychology, 13,* 666–672.

MASATAKA, N. (1993). Effects of contingent and noncontingent maternal stimulation on the social behavior of three- to four-month-old Japanese infants. *Journal of Child Language, 20,* 303–312.

MASATAKA, N. (1996). Perception of motherese in a signed language by 6-month-old deaf infants. *Developmental Psychology, 32,* 874–879.

MASSEY, C. M., & GELMAN, R. (1988). Preschoolers' ability to decide whether a photographed unfamiliar object can move itself. *Developmental Psychology, 24,* 307–317.

MASTERS, J. C., FORD, M. E., AREND, R., GROTEVANT, H. D., & CLARK, L. V. (1979). Modeling and labeling as integrated determinants of children's sex-typed imitative behaviors. *Child Development, 50,* 364–371.

MASTERS, J. C., & FURMAN, W. (1981). Popularity, individual friendship selection, and specific peer interaction among children. *Developmental Psychology, 17,* 344–350.

MASTERS, M. S., & SANDERS, B. (1993). Is the gender difference in mental rotation disappearing? *Behavior Genetics, 23,* 337–341.

MASUR, E. F. (1982). Mothers' responses to infants' object-related gestures: Influences on lexical development. *Journal of Child Language, 9,* 23–30.

MATAS, L., AREND, R., & SROUFE, L. A. (1978). Continuity of adaptation in the second year: The relationship between quality of attachment and later competence. *Child Development, 49,* 547–556.

MATEFY, R. E., & ACKSEN, B. A. (1976). The effect of role-playing discrepant positions on change in moral judgments and attitudes. *Journal of Genetic Psychology, 128,* 189–200.

MATHENY, A. P., JR. (1986). Stability and change of infant temperament: Contributions from infant, mother, and family environment. In G. Kohnstamm (Ed.), *Temperament discussed.* Berwyn, PA: Swets North America.

MATHENY, A. P., JR. (1989). Children's behavioral inhibition over age and across situations: Genetic similarity for a trait during change. Long-term stability and change in personality [Special issue]. *Journal of Personality, 57,* 215–235.

MATSUMOTO, D., HAAN, N., YABROVE, G., THEODOROU, P., & CARNEY, C. C. (1986). Pre-schoolers' moral actions and emotions in Prisoner's Dilemma. *Developmental Psychology, 22,* 663–670.

MAURER, D., & SALAPATEK, P. (1976). Developmental changes in the scanning of faces by young infants. *Child Development, 47,* 523–527.

MAYER, N. K., & TRONICK, E. Z. (1985). Mothers' turn-giving signals and infant turn-taking in mother–infant interaction. In T. M. Field & N. A. Fox (Eds.), *Social perception in infants.* Norwood, NJ: Ablex.

MAYES, L. C. (1992). Prenatal cocaine exposure and young children's development. *Annals, AAPSS, 521,* 11–27.

MAYES, L. C., CARTER, A. S., & STUBBE, D. (1993). Individual differences in exploratory behavior in the second year of life. *Infant Behavior and Development, 16,* 269–284.

MAYNARD SMITH, J. (1976). Group selection. *Quarterly Review of Biology, 51,* 277–283.

MAZZELLA, C., DURKIN, K., CERINI, E., & BURALLI, P. (1992). Sex-role stereotyping in Australian television advertisements. *Sex Roles, 26,* 243–259.

McANINCH, C. B., MANOLIS, M. B., MILICH, R., & HARRIS, M. J. (1993). Impression formation in children: Influence of gender and expectancy. *Child Development, 64,* 1492–1506.

McBRIDE, S. (1990). Maternal modulators of child care: The role of maternal separation anxiety. In K. McCartney (Ed.), *New directions for child development: No. 49. Child care and maternal employment: A social ecology approach.* San Francisco: Jossey-Bass.

McBRIDE-CHANG, C. (1995). What is phonological awareness? *Journal of Educational Psychology, 87,* 179–192.

McCABE, A., & LIPSCOMB, T. J. (1988). Sex differences in children's verbal aggression. *Merrill-Palmer Quarterly, 34,* 389–401.

McCABE, A. E. (1989). Differential language learning styles in young children: The importance of context. *Developmental Review, 9,* 1–20.

McCALL, R. B. (1977). Challenges to a science of developmental psychology. *Child Development, 48,* 333–344.

McCALL, R. B. (1981). Early predictors of later IQ: The search continues. *Intelligence, 5,* 141–148.

McCALL, R. B. (1994). What process mediates predictions of childhood IQ from infant habituation and recognition memory? Speculations on the roles of inhibition and rate of information processing. *Intelligence, 18,* 107–125.

McCALL, R. B., APPLEBAUM, M. I., & HOGARTY, P. S. (1973). Developmental changes in mental performance. *Monographs of the Society for Research in Child Development, 38* (3, Serial No. 150).

McCALL, R. B., & CARRIGER, M. S. (1993). A meta-analysis of infant habituation and recognition memory as predictors of later IQ. *Child Development, 64,* 57–79.

McCALL, R. B., & MASH, C. W. (1994). Infant cognition and its relation to mature intelligence. In R. Vasta (Ed.), *Annals of child development* (Vol. 10). London: Kingsley.

McCARTNEY, K. (Ed.). (1990). *New directions for child development: No. 49. Child care and maternal employment: A social ecology approach.* San Francisco: Jossey-Bass.

McCARTNEY, K., & NELSON, K. (1981). Children's use of scripts in story recall. *Discourse Processes, 4,* 59–70.

McCORD, J., & TREMBLAY, R. E. (1992). *Preventing antisocial behavior: Interventions from birth through adolescence.* New York: Guilford.

McCORMICK, C. M., & WITELSON, S. F. (1991). A cognitive profile of homosexual men compared to heterosexual men and women. *Psychoneuroendocrinology, 16,* 459–473.

McCOY, E. (1988). Childhood through the ages. In R. Finsterbusch (Ed.), *Sociology 88/89.* Guildford, CT: Dushkin.

McCUNE-NICOLICH, L. (1981). The cognitive bases of relational words in the single word period. *Journal of Child Language, 8,* 15–34.

McDANIEL, D., McKEE, C., & CAIRNS, H. S. (Eds.). (1997). *Methods for assessing children's syntax.* Cambridge: MIT Press.

McDONALD, J. L. (1997). Language acquisition: The acquisition of linguistic structure in normal and special populations. *Annual Review of Psychology, 48,* 215–241.

McDONOUGH, L., & MANDLER, J. M. (1994). Very long-term recall in infants: Infantile amnesia reconsidered. *Memory, 2,* 339–352.

McEWEN, B. S. (1987). Observations on brain sexual differentiation: A biochemist's view. In J. M. Reinisch, L. A. Rosenblum, & S. A. Sanders (Eds.), *Masculinity/femininity: Basic properties.* New York: Oxford University Press.

McFAYDEN-KETCHUM, S. A., BATES, J. E., DODGE, K. A., & PETTIT, G. S. (1996). Patterns of change in early childhood aggressive-disruptive behavior: Gender differences in predictions from early coercive and affectionate mother-child interactions. *Child Development, 67,* 2417–2433.

McGEE, L. M., & RICHGELS, D. J. (1990). *Literacy's beginnings: Supporting young readers and writers.* Boston: Allyn & Bacon.

McGEE, M. G. (1982). Spatial abilities: The influence of genetic factors. In M. Potegal (Ed.), *Spatial abilities: Development and physiological foundations.* New York: Academic Press.

McGHEE, P. E., & FRUEH, T. (1980). Television viewing and the learning of sex-role stereotypes. *Sex Roles, 6,* 179–188.

McGILLICUDDY-DE LISI, A. V. (1988). Sex differences in parental teaching behaviors. *Merrill-Palmer Quarterly, 34,* 147–162.

McGLONE, J. (1980). Sex differences in human brain asymmetry: Critical survey. *Behavioral and Brain Sciences, 3,* 215–227.

McGRAW, M. B. (1935). *Growth: A study of Johnny and Jimmy.* New York: Appleton-Century-Crofts.

McGRAW, M. B. (1940). Suspension grasp behavior of the human infant. *American Journal of the Disabled Child, 60,* 799–811.

McGUE, M., BOUCHARD, T. J., JR., IACONO, W., & LYKKEN, D. T. (1993). Behavioral genetics of cognitive ability: A life-span perspective. In R. Plomin & G. McLearn (Eds.), *Nature, nurture, and psychology.* Washington, DC: American Psychological Association.

McGUE, M., BOUCHARD, T. J., JR., IACONO, W. G., & LYKKEN, D. T. (1993). Behavior genetics of cognitive ability: A life-span perspective. In R. Plomin & G. E. McClearn (Eds.), *Nature, nurture, and psychology.* Washington, DC: American Psychological Association.

McGUE, M., & LYKKEN, D. T. (1992). Genetic influences on risk of divorce. *Psychological Science, 3,* 368–373.

McHALE, S. M., BARTKO, W. T., CROUTER, A. C., & PERRY-JENKINS, M. (1990). Children's housework and psychosocial functioning: The mediating effects of parents' sex-role behaviors and attitudes. *Child Development, 61,* 1413–1426.

McKNIGHT, C. C., CROSSWHITE, F. J., DOSSEY, J. A., KIFER, E., SWAFFORD, J. O., TRAVERS, K. J., & COONEY, T. J. (1987). *The uderachieving curriculum: Assessing U.S. school mathematics from an international perspective.* Champaign, IL: Stipes.

McKUSICK, V. A. (1994). *Mendelian inheritance in man* (11th ed.). Baltimore: Johns Hopkins University Press.

McLANAHAN, S., & SANDEFUR, G. (1994). *Growing up with a single parent: What hurts, what helps?* Cambridge: Harvard University Press.

McLAUGHLIN, B., WHITE, D., McDEVITT, T., & RASKIN, R. (1983). Mothers' and fathers' speech to their young children: Similar or different? *Journal of Child Language, 10,* 245–252.

McLOYD, V. C. (1998). Poverty. In W. Damon (Ed.), *Handbook of child psychology: Vol 4. Child psychology in practice.* New York: Wiley.

McNEILL, D. (1992). *Hand and mind: What gestures reveal about thought.* Chicago: University of Chicago Press.

MEAD, M. (1935). *Sex and temperament in three primitive societies.* New York: William Morrow.

MEAD, M., & NEWTON, N. (1967). Cultural patterning of perinatal behavior. In S. A. Richardson & A. F. Guttmacher (Eds.), *Childbearing: Its social and psychological factors.* Baltimore: Williams & Wilkins.

MEBERT, C. J. (1989). Stability and change in parents' perceptions of infant temperament: Early pregnancy to 13.5 months postpartum. *Infant Behavior and Development, 2,* 237–244.

MEBERT, C. J. (1991). Dimensions of subjectivity in parents' ratings of infant temperament. *Child Development, 62,* 352–361.

MEDOFF-COOPER, B., CAREY, W. B., & McDEVITT, S. C. (1993). The Early Infancy Temperament Questionnaire. *Journal of Developmental and Behavioral Pediatrics, 14,* 230–235.

MEDRICH, E. A., ROIZEN, J. A., RUBIN, V., & BUCKLEY, S. (1982). *The serious business of growing up: A study of children's lives outside school.* Berkeley: University of California Press.

MEHLER, J., BERTONCINI, J., BARRIERE, M., & JASSIK-GERSHENFELD, D. (1978). Infant recognition of mother's voice. *Perception, 7,* 491–497.

MEHLER, J., JUSCZYK, P. W., LAMBERTZ, G., HALSTED, N., BERTONCINI, J., & AMIEL-TISON, C. (1988). A precursor of language acquisition in young infants. *Cognition, 29,* 143–178.

MEICHENBAUM, D., & GOODMAN, S. (1979). Clinical use of private speech and critical questions about its study in natural settings. In G. Zivin (Ed.), *The development of self-regulation through private speech.* New York: Wiley.

MEIER, R. P., & NEWPORT, E. L. (1990). Out of the hands of babes: On a possible sign advantage in language acquisition. *Language, 66,* 1–23.

MELOT, A.-M., & CORROYER, D. (1992). Organization of metacognitive knowledge: A condition for strategy use in memorization. *European Journal of Psychology of Education, 7,* 23–38.

MELTZOFF, A. N. (1988a). Infant imitation after a 1-week delay: Long-term memory for novel and multiple stimuli. *Developmental Psychology, 24,* 470–476.

MELTZOFF, A. N. (1988b). Infant imitation and memory: Nine-month-olds in immediate and deferred tests. *Child Development, 59,* 217–225.

MELTZOFF, A. N. (1990). Foundations for developing a concept of self: The role of imitation in relating self to other and the value of social mirroring, social modeling, and self practice in infancy. In D. Cicchetti & M. Beeghly (Eds.), *The self in transition: Infancy to childhood.* Chicago: University of Chicago Press.

MELTZOFF, A. N., & BORTON, R. W. (1979). Intermodal matching by human neonates. *Nature, 282,* 403–404.

MELTZOFF, A. N., & MOORE, M. K. (1977). Imitation of facial and manual gestures by human neonates. *Science, 198,* 75–78.

MELTZOFF, A. N., & MOORE, M. K. (1983). Newborn infants imitate adult facial gestures. *Child Development, 54,* 702–709.

MELTZOFF, A. N., & MOORE, M. K. (1985). Cognitive foundations and social functions of imitation and intermodal representation in infancy. In J. Mehler & R. Fox (Eds.), *Neonate cognition: Beyond the blooming buzzing confusion.* Hillsdale, NJ: Erlbaum.

MELTZOFF, A. N., & MOORE, M. K. (1989). Imitation in newborn infants: Exploring the range of gestures imitated and the underlying mechanisms. *Developmental Psychology, 25,* 954–962.

MELTZOFF, A. N., & MOORE, M. K. (1994). Imitation, memory, and the representation of persons. *Infant Behavior and Development, 17,* 83–99.

MELTZOFF, A. N., & MOORE, M. K. (1995). A theory of the role of imitation in the emergence of self. In P. Rochat (Ed.), *The self in infancy: Theory and research.* Amsterdam: Elsevier.

MENARD, S. (1991). *Longitudinal research.* Newbury Park, CA: Sage.

MENDELSON, M. J. (1990). *Becoming a brother.* Cambridge: MIT Press.

MENIG-PETERSON, C. L. (1975). The modification of communicative behaviors in preschool-aged children as a function of the listener's perspective. *Child Development, 46,* 1015–1018.

MEREDITH, H. V. (1963). Change in the stature and body weight of North American boys during the last 80 years. In L. P. Lipsitt & C. C. Spiker (Eds.), *Advances in child development and behavior* (Vol. 1). New York: Academic Press.

MERRIMAN, W. E. (1997). CALLED: A model of early word learning. In R. Vasta (Ed.), *Annals of child development* (Vol. 13). London: Kingsley.

MERVIS, C. B. (1987). Child-basic object categories and early lexical development. In U. Neisser (Ed.), *Concepts and conceptual development: Ecological and intellectual factors in categorization.* New York: Cambridge University Press.

MESSER, D. J. (1980). The episodic structure of maternal speech to young children. *Journal of Child Language, 7,* 29–40.

MESSER, D. J., McCARTHY, M. E., McQUISTON, S., MacTURK, R. H., YARROW, L. J., & VIETZE, P. M. (1986). Relation between mastery motivation in infancy and competence in early childhood. *Developmental Psychology, 22,* 366–372.

METTETAL, G. (1983). Fantasy, gossip, and self-disclosure: Children's conversations with friends. In R. N. Bostrom (Ed.), *Communication yearbook* (Vol. 7). Beverly Hills, CA: Sage.

MEYER-BAHLBERG, H. F. L. (1993). Psychobiologic research on homosexuality. *Child and Adolescent Psychiatric Clinics of North America, 2,* 489–500.

MEYER-BAHLBERG, H. F. L., EHRHARDT, A. A., ROSEN, L. R., GRUEN, R. S., VERIDIANO, N. P., VANN, F. H., & NEUWALDER, H. F. (1995). Prenatal estrogens and the development of homosexual orientation. *Developmental Psychology, 31,* 12–21.

MICHAEL, J. (1984). Verbal behavior. *Journal of the Experimental Analysis of Behavior, 42,* 363–376.

MIDGLEY, C., FELDLAUFER, H., & ECCLES, J. (1988a). Student/teacher relations and attitudes towards mathematics before and after the transition to junior high school. *Child Development, 60,* 375–395.

MIDGLEY, C., FELDLAUFER, H., & ECCLES, J. (1988b). The transition to junior high school: Beliefs of pre- and post-transition teachers. *Journal of Youth and Adolescence, 17,* 543–562.

MIDLARSKY, E., & HANNAH, M. E. (1985). Competence, reticence, and helping by children and adolescents. *Developmental psychology, 21,* 534–541.

MILLER, L. T., & VERNON, P. A. (1997). Developmental changes in speed of information processing in young children. *Developmental Psychology, 23,* 549–554.

MILLER, N., & MARUYAMA, G. (1976). Ordinal position and peer popularity. *Journal of Personality and Social Psychology, 33,* 123–131.

MILLER, P. A., EISENBERG, N., FABES, R. A., & SHELL, R. (1996). Relations of moral reasoning and vicarious emotion to young children's prosocial behavior toward peers and adults. *Developmental Psychology, 32,* 210–219.

MILLER, P. H. (1990). The development of strategies of selective attention. In D. F. Bjorklund (Ed.), *Children's strategies: Contemporary views of cognitive development.* Hillsdale, NJ: Erlbaum.

MILLER, P. H. (1993). *Theories of developmental psychology* (3rd ed.). New York: W. H. Freeman.

MILLER, P. H., & DeMARIE-DREBLOW, D. (1990). Social-cognitive correlates of children's understanding of displaced aggression. *Journal of Experimental Child Psychology, 49,* 488–504.

MILLER, P. H., & SEIER, W. L. (1994). Strategy utilization deficiencies in children: When, where, and why? In H. W. Reese (Ed.), *Advances in child development and behavior* (Vol. 25). New York: Academic Press.

MILLER, P. J. (1994). Narrative practices: Their role in socialization and self-construction. In U. Neisser & R. Fivush (Eds.), *The remembering self: Construction and accuracy in the self-narrative.* New York: Cambridge University Press.

MILLER, P. M., DANAHER, D. L., & FORBES, D. (1986). Sex-related strategies for coping with interpersonal conflict in children aged five to seven. *Developmental Psychology, 22,* 543–548.

MILLER, S. A. (1976). Nonverbal assessment of Piagetian concepts. *Psychological Bulletin, 83,* 405–430.

MILLER, S. A. (1982). Cognitive development: A Piagetian perspective. In R. Vasta (Ed.), *Strategies and techniques of child study.* New York: Aca-demic Press.

MILLER, S. A. (1986). Certainty and necessity in the understanding of Piagetian concepts. *Developmental Psychology, 22,* 3–18.

MILLER, S. A. (1998). *Developmental research methods* (2nd ed.). Englewood Cliffs, NJ: Prentice-Hall.

MILLER, S. A., & DAVIS, T. L. (1992). Beliefs about children: A comparative study of mothers, teachers, peers, and self. *Child Development, 63,* 1251–1265.

MILLER, S. A., SHELTON, J., & FLAVELL, J. H. (1970). A test of Luria's hypotheses concerning the development of verbal self-regulation. *Child Development, 41,* 651–665.

MILLS, R. S. L., & GRUSEC, J. E. (1988). Socialization from the perspective of the parent–child relationship. In S. Duck (Ed.), *Handbook of personal relationships.* Chichester, England: Wiley.

MILLS, R. S. L., & GRUSEC, J. E. (1989). Cognitive, affective, and behavioral consequences of praising altruism. *Merrill-Palmer Quarterly, 35,* 299–326.

MINDE, K. (1993). Prematurity and illness in infancy: Implications for development and intervention. In C. H. Zeanah, Jr. (Ed.), *Handbook of infant mental development.* New York: Guilford.

MINUCHIN, P. (1985). Families and individual development: Provocations from the field of family therapy. *Child Development, 56,* 289–302.

MISCHEL, W., SHODA, Y., & PEAKE, P. K. (1988). The nature of adolescent competencies predicted by preschool delay of gratification. *Journal of Personality and Social Psychology, 54,* 687–696.

MISCHEL, W., SHODA, Y., & RODRIGUEZ, M. L. (1989). Delay of gratification in children. *Science, 244,* 933–938.

MITCHELL, P. (1996). *Introduction to theory of mind.* New York: Arnold.

MITZENHEIM, P. (1985). The importance of Rousseau's developmental thinking for child psychology. In G. Eckardt, W. G. Bringmann, & L. Sprung (Eds.), *Contributions to a history of developmental psychology.* Berlin: Mouton.

MIYAKE, K., CHEN, S. J., & CAMPOS, J. J. (1985). Infant temperament, mother's mode of interaction, and attachment in Japan: An interim report. In I. Bretherton & E. Waters (Eds.), Growing points of attachment theory and research. *Monographs of the Society for Research in Child Development, 50*(1–2, Serial No. 209).

MIYAWAKI, K., STRANGE, W., VERBRUGGE, R., LIBERMAN, A. M., JENKINS, J. J., & FUJIMURA, O. (1975). An effect of linguistic experience: The discrimination of the [r] and [l] by native speakers of Japanese and English. *Perception and Psychophysics, 18,* 331–340.

MIZE, J., & LADD, G. W. (1990). A cognitive-social learning approach to social skill training with low-status preschool children. *Developmental Psychology, 26,* 388–397.

MODGIL, S., & MODGIL, C. (1976). *Piagetian research: Compilation and commentary* (Vols. 1–8). Windsor, England: NFER.

MOELY, B. E., HART, S. S., SANTULLI, K. A., LEAL, L., JOHNSON, T., RAO, N., & BURNEY, L. (1986). How do teachers teach memory skills? *Educational Psychologist, 21,* 55–71.

MOELY, B. E., SANTULLI, K. A., & OBACH, M. S. (1995). Strategy instruction, metacognition, and motivation in the elementary school classroom. In F. E. Weinert & W. Schneider (Eds.), *Memory performance and competencies: Issues in growth and development.* Mahwah, NJ: Erlbaum.

MOEN, P., ELDER, G. H., JR., LUSCHER, K. (Eds.). (1995). *Examining lives in context: Perspectives on the ecology of human development.* Washington, DC: American Psychological Association.

MOERK, E. L. (1996). Input and learning processes in first language acquisition. In H. W. Reese (Ed.), *Advances in child development and behavior* (Vol. 26). San Diego: Academic Press.

MOFFITT, A. R. (1973). Intensity discrimination and cardiac reaction in young infants. *Developmental Psychology, 8,* 357–359.

MOFFITT, T. E., CASPI, A., HARKNESS, A. R., & SILVA, P. A. (1993). The natural history of change in intellectual performance: Who changes? How much? Is it meaningful? *Journal of Child Psychology and Psychiatry and Allied Disciplines, 34,* 455–506.

MOLFESE, D. L., & MOLFESE, V. J. (1979). Hemispheric and stimulus differences as reflected in the cortical responses of newborn infants to speech stimuli. *Developmental Psychology, 15,* 505–511.

MOLFESE, D. L., & SEGALOWITZ, S. J. (1989). *Brain lateralization in children: Developmental implications.* New York: Guilford.

MOLLER, L. C., & SERBIN, L. A. (1996). Antecedents of toddler gender segregation: Cognitive consonance, gender-typed toy preferences and behavioral compatibility. *Sex Roles, 26,* 331–353.

MONAHAN, S. C., BUCHANAN, C. M., MACCOBY, E. E., & DORNBUSCH, S. M. (1993). Sibling differences in divorced families. *Child Development, 64,* 152–168.

MONEY, J. (1975). Ablatio penis: Normal male infant sex-reassigned as a girl. *Archives of Sexual Behavior, 4,* 65–71.

MONEY, J. (1991). *Biographies of gender and hermaphroditism in paired comparisons.* Amsterdam: Elsevier.

MONEY, J. (1993). *The Adam principle. Genes, genitals, hormones, and gender: Selected readings in sexology.* Buffalo, NY: Prometheus Books.

MONEY, J. (1994). The concept of gender identity disorder in childhood and adolescence after 39 years. *Journal of Sex and Marital Therapy, 20,* 163–177.

MONEY, J. C., & ANNECILLO, C. (1987). Crucial period effect in psychoendocrinology: Two syndromes, abuse dwarfism and female (CVAH) hermaphroditism. In M. H. Bornstein (Ed.), *Sensitive periods in development: Interdisciplinary perspectives.* Hillsdale, NJ: Erlbaum.

MONEY, J., DEVORE, H., & NORMAN, B. F. (1986). Gender identity and gender transposition: Longitudinal outcome study of 32 male hermaphrodites assigned as girls. *Journal of Sex and Marital Therapy, 12,* 165–181.

MONEY, J. C., & EHRHARDT, A. A. (1972). *Man and woman, boy and girl.* Baltimore: Johns Hopkins University Press.

MONTAGUE, M. F. A. (1968). *Man and aggression.* New York: Oxford University Press.

MONTEMAYOR, R. (1974). Children's performance in a game and their attraction to it as a function of sex-typed labels. *Child Development, 45,* 152–156.

MONTGOMERY, D. E. (1993). Young children's understanding of interpretive diversity between different-age listeners. *Developmental Psychology, 29,* 337–345.

MOON, C., COOPER, R. P., & FIFER, W. P. (1993). Two-day-olds prefer their native language. *Infant Behavior and Development, 16,* 495–500.

MOORE, B. S., & EISENBERG, N. (1984). The development of altruism. In G. J. Whitehurst (Ed.), *Annals of child development* (Vol. 1). Greenwich, CT: JAI Press.

MOORE, L., HUGHES, J., & ROBINSON, M. (1992). A comparison of the social information-processing abilities of rejected and accepted hyperactive children. *Journal of Clinical Child Psychology, 21,* 123–131.

MORAN, G. F., & VINOVSKIS, M. A. (1985). The great care of godly parents: Early childhood in Puritan New England. In A. B. Smuts & J. W. Hagen (Eds.), History and research in child development. *Monographs of the Society for Research in Child Development, 50*(4–5, Serial No. 211).

MORAN, J. D., III, & McCULLERS, J. C. (1984). The effects of recency and story content on children's moral judgments. *Journal of Experimental Child Psychology, 38,* 447–455.

MORELL, V. (1993). The puzzle of the triple repeats. *Science, 260,* 1422–1423.

MORELLI, G., ROGOFF, B., OPPENHEIM, D., & GOLDSMITH, D. (1992). Cultural variations in infants' sleeping arrangements: Questions of independence. *Developmental Psychology, 28,* 604–613.

MORETTI, M. M., & HIGGINS, E. T. (1990). The development of self-esteem vulnerabilities: Social and cognitive factors in developmental psychopathology. In R. J. Sternberg & J. Kolligian, Jr. (Eds.), *Competence considered.* New Haven, CT: Yale University Press.

MORGAN, B., & GIBSON, K. R. (1991). Nutritional and environmental interactions in brain development. In K. R. Gibson and A. C. Petersen (Eds.), *Brain maturation and cognitive development.* New York: Aldine de Gruyter.

MORGAN, J. L. (1986). *From simple input to complex grammar.* Cambridge: MIT Press.

MORGAN, J. L., BONAMO, K. M., & TRAVIS, L. L. (1995). Negative evidence on negative evidence. *Developmental Psychology, 31,*180–197.

MORGANE, P. J., AUSTIN-LaFRANCE, R., BRONZINO, J., TONKISS, J., DIÁZ-CINTRA, S., CINTRA, L., KEMPER, T., & GALLER, J. R. (1993). Prenatal malnutrition and development of the brain. *Neuroscience and Biobehavioral Reviews, 17,* 91–128.

MORO, E. (1918). Das erste Trimenon. *Munch. med. Wschr., 65,* 1147–1150.

MORRISON, F. J., GRIFFITH, E. M., & ALBERTS, D. M. (1997). Nature–nurture in the classroom: Entrance age, school readiness, and learning in children. *Developmental Psychology, 33,* 254–262.

MORRISON, F. J., SMITH, L., & DOW-EHRENSBERGER, M. (1995). Education and cognitive development: A natural experiment. *Developmental Psychology, 31,* 789–799.

MORRISON, H., & KUHN, D. (1983). Cognitive aspects of preschoolers' peer imitation in a play situation. *Child Development, 54,* 1054–1063.

MORRONGIELLO, B. A. (1988). Infants' localization of sounds along two spatial dimensions: Horizontal and vertical axes. *Infant Behavior and Development, 11,* 127–143.

MORRONGIELLO, B. A. (1994). Effects of colocation on auditory-visual interactions and cross-modal perception in infants. In D. J. Lewkowicz & R. Lickliter (Eds.), *The development of intersensory perception: Comparative perspectives.* Hillsdale, NJ: Erlbaum.

MORRONGIELLO, B. A., FENWICK, K. D., HILLIER, L., & CHANCE, G. (1994). Sound localization in newborn human infants. *Developmental Psychobiology, 27,* 519–538.

MOSHMAN, D. (1998). Cognitive development beyond childhood. In W. Damon (Series Ed.) & D. Kuhn & R. S. Siegler (Vol. Eds.), *Handbook of child psychology: Vol. 2. Cognition, perception, and language* (5th ed.). New York: Wiley.

MOUNTEER, C. A. (1987). Roman childhood, 200 B.C. to A.D. 600. *Journal of Psychohistory, 14,* 233–254.

MOUNTS, N. S., & STEINBERG, L. (1995). An ecological analysis of peer influence on adolescent grade point average and drug use. *Developmental Psychology, 31,* 915–922.

MRAZEK, P. J. (1993). Maltreatment and infant development. In C. H. Zeanah, Jr. (Ed.), *Handbook of infant mental development.* New York: Guilford.

MUELLER, C. (1996). Multidisciplinary research of multimodal stimulation of premature infants: An integrative review of the literature. *Maternal-Child Nursing Journal, 24,* 18–31.

MUELLER, E., & SILVERMAN, N. (1989). Peer relations in maltreated children. In D. Cicchetti & V. Carlson (Eds.), *Child maltreatment: Theory and research on the causes and consequences of child abuse and neglect.* New York: Cambridge University Press.

MUELLER, W. H. (1986). The genetics of size and shape in children and adults. In F. Falkner & J. M. Tanner (Eds.), *Human growth: A comprehensive treatise* (2nd ed., Vol. 3). New York: Plenum.

MUIR, D., & CLIFTON, R. K. (1985). Infants' orientation to the location of sound sources. In G. Gottlieb & N. A. Krasnegor (Eds.), *Measurement of audition and vision in the first year of postnatal life: A methodological overview.* Norwood, NJ: Ablex.

MULLEN, M. K. (1994). Earliest recollections of childhood: A demographic analysis. *Cognition, 52,* 55–79.

MULLEN, M. K., & YI, S. (1995). The cultural context of talk about the past: Implications for the development of autobiographical memory. *Cognitive Development, 10,* 407–419.

MUMME, D. L., FERNALD, A., & HERRERA, C. (1996). Infants' responses to facial and vocal emotional signals in a social referencing paradigm. *Child Development, 67,* 3219–3237.

MUNAKATA, Y., McCLELLAND, J. L., JOHNSON, M. H., & SIEGLER, R. S. (1997). Rethinking infant knowledge: Toward an adaptive process account of successes and failures in object permanence tasks. *Psychological Review, 104,* 686–713.

MUNRO, D. J. (1977). *The concept of man in contemporary China.* Ann Arbor: University of Michigan Press.

MUNROE, R. H., SHIMMIN, H. S., & MUNROE, R. L. (1984). Gender understanding and sex role preference in four cultures. *Developmental Psychology, 20,* 673–682.

MURATA, P. J., McGLYNN, E. A., SIU, A. L., & BROOK, R. H. (1992). *Prenatal care.* Santa Monica, CA: Rand.

MURPHEY, D. A. (1992). Constructing the child: Relations between parents' beliefs and child outcomes. *Developmental Review, 12,* 199–232.

MURRAY, A. D., JOHNSON, J., & PETERS, J. (1990). Fine-tuning of utterance length to preverbal infants: Effects on later language development. *Journal of Child Language, 17,* 511–525.

MURRAY, F. B. (1982). Learning and development through social interaction and conflict: A challenge to social learning theory. In L. Liben (Ed.), *Piaget and the foundation of knowledge.* Hillsdale, NJ: Erlbaum.

MURRAY, L., FIORI-COWLEY, A., HOOPER, R., & COOPER, P. (1996). The impact of postnatal depression and associated adversity on early mother-infant interactions and later outcome. *Child Development, 67,* 2512–2526.

MWAMWENDA, T. S. (1992). Cognitive development in African children. *Genetic, Social, and General Psychology Monographs, 118,* 5–72.

MYERS, B. J. (1987). Mother–infant bonding as a critical period. In M. H. Bornstein (Ed.), *Sensitive periods in development: Interdisciplinary perspectives.* Hillsdale, NJ: Erlbaum.

NADEL, J., & FONTAINE, A. (1989). Communicating by imitation: A developmental and comparative approach to transitory social competence. In B. H. Schneider, G. Attili, J. Nadel, & R. P. Weissberg (Eds.), *Social competence in developmental perspective.* Dordrecht, Netherlands: Kluwer.

NAEYE, R. L., DIENER, M. M., & DELLINGER, W. S. (1969). Urban poverty: Effects on prenatal nutrition. *Science, 166,* 1026.

NAIGLES, L. G., & GELMAN, S. A. (1995). Overextensions in comprehension and production revisited: Preferential-looking in a study of dog, cat, and cow. *Journal of Child Language, 22,* 19–46.

NAKAHARA, T., UOZUMI, T., MONDEN, S., MUTTAGIN, Z., KURISU, K., ARITA, K., KUWABARA, S., OHAMA, K., KUMAGAI, M., & NAKAHARA, K. (1993). Prenatal diagnosis of open spina bifida by MRI and ultrasonography. *Brain and Development, 15,* 75–78.

NATHANIELSZ, P. W. (1995). The role of basic science in preventing low birth weight. *The future of children* (Vol. 5, No. 1). Los Angeles: Packard Foundation.

NATIONAL INSTITUTES OF HEALTH. (1993). The human genome: A race to the 3 billionth base. *Journal of NIH Research, 5,* 44.

NEEDHAM, J. (1959). *A history of embryology.* Cambridge: Cambridge University Press.

NEEDLEMAN, H. L., SCHELL, A. S., BELLINGER, D., LEVITON, A., & ALLDRED, E. N. (1990). The long-term effects of exposure to low doses of lead in childhood: An 11-year follow-up report. *New England Journal of Medicine, 322,* 83.

NEISSER, U. (Ed.). (1993). *Ecological and interpersonal knowledge of self.* New York: Cambridge University Press.

NEISSER, U. (1995). Criteria for an ecological self. In P. Rochat (Ed.), *The self in infancy: Theory and research.* Amsterdam: Elsevier.

NEISSER, U., BOODOO, G., BOUCHARD, T. J., JR., BOYKIN, A. W., BRODY, N., CECI, S. J., HALPERN, D. F., LOEHLIN, J. C., PERLOFF, R., STERNBERG, R. J., & URBINA, S. (1996). Intelligence: Knowns and unknowns. *American Psychologist, 51,* 77–101.

NELSON, C. A. (1987). The recognition of facial expressions in the first two years of life: Mechanisms of development. *Child Development, 58,* 889–909.

NELSON, C. A., & HOROWITZ, F. D. (1987). Visual motion perception in infancy: A review and synthesis. In P. Salapatek & L. Cohen (Eds.), *Handbook of infant perception: Vol. 2. From perception to cognition.* New York: Academic Press.

NELSON, K. (1973). Structure and strategy in learning to talk. *Monographs of the Society for Research in Child Development, 38*(1–2, Serial No. 149).

NELSON, K. (1985). *Making sense: The acquisition of shared meaning.* Orlando, FL: Academic Press.

NELSON, K. (1986). *Event knowledge: Structure and function in development.* Hillsdale, NJ: Erlbaum.

NELSON, K. (1988). Constraints on word learning? *Cognitive Development, 3,* 221–246.

NELSON, K. (1993a). Events, narratives, memory: What develops? In C. A. Nelson (Ed.), *Minnesota symposia on child psychology: Vol. 26. Memory and affect in development.* Hillsdale, NJ: Erlbaum.

NELSON, K. (1993b). The psychological and social origins of autobiographical memory. *Psychological Science, 4,* 7–14.

NELSON, K. (1996). *Language in cognitive development.* New York: Cambridge University Press.

NELSON, K., HAMPSON, J., & SHAW, L. K. (1993). Nouns in early lexicons: Evidence, explanations, and implications. *Journal of Child Language, 20,* 61–84.

NELSON, S. A. (1980). Factors influencing young children's use of motives and outcomes as moral criteria. *Child Development, 51,* 823–829.

NELSON, S. A., & DWECK, C. S. (1977). Motivation and competence as determinants of young children's reward allocation. *Developmental Psychology, 13,* 192–197.

NEVILLE, B., & PARKE, R. D. (1997). Waiting for paternity: Interpersonal and contextual implications of the timing of fatherhood. *Sex Roles, 37,* 45–59.

NEWCOMB, A. F., & BAGWELL, C. L. (1995). Children's friendship relations: A meta-analytic review. *Psychological Bulletin, 117,* 306–347.

NEWCOMB, A. F., BUKOWSKI, W. M., & PATTEE, L. (1993). Children's peer relations: A meta-analytic review of popular, rejected, neglected, controversial, and average sociometric status. *Psychological Bulletin, 113,* 99–128.

NEWCOMBE, N. (1989). The development of spatial perspective taking. In H. W. Reese (Ed.), *Advances in child development and behavior* (Vol. 22). San Diego: Academic Press.

NEWCOMBE, N., & DUBAS, J. S. (1992). A longitudinal study of predictors of spatial ability in adolescent females. *Child Development, 63,* 37–46.

NEWCOMER, S., & UDRY, J. R. (1987). Parental marital status effects on adolescent sexual behavior. *Journal of Marriage and the Family, 48,* 235–240.

NEWMAN, D. L., CASPI, A., MOFFITT, T. E., & SILVA, P. A. (1997). Antecedents of adult interpersonal functioning: Effects of individual differences in age 3 temperament. *Developmental Psychology, 33,* 206–217.

NEWMAN, P. R. (1982). The peer group. In B. B. Wolman (Ed.), *Handbook of developmental psychology.* Engelwood Cliffs, NJ: Prentice-Hall.

NEWPORT, E. L. (1977). Motherese: The speech of mothers to young children. In N. J. Castellan, D. B. Pisoni, & G. Potts (Eds.), *Cognitive theory* (Vol. 2). Hillsdale, NJ: Erlbaum.

NEWPORT, E. L. (1991). Contrasting concepts of the critical period for language. In S. Carey & R. Gelman (Eds.), *The epigenesis of mind: Essays on biology and cognition.* Hillsdale, NJ: Erlbaum.

NICHD EARLY CHILD CARE RESEARCH NETWORK. (1997a). Child care in the first year of life. *Merrill-Palmer Quarterly, 43,* 340–360.

NICHD EARLY CHILD CARE RESEARCH NETWORK. (1997b). The effects of infant child care on infant-mother attachment security: Results of the NICHD study of early child care. *Child Development, 68,* 860–879.

NICHOLS, R. C. (1978). Heredity and environment: Major findings from twin studies of ability, personality, and interests. *Homo, 29,* 158–173.

NINIO, A. (1992). The relation of children's single-word utterances to single-word utterances in the input. *Journal of Child Language, 19,* 87–110.

NINIO, A., & BRUNER, J. (1978). The achievement and antecedents of labeling. *Journal of Child Language, 5,* 1–15.

NINIO, A., & SNOW, C. E. (1988). Language acquisition through language use: The functional sources of children's early utterances. In Y. Levy, I. M. Schlesinger, & M. D. S. Braine (Eds.), *Categories and processes in language acquisition.* Hillsdale, NJ: Erlbaum.

NINIO, A., & SNOW, C. E. (1996). *Pragmatic development.* Boulder, Co: Westview Press.

NINIO, A., & WHEELER, P. (1984). Functions of speech in mother–infant interaction. In L. Feagans, C. Garvey, & R. Golinkoff (Eds.), *The origins and growth of communication.* Norwood, NJ: Ablex.

NISAN, M. (1984). Distributive justice and social norms. *Child Development, 55,* 1020–1029.

NOLEN-HOEKSEMA, S., GIRGUS, J. S., & SELIGMAN, M. E. P. (1986). Learned helplessness in children: A longitudinal study of depression, achievement, and explanatory style. *Journal of Personality and Social Psychology, 51,* 435–442.

NORCINI, J. J., & SNYDER, S. S. (1986). Effects of modeling and cognitive induction on moral reasoning. In G. L. Sapp (Ed.), *Handbook of moral development: Models, processes, techniques, and research.* Birmingham, AL: Religious Education Press.

NOTTLEMAN, E. D. (1987). Competence and self-esteem during transition from childhood to adolescence. *Developmental Psychology, 23,* 441–450.

NOVICK, N., CAUCE, A. M., & GROVE, K. (1996). Competence self-concept. In B. A. Bracken (Ed.), *Handbook of self-concept: Developmental, social, and clinical considerations.* New York: Wiley.

NUNES, T., CARRAHER, D. W., & SCHLIEMANN, A. D. (1993). *Street mathematics and school mathematics.* New York: Cambridge University Press.

NUNNALLY, J. C. (1982). The study of human change: Measurement, research strategies, and methods of analysis. In B. B. Wolman (Ed.), *Handbook of developmental psychology.* Englewood Cliffs, NJ: Prentice Hall.

NUNNER-WINKLER, G., & SODIAN, B. (1988). Children's understanding of moral emotions. *Child Development, 59,* 1323–1338.

NYITI, R. M. (1982). The validity of "cultural differences explanations" for cross-cultural variation in the rate of Piagetian cognitive development. In D. A. Wagner & H. W. Stevenson (Eds.), *Cultural perspectives on child development.* San Francisco: W. H. Freeman.

OAKES, L. M., & COHEN, L. B. (1995). Infant causal perception. In C. K. Rovee-Collier & L. P. Lipsitt (Eds.), *Advances in infancy research* (Vol. 9). Norwood, NJ: Ablex.

O'BRIEN, M., & HUSTON, A. C. (1985). Development of sex-typed play behavior in toddlers. *Developmental Psychology, 21,* 866–871.

O'BRIEN, M., & NAGLE, K. (1987). Parents' speech to toddlers: The effect of play context. *Journal of Child Language, 14,* 269–279.

OCHS, E. (1982). Talking to children in western Samoa. *Language in Society, 11,* 77–104.

O'CONNOR, B. (1993). The home birth movement in the United States. *The Journal of Medicine and Philosophy, 18,* 147–174.

O'CONNOR, R. D. (1969). Modification of social withdrawal through symbolic modeling. *Journal of Applied Behavior Analysis, 2,* 15–22.

O'CONNOR, R. D. (1972). Relative efficacy of modeling, shaping, and the combined procedures for modification of social withdrawal. *Journal of Abnormal Psychology, 79,* 327–334.

ODOM, S. L., & STRAIN, P. S. (1984). Peer-mediated approaches to promoting children's social interaction: A review. *American Journal of Orthopsychiatry, 54,* 544–557.

OEHLER, J. M., & ECKERMAN, C. D. (1988). Regulatory effects of human speech and touch in premature infants prior to term age. *Infant Behavior and Development, 11,* 249.

OHLENDORF-MOFFAT, P. (1991, February). Surgery before birth. *Discover,* pp. 59–65.

OLLER, D. K., & EILERS, R. E. (1982). Similarity of babbling in Spanish- and English-learning babies. *Journal of Child Language, 9,* 565–577.

OLLER, D. K., & EILERS, R. E. (1988). The role of audition in infant babbling. *Child Development, 59,* 441–449.

OLSON, G. M., & SHERMAN, T. (1983). Attention, learning, and memory in infants. In P. H. Mussen (Series Ed.) & M. M. Haith & J. J. Campos (Vol. Eds.), *Handbook of child psychology: Vol. 2. Infancy and developmental psychobiology.* New York: Wiley.

OLSON, H. (1994). The effects of prenatal alcohol exposure on child development. *Infants and Young Children, 6,* 10–25.

OLSON, S. L., BATES, J. E., & KASKIE, B. (1992). Caregiver–infant interaction antecedents of children's school-age cognitive ability. *Merrill-Palmer Quarterly, 38,* 309–330.

OLVERA-EZZELL, N., POWER, T. G., & COUSINS, J. H. (1990). Maternal socialization of children's eating habits: Strategies used by obese Mexican-American mothers. *Child Development, 61,* 395–400.

OLWEUS, D., MATTISON, A., SCHALLING, D., & LOW, H. (1988). Circulating testosterone levels and aggression in adolescent males: A causal analysis. *Psychosomatic Medicine, 50,* 261–272.

OMARK, D. R., STRAYER, F. F., & FREEDMAN, D. G. (1980). *Dominance relations: An ethological view of human conflict and social interaction.* New York: Garland.

O'NEILL, D. K. (1996). Two-year-olds' sensitivity to a parent's knowledge state when making requests. *Child Development, 51,* 659–677.

O'NEILL, D. K., ASTINGTON, J. W., & FLAVELL, J. H. (1992). Young children's understanding of the role that sensory experiences play in knowledge acquisition. *Child Development, 63,* 474–490.

O'NEILL, D. K., & GOPNIK, A. (1991). Young children's ability to identify the sources of their beliefs. *Developmental Psychology, 27,* 390–397.

OOSTERWEGEL, A., & OPPENHEIMER, L. (1993). *The self-system: Developmental changes between and within self-concepts.* Hillsdale, NJ: Erlbaum.

O'REILLY, A. W., & BORNSTEIN, M. (1993). Caregiver–child interaction in play. In M. H. Bornstein & A. W. O'Reilly (Eds.), *New directions for child development: No. 59. The role of play in the development of thought.* San Francisco: Jossey-Bass.

ORLOFSKY, J. L., & O'HERON, C. A. (1987). Stereotypic and nonstereotypic sex-role trait and behavior orientations: Implications for personal adjustment. *Journal of Personality and Social Psychology, 52,* 1034–1042.

ORNSTEIN, P. A., NAUS, M. J., & LIBERTY, C. (1975). Rehearsal and organizational processes in children's memory. *Child Development, 46,* 818–830.

OSHERSON, D. N. (1990). *An invitation to cognitive science.* Cambridge: MIT Press.

OSOFSKY, J. (1995a). Children who witness domestic violence: The invisible victims. *Social Policy Report: Society for Research in Child Development, 18,* 1–16.

OSOFSKY, J. (1995b). The effects of exposure to violence on young children. *American Psychologist, 50,* 782–788.

OSTER, H., HEGLEY, D., & NAGEL, L. (1992). Adult judgments and fine-grained analysis of infant facial expressions: Testing the validity of a priori coding formulas. *Developmental Psychology, 28,* 1115–1131.

OWEN, D. R. (1972). The 47,XYY male: A review. *Psychological Bulletin, 78,* 209–233.

OWEN, D. R. (1979). Psychological studies in XYY men. In H. L. Vallet & I. H. Porter (Eds.), *Genetic mechanisms of sexual development.* New York: Academic Press.

PAGE, R. A. (1981). Longitudinal evidence for the sequentiality of Kohlberg's stages of moral judgment in adolescent males. *Journal of Genetic Psychology, 139,* 3–9.

PAIK, H., & COMSTOCK, G. (1994). The effects of television violence on antisocial behavior: A meta-analysis. *Communication Research, 21,* 516–546.

PAIKOFF, R. L., & BROOKS-GUNN, J. (1990). Physiological processes: What role do they play during the transition to adolescence? In R. Montemayor, G. R. Adams, & T. Gullotta (Eds.), *From childhood to adolescence: Vol. 2. Advances in adolescent development.* London: Sage.

PAINE, P., DOREA, J. G., PASQUALI, L., & MONTEIRO, A. M. (1992). Growth and cognition in Brazilian school children: A spontaneously occurring intervention. *International Journal of Child Development, 15,* 169–183.

PALCA, J. (1990). AIDS and the future. *Science, 248,* 1484.

PALINCSAR, A. S. (1992, April). *Beyond reciprocal teaching: A retrospective and prospective view.* Address presented at the meeting of the American Educational Research Association, San Francisco.

PALKOVITZ, R. (1984). Parental attitudes and fathers' interactions with their 5-month-old infants. *Developmental Psychology, 20,* 1054–1060.

PANETH, N. S. (1995). The problem of low birth weight. *The future of children* (Vol. 5. No. 1). Los Angeles: Packard Foundation.

PAREKH, V. C., PHERWANI, A., UDANI, P. M., & MUKKERJIE, S. (1970). Brain weight and head circumference in fetus, infant, and children of different nutritional and socioeconomic groups. *Indian Pediatrics, 7,* 347–358.

PARIKH, B. (1980). Development of moral judgment and its relation to family environment factors in Indian and American families. *Child Development, 51,* 1030–1039.

PARIS, S. G., & CROSS, D. R. (1988). The zone of proximal development: Virtues and pitfalls of a metaphorical representation of children's learning. *Genetic Epistemologist, 16*(1), 27–37.

PARIS, S. G., & LINDAUER, B. K. (1976). The role of inference in children's comprehension and memory for sentences. *Cognitive Psychology, 8,* 217–227.

PARIS, S. G., & OKA, E. R. (1986). Children's reading strategies, meta-cognition, and motivation. *Developmental Review, 6,* 25–56.

PARKE, R. D. (1977). Some effects of punishment on children's behavior—revisited. In E. M. Hetherington & R. D. Parke (Eds.), *Contemporary readings in child psychology.* New York: McGraw-Hill.

PARKE, R. D. (1994). Progress, paradigms, and unresolved problems: Recent advances in our understanding of children's emotions. *Merrill-Palmer Quarterly, 40,* 157–169.

PARKE, R. D. (1995). Fathers and families. In M. H. Bornstein (Ed.), *Handbook of parenting: Vol. 3. Status and social conditions of parenting.* Hillsdale, NJ: Erlbaum.

PARKE, R. D. (1996). *Fatherhood.* Cambridge: Harvard University Press.

PARKE, R. D., & BURIEL, R. (1998). Socialization in the family: Ethnic and ecological perspectives. In W. Damon (Ed.), *Handbook of child psychology: Vol. 3. Social, emotional, and personality development.* New York: Wiley.

PARKE, R. D., CASSIDY, J., BURKS, V. M., CARSON, J. L., & BOYUM, L. (1992). Familial contribution to peer competence among young children: The role of interactive and affective processes. In R. D. Parke & G. W. Ladd (Eds.), *Family-peer relationships: Modes of linkage.* Hillsdale, NJ: Erlbaum.

PARKE, R. D., & LADD, G. W. (Eds.). (1992). *Family-peer relationships: Modes of linkage.* Hillsdale, NJ: Erlbaum.

PARKE, R. D., & SLABY, R. G. (1983). The development of aggression. In E. M. Hetherington (Ed.), *Handbook of child psychology: Vol. 4. Socialization, personality, and social development.* New York: Wiley.

PARKER, J. G., & ASHER, S. R. (1987). Peer relations and later personal adjustment: Are low-accepted children at risk? *Psychological Bulletin, 102,* 357–389.

PARKER, J. G., RUBIN, K. H., PRICE, J. M., & DEROSIER, M. E. (1995). Peer relationships, child development, and adjustment: A developmental psychopathology perspective. In D. Cicchetti & D. J. Cohen (Eds.), *Developmental psychopathology: Vol. 2. Risk, disorder, and adaptation.* New York: Wiley.

PARMELEE, A. H., & GARBANATI, J. (1987). Clinical neurobehavioral aspects of state organization in newborn infants. In A. Kobayashi (Ed.), *Neonatal brain and behavior.* Nagoya, Japan: University of Nagoya Press.

PARMELEE, A. H., & SIGMAN, M. D. (1983). Perinatal brain development and behvior. In P. H. Mussen (Series Ed.) & M. M. Haith & J. J. Campos (Vol. Eds.), *Handbook of child psychology: Vol. 2. Infancy and developmental psychobiology.* New York: Wiley.

PARSONS, C. (1960). Inhelder and Piaget's "The growth of logical thinking": II. A logician's viewpoint. *British Journal of Psychology, 51,* 75–84.

PARTEN, M. B. (1932). Social participation among preschool children. *Journal of Abnormal and Social Psychology, 27,* 243–269.

PASCALIS, O., DE SCHONEN, S., MORTON, J., & DERUELLE, C. (1995). Mother's face recognition by neonates: A replication and an extension. *Infant Behavior and Development, 18,* 79–85.

PATCHENS, M. (1982). *Black-white contact in the schools: Its social and academic effects.* West Lafayette, IN: Purdue University Press.

PATTERSON, C. J. (1982). Self-control and self-regulation in childhood. In T. M. Field, A. Huston, H. C. Quay, L. Troll, & G. E. Finley (Eds.), *Review of human development.* New York: Wiley.

PATTERSON, C. J. (1992). Children of lesbian and gay parents. *Child Development, 63,* 1025–1042.

PATTERSON, C. J. (1994). Lesbian and gay families. *Current Directions in Psychological Science, 3,* 62–64.

PATTERSON, C. J. (1994a). Children of the lesbian baby boom: Behavioral adjustment, self-concepts, and sex-role identity. In B. Greene & G. Herek (Eds.), *Contemporary perspectives on lesbian and gay psychology: Theory, research, and application.* Beverly Hills, CA: Sage.

PATTERSON, C. J. (1994b). Lesbian and gay families. *Current Directions in Psychological Science, 3,* 62–64.

PATTERSON, C. J. (1995a). Families of the lesbian baby boom: Parents' division of labor and children's adjustment. *Developmental Psychology, 31,* 115–123.

PATTERSON, C. J. (1995b). Lesbian and gay parenthood. In M. H. Bornstein (Ed.), *Handbook of parenting: Vol. 3. Status and social conditions of parenting.* Mahwah, NJ: Erlbaum.

PATTERSON, C. J. (1995c). Sexual orientation and human development: An overview. *Developmental Psy-chology, 31,* 3–11.

PATTERSON, G. R. (1982). *Coercive family process.* Eugene, OR: Castalia.

PATTERSON, G. R. (1995). Coercion—A basis for early age of onset of arrest. In J. McCord (Ed.), *Coercion and punishment in long-term per-spective.* New York: Cambridge University Press.

PATTERSON, G. R., LITTMAN, R. A., & BRICKER, W. (1967). Assertive behavior in children: A step toward a theory of aggression. *Monographs of the Society for Research in Child Development, 32* (5, Serial No. 113).

PATTERSON, G. R., REID, J. B., & DISHION, T. J. (1992). *Antisocial boys.* Eugene, OR: Castalia.

PAUL, R., & MILLER, D. (1995). Cesarean delivery: How to reduce the rate. *American Journal of Obstetrics and Gynecology, 172,* 1903–1911.

PAYNE, A. C., WHITEHURST, G. J., & ANGELL, A. A.(1994). The role of home literacy environment in the development of language ability in preschool children from low-income families. *Early Childhood Research Quarterly, 9,* 427–440.

PEARL, D. (1987). Familial, peer, and television influences on aggressive and violent behavior. In D. H. Crowell, I. M. Evans, & C. R. O'Donnell (Eds.), *Childhood aggression and violence: Sources of influence, prevention, and control.* New York: Plenum.

PECHEUX, M., LEPECQ, J., & SALZARULO, P. (1988). Oral activity and exploration in 1–2-month-old infants. *British Journal of Developmental Psychology, 6,* 245–256.

PEDERSON, D. R., & MORAN, G. (1995). A categorical description of infant-mother relationships in the home and its relation to Q-sort measures of infant-mother interaction. In E. Waters, B. E. Vaughn, G. Posada, & K. Kondo-Ikemura (Eds.), Caregiving, cultural, and cognitive perspectives on secure-base behavior and working models. *Monographs of the Society for Research in Child Development, 60* (2–3, Serial No. 244).

PEDERSON, D. R., & MORAN, G. (1996). Expressions of the attachment relationship outside of the Strange Situation. *Child Development, 67,* 915–927.

PEDERSON, D. R., & TER VRUGT, D. (1973). The influence of amplitude and frequency of vestibular stimulation on the activity of two-month-old infants. *Child Development, 44,* 122–128.

PEDERSON, N. L., FRIBERG, L., FLODERUS-MYRHED, B., McCLEARN, G. E., & PLOMIN, R. (1984). Swedish early-separated twins: Identification and characterization. *Acta Geneticae Medicae et Gemellogiae, 33,* 243–250.

PEDLOW, R., SANSON, A., PRIOR, M., & OBERKLAID, F. (1993). Stability of maternally reported temperament from infancy to 8 years. *Developmental Psychology, 29,* 998–1007.

PEGG, J. E., WERKER, J. F., & McLEOD, P. J. (1992). Preferences for infant-directed over adult-directed speech: Evidence from 7-week-old infants. *Infant Behavior and Development, 15,* 325–345.

PEIPER, A. (1963). *Cerebral function in infancy and adulthood.* New York: Consultants Bureau.

PELAEZ-NOGUERAS, M., FIELD, T., CIGALES, M., GONZALEZ, A., & CLASKY, S. (1994). Infants of depressed mothers show less "depressed" behavior with their nursery teachers. *Infant Mental Health Journal, 15,* 358–367.

PELHAM, W. E., & HINSHAW, S. P. (1992). Behavior intervention for attention-deficit hyperactivity disorder. In S. M. Turner, K. S. Calhoun, & H. E. Adams (Eds.), *Handbook of clinical behavior therapy* (2nd ed.). New York: Wiley.

PENNER, S. G. (1987). Parental responses to grammatical and ungrammatical child utterances. *Child Development, 58,* 376–384.

PEPLER, D. J., KING, G., & BYRD, W. (1991). A social-cognitively based social skills training program for aggressive children. In D. J. Pepler & K. H. Rubin (Eds.), *The development and treatment of childhood aggression.* Hillsdale, NJ: Erlbaum.

PERFETTI, C. A. (1991). The psychology, pedagogy, and politics of reading. *Psychological Science, 2,* 70–76.

PERNER, J., RUFFMAN, T. K., & LEEKAM, S. R. (1994). Theory of mind is contagious: You catch it from your sibs. *Child Development, 65,* 1228–1238.

PERRY, D. G., & BUSSEY, K. (1979). The social learning theory of sex differences: Imitation is alive and well. *Journal of Personality and Social Psychology, 37,* 1699–1712.

PERRY, D. G., & BUSSEY, K. (1984). *Social development.* Englewood Cliffs, NJ: Prentice Hall.

PERRY, D. G., & PERRY, L. C. (1983). Social learning, causal attribution, and moral internalization. In J. Bizanz, G. L. Bizanz, & R. Kail (Eds.), *Learning in children: Progress in cognitive development research.* New York: Springer-Verlag.

PERRY, D. G., PERRY, L. C., & WEISS, R. J. (1989). Sex differences in the consequences that children anticipate for aggression. *Developmental Psychology, 25,* 312–319.

PERRY, D. G., WHITE, A. J., & PERRY, L. C. (1984). Does early sex typing result from children's attempts to match their behavior to sex role stereotypes? *Child Development, 55,* 2114–2121.

PERRY, M., CHURCH, R. B., & GOLDIN-MEADOW, S. (1988). Transitional knowledge in the acquisition of concepts. *Cognitive Development, 3,* 359–400.

PERRY, M., & ELDER, A. D. (1997). Knowledge in transition: Adults' developing understanding of a principle of physical causality. *Cognitive Development, 12,* 131–157.

PERRY, M., WOOLLEY, J., & IFCHER, J. (1995). Adults' abilities to detect children's readiness to learn. *International Journal of Behavioral Development, 18,* 364–381.

PETERS, D. P. (1991). The influence of stress and arousal on the child witness. In J. Doris (Ed.), *The suggestibility of children's recollections.* Washington, DC: American Psychological Association.

PETERSEN, A. C. (1987). The nature of biological-psychosocial interactions: The sample case of early adolescence. In R. M. Lerner & T. L. Foch (Eds.), *Biological-psychosocial interactions in early adolescence.* Hillsdale, NJ: Erlbaum.

PETERSON, L. (1983). Role of donor competence, donor age, and peer presence on helping in an emergency. *Developmental Psychology, 19,* 873–880.

PETITTO, L. A. (1992). Modularity and constraints in early lexical acquisition: Evidence from children's early language and gesture. In M. R. Gunnar & M. Maratsos (Eds.), *Minnesota symposia on child psychology: Vol. 25. Modularity and constraints in language and cognition.* Hillsdale, NJ: Erlbaum.

PETITTO, L. A., & MARENTETTE, P. F. (1991). Babbling in the manual mode: Evidence for the ontogeny of language. *Science, 251,* 1493–1496.

PETTIT, G. S., BAKSHI, A., DODGE, K. A., & COIE, J. D. (1990). The emergence of social dominance in young boys' play groups: Developmental differences and behavioral correlates. *Developmental Psychology, 26,* 1017–1025.

PHARES, V. (1992). Where's Poppa?: The relative lack of attention to the role of fathers in child and adolescent psychopathology. *American Psychologist, 47,* 656–664.

PHARES, V., & COMPAS, E. (1992). The role of fathers in child and adolescent psychopathology: Make room for daddy. *Psychological Bulletin, 111,* 387–412.

PHELPS, E., & DAMON, W. (1991). Peer collaboration as a context for cognitive growth. In L. T. Landsmann (Ed.), *Culture, schooling, and psychological development.* Norwood, NJ: Ablex.

PHILLIPS, D. A. (1984). The illusion of incompetence among academically competent children. *Child Development, 55,* 2000–2016.

PHILLIPS, D. A. (1987). Socialization of perceived academic competence among highly competent children. *Child Development, 58,* 1308–1320.

PHILLIPS, D. A., & ZIMMERMAN, M. (1990). The developmental course of perceived competence and incompetence among competent children. In R. J. Sternberg & J. Kolligian (Eds.), *Competence considered.* New Haven, CT: Yale University Press.

PHILLIPS, R. B., SHARMA, R., PREMACHANDRA, B. R., VAUGHN, A. J., & REYES-LEE, M. (1996). Intrauterine exposure to cocaine: Effect on neurobehavior of neonates. *Infant Behavior and Development, 19,* 71–81.

PHILLIPS, S., KING, S., & DUBOIS, L. (1978). Spontaneous activities of female versus male newborns. *Child Development, 49,* 590–597.

PIAGET, J. (1926). *The language and thought of the child.* New York: Harcourt Brace.

PIAGET, J. (1929). *The child's conception of the world.* London: Routledge & Kegan Paul.

PIAGET, J. (1932). *The moral judgment of the child.* London: Routledge & Kegan Paul.

PIAGET, J. (1950). *The psychology of intelligence.* New York: Harcourt Brace.

PIAGET, J. (1951). *Plays, dreams, and imitation in childhood.* New York: Norton.

PIAGET, J. (1952). *The origins of intelligence in children.* New York: International Universities Press.

PIAGET, J. (1954). *The construction of reality in the child.* New York: Basic Books.

PIAGET, J. (1957). Logique et equilibre dans les comportements du sujet. In L. Apostel, B. Mandelbrot, & J. Piaget (Eds.), *Etudes d'epistemologie genetique* (Vol. 2). Paris: Presses Universitaires de France.

PIAGET, J. (1964). Development and learning. In R. E. Ripple & V. N. Rockcastle (Eds.), *Piaget rediscovered.* Ithaca, NY: Cornell University Press.

PIAGET, J. (1967). *Six psychological studies.* New York: Random House.

PIAGET, J. (1968). *On the development of memory and identity.* Barre, MA: Clark University Press and Barre Publishers.

PIAGET, J. (1969). *The child's conception of time.* London: Routledge & Kegan Paul.

PIAGET, J. (1970). *The child's conception of movement and speed.* London: Routledge & Kegan Paul.

PIAGET, J. (1971). *Science of education and the psychology of the child.* New York: Viking.

PIAGET, J. (1972). Intellectual evolution from adolescence to adulthood. *Human Development, 15,* 1–12.

PIAGET, J. (1976). *To understand is to invent: The future of education.* New York: Penguin.

PIAGET, J. (1977). *The development of thought: Equilibration of cognitive structures.* New York: Viking.

PIAGET, J. (1979). Correspondence and transformation. In F. B. Murray (Ed.), *The impact of Piagetian theory.* Baltimore: University Park Press.

PIAGET, J. (1980). Recent studies in genetic epistemology. *Cashiers Foundation Archives, Jean Piaget, No. 1.*

PIAGET, J. (1983). Piaget's theory. In P. H. Mussen (Series Ed.) & W. Kessen (Vol. Ed.), *Handbook of child psychology: Vol. 1. History, theory, and methods.* New York: Wiley.

PIAGET, J., & INHELDER, B. (1956). *The child's conception of space.* London: Routledge & Kegan Paul.

PIAGET, J., & INHELDER, B. (1969). *The psychology of the child.* New York: Basic Books.

PIAGET, J., & INHELDER, B. (1973). *Memory and intelligence.* New York: Basic Books.

PIAGET, J., & INHELDER, B. (1974). *The child's construction of quantities.* London: Routledge & Kegan Paul.

PIAGET, J., INHELDER, B., & SZEMINSKA, A. (1960). *The child's conception of geometry.* New York: Basic Books.

PIAGET, J., & SZEMINSKA, A. (1952). *The child's conception of number.* New York: Basic Books.

PICARIELLO, M. L., GREENBERG, D. N., & PILLEMER, D. B. (1990). Children's sex-related stereotyping of colors. *Child Development, 61,* 1453–1460.

PICK, H. L., JR., (1992). Eleanor J. Gibson: Learning to perceive and perceiving to learn. *Developmental Psychology, 28,* 787–794.

PICKENS, J., & FIELD, T. (1993). Facial expressivity in infants of depressed mothers. *Developmental Psychology, 29,* 986–988.

PIERCE, K., & EDWARDS, E. D. (1988). Children's construction of fantasy stories: Gender differences in conflict resolution strategies. *Sex Roles, 18,* 393–404.

PIERCE, K. A., & COHEN, R. (1995). Aggressors and their victims: Toward a contextual framework for understanding children's aggressor-victim relationships. *Developmental Review, 15,* 292–310.

PINE, J. M., LIEVEN, E. V. M., & ROWLAND, C. F. (1997). Stylistic variation at the "single-word stage": Relations between maternal speech characteristics and children's vocabulary composition and usage. *Child Development, 68,* 807–819.

PINKER, S. (1984). *Language learnability and language development.* Cambridge: Harvard University Press.

PINKER, S. (1987). The bootstrapping problem in language acquisition. In B. MacWhinney (Ed.), *Mechanisms of language acquisition.* Hillsdale, NJ: Erlbaum.

PINKER, S. (1989). *Learnability and cognition: The acquisition of argument structure.* Cambridge: MIT Press.

PINKER, S. (1994). *The language instinct: How the mind creates language.* New York: William Morrow.

PIPP, S. (1990). Sensorimotor and representational internal working models of self, other, and relationship: Mechanisms of connection and separation. In D. Cicchetti & M. Beeghly (Eds.), *The self in transition: Infancy to childhood.* Chicago: University of Chicago Press.

PIPP, S. (1993). Infants' knowledge of self, other, and relationship. In U. Neisser (Ed.), *Ecological and interpersonal knowledge of self.* New York: Cambridge University Press.

PIPP, S., EASTERBROOKS, M. A., & HARMON, R. J. (1992). The relation between attachment and knowledge of self and mother in one- to three-year-old infants. *Child Development, 63,* 738–750.

PIPP, S., FISCHER, K. W., & JENNINGS, S. (1987). Acquisition of self- and mother knowledge in infancy. *Developmental Psychology, 23,* 86–96.

PIPP-SIEGEL, S., & FOLTZ, C. (1997). Toddlers' acquisition of self/other knowledge: Ecological and interpersonal aspects of self and other. *Child Development, 68,* 69–79.

PLOMIN, R. (1990). *Nature and nurture.* Belmont, CA: Wadsworth.

PLOMIN, R. (1994). *Genes and experience: The interplay between nature and nurture.* Thousand Oaks, CA: Sage.

PLOMIN, R. (1995). Molecular genetics and psychology. *Current Directions in Psychological Science, 4,* 114–117.

PLOMIN, R., & DeFRIES, J. C. (1985). *Origins of individual differences in infancy: The Colorado Adoption Project.* Orlando, FL: Academic Press.

PLOMIN, R., DeFRIES, J. C., & FULKER, D. W. (1988). *Nature and nurture during infancy and early childhood.* Cambridge: Cambridge University Press.

PLOMIN, R., DeFRIES, J. C., McCLEARN, G. E., & RUTTER, M. (1997). *Behavioral genetics* (3rd ed.). New York: W. H. Freeman.

PLOMIN, R., EMDE, R. N., BRAUNGART, J. M., CAMPOS, J., CORLEY, R., FULKER, D. W., KAGAN, J., REZNICK, J. S., ROBINSON, J., ZAHN-WAXLER, C., & DeFRIES, J. C. (1993). Genetic change and continuity from fourteen to twenty months: The MacArthur Longitudinal Twin Study. *Child Development, 64,* 1354–1376.

PLOMIN, R., FULKER, D. W., CORLEY, R., & DeFRIES, J. C. (1997). Nature, nurture, and cognitive development from 1 to 16 years: A parent-offspring adoption study. *Psychological Science, 8,* 442–447.

PLOMIN, R., & McCLEARN, G. E. (Eds.). (1993). *Nature, nurture, and psychology.* Washington, DC: American Psychological Association.

PLOMIN, R., & NEIDERHISER, J. M. (1992). Genetics and experience. *Current Directions in Psychological Science, 1,* 160–164.

PLOMIN, R., REISS, D., HETHERINGTON, E. M., & HOWE, G. W. (1994). Nature and nurture: Genetic contributions to measures of the family environment. *Developmental Psychology, 30,* 32–43.

PLUMERT, J. M. (1995). Relations between children's overestimation of their physical abilities and accident proneness. *Developmental Psychology, 31,* 866–876.

POLLITT, E., GOLUB, M., GORMAN, K., GRANTHAM-McGREGOR, S., LEVITSKY, D., SCHURCH, B., STRUPP, B., & WACHS, T. (1996). A reconceptualization of the effects of undernutrition on children's biological, psychosocial, and behavioral development. *Social Policy Report: Society for Research in Child Development, 10,* 1–31.

POLLITT, E., GORMAN, K., ENGLE, P., MARTORELL, R., & RIVERA, J. (1993). Early supplementary feeding and cognition: Effects over two decades. *Monographs of the Society for Research in Child Development, 58*(6, Serial No. 235).

POLLOCK, L. (1983). *Forgotten children: Parent–child relations from 1500 to 1900.* Cambridge: Cambridge University Press.

POLLOCK, L. (1987). *A lasting relationship: Parents and children over three centuries.* London: Fourth Estate.

POMERANTZ, E. M., RUBLE, D. N., FREY, K. S., & GREULICH, F. (1995). Meeting goals and confronting conflict: Children's changing perceptions of social comparison. *Child Development, 66,* 723–738.

POMERLEAU, A., BOLDUC, D., MALCUIT, G., & COSSETTE, L. (1990). Pink or blue: Environmental gender stereotypes in the first two years of life. *Sex Roles, 22,* 359–367.

PORTER, R. H., BALOGH, R. D., & MAKIN, J. W. (1988). Olfactory influences on mother-infant interaction. In C. Rovee-Collier & L. P. Lipsitt (Eds.), *Advances in infancy research* (Vol. 5). Norwood, NJ: Ablex.

PORTER, R. H., & LANEY, M. D. (1980). Attachment theory and the concept of inclusive fitness. *Merrill-Palmer Quarterly, 26,* 35–51.

POSADA, G., WATERS, E., CROWELL, J. A., & LAY, K. (1995). Is it easier to use a secure mother as a secure base? Attachment Q-sort correlates of the Adult Attachment Interview. In E. Waters, B. E. Vaughn, G. Posada, & K. Kondo-Ikemura (Eds.), Caregiving, cultural, and cognitive perspectives on secure-base behavior and working models. *Monographs of the Society for Research in Child Development, 60*(2–3, Serial No. 244).

POSNER, M. C., PETERSEN, S. E., FOX, P. T., & RAICHLEY, M. E. (1988). Localization of cognitive operations in the human brain. *Science, 240,* 1627–1631.

POULIN, F., CILLESSEN, A. H. N., HUBBARD, J. A., COIE, J. D., DODGE, K. A., & SCHWARTZ, D. (1997). Children's friends and behavioral similarity in two social contexts. *Social Development, 6,* 224–236.

POULIN-DUBOIS, D., GRAHAM, S., & SIPPOLA, L. (1995). Early lexical development: The contribution of parental labeling and infants' categorization abilities. *Journal of Child Language, 22,* 325–343.

POULIN-DUBOIS, D., SERBIN, L. A., KENYON, B., & DERBYSHIRE, A. (1994). Infants' intermodal knowledge about gender. *Developmental Psychology, 30,* 436–442.

POULSON, C. L., & NUNES, L. R. P. (1988). The infant vocal-conditioning literature: A theoretical and methodological review. *Journal of Experimental Child Psychology, 46,* 438–450.

POVINELLI, D. J. (1995). The unduplicated self. In P. Rochat (Ed.), *The self in infancy: Theory and research.* Amsterdam: Elsevier.

POWELL, G. F., BRASEL, J. A., & BLIZZARD, R. M. (1967). Emotional deprivation and growth retardation simulating ideopathic hypopituitarism: I. Clinical evaluation of the syndrome. *New England Journal of Medicine, 276,* 1271–1278.

POWLISHTA, K. K. (1995). Intergroup processes in childhood: Social categorization and sex role development. *Developmental Psychology, 31,* 781–788.

POWLISHTA, K. K., SERBIN, L. A., & MOLLER, L. C. (1993). The stability of individual differences in gender typing: Implications for understanding gender segregation. *Sex Roles, 29,* 723–737.

PRADER, A., TANNER, J. M., & VON HARNACK, G. A. (1963). Catch up growth following illness or starvation. *Journal of Paediatrics, 62,* 646–659.

PRATT, M. W., KERIG, P., COWAN, P. A., & COWAN, C. P. (1988). Mothers and fathers teaching 3-year-olds: Authoritative parenting and adult scaffolding of young children's learning. *Developmental Psychology, 24,* 832–839.

PRECHTL, H. F. R. (1968). Neurological findings in newborn infants after pre- and paranatal complications. In J. H. P. Jonxis, H. K. A. Visser, & J. A. Troelstra (Eds.), *Aspects of prematurity and dysmaturity.* Springfield, IL: Charles C. Thomas.

PRECHTL, H. F. R. (1977). *The neurological examination of the full-term newborn infant* (2nd ed.). London: Heinemann.

PRECHTL, H. F. R., & BEINTEMA, D. (1964). *The neurological examination of the full-term newborn infant.* London: Heinemann.

PRESSLEY, M. (1992). How not to study strategy discovery. *American Psychologist, 47,* 1240–1241.

PRESSLEY, M., BORKOWSKI, J. G., & O'SULLIVAN, J. (1985). Children's metamemory and the teaching of memory strategies. In D. L. Forrest-Pressley, G. E. MacKinnon, & T. G. Waller (Eds.), *Metacognition, cognition, and human performance: Vol. 1. Theoretical perspectives.* New York: Academic Press.

PRESSLEY, M., FORREST-PRESSLEY, D., & ELLIOT-FAUST, D. J. (1988). What is strategy instructional enrichment and how to study it: Illustrations from research on children's prose memory and comprehension. In F. E. Weinert & M. Perlmutter (Eds.), *Memory development: Universal changes and individual differences.* Hillsdale, NJ: Erlbaum.

PRESSLEY, M., LEVIN, J. R., & BRYANT, S. L. (1983). Memory and strategy instruction during adolescence: When is explicit instruction needed? In M. Pressley & J. R. Levin (Eds.), *Cognitive strategy research: Psychological foundations.* New York: Springer-Verlag.

PRIEL, B., & de SCHONEN, S. (1986). Self-recognition: A study of a population without mirrors. *Journal of Experimental Child Psychology, 41,* 237–250.

PUKA, B. (1991). Interpretive experiments: Probing the care-justice debate in moral development. *Human Development, 34,* 61–80.

PULLYBANK, J., BISANZ, J., SCOTT, C., & CHAMPION, M. A. (1985). Developmental invariance in the effects of functional self-knowledge on memory. *Child Development, 56,* 1447–1454.

PURCELL, P., & STEWART, L. (1990). Dick and Jane in 1989. *Sex Roles, 22,* 177–185.

PUTALLAZ, M., & HEFLIN, A. H. (1990). Parent–child interaction. In S. R. Asher & J. D. Coie (Eds.), *Peer rejection in childhood.* New York: Cambridge University Press.

PUTALLAZ, M., & WASSERMAN, A. (1990). Children's entry behavior. In S. R. Asher & J. D. Coie (Eds.), *Peer rejection in childhood.* New York: Cambridge University Press.

PYE, C. (1986). One lexicon or two? An alternative interpretation of early bilingual speech. *Journal of Child Language, 13,* 591–593.

QUIGGLE, N. L., GARBER, J., PANAK, W. F., & DODGE, K. A. (1992). Social information processing in aggressive and depressed children. *Child Development, 63,* 1305–1320.

QUINN, P. C., & EIMAS, P. D. (1996). Perceptual organization and categorization in young infants. In C. Rovee-Collier & L. P. Lipsitt (Eds.), *Advances in infancy research* (Vol. 10). Norwood, NJ: Ablex.

RACK, J. P., HULME, C., & SNOWLING, M. J. (1993). Learning to read: A theoretical synthesis. In H. W. Reese (Ed.), *Advances in child development and behavior* (Vol. 24). San Diego: Academic Press.

RADFORD, A. (1990). *Syntactic theory and the acquisition of English syntax: The nature of early child grammars of English.* Oxford, England: Blackwell.

RADKE-YARROW, M., & ZAHN-WAXLER, C. (1984). Roots, motives, and patterns in children's prosocial behavior. In E. Staub, D. Bar-Tal, J. Karylowski, & J. Reykowski (Eds.), *Development and maintenance of prosocial behavior.* New York: Plenum.

RADKE-YARROW, M., & ZAHN-WAXLER, C. (1986). The role of familial factors in the development of prosocial behavior: Research findings and questions. In D. Olweus, J. Block, & M. Radke-Yarrow (Eds.), *Development of antisocial and prosocial behavior.* Orlando, FL: Academic Press.

RADKE-YARROW, M., ZAHN-WAXLER, C., & CHAPMAN, M. (1983). Children's prosocial dispositions and behavior. In E. M. Hetherington (Ed.), *Handbook of child psychology: Vol. 4. Socialization, personality, and social development.* New York: Wiley.

RAFF, M. C., BARRES, B. A., BURNE, J. F., COLES, H. S., ISHIZAKI, Y., & JACOBSON, M. D. (1993). Programmed cell death and the control of cell survival: Lessons from the nervous system. *Science, 262,* 695–700.

RAKIC, P. (1988). Specification of cerebral cortical areas. *Science, 241,* 170–176.

RAMSEY, P. G. (1991). *Making friends in school: Promoting peer relationships in early childhood.* New York: Teachers College Press.

RAPOPORT, J. L., BUCHSBAUM, M. S., ZAHN, T. P., WEINGARTNER, H., LUDLOW, D., & MIKKELSON, E. J. (1978). Dextroamphetamine: Cognitive and behavioral effects in normal prepubertal boys. *Science, 199,* 560–563.

RASKIN, P. A., & ISRAEL, A. C. (1981). Sex-role imitation in children: Effects of sex of child, sex of model, and sex-role appropriateness of modeled behavior. *Sex Roles, 7,* 1067–1077.

RATCLIFFE, S. G., & FIELD, M. A. S. (1982). Emotional disorder in XYY children: Four case reports. *Journal of Child Psychology and Psychiatry, 23,* 401–406.

RATNER, N. B. (1988). Patterns of parental vocabulary selection in speech to very young children. *Journal of Child Language, 15,* 481–492.

RAVN, K. E., & GELMAN, S. A. (1984). Rule usage in children's understanding of "big" and "little." *Child Development, 55,* 2141–2150.

RAWLINS, W. K. (1992). *Friendship matters: Communication, dialectics, and the life course.* New York: Aldine de Gruyter.

RAYMOND, C. L., & BENBOW, C. P. (1986). Gender differences in mathematics: A function of parental support and student sex typing? *Developmental Psychology, 22,* 808–819.

RECHT, D. R., & LESLIE, L. (1988). Effect of prior knowledge on good and poor readers' memory of text. *Journal of Educational Psychology, 80,* 16–20.

REDLINGER, W. E., & PARK, T. (1980). Language mixing in young bilinguals. *Journal of Child Language, 7,* 337–352.

REES, J. M., & TRAHMS, C. M. (1989). Nutritional influences on physical growth and behavior in adolescence. In G. R. Adams, R. Montemayor, & T. P. Gullotta (Eds.), *Biology of adolescent behavior and development.* Newbury Park, CA: Sage.

REGALADO, M. G., SCHECHTMAN, V. L., DEL ANGEL, A. P., & BEAN, X. D. (1995). Sleep disorganization in cocaine-exposed neonates. *In-fant Behavior and Development, 18,* 319–327.

REID, J. B. (1993). Prevention of conduct disorder before and after school entry: Relating interventions to developmental findings. *Development and Psychopathology, 5,* 243–262.

REID, M., LANDESMAN, S., TREDER, R., & JACCARD, J. (1989). "My Family and Friends": Six- to twelve-year-old children's perceptions of social support. *Child Development, 60,* 896–910.

REINISCH, J. M., ZIEMBA-DAVIS, M., & SANDERS, S. A. (1991). Hormonal contributions to sexual dimorphic behavioral development in humans. *Psychoneuroendocrinology, 16,* 213–278.

REISMAN, J. E. (1987). Touch, motion and perception. In P. Salapatek & L. Cohen (Eds.), *Handbook of infant perception: Vol. 1. From sensation to perception.* New York: Academic Press.

REISSLAND, N. (1988). Neonatal imitation in the first hour of life: Observations in rural Nepal. *Developmental Psychology, 24,* 464–469.

RENNINGER, K. A. (1998). Developmental psychology and instruction: Issues from and for practice. In W. Damon (Series Ed.) & I. E. Sigel & K. A. Renninger (Vol. Eds.), *Handbook of child psychology: Vol. 4. Child psychology in practice* (5th ed.). New York: Wiley.

REPETTI, R. L. (1996). The effects of perceived daily social and academic failure experiences on school-age children's subsequent interactions with parents. *Child Development, 67,* 1467–1482.

RESCORLA, L. A. (1980). Overextension in early language development. *Journal of Child Language, 7,* 321–335.

RESCORLA, L. A. (1981). Category development in early language. *Journal of Child Language, 8,* 225–238.

REST, J. R. (1983). Morality. In J. H. Flavell & E. M. Markman (Eds.), *Handbook of child psychology: Vol. 3. Cognitive development.* New York: Wiley.

REZNICK, J. S., GIBBONS, J. L., JOHNSON, M. O., & McDONOUGH, P. M. (1989). Behavioral inhibition in a normative sample. In J. S. Reznick (Ed.), *Perspectives on behavioral inhibition.* Chicago: University of Chicago Press.

REZNICK, J. S., KAGAN, J., SNIDMAN, N., GERSTEN, M., BAAK, K., & ROSENBERG, A. (1986). Inhibited and uninhibited behavior: A follow-up study. *Child Development, 51,* 660–680.

RHEINGOLD, H. L. (1982a). Ethics as an integral part of research in child development. In R. Vasta (Ed.), *Strategies and techniques of child study.* New York: Academic Press.

RHEINGOLD, H. L. (1982b). Little children's participation in the work of adults: A nascent prosocial behavior. *Child Development, 53,* 114–125.

RHEINGOLD, H. L. (1988). The infant as a member of society. *Acta Paediatrica Scandinavica, 77,* 9–20.

RHEINGOLD, H. L., & COOK, K. (1975). The contents of boys' and girls' rooms as an index of parents' behavior. *Child Development, 46,* 459–463.

RHEINGOLD, H. L., & EMERY, G. N. (1986). The nurturant acts of very young children. In D. Olweus, J. Block, & M. Radke-Yarrow (Eds.), *Development of antisocial and prosocial behavior.* Orlando, FL: Academic Press.

RHEINGOLD, H. L., HAY, D. F., & WEST, M. J. (1976). Sharing in the second year of life. *Child Development, 47,* 1148–1158.

RHOLES, W. S., & LANE, J. W. (1985). Consistency between cognitions and behavior: Cause and consequence of cognitive moral development. In J. B. Pryor & J. D. Day (Eds.), *The development of social cognition.* New York: Springer-Verlag.

RICCIO, C. A., HYND, G. W., COHEN, M. J., & GONZALEZ, J. J. (1993). Neurological basis of attention deficit hyperactivity disorder. *Exceptional Children, 60,* 118–124.

RICCIUTI, H. N. (1993). Nutrition and mental development. *Current Directions in Psychological Science, 2,* 43–46.

RICE, M. L. (1989). Children's language acquisition. *American Psychologist, 44,* 149–156.

RICE, M. L., & WOODSMALL, L. (1988). Lessons from television: Children's word learning when viewing. *Child Development, 59,* 420–429.

RICHARDS, D. S., FRENTZEN, B., GERHARDT, K. J., McCANN, M. E., & ABRAMS, R. M. (1992). Sound levels in the human uterus. *Obstetrics and Gynecology, 80,* 186–190.

RICHTERS, J. E. (1993). Community violence and children's development: Toward a research agenda for the 1990s. In D. Reiss, J. E. Richters, M. Radke-Yarrow, & D. Scharf, (Eds.), *Children and violence.* New York: Guilford.

RIESE, M. L. (1987). Temperament stability between the neonatal period and 24 months. *Developmental Psychology, 23,* 216–222.

RIESER, J., YONAS, A., & WIKNER, K. (1976). Radial localization of odors by human newborns. *Child Development, 47,* 856–859.

RITTS, V., PATTERSON, M. L., & TUBBS, M. E. (1992). Expectations, impressions, and judgments of physically attractive students: A review. *Review of Educational Research, 62,* 413–426.

RIZZO, T. A., & CORSARO, W. A. (1988). Toward a better understanding of Vygotsky's process of internalization: Its role in the development of the concept of friendship. *Developmental Review, 8,* 219–237.

ROBERTS, C. W., GREEN, R., WILLIAMS, K., & GOODMAN, M. (1987). Boyhood gender identity development: A statistical contrast of two family groups. *Developmental Psychology, 23,* 544–557.

ROBERTS, L. (1990). To test or not to test? *Science, 247,* 17–19.

ROBERTS, R. J., BROWN, D., WIEBKE, S., & HAITH, M. M. (1991). A computer-automated laboratory for studying complex perception-action skills. *Behavior Research Methods and Instrumentation, 23,* 493–504.

ROBERTS, R. N., NELSON, R. O., & OLSON, T. W. (1987). Self-instruction: An analysis of the differential effects of instruction and reinforcement. *Journal of Applied Behavior Analysis, 20,* 235–242.

ROBERTS, W., & STRAYER, J. (1996). Empathy, emotional expressiveness, and prosocial behavior. *Child Development, 67,* 449–470.

ROBINSON, C. C., & MORRIS, J. T. (1986). The gender-stereotyped nature of Christmas toys received by 36-, 48-, and 60-month old children: A comparison between nonrequested vs. requested toys. *Sex Roles, 15,* 21–32.

ROBINSON, E. J. (1981). The child's understanding of inadequate messages and communication failure: A problem of ignorance or egocentrism? In W. P. Dickson (Ed.), *Children's oral communication skills.* New York: Academic Press.

ROBINSON, J. L., REZNICK, J. S., KAGAN, J., & CORLEY, R. (1992). The heritability of inhibited and uninhibited behavior: A twin study. *Developmental Psychology, 28,* 1030–1037.

ROBINSON, J., LITTLE, C., & BIRINGEN, Z. (1993). Emotional communication in mother–toddler relationships: Evidence for early gender differentiation. *Merrill-Palmer Quarterly, 39,* 496–517.

ROCHAT, P. (1989). Object manipulation and exploration in 2- to 5-month-old infants. *Developmental Psychology, 25,* 871–884.

ROCHAT, P. (1993). Hand–mouth coordination in the newborn: Morphology, determinants, and early development of a basic act. In G. J. P. Savelsbergh (Ed.), *The development of coordination in infancy.* London: Elsevier.

ROCHAT, P. (Ed.). (1995). *The self in infancy: Theory and research.* Amsterdam: Elsevier.

ROCHAT, P., & MORGAN, R. (1995). Spatial determinants in the perception of self-produced leg movements by 3- to 5-month-old infants. *Developmental Psychology, 31,* 626–636.

RODE, S., CHANG, P., FISCH, R., & SROUFE, L. A. (1981). Attachment patterns of infants separated at birth. *Developmental Psychology, 17,* 188–191.

ROFF, M., SELLS, S. B., & GOLDEN, M. M. (1972). *Social adjustment and personality development in children.* Minneapolis: University of Minnesota Press.

ROGAN, W. J. (1982). PCB's and cola-colored babies: Japan, 1968, and Taiwan, 1979. *Teratology, 26,* 259–261.

ROGOFF, B. (1981). Schooling and the development of cognitive skills. In H. C. Triandis & A. Heron (Eds.), *Handbook of cross-cultural psychology: Vol. 4. Developmental psychology.* Boston: Allyn & Bacon.

ROGOFF, B. (1990). *Apprenticeship in thinking: Cognitive development in social context.* New York: Oxford University Press.

ROGOFF, B. (1991). The joint socialization of development by young children and adults. In M. Lewis & S. Feinman (Eds.), *Social influences and socialization in infancy.* New York: Plenum.

ROGOFF, B. (1998). Cognition as a collaborative process. In W. Damon (Series Ed.) & D. Kuhn & R. S. Siegler (Vol. Eds.), *Handbook of child psychology: Vol. 2. Cognition, perception, and language* (5th ed.). New York: Wiley.

ROGOFF, B., & MISTRY, J. (1990). The social and functional context of children's remembering. In R. Fivush & J. A. Hudson (Eds.), *Knowing and remembering in young children.* New York: Cambridge University Press.

ROGOFF, B., MISTRY, J., GONCU, A., & MOSIER, C. (1991). Cultural variation in the role relations of toddlers and their families. In M. H. Bornstein (Ed.), *Cultural approaches to parenting.* Hillsdale, NJ: Erlbaum.

ROGOFF, B., MISTRY, J., GONCU, A., & MOSIER, C. (1993). Guided participation in cultural activity by toddlers and caregivers. *Monographs of the Society for Research in Child Development, 58* (Serial No. 236).

ROGOFF, B., MISTRY, J., RADZISZEWSKA, B., & GERMOND, J. (1992). Infants' instrumental social interaction with adults. In S. Feinman (Ed.), *Social referencing and the social construction of reality in infancy.* New York: Plenum.

ROGOFF, B., & WADDELL, K. J. (1982). Memory for information organized in a scene by children from two cultures. *Child Development, 53,* 1224–1228.

ROGOSCH, F. A., CICCHETTI, D., SHIELDS, A., & TOTH, S. L. (1995). Parenting dysfunction in child maltreatment. In M. H. Bornstein (Ed.), *Handbook of parenting: Vol. 4. Applied and practical parenting.* Mahwah, NJ: Erlbaum.

ROOPNARINE, J. L. (1984). Sex-typed socialization in mixed-age preschool classrooms. *Child Development, 55,* 1078–1084.

ROSALES-RUIZ, J., & BAER, D. M. (1996). A behavior-analytic view of development. In S. W. Bijou & E. Ribes (Eds.), *New directions in behavior development.* Reno, NV: Context Press.

ROSE, S. A. (1994). From hand to eye: Findings and issues in infant cross-modal transfer. In D. J. Lewkowicz & R. Lickliter (Eds.), *The development of intersensory perception: Comparative perspectives.* Hillsdale, NJ: Erlbaum.

ROSE, S. A., & FELDMAN, J. F. (1995). Prediction of IQ and specific cognitive abilities at 11 years from infancy measures. *Developmental Psychology, 31,* 685–696.

ROSE, S. A., GOTTFRIED, A. W., & BRIDGER, W. H. (1981). Cross-modal transfer and information processing by the sense of touch in infancy. *Developmental Psychology, 17,* 90–98.

ROSE, S. A., & ORLIAN, E. K. (1991). Asymmetries in cross-modal transfer. *Child Development, 62,* 706–718.

ROSE, S. A., & RUFF, H. A. (1987). Cross-modal abilities in human infants. In J. D. Osofsky (Ed.), *Handbook of infant development* (2nd ed.). New York: Wiley.

ROSEN, K. S., & ROTHBAUM, F. (1993). Quality of parental caregiving and security of attachment. *Developmental Psychology, 29,* 358–367.

ROSEN, W. D., ADAMSON, L. B., & BAKEMAN, R. (1992). An experimental investigation of infant social referencing: Mothers' messages and gender differences. *Developmental Psychology, 28,* 1172–1178.

ROSENBAUM, M. S., & DRABMAN, R. S. (1979). Self-control training in the classroom: Review and critique. *Journal of Applied Behavior Analysis, 12,* 467–485.

ROSENBERG, M. (1985). Self-concept and psychological well-being in adolescence. In R. L. Leahy (Ed.), *The development of the self.* Orlando, FL: Academic Press.

ROSENBERG, M. (1986a). *Conceiving the self.* Melbourne, FL: Krieger.

ROSENBERG, M. (1986b). Self-concept from middle childhood through adolescence. In J. Suls (Ed.), *Psychological perspectives on the self* (Vol. 3). Hillsdale, NJ: Erlbaum.

ROSENGREN, K. S., GELMAN, S. A., KALISH, C. W., & McCORMICK, M. (1991). As time goes by: Children's early understanding of growth in animals. *Child Development, 62,* 1302–1320.

ROSENSTEIN, D., & OSTER, H. (1988). Differential facial responses to four basic tastes in newborns. *Child Development, 59,* 1555–1568.

ROSENTHAL, R. (1976). *Experimenter effects in behavioral research* (enl. ed.). New York: Halsted Press.

ROSENTHAL, R., & JACOBSON, L. (1968). *Pygmalion in the classroom.* New York: Holt, Rinehart & Winston.

ROSENTHAL, R., & VANDELL, D. L. (1996). Quality of care at school-aged child-care programs: Regulatable features, observed experiences, child perspectives, and parent perspectives. *Child Development, 67,* 2434–2445.

ROSS, D. S. (1972). *G. Stanley Hall: The psychologist as prophet.* Chicago: University of Chicago Press.

ROSS, G. (1980). Categorization in 1- to 2-year-olds. *Developmental Psychology, 16,* 391–396.

ROSS, J. B., & McLAUGHLIN, M. M. (Eds.). (1949). *The portable medieval reader.* New York: Viking Press.

ROSS, H. S., & LOLLIS, S. P. (1987). Communication within infant social games. *Developmental Psychology, 23,* 241–248.

ROSS, H. S., & LOLLIS, S. P. (1989). A social relations analysis of toddler peer relationships. *Child Development, 60,* 1082–1091.

ROSS, S. A. (1971). A test of the generality of the effects of deviant preschool models. *Developmental Psychology, 4,* 262–267.

ROSSO, P. (1990). *Nutrition and metabolism in pregnancy.* New York: Oxford University Press.

ROTENBERG, K. J. (1980). Children's use of intentionality in judgments of character and disposition. *Child Development, 51,* 282–284.

ROTENBERG, K. J., & SLIZ, D. (1988). Children's restrictive disclosure to friends. *Merrill-Palmer Quarterly, 34,* 203–215.

ROTHBART, M. K., AHADI, S. A., & HERSHEY, K. L. (1994). Temperament and social behavior in childhood. *Merrill-Palmer Quarterly, 40,* 21–39.

ROTHBART, M. K., & BATES, J. E. (1998). Temperament. In W. Damon (Ed.), *Handbook of child psychology: Vol. 3. Social, emotional, and personality development.* New York: Wiley.

ROTHBART, M. K., & GOLDSMITH, H. H. (1985). Three approaches to the study of infant temperament. *Developmental Review, 5,* 237–260.

ROTHBART, M. K., & POSNER, M. I. (1985). Temperament and the development of self-regulation. In L. C. Hartledge & C. F. Telzrow (Eds.), *The neuropsychology of individual differences: A developmental perspective.* New York: Plenum.

ROTHBART, M. K., POSNER, M. I., & HERSHEY, K. L. (1995). Temperament, attention, and developmental psychopathology. In D. Cicchetti & D. J. Cohen (Eds.), *Manual of developmental psychopathology* (Vol. 1). New York: Wiley.

ROTMAN, B. (1977). *Jean Piaget: Psychologist of the real.* Hassocks, England: Harvester Press.

ROVEE-COLLIER, C. K. (1987). Learning and memory in infancy. In J. D. Osofsky (Ed.), *Handbook of infant development* (2nd ed.). New York: Wiley.

ROVEE-COLLIER, C. K., & BHATT, R. S. (1993). Evidence of long-term memory in infancy. In R. Vasta (Ed.), *Annals of child development* (Vol. 9). London: Kingsley.

ROVEE-COLLIER, C. K., & HAYNE, H. (1987). Reactivation of infant memory: Implications for cognitive development. In H. W. Reese (Ed.), *Advances in child development and behavior* (Vol. 20). New York: Academic Press.

ROVEE-COLLIER, C. K., & SHYI, G. (1992). A functional and cognitive analysis of infant long-term retention. In M. L. Howe, C. J. Brainerd, & V. F. Reyna (Eds.), *Development of long-term retention.* New York: Springer-Verlag.

ROVET, J. F. (1991). The cognitive and neuropsychological characteristics of females with Turner syndrome. In B. Bender & D. Berch (Eds.), *Sex chromosome abnormalities and behavior: Psychological studies.* Boulder, CO: Westview.

ROWE, I., & MARCIA, J. E. (1980). Ego identity status, formal operations, and moral development. *Journal of Youth and Adolescence, 9,* 87–99.

RUBENSTEIN, J., & HOWES, C. (1976). The effect of peers on toddler interaction with mother and toys. *Child Development, 47,* 597–605.

RUBIN, J. Z., PROVENZANO, F. J., & LURIA, Z. (1974). The eye of the beholder: Parents' views on sex of newborns. *American Journal of Orthopsychiatry, 44,* 512–519.

RUBIN, K. H. (1977). The social and cognitive value of preschool toys and activities. *Canadian Journal of Behavioral Science/Review of Canadian Science, 9,* 382–385.

RUBIN, K. H. (1989). *The Play Observation Scale (POS).* Unpublished manuscript. University of Waterloo, Waterloo, Ontario.

RUBIN, K. H. (1993). The Waterloo Longitudinal Project: Correlates and consequences of social withdrawal from childhood to adolescence. In K. H. Rubin & J. B. Asendorpf (Eds.), *Social withdrawal, inhibition, and shyness in childhood.* Hillsdale, NJ: Erlbaum.

RUBIN, K. H., & ASENDORPF, J. B. (Eds.). (1993). *Social withdrawal, inhibition, and shyness in childhood.* Hillsdale, NJ: Erlbaum.

RUBIN, K. H., BREAM, L., & ROSE-KRASNOR, L. (1991). Social problem solving and aggression in childhood. In D. J. Pepler & K. H. Rubin (Eds.), *The development and treatment of childhood aggression.* Hillsdale, NJ: Erlbaum.

RUBIN, K. H., & KRASNOR, L. R. (1986). Social-cognitive and social behavioral perspectives on problem solving. In M. Perlmutter (Ed.), *Minnesota symposia on child psychology: Vol. 19. Cognitive perspectives on children's social and behavioral development.* Hillsdale, NJ: Erlbaum.

RUBIN, K. H., & MAIONI, T. L. (1975). Play preference and its relationship to egocentrism, popularity and classification skills in preschoolers. *Merrill-Palmer Quarterly, 21,* 171–179.

RUBIN, K. H., & ROSE-KRASNOR, L. (1992). Interpersonal problem solving and social competence in children. In W. B. Van Hasselt & M.

Hersen (Eds.), *Handbook of social development.* New York: Plenum.

RUBIN, K. H., BUKOWSKI, W., & PARKER, J. G. (1998). Peer interactions, relationships, and groups. In W. Damon (Series Ed.) & N. Eisenberg (Vol. Ed.), *Handbook of child psychology: Vol. 3. Social, emotional, and personality development* (5th ed.). New York: Wiley.

RUBIN, K. H., FEIN, G. G., & VANDENBERG, B. (1983). Play. In P. H. Mussen (Series Ed.) & E. M. Hetherington (Vol. Ed.), *Handbook of child psychology: Vol. 4. Socialization, personality, and social development.* New York: Wiley.

RUBIN, K. H., LeMARE, L. J., & LOLLIS, S. (1990). Social withdrawal in childhood: Developmental pathways to peer rejection. In S. R. Asher & J. D. Coie (Eds.), *Peer rejection in childhood.* New York: Cambridge University Press.

RUBIN, K. H., LYNCH, D., COPLAN, R., ROSE-KRASNOR, L., & BOOTH, C. L. (1994). "Birds of a feather . . .": Behavioral concordances and preferential personal attraction in children. *Child Development, 65,* 1778–1785.

RUBIN, K. H., STEWART, S. L., & CHEN, X. (1995). Parents of aggressive and withdrawn children. In M. H. Bornstein (Ed.), *Handbook of parenting. Vol. 1. Children and parenting.* Mahwah, NJ: Erlbaum.

RUBIN, K. H., WATSON, K. S., & JAMBOR, T. W. (1978). Free-play behaviors in preschool and kindergarten children. *Child Development, 49,* 534–536.

RUBIN, Z. (1980). *Children's friendships.* Cambridge: Harvard University Press.

RUBLE, D. N. (1994). A phase model of transitions: Cognitive and motivational consequences. In M. Zanna (Ed.), *Advances in experimental social psychology.* New York: Academic Press.

RUBLE, D. N., & DWECK, C. S. (1995). Self-conceptions, person conception, and their development. In N. Eisenberg (Ed.), *Review of personality and social psychology: Vol. 15. Development and social psychology: The interface.* Thousand Oaks, CA: Sage.

RUBLE, D. N., & FLETT, G. L. (1988). Conflicting goals in self-evaluative information seeking: Developmental and ability level analyses. *Child Development, 59,* 97–106.

RUBLE, D. N., & FREY, K. S. (1987). Social comparison and outcome evaluation in group contexts. In J. C. Masters & W. P. Smith (Eds.), *Social comparison, social justice, and relative deprivation.* Hillsdale, NJ: Erlbaum.

RUBLE, D. N., & FREY, K. S. (1991). Changing patterns of behavior as skills are acquired: A functional model of self-evaluation. In J. Suls & T. A. Wills (Eds.), *Social comparison: Contemporary theory and research.* Hillsdale, NJ: Erlbaum.

RUBLE, D. N., & MARTIN, C. A. (1998). Gender development. In W. Damon (Ed.), *Handbook of child psychology: Vol. 3. Social, emotional, and personality development.* New York: Wiley.

RUBLE, D. N., GROSOVSKY, E. H., FREY, K. S., & COHEN, R. (1990). Developmental changes and competence assessment. In A. K. Boggiano & T. S. Pittman (Eds.), *Achievement motivation,* New York: Cambridge University Press.

RUDDY, M. G. (1993). Attention shifting and temperament at 5 months. *Infant Behavior and Development, 16,* 255–259.

RUFF, H. A., & KOHLER, C. J. (1978). Tactual-visual transfer in six-month-old infants. *Infant Behavior and Development, 1,* 259–264.

RUFF, H. A., & ROTHBART, M. K. (1996). *Attention in early development.* New York: Oxford University Press.

RUFFMAN, T., PERNER, J., NAITO, M., PARKIN, L., & CLEMENTS, W. A. (1998). Older (but not younger) siblings facilitate false belief understanding. *Developmental Psychology, 34,*161–174.

RUFFMAN, T., PERNER, J., OLSON, D. R., & DOHERTY, M. (1993). Reflecting on scientific thinking: Children's understanding of the hypothesis-evidence relation. *Child Development, 64,* 1617–1636.

RUSHTON, J. P., FULKER, D. W., NEALE, M. C., NIAS, D. K. B., & EYSENCK, H. J. (1986). Altruism and aggression: The heritability of individual differences. *Journal of Personality and Social Psychology, 50,* 1192–1198.

RUSSELL, A., & SAEBEL, J. (1997). Mother-son, mother-daughter, father-son, father-daughter: Are they distinct relationships? *Developmental Review, 17,* 111–147.

RUSSELL, G., & RADOJEVIC, M. (1992). The changing role of fathers? Current directions and future directions for research and practice. *Infant Mental Health Journal, 13,* 296–311.

RUTTER, M. (1983). School effects on pupil progress: Research findings and policy implications. *Child Development, 54,* 1–29.

RUTTER, M. (1987). Continuities and discontinuities from infancy. In J. D. Osofsky (Ed.), *Handbook of infant development* (2nd ed.). New York: Wiley.

RUTTER, M., & CAESAR, P. (Eds.). (1991). *Biological risk factors for psychosocial disorders.* Cambridge: Cambridge University Press.

RUTTER, M., MacDONALD, H., LECOUTEUR, A., HARRINGTON, R., BOLTON, P., & BAILEY, A. (1990). Genetic factors in child psychiatric disorders: II. Empirical findings. *Journal of Child Psychology and Psychiatry, 31,* 39–84.

SAARNI, C. (1984). An observational study of children's attempts to monitor their expressive behavior. *Child Development, 55,* 1504–1513.

SAARNI, C. (1989). Children's understanding of strategic control of emotional expression in social transactions. In C. Saarni & P. L. Harris (Eds.), *Children's understanding of emotion.* Cambridge: Cambridge University Press.

SAARNI, C. (1990). Emotional competence: How emotions and relationships become integrated. In R. A. Thompson (Ed.), *Nebraska symposium on motivation: Vol. 36. Socioemotional development.* Lincoln: University of Nebraska Press.

SAARNI, C., MUMME, D., & CAMPOS, J. J. (1998). Emotional development: Action, communication, and understanding. In W. Damon (Ed.), *Handbook of child psychology: Vol. 3. Social, emotional, and personality development.* New York: Wiley.

SACHS, J., & DEVIN, J. (1976). Young children's use of age-appropriate speech styles in social interaction and role-playing. *Journal of Child Language, 3,* 81–98.

SACHS, O. (1993, May 10) A neurologist's notebook: To see and not see. *New Yorker,* pp. 59–73.

SADEH, A., & ANDERS, T. F. (1993). Sleep disorders. In C. H. Zeanah, Jr. (Ed.), *Handbook of infant mental development.* New York: Guilford.

SADKER, M., & SADKER, D. (1994). *Failing at fairness: How America's schools cheat girls.* New York: Scribner.

SAGI, A. (1990). Attachment theory and research from a cross-cultural perspective. *Human Development, 33,* 10–22.

SAGI, A., & LEWKOWICZ, K. S. (1987). A cross-cultural evaluation of attachment research. In L. W. C. Tavecchio & M. H. van IJzendoorn (Eds.), *Attachment in social networks. Contributions to the Bowlby–Ainsworth attachment theory.* Amsterdam: Elsevier.

SAGI, A., VAN IJZENDOORN, M. H., AVIEZER, O., DONNELL, F., KOREN-KARIE, N., JOELS, T., & HAREL, Y. (1995). Attachments in multiple-caregiver and multiple-infant environments: The case of the Israeli kibbutzim. In E. Waters, B. E. Vaughn, G. Posada, & K. Kondo-Ikemura (Eds.), Caregiving, cultural, and cognitive perspectives on secure-base behavior and working models. *Monographs of the Society for Research in Child Development, 60*(2–3, Serial No. 244).

St. PETERS, M., FITCH, M., HUSTON, A. C., WRIGHT, J. C., & EAKINS, D. J. (1991). Television and families: What do young children watch with their parents? *Child Development, 62,* 1409–1423.

SALTZ, E., CAMPBELL, S., & SKOTKO, D. (1983). Verbal control of behavior: The effects of shouting. *Developmental Psychology, 19,* 461–464.

SALTZSTEIN, H. D., SANVITALE, D., & SUPRANER, A. (1978). Social influence on children's standards for judging criminal culpability. *Developmental Psychology, 14,* 125–131.

SALTZSTEIN, H. D., WEINER, A. S., MUNK, J. J., SUPRANER, A., BLANK, R., & SCHWARZ, R. P. (1987). Comparison between children's own moral judgments and those they attribute to adults. *Merrill-Palmer Quarterly, 33,* 33–51.

SALZINGER, S., FELDMAN, R. S., HAMMER, M., & ROSARIO, M. (1993). The effects of physical abuse on children's social relationships. *Child Development, 64,* 169–187.

SAMARAPUNGAVAN, A., VOSNIADOU, S., & BREWER, W. F. (1996). Mental models of the earth, sun, and moon: Indian children's cosmologies. *Cognitive Development, 11,* 491–521.

SAMEROFF, A. J., SEIFER, R., BALDWIN, A., & BALDWIN, C. (1993). Stability of intelligence from pre-school to adolescence: The influence of social and family risk factors. *Child Development, 64,* 80–97.

SAMUELS, C. A. (1986). Bases for the infant's developing self-awareness. *Human Development, 29,* 36–48.

SANDER, L. W., SNYDER, P. A., ROSETT, H. L., LEE, A., GOULD, J. B., & OUELLETTE, E. (1977). Effects of alcohol intake during pregnancy on newborn state regulation: A progress report. *Alcoholism: Clinical and Experimental Research, 1,* 233–241.

SANSON, A., PRIOR, M., & KYRIOS, M. (1990). Contamination of measures in temperament research. *Merrill-Palmer Quarterly, 36,* 179–192.

SANSON, A., & ROTHBART, M. K. (1995). Child temperament and parenting. In M. H. Bornstein (Ed.), *Handbook of parenting: Vol. 4. Applied and practical parenting.* Mahwah, NJ: Erlbaum.

SANVITALE, D., SALTZSTEIN, H. D., & FISH, M. C. (1989). Moral judgments by normal and conduct-disordered preadolescent and adolescent boys. *Merrill-Palmer Quarterly, 35,* 463–481.

SARASWATHI, T. S., & SUNDARESAN, J. (1980). Perceived maternal disciplinary practices and their relations to development of moral judgment. *International Journal of Behavioral Development, 3,* 91–104.

SASANUMA, S. (1980). Do Japanese show sex differences in brain asymmetry? Supplementary findings. *Behavioral and Brain Sciences, 3,* 247–248.

SAUDINO, K. J., & PLOMIN, R. (1997). Cognitive and temperamental mediators of genetic contributions to the home environment during infancy. *Merrill-Palmer Quarterly, 43,* 1–23.

SAVIN-WILLIAMS, R. C. (1979). Dominance hierarchies in groups of early adolescents. *Child Development, 50,* 923–935.

SAVIN-WILLIAMS, R. C. (1987). *Adolescence: An ethological perspective.* New York: Springer-Verlag.

SAVIN-WILLIAMS, R. C., & BERNDT, T. J. (1990). Friendship and peer relations. In S. S. Feld-man & G. R. Elliott (Eds.), *At the threshold: The developing adolescent.* Cambridge: Harvard University Press.

SAWIN, D. G. (1990). Aggressive behavior among children in small playgroup settings with violent television. In K. D. Gadow (Ed.), *Advances in learning and behavioral disabilities* (Vol. 6). Greenwich, CT: JAI Press.

SAXE, G. B. (1988). The mathematics of child street vendors. *Child Development, 59,* 1415–1425.

SAXE, G. B. (1991). *Culture and cognitive development: Studies in mathematical understanding.* Hillsdale, NJ: Erlbaum.

SAYEGH, Y., & DENNIS, W. (1965). The effect of supplementary experiences upon the behavioral development of infants in institutions. *Child Development, 36,* 81–90.

SAYWITZ, K. J., GOODMAN, G. S., NICHOLAS, E., & MOAN, S. F. (1991). Children's memories of a physical examination involving genital touch: Implications for reports of child sexual abuse. *Journal of Consulting and Clinical Psyhology, 59,* 682–691.

SCARBOROUGH, H., & WYCKOFF, J. (1986). Mother, I'd still rather do it myself: Some further non-effects of "motherese." *Journal of Child Language, 13,* 431–437.

SCARR, S. (1981). *Race, social class, and individual differences in IQ: New studies of old problems.* Hillsdale, NJ: Erlbaum.

SCARR, S. (1983). An evolutionary perspective on infant intelligence: Species patterns and individual variations. In M. Lewis (Ed.), *Origins of intelligence: Infancy and early childhood* (2nd ed.). New York: Plenum.

SCARR, S. (1992). Developmental theories for the 1990s: Development and individual differences. *Child Development, 63,* 1–19.

SCARR, S. (1993). Biological and cultural diversity: The legacy of Darwin for development. *Child Development, 64,* 1333–1353.

SCARR, S. (1998). American child care today. *American Psychologist, 53,* 95–108.

SCARR, S., & KIDD, K. K. (1983). Developmental behavior genetics. In P. H. Mussen (Series Ed.) & M. M. Haith & J. J. Campos (Vol. Eds.), *Handbook of child psychology: Vol. 2. Infancy and developmental psychobiology.* New York: Wiley.

SCARR, S., & McCARTNEY, K. (1983). How people make their own environments: A theory of genotype–environment effects. *Child Development, 54,* 424–435.

SCARR, S., PAKSTIS, A. J., KATZ, S. H., & BARKER, W. B. (1977). Absence of a relationship between degree of white ancestry and intellectual skills within a black population. *Human Genetics, 39,* 69–86.

SCARR, S., & WEINBERG, R. A. (1983). The Minnesota Adoption Studies: Genetic differences and malleability. *Child Development, 54,* 260–267.

SCHACTER, F. F., SHORE, E., HODAPP, R., CHALFIN, S., & BUNDY, C. (1978). Do girls talk earlier? Mean length of utterance in toddlers. *Developmental Psychology, 14,* 388–392.

SCHAFFER, C. E., & BLATT, S. J. (1990). Interpersonal relationships and the experience of perceived efficacy. In R. J. Sternberg & J. Kolligian (Eds.), *Competence considered.* New Haven, CT: Yale University Press.

SCHAFFER, H. R. (1986). Some thoughts of an ordinologist. *Developmental Review, 6,* 115–121.

SCHAFFER, H. R., & EMERSON, P. E. (1964). The development of social attachments in infancy. *Monographs of the Society for Research in Child Development, 29*(3, Serial No. 94).

SCHIEFFELIN, B. (1985). The acquisition of Kaluli. In D. I. Slobin (Ed.), *The crosslinguistic study of language acquisition: Vol. 1. The data.* Hillsdale, NJ: Erlbaum.

SCHLEIDT, M. (1991). An ethological perspective on infant development. In M. E. Lamb & H. Keller (Eds.), *Infant development: Perspectives from German-speaking countries.* Hillsdale, NJ: Erlbaum.

SCHLESINGER, I. M. (1988). The origin of relational categories. In Y. Levy, I. M. Schlesinger, & M. D. S. Braine (Eds.), *Categories and processes in language acquisition.* Hillsdale, NJ: Erlbaum.

SCHMIDT, C. R., OLLENDICK, T. H., & STANOWICZ, L. B. (1988). Developmental changes in the influence of assigned goals on cooperation and competition. *Developmental Psychology, 24,* 574–579.

SCHMIDT, L. A., & FOX, N. A. (1998). The development and outcomes of childhood shyness: A multiple psychophysiologic measure approach. In R. Vasta (Ed.), *Annals of child development* (Vol. 13). London: Kingsley.

SCHMUCKLER, M. A. (1995). Self-knowledge of body position: Integration of perceptual and action system information. In P. Rochat (Ed.), *The self in infancy: Theory and research.* Amsterdam: Elsevier.

SCHNEIDER, B. A., & TREHUB, S. E. (1985a). Behavioral assessment of basic capabilities. In S. E. Trehub & B. A. Schneider (Eds.), *Auditory development in infancy.* New York: Plenum.

SCHNEIDER, B. A., & TREHUB, S. E. (1985b). Infant auditory psychophysics: An overview. In G. Gottlieb & N. A. Krasnegor (Eds.), *Measurement of audition and vision in the first year of postnatal life: A methodological overview.* Norwood, NJ: Ablex.

SCHNEIDER, B. H., & BYRNE, B. M. (1985). Children's social skills training: A meta-analysis. In B. H. Schneider, K. H. Rubin, & J. E. Ledingham (Eds.), *Children's peer relations: Issues in assessment and intervention.* New York: Springer-Verlag.

SCHNEIDER, B. H., RUBIN, K. H., & LEDINGHAM, J. E. (Eds.). (1985). *Children's peer relations: Issues in assessment and intervention.* New York: Springer-Verlag.

SCHNEIDER, W., & BJORKLUND, D. F. (1998). Memory. In W. Damon (Series Ed.) & D. Kuhn & R. S. Siegler (Vol. Eds.), *Handbook of child psychology: Vol. 2. Cognition, perception, and language* (5th ed.). New York: Wiley.

SCHNEIDER, W., GRUBER, H., GOLD, A., & OPWIS, K. (1993). Chess expertise and memory for chess positions in children and adults. *Journal of Experimental Child Psychology, 56,* 328–349.

SCHNEIDER, W., & PRESSLEY, M. (1989). *Memory development between 2 and 20.* New York: Springer-Verlag.

SCHNEIDER, W., KORKEL, J., & WEINERT, F. E. (1987). *The knowledge base and memory per-*

formance: A comparison of academically successful and unsuccessful learners. Paper presented at the meeting of the American Educational Research Association, Washington, DC.

SCHNEIDER-ROSEN, K., & CICCHETTI, D. (1984). The relationship between affect and cognition in maltreated infants: Quality of attachment and the development of visual self-recognition. *Child Development, 55,* 648–658.

SCHNEIDER-ROSEN, K., & CICCHETTI, D. (1991). Early self-knowledge and emotional development: Visual self-recognition and affective reactions to mirror self-image in maltreated and nonmaltreated toddlers. *Developmental Psychology, 27,* 471–478.

SCHULMAN, A. H., & KAPLOWITZ, C. (1977). Mirror-image response during the first two years of life. *Developmental Psychobiology, 10,* 133–142.

SCHUNK, D. H. (1983). Reward contingencies and the development of children's skills and self-efficacy. *Journal of Educational Psychology, 75,* 511–518.

SCHUNK, D. H. (1984). Self-efficacy perspective on achievement behavior. *Educational Psychologist, 19,* 48–58.

SCHUNK, D. H. (1987). Peer models and children's behavioral change. *Review of Educational Research, 57,* 159–174.

SCHWARTZ, B. (1990). The creation and destruction of value. *American Psychologist, 45,* 7–15.

SCHWARTZ, D., DODGE, K. A., PETTIT, G. S., & BATES, J. E. (1997). The early socialization of aggressive victims of bullying. *Child Development, 68,* 665–675.

SCHWARTZ, R. G., & CAMARATA, S. (1985). Examining relationships between input and language development: Some statistical issues. *Journal of Child Language, 12,* 199–207.

SCHWARTZ, R. G., LEONARD, L. B., FROME-LOEB, D. M., & SWANSON, L. A. (1987). Attempted sounds are sometimes not: An expanded view of phonological selection and avoidance. *Journal of Child Language, 14,* 411–418.

SCHWEINHART, L. J., & WEIKART, D. P. (1991). Response to "Beyond IQ in Preschool Programs?" *Intelligence, 15,* 313–315.

SCOTT, J. P. (1987). Critical periods in the processes of social organization. In M. H. Bornstein (Ed.), *Sensitive periods in development: Interdisciplinary perspectives.* Hillsdale, NJ: Erlbaum.

SCOTT, M. M. (1997, April). *Children's problems and solution strategies in the natural habitat.* Paper presented at the meeting of the Society for Research in Child Development, Washington, DC.

SEARS, R. R. (1977). Sources of life satisfactions of the Terman gifted men. *American Psychologist, 32,* 119–128.

SEASHORE, M. J., LEIFER, A. D., BARNETT, C. R., & LEIDERMAN, P. H. (1973). The effects of denial of early mother–infant interaction on maternal self-confidence. *Journal of Personality and Social Psychology, 26,* 369–378.

SEBALD, H. (1989). Adolescent peer orientation: Changes in the support system during the last three decades. *Adolescence, 24,* 937–945.

SEGAL, L. B., OSTER, H., COHEN, M., CASPI, B., MYERS, M., & BROWN, D. (1995). Smiling and fussing in seven-month-old preterm and full-term black infants in the still-face situation. *Child Development, 66,* 1829–1843.

SEIDMAN, E., ALLEN, L., ABER, J. L., MITCHELL, C., & FEINMAN, J. (1994). The impact of school transition in early adolescence on the self-system and perceived social context of poor urban youth. *Child Development, 65,* 507–522.

SEIFER, R., & SCHILLER, M. (1995). The role of parenting sensitivity, infant temperament, and dyadic interaction in attachment theory and assessment. In E. Waters, B. E. Vaughn, G. Posada, & K. Kondo-Ikemura (Eds.), Caregiving, cultural, and cognitive perspectives on secure-base behavior and working models. *Monographs of the Society for Research in Child development, 60* (2–3, Serial No. 244).

SEIFER, R., SCHILLER, M., SAMEROFF, A. J., RESNICK, S., & RIORDAN, K. (1996). Attachment, maternal sensitivity, and infant temperament during the first year of life. *Developmental Psychology, 32,* 12–25.

SELMAN, R. L. (1980). *The growth of interpersonal understanding: Development and clinical analyses.* New York: Academic Press.

SELMAN, R. L., & JAQUETTE, D. (1977). *The development of interpersonal awareness.* Unpublished manuscript.

SERBIN, L. A., & SPRAFKIN, C. (1986). The salience of gender and the process of sex typing in three- to seven-year-old children. *Child Development, 57,* 1188–1199.

SERBIN, L. A., POWLISHTA, K. K., & GULKO, J. (1993). The development of sex typing in middle childhood. *Monographs of the Society for Research in Child Development, 58*(Serial No. 232).

SERBIN, L. A., SPRAFKIN, C., ELMAN, M., & DOYLE, A. (1994). The early development of sex differentiated patterns of social influence. *Canadian Journal of Social Science, 14,* 350–363.

SERBIN, L. A., TONICK, I. J., & STERNGLANZ, S. H. (1977). Shaping cooperative cross-sex play. *Child Development, 48,* 924–929.

SHAKIN, M., SHAKIN, D., & STERNGLANZ, S. H. (1985). Infant clothing: Sex labeling for strangers. *Sex Roles, 12,* 955–963.

SHANTZ, C. U. (1983). Social cognition. In P. H. Mussen (Series Ed.) & J. H. Flavell & E. M. Markman (Vol. Eds.), *Handbook of child psychology: Vol. 3. Cognitive development.* New York: Wiley.

SHANTZ, C. U. (1987). Conflicts between children. *Child Development, 58,* 283–305.

SHANTZ, C. U., & HARTUP, W. W. (Eds.). (1995). *Conflict in child and adolescent development.* New York: Cambridge University Press.

SHARPE, R. M., & SKAKKEBAEK, N. E. (1993). Are oestrogens involved in falling sperm counts and disorders of the male reproductive tract? *Lancet, 341,* 1392–1395.

SHATZ, M. (1983). On transition, continuity, and coupling: An alternative approach to communicative development. In R. M. Golinkoff (Ed.), *The transition from prelinguistic to linguistic communication.* Hillsdale, NJ: Erlbaum.

SHATZ, M. (1991). Using cross-cultural research to inform us about the role of language development: Comparisons of Japanese, Korean, and English, and of German, American English, and British English. In M. H. Bornstein (Ed.), *Cultural approaches to parenting.* Hillsdale, NJ: Erlbaum.

SHATZ, M., & GELMAN, R. (1973). The development of communication skills: Modifications in the speech of young children as a function of the listener. *Monographs of the Society for Research in Child Development, 38* (5, Serial No. 152).

SHATZ, M., & McCLOSKEY, L. (1984). Answering appropriately: A developmental perspective on conversational knowledge. In S. A. Kuczaj (Ed.), *Discourse development: Progress in cognitive developmental research.* New York: Springer-Verlag.

SHAYER, M., KUCHEMAN, D. E., & WYLAM, H. (1976). The distribution of Piagetian stages of thinking in British middle and secondary school children. *British Journal of Educational Psychology, 46,* 164–173.

SHAYER, M., & WYLAM, H. (1978). The distribution of Piagetian stages of thinking in British middle and secondary school children: II. 14 to 16 year old and sex differentials. *British Journal of Educational Psychology, 48,* 62–70.

SHELDON, A. (1990). Pickle fights: Gendered talk in preschool disputes. *Discourse Processes, 13,* 5–31.

SHELDON, A. (1992). Conflict talk: Sociolinguist challenges to self-assertion and how young girls meet them. *Merrill-Palmer Quarterly, 38,* 95–117.

SHEPARD, T. H. (1986). Human teratogenicity. *Advances in Pediatrics, 33,* 225–268.

SHERIF, M., HARVEY, O. J., WHITE, B. J., HOOD, W. R., & SHERIF, C. W. (1961). *Intergroup conflict and cooperation: The Robbers Cave experiment.* Norman: University of Oklahoma Press.

SHIGETOMI, C. C., HARTMANN, D. P., & GELFAND, D. M. (1981). Sex differences in children's altruistic behavior and reputations for helpfulness. *Developmental Psychology, 17,* 434–437.

SHORE, C. M. (1995). *Individual differences in language development.* Thousand Oaks, CA: Sage.

SHUCARD, J. L., & SHUCARD, D. W. (1990). Auditory evoked potentials and hand preference in 6-month-old infants: Possible gender-related differences in cerebral organization. *Developmental Psychology, 26,* 923–930.

SHUCARD, J. L., SHUCARD, D. W., CUMMINS, K. R., & CAMPOS, J. J. (1981). Auditory evoked potentials and sex-related differences in brain development. *Brain and Language, 13,* 91–102.

SHULMAN, S., & COLLINS, W. A. (Eds.). (1997). *New directions for child development: No. 78. Romantic relationships in adolescence: Developmental perspectives.* San Francisco: Jossey-Bass.

SHULTZ, T. R., & DARLEY, J. M. (1991). An information-processing model of retributive moral judgments based on "legal reasoning." In W. M. Kurtines & J. L. Gewirtz (Eds.), *Handbook of moral behavior and development: Vol. 2. Research.* Hillsdale, NJ: Erlbaum.

SHULTZ, T. R., & WRIGHT, K. (1985). Concepts of negligence and intention in the assignment of moral responsibility. *Canadian Journal of Behavioural Science, 17,* 97–108.

SHULTZ, T. R., WRIGHT, K., & SCHLEIFER, M. (1986). Assignment of moral responsibility and punishment. *Child Development, 57,* 177–184.

SHURE, M. B. (1989). Interpersonal competence training. In W. Damon (Ed.), *Child development today and tomorrow.* San Francisco: Jossey-Bass.

SHURKIN, J. N. (1992). *Terman's kids: The groundbreaking study of how the gifted grow up.* Boston: Little, Brown.

SHWE, H. I., & MARKMAN, E. M. (1997). Young children's appreciation of the mental impact of their communicative signals. *Developmental Psychology, 33,* 630–636.

SHWEDER, R. A., GOODNOW, J., HATANO, G., LEVINE, H. M., & MILLER, P. (1998). The cultural psychology of development: One mind, many mentalities. In W. Damon (Ed.), *Handbook of child psychology: Vol. 1. Theoretical models of human development.* New York: Wiley.

SHWEDER, R. A., MAHAPATRA, M., & MILLER, J. (1987). Culture and moral development. In J. Kagan & S. Lamb (Eds.), *The emergence of morality in young children.* Chicago: University of Chicago Press.

SHWEDER, R. A., & MUCH, M. C. (1987). Determinations of meaning: Discourse and moral socialization. In W. M. Kurtines & J. L. Gewirtz (Eds.), *Moral development through social interaction.* New York: Wiley.

SIEBER, J. E. (1992). *Planning ethically responsible research: A guide for students and internal review boards.* Newbury Park, CA: Sage.

SIEGAL, M. (1987). Are sons and daughters treated more differently by fathers than by mothers? *Developmental Review, 7,* 183–209.

SIEGAL, M. (1991). *Knowing children: Experiments in conversation and cognition.* Hillsdale, NJ: Erlbaum.

SIEGEL, L. S. (1984). Home environment influences on cognitive development in preterm and full-term children during the first 5 years. In A. W. Gottfried (Ed.), *Home environment and early cognitive development.* New York: Academic Press.

SIEGEL, L. S. (1989). A reconceptualization of prediction from infant test scores. In M. H. Bornstein & N. Krasnegor (Eds.), *Stability and continuity in mental development.* Hillsdale, NJ: Erlbaum.

SIEGEL, L. S. (1992). Infant, motor, and language behaviors as predictors of achievement at school age. In C. Rovee-Collier & L. P. Lipsitt (Eds.), *Advances in infancy research* (Vol. 7). Norwood, NJ: Ablex.

SIEGEL, L. S. (1993a). The development of reading. In H. W. Reese (Ed.), *Advances in child development and behavior* (Vol. 24). San Diego: Academic Press.

SIEGEL, L. S. (1993b). Phonological processing deficits as the basis of a reading disability. *Developmental Review, 13,* 246–257.

SIEGLER, R. S. (1976). Three aspects of cognitive development. *Cognitive Psychology, 8,* 481–520.

SIEGLER, R. S. (1978). The origins of scientific reasoning. In R. S. Siegler (Ed.), *Children's thinking: What develops?* Hillsdale, NJ: Erlbaum.

SIEGLER, R. S. (1981). Developmental sequences within and between concepts. *Monographs of the Society for Research in Child Development, 46* (2, Serial No. 189).

SIEGLER, R. S. (1988). Individual differences in strategy choices: Good students, not-so-good students, and perfectionists. *Child Development, 59,* 833–851.

SIEGLER, R. S. (1995). How does change occur?: A microgenetic study of number conservation. *Cognitive Psychology, 28,* 225–273.

SIEGLER, R. S. (1996a). *Emerging minds: The process of change in children's thinking.* New York: Oxford University Press.

SIEGLER, R. S. (1996b). A grand theory of development. *Monographs of the Society for Research in Child Development, 61* (1–2, Serial No. 246).

SIEGLER, R. S. (1998). *Children's thinking* (3rd ed.). Englewood Cliffs, NJ: Prentice Hall.

SIEGLER, R. S., & JENKINS, E. (1989). *How children discover new strategies.* Hillsdale, NJ: Erlbaum.

SIEGLER, R. S., & SHIPLEY, C. (1995). Variation, selection, and cognitive change. In T. J. Simon & G. S. Halford (Eds.), *Developing cognitive competence: New approaches to process modeling.* Hillsdale, NJ: Erlbaum.

SIEGLER, R. S., & SHRAGER, J. (1984). Strategy choices in addition and subtraction: How do children know what to do? In C. Sophian (Ed.), *Origins of cognitive skills.* Hillsdale, NJ: Erlbaum.

SIGELMAN, C. K., & WAITZMAN, K. A. (1991). The development of distributive justice orientations: Contextual influences of children's resource allocations. *Child Development, 62,* 1367–1378.

SIGMAN, M. (1995). Nutrition and child development: More food for thought. *Current Directions in Psychological Science, 4,* 52–55.

SIGNORELLA, M. L. (1987). Gender schemata: Individual differences and context effects. In L. S. Liben & M. L. Signorella (Eds.), *New directions for child development: No. 38. Children's gender schemata.* San Francisco: Jossey-Bass.

SIGNORELLA, M. L., BIGLER, R. S., & LIBEN, L. S. (1993). Developmental differences in children's gender schemata about others: A meta-analytic review. *Developmental Review, 13,* 147–183.

SIGNORELLA, M. L., & LIBEN, L. S. (1984). Recall and reconstruction of gender-related pictures: Effects of attitude, task difficulty, and age. *Child Development, 55,* 393–405.

SIGNORIELLI, N. (1993). Television, the portrayal of women, and children's attitudes. In G. Berry & J. K. Asamen (Eds.), *Children and television: Images in a changing sociocultural world.* Newbury Park, CA: Sage.

SILVER, L. B. (1992). *Attention-deficit hyperactivity disorder.* Washington, DC: American Psychiatric Association.

SILVERMAN, I., & EALS, M. (1992). Sex differences in spatial abilities: Evolutionary theory and data. In J. H. Barkow, L. Cosmides, & J. Tooby (Eds.), *The adapted mind: Evolutionary psychology and the generation of culture.* New York: Oxford University Press.

SIMMONS, R. G., & BLYTH, D. A. (1987). *Moving into adolescence: The impact of pubertal change and social context.* Hawthorne, NY: Aldine de Gruyter.

SIMMONS, R. G., CARLTON-FORD, S. L., & BLYTH, D. A. (1987). Predicting how a child will age with the transition to junior high school. In R. M. Lerner & T. M. Foch (Eds.), *Biological-psychosocial interactions in early adolescence.* Hillsdale, NJ: Erlbaum.

SIMON, T. J. (1997). Reconceptualizing the origins of number knowledge: A "non-numerical" account. *Cognitive Development, 12,* 349–372.

SIMON, T. J., & HALFORD, G. S. (Eds.). (1995). *Developing cognitive competence: New approaches to process modeling.* Hillsdale, NJ: Erlbaum.

SIMON, T. J., HESPOS, S. J., & ROCHAT, P. (1995). Do infants understand simple arithmetic? A replication of Wynn. *Cognitive Development, 10,* 253–269.

SKINNER, B. F. (1953). *Science and human behavior.* New York: Macmillan.

SKINNER, B. F. (1957). *Verbal behavior.* New York: Appleton-Century-Crofts.

SKOWRONSKI, J. J., BETZ, A. L., THOMPSON, C. P., & LARSEN, S. F. (1995). Long-term performance in autobiographical event dating: Patterns of accuracy and error across a two-and-a-half year time span. In A. L. Healy & L. B. Bourne (Eds.), *Acquisition and long-term re-*

tention of knowledge and skills: The durability and specificity of cognitive procedures. Newbury Park, CA: Sage.

SLABY, R. G., & FREY, K. S. (1975). Development of gender constancy and selective attention to same-sex models. *Child Development, 46,* 849–856.

SLADE, A. (1987). Quality of attachment and early symbolic play. *Developmental Psychology, 23,* 78–85.

SLATER, A. (1995a). Individual differences in infancy and later IQ. *Journal of Child Psychology and Psychiatry and Allied Disciplines, 36,* 69–112.

SLATER, A. (1995b). Visual perception and memory at birth. In C. Rovee-Collier & L. P. Lipsitt (Eds.), *Advances in infancy research* (Vol. 9). Norwood, NJ: Ablex.

SLATER, A., & MORISON, V. (1985). Shape constancy and slant perception at birth. *Perception, 14,* 337–344.

SLATER, A., COOPER, R., ROSE, D., & MORISON, V. (1989). Prediction of cognitive performance from infancy to early childhood. *Human Development, 32,* 137–147.

SLATER, A., JOHNSON, S. P., BROWN, E., & BADENOCH, M. (1996). Newborn infants' perception of partly occluded objects. *Infant Behavior and Development, 19,* 145–148.

SLATER, A., JOHNSON, S. P., KELLMAN, P. J., & SPELKE, E. S. (1994). The role of three dimensional depth cues in infants' perception of partly occluded objects. *Early Development and Parenting, 3,* 187–191.

SLATER, A., MATTOCK, A., & BROWN, E. (1990). Size constancy at birth: Newborn infant's responses to retinal and real size. *Journal of Experimental Child Psychology, 49,* 314–322.

SLATER, A., MATTOCK, A., BROWN, E., & BREMNER, J. G. (1991). Form perception at birth: Cohen and Younger (1984) revisited. *Journal of Experimental Child Psychology, 51,* 395–406.

SLAUGHTER-DeFOE, D. T., NAKAGAWA, K., TAKANISHI, R., & JOHNSON, D. J. (1990). Toward cultural/ecological perspectives on schooling and achievement in African- and Asian-American children. *Child Development, 61,* 363–383.

SLOBIN, D. I. (1982). Universal and particular in the acquisition of language. In E. Wanner & L. R. Gleitman (Eds.), *Language acquisition: The state of the art.* Cambridge: Cambridge University Press.

SLOBIN, D. I. (Ed.). (1985). *The cross-linguistic study of language* (Vols. 1 and 2). Hillsdale, NJ: Erlbaum.

SLOMKOWSKI, C., & DUNN, J. (1993, March). *Conflict in close relationships.* Paper presented at the meeting of the Society for Research in Child Development, New Orleans.

SLOMKOWSKI, C. L., & KILLEN, M. (1992). Young children's conceptions of transgressions with friends and nonfriends. *International Journal of Behavioral Development, 15,* 247–258.

SLUCKIN, A. (1980). Dominance relationships in preschool children. In D. R. Omark, F. F. Strayer, & D. G. Freedman (Eds.), *Dominance relations: An ethological view of human conflict and social interaction.* New York: Garland.

SMETANA, J. G. (1986). Preschool children's conceptions of sex-role transgressions. *Child Development, 57,* 862–871.

SMETANA, J. G. (1989). Toddlers' social interactions in the context of moral and conventional transgressions in the home. *Developmental Psychology, 25,* 499–508.

SMETANA, J. G. (1994). Morality in context: Abstractions, ambiguities, and applications. In R. Vasta (Ed.), *Annals of child development.* (Vol. 10). London: Kingsley.

SMETANA, J. G., & BRAEGES, J. L. (1990). The development of toddlers' moral and conventional judgments. *Merrill-Palmer Quarterly, 36,* 329–346.

SMETANA, J. G., KILLEN, M., & TURIEL, E. (1991). Children's reasoning about interpersonal and moral conflicts. *Child Development, 62,* 629–644.

SMETANA, J. G., SCHLAGMAN, N., & ADAMS, P. (1993). Preschoolers' judgments about hypothetical and actual transgressions. *Child Development, 64,* 202–214.

SMILEY, P., & HUTTENLOCHER, J. (1989). Young children's acquisition of emotion concepts. In C. Saarni & P. L. Harris (Eds.), *Children's understanding of emotion.* Cambridge: Cambridge University Press.

SMILEY, P. A., & DWECK, C. S. (1994). Individual differences in achievement goals among young children. *Child Development, 65,* 1723–1743.

SMITH, B. A., & BLASS, E. M. (1996). Taste-mediated calming in premature, preterm, and full-term human infants. *Developmental Psychology, 32,* 1084–1089.

SMITH, B. A., STEVENS, K., TORGERSON, W. S., & KIM, J. H. (1992). Diminished reactivity of postmature human infants to sucrose compared with term infants. *Developmental Psychology, 28,* 811–820.

SMITH, C. L. (1979). Children's understanding of natural language hierarchies. *Journal of Experimental Child Psychology, 27,* 437–458.

SMITH, E. A. (1989). A biosocial model of adolescent sexual behavior. In G. R. Adams, R. Montemayor, & T. P. Gullota (Eds.), *Biology of adolescent behavior and development.* Newbury Park, CA: Sage.

SMITH, P. K. (1978). A longitudinal study of social participation in preschool children: Solitary and parallel play reexamined. *Developmental Psychology, 14,* 517–523.

SMITH, P. K. (1995). Grandparenthood. In M. H. Bornstein (Ed.), *Handbook of parenting: Vol. 3. Status and social conditions of parenting.* Mahwah, NJ: Erlbaum.

SMITH, P. K., & CONNOLLY, K. J. (1981). *The ecology of preschool behavior.* Cambridge: Cambridge University Press.

SNAREY, J. R. (1985). Cross-cultural universality of social-moral development: A critical review of Kohlbergian research. *Psychological Bulletin, 97,* 202–232.

SNAREY, J. R., & KELJO, K. (1991). In a *Gemeinschaft* voice: The cross-cultural expansion of moral development theory. In W. M. Kurtines & J. L. Gewirtz (Eds.), *Handbook of moral behavior and development: Vol. 1. Theory.* Hillsdale, NJ: Erlbaum.

SNAREY, J. R., REIMER, J., & KOHLBERG, L. (1985). Development of social-moral reasoning among kibbutz adolescents: A longitudinal cross-cultural study. *Developmental Psychology, 21,* 3–17.

SNOW, C. E. (1981). The uses of imitation. *Journal of Child Language, 8,* 205–212.

SNOW, C. E. (1983). Saying it again: The role of expanded and deferred imitations in language acquisition. In K. E. Nelson (Ed.), *Children's language* (Vol. 4). Hillsdale, NJ: Erlbaum.

SNOW, C. E., & FERGUSON, C. (1977). *Talking to children: Language input and acquisition.* Cambridge: Cambridge University Press.

SNOW, C. E., & GOLDFIELD, B. A. (1983). Turn the page please: Situation-specific language acquisition. *Journal of Child Language, 10,* 551–569.

SNOW, C. E., PAN, B. E., IMBENS-BAILEY, A., & HERMAN, J. (1996). Learning how to say what one means: A longitudinal study of children's speech act use. *Social Development, 5,* 56–84.

SNOW, C. E., PERLMAN, R., & NATHAN, D. (1987). Why routines are different: Toward a multiple-factors model of the relation between input and language acquisition. In K. E. Nelson & A. VanKleeck (Eds.), *Children's language* (Vol. 6). Hillsdale, NJ: Erlbaum.

SNOW, R. E., & YALOW, E. (1982). Education and intelligence. In R. J. Sternberg (Ed.), *Handbook of human intelligence.* Cambridge: Cambridge University Press.

SNYDER, J. J., & PATTERSON, G. R. (1995). Individual differences in social aggression: A test of a reinforcement model of socialization in the natural environment. *Behavior Therapy, 26,* 371–391.

SNYDER, J., WEST, L., STOCKEMER, V., & GIBBONS, S. (1996). A social learning model of peer choice in the natural environment. *Journal of Applied Developmental Psychology, 17,* 215–237.

SOKOLOV, E. N. (1960). *Perception and the conditioned reflex.* New York: Macmillan.

SOLOMON, G. E. A., JOHNSON, S. C., ZAITCHIK, D., & CAREY, S. (1996). Like father, like son: Young children's understanding of how and why offspring resemble their parents. *Child Development, 67,* 151–171.

SOMMERVILLE, J. (1978). English Puritans and children: A social-cultural explanation. *Journal of Psychohistory, 6,* 113–137.

SOMMERVILLE, J. (1982). *The rise and fall of childhood.* Beverly Hills, CA: Sage.

SONNENSCHEIN, S. (1988). The development of referential communication: Speaking to different listeners. *Child Development, 59,* 694–702.

SONTAG, L. W. (1944). War and fetal maternal relationship. *Marriage and Family Living, 6,* 1–5.

SONTAG, L. W. (1966). Implications of fetal behavior and environment for adult personalities. *Annals of the New York Academy of Sciences, 134,* 782–786.

SOPHIAN, C. (1995). *Children's numbers.* Madison, WI: Brown & Benchmark.

SORCE, J. F., EMDE, R. N., CAMPOS, J. J., & KLINNERT, M. D. (1985). Maternal emotional signaling: Its effect on the visual cliff behavior of 1-year-olds. *Developmental Psychology, 21,* 195–200.

SOSTEK, A. M., SMITH, Y. F., KATZ, K. S., & GRANT, E. G. (1987). Developmental outcome of preterm infants with intraventricular hemorrhage at one and two years of age. *Child Development, 58,* 779–786.

SPEARMAN, C. (1927). *The abilities of man.* New York: Macmillan.

SPEER, J. R., & FLAVELL, J. H. (1979). Young children's knowledge of the relative difficulty of recognition and recall memory tasks. *Developmental Psychology, 15,* 214–217.

SPELKE, E. S. (1976). Infants' intermodal perception of events. *Cognitive Psychology, 8,* 533–560.

SPELKE, E. S. (1985). Perception of unity, persistence, and identity: Thoughts on infants' conceptions of objects. In J. Mehler & R. Fox (Eds.), *Neonate cognition: Beyond the blooming buzzing confusion.* Hillsdale, NJ: Erlbaum.

SPELKE, E. S. (1988). Where perceiving ends and thinking begins: The apprehension of objects in infancy. In A. Yonas (Ed.), *Minnesota symposia on child psychology: Vol. 20. Perceptual development in infancy.* Hillsdale, NJ: Erlbaum.

SPELKE, E. S. (1991). Physical knowledge in infancy: Reflections on Piaget's theory. In S. Carey & R. Gelman (Eds.), *The epigenesis of mind.* Hillsdale, NJ: Erlbaum.

SPELKE, E. S., BREINLINGER, K., MACOMBER, J., & JACOBSON, K. (1992). Origins of knowledge. *Psychological Review, 99,* 605–632.

SPELKE, E. S., & HERMER, L. (1996). Early cognitive development: Objects and space. In R. Gelman & T. Au (Eds.), *Perceptual and cognitive development.* San Diego: Academic Press.

SPELKE, E. S., & OWSLEY, C. J. (1979). Intermodal exploration and knowledge in infancy. *Infant Behavior and Development, 2,* 13–28.

SPENCE, J. T. (1985). Gender identity and its implications for concepts of masculinity and feminity. In T. B. Sonderegger (Ed.), *Nebraska symposium on motivation: Psychology and gender* (Vol. 32). Lincoln: University of Nebraska Press.

SPENCE, J. T., & HELMREICH, R. L. (1978). *Masculinity and femininity: Their psychological dimensions, correlates, and antecedents.* Austin: University of Texas Press.

SPENCE, J. T., HELMREICH, R. L., & HOLAHAN, C. K. (1979). Negative and positive components of psychological masculinity and femininity and their relationships to self-reports of neurotic and acting out behaviors. *Journal of Personality and Social Psychology, 37,* 1673–1682.

SPERGEL, I. A., CHANCE, R. I., & CURRY, G. (1990, June). *National Youth Gang Suppression and Intervention Program* (National Institute of Justice Reports, No. 222, pp. 1–4).

SPERGEL, I. A., & CURRY, G. D. (1993). The National Youth Gang Survey: A research and development process. In A. P. Goldstein & C. R. Huff (Eds.), *The gang intervention handbook.* Champaign, IL: Research Press.

SPERRY, L. L., & SPERRY, D. E. (1995). Young children's presentations of self in conversational narration. In L. L. Sperry & P. A. Smiley (Eds.), *Exploring young children's concepts of self and other through conversation.* San Francisco: Jossey-Bass.

SPIEKER, S. J., & BENSLEY, L. (1994). Roles of living arrangements and grandmother social support in adolescent mothering and infant attachment. *Developmental Psychology, 30,* 102–111.

SPITZ, R. (1945). Hospitalism: An inquiry into the genesis of psychiatric conditions in early childhood. *Psychoanalytic Study of the Child, 1,* 53–74.

SPRINGER, K. (1996). Young children's understanding of a biological basis for parent-offspring relations. *Child Development, 67,* 2841–2856.

SPRINGER, K., & KEIL, F. C. (1991). Early differentiation of causal mechanisms appropriate to biological and nonbiological kinds. *Child Development, 62,* 767–781.

SPRINGER, S. P., & DEUTSCH, G. (1989). *Left brain, right brain* (3rd ed.). New York: W. H. Freeman.

SROUFE, L. A. (1986). Bowlby's contribution to psychoanalytic theory and developmental psychology: Attachment: Separation: Loss. *Journal of Child Psychology and Psychiatry, 27,* 841–849.

SROUFE, L. A. (1990). An organizational perspective on the self. In D. Cicchetti & M. Beeghly (Eds.), *The self in transition: Infancy to childhood.* Chicago: University of Chicago Press.

SROUFE, L. A. (1996). *Emotional development.* New York: Cambridge University Press.

SROUFE, L. A., BENNETT, C., ENGLUND, M., URBAN, J., & SHULMAN, S. (1993). The significance of gender boundaries in preadolescence: Contemporary correlates and antecedents of boundary violation and maintenance. *Child Development, 64,* 455–466.

STACK, D. M., & MUIR, D. W. (1992). Adult tactile stimulation during face-to-face interactions modulates five-month-olds' affect and attention. *Child Development, 63,* 1509–1525.

STAKE, J. E. (1997). Integrating expressiveness and instrumentality in real-life settings: A new perspective on the benefits of androgyny. *Sex Roles, 37,* 541–564.

STAMBAK, M., & SINCLAIR, H. (1993). *Pretend play among 3-year-olds.* Hillsdale, NJ: Erlbaum.

STANGOR, C., & RUBLE, D. N. (1987). Development of gender role knowledge and gender constancy. In L. S. Liben & M. L. Signorella (Eds.), *New directions for child development: No. 38. Children's gender schemata.* San Francisco: Jossey-Bass.

STANHOPE, R. (1989). The endocrine control of puberty. In J. M. Tanner & M. A. Preece (Eds.), *The physiology of human growth.* London: Cambridge University Press.

STANOVICH, K. E. (Ed.). (1993a). The development of rationality and critical thinking [Special issue]. *Merrill-Palmer Quarterly, 39* (1).

STANOVICH, K. E. (1993b). Does reading make you smarter? Literacy and the development of verbal intelligence. In H. W. Reese (Ed.), *Advances in child development and behavior* (Vol. 24). San Diego: Academic Press.

STARK, R. E. (1986). Prespeech segmental feature development. In P. Fletcher & M. Garman (Eds.), *Language acquisition: Studies in first language development* (2nd ed.). New York: Cambridge University Press.

STARKEY, P., & COOPER, R. (1980). Perception of numbers by human infants. *Science, 210,* 1033–1034.

STAUB, E. (1996). Cultural-societal roots of violence: Examples of genocidal violence and of contemporary youth violence in the United States. *American Psychologist, 51,* 117–132.

STEELE, H., STEELE, M., & FONAGY, P. (1996). Associations among attachment classifications of mothers, fathers, and their infants. *Child Development, 67,* 541–555.

STEIN, A. H., & FRIEDRICH, L. K. (1975). The impact of television on children and youth. In E. M. Hetherington (Ed.), *Review of child development research* (Vol. 5). Chicago: University of Chicago Press.

STEINBERG, L. D. (1988). Pubertal maturation and family relations: Evidence for the distancing hypothesis. In G. Adams, R. Montemayor, & T. Gullotta (Eds.), *Advances in adolescent development.* Beverly Hills, CA: Sage.

STEINBERG, L., DARLING, N. E., FLETCHER, A. C., BROWN, B. B., & DORNBUSCH, S. M. (1995). Authoritative parenting and adolescent adjustment: An ecological journey. In P. Moen, G. H. Elder, Jr., & K. Luscher (Eds.), *Examining lives in context: Perspectives on the ecology of human development.* Washington, DC: American Psychological Association.

STEINBERG, L., LAMBORN, S. D., DARLING, N., MOUNTS, N. S., & DORNBUSCH, S. M. (1994). Over-time changes in adjustment and competence among adolescents from authoritative, authoritarian, indulgent, and neglectful families. *Child Development, 65,* 754–770.

STEINER, J. E. (1979). Human facial expressions in response to taste and smell stimulation. In H. W. Reese & L. P. Lipsitt (Eds.), *Advances in child development and behavior* (Vol. 13). New York: Academic Press.

STENBERG, C. R., CAMPOS, J. J., & EMDE, R. N. (1983). The facial expression of anger in seven-month-old infants. *Child Development, 54,* 178–184.

STEPHENS, T. (1990). Blocking fetal AIDS: Immune intervention paces science. *Journal of NIH Research, 3,* 53–54.

STERN, M., & KARRAKER, K. (1989). Sex stereotyping of infants: A review of gender labeling studies. *Sex Roles, 20,* 501–522.

STERN, M., & KARRAKER, K. (1992). Modifying the prematurity stereotype in matters of premature and ill full-term infants. *Journal of Clinical Child Psychology, 21,* 76–82.

STERNBERG, R. J., & POWELL, J. S. (1983). The development of intelligence. In P. H. Mussen (Series Ed.) & J. H. Flavell & E. M. Markman (Vol. Eds.), *Handbook of child psychology: Vol. 3. Cognitive development.* New York: Wiley.

STERNBERG, R. J. (1985). *Beyond IQ: A triarchic theory of human intelligence.* New York: Cambridge University Press.

STERNBERG, R. J. (1991). Death, taxes, and bad intelligence tests. *Intelligence, 15,* 257–269.

STEVENSON, H. W., & STIGLER, J. W. (1992). *The learning gap: Why our schools are failing and what we can learn from Japanese and Chinese education.* New York: Summit Books.

STEVENSON, H. W., CHEN, C., & LEE, S. Y. (1993). Mathematics achievement of Chinese, Japanese, and American children: Ten years later. *Science, 259,* 53–58.

STEVENSON, H. W., LEE, S., CHEN, C., STIGLER, J. W., HSU, C., & KITAMURA, S. (1990). Contexts of achievement: A study of American, Chinese, and Japanese children. *Monographs of the Society for Research in Child Development, 55* (1–2, Serial No. 221).

STEVENSON, H. W., LEE S. Y., & STIGLER, J. W. (1986). Mathematics achievement of Chinese, Japanese, and American children. *Science, 231,* 693–699.

STEVENSON, M. R., & BLACK, K. N. (1988). Paternal absence and sex-role development: A meta-analysis. *Child Development, 59,* 793–814.

STEWART, S. L., & RUBIN, K. H. (1995). The social problem solving skills of anxious-withdrawn children. *Development and Psychopathology, 7,* 323–336.

STIFTER, C. A., & BRAUNGART, J. M. (1995). The regulation of negative reactivity in infancy: Function and development. *Developmental Psychology, 31,* 448–455.

STIFTER, C. A., COULEHAN, C. M., & FISH, M. (1993). Linking employment to attachment: The mediating effects of maternal separation anxiety and interactive behavior. *Child Development, 64,* 1451–1460.

STIFTER, C. A., & FOX, N. A. (1990). Infant reactivity: Physiological correlates of newborn and 5-month temperament. *Developmental Psychology, 26,* 582–588.

STIGLER, J. W., & FERNANDEZ, C. (1995). Learning mathematics from classroom instruction: Cross-cultural and experimental perspectives. In C. A. Nelson (Ed.), *Minnesota symposia on child psychology: Vol. 28. Basic and applied perspectives on learning, cognition, and development.* Mahwah, NJ: Erlbaum.

STIPEK, D. (1992). The child at school. In M. E. Lamb & M. H. Bornstein (Eds.), *Developmental psychology: An advanced textbook* (3rd ed.). Hillsdale, NJ: Erlbaum.

STIPEK, D., GRALINSKI, J. H., & KOPP, C. B. (1990). Self-concept development in the toddler years. *Developmental Psychology, 26,* 972–977.

STIPEK, D., & MacIVER, D. (1989). Developmental change in children's assessment of intellectual competence. *Child Development, 60,* 521–538.

STIPEK, D., RECCHIA, S., & McCLINTIC, S. (1992). Self-evaluation in young children. *Monographs of the Society for Research in Child Development, 57*(1, Serial No. 226).

STIPEK, D., & TANNATT, L. (1984). Children's judgments of their own and their peers' academic competence. *Journal of Educational Psychology, 76,* 75–84.

STJERNFELDT, M., BERGLUND, K., LINDSTEN, J., & LUDVIGSSON, J. (1986). Maternal smoking during pregnancy and risk of childhood cancer. *Lancet, 1,* 1350–1352.

STOCKER, C., & DUNN, J. (1990). Sibling relationships in childhood: Links with friendships and peer relationships. *British Journal of Developmental Psychology, 8,* 227–244.

STOCKER, C. M., & MANTZ-SIMMONS, L. M. (1993). *Children's friendship and peer status: Links with family relationships, temperament, and social skills.* Unpublished manuscript.

STODDART, T., & TURIEL, E. (1985). Children's concepts of cross-gender activities. *Child Development, 56,* 1241–1252.

STOLL, C., DOTT, B., ALEMBIK, Y., & ROTH, M. (1993). Evaluation of routine prenatal ultrasound examination in detecting fetal chromosomal abnormalities in a low risk population. *Human Genetics, 91,* 37–41.

STONE, C. A., & DAY, M. C. (1978). Levels of availability of a formal operational strategy. *Child Development, 49,* 1054–1065.

STOTT, D. H. (1969). The child's hazards *in utero.* In J. G. Howells (Ed.), *Modern perspectives in international child psychiatry.* Edinburgh: Oliver & Boyd.

STRAKER, G. (1992). *Faces in the revolution.* Cape Town, South Africa: David Philip.

STRAUGHAN, R. (1986). Why act on Kohlberg's moral judgments? (Or how to reach Stage 6 and remain a bastard). In S. Modgil & C. Modgil (Eds.), *Lawrence Kohlberg: Consensus and controversy.* Philadelphia: Falmer.

STRAYER, F. F. (1980). Social ecology of the preschool peer group. In W. A. Collins (Ed.), *Minnesota symposia on child psychology: Vol. 13. Development of cognition, affect, and social relations.* Hillsdale, NJ: Erlbaum.

STRAYER, F. F., & NOEL, J. M. (1986). The prosocial and antisocial functions of preschool aggression: An ethological study of triadic conflict among young children. In C. Zahn-Waxler, E. M. Cummings, & R. Iannotti (Eds.), *Altruism and aggression: Biological and social origins.* Cambridge: Cambridge University Press.

STRAYER, F. F., & STRAYER, J. (1976). An ethological analysis of social agonism and dominance relations among preschool children. *Child Development, 47,* 980–989.

STREISSGUTH, A. P., BARR, H. M., JOHNSON, J. C., MARTIN, D. C., & KIRCHNER, G. L. (1985). Attention and distraction at age 7 years related to maternal drinking during pregnancy. *Alcoholism: Clinical and Experimental Research, 9,* 195.

STREISSGUTH, A. P., SAMPSON, P. D., & BARR, H. M. (1989). Neurobehavioral dose-response effects of prenatal alcohol exposure in humans from infancy to adulthood. *Annals of the New York Academy of Sciences, 562,* 145–158.

STUDDERT-KENNEDY, M. (1986). Sources of variability in early speech in infancy. In G. Yeni-Konshian, C. Kavanaugh, & C. Ferguson (Eds.), *Child phonology: Perception and production.* New York: Academic Press.

SUE, S., & OZAKI, S. (1990). Asian-American educational achievements: A phenomenon in search of an explanation. *American Psychologist, 45,* 913–920.

SULLIVAN, M. W. (1982). Reactivation: Priming forgotten memories in human infants. *Child Development, 53,* 516–523.

SULLIVAN, M. W., LEWIS, M., & ALESSANDRI, S. M. (1992). Cross-age stability in emotional expressions: During learning and extinction. *Developmental Psychology, 28,* 58–63.

SULS, J., & WILLS, T. A. (Eds.). (1991). *Social comparison: Contemporary theory and research.* Hillsdale, NJ: Erlbaum.

SUN, M. (1988). Anti-acne drug poses dilemma for FDA. *Science, 240,* 714–715.

SUOMI, S. J., & HARLOW, H. F. (1975). The role and reason of peer relationships in rhesus monkeys. In M. Lewis & L. A. Rosenblum (Eds.), *Friendship and peer relations.* New York: Wiley.

SUPER, C. M. (1981). Cross-cultural research on infancy. In H. C. Triandis & A. Heron (Eds.), *Handbook of cross-cultural psychology: Vol. 4. Developmental psychology.* Boston: Allyn & Bacon.

SUPER, C. M., HERRERA, M. G., & MORA, J. O. (1990). Long-term effects of food supplementation and psychosocial intervention on the physical growth of Colombian infants at risk of malnutrition. *Child Development, 61,* 29–49.

SURBER, C. F. (1982). Separable effects of motives, consequences, and presentation order on children's moral judgments. *Developmental Psychology, 18,* 257–266.

SUSMAN, E. J., INOFF-GERMAIN, G., NOTTELMANN, E. D., LORIAUX, L., CUTLER, G. B., & CHROUSOS, G. P. (1987). Hormones, emotional dispositions, and aggressive attributes in young adolescents. *Child Development, 58,* 1114–1134.

SUZUKI, L. A., & VALENCIA, R. (1997). Race-ethnicity and measured intelligence. *American Psychologist, 52,* 1103–1114.

SVARE, B. (1983). Psychobiological determinants of maternal aggressive behavior. In E. C. Simmel, M. E. Hahn, & J. K. Walters (Eds.), *Aggressive behavior: Genetic and neural approaches.* Hillsdale, NJ: Erlbaum.

SVEJDA, M. J., PANNABECKER, B. J., & EMDE, R. N. (1982). Parent-to-infant attachment: A critique of the early "bonding" model. In R. N. Emde & R. J. Harmon (Eds.), *The development of attachment and affiliative systems.* New York: Plenum.

SWAAB, D. F., GOOREN, L. J. G., & HOFMAN, M. A. (1992). The human hypothalamus in relation to gender and sexual orientation. *Progress in Brain Research, 93,* 205–219.

SWAIN, I. U., ZELAZO, P. R., & CLIFTON, R. K. (1993). Newborn infants' memory for speech sounds retained over 24 hours. *Developmental Psychology, 29,* 313–323.

SWAIN, M. (1977). Bilingualism, monolingualism, and code acquisition. In W. Mackey & T. Andersson (Eds.), *Bilingualism in early childhood.* Rowley, MA: Newbury House.

SWANSON, H. L. (1996). *Swanson Cognitive Processing Test.* Austin, TX: PRO-ED.

St. PETERS, M., FITCH, M., HUSTON, A. C., WRIGHT, J. C., & EAKINS, D. J. (1991). Television and families: What do young children watch with their parents? *Child Development, 62,* 1409–1423.

TAGER-FLUSBERG, H., & CALKINS, S. (1990). Does imitation facilitate the acquisition of grammar? Evidence from a study of autistic, Down's syndrome and normal children. *Journal of Child Language, 17,* 591–606.

TAKAHASHI, K. (1986). Examining the Strange Situation procedure with Japanese mothers and 12-month-old infants. *Developmental Psychology, 22,* 265–270.

TAKAHASHI, K. (1990). Are the key assumptions of the "Strange Situation" procedure universal? A view from Japanese research. *Human Development, 33,* 23–30.

TAMIS-LEMONDA, C. S., & BORNSTEIN, M. H. (1994). Specificity in mother–toddler language-play relations across the second year. *Developmental Psychology, 30,* 283–292.

TANGNEY, J., & FISCHER, K. (Eds.). (1995). *Self-conscious emotions: The psychology of shame, guilt, embarrassment, and pride.* New York: Guilford.

TANNER, J. M. (1963). The regulation of human growth. *Child Development, 34,* 817–847.

TANNER, J. M. (1974). Variability of growth and maturity in newborn infants. In M. Lewis & L. A. Rosenblum (Eds.), *The effect of the infant on its caregiver.* New York: Wiley.

TANNER, J. M. (1987). Issues and advances in adolescent growth and development. *Journal of Adolescent Health Care, 8,* 470–478.

TANNER, J. M. (1990). *Fetus into man: Physical growth from conception to maturity* (2nd ed.). Cambridge: Harvard University Press.

TAPPAN, M. B. (1997) Language, culture, and moral development: A Vygotskian perspective. *Developmental Review, 17,* 78–100.

TATE, D. C., REPPUCCI, N. D., & MULVEY, E. P. (1995). Violent juvenile delinquents: Treatment effectiveness and implications for future action. *American Psychologist, 50,* 777–781.

TAYLOR, H. J. (1980). *The IQ game: A methodological inquiry into the heredity-environment controversy.* New Brunswick, NJ: Rutgers University Press.

TAYLOR, M. (1996). A theory of mind perspective on social cognitive development. In R. Gelman & T. Au (Eds.), *Perceptual and cognitive development.* San Diego: Academic Press.

TAYLOR, M., CARTWRIGHT, B. S., & BOWDEN, T. (1991). Perspective taking and theory of mind: Do children predict interpretive diversity as a function of differences in observers' knowledge? *Child Development, 62,* 1334–1351.

TAYLOR, M., ESBENSEN, B. M., & BENNETT, R. T. (1994). Children's understanding of knowledge acquisition: The tendency for children to report that they have always known what they have just learned. *Child Development, 65,* 1581–1604.

TAYLOR, M. G. (1996). The development of children's beliefs about social and biological aspects of gender differences. *Child Development, 67,* 1555–1571.

TELLER, D. Y., & BORNSTEIN, M. H. (1987). Infant color vision and color perception. In P. Salapatek & L. Cohen (Eds.), *Handbook of infant perception: Vol. 1. From sensation to perception.* New York: Academic Press.

TELZROW, R., CAMPOS, J., ATWATER, S., BERTENTHAL, B., BENSON, J., & CAMPOS,. (1988). Delays and spurts in spatial cognitive development in locomotor-handicapped infants. *Infant Behavior and Development, 11,* 312.

TEO, T., BECKER, G., & EDELSTEIN, W. (1995). Variability in structured wholeness: Context factors in L. Kohlberg's data on the development of moral judgment. *Merrill-Palmer Quarterly, 41,* 381–393.

TERMAN, L. M. (1925). *Genetic studies of genius: Vol. 1. Mental and physical traits of a thousand gifted children.* Stanford, CA: Stanford University Press.

TERRY, R., & COIE, J. D. (1991). A comparison of methods for defining sociometric status among children. *Developmental Psychology, 27,* 867–880.

TESSER, A. (1984). Self-evaluation maintenance processes: Implications for relationships and for development. In J. C. Masters & K. Yarkin-Levin (Eds.), *Boundary areas in social and developmental psychology.* New York: Academic Press.

TETI, D. M. (1992). Sibling interaction. In V. B. Van Hasselt & M. Hersen (Eds.), *Handbook of social development.* New York: Plenum.

THARP, R. G. (1989). Psychocultural variables and constants: Effects on teaching and learning in schools. *American Psychologist, 44,* 349–359.

THELEN, E. (1994). Three-month-old infants can learn task-specific patterns of interlimb coordination. *Psychological Science, 5,* 280–285.

THELEN, E. (1995). Motor development: A new synthesis: *American Psychologist, 50,* 79–95.

THELEN, E., & ADOLPH, K. E. (1992). Arnold L. Gesell: The paradox of nature and nurture. *Developmental Psychology, 28,* 368–380.

THELEN, E., CORBETTA, D., & SPENCER, J. (1996). The development of reaching during the first year: The role of movement speed. *Journal of Experimental Psychology: Human Perception and Performance, 22,* 1059–1076.

THELEN, E., & FISHER, D. M. (1982). Newborn stepping: An explanation for a "disappearing reflex." *Developmental Psychology, 18,* 760–775.

THELEN, E., & FISHER, D. M. (1983). The organization of spontaneous leg movements in newborn infants. *Journal of Motor Behavior, 15,* 353–377.

THELEN, E., & SMITH, L. B. (1998). Dynamic systems theories. In W. Damon (Ed.), *Handbook of child psychology: Vol. 1. Theoretical models of human development.* New York: Wiley.

THOMA, S. J. (1986). Estimating gender differences in the comprehension and preference of moral issues. *Developmental Review, 6,* 165–180.

THOMAN, E. B. (1990). Sleeping and waking states in infants: A functional perspective. *Neuroscience and Behavioral Reviews, 14,* 93–107.

THOMAN, E. B. (1993). Obligation and option in the premature nursery. *Developmental Review, 13,* 1–30.

THOMAN, E. B., INGERSOLL, E. W., & ACEBO, C. (1991). Premature infants seek rhythmic stimulation, and the experience facilitates neurobehavioral development. *Journal of Developmental and Behavioral Pediatrics, 12,* 11–18.

THOMAS, A., & CHESS, S. (1977). *Temperament and development.* New York: Bruner/Mazel.

THOMAS, A., & CHESS, S. (1984). Genesis and evaluation of behavioral disorder: From infancy to early adult life. *American Journal of Psychiatry, 141,* 1–9.

THOMAS, A., & CHESS, S. (1986). The New York Longitudinal Study: From infancy to early adult life. In R. Plomin & J. Dunn (Eds.), *The study of temperament: Changes, continuities and challenges.* Hillsdale, NJ: Erlbaum.

THOMAS, A., CHESS, S., & BIRCH, H. G. (1968). *Temperament and behavior disorders in children.* New York: New York University Press.

THOMAS, H. (1983). Familial correlational analyses, sex differences, and the X-linked gene hypothesis. *Psychological Bulletin, 93,* 427–440.

THOMAS, H. (1993). A theory explaining sex differences in high mathematical ability has been around for some time. *Behavioral and Brain Sciences, 16,* 187–215.

THOMAS, R. M. (1979). *Comparing theories of child development.* Belmont, CA: Wadsworth.

THOMPSON, C. P., SKOWRONSKI, J. J., LARSEN, S. F., & BETZ, A. L. (1996). *Autobiographical memory: Remembering what and remembering when.* Mahwah, NJ: Erlbaum.

THOMPSON, R. A. (1998). Early sociopersonality development. In W. Damon (Ed.), *Handbook of child psychology: Vol. 3. Social, emotional, and personality development.* New York: Wiley.

THOMPSON, R. A., CONNELL, J. P., & BRIDGES, L. J. (1988). Temperament, emotion, and social interactive behavior in the Strange Situation: A component process analysis of attachment system functioning. *Child Development, 59,* 1102–1110.

THOMPSON, R. A., FLOOD, M. F., & LUNDQUIST, L. (1995). Emotion regulation: Its relations to attachment and developmental psychopathology. In D. Cicchetti & S. L. Toth (Eds.), *Emotion, cognition, and representation. Rochester Symposium on Developmental Psychopathology* (Vol. 6). Rochester, NY: University of Rochester Press.

THOMPSON, R. A., & LIMBER, S. (1990). "Social anxiety" in infancy: Stranger wariness and separation distress. In H. Leitenberg (Ed.), *Handbook of social and evaluation anxiety.* New York: Plenum.

THOMPSON, T. L., & ZERBINOS, E. (1995). Gender roles in animated cartoons: Has the picture changed in 20 years? *Sex Roles, 32,* 651–674.

THOMPSON, T. L., & ZERBINOS, E. (1997). Television cartoons: Do children notice it's a boy's world? *Sex Roles, 37,* 415–432.

THOMPSON, W. R., & GRUSEC, J. E. (1970). Studies of early experience. In P. H. Mussen (Ed.), *Carmichael's manual of child psychology* (3rd ed., Vol. 1). New York: Wiley.

THOMSON, J. R., & CHAPMAN, R. S. (1977). Who is "Daddy" revisited: The status of two-year-olds' over-extended words in use and comprehension. *Journal of Child Language, 4,* 359–375.

THORNDIKE, R. L., HAGEN, E. P., & SATTLER, J. M. (1986). *Stanford–Binet Intelligence Scale* (4th ed.). Chicago: Riverside Publishing Company.

THORNE, B. (1986). Girls and boys together . . . but mostly apart: Gender arrangements in elementary schools. In W. W. Hartup & Z. Rubin (Eds.), *Relationships and development.* Hillsdale, NJ: Erlbaum.

THURSTONE, L. L. (1938). *Primary mental abilities.* Chicago: University of Chicago Press.

THURSTONE, L. L., & THURSTONE, T. G. (1962). *SRA Primary Mental Abilities.* Chicago: Science Research Associates.

TIESZEN, H. R. (1979). Children's social behavior in a Korean preschool. *Journal of Korean Home Economics Association, 17,* 71–84.

TIETJEN, A. M., & WALKER, L. J. (1985). Moral reasoning and leadership among men in Papua New Guinea society. *Developmental Psychology, 21,* 982–992.

TINBERGEN, N. (1973). *The animal in its world: Explorations of an ethologist, 1932–1972* (Vols. 1 and 2). Cambridge: Harvard University Press.

TINSLEY, B. J., & PARKE, R. D. (1988). The role of grandfathers in the context of the family. In P. Bronstein & C. P. Cowan (Eds.), *Fatherhood today: Men's changing roles in the family.* New York: Wiley.

TISAK, M. S. (1995). Domains of social reasoning and beyond. In R. Vasta (Ed.), *Annals of child development* (Vol. 11). London: Kingsley.

TISAK, M. S., & TURIEL, E. (1988). Variation in seriousness of transgressions and children's immoral and conventional concepts. *Developmental Psychology, 24,* 352–357.

TITTLE, C. K. (1986). Gender research in education. *American Psychologist, 41,* 1161–1168.

TOBEY, A. E., & GOODMAN, G. S. (1992). Children's eyewitness memory: Effects of participation and forensic context. *Child Abuse and Neglect, 16,* 779–796.

TODA, S., & FOGEL, A. (1993). Infant response to the still-face situation at 3 and 6 months. *Developmental Psychology, 29,* 532–538.

TOMADA, G., & SCHNEIDER, B. H. (1997). Relational aggression, gender, and peer acceptance: Invariance across culture, stability over time, and concordance among informants. *Developmental Psychology, 33,* 601–609.

TOMASELLO, M. (1996). Piagetian and Vygotskian approaches to language acquisition. *Human Development, 39,* 269–276.

TOMASELLO, M., CONTI-RAMSDEN, G., & EWERT, B. (1990). Young children's conversations with their mothers and fathers: Differences in breakdown and repair. *Journal of Child Language, 17,* 115–130.

TOMASELLO, M., & FARRAR, M. J. (1986). Joint attention and early language. *Child Development, 57,* 1454–1463.

TOMASELLO, M., & MERRIMAN, W. E. (Eds.). (1995). *Beyond names for things: Young children's acquisition of verbs.* Hillsdale, NJ: Erlbaum.

TORRANCE, E. P. (1970). Influence of dyadic interaction on creative functioning. *Psychological Reports, 26,* 391–394.

TOUCHETTE, N. (1990). Evolutions: Fertilization. *Journal of NIH Research, 2,* 94–97.

TRACY, D. M. (1987). Toys, spatial ability, and science and mathematics achievement: Are they related? *Sex Roles, 17,* 115–138.

TRACY, R. L., & AINSWORTH, M. D. S. (1981). Maternal affectionate behavior and infant–mother attachment patterns. *Child Development, 52,* 1341–1343.

TRAUTNER, H. M. (1992). The development of sex-typing in children: A longitudinal analysis. *German Journal of Psychology, 16,* 183–199.

TRAVERS, J. R., & LIGHT, R. J. (Eds.). (1982). *Learning from experience: Evaluating early childhood demonstration programs.* Washington, DC: National Academy Press.

TREHUB, S. E. (1976). The discrimination of foreign speech contrasts by infants and adults. *Child Development, 47,* 466–472.

TREHUB, S. E., & HENDERSON, J. (1994, July). Caregivers' songs and their effect on infant listeners. *Proceedings of the Meeting of the International Conference for Music Perception and Cognition.* Liege, Belgium.

TREHUB, S. E., & SCHELLENBERG, E. G. (1995). Music: Its relevance to infants. In R. Vasta (Ed.), *Annals of child development* (Vol. 11). London: Kingsley.

TREHUB, S. E., & SCHNEIDER, B. A. (1983). Recent advances in the behavioral study of infant audition. In S. E. Gerber & G. T. Mencher (Eds.), *Development of auditory behavior.* New York: Grune & Stratton.

TREHUB, S. E., SCHNEIDER, B. A., MORRONGIELLO, B. A., & THORPE, L. A. (1988). Auditory sensitivity in school-age children. *Journal of Experimental Child Psychology, 46,* 273–285.

TREHUB, S. E., THORPE, L. A., & COHEN, A. J. (1991, April). *Infants' auditory processing of numerical information.* Paper presented at the meeting of the Society for Research in Child Development, Seattle.

TREXLER, R. C. (1973). The foundlings of Florence, 1395–1455. *History of Childhood Quarterly, 1,* 259–284.

TRICKETT, P. K., & McBRIDE-CHANG, C. (1995). The developmental impact of different forms of child abuse and neglect. *Developmental Review, 15,* 311–337.

TRIVERS, R. L. (1971). The evolution of reciprocal altruism. *Quarterly Review of Biology, 46,* 35–57.

TRIVERS, R. L. (1983). The evolution of cooperation. In D. L. Bridgeman (Ed.), *The nature of prosocial development.* New York: Academic Press.

TRONICK, E. Z. (1989). Emotions and emotional communication in infants. *American Psychologist, 44,* 112–119.

TSUSHIMA, T., TAKIZAWA, O., SASAKI, M., SIRAKI, S., NUSHI, K., KOHNO, M., MENYUK, P., & BEST, C. (1994). *Discrimination of English /r-l/ and /w-y/ by Japanese infants at 6–12 months: Language specific developmental changes in speech perception abilities.* Paper presented at the International Conference on Spoken Language Processing, 4, Yokahama, Japan.

TUBMAN, J. G., LERNER, R. M., LERNER, J. V., & VON EYE, A. (1992). Temperament and adjustment in young adulthood: A 15-year longitudinal analysis. *American Journal of Orthopsychiatry, 62,* 564–574.

TUDGE, J., & ROGOFF, B. (1989). Peer influences on cognitive development: Piagetian and Vygotskian perspectives. In M. H. Bornstein & J. S. Bruner (Eds.), *Interaction in human development.* Hillsdale, NJ: Erlbaum.

TURIEL, E. (1966). An experimental test of the sequentiality of developmental stages in the child's moral judgments. *Journal of Personality and Social Psychology, 3,* 611–618.

TURIEL, E. (1987). Potential relations between the development of social reasoning and childhood aggression. In D. H. Crowell, I. M. Evans, & C. R. O'Donnell (Eds.), *Childhood aggression and violence: Sources of influence, prevention, and control.* New York: Plenum.

TURIEL, E. (1998). The development of morality. In W. Damon (Ed.), *Handbook of child psychology: Vol. 3. Social, emotional, and personality development.* New York: Wiley.

TURIEL, E., HILDEBRANDT, C., & WAINRYB, C. (1991). Judging social issues. *Monograph of the Society for Research in Child Development, 56*(Serial No. 224).

TURIEL, E., KILLEN, M., & HELWIG, C. C. (1987). Morality: Its structure, functions, and vagaries. In J. Kagan & S. Lamb (Eds.), *The emergence of moral concepts in young children.* Chicago: University of Chicago Press.

TURIEL, E., & WAINRYB, C. (1994). Social reasoning and the varieties of social experiences in cultural contexts. In H. W. Reese (Ed.), *Advances in child development and behavior* (Vol. 25). San Diego: Academic Press.

TURKHEIMER, E. (1991). Individual and group differences in adoption studies of IQ. *Psychological Bulletin, 110,* 392–405.

TURNER, P. J., & GERVAI, J. (1995). A multidimensional study of gender typing in preschool children and their parents: Personality, attitudes, preferences, behavior, and cultural differences. *Developmental Psychology, 31,* 759–772.

TURNER-BOWKER, D. M. (1996). Gender stereotyped descriptors in children's picture books: Does "Curious Jane" exist in the literature? *Sex Roles, 35,* 461–488.

U. S. BUREAU OF THE CENSUS. (1990). *Current population reports.* Washington, DC: U.S. Government Printing Office.

UMBEL, V. M., PEARSON, B. Z., FERNANDEZ, M. C., & OLLER, D. K. (1992). Measuring bilingual children's receptive vocabularies. *Child Development, 63,* 1012–1020.

UNDERWOOD, B., & MOORE, B. (1982). Perspective-taking and altruism. *Psychological Bulletin, 91,* 143–173.

UNDERWOOD, M. K., COIE, J. D., & HERBSMAN, C. R. (1992). Display rules for anger and aggression in school-age children. *Child Development, 63,* 366–380.

UNGER, D., & COOLEY, M. (1992). Partner and grandmother contact in black and white teen parent families. *Journal of Adolescent Health, 13,* 546–552.

UNGERER, J. A., DOLBY, R., WATERS, B., BARNETT, B., KEIK, N., & LEWIN, V. (1990). The early development of empathy: Self-regulation and individual differences in the first year. *Motivation and Emotion, 14,* 93–106.

URBAIN, E. S., & KENDELL, P. C. (1980). Review of social-cognitive problem-solving interventions with children. *Psychological Bulletin, 88,* 109–143.

URBERG, K. A., DEGIRMENCIOUGLU, S. M., & PILGRIM, C. (1997). Close friend and group influence on adolescent cigarette smoking and alcohol use. *Developmental Psychology, 33,* 834–844.

UZGIRIS, I. C., & HUNT, J. McV. (1975). *Assessment in infancy: Ordinal scales of psychological development.* Urbana: University of Illinois Press.

VALDEZ-MENCHACA, M. C., & WHITEHURST, G. J. (1992). Accelerating language development through picture book reading: A systematic extension to Mexican day-care. *Developmental Psychology, 28,* 1106–1114.

VALIAN, V. (1996). *Parental replies: Linguistic status and didactic role.* Cambridge: MIT Press.

VALSINER, J. (1998). The development of the concept of development: Historical and epistemological perspectives. In W. Damon (Ed.), *Handbook of child psychology: Vol. 1. Theoretical models of human development.* New York: Wiley.

VAN DEN BOOM, D. C. (1994). The influence of temperament and mothering on attachment and exploration: An experimental manipulation of sensitive responsiveness among lower-class mothers with irritable infants. *Child Development, 65,* 1457–1477.

VAN DEN BOOM, D. C. (1995). Do first-year intervention effects endure? Follow-up during toddlerhood of a sample of Dutch irritable infants. *Child Development, 66,* 1798–1816.

VAN DER VEER, R., & VALSINER, J. (1988). Lev Vygotsky and Pierre Janet: On the origin of the concept of sociogenesis. *Developmental Review, 8,* 52–65.

VAN GIFFEN, K., & HAITH, M. M. (1984). Infant visual response to gestalt geometric forms. *Infant Behavior and Development, 7,* 335–346.

VAN IJZENDOORN, M. H. (1992). Intergenerational transmission of parenting: A review of studies in nonclinical populations. *Developmental Review, 12,* 76–99.

VAN IJZENDOORN, M. H. (1995). Associations between adult attachment representations and parent-child attachment, parent responsiveness, and clinical status: A meta-analysis on the predictive validity of the Adult Attachment Interview. *Psychological Bulletin, 117,* 387–403.

VAN IJZENDOORN, M. H., & De WOLFF, M. S. (1997). In search of the absent father—Meta-analyses of infant-father attachment: A rejoinder to our discussants. *Child Development, 68,* 604–609.

VAN IJZENDOORN, M. H., GOLDBERG, S., KROONENBERG, P. M., & FRENKEL, O. J. (1992). The relative effects of maternal and child problems on the quality of attachment: A meta-analysis of attachment in clinical samples. *Child Development, 63,* 840–858.

VAN IJZENDOORN, M. H., JUFFER, F., & DUYVESTEYN, M. G. C. (1995). Breaking the intergenerational cycle of insecure attachment: A review of the effects of attachment-based interventions on maternal sensitivity and infant security. *Journal of Child Psychology and Psychiatry, 36,* 225–248.

VAN IJZENDOORN, M. H., & KROONENBERG, P. M. (1988). Cross-cultural patterns of attachment: A meta-analysis of the Strange Situation. *Child Development, 59,* 147–156.

VAN LOOSBROEK, E., & SMITSMAN, A. W. (1990). Visual perception of numerosity in infancy. *Developmental Psychology, 26,* 916–922.

VAN TUINEN, I., & WOLFE, S. M. (1993). *Unnecessary cesarean sections: Halting a national epidemic.* Washington, DC: Public Citizens' Health Research Group.

VANDELL, D. L., MINNET, A. M., JOHNSON, B. S., & SANTROCK, J. W. (1990). *Siblings and friends: Experiences of school-aged children.* Unpublished manuscript, University of Texas at Dallas.

VANDELL, D. L., WILSON, K. S., & BUCHANAN, N. R. (1980). Peer interaction in the first year of life: An examination of its structure, content, and sensitivity to toys. *Child Development, 51,* 481–488.

VARGAS, E. A. (1986). Intraverbal behavior. In P. N. Chase & L. J. Parrott (Eds.), *Psychological aspects of language: The West Virginia Lectures.* Springfield, IL: Thomas.

VASTA, R. (1982a). Child study: Looking toward the eighties. In R. Vasta (Ed.), *Strategies and techniques of child study.* New York: Academic Press.

VASTA, R. (Ed.). (1982b). *Strategies and techniques of child study.* New York: Academic Press.

VASTA, R., & GREEN, P. J. (1982). Differential cue utilization by males and females in pattern copying. *Child Development, 53,* 1102–1105.

VASTA, R., & LIBEN, L. S. (1996). The water-level task: An intriguing puzzle. *Current Directions in Psychological Science, 5,* 171–177.

VAUGHN, B. E., BRADLEY, C. F., JOFFE, L. S., SEIFER, R., & BARGLOW, P. (1987). Maternal characteristics measured prenatally are predictive of ratings of temperamental "difficulty" on the Carey Infant Temperament Questionnaire. *Developmental Psychology, 23,* 152–161.

VAUGHN, B. E., KOPP, C. B., & KRAKOW, J. B. (1984). The emergence and consolidation of self-control from eighteen to thirty months of age: Normative trends and individual differences. *Child Development, 55,* 990–1004.

VAUGHN, B. E., & WATERS, E. (1990). Attachment behavior at home and in the laboratory: Q-sort observations and Strange Situation classifications of one-year-olds. *Child Development, 61,* 1965–1990.

VAUGHN, V. C., McKAY, J. R., & BEHRMAN, R. E. (1984). *Nelson textbook of pediatrics* (12th ed.). Philadelphia: Saunders.

VEDAM, S., & KOLODJII, Y. (1995). Guidelines for client selection in the home birth midwifery practice. *Journal of Nurse-Midwifery, 40,* 508–521.

VENTURA, S. J. (1989). Trends and variations in first births to older women, United States, 1970–1986 (Vital and Health Statistics Series 21, No. 47). Bethesda, MD: National Center for Health Statistics.

VERNON, P. A. (1993). *Biological approaches to the study of human intelligence.* Norwood, NJ: Ablex.

VERSCHUEREN, K., MARCOEN, A., & SCHOEFS, V. (1996). The internal working model of the self, attachment, and competence in five-year-olds. *Child Development, 67,* 2493–2511.

VESPO, J. E., & CAPLAN, M. (1993). Preschoolers' differential conflict behavior with friends and acquaintances. *Early Education and Development, 4,* 45–58.

VIETZE, P. M., & VAUGHAN, H. G. (1988). *Early identification of infants with developmental disabilities.* Philadelphia: Grune & Stratton.

VIHMAN, M. M. (1985). Language differentiation by the bilingual infant. *Journal of Child Language, 12,* 297–324.

VIHMAN, M. M., FERGUSON, C. A., & ELBERT, M. (1986). Phonological development from babbling to speech: Common tendencies and individual differences. *Applied Psycholinguistics, 7,* 3–40.

VIHMAN, M. M., & MILLER, R. (1988). Words and babble at the threshold of language acquisition. In M. D. Smith & J. L. Locke (Eds.), *The emergent lexicon.* Orlando, FL: Academic Press.

VINCENT, K. R. (1991). Black/White IQ differences: Does age make the difference? *Journal of Clinical Psychology, 47,* 266–270.

VINDEN, P. G. (1996). Junin Quechua children's understanding of mind. *Child Development, 67,* 1707–1716.

VOCATE, D. R. (1987). *The theory of A. R. Luria.* Hillsdale, NJ: Erlbaum.

VOLLING, B. L., & BELSKY, J. (1991). Multiple determinants of father involvement during infancy in dual-earner and single-earner families. *Journal of Marriage and the Family, 53,* 461–474.

VOLLING, B. L., YOUNGBLADE, L. M., & BELSKY, J. (1997). Young children's social relationships with siblings and friends. *American Journal of Orthopsychiatry, 67,* 102–111.

VOLTERRA, V., & TAESCHNER, T. (1978). The acquisition and development of language by bilingual children. *Journal of Child Language, 5,* 311–326.

VON HOFSTEN, C. (1982). Eye-hand coordination in the newborn. *Developmental Psychology, 18,* 450–461.

VON SENDEN, M. (1960). *Space and sight.* New York: Free Press.

VOORHEES, C. V., & MOLLNOW, E. (1987). Behavioral teratogenesis: Long-term influences on behavior from early exposure to environmental agents. In J. D. Osofsky (Ed.), *Handbook of infant development* (2nd ed.). New York: Wiley.

VOSNIADOU, S., & BREWER, W. F. (1992). Mental models of the earth: A study of conceptual change in childhood. *Cognitive Psychology, 24,* 535–585.

VOSNIADOU, S., & BREWER, W. F. (1994). Mental models of the day/night cycle. *Cognitive Science, 18,* 123–183.

VOYER, D., VOYER, S., & BRYDEN, M. P. (1995). Magnitude of sex differences in spatial abilities: A meta-analysis and consideration of critical variables. *Psychological Bulletin, 117,* 250–270.

VUCHINICH, S., BANK, L., & PATTERSON, G. R. (1992). Parenting, peers, and the stability of antisocial behavior in preadolescent boys. *Developmental Psychology, 28,* 510–521.

VURPILLOT, E. (1968). The development of scanning strategies and their relation to visual differentiation. *Journal of Experimental Child Psychology, 6,* 632–650.

VURPILLOT, E., & BALL, W. A. (1979). The concept of identity and children's selective attention. In G. A. Hale & M. Lewis (Eds.), *Attention and cognitive development.* New York: Plenum.

VYGOTSKY, L. S. (1962). *Thought and language.* Cambridge: MIT Press. (Original work published 1934).

VYGOTSKY, L. S. (1978). *Mind in society: The development of higher psychological processes.* Cambridge: Harvard University Press.

VYGOTSKY, L. S. (1987). *The collected works of L. S. Vygotsky: Vol. 1. Problems of general psychology.* New York: Plenum.

WAAS, G. A. (1988). Social attributional biases of peer-rejected and aggressive children. *Child Development, 59,* 969–975.

WACHS, T. D. (1988). Relevance of physical environment influences for toddler temperament. *Infant Behavior and Development, 11,* 431–445.

WACHS, T. D. (1992). *The nature of nurture.* Newbury Park, CA: Sage.

WACHS, T. D. (1994). Fit, context, and the transition between temperament and personality. In C. F. Halverson, Jr., G. A. Kohnstamm, & R. P. Martin (Eds.), *The developing structure of temperament and personality from infancy to adulthood.* Hillsdale, NJ: Erlbaum.

WAGHORN, L., & SULLIVAN, E. V. (1970). The exploration of transition rules in conservation of quantity (substance) using film mediated modeling. *Acta Psychologica, 32,* 65–80.

WAGNER, B. M., & PHILLIPS, D. A. (1992). Beyond beliefs: Parent and child behaviors and children's perceived academic competence. *Child Development, 63,* 1380–1391.

WAGNER, R. K., & McBRIDE-CHANG, C. (1996). The development of reading-related phonological processing abilities. In R. Vasta (Ed.), *Annals of child development* (Vol. 12). London: Kingsley.

WAINRYB, C. (1993). The application of moral judgments to other cultures: Relativism and universality. *Child Development, 64,* 924–933.

WALDMAN, I. D. (1996). Aggressive boys' hostile perceptual and response biases: The role of attention and impulsivity. *Child Development, 67,* 1015–1033.

WALDMAN, I. D., WEINBERG, R. A., & SCARR, S. (1994). Racial-group differences in IQ in the Minnesota Transracial Adoption Study: A reply to Levin and Lynn. *Intelligence, 19,* 29–44.

WALDROP, M. F., & HALVERSON, C. F., JR. (1975). Intensive and extensive peer behavior: Longitudinal and cross-sectional analyses. *Child Development, 46,* 19–26.

WALKER, A. S. (1982). Intermodal perception of expressive behaviors by human infants. *Journal of Experimental Child Psychology, 33,* 514–535.

WALKER, L. J. (1980). Cognitive and perspective-taking prerequisites for moral development. *Child Development, 51,* 131–139.

WALKER, L. J. (1983). Sources of cognitive conflict for stage transition in moral development. *Developmental Psychology, 19,* 103–110.

WALKER, L. J. (1986). Cognitive processes in moral development. In G. L. Sapp (Ed.), *Handbook of moral development: Models, processes, techniques, and research.* Birmingham, AL: Religious Education Press.

WALKER, L. J. (1988). The development of moral reasoning. In R. Vasta (Ed.), *Annals of child development* (Vol. 5). Greenwich, CT: JAI Press.

WALKER, L. J. (1989). A longitudinal study of moral reasoning. *Child Development, 60,* 157–166.

WALKER, L. J. (1991). Sex differences in moral reasoning. In W. M. Kurtines & J. L. Gewirtz (Eds.), *Handbook of moral behavior and development: Vol. 2. Research.* Hillsdale, NJ: Erlbaum.

WALKER, L. J. (1995). Sexism in Kohlberg's moral psychology? In W. M. Kurtines & J. L. Gewirtz (Eds.), *Moral development: An introduction.* Needham Heights, MA: Allyn & Bacon.

WALKER, L. J., DeVRIES, B., & BICHARD, S. L. (1984). The hierarchical nature of stages of moral development. *Developmental Psychology, 20,* 960–966.

WALKER, L. J., DeVRIES, B., & TREVARTHEN, S. D. (1987). Moral stages and moral orientations in real-life and hypothetical dilemmas. *Child Development, 58,* 842–858.

WALKER, L. J., & RICHARDS, B. S. (1979). Stimulating transitions in moral reasoning as a function of stage of cognitive development. *Developmental Psychology, 15,* 95–103.

WALKER, L. J., & TAYLOR, J. H. (1991a). Family interactions and the development of moral reasoning. *Child Development, 62,* 264–283.

WALKER, L. J., & TAYLOR, J. H. (1991b). Stage transitions in moral reasoning: A longitudinal study of developmental processes. *Developmental Psychology, 27,* 330–337.

WALKER-ANDREWS, A. S. (1997). Infants' perception of expressive behaviors: Differentiation of multimodal information. *Psychological Bulletin, 121,* 437–456.

WALKER-ANDREWS, A. S., BAHRICK, L. E., RAGLIONI, S. S., & DIAZ, I. (1991). Infants' bimodal perception of gender. *Ecological Psychology, 3,* 55–75.

WALLACH, L., WALL, A. J., & ANDERSON, L. (1967). Number conservation: The role of reversibility, addition-subtraction, and misleading perceptual cues. *Child Development, 38,* 425–442.

WALLER, N. G., KOJETIN, B. A., BOUCHARD, T. J., JR., LYKKEN, D. T., & TELLEGEN, A. (1990). Genetic and environmental influences on religious interests, attitudes, and values: A study of twins reared apart and together. *Psychological Science, 1,* 138–142.

WALLERSTEIN, J. S., CORBIN, S. B., & LEWIS, J. M. (1988). Children of divorce: A 10-year study. In E. M. Hetherington & J. D. Arasteh (Eds.), *Impact of divorce, single parenting, and stepparenting on children.* Hillsdale, NJ: Erlbaum.

WALTON, G. E., BOWER, N. J., & BOWER, T. G. (1992). Recognition of familiar faces by newborns. *Infant Behavior and Development, 15,* 265–269.

WARD, M. J., & CARLSON, E. A. (1995). Associations among adult attachment representations, maternal sensitivity, and infant-mother attachment in a sample of adolescent mothers. *Child Development, 66,* 69–79.

WARK, G. R., & KREBS, D. L. (1996). Gender and dilemma differences in real-life moral judgment. *Developmental Psychology, 32,* 220–230.

WARKANY, J. (1977). History of teratology. In J. G. Wilson & F. C. Fraser (Eds.), *Handbook of teratology: Vol. 1. General principles and etiology.* New York: Plenum.

WARKANY, J. (1981). Prevention of congenital malformations. *Teratology, 23,* 175–189.

WARREN, K. R., & BAST, R. J. (1988). Alcohol-related birth defects: An update. *Public Health Reports, 103,* 638–642.

WARREN-LEUBECKER, A., & BOHANNON, J. N. (1989). *Pragmatics: Language in social contexts.* In J. B. Gleason (Ed.), *The development of language* (2nd ed.). Columbus, OH: Chas E. Merrill.

WARTNER, U. G., GROSSMANN, K., FREMMER-BOMBIK, E., & SUESS, G. (1994). Attachment patterns at age six in south Germany: Predictability from infancy and implications for preschool behavior. *Child Development, 65,* 1014–1027.

WASHINGTON, J., MINDE, K., & GOLDBERG, S. (1986). Temperament in premature infants: Style and stability. *Journal of the American Academy of Child Psychiatry, 25,* 493–502.

WASSERMAN, G. A., & LEWIS, M. (1985). Infant sex differences: Ecological effects. *Sex Roles, 12,* 665–675.

WASSERMAN, P. M. (1988). Fertilization in mammals. *Scientific American, 259,* 78–84.

WASZ-HOCKERT, O., MICHELSSON, K., & LIND, J. (1985). Twenty-five years of Scandinavian cry research. In B. M. Lester & C. Z. Boukydis (Eds.), *Infant crying: Theoretical and research perspectives.* New York. Plenum.

WATERS, E. (1995). The Attachment Q-Set (Version 3.0) (Appendix A). In E. Waters, B. E. Vaughn, G. Posada, & K. Kondo-Ikemura (Eds.), Caregiving, cultural, and cognitive perspectives on secure-base behavior and working models. *Monographs of the Society for Research in Child Development, 60*(2–3, Serial No. 244).

WATERS, E., & DEANE, K. E. (1985). Defining and assessing individual differences in attachment relationships: Q-methodology and the organization of behavior in infancy and early childhood. In I. Bretherton & E. Waters (Eds.), Growing points of attachment theory and research. *Monographs of the Society for Research in Child Development, 50*(1–2, Serial No. 209).

WATERS, E., VAUGHN, B. E., POSADA, G., & KONDO-IKEMURA, K. (Eds.). (1995). Caregiving, cultural, and cognitive perspectives on secure-base behavior and working models. *Monographs of the Society for Research in Child Development, 60*(2–3, Serial No. 244).

WATERS, H. S. (1981). Organization strategies in memory for prose: A developmental analysis. *Journal of Experimental Child Psychology, 32,* 223–246.

WATERS, H. S., & SCHREIBER, L. L. (1991). Sex differences in elaborative strategies: A developmental analysis. *Journal of Experimental Child Psychology, 52,* 319–335.

WATERS, H. S., & TINSLEY, V. S. (1982). The development of verbal self-regulation: Relationships between language, cognition, and behavior. In S. Kuczaj (Ed.), *Language development: Language, cognition, and culture.* Hillsdale, NJ: Erlbaum.

WATSON, J. B., & RAYNER, R. (1920). Conditioned emotional reactions. *Journal of Experimental Psychology, 3,* 1–14.

WATSON, J. D. (1968). *The double helix: A personal account of the discovery of the structure of DNA.* New York: Atheneum.

WATSON, J. D. (1990). The Human Genome Project: Past, present, and future. *Science, 248,* 44–49.

WATSON, J. D., & CRICK, F. H. C. (1953). Molecular structure of nucleic acid: A structure for deoxyribose nucleic acid. *Nature, 171,* 737–738.

WAXMAN, S. R. (1990). Linguistic biases and the establishment of conceptual hierarchies. *Cognitive Development, 5,* 123–150.

WECHSLER, D. (1989). *Wechsler Preschool and Primary Scale of Intelligence—Revised.* New York: The Psychological Corporation.

WECHSLER, D. (1991). *Wechsler Intelligence Scale for Children—Third Edition.* New York: The Psychological Corporation.

WEGMAN, M. E. (1994). Annual summary of vital statistics—1993. *Pediatrics, 94,* 792–803.

WEINRAUB, M., & BROWN, L. M. (1983). The development of sex-role stereotypes in children: Crushing realities. In V. Franks & E. D. Rothblum (Eds.), *The stereotyping of women: Its effects on mental health.* New York: Springer.

WEINRAUB, M., CLEMENS, L. P., SOCKLOFF, A., ETHRIDGE, T., GRACELY, E., & MYERS, B. (1984). The development of sex role stereotypes in the third year: Relationships to gender labeling, gender identity, sex-typed toy preference, and family characteristics. *Child Development, 55,* 1493–1503.

WEINRAUB, M., & JAEGER, E. (1990). The timing of mothers' return to the workplace: Effects on the developing mother–infant relationship. In J. S. Hyde & M. J. Essex (Eds.), *Parental leave and child care: Setting a research and policy agenda.* Philadelphia: Temple University Press.

WEISNER, T. S., & EIDUSON, B. T. (1986). Children of the '60's as parents. *Psychology Today, 20,* 60–66.

WEISNER, T. S., & WILSON-MITCHELL, J. E. (1990). Nonconventional family life styles and sex typing in six-year-olds. *Child Development, 61,* 1915–1933.

WEISS, B., DODGE, K. A., BATES, J. E., & PETTIT, G. S. (1992). Some consequences of early harsh discipline: Child aggression and a maladaptive social information processing style. *Child Development, 63,* 1321–1335.

WEISS, M. G., & MILLER, P. H. (1983). Young children's understanding of displaced aggression. *Journal of Experimental Child Psychology, 35,* 529–539.

WEISSBERG, R. P. (1985). Designing effective social problem-solving programs for the classroom. In B. H. Schneider, K. H. Rubin, & J. E. Ledingham (Eds.), *Children's peer relations: Issues in assessment and intervention.* New York: Springer-Verlag.

WEISZ, J. R., CHAIYASIT, W., WEISS, B., EASTMAN, K. L., & JACKSON, E. W. (1995). A multimethod study of problem behavior among Thai and American children in school: Teacher reports versus direct observations. *Child Development, 66,* 402–415.

WEISZ, J. R., SIGMAN, M., WEISS, B., & MOSK, J. (1993). Parent reports of behavioral and emotional problems among children in Kenya, Thailand, and the United States. *Child Development, 64,* 98–109.

WEITZMAN, N., BIRNS, B., & FRIEND, R. (1985). Traditional and nontraditional mothers' communication with their sons and daughters. *Child Development, 56,* 894–898.

WEKSELMAN, K., SPIERING, K., HETTEBERG, C., KENNER, C., & FLANDERMEYER, A. (1995). Fetal alcohol syndrome from infancy to childhood: A review of the literature. *Journal of Pediatric Nursing, 10,* 296–303.

WELCH-ROSS, M. K. (1995). An integrative model of the development of autobiographical memory. *Developmental Review, 15,* 338–365.

WELCH-ROSS, M. K. (1997). Mother-child participation in conversation about the past: Relationships to preschoolers' theory of mind. *Developmental Psychology, 33,* 618–629.

WELCH-ROSS, M. K., & SCHMIDT, E. R. (1996). Gender schema development and children's constructive story memory: Evidence for a developmental model. *Child Development, 67,* 820–835.

WELD, N. (1968). Some possible genetic implications of Carthaginian child sacrifice. *Perspectives in Biology and Medicine, 12,* 69–78.

WELLMAN, H. M. (1977). Preschoolers' understanding of memory-relevant variables. *Child Development, 48,* 1720–1723.

WELLMAN, H. M. (1988). The early development of memory strategies. In F. E. Weinert & M. Perlmutter (Eds.), *Memory development: Universal changes and individual differences.* Hillsdale, NJ: Erlbaum.

WELLMAN, H. M., & GELMAN, S. A. (1998). Knowledge acquisition in foundational domains. In W. Damon (Series Ed.) & D. Kuhn & R. S. Siegler (Vol. Eds.) *Handbook of child psychology: Vol. 2. Cognition, perception, and language* (5th ed.). New York: Wiley.

WELLMAN, H. M., RITTER, K., & FLAVELL, J. H. (1975). Deliberate memory behavior in the delayed reactions of very young children. *Developmental Psychology, 11,* 780–787.

WENTZEL, K. R. (1988). Gender differences in math and English achievement: A longitudinal study. *Sex Roles, 18,* 691–699.

WENTZEL, K. R., & ERDLEY, C. A. (1993). Strategies for making friends: Relations to social behavior and peer acceptance in early adolescence. *Developmental Psychology, 29,* 819–826.

WERKER, J. F., & DESJARDINS, R. N. (1995). Listening to speech in the 1st year of life: Experiential influences on phoneme perception. *Current Directions in Psychological Science, 4,* 76–81.

WERNER, L. A., & BARGONES, J. Y. (1992). Psychoacoustic development of human infants. In C. Rovee-Collier & L. P. Lipsitt (Eds.), *Advances in infancy research* (Vol. 7). Norwood, NJ: Ablex.

WERTHEIMER, M. (1985). The evolution of the concept of development in the history of psychology. In G. Eckardt, W. G. Bringmann, & L. Sprung (Eds.), *Contributions to a history of developmental psychology.* Berlin: Mouton.

WERTSCH, J. V., & TULVISTE, P. (1992). L. S. Vygotsky and contemporary developmental psychology. *Developmental Psychology, 28,* 548–557.

WESTINGHOUSE LEARNING CENTER. (1969). *The impact of Head Start: An evaluation of the effects of Head Start on children's cognitive and affective development.* Washington, DC: Clearinghouse for Federal Scientific and Technical Information.

WHITAM, F. L., DIAMOND, M., & MARTIN, J. (1993). Homosexual orientation in twins: A report on 61 pairs and three triplet sets. *Archives of Sexual Behavior, 22,* 187–206.

WHITE, B. L., CASTLE, P., & HELD, R. (1964). Observations on the development of visually directed reaching. *Child Development, 35,* 349–364.

WHITE, B. L., KABAN, B. T., ATTANUCCI, J., & SHAPIRO, B. B. (1978). *Experience and environment: Major influences on the development of the young child* (Vol. 2). Englewood Cliffs, NJ: Prentice Hall.

WHITE, P. C., NEW, M. I., & DUPONT, B. (1987). Congenital adrenal hyperplasia. *New England Journal of Medicine, 316,* 1519–1524.

WHITE, S., & THARP, R. G. (1988, April). *Questioning and wait-time: A cross-cultural analysis.* Paper presented at the meeting of the American Educational Research Association, New Orleans.

WHITE, S. H. (1992). G. Stanley Hall: From philosophy to developmental psychology. *Developmental Psychology, 28,* 25–34.

WHITE, T. G. (1982). Naming practices, typicality, and underextension in child language. *Journal of Experimental Child Psychology, 33,* 324–346.

WHITEHURST, G. J. (1997). Language processes in context: Language learning in children reared in poverty. In L. B. Adamson & M. A. Romski (Eds.), *Research on communication and language disorders: Contributions to theories of language development.* Baltimore: Brookes.

WHITEHURST, G. J., ARNOLD, D. H., EPSTEIN, J. N., ANGELL, A. L., SMITH, M., & FISCHEL, J. E. (1994). A picture book reading intervention in daycare and home for children from low-income families. *Developmental Psychology, 30,* 679–689.

WHITEHURST, G. J., & DeBARYSHE, B. D. (1989). Observational learning and language acquisition: Principles of learning, systems, and tasks. In G. E. Speidel & K. E. Nelson (Eds.), *The many faces of imitation in language learning.* New York: Springer-Verlag.

WHITEHURST, G. J., EPSTEIN, J. N., ANGELL, A. L., PAYNE, A. C., CRONE, D., & FISCHEL, J. E. (1994). Outcomes of an emergent literacy intervention in Head Start. *Journal of Educational Psychology, 84,* 541–556.

WHITEHURST, G. J., FISCHEL, J. E., CAULFIELD, M., DeBARYSHE, B., & VALDEZ-MENCHACA, M. C. (1989). Assessment and treatment of early expressive language delay. In P. Zelazo & R. Barr (Eds.), *Challenges to developmental paradigms: Implications for theory, assessment, and treatment.* Hillsdale, NJ: Erlbaum.

WHITEHURST, G. J., & LONIGAN, C. J. (in press). Child development and emergent literacy. *Child Development.*

WHITEHURST, G. J., & NOVAK, G. (1973). Modeling, imitation training, and the acquisition of sentence phrases. *Journal of Experimental Child Psychology, 16,* 332–345.

WHITEHURST, G. J., & SONNENSCHEIN, S. (1985). The development of communication: A functional analysis. In G. J. Whitehurst (Ed.), *Annals of child development* (Vol. 2). Greenwich, CT: JAI Press.

WHITEHURST, G. J., & VALDEZ-MENCHACA, M. C. (1988). What is the role of reinforcement in language acquisition? *Child Development, 59,* 430–440.

WHITELY, B. E. (1985). Sex-role orientation and psychological well-being: Two meta-analyses. *Sex Roles, 12,* 207–225.

WHITING, B. B. (1983). The genesis of prosocial behavior. In D. Bridgeman (Ed.), *The nature of prosocial development: Interdisciplinary theories and strategies.* London: Academic Press.

WHITING, B. B., & EDWARDS, C. P. (1988). *Children of different worlds: The formation of social behavior.* Cambridge: Harvard University Press.

WHITLEY, R., & GOLDENBERG, R. (1990). Infectious disease in the prenatal period and the recommendations for screening. In I. R. Merkatz & J. E. Thompson (Eds.), *New perspectives on prenatal care.* New York: Elsevier.

WHYTE, M., & PARISH, W. (1984). *Urban life in contemporary China.* Chicago: University of Chicago Press.

WIDAMAN, K. F., LITTLE, T. D., GEARY, D. C., & CORMIER, P. (1992). Individual differences in the development of skill in mental addition: Internal and external validation of chronometric models. *Learning and Individual Differences, 4,* 167–213.

WIGFIELD, A., ECCLES, J. S., MacIVER, D., REUMAN, D. A., & MIDGLEY, C. (1991). Transitions during early adolescence: Changes in children's domain-specific self-perceptions and general self-esteem across the transition to junior high school. *Developmental Psychology, 27,* 552–565.

WILCOX, A. J., & SKJOERVEN, R. (1992). Birthweight and perinatal mortality: The effect of gestational age. *American Journal of Public Health, 82,* 378–382.

WILDER, G., MACKIE, D., & COOPER, J. (1985). Gender and computers: Two surveys of computer-related attitudes. *Sex Roles, 13,* 215–228.

WILLIAMS, J. (1987). *Psychology of women: Behavior in a biosocial context.* New York: Norton.

WILLIAMS, J. E., & BEST, D. L. (1990). *Measuring sex stereotypes: A multinational study.* Newbury Park, CA: Sage.

WILLIAMS, T. M. (1986). *The impact of television.* New York: Academic Press.

WILLINGER, M. (1995). SIDS prevention. *Pediatric Annals, 24,* 358–364.

WILLINGER, M., JAMES, L., & CATZ, C. (1991). Defining sudden infant death syndrome (SIDS). *Developmental Pediatric Pathology, 11,* 677–684.

WILSON, E. O. (1975). *Sociobiology: The new synthesis.* Cambridge: Harvard University Press.

WILSON, R. S. (1983). The Louis-ville Twin Study: Developmental synchronies in behavior. *Child De-velopment, 54,* 298–316.

WILSON, R. S. (1986). Growth and development of human twins. In F. Falkner & J. M. Tanner (Eds.), *Human growth: A comprehensive treatise.* New York: Plenum.

WINDLE, M., & LERNER, R. M. (1986). The "goodness-of-fit" model of temperament-context relations: Interaction or correlation? In J. V. Lerner & R. M. Lerner (Eds.), *New directions for child development: No. 31. Temperament and social interaction in infants and children.* San Francisco: Jossey-Bass.

WINDSOR, J. (1993). The functions of novel word compounds. *Journal of Child Language, 20,* 119–138.

WINEBERG, S. S. (1987). The fulfillment of the self-fulfilling prophecy. *Educational Researcher, 16,* 28–36.

WINSTON, R. M. L., & HANDYSIDE, A. H. (1993). New challenges in human in vitro fertilization. *Science, 260,* 932–936.

WITELSON, S. F. (1976). Sex and the single hemisphere: Specialization of the right hemisphere for spatial processing. *Science, 193,* 425–427.

WITELSON, S. F., & KIGAR, S. (1989). Anatomical development of the corpus callosum in humans: A review with reference to sex and cognition. In D. L. Molfese & S. J. Segalowitz (Eds.), *Brain lateralization in children: Developmental implications.* New York: Guilford.

WOLFF, P. H. (1959). Observations on newborn infants. *Psychosomatic Medicine, 21,* 110–118.

WOLFF, P. H. (1966). The causes, controls and organization of behavior in the neonate. *Psychological Issues, 5* (17).

WOLFF, P. H. (1969). The natural history of crying and other vocalizations in early infancy. In B. Foss (Ed.), *Determinants of infant behavior* (Vol. 4). London: Methuen.

WOLFNER, G. D., & GELLES, R. J. (1993). A profile of violence toward children: A national study. *Child Abuse and Neglect, 17,* 197–212.

WOODWARD, A. L., & MARKMAN, E. M. (1998). Early word learning. In W. Damon (Series Ed.) & D. Kuhn & R. S. Siegler (Vol. Eds.), *Handbook of child psychology: Vol. 2. Cognition, perception, and language* (5th ed.). New York: Wiley.

WOOLLETT, A., WHITE, D., & LYON, L. (1982). Observations of fathers at birth. In N. Beail & J. McGuire (Eds.), *Fathers: Psychological perspectives.* London: Junction Books.

WOROBEY J., & BLAJDA, V. M. (1989). Temperament ratings at 2 weeks, 2 months, and 1 year: Differential stability of activity and emotionality. *Developmental Psychology, 25,* 257–263.

WYNN, K. (1992). Addition and subtraction by human infants. *Nature, 358,* 749–750.

WYNN, K. (1995). Origins of numerical knowledge. *Mathematical Cognition, 1,* 36–60.

YANG, B., OLLENDICK, T. H., DONG, Q., XIA, Y., & LIN, L. (1995). Only children and children with siblings in the People's Republic of China: Levels of fear, anxiety, and depression. *Child Development, 66,* 1301–1311.

YATES, G. C. R., YATES, S. M., & BEASLEY, C. J. (1987). Young children's knowledge of strategies in delay of gratification. *Merrill-Palmer Quarterly, 33,* 159–169.

YEATES, K. O., SCHULTZ, L. H., & SELMAN, R. L. (1991). The development of interpersonal negotiation strategies in thought and action: A social-cognitive link to behavioral adjustment and social status. *Merrill-Palmer Quarterly, 37,* 369–406.

YONAS, A. (1981). Infants' responses to optical information for collision. In R. N. Aslin, J. R. Alberts, & M. R. Peterson (Eds.), *Development of perception: Psychobiological perspectives: Vol. 2. The visual system.* New York: Academic Press.

YONAS, A., & OWSLEY, C. (1987). Development of visual space perception. In P. Salapatek & L. Cohen (Eds.), *Handbook of infant perception: Vol. 2. From perception to cognition.* New York: Academic Press.

YOUNGBLADE, L. M., & BELSKY, J. (1992). Parent–child antecedents of 5-year-olds' close friendships: A longitudinal analysis. *Developmental Psychology, 28,* 700–713.

YOUNGER, A. J., & PICCININ, A. M. (1989). Children's recall of aggressive and withdrawn behaviors: Recognition memory and likability judgments. *Child Development, 60,* 580–590.

YOUNGER, A. J., SCHWARTZMAN, A. E., & LEDINGHAM, J. E. (1985). Age-related changes in children's perceptions of aggression and withdrawal in their peers. *Developmental Psychology, 21,* 70–75.

YOUNISS, J., & VOLPE, J. (1978). A relational analysis of children's friendship. In W. Damon (Ed.), *New directions for child development: No. 1. Social cognition.* San Francisco: Jossey-Bass.

YUILL, N., & PERNER, J. (1988). Intentionality and knowledge in children's judgments of actor's responsibility and recipient's emotional reaction. *Developmental Psychology, 24,* 358–365.

YUSSEN, S. R., & LEVY, V. M. (1975). Developmental changes in predicting one's own span of short-term memory. *Journal of Experimental Child Psychology, 19,* 502–508.

ZABRISKI, A. L., & COIE, J. D. (1996). A comparison of aggressive-rejected and nonaggressive-rejected children's interpretations of self-directed and other-directed rejection. *Child Development, 67,* 1048–1070.

ZAHN-WAXLER, C., CUMMINGS, E. M., & IANNOTTI, R. (Eds.). (1986). *Altruism and aggression: Biological and social origins.* Cambridge: Cambridge University Press.

ZAHN-WAXLER, C., RADKE-YARROW, M., WAGNER, E., & CHAPMAN, M. (1992). Development of concern for others. *Developmental Psychology, 28,* 126–136.

ZAHN-WAXLER, C., ROBINSON J. L., & EMDE, R. N. (1992). The development of empathy in twins. *Developmental Psychology, 28,* 1038–1047.

ZAMETKIN, A. J., NORDAHL, T. E., GROSS, M., KING, A. C., SEMPLE, W. E., RUMSEY, J., HAMBURGER, S., & COHEN, R. M. (1990). Cerebral glucose metabolism in adults with hyperactivity of childhood onset. *The New England Journal of Medicine, 20,* 1361–1366.

ZARBATANY, L., HARTMANN, D. P., & GELFAND, D. M. (1985). Why does children's generosity increase with age: Susceptibility to experimenter influence or altruism? *Child Development, 56,* 746–756.

ZARBATANY, L., HARTMANN, D. P., GELFAND, D. M., & VINCIGUERRA, P. (1985). Gender differences in altruistic reputation: Are they artifactual? *Developmental Psychology, 21,* 97–101.

ZELAZO, N. A., ZELAZO, P. R., COHEN, K. M., & ZELAZO, P. D. (1993). Specificity of practice effects on elementary neuromotor patterns. *Developmental Psychology, 29,* 686–691.

ZELAZO, P. D., HELWIG, C. C., & LAU, A. (1996). Intention, act, and outcome in behavioral prediction and moral judgment. *Child Development, 67,* 2478–2492.

ZELAZO, P. R. (1971). Smiling to social stimuli: Eliciting and conditioning effects. *Developmental Psychology, 4,* 32–42.

ZELAZO, P. R., WEISS, M. J. S., & TARQUINO, N. (1991). Habituation and recovery of neonatal orienting to auditory stimuli. In M. J. S. Weiss & P. R. Zelazo (Eds.), *Newborn attention: Biological constraints and the influence of experience.* Norwood, NJ: Ablex.

ZELAZO, P. R., ZELAZO, N., & KOLB, S. (1972). "Walking" in the newborn. *Science, 177,* 314–315.

ZESKIND, P. S. (1983). Production and spectral analysis of neonatal crying and its relation to other biobehavioral systems in the infant at risk. In T. Field & A. Sostek (Eds.), *Infants born at risk: Psychological and perceptual processes.* New York: Grune & Stratton.

ZESKIND, P. S., & MARSHALL, T. R. (1988). The relation between variations in pitch and maternal perceptions of infant crying. *Child Development, 59,* 193–196.

ZESKIND, P. S., & RAMEY, C. T. (1981). Preventing intellectual and interactional sequelae of fetal malnutrition: A longitudinal, transactional and synergistic approach to development. *Child Development, 52,* 213–218.

ZESKIND, P. S., KLEIN, L., & MARSHALL, T. R. (1992). Adults' perceptions of experimental modifications of durations of pauses and expiratory sounds in infant crying. *Developmental Psychology,* 28, 1153–1162.

ZIGLER, E. F., & FINN-STEVENSON, M. (1992). Applied developmental psychology. In M. H. Bornstein & M. E. Lamb (Eds.), *Developmental psychology: An advanced textbook* (3rd ed.). Hillsdale, NJ: Erlbaum.

ZIGLER, E. F., HOPPER, P., & HALL, N. W. (1993). Infant mental health and social policy. In C. H. Zeanah, Jr. (Ed.), *Handbook of infant mental health.* New York: Guilford.

ZIGLER, E. F., & MUENCHOW, S. (1992). *Head Start: The inside story of America's most successful educational experiment.* New York: Basic Books.

ZIGLER, E. F., & STYFCO, S. J. (Eds.). (1993). *Head Start and beyond: A national plan for extended childhood intervention.* New Haven, CT: Yale University Press.

ZILL, N., MORRISON, D. R., & COIRO, M. J. (1993). Long-term effects of parental divorce on parent-child relationships, adjustment, and achievement in young adulthood. *Journal of Family Psychology, 7,* 1–13.

ZIMMERMAN, B. J. (1983). Social learning theory: A contextualist account of cognitive functioning. In C. J. Brainerd (Ed.), *Recent advances in cognitive-developmental theory: Progress in cognitive development research.* New York: Springer-Verlag.

ZIMMERMAN, B. J., & BLOM, D. E. (1983). Toward an empirical test of the role of cognitive conflict in learning. *Developmental Review, 3,* 18–38.

ZINOBER, B., & MARTLEW, M. (1985). The development of communicative gestures. In M. D. Barrett (Ed.), *Children's single-word speech.* New York: Wiley.

ZIVIN, G. (1979). Removing common confusions about egocentric speech, private speech, and self-regulation. In G. Zivin (Ed.), *The development of self-regulation through private speech.* New York: Wiley.

ZUCKER, K. J. (1992). Gender identity disorder. In S. R. Hooper, G. W. Hynd, & R. E. Mattison (Eds.), *Child psychopathology: Diagnostic criteria and clinical assessment.* Hillsdale, NJ: Erlbaum.

ZUCKER, K. J., & BRADLEY, S. J. (Eds.). (1995). *Gender identity disorder and psychosexual problems in children and adolescents.* New York: Guilford.

ZUCKER, K. J., BRADLEY, S. J., & IPP, M. (1993). Delayed naming of a newborn boy: Relationship to the mother's wish for a girl and subsequent cross-gender identity in the child by the age of two. *Journal of Psychology and Human Sexuality, 6,* 57–68.

ZUCKER, K. J., WILD, J., BRADLEY, S. J., & LOWRY, C. B. (1993). Physical attractiveness of boys with gender identity disorder. *Archives of Sexual Behavior, 22,* 23–34.

ZUKOW, P. G. (Ed.). (1989). *Sibling interaction across cultures.* New York: Springer-Verlag.

ZUPAN, B. A., HAMMEN, C., & JAENICKE, C. (1987). The effects of current mood and prior depressive history on self-schematic processing in children. *Journal of Experimental Child Psychology, 43,* 149–158.

Chapter 1 Page 2: ©Gaillard/Jerrican/Photo Researchers. Page 4: ©Ursula Markus/Photo Researchers. Page 5: PEANUTS reprinted by permission of United Features Syndicate, Inc. Page 8 (top): Courtesy New York Public Library Picture Collection. Page 8 (bottom): ©Corbis-Bettmann. Page 9: Courtesy National Library of Medicine. Page 11: Culver Pictures, Inc. Page 14: ©Margaret Miller/Photo Researchers. Page 15: Herb Gehr/LIFE Magazine/©Time Warner, Inc. Page 16: ©Conklin/Monkmeyer Press Photo. Page 17: Courtesy Jean Piaget Society. Page 19: Courtesy Michael Cole. Page 21: Comstock, Inc. Page 23: ©Anne Nielsen/Tony Stone Images/New York, Inc.

Chapter 2 Page 26: ©Laurence Monneret/Tony Stone Images/New York, Inc. Page 29: ©Rosanne Olson/Tony Stone Images/New York, Inc. Page 31: Comstock, Inc. Page 33: ©Lawrence Migdale/Photo Researchers. Page 35: ©Falk/Monkmeyer Press Photo. Page 36: ©Griffin/The Image Works. Page 39 (top): ©David M. Grossman/Photo Researchers. Page 39 (bottom): ©Jeff Greenberg/Photo Researchers. Page 41 (top): ©Jeff Greenberg/Photo Researchers. Page 41 (bottom): Courtesy Albert Bandura, Stanford University. Page 47 (top): Nina Leen/LIFE Magazine/©Time Warner, Inc. Page 47 (bottom): ©Jan Halaska/Photo Researchers. Page 50 (top): Courtesy Cornell University. Page 50 (bottom left): ©Gish/Monkmeyer Press Photo. Page 50 (bottom right): ©Mathieu Jacob/The Image Works.

Chapter 3 Page 56: ©Mark Richards/PhotoEdit. Page 59: ©Lawrence Migdale/Photo Researchers. Page 67: ©Elizabeth Crews. Page 69: ©UPI/Newsphoto/Corbis-Bettmann. Page 73: ©Leonide Principe/Photo Researchers. Page 74 (left): ©J. Gerard Smith/Monkmeyer Press Photo. Page 74 (right): ©Ralph A. Reinhold/Animals Animals. Page 75: ©Andrew M. Levine/Photo Researchers.

Chapter 4 Page 82: ©Stuart Westmorland/Tony Stone Images/New York, Inc. Page 88: ©Joel Gordon 1989. Page 90: Culver Pictures, Inc. Page 94: ©Bill Longcore/Science Source/Photo Researchers. Page 95 (top): ©Sylvain Grandadam/Photo Researchers. Page 95 (bottom): ©Gary Parker/Photo Researchers. Page 99 (left): ©Larry S. Voigt/Photo Researchers. Page 99 (right): ©Jeff Isaac Greenberg/Photo Researchers. Page 105: ©Camille Tokerud/Photo Researchers.

Chapter 5 Pages 112, 117 and 119: ©Petit Format/Nestle/Photo Researchers. Page 116: ©Francis Leroy, Biocosmos/Photo Researchers. Page 131: ©David Young Wolff/Tony Stone Images/New York, Inc. Page 133: ©John Giordano/SABA. Page 136: ©James W. Hanson. Page 138: Courtesy The New York State Office of Alcoholism and Substance Abuse Services. Page 140: ©Kindra Clineff/The Picture Cube. Page 143: ©Alexander Tsiaras/Stock, Boston.

Chapter 6 Page 148: ©Suzanne Szasz/Photo Researchers. Page 153: ©SIU Science Source/Photo Researchers. Page 158: ©Rick Friedman/Black Star. Page 160: Courtesy Evelyn B.Thoman. Page 165 (top left): ©Petit Format/Photo Researchers. Page 165 (top right): ©Elizabeth Crews/The Image Works. Page 165 (bottom): ©Laura Dwight Photography. Page 173: Reproduced with permission of Dr. Charles Super, Pennsylvania State University. Page 176: ©Lori Adamski Peek/Tony Stone Images/New York, Inc. Page 180: ©B. Daemmrich/The Image Works. Page 182: ©Bob Daemmrich/Stock, Boston. Page 186: ©Ron Giling/LINEAIR. Page 187: ©Oscar Burriel/Latin Stock/Science Photo Library/Photo Researchers. Page 190: ©M. Siluk/The Image Works.

Chapter 7 Page 194: ©Grantpix/Photo Researchers. Page 197: ©Penny Gentieu/Tony Stone Images/New York, Inc. Page 199: Courtesy R.C. James. Page 201: ©Joseph Nettis/Photo Researchers. Page 202: From *Differential Facial Responses to Four Basic Tastes in Newborns* by D. Rosenstein and H. Oster, 1988, *Child Development*, **59**, pp. 1561-1563. ©1988 by The Society for Research in Child Development, Inc. Reprinted by permission. Page 210: From *The Recognition of Facial Expressions in the First Two Years of Life: Mechanisms of Development* by Charles A. Nelson, *Child Development*, **58**, p. 892, Figure 1. ©1987 by the Society for Research in Child Development, Inc. Reprinted by permission. These photos were made available by Martin Banks and Arthur Ginsburg. Page 214: ©Merrim/Monkmeyer Press Photo. Page 219: From *Size Constancy at Birth: Newborn Infants' Responses to Retinal and Real Size*, by A. Slater, A. Mattock, and E. Brown, 1990, *Journal of Experimental Child Psychology*, **49**, pp. 317 and 318. ©1990 by Academic Press. Reproduced with permission. Page 221: ©Topham/The Image Works. Page 222: Tony Stone Images/New York, Inc. Page 225: ©Erika Stone/Photo Researchers. From *The World of the Newborn* by Daphne Maurer and Charles Maurer. ©1988 by

Daphne Maurer and Charles Maurer. Photographs by Charles Maurer. Reproduced with permission. Page 230: ©Elizabeth Crews.

Chapter 8 Page 240: ©Elizabeth Crews. Page 246: ©Yves de Braine/Black Star. Page 249 (top left): ©Richard Hutchings/Photo Researchers. Page 249 (center): ©David Young-Wolff/PhotoEdit. Page 249 (right): ©Elizabeth Crews. Page 257: Reprinted with permission from *Imitation of Social and Manual Gestures by Human Neonates* by A.N. Meltzoff and M.K. Moore, *Science*, **298**, p. 75 (1977). ©1977 by the American Association for the Advancement of Science. Reproduced with pemission. Page 259: ©Hank Morgan/Rainbow. Page 261: From "Constancy of Generic Identity in the Years Three to Six" by R. De Vries, 1969, *Monographs of the Society for Research in Child Development*, **34** (3, Serial No. 127), p. 8. ©1969 by the Society for Research in Child Development. Reproduced with permission. Page 264: ©Elizabeth Crews. Page 268: ©Blair Seitz/Photo Researchers. Page 275: ©Momatiuk/Eascott/Woodfin Camp & Associates. Page 279: ©Steve Thomas, The Last Navigator. Page 283: ©Bob Daemmrich/The Image Works.

Chapter 9 Page 294: ©D. E. Cox/Tony Stone Images/New York, Inc. Page 297: ©Elizabeth Crews. Page 303: ©Elizabeth Crews. Page 305: ©Michael Newman/PhotoEdit. Page 309: From *Apprenticeship in Thinking* by B. Rogoff, 1990, p. 49, New York: Oxford University Press. ©1990 by Barbara Rogoff. Reproduced with permission. Page 310: ©Mike & Carol Werner/Comstock, Inc. Page 320: ©Gale Zucker/Stock, Boston. Page 321: ©David Harry Stewart/Tony Stone Images/New York, Inc. Page 331: ©Lawrence Migdale/Tony Stone Images/New York, Inc. Page 334: ©Jeff Isaac Greenberg/Photo Researchers.

Chapter 10 Page 344: ©Bob Daemmrich/The Image Works. Page 348: Culver Pictures, Inc. Page 352: ©R. Rowan/Photo Researchers. Page 357: From *Predictive Validity of the Fagan Test of Infant Intelligence* by J.F. Fagan III, p. Shephard, & C. Knevel, 1991, *Meeting of the Society for Research in Child Development,* ©1993 by J.F. Fagan III. Reproduced with permission. Page 360: ©Jodi Buren. Page 365: ©F. Paolini/Sygma. Page 372: ©Lawrence Migdale/Photo Researchers. Page 375: ©Blair Seitz/Photo Researchers. Page 378: ©Ralf-Finn Hestoft/SABA. Page 382: ©Joseph Nettis/Photo Researchers. Page 383: ©Sean Sprague/LINEAIR. Page 389 (left): Courtesy Harlow Primate Laboratory, University of Wisconsin. Page 389 (right): ©Elizabeth Crews/The Image Works.

Chapter 11 Page 394: ©Charles Thatcher/Tony Stone Images/New York, Inc. Page 399: Courtesy M.I.T. Page 401: ©Elizabeth Crews. Page 405: ©Novastock/Photo Researchers. Page 406: ©Tom Armstrong/King Features Syndicate. Reprinted with special permission of North America Syndicate. Page 407: ©Robert Brenner/PhotoEdit. Page 410: ©Elizabeth Crews. Page 412: ©Emily Stong/The Picture Cube. Page 415: ©David J. Sams/Tony Stone Images/New York, Inc. Page 417: ©Bob Thaves/United Media (NEA). FRANK & ERNEST reprinted by permission of Newspaper Enterprise Association, Inc. Page 424: ©Elizabeth Crews. Page 428: ©Erika Stone/Photo Researchers. Page 433: ©Frank Siteman/The Picture Cube. Page 435: ©Elizabeth Crews.

Chapter 12 Page 440: ©John Carter/Photo Researchers. Page 443: ©Camille Tokerud/Photo Researchers. Pages 445 and 452: ©Laura Dwight Photography. Page 459: ©Jeffrey W. Myers/Stock, Boston. Page 460: ©Stephanie Maze/Woodfin Camp & Associates. Page 465: ©Carolyn A. McKeone/Photo Researchers. Page 468 (top): Courtesy Harlow Primate Laboratory, University of Wisconsin. Page 468 (bottom): ©John Fortunato/Tony Stone Images/New York, Inc. Page 473: ©Margaret Miller/Photo Researchers. Page 478: ©Dorothy Littell Greco/Stock, Boston. Page 480: ©Bob Daemmrich/Stock, Boston.

Chapter 13 Page 486: ©Richard Hutchings/Photo Researchers. Page 493: ©Elizabeth Crews. Page 497: ©Joseph Pobereskin/Tony Stone Images/New York, Inc. Page 505: ©The Photo Works/Photo Researchers. Page 507: ©Chris Cheadle/Tony Stone Images/New York, Inc. Page 508: ©Spencer Grant/Monkmeyer Press Photo. Page 509: CALVIN AND HOBBES, ©1993 Watterson. Reprinted with permission of UNIVERSAL PRESS SYNDICATE. All rights reserved. Page 512: ©Bachmann/Photo Researchers. Page 518: ©Janeart Ltd./The Image Bank.

Chapter 14 Page 524: ©David Young-Wolff/PhotoEdit. Page 528: ©Donald Dietz/Stock, Boston. Page 529: PEANUTS reprinted by permission of United Features Syndicate, Inc. Page 540: ©Charles Thatcher/Tony Stone Images/New York, Inc. Page 544: ©Charles D. Winters/Photo Researchers. Page 550: ©P. Davidson/The Image Works. Page 551: ©Jeff Isaac Greenberg/Photo Researchers. Page 555 (top): ©The Photo Works/Photo Researchers. Page 555 (bottom): ©Melanie Carr/Zephyr Pictures. Page 560: ©Etta Hulme/United Media (NEA). Reprinted by permission of Newspaper Enterprise Association, Inc.

Chapter 15 Page 570: ©Lori Adamski Peek/Tony Stone Images/New York, Inc. Page 575: ©Donald Dietz/Stock, Boston. Page 580: ©J. Koontz/The Picture Cube. Page

581: ©Matusow/Monkmeyer Press Photo. Page 583: ©Paul Gish/Monkmeyer Press Photo. Page 594: ©Bill Bachmann/Photo Researchers. Page 596: ©Will & Deni McIntyre/Photo Researchers. Page 608: ©Tim Davis/Photo Researchers.

Chapter 16 Page 612: ©Richard Hutchings/Photo Researchers. Page 619: Comstock, Inc. Page 621: ©Mike Mazzaschi/Stock, Boston. Page 622: ©Lawrence Migdale/Photo Researchers. Page 625 (top): ©Lawrence Migdale/Photo Researchers. Page 625 (bottom left): ©Elizabeth Crews. Page 625 (bottom right): ©Laura Dwight Photography. Page 627: From *The Robbers Cave Experiment: Intergroup Conflict and Cooperation*, p. 103, ©1988 Muzafer Sherif, Wesleyan University Press. Reproduced with permission of the University Press of New England. Page 629: From Two Worlds of Childhood, 1970, pp. 45, 48, by U. Bronfenbrenner, Russell Sage Foundation, New York. Page 638: ©Gallant/The Image Bank. Page 641: ©Richard Hutchings/Photo Researchers. Page 653 (left): ©Jeff Greenberg/Photo Researchers. Page 653 (right): ©Carolyn A. McKeone/Photo Researchers. Page 655 (left): ©Elizabeth Crews. Page 655 (right): ©Eduardo Gill/Black Star.

Sources for Chapter-Opening Vignettes

Chapter 5 David Holmstrom, "U.S. Hospitals Are Flooded with Babies Abandoned by Alcohol and Drug Abusers," *Christian Science Monitor*, September 17, 1992; Donna O'Neal and Debbie Salamone, "Cocaine Mom's Case Thrown Out," *Orlando Sentinel*, July 24, 1992, p. B1; Mimi Hall, "Cocaine-Babies Case Appealed," *USA Today*, March 6, 1992, p. 3A; Andrew Stone, "Prosecutors Focus on Drug Use, Pregnancy," *USA Today*, February 26, 1990, p. 3A; Catherine Foster, "Fetal Endangerment Cases Increase," *Christian Science Monitor*, Ocober 10, 1989; Andrea Stone, "It's 'Tip of Iceberg' in Protecting Infants," *USA Today*, August 25, 1989, p. 3A.

Chapter 6 Brendan I. Koerner, "Outlook: Baby Talk," *U.S. News & World Report*, December 8, 1997; Linda Kulman, "Outlook: Cigars All Around," *U.S. News & World Report*, December 1, 1997; Jordan Lite, "Breaking News: Iowa Septuplets Are Doing Well," *U.S. News & World Report*, November 20, 1997; Pam Belluck, "Iowa Woman Gives Birth to 7 Children," *New York Times*, November 20, 1997.

Chapter 8 Debra Rosenberg and Larry Reibstein, "Pots, Blocks and Socks," *Newsweek Special Edition: Your Child*, Spring/Summer 1997, pp. 34–35; Doris Iarovici, "More!" *Parents*, November 1996, pp. 102–104; Karen S. Peterson, "Quest for Superkids," *USA Today*, August 22, 1988, p. 1D.

Chapter 9 Pam Belluck, "Woman Wins Suit Claiming Therapists Invoked Traumatic Memories," *New York Times*, November 6, 1997; Amy Argetsinger, "Maryland Court Rejects 'Repressed Memory' Argument," *Washington Post*, July 30, 1996, p. A7; Dan Morain, "Retrial in California Case Would Test Recovered Memory," *Washington Post*, December 27, 1995, p. A12; James H. Andrews, "Dredging the Past: Recovered Memory or False Memory?" *Christian Science Monitor*, July 25, 1994.

Chapter 12 Charmagne Helton, "Mom Loses Custody over Day Care," *USA Today*, July 27, 1994, p. 1A; Elizabeth Kastor, "The Maranda Decision," *Washington Post*, July 30, 1994, p. D1; Associated Press, "Court Gives Daughter Back to Mom: Ruling Overturned in Day Care Case," November 9, 1995; Jeanne May, "Parents to Share Maranda Equally: Long Custody Battle Ends with Settlement," *Detroit Free Press*, October 17, 1996, p. 1A.

Chapter 14 Blaine Harden, "Prom Night Mother Charged with Murder," *Washington Post*, June 25, 1997, p. A3; Faye Bowers, "Behind the Tragedy of Discarded Babies," *Christian Science Monitor*, June 18, 1997, p. 3; Laurie Goodstein and Blaine Harden, "Of Birth, Death and the Prom," *Washington Post*, June 10, 1997, p. A3; Marc Peyser, "Death in a Dumpster," *Newsweek*, December 2, 1996, pp. 92–94; Kari Vick, "Young Love and a Dead Baby Tear at the Heart of Delware," *Washington Post*, November 22, 1996, p. A1.

Chapter 16 Lucia Mouat, "Teens Take the Lead in Keeping Intoxicated Friends Off the Road," *Christian Science Monitor*, January 19, 1984, p. 7; Victoria Benning, "Bringing Peer Pressure to Bear on School Problems," *Washington Post*, September 20, 1997, p. A14; "News in Brief," *Christian Science Monitor*, October 9, 1997, p. 2.

Author Index

Subject Index

Chapter 11: Language Development

This chapter discusses the role of parents in language learning in several sections:

- (p. 400) Introduces the speech style known as "motherese."
- (pp. 410–411) Considers parents' contribution to early individual differences in language.
- (pp. 415–416) Discusses the role of parents' labeling practices in semantic development.
- (pp. 424–426) Evaluates the role of modeling and feedback in grammatical development.
- (pp. 434–437) ■ *Development in School Context:* Bilingualism: Teaching (and Learning) One Language or Two?
- (pp. 426–427) ■ *Development in Cultural Context:* Cultural Variations in Language Learning Experiences

Chapter 12: Early Social and Emotional Development

- (pp. 451–454) Examines parents' contribution to early emotional development.
- (pp. 467–470) Discusses the child-rearing antecedents of different forms of attachment.
- (pp. 473–481) "Family Influences"—Considers research on different styles of child rearing, issues of maternal employment and infant day care, the role of fathers, and the consequences of child abuse.
- (pp. 461–462) ■ *Development in Cultural Context:* Ethnic Differences in Temperament: Biology or Culture?
- (pp. 471–472) ■ *Development in Cultural Context:* Attachment Across Cultures
- (pp. 478–479) ■ *Development in Cultural Context:* The Changing Roles of Fathers in China

Chapter 13: Development of the Self

- (pp. 491–492) Provides an application of the Vygotskian approach in a section on parental directives as a source of children's self-regulation.
- (pp. 495–496) Discusses the contribution of parents' caregiving to working models of the self.
- (p. 510) Examines the relation between parenting styles and children's self-concept.
- (pp. 510–511) Considers schools as one contributor to self-concept.
- (pp. 506–507) Discusses academic self-concept and academic motivation.
- (pp. 506–507) ■ *Development in Family Context:* Children's Self-Evaluation in Single-Parent Families
- (pp. 511–512) ■ *Development in School Context:* Do Schools Depress Adolescents' Academic Self-Concept?
- (pp. 500–501) ■ *Development in Cultural Context:* Self-Understanding Among Exceptional Inner-City Adolescents

Chapter 14: Moral Development

This chapter considers the contribution of the family to each of the major outcomes reviewed:

- (pp. 545–546) Moral reasoning
- (p. 552) Prosocial behavior
- (pp. 557–558) Variations in levels of aggression

Similarly, the chapter includes discussions of culture with respect to each of the main topics:

- (pp. 542–543) Moral reasoning
- (pp. 552–553) Prosocial behavior
- (p. 560) Aggression
- (pp. 558–559) "Cutting Edge" box—Covers research on real-life violence in different cultural settings.
- (pp. 535–536) ■ *Development in Family Context:* An Evolutionary Account of the Development of Antisocial Behavior
- (p. 562) ■ *Development in Cultural Context:* Does Being Aggressive Mean Being Rejected?

Chapter 15: Gender Role Development and Sex Differences

Parents' contribution to gender role development is considered throughout the chapter:

- (pp. 576–577) "Classics of Research" box—Discusses Margaret Mead's cross-cultural work.
- (pp. 580–582) Early differential treatment of boys and girls
- (pp. 582–584) Parental modeling of sex-typed behavior
- (p. 584) Role of fathers in gender role socialization
- (pp. 588–591) Extensive "Family Influences" section
- (pp. 606–607) Gay and lesbian families
- (pp. 590–591) ■ *Development in Family Context:* Growing up in a Single-Parent Household
- (pp. 596–597) ■ *Development in School Context:* Do Schools Cheat Girls?

Chapter 16: Peer Relations

- (pp. 628–629) "Classics of Research" box—Discusses Bronfenbrenner's comparison of Soviet-American cultures.
- (p. 642) Discusses contributors to children's collaborative problem-solving.
- (p. 644) Reviews evidence on the effects of friendship on adjustment to school.
- (pp. 652–657) "The Family"—Provides extended treatment of the interrelations between family life and experience with peers.
- (pp. 622–624) ■ *Development in Cultural Context:* Cross-Cultural Variations in Early Play
- (pp. 650–651) ■ *Development in Cultural Context:* Cross-Cultural Studies of Sociometric Status